GROUSE
of the
WORLD

This edition published in 2013 by New Holland Publishers
London • Cape Town • Sydney • Auckland
www.newhollandpublishers.com

The Chandlery, Unit 114, 40 Westminster Bridge Road, London SE1 7QY
Unit 1, 66 Gibbes Street, Chatswood, NSW 2067, Australia
Wembley Square, First Floor, Solan Road Gardens, Cape Town, 8001, South Africa
218 Lake Road, Northcote, Auckland, New Zealand

10 9 8 7 6 5 4 3 2 1

A record of this book is held at the British Library and the National Library of Australia.

ISBN 978 1 78009 250 8

Senior Editor: Sally McFall
Designer: Keisha Galbraith
Production: Olga Dementiev
Publisher: Simon Papps

Printed and bound in China by Toppan Leefung Printing Ltd

Photographs by: **Christian Artuso** (pp. 8, 73), **Jeff Banke**/shutterstock.com (p. 350), **Soner Bekir**/ *Top 100 Birding Sites of the World* (p. 318), **Julia Biblichenko** (pp. 82 [top & bottom], 185, 203), **Paul Binet** /fotolia.com (p. 61), **Double Brow Imagery**/shutterstock.com (p. 127), **Ronnie Howard**/fotolia.com (p. 144), **Vitaly Ilyasov**/shutterstock.com (p. 296), **Zura Javakhishvili** (p. 315), **Tang Jun** (p. 77), **Yuri Kokovin** (p. 102), **Christopher Kolaczan**/shutterstock.com (p. 284), **A.V. Krechmar** (pp. 211, 221), **Greg W. Lasley**/www.greglasley.net (pp. 6, 116 [top & bottom], 149, 338, 343, 348), **Per Michelson** (front and back covers, pp. 189, 251, 268, 270, 271, 362), **mihalizhukov**/fotolia.com (pp. 217, 219), **Noppadol Paothong**/www.nopnatureimages.com (p. 165), **Eugene Potapov** (pp. 69, 70), **Roald Potapov** (p. 324), **Tom Reichner**/shutterstock.com (pp. 63, 140, 152, 167, 168, 359), **Richard Sale** (pp. 115, 235, 236, 244, 257, 268), **Bill Schmoker** (p. 337), **Bob Shade** (pp. 282, 339), **Shattil & Rozinski**/naturepl.com (p. 173), **Yuri Shibnev** (p. 101), **BGSmith**/shutterstock.com (p. 130), **Sergey Uryadnikov**/shutterstock.com (pp. 303, 305), **voevodin voevodin**/fotolia.com (p. 81). **Front cover:** Willow Grouse in spring moult, NWT, Canada. **Back cover:** male Western Capercaillie, Norway.

GROUSE
of the
WORLD

ROALD POTAPOV AND RICHARD SALE

NEW HOLLAND

ACKNOWLEDGEMENTS

The authors express their thanks to all those who have generously helped in the preparation of this book, with illustrations, specimens, information and during the course of personal discussions on all aspects of the grouse family. But particular mention must be made of the contributions of Per Angelstam, James Bendell, David Boag, Javier Castroviejo, Marcel and Andree Couturier, Laurence Ellison, Alexey Estafiev, David Jenkins, Hans Johansen, Sergey Kirpichev, Harto Linden, Harry Lumsden, Alexey Malchevsky, Sergey Matvejev, Per Michelsen, Robert Moss, Eugene Potapov, Yuriy Pukinsky, Boris Stegmann, Jon Swennson, Oleg Vitowich, Mike Wilson and Adam Watson.

The collections of grouse specimens in several museums and institutes were used during production of the book, and we thank the staff of these for their cooperation, particularly at the Zoological Institute of Russian Academy of Science, St Petersburg (COLL ZIN RAN), the Zoological Museum of Moscow State University, collections of the local Museums of Nature in Petrozavodsk (Karelian Republic) and Teberda State Reserve in the North Caucasus, the Zoological Institute of the Estonian Academy of Sciences (Tallinn), the Institute of Zoology and Parasitology of Kazakhstan Academy of Sciences (Alma-Ata), the British Natural History Museum (Tring) and the Yamashina Institute of Ornithology (Tokio). Specimens were also received from Canada (Alberta), USA (Alaska), Norway (Bergen), Sweden (Uppsala University) and Finland (Helsinki University), and for these we thank Drs Robert Weeden, David Archibald and Harry Lumsden. In all, over 4,500 collection specimens were studied in the course of preparing this book.

In addition to the examination of specimens in collection, specimens were collected and studied by Roald Potapov (nearly 400 in total) during field trips over a period of more than 40 years from 1967, throughout Russia (including the North-eastern Magadan State Reserve, the Caucasus, Tan-Shan, and Altai mountain ranges, the northern Urals, the Karelian Republic, and Leningrad, Novgorod, and Pskov Provinces), in the western and northern areas of the Mongolian Republic, in the Zinchay Region of China, in Scotland, central Sweden, the mountains of southern Germany and northern Italy, in central Japan, and in the American states of Pennsylvania, South Dakota, Montana and Wyoming. During these trips, grouse behaviour – the courtship displays of males, habitat preferences, nutrition, nesting, life of the broods, etc – was studied, with particular attention being paid to the winter life of the birds, especially their diet and use of snow burrows. The data also includes that from studies made by Richard Sale throughout the Arctic.

CONTENTS

INTRODUCTION

The grouse are a wonderful group of birds, familiar to most dwellers of the northern hemisphere, not least because of their distribution, abundance and size. Grouse range from the Gulf of Mexico to the high Arctic, reaching above 83°N in northern Greenland. They are found throughout the Nearctic and Palearctic, in a range of habitats. They inhabit Arctic tundra, the Russian steppes and North American prairies, the Siberian taiga, and mountain forests of Central Asia and the Rocky Mountains. The natural conditions of these regions are very different, but they are similar in one important feature – they all exhibit strongly defined climatic seasons, with winters during which there is persistent snow cover, prevailing sub-zero temperatures, short days and long, dark nights. The majority of other birds breeding in the northern hemisphere leave their breeding grounds to avoid these unfavourable conditions, migrating to warmer regions. Only a few dozen birds, of differing families, have the adaptations necessary to survive the northern winter as residents. However, there is only one particular family of terrestrial birds in the world whose members are all winter residents – the grouse. Some members of the family may move short distances to different habitats, but even then they remain within a range of which the winter season is climatically severe.

Grouse, the Tetraonidae family, belong to the order Galliformes, a well-known order because it includes domestic fowls – hens, turkeys, guinea fowls – as well as other game birds such as partridges, pheasants, peacocks, etc. Most of the species of the order are birds of tropical or subtropical zones, the ancestors of the Galliformes that appeared about 60 million years ago during the Eocene epoch. The Tetraonidae are the youngest family of the order, appearing only 7–8 millions years ago during the Miocene, at the beginning of a time of global cooling. The cooling was slow, providing the Tetraonidae family with an opportunity to remain in its original habitat and evolve for survival in a cooler climate. This steady adaptation has enabled the grouse to effectively climb through a window of survivability that became smaller as the winters became steadily harsher with time. The efficiency with which the grouse survives modern winters is the result of millions of years of evolution.

In this book we describe all the representatives of the Tetraonidae family, as well as their morphology and life histories. Following the example of great ornithological authorities, we consider all grouse to be a separate family in the subfamily Phasianoidea – the Tetraonidae (Elliot, 1865; Aldrich, 1963; Hjorth, 1970; Peters, 1934; Short, 1967; Snow and Perrins, 1998 and many others – see Chapter 1). We also evaluate the theories regarding the time and place of origin of the family as a whole, and its spread across the northern hemisphere. Special attention is given to the problems associated with the role of grouse as a human food source. Hunting, especially by professional, market-driven hunters, threatened the survival of species in many regions over the last two centuries. But now other problems that threaten species numbers have arisen – the disappearance of habitats by deforestation and the drainage of bogs, as well as pollution by the gas and oil industries, to say nothing of human population growth and expansion. Yet despite these serious problems, there is now, thankfully, positive evidence that grouse are surviving in heavily populated areas. That, and the fact that for some species the remoteness of their ranges means that conservation is much less of an issue, encourages us to believe that the Tetraonidae will continue to captivate humans for generations to come.

Note: The literature sources on the different species of the Tetraonidae are so numerous that it is unrealistic to cite all, or even a large sample, in this one book. As a consequence, the authors have paid more attention to sources published in Russian, as these papers – often in obscure or rare journals, proceedings and collections – are not available for scientists outside that country. For Western sources, we have paid the most attention to key publications, especially those that have appeared after the last general review of the Tetraonidae (Johnsgard, 1973, 1983), including those regarding the newly identified Gunnison Sage-Grouse.

Female Gunnison Sage-Grouse

CHAPTER 1
Overview of the Grouse

1. SYSTEMATIC REVIEW

The Tetraonidae family was first described by Vigors (1825), who included only the nine species known at the time, the same nine species that had appeared in the work of Linnaeus (Linnaeus, 1758, 1766) in the 10th and 12th editions of his *Systema Naturae* under the genus *Tetrao*. Those nine were *Tetrao umbellus* (now *Bonasa umbellus*), *T. togatus* (now *Bonasa umbellus togata*), *T. bonasia* (now *Bonasa bonasia*), *T. canadensis* (now *Falcipennis canadensis*), *T. urogallus*, *T. lagopus* (now *Lagopus lagopus*), *T. tetrix* (now *Lyrurus tetrix*), *T. cupido* (now *Tympanuchus cupido*) and *T. phasianellus* (now *Tympanuchus phasianellus*). *T. togatus* was reclassified as a subspecies by Ridgway (1885). However, Vigors did not include two other species in the Tetraonidae family that had already been described by 1825 – *T. mutus* (Montin, 1791) and *T. obscurus* (say, 1823). The classification of new grouse species followed, with the addition of *Centrocercus urophasianus* in 1828, *Falcipennis (Canachites) franklinii* in 1829, *Lagopus leucurus* in 1831, *Tetrao parvirostris* in 1851, *Falcipennis falcipennis* in 1855, *Dendragapus fuliginosus* in 1873, *Tympanuchus pallidicinctus* in 1873, *Lyrurus mlokosiewiczi* in 1875, *Bonasa sewerzowi* in 1876, and, the last to date, *Centrocercus minimus* in 1999.

Most of the new species identified after Linnaeus (1758) were described as species under the generic name *Tetrao* (*Tetrao falcipennis*, *Tetrao franklinii*, etc), though at the same time a more detailed classification began. Vigors was the first to use the name Tetraonidae, pointing out that this family coincided with the Linnaean genus *Tetrao* and that the species in the family differed from those of the Phasianidae by their simpler plumage colouration and the absence of different forms of carunculates on the head (Vigors, 1825).

The Tetraonidae family belongs to the superfamily Phasianoidea that differs from another super-family of Galliformes, the Cracoidea, primarily by the position of the hallux in the tarsi. The taxonomic subdivision of this superfamily is rather complex, and to the present day authors have argued, with varying degrees of conviction, the taxonomical status of the groups – turkeys, guinea fowl, peafowl, pheasants, Old World quails (partridges), New World quails, and grouse – that comprise the Phasianoidea. During the last two centuries, all possible combinations appear to have been tried in an attempt to classify these groups, which have been variously given the rank of subfamilies within the single family Phasianidae or treated as separate families altogether. The most realistic classification treated the Phasianidae (comprising the subfamilies Odontophorinae, Perdicinae, Phasianinae and Numidinae), the Meleagridae and the Tetraonidae as separate families, but new evidence has now been produced suggesting that the guinea fowl should be elevated to family rank as well (Sibley, Ahlquist, 1990; Sych, 1999). That said, most authors stick with the tradition of treating the grouse as a subfamily of Phasianidae, usually without reference or argument, the tradition being more a memory reflex, without real support: we suggest it is enough merely to point out that in the main works of professional ornithologists, grouse are given the status of a family – the Tetraonidae (Elliot, 1865; Aldrich, 1963; Hjorth, 1970; Peters, 1934; Short, 1967; Potapov, 1992; Snow and Perrins, 1998 and many others).

The diversity of opinion with respect to the classification of the Phasianoidea points, above all, to the low degree of divergence within the superfamily. It may further reflect the universal nature of phasianid morphology, which permits adaptation to a variety of environmental conditions. Our research indicates that some of those adaptations can produce new forms in new conditions and, therefore, the possibility of the evolutionary development of some groups of taxon members in new directions as a consequence of global, natural changes. Because of this, following the arguments of evolutionary trends so prominently expressed by Simpson (1969), we completely support his opinion that the size of a new zone occupied by a newly appeared taxon is determined by its taxonomical status: more waste space – higher status (Simpson, 1969). Our revision undoubtedly shows the status of this group as a clearly expressed family taxon (Potapov, 1985; 1992): there is no publication with any specific argument against this position, and no single work that backs up its inherent assumptions regarding the subfamily status of the grouse.

Attempts to separate different genera inside the family began in 1819 when the genus *Bonasa* was described (Stephens, 1819) and continued until 1885, when the last genus was described (*Canachites* by Steineger, 1885). These genera are still the subject of discussion among taxonomists to the present day. One of the most important aims of taxonomy is to reflect the levels of divergence between the members of one or another taxon and it is obvious that these levels differ even within a genus. As a consequence, taxonomists use the subgenus category to reflect more clearly the differences of the levels of divergence between congeneric species. For the Tetraonidae family, this taxonomic categorization was applied by Potapov (Potapov, 1985) and is described in the chapters dedicated to each genus.

2. DISTRIBUTION

Distribution maps for each of the Tetraonidae are given in the genus chapters. Here we note that only two species are common to both Eurasia and North America – the Willow and Rock Ptarmigan (the latter known in Eurasia simply as Ptarmigan) of the genus *Lagopus*. A third species of this genus, the White-tailed Ptarmigan, is confined to the Nearctic. Two further genera are represented on the continents by different species: the genus *Bonasa* by the Ruffed Grouse in North America, and by the Hazel Grouse and Severtzov's Grouse in Eurasia; and the genus *Falcipennis* with two North American species, the Canadian Spruce Grouse and Franklin's Spruce Grouse, and one Eurasian species, the Asian Spruce Grouse. All other tetraonids are represented on the two continents by different genera. In North America, there are three genera: *Dendragapus* (2 species); *Centrocercus* (2 species); and *Tympanuchus* (3 species), while in Eurasia there are two genera: *Tetrao* (2 species) and *Lyrurus* (2 species). The 20 species therefore include 2 species common to both continents, a further 7 species peculiar to Eurasia and 11 peculiar to North America.

The Tetraonidae inhabit a significant proportion of all lands in the northern hemisphere from middle to high latitudes, including mountains up to the snowline. The northern limit of the family's distribution is the northern shore of Greenland (83°30'N, Rock Ptarmigan). The southern border is more complicated and is determined primarily by climatic characteristics: it is always a seasonal climate with a pronounced winter period involving snow cover, sub-zero temperatures and short days. Out of such areas grouse lose their adaptive advantages and fair poorly in competition with birds adapted to a warmer climate. The most southerly population in North America is that of the Greater Prairie-Chicken, which breeds as far south as the Gulf of Mexico, at about 27°40'N. In Eurasia the most southerly Tetraonidae population is that of Severtzov's Hazel Grouse (also, but we consider incorrectly, known as the Black-breasted, or Chinese, Hazel Grouse), which extends as far south as 27°35'N where favourable habitats of mixed boreal forests are situated above 4,000m (13,123ft) in the Sino-Tibetan mountains (He, Zeng, 1987). The population of Greater Prairie-Chicken on the shores of the Gulf of Mexico, with its subtropical climate, is explained by the occasional invasions of cold Arctic cyclones that bring both snowstorms and sub-zero temperatures. These events are catastrophic for most of the local birds, but not for prairie-chickens.

The other main feature of the grouse habitat is the presence of arboreal or bush vegetation, as these are the principal source of its winter nutrition (i.e. buds, twigs, catkins, needles, etc). Even in the Arctic tundra, ptarmigan prefer areas with dwarf willows and birches. In general, those species with a preference for open habitats (steppe and prairie) still need the presence of bush-arboreal vegetation, including heath brushes and sage bushes, to sustain them during the winter.

3. GENERAL CHARACTERISTICS

The Tetraonidae have common specific features in both morphology and ecology, these clearly differentiating them from all other Galliformes, and it is our view that these peculiarities are adaptations to winter conditions, i.e. to snow cover, cold and short days. The ability of the birds to survive harsh winters successfully has been well known for many years, but an understanding of all the adaptations that allow this has been identified and described in detail only recently (Potapov, 1974; 1985; 1992). These features are considered in details below.

3.1 Pectinated Toes

This feature is common to all but three species of the family and is not found in any other bird. The horny pectinates (appendages) along the sides of the toes (**Figure 1**) are, in form, miniature elongated scoops with blunt tips. Forming a single or double row on both sides of the toes, they break and fall off in spring, and are regrown each autumn before the onset of winter. Only in the genus *Lagopus*, which live under the most severe climatic conditions, are pectinates replaced by thick feathering, though traces of a rudimentary form of pectination in the White-tailed Ptarmigan and in some specimens of Willow Ptarmigan (*L. l. major*) give clear evidence that the feathering of the toes is a secondary feature, evolving in place of the pectinates. The pectinates more than double the surface area of the foot and are therefore clearly an important aid. The function of

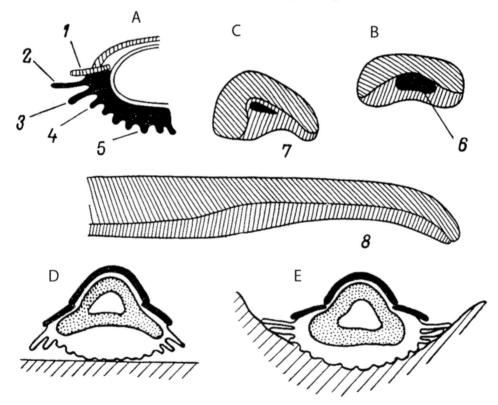

Figure 1. Horny pectinations

A − cross-section of the third phalange of Capercaillie central toe: 1 − the lateral scale covering the pectination from above, 2 − the first row of horny pectinations, 3 − the second row (more abundant in northern species), 4, 5 − horny knobs of the toe's sole. B − cross-section of the growing pectin at its base; 6 − the pulp. C − The horny pectination: 7 − transverse cross-section, 8 − longitudinal cross-section. D − position of the horny pectinations on the toe of a bird sitting on a branch (cross-section): the pectinations do not reach the branch except in a few birds of northern populations, and have no strength to stabilize the toe on the branch. E − the position of the horny pectinations during contact with the snow: the pectinations are held in place by the force of the snow pressing them against the rigid lateral scales.

the appendages has been much debated, with suggestions that they aid locomotion on the friable snow surface or aid perching. The latter idea was postulated despite pectinates being present in species that are not forest dwellers (sage-grouse), but are absent in Severtzov's Hazel Grouse (see Figure 32 in Chapter 2), which spends most of its life in trees. The position of the pectinates also indicates that improving the bird's ability to perch is not the reason for the adaptation. Each pectinate is a strongly elongated, horny knob extending from the lateral horny prominences that cover the toe's sole (i.e. the podotheca). The histological description of the pectinates has yet to be carried out, but from the external position and the movement potential it is clear that when the bird is perched (Figure 1), the pectinates either do not reach the branch, or have only soft contact with it. They cannot, we therefore contend, aid perching.

The scales that cover each outer pectinate on the toe also restrict its ability to lift above the horizontal. This 'stop' acts only when the bird's foot is resting on the snow (Figure 1). While this aids movement in deep snow (see Section 3.4 below for a further adaptation for snow walking), the scoop-shaped pectinates significantly increase the digging function of the foot and enable the bird to dig itself into the snow within a matter of seconds, and we consider this to be the main advantage of the adaptation, as the birds do not actually spend much time walking on snow. Snow burrows are refuges where the birds roost, and where they may spend most of the day during periods of very low temperatures (see Section 3.8) often constructing burrows up to three times each day in harsh weather. Pectinates attain maximal size in areas with the most severe winters, and, consequently, where the digging of burrows is needed most frequently, e.g. the Black-Billed Capercaillie of north-east Siberia, which has especially large pectinations. This, together with the fact that pectinates are not found in any other avian taxon, significantly increases the taxonomic value of this feature. Similar structures are found in some desert lizards inhabiting loose sand (Buxton, 1928), but these are not homologues of grouse pectinates, being transformed scales. Other birds may also occasionally bury themselves in friable snow overnight – for instance, three species of the Phasianid family (Grey Partridge, *Perdix perdix*, Bearded Partridge, *P. dauuricae*, and (Ring-necked) Pheasant, *Phasianus colchicus*) – but these species have no adaptations to aid regular under-snow roosting and, indeed, generally avoid wintering in their 'native' lands, migrating to snow-free areas. Other species also dig burrows in the soil for nesting – puffins, Manx Shearwaters, kingfishers and sand-martins – but do so using the bill and strong claws: in hard soils pectinations would be useless. Such burrow nesting is also, of course, a specific breeding strategy and is not carried out routinely, as snow burrowing is for grouse species.

3.2 Feathering of Nostrils, Tarsi and Toes

All species of the family have full and thick feathering of the nostrils and, perhaps as a consequence, a complete absence of the horny covering flap, the operculum. In

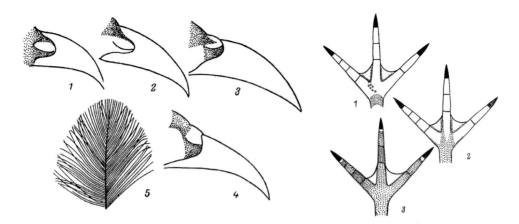

Figure 2. Feathering of the nostrils in some phasianid birds (dotted) *1* – Lerwa lerwa; *2* – Tragopan temmincki; *3* – Lophophorus impeyanus; *4* – L. lhuysi; *5* – *a nostril feather of male Western Capercaillie.*

Figure 3. Feathering of tarsi and toes of grouse (dots)
The circles indicate feathers seen only in northern populations. 1 – Lyrurus tetrix, *2* – Tetrao urogallus, *3* – Lagopus *spp.*

some members of the Phasianidae (e.g. the Snow Partridge (*Lerwa lerwa*), *Tragopan* spp., *Lophophorus* spp., *Tetraogallus* spp.) there is some feathering around and on the surface of the operculum, but the operculum itself is not reduced (**Figure 2**). While this thick feathering of the nostrils is an aid against severe cold, we consider its main purpose is to protect the bird from snow during the digging of snow burrows, and to aid the bird in avoiding high humidity during a long stay in the burrow, condensing exhaled moisture that is then returned to the bird and preventing icing of the internal walls of the burrow that could result in an oxygen shortage.

In all grouse, the tarsi are thickly feathered, apart from a narrow strip along the rear. Most grouse have lateral feathering extending to the base of the toes: only in *Lagopus* species are the toes completely feathered (except for the upper part of the extreme tips) (**Figure 3**). While many phasianids, especially northern or mountain species, have feathering on the upper part of the tarsus, this never extends to the lower third. With one exception, in all grouse apart from the *Bonasa* species, the tarsi are feathered to the base, even in southerly populations of those species living in a warmer climate than the *Bonasa*. The one exception is the southern subspecies of the Greater Prairie-Chicken (*T. c. attwateri*), which inhabits the shores of the Gulf of Mexico. That these birds have tarsi on which the feathering does not reach the base indicates natural selection operating to alter a structure adapted to colder habitats and epochs. In northern populations of Hazel Grouse, which inhabit areas with severe winters, the tarsi have a greater area of feathering: the feathers are more elongated, fluffier and cover the entire naked part of the tarsi, reaching the toes. As would be expected, the more northerly the species, the more extensive the tarsi feathering.

The feathers of the tarsi are specific (**Figure 4**). The front surface is covered by small feathers with solid, resilient fans that closely contact each other. These feathers create a solid, smooth cover that permits the bird to move easily through snow. The feathers of the sides of the tarsi are progressively longer and fluffier, with the longest ones situated close to both sides of the narrow, unfeathered strip along the back of the tarsi. These feathers act in a similar fashion to warm trousers and are very important, not only in keeping the bird's legs warm but in creating warm bedding, a mattress that isolates the bird's body from the burrow's snow floor, as the reposing position is with the feet tucked under the body (see Figure 19). As the bird may sit for many hours, sometimes up to 22 hours, this is critical for the bird's well-being. That the feathering is a winter

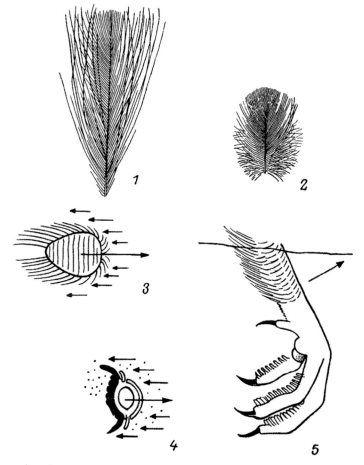

Figure 4. Feathers and tarsi movement
Feathers from the back (1) and front (2) of the tarsi; Movement of the leg through snow: 3 – cross section of the tarsi and position of feathers during forward motion (long arrow) through snow resistance (short arrows), 4 – cross-section from the central phalange of the toe and position of the horny pectinations during the same process; 5 – side view of the leg during its movement through the snow cover (long arrow).

adaptation is clear from the fact that the tarsi feathering moults in the spring and is replaced completely in the autumn.

3.3 Feathers (Pterylosis)

While the feathering of nostrils, tarsi and toes is the main feature of the grouse family, there are other feather peculiarities that differentiate the species from phasianids, and which represent an adaptation to low air temperatures during the long winter, and short periods of higher temperatures in mid-summer. The general configuration of pterilias and apterias in both families are practically the same (**Figure 5**), but the apteria of tetraonids are covered by specific downy feathers that have partially reduced stems and long, fluffy branches. These feathers appear only during the autumn moult. They are situated at some distance from each other, but because of the long branches cover practically all the surface of the apteria, forming a downy blanket. In contrast to some northern phasianids, such as partridges and pheasants, tetraonids of the same size have many more feathers, and among this number, more than twice as many with fluffy, or hair-like, constructions. An additional rod, with a downy fan, covers the central part of the feather and is significantly more expressed in tetraonids: its length is 70–79% of the main rod, as compared to 54–65% in phasianid birds. In tetraonids, the rod's thickness is also 1.5 to 2 times larger.

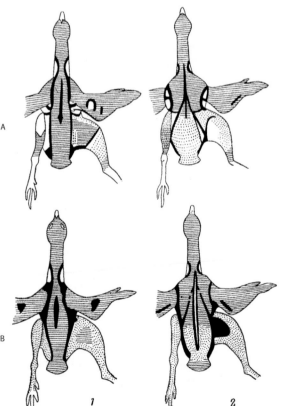

Another specificity of tetraonid feathering is the presence of seasonal colouration in all ptarmigan (and also, to an extent, black grouse), which is possible because most of the feather follicles can produce two or even three feathers during the year.

The general moult process of grouse is illustrated in **Figure 6**.

3.4 Skeletal Features

The main specificity of the grouse skeleton in comparison to phasianids is the wide and flat (shallow) pelvis (**Figure 7**). The main reason for the development of this feature is the large volume of grouse intestines. The

Figure 5. Pterylosis
A – a phasianid bird, Alectoris chukar, *and B –* Lagopus lagopus. *1 – from above, 2 – from below. Hatched parts – covered by contour feathers, dotted parts – covered by hair-like feathers, solid black – covered by downy feathers, uncoloured – apteria (naked skin).*

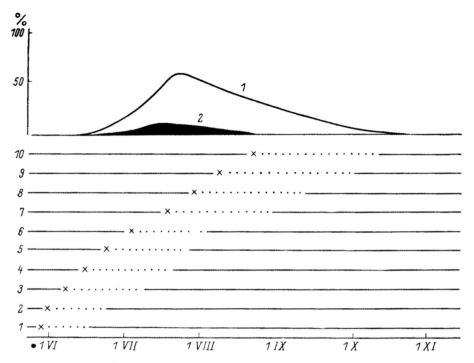

Figure 6. Grouse moult process

Vertical axis: upper part – % of molted feathers, lower part –number of primaries. Horizontal axis – calendar. 1 – feathers that grow simultaneously; 2 – growing summer feathers. X – moment of molt, '......' – time of feather growth, solid line – finished feathers.

ratio of the pelvis width to length in the tetraonids is 75–95%, in comparison to 48–67% in phasianids (**Table 1**).

Equally prominent is the construction of the grouse skull (**Figure 8**). It is shorter in comparison to phasianids, especially the bill. The prokinethic zone (the zone of contact between the nasal and frontal, or prefrontal, bones) is also more vertically arranged than in phasianids and is a development resulting from bill usage during feeding on harder parts of trees and bushes (Gambarian, 1978). A further development resulting from this bill work is another specific feature of the skull – the large opening in the lower mandible, the *foramen mandibularis* (**Figure 9**), the presence of which is related to the strongly developed adductor muscle, the *mandibulare externa*, which raises the lower mandible and requires a firmer attachment to

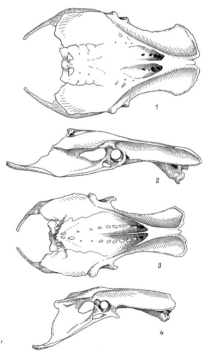

Figure 7. Pelvis

Pelvis of grouse (Tetrao urogallus, 1, 2) and phasianid (Phasianus colchicus, 3, 4) birds.

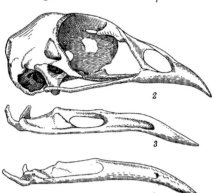

Figure 8. Skulls
*The skulls of grouse (*Lyrurus tetrix, *1, 3) and phasianid (*Phasianus colchicus, *2, 4) birds.*

the external surface. This adaptation is particularly important during feeding on the harder parts of twigs and on bunches of needles, when the loading of the lower mandible is extremely high.

The other important peculiarity of the grouse skeleton is the increased angle between the digit condyles. These also noticeably protrude outwards, forming almost an arch, which is lacking in the taxonomically similar phasianids. The grouse

Table 1. Skeletal Features of Species

Species	Number of specimens	Pelvis length (mm)		Pelvis width as percentage of length between lateral edges of processa pars acetabularis		Maximum width between lateral edges of the os pubis		Pelvis height	
		Average	Range	Average	Range	Average	Range	Average	Range
Bonasa umbellus m.,f.	2	52	51.7-52.3	83.7	82.2-85.3	95.2	93.7-96.7	22.9	21.2-24.7
Bonasa bonasia m.,f.	10	50.2	48.8-53.8	79.9	74.8-85.6	84.9	76.4–91.2	17.4	14.8-19.4
Falcipennis canadensis m.	1	59		79.8		85.6		17.6	
F. falcipennis m.	1	58.2		78		82.1		17.2	
Dendragapus obscurus m.	2	81.5	81-82	71.8	71.6-71.9	76.3	75.3-77.3	18.4	17.3-19.5
Tetrao urogallus m.	16	112.6	106.3-119	77.2	74.8-79.9	84.3	79.6-90.5	17.1	15-19
T. parvisostris m.	1	106.3		76.3		84.8		17.2	
T. parvirostris f.	2	99.1	93-106.3	74.5	71.6-77.4	79.5	76.9-82	16.6	16.4-16.8
Lyrurus tetrix m.	3	79.4	76.5-81.5	73.4	.71.4-74.8	76.6	75-78.3	15.9	14.3-17
L. tetrix f.	5	71.1	68.2-73	74.8	73.7-77	78.2	77-80.2	16.6	16.1-17.8
L. mlokosiewiczi m.	1	67.7		74.1		78.4		18.5	
Lagopus lagopus m.,f.	7	57.7	52-65	86	79- 92.7	84.8	77.5-91.6	22.2	18.5-26.7
L. mutus m., f.	2	55.6	52-59.3	88.3	85.6-91.1	87.6	85.6-89.6	201	19-21.3
L. leucurus m.	1	47.3		84.6		87.7		21.1	
Tympanuchus phasianellus m.,f.	2	69.8	69.6-70	76.9	75.7-78	76.9	76-77.6	17.1	
Centrocercus urophasianus m.	1	114.5		65		69		14.1	
C. urophasianus f.	1	99.1		57.6		70.6		16.2	
Megapodiidae									
Macicehpalon maleo	1	100.4		62.6		56		25	
Cracidae									
Crax nigra	1	118		51.7		46		20.2	
Crax globulosa	1	117.5		61.1		52.8		22.5	
Crax sp.	1	119		57.2		44.5		20.5	
Ortalis motmot ruficeps	1	67		58.2		52.4		25.4	
Ortalis vetula	1	58		65.9		58.8		29	
Meleagridae									
Meleagris gallopavo	1	127		65.5		58.2		66.9	
Phasianidae									
Numida sp..	1	82.8		61.9		65.8		33.7	
Numida sp..	1	84.2		61		56.8		37.6	
Coturnix coturnix,	3	31.4	30-32.9	53.3	52.3-54.3	48.3	42.8 - 51.4	24.2	23.3-24.7
Coturnix japonicus	4	30.65	30.1-31.4	55.9	51 - 58.3	49	48.6 - 49.6	24.2	23.3-24.9
Perdix perdix	5	45.9	43.4 - 49	68.3	65.1-70.7	65.6	62.6-67.3	29	26.9-30.2
Ammoperdix griseogularis	2	35.5	35-36	69.1	65.7-70.8	67.7	66.6-68.8	25.5	225.3-25.7
Alectoris kakelik	11	53.9	52.2-55.3	66.6	62.1-7o.9	61.2	58.7-65.8	28.6	26.8-30.9
Tetraogallus himalayensis m.	1	90		75.8		71.1		37.7	
Tetraogallus himalayensis f..	3	90.6	89.3-91.3	73.5	70.4-76.3	66	64-67	33	30.8-34.6
Tetraogallus altaicus m.	2	95.1	94.5-95.7	71.9	70.7-73.1	66.2	66.1-66.6	37.4	36-38.8
T. caucasicus m.	1	79.5		72.9		67.8		35.8	
Francolinus francolinus m.	1	56		55.9		52		22.1	
Colinus m.	1	37.2		66.2		62.2		24.9	
Phasianus colchicus m.	7	68.7	66.3-70	60.7	58.6-64.9	56.5	49.6-59.8	32.1	28.4-33.2
Phasianus colchicus f.	2	67.7	65.5-70	61.7	60.6-62.9	56.8	53.6-60	29.4	28.4-30.5
Crossoptilon crossoptilon m.	1	98.3		64		56.9		29	

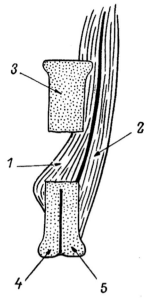

Figure 9. Lower mandibula
Cross section of lower mandibula of Tetrao urogallus *through* foramen mandibularis:
1 – m. adductor mandibulae externa medialis; *2* – m. mandibulae externa superficialis, *3* – os supraangulare, *4* – os angulare, *5* – os dentale.

morphology allows all the digits connected to the condyles to be especially widely spread, allowing the birds to walk in deep snow without losing their perching skills. Grouse digits diverge to an angle of 149° during walking, in comparison to the 80–115° of phasianids (**Figure 10**).

Among other skeletal peculiarities, the prominent humerus (elbow) projection must be mentioned. The functional significance of the projection is still unclear, but it is undoubtedly connected with the species' arboreal mode of life: it is also well expressed in other Galliformes and in the Cracidae family, but is absent in the Phasianidae (**Figure 11**).

Figure 10. Legs and toes
Tarsometatharsus *bones of* Lyrurus tetrix *(1–3) and* Phasianus colchicus *(4–6) and the divergence of the toes of* Lyrurus tetrix *(7) and* Tetraogallus himalayensis *(8) illustrated by footprints in snow, and of the toes of* Phasianus colchicus *(9) illustrated by a footprint in muddy soil.*

Figure 11. Humerus bones of Galliforme birds
1 – Lagopus lagopus; *2* – Tympanuchus phasianellus; *3* – Tetrao urogallus; *4* – Crax sp.; *5* – Tetraogallus himalayensis; *6* – Phasianus colchicus.

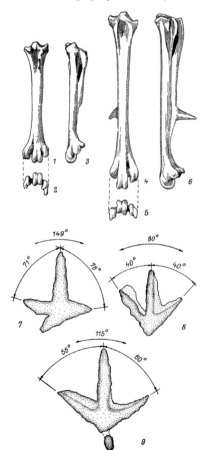

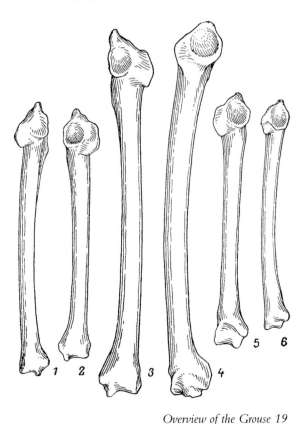

3.5 Rhamphotecae

The horny covers of the upper and lower mandibles that form the bill have sharp, cutting edges on both mandibles in all grouse species. Grouse have a hard, horny palate with three prolonged, rolled combs and a shoot that goes along the inner edge of the upper mandible. The main task of the combs is to fix the position of the subject within the bill during the process of tearing a piece from a tree or bush. When the bird wishes to separate a bud or catkin, it simply bites, the sharp cutting edges of the mandibles acting in the same way as mammalian teeth. However, the task is more complicated when there is a need to separate a large portion of pine needles in one go (as would be the case for capercaillie) or to separate the hard ends of the twigs of willow, birch, larch, etc in the case of most other grouse species. With pine needles, the bird squeezes the whole bunch of needles between its mandibles and then tears it off with a sharp jerk of the head, directed away from the branch. Some ornithologists believe capercaillie actually cut the needles away using the mandibles as scissors. However, analysis of the needles from the crops suggests that more than half the needles (50.7%) were completely intact, including the base, while most of the remainder was broken, partly or completely (Potapov, 1974).

In all other situations the bird removes pieces of twig using the mandibles as nippers rather than scissors, beginning from the tip of the twig (**Figure 12**). The bill of some phasianids shows a similar construction to that of grouse and some also feed on the

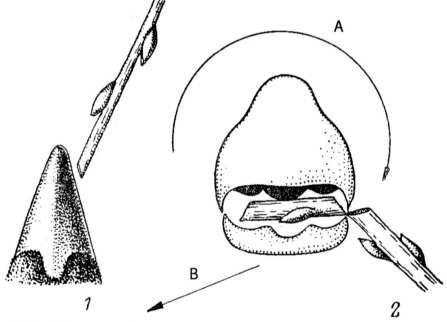

Figure 12. The biting process of grouse
1 – Position of the bill and twig; 2 – position of twig inside the bill at the moment of biting, A – direction of the head's rotation simultaneous with the sharp jerk aside (B).

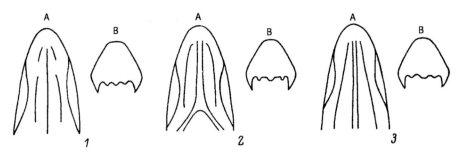

Figure 13. Rhamphotheca of some phasianid birds
The position of horny ridges in the palate (A) and cross section through the upper jaw (B). 1 – Lophura leucomelanos; *2 –* Tragopan satyra; *3 –* Ithaginis cruentus.

same sort of material (e.g. the Blood Pheasant [*Ithaginis cruentes*] – see **Figure 13**). But even here there is a difference in the character of the moult of the horny bill cover. In grouse, moult of the rhamphotecae has a seasonal character, starting in mid-summer, i.e. at a time when the need for arboreal-type food is minimal, and finishing in September. This means that the rhamphotecae are renewed completely by the beginning of winter when arboreal food sources become the principal food resource (Snigirewsky, 1950). By contrast, the moult of rhamphotecae in those phasianids for which there have been studies (species of the genera *Phasianus*, *Tetraogallus* and *Alectoris*) is a constant process, the rhamphotecae growing continuously to compensate for wear (Kuzmina, 1968).

3.6 Digestive System

One of the main features of the grouse digestive system is the exceptionally strong development of the caeca. This is seen in all species, though it is most pronounced in *Lagopus* birds. Generally, the length of the two caeca in grouse varies from *c.*60–139% of the length of the small and large intestine. In phasianids, the ratio is up to 50%, though in a few extreme cases it may be up to 64% (Potapov, 1985). The length of caeca is directly correlated with the duration of the winter and its severity, a trend that is evident even within different populations of a single species. The length of the caeca is not constant, varying with the age of the bird, the nature of its diet, the season and, to some extent, the severity of the climate (Levin, 1963; Pendergast, 1969; Pendergast, Boag, 1973; Fenna, Boag, 1974). Experiments with caged grouse (*Lagopus lagopus scoticus*) showed that with well-assimilated food, caeca length almost halved in three to four generations (Moss, 1972). What is also important from Moss's study was that the shallow, wide pelvis, itself such a feature of grouse, remained constant, showing no variation with caeca length.

The main, basal adaptation of tetraonids to survive the northern winter season is the ability to survive on plant food of low nutritional value, but high abundance, making it available at low cost in both time and energy. In turn, this ability is based on the presence of a well-developed gut, including the caeca, into which passes the liquid digestive extract (*chyme*) containing the main nutritionally valuable material (fat, protein and

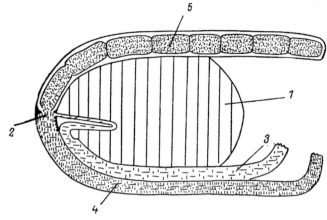

Figure 14. Position of the 'distributor' in the bird's body
1 – gizzard; 2 – distributive device; 3 – caeca; 4 – small intestine; 5 – large intestine.

micro-elements), as well as some less useful, and even poisonous, substances extracted from the forage during the grinding process in the gizzard. This extract remains in the caeca for not less than 24 hours (usually nearer 48 hours per portion), significantly prolonging the digestive process. The passage of food through the alimentary canal takes about a further four hours (Bump *et al.*, 1947). The chemistry of the digestive process in the caeca requires further research, but it is known that there is intensive secretary activity, with an exceptionally well-developed absorbent surface of the epithelium, the area and efficiency of which is considerably increased by the existence of well-developed ridges extending along the caeca. The caeca are thus a special kind of reactor, working uninterruptedly throughout the winter to provide the bird with a constant supply of energy and nutrients.

The general construction of caeca is the same in all grouse species, consisting of a 'reception capsule' (Potapov, 1974), a narrow muscular 'neck' and a large 'balloon' cylinder with soft and extensible walls, finishing with a short, oval bottom (**Figure 14**) (Schumacher, 1922). The 'reception capsule' (**Figure 15**) has a narrow entrance that can be closed by a muscular sphincter, and filter system formed by thick, three-cornered protuberances. The inner surface is completely covered by long, club-shaped vilii. The space between the vilii is filled with a specific mucus. All these structures need further research by histologists, as nothing further is available from Schumacher's work.

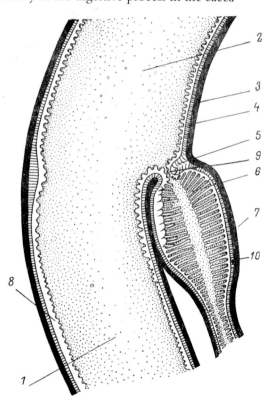

Figure 15. Reception capsule of Capercaillie caeca
1 – small intestine; 2 – large intestine; 3 – outer layer of longitudinal musculature; 4 – fibres of the large intestine; 5 – muscular sphincters; 6 – fibres of the capsule; 7 – reception capsule; 8 – fibres of the small intestine; 9 – filter mechanism of the reception capsule entrance; 10 – inside layer of the cross musculature

The construction of the 'neck' is less complicated. It forms 1/7–1/4 of the caecum, the walls consisting of two thick layers of longitudinal and circular muscles. The entire inner surface of the 'neck' is covered by long fibres similar to those of the 'reception capsule' but only half the length. The presence of the vilii's epithelium here is very important. It covers the fibres and the space between them, but to a different degree in different species. For example, it is much more prominent in capercaillie and Willow Grouse, and much less so in Hazel Grouse (Schumacher, 1922).

The main part of the caecum is the 'balloon'. Its diameter is many times that of the 'neck', while its length varies in different species, in different conspecific populations and even with the season. In contrast to the caeca of phasianids, the grouse caeca is almost twice the length and is longer that the length of the small intestine (**Table 2**). As a consequence, the grouse caeca are positioned along the small intestine forming two loops, in contrast to phasianids, where it simply lies parallel to the small intestine (**Figure 16**). The length of the balloon is maximal in midwinter and minimal in summer, the system's efficiency also being minimal at that time.

The walls of the 'balloon' are soft, thin and tensile. The main feature is a series of 7–10 ridges formed by connective tissue along the inner side. The ridges continue along the entire length of the balloon, and vary in height from 1–2mm in Hazel Grouse to 3–4mm in capercaillie. The surface of the ridges includes a number of small, strongly ramified protuberances, covered by a well-developed suction-epithelium: in total, the caeca suction-epithelium comprise 63–66% of the grouse digestive tract (Table 2), though the effect of the uninterrupted working of the caeca means that it is effectively a much higher percentage, as the intestines work for only a few hours.

The position of the 'distributor', where the caeca connect to the small intestine, is not accidental (Potapov, 1974). It is located at the end of the small intestine, where it is orientated vertically and joins the large intestine (Figures 14 and 15). The entrances to

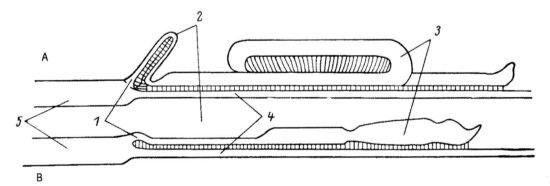

Figure 16. Caeca and small intestine
Junction of the caeca and small intestine in grouse (A) and phasianid birds (B). 1 – reception capsule; 2 – neck part of the caeca; 3 – the 'balloon'; 4 – small intestine; 5 – large intestine.

Table 2. Caeca and Intestines in Some Species of Grouse (in cm³)

Species	Sex and age	Number of specimens	Length of intestines (mm) caeca	small + large intestine	Caeca as % of large and small intestines	Volume Caeca	% of small intestine	Place	Reference
Bonasa bonasia	m.,f., ad.	7	860	1110	85.1	-	-	Kola Peninsula	Semenov-Tiansansky, 1959
	m.,ad.	5	979	1052	93.7	81.6	144.1	Leningrad Prov.	Potapov, 1985
	m., sad.	14	911	1008.3	86.9	106.3	159.8	Northern Ural	Potapov, 1985
	m., ad.	12	857	993	86.3	109.5	146.9	Northern Ural	Potapov, 1985
	f., sad.	7	906	1009.5	80.1	123	181.4	Northern Ural	Potapov, 1985
	f. ad.	7	847	1005.9	80	128.4	180.5	Northern Ural	Potapov, 1985
	m., ad.	1	760	860	88.3	-	-	Lower Amur	Potapov, 1985
Bonasa umbellus	m.,f., ad.	16	649	1030	63	-	-	N.E.USA	Bump et al.,1947
	m.,ad.	1	640	910	68.1	-	-	Ontario, Canada	Potapov, 1985
	f., ad.	1	680	990	68.6	-	-	Ontario, Canada	potapov, 1985
	m., ad.	2	860	953	-	-	-	Wisconsin, USA	Leopold, 1953
Falcipennis canadensis	m., sad.	2	560	780	71.8	-	-	Ontario, Canada	Potapov, 1985
	m., sad.	1	810	1075	75.3	-	-	Alaska	Potapov,1985
	f., sad.	1	675	1010	66.8	-	-	Alaska	Potapov, 1985
	m.?	1	800	1160	69	-	-	Alaska	Leopold, 1953
	m., ad.	1	820	1030	79.6	-	-	Alberta, Canada	Pendergast, Boag, 1973
Falcipennis falcipennis	m.,ad.	1	750	1090	72.5	-	-	Lower Amur	Potapov, 1985
Dendragapus fuliginosus	m.?	2	1000	1380	72.5	-	-	California, USA	Leopold, 1953
	m., ad.	2	752.5	997.5	77.5	-	-	Vancouver,Canada	Potapov, 1985
D. obscurus	m.?	10	740	1240	59.6	-	-	?	Beer, 1955
	f.,?	31	630	1040	60.5	-	-	?	Beer, 1955
Tetrao urogallus	m., ad.	8	1840	2370	77.6	-	-	Kola Peninsula	Semenov-Tianshansky, 1959
	f., ad.	9	1360	1970	71.2	-	-	Kola Peninsula	Semenov-Tianshansky, 1959
	f., ad..	7	1457	1834	79.4	-	-	Northern Ural	Semenov-Tianshansky, 1959
	m., ad.	10	1843	2281	80.7	453.1	108.6	Leningrad Prov.	Potapov, 1985
	f.,ad.	3	1542	1953	78.8	340.9	126.7	Leningrad Prov.	Potapov, 1985
	m., ad.	3	1850	2253	82.1	445.8	108	N.Karelia,Russia	Potapov, 1985
Tetrao parvirostris	m.,ad.	14	1396	1784	78.2	173	137.3	Kolyma,Russia	Andreev, 1980
	f.,ad.	10	1218	1610	75.6	93	77.5	Kolyma,Russia	Andreev, 1980
	m.,ad.	4	1541	2025	76.2	-	-	N. Mongolia	Potapov, 1985
	f., ad..	2	1260	1706	73.8	-	-	N. Mongolia	Potapov, 1985
	m., ad.	1	1160	1845	90	198.8	143	Kamchatka	Potapov, 1985
	f.,ad.	1	1230	1440	85.4	73.8	131.5	Kamchatka	Potapov, 1985
Lyrurus tetrix	ad.?	4	1100	1580	76.2	-	-	Kola Peninsula	Semenov-Tianshansky, 1959
	m., ad.	5	1196	1631	81.3	85.6	110.3	Leningrad Prov.	Potapov, 1985
	f. ad.	3	1047	1436	72.8	64.3	108	Leningrad Prov.	Potapov, 1985
	f.,ad.	2	970	1360	71	53.8	86.7	N. Mongolia	Potapov, 1985
Lyrurus mlokosiewiczi	m., ad	1	815	1440	71.5	-	-	N. Caucasus	Potapov, 1985
Lagopus lagopus	m.,ad.	11	1290	990	133.3	-	-	Kola Peninsula	Semenov-Tianshansky, 1959
	f.,ad.	8	1320	950	138.9	-	-	Kola Peninsula	Semenov-Tianshansky, 1959
	m., f.,ad.	12	1198	851	140.7	64	118.5	Kolyma,Russia	Andreev, 1980
	m., ad.,	62	1297	971	133.6	-	-	N.Finland	Pulliainen,1976
	m.,sad.,	81	1312	979	-	-	-	N.Finland	Pulliainen,1976
	f.,ad.,	46	1271	933	-	-	-	N.Finland	Pulliainen,1976
	f.,sad.,	93	1245	938	-	-	-	N.Finland	Pulliainen,1976
	m./f., ad.	6	940	1035	90.8	-	-	Alaska, USA	Leopold, 1953
	m., f.,	69	1056	808	-	-	-	Alaska, USA	Moss, 1974
	m., f.,	?	840	1160	72.4	-	-	Great Britian	Wilson, 1911
Lagopus mutus	m., ad.	6	960	1160	82.7	-	-	Kola Peninsula	Semenov-Tianshansky, 1959
	m., ad.	1	1180	1133	104.1	94.5	225.7	Kola Peninsula	Potapov, 1985
	m., f.,	90	879	960	-	-	-	Alaska, USA	Moss, 1974
	m.,f., ad.,	10	996	1016	92	59.2	135.3	Kolyma,Russia	Andreev, 1980
	m.,f.,	?	960	1100	-	-	-	Alps, Europa	Couturier, 1964
Lagopus leucurus	m., f.,	27	887	915	-	-	-	Alaska, USA	Moss, 1974
Tympanuchus phasianellus	m.,?	4	980	1355	72.3	-	-	Wisconsin, USA	Leopold, 1953
	m.,sad.,	1	665	1005	66.1	-	-	S. Canada	Potapov, 1985
	f. sad.	1	635	1012	62.7	-	-	S. Canada	Potapov, 1985
Tympanuchus cupido	m.?	3	900	1310	68.7	-	-	Wisconsin, USA	Leopold, 1953
	f.?	3	820	1300	63.1	-	-	Wisconsin, USA	Leopold, 1953
Centrocercus urophasianus	m.,	3	730	1485	49.2	-	-	California,USA	Leopold, 1953
Colinus virginianus	m.,f.,	2	280	703	39.8	-	-	Wisconsin, USA	Leopold, 1953
Gallipepla squamata	m.,f., ad	2	210	685	30.6	-	-	Mexico	Leopold, 1953
Lophortyx gambelli	m.,f., ad.	2	226	895	25.2	-	-	Nevada, USA	Leopold, 1953
L.californicus	m.,f., ad.	28	278	860	32.3	-	-	California, USA	Leopold, 1953
Oreortyx picta	m.,f., ad.	5	350	880	39.5	-	-	California, USA	Leopold, 1953
Cyrtonyx montezumae	m., ad	1	230	535	42.9	-	-	Mexico	Leopold, 1953
Perdix perdix	?	2	300	730	41	-	-	?	Kuzmina, 1968
	m.,f., ad.	2	290	673	43	-	-	Wisconsin, USA	Leopold, 1953
P. dauurica	m., ad	4	360	695	54.7	-	-	Kazakhstan	Potapov, 1985
Ammoperdix griseogularis	m., f., ad.	4	220	586	37.5	-	-	Tajikistan	Potapov, 1985
Alectoris kakelik	m., f., ad.	2	350	890	39.3	-	-	N. Caucasus	Semenov-Tianshansky, 1959
A. graeca	m., f., ad.	?	640	1127	56.8	-	-	Alps, Europa	Couturier, 1964
Tetraogallus himalayensis	f., ad.	1	900	1420	63.4	-	-	Tajikistan	Potapov, 1985
	m., juv.	1	630	770	81.8	-	-	Tajikistan	Potapov, 1985
T. altaicus	f.,ad.	1	840	1360	61.7	-	-	Mongolian Altai	Potapov, 1985
	m., sad.	1	699	1147	60.8	-	-	Mongolian Altai	Potapov, 1985
	m., juv.	1	681	1030	66.1	-	-	Mongolian Altai	Potapov, 1985
Coturnix coturnix	m., ad.	1	160	426	37.5	-	-	N. Ukraine	Potapov, 1985
C. coromandelica	m., ad.	1	70	280	25	-	-	Bombay, India	Potapov, 1985
Perdicula asiatica	m.,f., ad.	5	88	276	31.9	-	-	Bombay, India	Potapov, 1985
Francolinus pictus	m., ad.	1	167	485	34.4	-	-	Bombay, India	Potapov, 1985
Phasianus colchicus	m., ad.	1	596	1140	47.5	-	-	Tajikistan	Sapojnicov, in lit.
	f., ad..	1	480	970	44.5	-	-	Tajikistan	Sapojnicov, in lit.
	m.,ad.	2	780	1460	53.4	-	-	Kazakhstan	Semenov-Tianshansky, 1959
Meleagris gallopavo	m., ad.	2	840	2440	34.4	-	-	Mexico	Leopold, 1953

the reception capsules are placed above the inner parts of the caeca. The liquid parts of the digestive mixture enter the narrow opening of the reception capsule of the caecum under gravity, and pressure is created by intestinal peristalsis (Potapov, 1974, 1985). The opposing directions of peristalsis in the small and large intestines also helps the process of filling the caecum (Fenna, Boag, 1974). Solid parts of the digestive masses cannot pass through the narrow entrance of the caecum because of the presence of the filter (as described above). As a result, most of the cellulose, which is the main constituent of the bird's winter nutrition, passes the caeca entrances straight into the large intestine. Here the solids are pressed into droppings with simultaneous absorption of all moisture, so that the droppings come out from the cloaca dry, and thus do not form a melting mass, which is important in snow burrows. Our studies of fresh droppings show that they consist mainly of cellulose F (for more details on the form of droppings, see Chapter 2, Hazel Grouse, Wintering).

Excretion from the caeca usually takes place once daily (only once every two days in extreme situations), as a rule, in the morning when the bird leaves its roost. Usually at this time, digestion is complete, and the gut, apart from the caeca, is empty. Before excretion from the caeca, any movement from the small intestine to the large is terminated by contraction of the muscular sphincter. Excretion results from three to four constrictions of the caeca's (intestinal) muscles, these producing the same number of excreta portions. It is important to note that caecal excrements have a viscous consistency and a specific, heavy smell that could betray the roost, especially if it was under snow. The excrement can also seriously dirty the bird's feathers. Caecal excretion may not happen on a daily basis in extreme low temperatures (*Bonasa bonasia*, Andreev, 1980), but under temperate conditions, the caeca may be not used in full capacity (**Table 3**) (Potapov, 1974; 1985).

Another important function of the grouse caeca is its ability to function according to local conditions: when the weather conditions are poor (hard frost, snowstorm, etc), the bird might not be able to leave its snow burrow for 48 hours or even longer, during which time it cannot feed.

Table 3. Volume of Caeca and its Excreta in Some Species of Grouse (in cm³)(from Potapov, 1974)

Species	Caeca	Excreta	
		Max.	Min.
Tetrao urogallus, ♂	154	116	24.7
Lyrurus tetrix, ♂	55	53	45.4
Bonasa bonasia, ♂♀	28	25	0.8
Lagopus lagopus, ♂♀	40	7	4.2

The widely held opinion that the main process in the caeca is the decomposition of the cellulose with the help of the specific bacterial flora (Semenow-Tianshansky, 1959; Kuzmina, 1968) is not confirmed by the evidence. Most of the cellulose bypasses the caeca and continues into the large intestine where the water is absorbed. The xylem and cambium are filtered into the caeca where they undergo digestion. It is believed that the microbial flora responsible for decomposition is present in equal amounts both in the caeca and the small intestine (Suomalainen, Arhimo, 1945). However, there are no recent studies on the matter.

The chemistry of the digestive process in the caeca requires further research. What is known, from chromatographic analysis of fresh caecal excreta from a male capercaillie, is that it comprises (in %): lipids 48.1 (phospholipids 40 ± 8.1; cholesterol 8.1 ± 1.2; cholesterol ethers 1.8 ± 0.03; monoglyserines 17.5 ± 2.4; diglycerines 5 ± 0.6; triglycerines 7.5 ± 1.2; free lipid acids 9.3 ± 1.8; not determined 10 ± 1.9), proteins 10.4; carbohydrates 38.5; ash 3.0 (Potapov, 1985). Fat compounds constitute about a half of caeca's excreta and have a high caloric value – 6.95 kcal/g (Potapov, Andreev, 1973).

The caeca of phasianids are maximal in Snowcocks (genus *Tetraogallus*), which inhabit subalpine and alpine zones where winters are cold. Here the caecal length is close to that of Dusky Grouse (see Table 2), but if the length is considered as a ratio of bird body weight, then a substantial difference is apparent, 260mm/kg for the *Tetraogallus* against 600mm/kg for the Dusky Grouse. Little is known about the functions of the caeca in phasianid birds.

Ablation of the caeca in domestic chickens produces a significant decrease in the ability to assimilate cellulose (Radeff, 1928). Vitamin synthesis ability was found in the caeca of domestic hens (Cough *et al.*, 1950). However, ablation of the caeca in both chickens and domestic turkeys did not influence their survival (Farner, 1960). Experiments with the Common Quail (*Coturnix coturnix*) showed that the length of all intestines increased under the influence of low temperatures, particularly the length of the caeca. Diet did not have a similar effect on the length of the gut (Fenna, Boag, 1974).

Other features of the grouse digestive system include the absence of a gall bladder (Semenow-Tianshansky, 1959), which is well developed in other Galliformes. There is only one reference claiming the presence of a gall bladder in grouse: this reports that it functions only in summer and is not detectable in other seasons (Efremov, 1940). However, our studies in all seasons, including summer, have never identified a gall bladder, only a marked widening of the gall-ducts in the liver of some specimens of Hazel Grouse in the autumn. Despite the lack of a gall bladder, bile is produced constantly by the liver with maximal intensity in winter, and is included with the intestine liquid fractions that pass to the caeca. The bile gives caeca excreta a special colour, though this changes rapidly from brown-yellow to black once exposed to the air.

3.7 Nutrition

The nutrition of all tetraonids has been well studied. While each species has its own diet, some general characteristics can be set down. Firstly, the diet is predominantly a vegetable one. The percentage of animal food (mainly invertebrates) is higher in southerly populations, but in adult birds never exceeds 48.6% (*Tympanuchus pallidicinctus*, Jones, 1963). The percentage of animal food is highest in the diet of chicks from the first days of life to an age of four to eight weeks, after which the percentage decreases rapidly to the adult level. In some species, even in northern populations, the amount of animal food in the diet of two-week-old chicks reaches 60% (Willow Grouse on the Kola Peninsula, Semenov-Tianshansky, 1959). In one southern population of Ruffed Grouse, the chicks were predominantly insectivorous (70% of diet) during the first two weeks of life, but by the age of one month this fraction had fallen to 30% (Bump *et al.*, 1947). This was also noted in the chicks of Sooty Grouse, whose nutrition in their first weeks (in June) was 70% animal food, this fraction decreasing to 10% in August (Zwickel, Bendell, 2004). However, in some populations inhabiting deep spruce forests (for instance the Siberian Spruce Grouse) the fraction of animal food in the chick diet is very low. The proportion of insects in the diet clearly depends on the local abundance of the insects: as an example, during periods of high Orthoptera numbers, the diet of prairie-chickens mainly comprised the insects (Bent, 1932). For captive Greater Sage-Grouse chicks, forage including insects was necessary for survival during the first three weeks of life (Johnson, Boyce, 1992)

The vegetable foodstuff taken by grouse is diverse, but can be divided into two main groups: 'twig feed' – buds, catkins, needles, and the twigs of deciduous and coniferous trees and shrubs – that form the main part of the diet of all grouse species during the winter; and vegetative parts – the flowers and seeds of herbaceous plants, berries and fruits – that are the main source of grouse nutrition during warmer seasons. A schematic of the seasonal changes in grouse nutrition is shown in **Figure 17**, which indicates that there are three main seasonal periods in the yearly cycle – winter, summer and late summer to early autumn – and two shorter ones, the transition periods of spring and late autumn–early winter.

In winter, the main sources of food for all grouse (with minor exceptions) are the bushes and trees of the genera *Pinus, Picea, Abies, Pseudotsuga, Larix, Juniperus, Betula, Salix, Alnus* and *Populus*, with others to a much lesser degree. The nutritive value of these differ (**Table 4**), but all are the forest-forming species of the boreal forest (or taiga), so they are readily available and abundant. From this list, each grouse species has its own preferences and hence shows a different composition, implying that speciation was primarily due to winter feeding, with the differences arising from slow but prolonged changes of natural conditions in different places: to date, no other hypothesis has been proposed to account for the observed speciation.

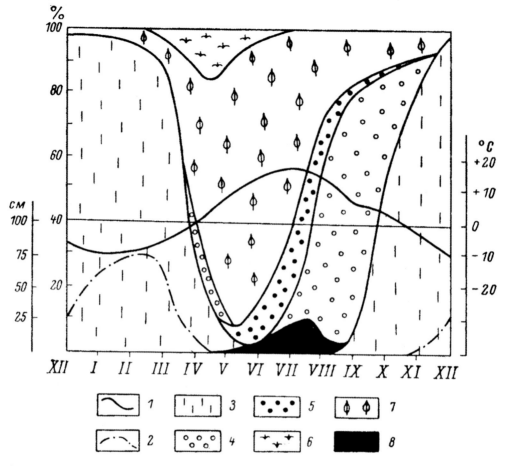

Figure 17. Seasonal changes in daily rations

Seasonal changes in the daily ration of a grouse during the year, as affected by changes in its environment: Left Vertical axis: % of forage (above) and the depth of snow cover in cm (below). Right Vertical axis – midday body temperature (°C). Horizontal axis – calendar. 1 – air T°C; 2 – depth of snow cover; 3 – twigs, catkins, buds etc.; 4 – berries; 5 – seeds; 6 – flowers, flower buds; 7 – fresh greenery (including leaves); 8 – animal.

The consistent availability of sufficient quantities of winter food is the reason grouse have no necessity to fatten prior to winter, fat reserves being found only in species that spend the winter in the most extreme conditions, such as Svalbard Ptarmigan and the grouse of north-eastern Asia. As an example, the Hazel Grouse inhabiting Russia's Kolyma Basin adds fat amounting to 11% of body weight prior to the onset of winter (Andreev, 1980), while the Black-billed Capercaillie of Russia's Verkhoyansk region (Earth's 'Pole of Coldness') have fat reserves of 16% of body weight (Egorov et al., 1959). Weight changes are seen in both males and females, the latter being more pronounced **(Figure 18)**.

In spring, some vegetation that was hidden under a blanket of snow becomes available to the birds, and fresh green shoots sprout, an important source of vitamins and albumens for females who will soon be laying eggs. An important food source at this time is berries

Table 4. Main Sources of Grouse Food

Food		Composition of the dry weight in %					Caloric Value	References
		proteins	fat	NFEM	cellulose	ash		
Betula sp.: catkins	-	13.1	8.2	-	23.9	-	-	Gasaway, 1976b
		17.4	7.8		53.2	-	-	Pulliainen, 1970a
		12.6	8.8	-	19.9	2.7	21.7	Salo, 1973
	-	-	-	-	-	-	24.7	Potapov, Andreev, 1973
	-	13	18.6	-	21.9	-	-	Gasaway, 1976a
Betula buds	-	9.3-10.5	30.9	-	13.4	2.4	23.4-24.7	Salo, 1973
	31.3	9.3	2.5	39.1	33	3.7	15.5	Treischler et al., 1946
Betula nana: catkins	-	-	-	-	-	-	20.5	Salo, 1973
Betula nana: buds	-	-	-	-	-	-	22.2	Salo, 1973
Betula nana: twigs	-	-	-	-	-	-	23	Salo, 1973
Alnus sp.: catkins	-	-	-	-	-	-	23.4	Andreev, 1973
	49.4	16.6	12.8	49.8	17.2	3.7	20.5	Treischler et al., 1946
Populus tremula: buds	-	-	-	-	-	-	19.3-20.9	Treischler et al., 1946
P. tremuloides: buds	-	-	-	-	-	-	-	Gasaway, 1976a
		12.2	20.2	-	21.4	-	-	Doerr et al., 1974
		12.9	7.3	50	27	-	-	Doerr et al., 1974
Salix sp.: buds	-	14	6.1	57.1	20.6	-	-	West, 1968; Andreev, 1973
Salix sp.: buds, twigs	-	-	-	-	-	-	20.5	Treischler et al., 1946
Corylus sp.: catkins	52.7	15	2.4	58.7	18.4	5.5	17.8	Kovalina, 1971
Pinus sp.: needles	59	8.87	11.01	55.22	27	2.11	-	Andreev, 1973
	-	-	-	-	-	-	22.3	Bump et al., 1947
Pinus banksiana: needles	59.42	9.51	13.71	48.46	25.83	2.5	-	Pendergast, Boag, 1971b
Picea sp.: buds	-	16.8	-	-	30	-	20.5	Pendergast, Boag, 1971b
Picea mariana: needles	-	5.7	6.2	63.24	22.47	2.53	21.3	Pendergast, Boag, 1971b
Picea glauca: needles	-	6.32	3.34	63.51	23.5	3.27	20.7	Salo, 1973
Vaccinium myrtillus: berries	-	11.86	7	-	17.8	3.3	18.4-19.7	Salo, 1973
V. myrtillus: leaves	-	-	-	-	-	-	18-18.4	Salo, 1973
V. myrtillus: stems	-	-	-	-	-	-	18.4-19.3	Salo, 1973
V. myrtillus: stems		8.1	-	-	38.8	3.2	-	Pulliainen et al.,1968
V. uliginosum: berries	-	-	-	-	-	-	19.3-20.1	Salo, 1973
V. vitis-ideae: berries	-	7.6	6.9	-	10.8	2.2	18.8-22.6	Salo, 1973
V. membranaceum: berries	-	10.1	-	-	38	-	20.5	Pendergast, Boag, 1971b
V. membranaceum: leaves	-	14.3	-	-	23	-	20.5	Pendergast, Boag, 1971b
Sumach sp.: berries	-	4.1-6	11.2-14.5	46.7-58.5	17.9-34-9	2.4-3.6	-	Bump et al., 1947
Carex sp.: seeds	57.6	11	2.7	49.1	30	7.6	-	Bump et al., 1947
	-	-	-	-	-	-	21.3	Pendergast, Boag, 1971b
Cereals: seeds	21.5	7.9	4.3	46.9	36.8	4	-	Salo, 1973

from the previous autumn that have lain frozen through the winter. However, the most important food sources are flowers and catkins, to such an extent that their availability, or lack of it, is crucial to breeding success (Siivonen, 1957). Indeed, production of a full clutch can only be satisfied by the availability of food sources with high protein content: the manner in which the different grouse species solve this problem by the use of differing plant sources is explored in the species chapters.

In summer, the need is for nutrition sources with high levels of albumens. Adult birds need albumens for the moult, while nestlings need them to fuel growth. Insects now also become important, as do flowers, seeds and berries as the season progresses. At the same time, grouse feed on the leaves of trees and bushes, and even on the needles of some coniferous trees. In summer, the lack of difference between the diets of different species is remarkable, with similar foods being utilized to the same degree, the only two exceptions being sage-grouse (sagebrush all year round) and Red Grouse (heather).

In late summer/early autumn, grouse move to a diet primarily of berries of different kind. To the north, where this period is shorter, berries are relatively more plentiful and form the bulk of the diet, though green plants, grass seeds and insects are also taken.

In late autumn, the birds switch to their winter diet. For a long time, expert opinion maintained that the switch in diet was prompted by snow cover (Semenov–Tianshansky,

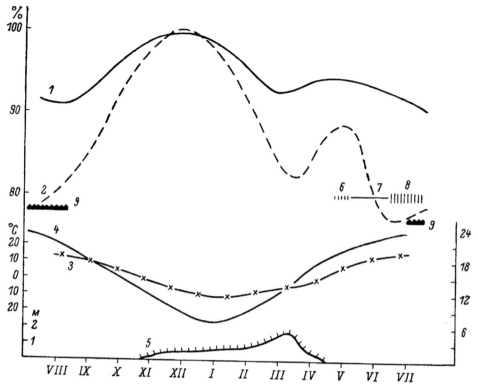

Figure 18. Seasonal body weight changes

Seasonal body weight changes (as percentage from maximum weight) in grouse: 1 – males; 2 – females; 3 – midday body temperature (°C); 4 – period of daylight; 5 – depth of snow cover; 6 – time of egg laying; 7 – incubation period; 8 – time of hatching; 9 – molt. Vertical line (down to up): to the left – depth of snow cover (m), temperature (°C), percentage of maximum body weight; to the right – time of day. Horizontal line – months.

1959; Zwickel *et al.*, 1974 and others). The simultaneous appearance of snow and change to arboreal food does occur, but there are now numerous observations in many different regions (see for instance Grange, 1936; Godfrey, 1967; Gullion, 1970; Svoboda, Gullion, 1972; Weeden, 1969; Keppie, 1977), including our own, that these events do not necessarily coincide. Our observations show clearly that there are two main reasons grouse change from their summer–autumn diet to their winter one. First is the shortening of the day (and corresponding lengthening of the night). Secondly, low air temperature: often air temperatures fall sharply, going below 0°C (32°F) long before the appearance of solid snow cover. As temperature falls, berries – which are 90% water – freeze, and offer significantly less caloric value than buds, catkins, etc (Table 4). It may still be possible for the birds to find seeds, but the search requires both time and energy input, and the nutritional value of the finds may not compensate for the searching. Although grouse can easily dig in snow, and do so regularly throughout the winter practically every day for roosting, and it might be expected that they would feed on ground vegetation, there are no observations of them doing so. Even in Western Europe, where snow-free winters are the norm, grouse have the same winter diet as in countries where snow cover is more usual. Most strikingly, during periods of prolonged thaws near St Petersburg, Russia, when large areas of bogs are freed from snow cover and cranberries become available, the local grouse (capercaillie, black grouse and Willow Grouse) maintain their normal winter diet, taking berries only as a minor addition. We believe low air temperature and lengthening hours of darkness began the process of both dietary shift and changes in the digestive system of ancestral grouse, and that those ancestors were forest phasianids, not specialized ground birds.

The most important aspect of the grouse winter diet, and the main distinction from the phasianids, is the birds' unique ability to survive on a monotonous plant diet throughout the severe and prolonged (6–8 months) winter. The winter arboreal diet is rich in cellulose and low in proteins and fats. However, its abundance means that the birds do not expend much time or energy in obtaining the amount necessary to sustain life. The food items also have the advantage of low thermal capacity, primarily because of its dryness.

3.8 Behavioural Characteristics

There are no fundamental differences between grouse and phasianids in respect of breeding strategy and timing, sex ratios, population dynamics, etc. The same general habitat types (open, bushy, forests, mountainous) are used by both groups, though grouse typically show a closer link with forest and bush vegetation, and the males of some species perform well-developed communal displays (leks). Open habitats inhabited by grouse are tundra (though this must have some woody vegetation, perhaps dwarf shrubs), steppe and semi-desert, but never true desert. Grouse are found in all types of boreal forest, but have not penetrated into subtropical, still less tropical, forests.

Adaptation to winter conditions has permitted grouse to follow the same sedentary mode of life as phasianids. Only some extreme northerly populations of ptarmigan display true, regular migrations. Some populations of other grouse species change habitats seasonally, though in general these movements are over short distances and are not regular. Studies have shown that some birds, mainly forest dwellers, spend their entire lives within an area of just a few square kilometres.

Bioenergetic studies have shown approximately equal energy requirements for all Galliforme birds of the same temperature and weight (Gavrilov, 1980), suggesting that the tetraonids have no specific adaptations in this respect at the tissue level, and that the successful survival of severe winter conditions that would be disastrous for phasianids is due only to morphological, physiological and behavioural adaptations.

The most remarkable feature of grouse behaviour is their ability to build snow burrows as thermal refuges for both nocturnal and diurnal roosting and, in our view, as noted above, most of the peculiarities of grouse morphology and physiology are closely connected with burrow construction. To create the burrow, the bird uses vigorous movements of both bill and feet to excavate a tunnel from 0.6-4m (2–21ft) long, at the end of which it prepares a roosting chamber large enough to accommodate itself comfortably, even if its feathers are ruffed, and positioned such that the bird can stretch up and poke its head through the snow in order to look around before leaving the burrow (**Figures 19, 20 and 21**). At moderately low temperatures (say -5°C to -9°C/23°F to 16°F), grouse spend the whole night in the burrow. If the temperature falls further, the bird may also spend most of the day in the burrow as well. Studies indicate that on average the burrow temperature stays at about -1.5°C (29°F), allowing the bird to roost comfortably. Even if the ambient temperature falls to -40°C (-40°F), or even colder, the burrow temperature does not go below about -3°C (27°F): the decrease in energy expenditure for thermoregulation as a consequence is 20–35%. In exceptionally low temperatures, the bird can spend up to 23 hours in the burrow, and has even been known to spend several days cooped up before being forced to emerge to feed. Because of the abundance of food, the bird can fill its crop with its entire daily ration within 30–40 minutes, though the time spent feeding is actually strongly dependent on air temperature (**Figure 22**). The crops of grouse have the same construction as phasianid birds, but their

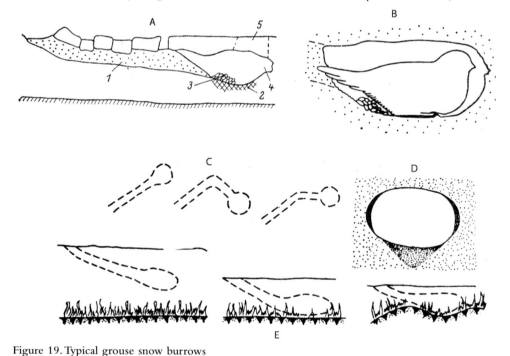

Figure 19. Typical grouse snow burrows

A – vertical longitudinal cross-section: 1 – tunnel chock-full of snow; 2 – 'platform' of compact and frozen snow; 3 – hard excrements; 4 – traces of snow eaten by the bird; 5 – section of snow ceiling through which grouse leaves the burrow. B – position of the bird in the snow burrow. C – plans of different types of tunnels excavated during preparation of a snow burrow. D – cross-section of the snow burrow: black colour – icing on walls (in rare cases); densely dotted part – the compact 'platform'. E – position of the snow burrow in snow of different depths.

Figure 20. Black-billed Capercaillie
Black-billed Capercaillie poking its head through the snow burrow roost chamber roof to scan for danger prior to leaving the burrow (Photo: E Potapov, Magadan State Nature Reserve).

volumes are increased because of this need to contain the entire daily ration at one time. As a consequence, the muscular support of the crop is more prominent (**Figure 23**). The bird's water needs are satisfied by pecking snow from the burrow wall, the tracks of such activity being visible in almost all investigated burrows.

The bird controls the depth of the tunnel by repeatedly thrusting its head through the roof. When the tunnel is complete, the bird prepares the chamber by pushing out the walls and by consolidating the snow of the roof, using its body in each case. When a satisfactory chamber has been prepared, the bird settles into a rest position, the thick feathering of the legs acting as an insulating layer between the body and the burrow's snow floor. Within the burrow there are three sources of heat. The first, of course, is the bird's body, though the insulation quality of its feathering reduces heat losses considerably. The second is exhaled air. The moisture in the bird's exhalations

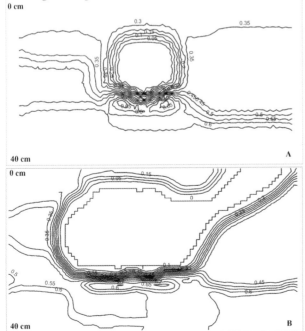

Figure 21. Density of snow around snow burrows of a Hazel Grouse
Isolines show density in g/cm3 (derived from E. Potapov, 1982). Figure B is a longitudinal section through a burrow, with the roost chamber to the left and the entrance to the right. Figure A is a transverse section, the entrance tunnel being normal to the image. In each case '0cm' indicates the snow surface, '40cm' snow depth. Distance along the horizontal axis of each drawing is not fixed. The isolines indicate the effect of the bird's movement during and after excavation in creating a stable platform on which to roost.

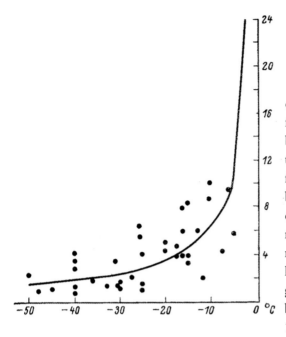

condenses as it passes through the cold, thick feathering of the nostrils and returns to the body, but the heat is lost to the burrow. The third heat source is the droppings excreted from the large intestine that are, of course, at body temperature. Excretion is more or less constant at about one dropping every 10–12 minutes (Potapov, 1982). (As a digression, this rate allows a good estimate of the time a bird has spent in a burrow or, for that matter, in any given place.) If the bird spends 22 hours in the burrow, the number of droppings will be 100–110, representing a significant heat input. The droppings are completely dry and form a solid heap beneath the tail of the resting bird. To an extent, the tail feathers isolate this source of heat, preventing some from reaching the burrow, but inevitably, some will be lost.

As a result of these heat sources the burrow air temperature remains more or less constant, perhaps fluctuating between -3°C (27°F) and -1°C (30°F). Maintenance of such a temperature is important, because the lower critical temperature of the bird's thermoneutral zone – i.e. when the expenditure of energy to support the body temperature is minimal – is -1.3°C (29.6°F) to -6.5°C (20.3°F) (West, 1972). Clearly, the higher the ambient air temperature, the less time the bird has to spend in the burrow (**Figure 22**), but during long occupations, a high burrow temperature reduces energy loss through thermoregulation. The bird also reduces energy loss because during its stay in the burrow it is practically motionless. However, there is one prominent energy expenditure requirement that cannot be avoided – the necessity to warm the daily ration of food from ambient air temperature to body temperature, a rise which could be from -40°C (-40°F) to +40°C (104°F). In rare cases, when the bird is in poor condition, or the temperature is very low and

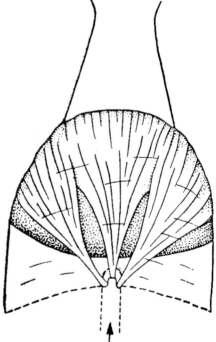

Figure 23. The position of muscular strands supporting the crop's surface
The arrow points to the end of fin of the breast's bone; the dots show the size of the full crop.

the snow layer inadequate to allow construction of a well-insulated burrow, the task of warming the food in the crop may be insoluble. This may explain the finding of dead birds with full crops in burrows after snow melt (Potapov, 2010).

It might, at first, be considered that a warmer burrow temperature would be beneficial for the bird, but if the temperature goes above 0°C (32°F), snow melt would occur, resulting in wet feathers and loss of insulation. To prevent this, if the bird senses a rise in temperature it will peck a small ventilation hole in the burrow roof so that the temperature falls again (Andreev, 1977b). Grouse also never make burrows during times of thaw, and should a thaw occur during occupation, the bird leaves immediately and roosts in a tree.

Each burrow is used once only, the bird constructing a new burrow after leaving to feed. When leaving its burrow, the bird thrusts its head through the snow roof to look for danger. If it considers that exiting is safe, it breaks through the burrow roof and, as it exits, excretes the viscous caecal droppings during its first steps. If a burrow is found without caecal droppings, then either the refuge was very temporary, or the bird left suddenly as a consequence of some threat (**Figure 24**).

The exact role of snow burrows as places of safety for the grouse is disputed. On occasions, fresh fox tracks can be seen close to a snow burrow, the bird not reacting to the approach and leaving the shelter later when the danger had passed. However, there are also instances when the tracks indicate that a predator located the grouse in the burrow by smell from a distance of several metres, calculated the position of the roosting bird and attempted capture (Semenow-Tianshansky, 1959). Evidence of successful hunts by fox, marten, sable and even wolf have been seen, and from this it would seem that success depends on the ability to smell the bird, which may be influenced by the experience of individual grouse in burrow construction. As far as avian predators are concerned, grouse burrows are without doubt protective, with reliable evidence from hunters suggesting that Black Grouse can avoid goshawk attacks by swiftly dropping to the snow and digging in.

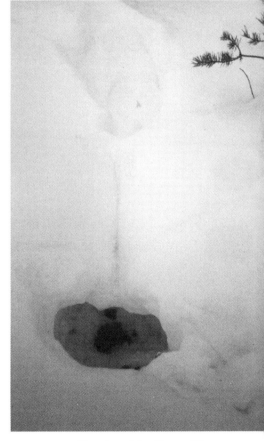

Figure 24. Grouse snow burrow
The droppings produced during occupation can be seen at the base of the roosting chamber. The bird has exited through the chamber roof. The line of the tunnel and tunnel entrance can be also be seen. The calm manner of the bird's exit from the burrow indicates an unhurried departure: the caecal droppings are just out of shot.

3.9 Reproduction

The ratio of the sexes in normal grouse populations is close to 1 to 1, but with a tendency for a bias towards males, though it needs to be kept in mind that males and females require different times to reach puberty. Although both male and female grouse reach maturity in their first spring, i.e. when they are 9–10 months old (Nemtzev *et al.*, 1973; Wiley, 1973; Kutovaya, 1976), in polygamous species the males do not, in general, mate at this age. In monogamous species they do mate, but not always successfully (Jenkins *et al.*, 1963; Wiley, 1974). In most cases young females also mate, but, as a rule, they start breeding 1–2 or even 3 weeks later than older females (Porat, Vohns, 1972; Potapov, 1985). The difference arises as a consequence of local conditions (weather, forage, etc) and of the hatch time of the younger females: those from early broods in the previous year are better able to breed in their first spring than females from later broods.

3.9a The role of the sexes

Reproduction in grouse is much as it is in phasianids. Most grouse species are polygamous (only *Bonasa bonasia, B. sewerzowi* and *Lagopus lagopus* are monogamous). The males of these monogamous species, as a rule, establish a nesting territory in which the female builds the nest and incubates the eggs. The male defends the territory and often takes an active part in rearing and defending the brood. Exceptionally, male *L. lagopus* may even help with incubation.

The polygamous species may be divided into two groups dependent on male behaviour. Males of the first group establish a personal lek place in which to fulfill their courtship displays and to mate with all the females they attract. This group comprises *B. umbellus,* the three *Falcipennis* species, two *Dendragapus* species, and the remaining two *Lagopus* species. Generally, females leave the lek after mating, nesting at a distance from it, though females nesting close to a lekking male has been described in *F. falcipennis*, and in the two polygamous *Lagopus* species, two or three females have been observed to nest within the male's territory.

Males of the second group use collective leks for their nuptial displays. In such collective leks each male has his own parcel of land in which he performs and in which he mates with any female he attracts. All species of *Centrocercus, Tetrao, Lyrurus* and *Tympanuchus* use collective leks. Interestingly, the two groups are defined by population density, which varies significantly (**Table 5**). Leks are traditional places where the males assemble in the spring, each male striving to achieve a position as close to the centre of the lek as possible, with success being dependent on the experience and strength of the male, each of which is age related. At any lek three groups of males can be observed. The first comprises fully sexually active birds with completely developed secondary-sexual characteristics (see below). The age of these males differs by species. In large grouse, such as capercaillie, black grouse or sage-grouse, they are 3–4 years old, with a maximum age

Table 5. Population Density by Species

Species	Density, individuals per 1000ha Average	Maximum	Place	Reference
Bonasa bonasia	110	230	Leningrad District	Potapov 1986
	160	488	Belorussia	Gavrin 1969b
	650	1200	Angara	Vladishevskiy, Shaparev, 1975
Bonasa umbellus	250.8	422	North Eastern USA	Bump et al. 1947
	350	702.5	Michigan	Robinson 1969
Falcipennis canadensis	231.7	386.1	Alaska	Palmer, Bennett 1963
Dendragapus fuliginosus	600	2550	Vancouver Island	Bergerud and Hemus 1975
Tetrao urogallus	79	290	Kola Peninsula	Semenov-Tianshanskiy 1959
	30	60	Leningrad District	Author data
	120	205	Kirov (Viatka) District	Romanov 1960
	187	232	North-Eastern Russia	Romanov 1979
Tetrao parvirostris	10-30	50	Kamchatka	Lobachev 1968 , Markov 1968
	15	83	Vitim and Stanovoy Mts	Benthen 1967, Izmailov and Pavlov 1975
Centrocercus urophasianus	119	192	Colorado	Johnsgard, 1973
	0.68		Washington State	Stinson et al. 2004.
Lagopus lagopus	33.9	64	Baraba, Siberia	Yurlov, 1960
	39	200	Kola Peninsula	Semenov-Tianshanskiy 1959
	180		Chroma-Indigirka Tundra	Perfiliev, 1975
	1159	2149	Bolshezemelskaya Tundra	Skrobov 1975
	100-140		Northern Taymir	Pavlov 1975
	300-400		Southern Taymir	Pavlov 1975
	24.3	82.6	Karelia	Ivanter 1974
		100	Finland	Rajala, 1966a, 1966b
	38	49	Leningrad District	Rodionov 1969
	57	120	Central Sweden	Recalculated from Aanes et al. 2002, Hörnell-Willebrand, 2005
		1612	Newfoundland	Mercer, MacGrath, 1963
Lagopus mutus	40-60	400	Kamchatka	Voronov 1968, Gizenko 1968
	25.8		North-Eastern Canada	Savile, 1951
Lagopus leucurus	20-103		Colorado: Mt. Evans	Braun et al. 1993
	45-135		Colorado: Rocky Mountain National Park	Braun et al. 1993
	670		Montana	Braun et al. 1993
	44-57		California	Braun et al. 1993
	31-66		California	Braun et al. 1993
Lyrurus tetrix	37	84	Baraba, Siberia	Yurlov, 1960
	7	30	Kola Peninsula	Semenov-Tianshanskiy 1959
	29±14		Estonia	Viht, 1974
	47	70	Kalinin District, Russia	Gibet, Voronov 1965
		170	Southern Karelia	Butiev et al. 1968
	134	286	Finland	Rajala, 1966a, 1966b
	20.5	120	Southern Karelia	Ivanter 1968
		1368	Guberlin Hills	Kirikov, 1975
	130-140		Switzerland	Pauli, 1974
Lyrurus mlokosiewizi	100		Teberda, Caucasus	Potapov 1986
Tympanuchus phasianellus	345		Alberta, Canada	Rippin, Boag 1974
Tympanuchus cupido	215		Illinois, Oklahoma	Jones, 1963
	147-191		Illinois, Oklahoma	Jones, 1963
Tympanuchus pallidicinctus	139-167		Oklahoma	Jones, 1963

of 5 years. In the other, smaller species they are 2–3 years old. This group occupies the top of the hierarchical stairs, staying close to the centre of the lek, each male defending its position from the constant attacks of neighbours. The females that visit the lek each morning firstly attempt to reach the centre and the males that occupy it, those males being responsible for most mating acts. The second group of males comprises younger or inexperienced birds, these occupying ground around the lek centre and, as a rule, having little mating success. The third group consists of yearling males taking part in the lek for the first time. In general, these males are completely ignored by females. The number of males in a lek depends strongly on population density: leks have been known to comprise hundreds of males (though, in general, such numbers are now a thing of the past), with some becoming so large that the lek splits into two or more smaller leks, each operating independently. In some species, e.g. black grouse and capercaillie, males will lek even if they are solitary – and in most cases successfully – because of low local population density: when the population density increases, collective leks reappear.

Males have secondary-sexual plumage characteristics connected with courtship displays, the males of most species showing richer colour, from the black neck patches of the *Bonasa* and *Falcipennis* species to the completely black feathering of the Caucasian Black Grouse. The males of some species have elongated feathers on the neck that create a brightly coloured collar during the lek, as in Ruffed Grouse. In the sage-grouse these elongated feathers are pennant-like and create an even more pronounced ruff. Differences between the sexes are especially prominent in the form, size and colour of the tail feathers because of the importance of the tail in nuptial performances. All male grouse raise their tails to a vertical position and strive for maximum opening during courtship displays. Because of this the tail feathers are longer and wider than those of females, or become sharp, or have the distinctly longer feathers in the central or side areas. In addition, there may be different forms of feather fans. The colour of the retrices may be completely black, or black with contrasting white marks, or with colour stripes across the feathers.

The naked skin patches, knobs, wattles, crests, large combs, etc, often brightly red-coloured, that are common in male phasianids are largely absent in grouse, almost certainly because populations inhabit northerly, cold areas. Only in some North American species are there naked skin patches, these being air sacs (of red, yellow-orange or even green-olive) situated at the sides of the neck that inflate during courtship displays. In general, only the combs above the eyes are well expressed in male grouse, but only during the breeding season. In winter, the comb size decreases, and it may also be covered by adjacent feathers.

Another prominent feature of leks, whether collective or comprising single birds, is sound – vocal or instrumental – made in an effort to attract females. As well as making various bubblings, poppings, barkings, cackles, hoots, whistles, etc, the males drum with their wings and feet, the sounds in some species being specific nuptial songs. Some of these sounds are quiet, audible over a distance of not more than 100m (109yd), but others are very loud, audible for up to 3.5km (2.2 miles) and sometimes over even longer distances. Further information on all the peculiarities of courtship display for individual species will be given later in the book.

3.9b Nesting

In their nesting, tetraonids reveal no essential differences from phasianids. The construction of the nest is very simple – just a shallow hole in the ground lined with a thin layer of dried grass, stems, leaves and feathers. The nest may be placed under the branches of a tree to disguise it from above, or between roots near the trunk. Very often, nests are made in open places, in longer grass or among tussocks. Occasionally, when the nest is placed in wet ground, the base is built up to create a low tower. Though the birds usually build their own nests, instances are known of grouse using the old nests of raptors or crows in trees, this having been noted in capercaillie, Hazel and Ruffed Grouse, all of which are forest dwellers. In all the observed cases of this behaviour, it was considered that the females had chosen elevated nests because of a high level of anxiety as a result of the proximity of people and dogs, or the danger of flooding. The fate of the chicks reared in such nests is known in only one case, in which they reached the ground safely: in the other known instances, the chicks left the nests unobserved. Instances of phasianids nesting in trees are very rare. Indeed, among all Galliformes tree nesting is only normal in the Cracidae family, though here the birds make their own nests rather than using old structures. Observations suggest female incubation behaviour in tree nests is no different from that of ground-nesting birds.

Clutch size in grouse is less than in phasianids, varying from 4–18 (usually 6–12), in comparison to the phasianid range of 6–22 (usually 12–17). This is not surprising when it is recalled that grouse females breed after a long winter survived with the help of a diet poor in the proteins essential for egg production. The weight of an entire grouse clutch reaches 43% of the weight of the female in rare cases: in phasianids, clutch weight is frequently 90% of female weight, and may even reach 100%. However, for those phasianids with a large body size that inhabit the upper forest, subalpine and alpine belts in high mountains, where the climate is cool or cold, clutch sizes are similar to those of grouse species. A good example is the Himalayan Snowcock (*Tetraogallus himalayensis*), an inhabitant of subalpine belts of high Asian mountains, in which the usual clutch size is 6–8 (Potapov, 1966).

In general, the female grouse produces, on average, about 2 eggs every 3 days. Incubation is 20–25 days, the actual time depending on the incubation intensity of the female, i.e. on the frequency of her feeding excursions or absences for other reasons. Old, experienced females tend to incubate 1–2 days shorter than younger birds. The incubation schedule is similar in all species, the female leaving the nest to feed 2–5 times each day and spending about 20 minutes away each time. Usually the female covers the clutch with dry leaves or grass when she leaves. Incubation begins after the laying of the last or penultimate egg, as a result of which hatching is more or less simultaneous and certainly completed in one day. After hatching, the female leads her brood away from the nest, to which the family never returns. The brood begins to break up after about 2.5–3 months. Young males leave first, young females usually preferring to remain with their mother for longer. In most species, the young, particularly lone young birds, form flocks in which they will stay throughout the winter. Usually males and females form separate flocks, particularly in spring, but the exact make-up of the flock depends on population density.

4. THE ORIGIN AND EVOLUTION OF THE GROUSE

Several information sources aid an exploration of the origins and evolution of grouse. First is the natural history of the species, their distribution, morphology, physiology, ecology and ethology. Second is an understanding of the climate, landscape, botany, etc in the Cenozoic period during which the earliest ancestors of the grouse appeared. Available from the paleontological record, such a study allows both an examination of fossil grouse, and morphological comparisons of recent and fossil species. Thirdly, cytogenetic studies of the relationships of living taxes, which have only been available during the last 20 years, allow species comparison at a genetic level. Though such comparisons have resulted in a plethora of papers, these have identified not only the great value of the methodology, but the caution that must be applied to the resulting data, some of which is contradictory and/or open to different interpretations. In this chapter, we explore each of these comparative tools in an attempt to piece together the history of grouse, a history that dates back several million years.

The Palaeontological Record

The characteristic features of grouse that distinguish them from other galliforms, as described in the species chapters, are the adaptations, directly or indirectly related to survival in the northern winter – adaptations that allow the birds to be year-round residents, with no recourse to migration. We believe it is clear that such a complex series of adaptations could appear and develop only in a climate with a winter combining low temperatures, short days/long nights and solid, stable snow cover, with forest (arboreal) vegetation to provide basal winter nutrition (Potapov, 1974; 1985; 1992). Such conditions were most clearly expressed at the time of global cooling that began at the end of the Oligocene epoch, about 25 million years ago. Before the cooling, the vegetation of Svalbard and Greenland, for example, was the 'Arcto-Tertiary flora', a mix of broad-leaved deciduous and coniferous forest (Christophovich, 1955; Tachtadjan, 1966; Budanzev, 1970, Boulterand Manum 1996, Birkenmajer and Zastawniak 2005, Uhl et al., 2007). Autumn leaf fall in these forests was the result of the long polar nights at high latitudes, not of low temperatures, the mid-year temperature of the Svalbard archipelago in the Miocene epoch being estimated as 5°C to 10°C (41°F–50°F) (Tolmachev, 1944), 8.4°C– 9.5°C (47°F–49°F) (Golovneva 2000) and 9.1°C–17°C (43°F–63°F) (Uhl et al., 2007) rather than the present -5.7°C to -6.4°C (21.7–20.4°F). The cooling was slow and non-uniform, with prolonged oscillations being superimposed on a gradual temperature decline.

The configuration of the northern hemisphere was different from that seen today. The Arctic Basin was more or less isolated from the Atlantic Ocean, completely isolated from the Pacific Ocean, and more oval, the long axis linking Canada and Svalbard through the North Pole. The overall temperature in the Arctic Ocean was exceptionally warm, reaching subtropical levels (Sluijs et al., 2006). The Canadian Arctic archipelago was a single land mass, linked to the Canadian mainland and Greenland, and much of the continental shelf of the basin was above the sea. The Atlantic Arctic sector was warmer than the Pacific sector. As the climate changed, the luxurious growth of the tropical and subtropical forests that cloaked the northern hemisphere altered, with heat-loving plants disappearing and cold-resistant plants (the 'Turgai flora') replacing them as the boreal forests that now characterize the taiga zone became established. The southern forest was still characterized by broad-leaved and coniferous trees that preferred a warmer climate (Tolmachev, 1954; Krischtofovich, 1955; Sinitzyn, 1962; Budanzev, 1970; Kojevnikov, 1996, Greenwood *et al.*, 2010), while to the north the cold-resistant deciduous (birches, willows, alders) and coniferous (pines, spruces, firs, larches) trees thrived (Vaskovsky, 1963; Budanzev, 1970). In addition to these changes at the Arctic fringe, there was equivalent change to the south, particularly in Central Asia where the Miocene's orogenic processes lifted forests to higher altitudes, reinforcing the influence of global cooling. As a result, the upper belts of mountain forest also saw heat-loving plants replaced by cold-resistant ones, resulting in a second centre of the taiga forest-type appearing in Central Asia (Tolmachev, 1954, Cronin, T. 2010).

At this time, it is now generally believed, ancestral grouse became established, though the exact time and place is still debated. The main source of information for this establishment is, of course, the fossils of ancient grouse, the earliest find to date of a tetraonid being *Tetrao rhodopensis Boev*, discovered in 1998 at Dorkovo, Bulgaria, which has been dated to about 4.5 million years ago (i.e. the early Pliocene/early Ruscinian epoch/ MN-14 – Boev, 1998 – see **Table 6**). This bird, a capercaillie, has been synonymized with the modern species, *Tetrao urogallus* from which it is '…inseparable' (Mlikovsky, 2002), although this view has to be considered doubtful, as such continuity of a modern species is unknown among avian species. However, fossils from the Pliocene also reveal bones with features similar across two genera (*Lagopus* and *Lyrurus*, or *Lyrurus* and *Tetrao* – Bochenski, 1991; Boev, 2002; Mlikovsky, 2002), possibly indicating that the divergence between these genera was not completed by the early Pliocene (Bochenski, 1991), although it might also be a result of hybridization, which is still occurring to this day.

In the Nearctic, there has been, to date, no find of a genuine tetraonid before the beginning of Pleistocene epoch. Indeed, there is little evidence of any vertebrate paleo-fauna from Holarctic forests because the wet forest soils are a poor preservation medium for fossil bones. There are fossils of other galliform birds dating from similar times from the Palearctic, but only a few from the Nearctic. Some of the latter, found in Miocene deposits, have been interpreted by several authors as tetraonids (*Archaeophasianus roberti, A. mioceanus, Tympanuchus stirtoni*, and *Palaeoalectoris incertus*), but since the 1980s serious doubts have been raised about these attributions (Olson, 1985). Moreover, it is believed that the morphology of the tarsi of *Tympanuchus stirtoni* is not grouse type, and that it may belong to a genus of Phasianidae or Odontopghorinae. It is also unclear why the

Table 6 The Earliest Data on Fossil Grouse

Species	Time (million years before present)	Place	Reference
Bonasa nini	1.0	N. Spain	Marco, 2009
Bonasa praebonasia	0.9	Poland	Bochenski, 1991
Falcipennis cf. canadensis	1.3–1.5	Rocky Mountains, USA	Emslie, 2004
Dendragapus cf. obscurus	1.2–1.5	Rocky Mountains, USA	Emslie, 2004
Dendragapus lucasi	0.3	Oregon, USA	Jehl, 1969
Dendragapus gilli	0.3	Oregon, USA	Brodkorb, 1964
Centrocercus urophasianus	1.2–1.5	Rocky Mountains, USA	Emslie, 2004
Tetrao rhodopensis[3]	4.5	Bulgaria	Boev, 2002
Lagopus sp.	4.2	Poland	Bochenski, 1991
	3.1–3.3	Bulgaria	Boev, 2002
L. lagopus atavus	3.2	Poland	Bochenski, 1991
L. leucurus	0.78	Rocky Mountains, USA	Emslie, 2004
Tetrao (Lyrurus) balcanicus[1]	2.5	Bulgaria	Boev, 1995
Lyrurus tetrix[2]	2.4	Bulgaria	Boev, 2002
Tympanuchus lulli	0.3	New Jersey, USA	Shufeldt, 1915

Notes:

[1] Described as *Lagopus balcanicus*, synonymized with *Tetrao tetrix* by Mlikowsky, 2002.

[2] *Tetrao tetrix* in Mlikowsky, 2002. Synonymized with *Lyrurus partium*, *Lyrurus tetrix longipes*, *Lagopus balcanicus*.

[3] Synonymized with *Tetrao urogallus* in Mlikowsky, 2002.

author of this view (Miller, 1944) did not compare the tarsus with other representatives of galliform birds found at the same site (O. Potapova, pers. com.). Additionally, it is clear that grouse are, primarily, birds adapted to a cold climate, and it is impossible to find any trace of such conditions in the early Miocene semitropical climate of Oregon and South Dakota where the fossils were discovered. There are also compelling reasons for assuming that the finds are fossil representatives of Cracidae (Johnsgard, 1973), galliform birds of tropical and subtropical forests. Reliable grouse fossils from North America date only from the Pleistocene, namely *Tympanuchus lulli Schufeldt, Palaeotetrix gilli Schufeldt* (*Dendragapus gilli* according to Jehl, 1969). *Dendragapus lucasi Schufeldt* (*D. nanus* described by Schufeldt) is not separable from *D. lucasi*, according to Jehl, 1969.

The latest Nearctic paleontological studies are very interesting, particularly the results from the Porcupine Cave, Colorado, USA, where the discovery of a North American grouse shifts the age of origin of some North American species to the beginning of Pleistocene, as they are the most ancient so far discovered. The age of the soil layers where the finds were made was determined as at least 780,000 years ago, and in some cases up to 1.3–1.5 million years (Emslie, 2004). This important finding confirms the early appearance of the group of Nearctic grouse characterized by the design of the inflatable parts of the neck (*Dendragapus, Centrocercus, Tympanuchus*). The unity of this group has been confirmed by molecular studies (Guttierez *et al.*, 2000: see also below), while the dating confirms the general scheme of inter-generic speciation proposed by Potapov (1985) without the need for any principal change apart from the time of divergence of the *Tympanuchus* branch from the general *Centrocercus* and *Dendragapus* stem.

But what can we say about the birds that were the ancestors of the first grouse? All the results of morphological, physiological and ecological analyses clearly show a phylogenetic connection with the Phasianidae family, mainly with the subfamily Perdicinae (Potapov, 1970; 1985). The oldest phasianids appeared in the Palearctic (France) during the Upper Eocene epoch, nearly 50 million years ago (Milne-Edwards, 1892; Mourer-Chauvire, 1992). In North America, phasianids appeared a little later, in the early Oligocene (Brodcorb, 1964), but were represented there only by species of the Odontophorinae, a specialized group of phasianids that inhabits only North and South America. No other representatives of the Phasianidae family have so far been found (Olson, 1985). The Odontophorinae (New World quails) are small, very specialized ground birds, and have never been considered as potential grouse ancestors. Because of this, it was recently suggested that grouse must have originated from turkeys (Drovetski, 2003; Pereira, Backer, 2006). This conclusion, based on chemical (cytogenetic) methods, makes no attempt to coordinate the sequencing results with paleontological data, comparative morphology and the adaptations to different natural conditions. For example, the authors did not link their results with the origin and development of the boreal forest belt. Turkeys and grouse are also dissimilar morphologically, the Meleagridae being strongly specialized terrestrial birds inhabiting an open forest landscape with no sign of adaptation to a cold climate. In addition, turkeys have many similarities to phasianids – low development of the caeca (the same as in Odontophorinae, Table 2) and the same proportions of the pelvis (Table 1). This is so clearly the case that 19th-century writers were already making the connection and placing turkeys in the Phasianidae family (Furbringer, 1888; Elliot, 1897).

To further disprove the idea that turkeys are the ancestors of grouse, it is enough to point out that the first appearance of these birds in the paleontology record is very early, in the lower Miocene, when the fossil Rhegminornis, dated to 16–20 million years ago, was found in Virginia. This fossil galliform had both pheasant- and turkey-like characteristics, which suggests that the Meleagridae originated from a pheasant-like (probably peafowl-like) ancestor of Asiatic origin that crossed the Beringian land-bridge, which was then isolated and evolved in the New World (Steadman, 1980; Olson, 1985).

We consider that there is no doubt that grouse originated from phasianids. As an example to support this contention, we note the plumage colouration during ontogenesis from nestling to adult male or female, data on which reflects the main stages of phylogenesis. In turn, the variability of colouration among all geographical forms of certain species demonstrates the same trends in colouration changes in recent species, dependent on specific environmental conditions. For example, the white colour of the adult Ruffed Grouse's throat can be considered as resulting from the retention of a colouration typical of ancestral grouse, and can also be seen in all Tympanachus species. The feature is found in the juvenile plumage of all grouse species, as well in other representatives of the Phasianoidea superfamily, including those in which a black throat patch appears in adult plumage. A black throat (gular) patch with white bordering (**Figure 25**) is well expressed in males of the subgenus *Tetrastes* and the genus *Falcipennis*, and traces are also present in Black Grouse (first adult plumage in the most primitive subspecies *Lyrurus tetrix viridanus*), in Sooty Grouse (*Dendragapus fuliginosus*), in both species of sage-grouse, and in both species of capercaillie. This black throat patch or its traces, in both Palearctic and Nearctic species, undoubtedly reflects a definite stage of colour development in grouse phylogeny. The throat patch, with other combinations of colour (rufous or white, with or without black bordering), or traces of throat patches are also present in the colouration of many species in different genera of the Phasianidae and Odonthophoridae families (*Alectoris, Coturnix, Exalfactoria, Tetraogallus, Cyrtonix, Lophortyx* and some others), and even in Megapodiidae (*Leipoa ocellata*). These data lead us to suppose that the white throat-patch was an ancestral characteristic of all these species (Potapov, 1983).

In support of our contention on the origins of grouse, we note the work of T.M. Crowe and co-authors (Crowe *et al.*, 2006a, 2006b) on the phylogenetics of, biogeography and classification of, and character evolution in, all groups of the order Galliformes, based on a study of 158 species representing all suprageneric galliform taxa and 65 genera. Data from the most important studies published in the last 50 years were also taken into account. The general result of this work is the taxonomical arrangement of Galliforme genera that confirms the current position, differing mainly by the inclusion of the partridges (genus *Perdix*) into the subfamily Meleagrinae on the basis of molecular data, despite this being a sharp contradiction to morphological, paleontological and biogeographical data.

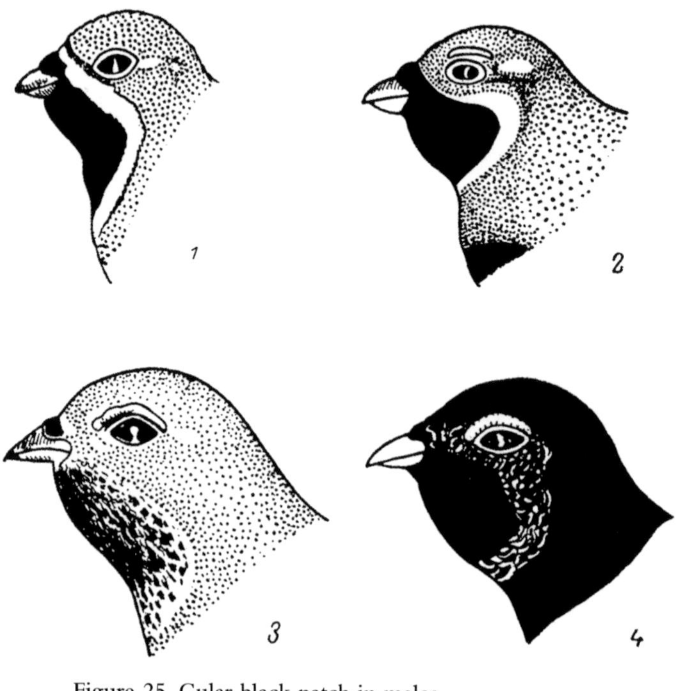

Figure 25. Gular black patch in males
1 – Bonasa bonasia; *2* – Falcipennis falcipennis; *3* – Dendragapus fuliginosus; *4* – Lyrurus tetrix viridanus, sub-adult.

Genetics

During the last 20 years, many investigations of bird phylogeny have appeared based on molecular phylogenetic studies (mitochondrial DNA sequences) and many publications based on the cladistic results of such studies have been produced, including some for Galliforme species (Ellsworth *et al.*, 1996; Luccini *et al.*, 2001; Dimichev *et al.*, 2002, etc).

However, these publications demonstrate some discrepancies between the results derived by genetical methods and data based on paleoenvironmental and paleontological evidence (Boev, 2002). At present, genetical studies suggest caution in the application of the mtDNA analysis in the evolutionary reconstruction of species, noting that the mtDNA is 'far from neutrally evolving and certainly not clock-like' (Galtier *et al.*, 2009) and 'that mtDNA evolves under both direct and indirect natural selection of mitochondria' (Ballard and Whitlock, 2004). Zink and Barrowclough (2007) also stress that the mitochondrial loci are generally a more sensitive indicator of population structure, since they have four times shorter coalescence times than that of nuclear genes, making the mtDNA-based methods more suitable for population studies than evolutionary analysis. Blind application of the mtDNA analysis to evolution might generate discrepancies, with the results generated by conventional systematics as well as to other mtDNA analyses approaches. This is not unexpected, as the genetical methods are relatively new and different sample sizes sometimes produce contradictory results. In **Figure 26** we give examples of two such studies that have resulted in different trees, placing the species in different clades. Both studies use similar taxa as an outgroup but, as can be seen, place, for example, *Dendrogapus canadensis* and *D. obscurus*, as well as *L. leucurus*, in different clades. Given that, in general,

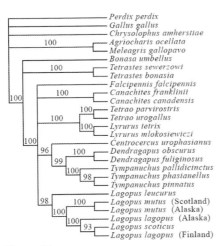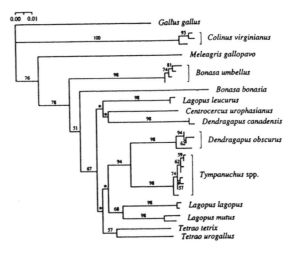

Figure 26

In genetical studies, different sample sizes may produce different results. Here we illustrate consensus trees depicting phylogenetic relationships based on (a) 500 bootstrap samples from the five complete mitochondrial genes (Gutiérrez et al., 2000) and (b) 609 nucleotides of the mitochondrial cytochrome-b gene (Ellsworth et al., 1996).

newer studies are very clearly dating older work on short timescales, we do not review the numerous genetical studies of Tetraonids here, believing that at present genetical methods cannot replace the traditional, well-developed methodology of morphological, ecological and behavioural research that we have used in this book. A good example of incorporating all the evidence is given in the work of Crowe *et al.* (2006a, b).

However, despite this decision, we have no doubt that, once matured, these new methods of study will provide new insights regarding the systematic position of certain groups. In particular, the techniques may be very useful in studies of micro-evolutional processes.

The Evolution of Grouse: A Hypothetical Structure

In considering the evolution of the grouse species, it is important to note that the adaptations for survival in severe northern winter are expressed to a practically equal degree in all family members, despite the different environmental conditions of their present habitats. This must mean that all modern genera and species of grouse originated from one ancestral form in which the whole complex of adaptations developed prior to dispersion. Evolution of the adaptations must have proceeded slowly, in step with the gradual climate cooling, the appearance of winter snow cover, and the transformation of forest vegetation. As the ancestral form spread north, it faced a lengthening of winter nights.

The appearance and first stages of evolution of ancestral grouse must have taken place long before the time of the first grouse fossils, as these already show the presence of different lineages of grouse, i.e. the intensive process of adaptive radiation was underway by the date of the oldest fossil (4.5 million years ago). We consider the ancestral grouse must have appeared by no later than 7 million years ago, in the Upper Miocene, when boreal forests covered huge areas of Eurasia and North America from (at least) 40°N up to the northern limits of land. We consider it probable that the first stages of this evolutionary process occurred mainly in deciduous forests, such as those now favored by Ruffed and Hazel Grouse, and the monophyletic origin of the grouse from a common ancestor is, we contend, indisputable at the present time.

It is well known that long-term preservation of animal bones in forest soil is impossible and it is difficult to find fossils on the continental shelf beneath the sea. But it is possible to find fossil bones in southerly parts of the forest zone in places where mountains, or the activity of predators, or other reasons allow preservation of skeletal remains transformed into fossils in caves or similar niches. It is from such places that numerous fossils of ancient galliform birds and the first true phasianids have been collected. The latter are of exceptional importance, as we believe the phasianids are ancestors of the Tetraonidae family.

The earliest phasianids to date were found in Eocene-Oligocene deposits in France (*Paraortyx* and *Pirortyx* spp.). Many of these partridges have also been described from other parts of Europe, from Oligocene to Pleistocene deposits, and most have been synonymized with *Coturnix gallica*, *Miogallus altus* and *Alectoris donnezani* (Mlikowsky, 2002). Several extinct species of *Alectoris* have also been described from the early and late Miocene, together with *Alectoris graeca* (from the Pleistocene) and *Perdix perdix* (from the late Pliocene), with which all extinct forms of Grey Partridge were synonymized (Mlikowsky, 2002). Besides the partridges, some extinct species of pheasants, gallinae birds, the enigmatic *Paraortygoides messelensis* (Mayr, 2000) and even peacocks have been described. Such abundance of different extinct forms of phasianids, together with the earliest appearance of Tetraonidae, is in sharp contrast with the position in North America, where the oldest fossil grouse appeared no earlier than the early Pleistocene (Emslie, 2004).

Our contention is that the ancestor of grouse was one of the lineages of phasianids, inhabiting the forested and semi-forested areas of central and northern Asia, Europe and North America in the Miocene[1]. By the Miocene-Pliocene, this forest zone almost entirely surrounded the Arctic Basin, the only major interruption being the north Atlantic (Sinitzyn, 1962): North America and Eurasia were connected, at least from the Eocene, by the wide land bridge of Beringia. Because of this continuity of forest, it is not possible to identify where, precisely, the ancestral grouse first appeared.

However, we contend that it is most likely that the ancestral grouse appeared in Eurasia. The biodiversity of Eurasia was rich, offering considerable scope for new forms. The same was also true of the Nearctic, of course, but in terms of land area, Eurasia is twice the size. In addition, inherited features of the birds' morphology that have no functional significance (and so were not influenced by natural selection and have therefore been preserved with little or no change) allow them to be used as phylogenetic markers. Tarsi scalation is one such. In grouse, tarsi scalation is strictly monotypical (**Figure 27**) and is

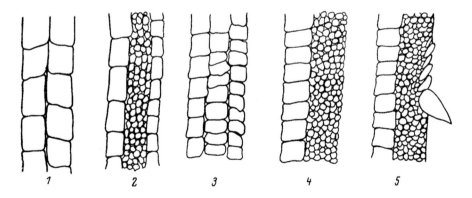

Figure 27. Types of tarsi scalation in grouse and phasianid birds
1 – Coturnix, Exalfactoria, Perdicula, Cryptoplectron, Trtopicoperdis; 2–3 Odontophorinae (all), Ammoperdix, Francolinus, Pternistes, Lobiophasis, Perdix, Synoicus, Bambusicola, Ithaginis, Crossoptilon, Gennaeus, Lophura, Phasianus, Gallus, Pucrasia, Catreus; 4 – Tetraonidae (all); 5 – Lerwa, Tetraogallus, Alectoris, Tetraophasis, Arborophila. Transitional between 4 and 5 are Tragopan (part) and Lophophorus.

[1]Drovetski (2003) erroneously claimed that Potapov (1985) dated the origin of grouse as Eocene. In fact, the Eocene was given as the date of origin of the ancestral phasianids (Potapov, 1985, p.107).

similar to that of several genera of the Perdicinae subfamily – *Lerwa, Alectoris, Tetraogallus, Tetraophasis, Arborophila, Tragopan* and *Lophophorus*. Most of these birds are inhabitants of Asian mountains, including high mountain forests, with a number having some grouse-like features, such as partly feathered tarsi (*Lerwa, Tetraophasis*) or nostrils (*Tragopan, Lophophorus*). However, there is no similarity with the tarsus scalation of turkeys or New World quails. There are also similarities between grouse and Eurasian mountain phasianid morphology and even with Cracidae birds (**Figures 28, 29 and 30**), but all these have strongly adaptive significance, parallel development being obvious.

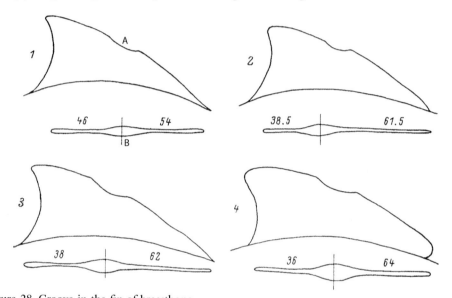

Figure 28. Groove in the fin of breastbone
The groove (A) in the fin of the breast bone and its form (B) in plan: 1 – Bonasa umbellus; 2 – Bonasa bonasia; 3 – Tetrao urogallus; 4 – Crax alector. The distance from the ends of the fin to the centre of the groove is given in cm.

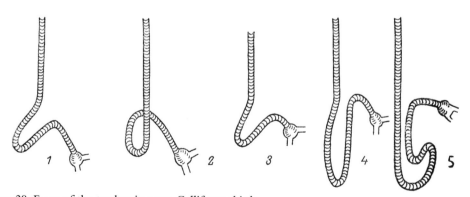

Figure 29. Form of the trachea in some Galliforme birds
1 – Tetrao urogallus; 2 – Tetrao parvirostris; 3 – Ortalis canicollis; 4 – Penelope superciliaris; 5 – Mitu mitu. 4 and 5 are from Taibel, 1976.

Figure 30. The sharpness of outer primaries (Nos 7–10) in some Galliforme birds
1 – Penelope superciliaris; 2 – Aburria carunculata; 3 – Pipile jacutinga; 4 – Chamaepetes goudoti; 5 – Falcipennis falcipennis.

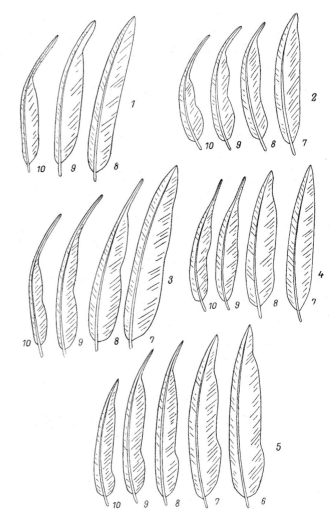

Such considerations, together with the diversity of fossil tetraonid birds, the history of appearance and distribution of its main habitats and the modern picture of grouse distribution, we maintain, support the contention that grouse originated in Eurasia. A scheme of the origin, dispersal and speciation of grouse, based on these considerations, was set down by Potapov (1985), but as this publication was in Russian only, it was not readily available to ornithologists in other countries. Since that work, important paleontological finds and new methodologies have appeared which, in general, support the scheme and offer the possibility of defining more exactly some of the details concerning the time and place of evolutionary events.

But regardless of the exact location in which that first ancestral grouse appeared, its descendants had time enough (from the end of the Miocene) to disperse within the boreal zone across both continents both east to west and vice versa.

There is no doubt that despite its continuity, conditions in these vast boreal forests (from Western Europe to eastern North America) were not homogenous. Ancient populations of ancestral grouse must therefore have evolved differently long before the final separation of the continental forest zones, with populations occupying different habitats within the boreal forest in accordance with adaptive radiation. However, it must be borne in mind that the major impetus to grouse evolution was adaptation to different winter forage. The first ancestral grouse inhabited deciduous or mixed forest types, as the Hazel and Ruffed Grouse do now, both being adapted to the use the catkins, buds and twigs of deciduous trees as the main source of winter food. The clear genetic similarity of all three species suggests the distribution of an ancestral form on both continents when forest zones were connected, mainly in the southern zone where deciduous trees dominated. We believe that the distributional range of the ancestral *Bonasa* was the oldest among the Tetraonidae, the antiquity of the genus being confirmed by the partially feathered tarsi, there being no basis for considering this feature to be the result of a reduction of tarsi feathering.

We believe the ancestral **Bonasa** form occupied territories close to the shores of the northern Pacific, mainly in river valleys cloaked with deciduous or mixed forest. A forested Beringia, linking the Palearctic and Nearctic, existed for much of the Miocene and Pliocene, disappearing only at the beginning of the Pleistocene when global cooling moved the northern limits of the taiga zone far south on both sides of the Pacific Ocean. The link between the Asiatic and North America boreal forest zones was lost and never remade, two branches of *Bonasa* ancestor being separated and developing independently.

In the Palearctic, the ancestral *Bonasa* was distributed widely through the boreal forest from the Pacific to the Atlantic. It penetrated north to Central Asian mountains with its taiga-forest types, where it evolved to a new species, Severtzov's Hazel Grouse. The connection of Central Asia's mountain forests with the solid Eurasian taiga zone may have ceased several times during cold and warm epochs of the Pleistocene. It is therefore difficult to estimate the age of this new species, but we consider it probable that it is the youngest grouse species (Potapov, 1985; 2005). Its colouration and morphology are very similar to the Hazel Grouse, with only the absence of winter pectinations and toe feathers distinguishing it from not only this species but from all other grouse species. Severtzov's Hazel Grouse also preserves some ancestral features because of its small distributional range and the more stable natural conditions peculiar to the mountain forests. By contrast to the Palearctic birds, the history of the Ruffed Grouse appears much simpler, though the size of its range during the Pleistocene may have changed significantly.

It is interesting to note the absence in Ruffed Grouse of the black gular patch, or any trace of it, despite it being so pronounced in many grouse species. The white Ruffed Grouse throat is a primitive colouration, still preserved in the juvenile plumage of all grouse and, in some cases, in the summer plumage of adults (for example, Black Grouse males). Moreover, among Hazel Grouse, individuals occasionally appear with aberrant colouration (grey-brown), a uniform pattern of cross-cut, thin blackish-ochre stripes and only one bright colour spot – the white throat. Such specimens were collected in different regions in northern European Russia, and have even been described as a new species, *Bonasa griseiventris* (Menzbier, 1895). Despite the sporadic appearance of these specimens, all those collected are absolutely similar in size and colour. This enigmatic Hazel Grouse seems to be a relic of the ancestral form, preserved in the genotype.

Further evolution of ancestral grouse stock was canalized by the search for new sources of winter food, particularly the needles of coniferous trees. Supplies of this forage were unlimited in both mixed or (and especially) pure coniferous forests and were assimilated by some ancient populations as a step in grouse evolution: two new forms of ancestral, needle-eating grouse appeared and were distributed widely through the belt of coniferous forests from Europe to Alaska. Based on the appearance of these first, specialized species of this evolutionary branch, the capercaillies, 4.5 million years ago, the branch could not have appeared later than the end of the Miocene, 5–7 million years ago. It is evident that the western and eastern representatives of this evolutionary branch developed independently, the western being adapted to a more southerly, drier form of forest belt – the pine forests. Later, during the Pliocene, this proto-urogallus form distributed slowly east where pine forests formed the southern border of the taiga zone. At the same time, ancestral larches appeared in the boreal forests. Originating from Central Asian mountain forests, the larches began to spread during the Pliocene-Pleistocene (Bobrov, 1972, Tarasov *et al.*, 2007) becoming especially numerous in the most continental areas of northern Asia, particularly in eastern Siberia. Dating from when the permafrost layer appeared here, ancestral larch, with the ability to grow in soils above permafrost, created a new form of forest – larch taiga – that spread across east Siberia and north-eastern Asia, replacing all other types of forest from the tundra to the steppe zones. The larch forest stopped the further distribution of ancestral capercaillie eastward: larch trees drop their needles in winter and so could not provide the birds with food. However, there is little doubt that during the early stages of development of the larch forest, ancestral capercaillie were familiar with the tree and fed on its needles in the autumn. The vast areas of larch forest then reactivated the process of natural selection and a new form of capercaillie evolved, the ancestor of the Black-billed Capercaillie, which expanded its range eastwards, reaching the Kamchatka Peninsula before the connection between the mainland and peninsular forests was broken 65,000 years ago. The differences between the Kamchatka subspecies and continental forms, and its close similarity with *T. urogallus*, indicate a relic character result from the very long isolation of the peninsula's population – an excellent example of long, complete isolation resulting in the preservation of ancestral features. Treeless tundra prevented the birds from reaching the Beringian land bridge and, hence, the Nearctic (Potapov, 1985), but the way of life of the two capercaillie species in the mountains is very similar to that of blue grouse: sedentary in all seasons (excluding some specific situations) and analogous displacements of populations, descending the mountain in summer and ascending in winter. There is also obvious similarity in colouration between Black-billed Capercaillie and Franklin's Spruce Grouse, while the gular patch of androgenic capercaillie females is very similar to blue grouse females.

The evolution of the second branch of needle-eating grouse, the **spruce grouse**, was more complicated, but details of both distribution and ecology, together with paleontological history, allow us to reconstruct a scenario. The ancestral form of this branch was adapted to winter feeding on spruce and fir needles in mountain forests of Miocene Beringia, occupying the same habitats along the shores of both sides of the Pacific Ocean. The ancestor of the Asian

Spruce Grouse spread south and had time to reach Sakhalin Island before it was separated from the mainland in the mid-Pleistocene. Further distribution southwards was prevented by warmer forests dominated by deciduous trees in which both spruce and fir were absent, while distribution westward was stopped by the appearance and rapid distribution of a new forest type – larch taiga – in which the main winter food of the birds, needles, was absent, larch being deciduous. The ancestor of the American spruce grouse spread south along the ridges of the Rocky Mountains to the Great Basin. Later, this ancestral form dispersed eastwards to the lowland forest belt where it evolved to the Canadian Spruce Grouse.

During the long period of dispersal to the south along the Rocky Mountains, a new form of grouse appeared, one adapted to winter feeding on the needles of the different firs that formed sparser forests during the warmer climatic conditions of the Pliocene in comparison to that of the Pleistocene. The main advantage of this new habitat was the presence of numerous clearings. Here a completely new morphological structure evolved – an inflatable oesophagus and elastic skin on the neck apteria of males that allowed inflation during courtship displays, forming two bubbles at the sides of the neck: the appearance of such large parts of naked skin in the cold climatic conditions previously inhabited by all grouse forms had been unlikely. The new form, ancestral to the genus of **blue grouse**, may have appeared in the late Miocene or early Pliocene, at approximately the same time the ancestral form of *Tetrao* appeared in western Eurasia. Though more adapted to an open landscape than the spruce grouse, blue grouse never lost the connection with coniferous forests, returning to them during the winter.

It is possible to hypothesize that two ancestral forms of **prairie-chickens** and **sage-grouse** also diverged from the ancestral blue grouse at an early stage of its evolution. The ancestor of prairie-chickens spread eastward to lowlands with arboreal vegetation, both deciduous and evergreen trees and bushes: such landscapes – open areas, grass-covered or with pine-oak, grassy woodland – existed in the eastern foothills of southern parts of the Rocky Mountains (Nebraska) at that time (MacGinitie, 1962), with true prairies appearing only at the beginning of Pleistocene (Leopold, Denton, 1987). The ancestral form of the sage-grouse reached the southern limits of the mountain forest, where it found a habitat that was completely new to grouse – sagebrush thickets set either below the forest margin or between areas of coniferous parkland, an ecological subzone in which competitors were minimal or absent, and pressure from raptors also minimal. Sagebrush offered the birds excellent shelter and unlimited food at all times. Specialization to this new food source was undoubtedly forced by this absence of a need to change diet in different seasons. The ability of the grouse digestive system to adapt to cope with unusual diets then allowed ancestral sage-grouse to develop a gut that could digest a food source rich in alkaloids, a richness that made sagebrush unavailable as forage to most animals. Increasing body size developed in response to a terrestrial way of life, while the decrease in the need for flight allowed flight structures to be adapted to courtship displays. As the displays evolved, male mobility decreased further, with attractive details in morphology and behaviour compensating for the loss of ability to perform attractive flights, jumps, etc. It must be taken in mind that the strongly developed lek system favors natural selection's process of increasing the body size of rivals.

The presence of the inflatable cervical sacs in blue grouse, sage-grouse and prairie-chickens, and the presence of similar morphological features in the representatives of these genera and of spruce grouse (such as the colouration of the hybrids), allows us to postulate that they all originate from an ancestral stem that differs from those of both *Bonasa* and *Lagopus*. That is, of course, a hypothetical scenario, but is consistent with there being Pleistocene representatives of the *Falcipennis*, *Dendragapus* and *Centrocercus* genera in the Rocky Mountains (Porcupine Cave, Colorado – Emslie, 2004). Zwickel, Bendell (2004) have also come to the same conclusion. It is interesting to note that in some molecular phylogenetic studies the group of North American genera (*Dendragapus*, *Centrocercus*, *Tympanuchus*) was obviously differentiated in general cladistic schemes (Ellsworth *et al*., 1996; Gutierrez *et al*., 2000; Luccini *et al*., 2001).

The paleontological history of the last two genera, the **ptarmigan** and black grouse, is, despite the availability of many fossil remains, not yet clear, particularly for the ptarmigan. The earliest ptarmigan fossils appear during the first half of the Pliocene epoch (4.2 million years ago) in central Europe (Bochenski, 1991). From the beginning of the Pleistocene, the number of such fossils increases rapidly, but again in Europe. Only during the later Pleistocene are fossils found elsewhere, and these are all very much younger – about 55,000–60,000 years bp (north-west Siberia, lower Irtysh River), 70,000 years bp (Altai Mountains, Yenisei River) and 50,000 years bp in north-eastern Asia (Kolyma Basin). Most of the fossils are of the Willow Ptarmigan, with the Rock Ptarmigan appearing significantly later, about 330,000 years bp and again in Europe (France, Mourer-Chauvire, 1975). From that time the species is found in many paleontological sites together with Willow Ptarmigan fossils. The first finding of representatives of *Lagopus* in North America were made in the Rocky Mountains and dated to 780,000bp (Emslie, 2004). The fossil was *L*. cf. *leucurus*, i.e. it was closest to the modern White-tailed Ptarmigan, a species which shows both deep specialization (the completely white winter feathering) and relict peculiarities such as the presence of rudimentary horny pectinations between the thick feathering of the toes, the pattern and colouration of the spring-summer breast feathers (which are similar to those of spruce grouse) and the evidently relict small distributional range. These features suggest the White-tailed Ptarmigan is a very ancient species. The positioning of the two oldest sites of the early *Lagopus* evolution at opposite ends of a huge, and practically uninterrupted, range seriously hampers any attempt to reconstruct the genus' evolutionary history, with links between them having either been destroyed by the numerous Pleistocene glaciations, or yet to be discovered. Nevertheless, the data we do have allow us to postulate a possible ptarmigan evolution scenario.

We consider that the ancestral ptarmigan was a mountain species, the ancestors of the Willow Ptarmigan descending from the mountains to the lowlands when forests disappeared from large areas of the Palaearctic during the glacial periods of the Pleistocene, which saw the creation of the 'tundra-steppe zone' that stretched from the Atlantic coast of Europe eastward to Alaska, an area now occupied by tundra, forest and steppe zones. Within this zone, the ancestral ptarmigan adapted to an existence in an open, bush-thicket but treeless landscape, with a severe winter season of permanent winds that created areas of snow-free, frozen ground. The dominance of these conditions allowed the ancestral form to spread across the entire Arctic, while the adaptations allowed the birds to utilize the food resources of an area where they were free from avian competition, the only other residents competing for food being vegetarian mammals. Within the zone, some birds would have preferred upland habitats, where food resources were scarcer but predators less numerous, while others preferred the lowlands, trading richer food resources for greater numbers of predators. The division formed the basis for the evolution of the Rock and Willow Ptarmigans.

The landscape forms of the zone in which the ancestral ptarmigans developed offered abundant food in the form of different grasses, moss and thickets of low bushes (willows, dwarf birch, etc), which were available as the wind scoured the ground free of snow, leaving the vegetation available for feeding. That the snow cover of the zone was, in the main, minimal is illustrated by the fact that the area was inhabited by herds of large mammals – mammoth, bison, horse, reindeer, etc – whose size precluded them from continuous occupation of an area of deep snow. But the thin or absent snow cover also meant that the ancestral grouse had no opportunity to excavate snow burrows for roosting, with natural selection resulting in better feathering of the feet, including the toes, while the role of horny pectinations was minimal or absent. The birds also accumulated reserves of fat, mainly in the under skin deposits and around internal organs. There is good evidence that ancient ptarmigan of Western Europe were heavier, though much the same size: weights calculated from the thickness of fossil tarsometatarsuses, which are larger, are 700–800g, a weight now seen in birds occupying the northern parts of the range (Svalbard, Taimyr) and in the forest-steppe zone of central Siberia.

A later warming episode locked a population that would evolve into the White-tailed Ptarmigan in an isolated area of tops and ridges in the Rocky Mountains. Interestingly, the last, Holocene, stage of the evolution of modern ptarmigan species was characterized by a rapid decrease in the ranges of both the Willow and Rock Ptarmigans. The species disappeared from most of Europe, with a large number of island and isolated mountain populations forming, this being a particular characteristic of Rock Ptarmigan. In theory, such isolated forms, especially if they are in very different natural zones, may give rise to new species in the remote future.

The ancestors of the **black grouse** developed from populations that inhabited the edges of the western Palearctic forest zone, and were probably closely related to the ancestral ptarmigan stock. The earliest black grouse fossils date from the Pliocene–Pleistocene boundary, i.e. 1.2–2.4 million years ago in the same southern part of central Europe as relatives of Willow Ptarmigan. By the mid-Pleistocene, ancestral black grouse were widely distributed throughout Europe and east to the Ural Mountains. One extinct form, *Lyrurus partium*, has been described from a site in the Carpathian Mountains and dated to the Early Pleistocene (Kretzoi, 1962). It was similar to *L. tetrix*, but smaller. *L. tetrix* is known from the Middle Pleisticene in France (extinct subspecies *L. tetrix longipes* dated to 550,000bp, Mourer-Chauvire, 1975). Another species, the Caucasian Black Grouse (*L. mlokosiewiczi*), appeared in the Caucasus no later than 350,000bp (Potapov, 1978; Pospelova *et al.*, 2001). The optimal habitats of the modern species are assumed to be as they were for these ancestral birds, i.e. forest-steppe dominated by birches and a subalpine belt above the timberline (also usually dominated by birches) for the Black Grouse, and the subalpine belt above the timberline for the Caucasian Black Grouse.

It must be noted that the conclusions stated here, based mainly on morphological and paleontological data, differ from the previously published scenarios (Potapov, 1985) only by an earlier divergence process as a consequence of new fossil evidence[2]. Because of scarce paleontological data regarding the first stages of divergence, it is, of course, possible to speculate on other grouse evolutionary paths, at least from the end of the Miocene. Hopefully this lack of a complete picture of grouse evolution is temporary, and that new paleontological finds will support our view or point to a different path.

[2]It is hard to use recent publications based on cladistic results of molecular phylogeny studies (Ellsworth *et al.*, 1996; Luccini *et al.*, 2001; Dimichev *et al.*, 2002) because of the absence of any connection between the results and data on the paleoenvironment, fossil finds, morphology, and because of significant disagreements between them and known paleontological data (Boev, 2002).

CHAPTER 2

Genus 1: *Bonasa* RUFFED AND HAZEL GROUSE

The genus *Bonasa* (Stephens, 1819) unites three species, the Ruffed Grouse (*Bonasa umbellus*) in the Nearctic, and the Hazel Grouse (*Bonasa bonasia*) and Severtzov's Grouse (*Bonasa sewerzowi*) in the Palearctic. All three are forest birds, with comparatively long tails and a crest on the head formed from a bunch of elongated feathers (which are less prominent in females). The principal difference of the genus from other tetraonids is the incomplete feathering of the tarsi, only the upper part being covered (**Figure 31**) except in very rare exceptions. *Bonasa sewerzowi* has digits with neither horny pectinations nor feathers in winter, the only example of this in the tetraonids (**Figure 32**).

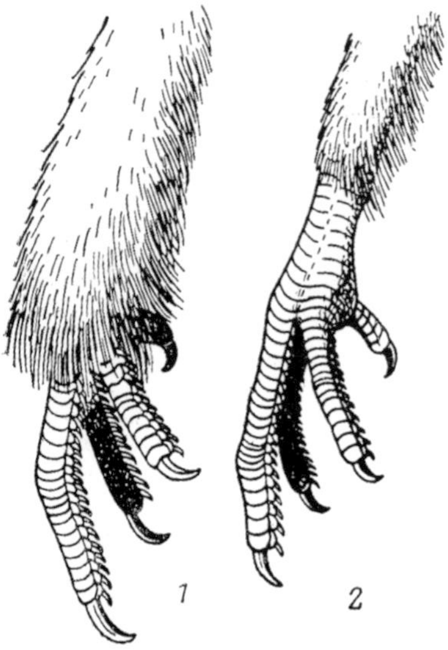

The plumage is predominantly mottled brown and grey. Sexual dimorphism in both colour and size is slight. Males are distinguished from females mainly by the colour of the head and neck. The dimensions of all three species are similar, with extreme values overlapping. The top of the wing is rounded: the longest primary feather is the 7th. Wing loading in Ruffed Grouse (male) is 0.98g/cm² (Poole, 1938), and in Hazel Grouse (N=10, males and females) it is 0.84–1.18g/cm² (Potapov, 1985). This wing construction is adapted primarily for quick, vertical flight, not for long distances: the maximum observed flight for a

Figure 31. Feathered tarsi of *Bonasa bonasia*
1 – in winter, 2 – in summer.

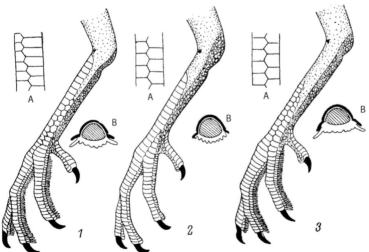

Figure 32. Tarsi scalation and feathering
(A) Tarsi scalation and feathering in Bonasa *species, and cross-sections through the middle toe (B) showing the development of the horny pectinations in winter in 1 –* Bonasa umbellus*; 2 –* Bonasa sewerzowi*; 3 –* Bonasa bonasia.

Ruffed Grouse is little more than 1km (0.6 mile) (Bump *et al.*, 1947). Because of this, all *Bonasa* species avoid open areas, spending their entire lives in forest cover. The form and colour of the tail is very similar in all species (**Figure 33**), the length being maximal in Ruffed Grouse males – up to 40% of body length, in comparison to 31–32% in Hazel Grouse.

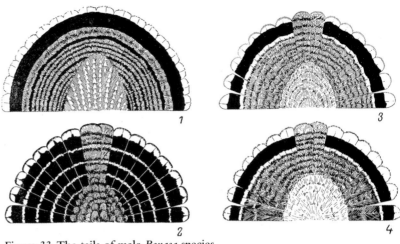

Figure 33. The tails of male *Bonasa* species
1 – Bonasa umbellus; 2 – Bonasa sewerzowi; 3, 4 – Bonasa bonasia (variations).

The colour of Palearctic males is very similar, differing from that of the Nearctic species mainly by the presence of a black guttural patch with white bordering, while in the Ruffed Grouse male the chin and ventral part of the neck are whitish. Male Ruffed Grouse also have bunches of brightly coloured, elongated feathers on both sides of the neck ('ruffs'). During courtship displays the ruffs are raised to form a brilliant standing collar beneath the head. Other differences between the Palearctic and Nearctic species are mainly in courtship displays.

The colouration of the three species shows the closer relationship between the two Palearctic species than between them and the Ruffed Grouse. As a consequence, the genus was originally divided into two subgenus (Potapov, 1985) on the basis of early designations – Ruffed Grouse (*Bonasa*: Stephens, 1819) and Hazel-Severtzov's Grouse (*Tetrastes*: Keyzerling and Blausius, 1840). The different levels of divergence were confirmed by later works, including studies of molecular phylogeny (Gutiérrez *et al.*, 2000; Luccini *et al.*, 2001).

All but two of the paleontological finds of *Bonasa* grouse are from Pleistocene deposits within the borders of the present distributional area of the species, the exceptions being the find of *Bonasa umbellus* in Florida in mid-Pleistocene layers (Brodkorb, 1959) and a find in the Pyrénées from the early Plesitocene (Marco, 2009). The earliest *Bonasa* find is from Early Pleistocene deposits dating back 1.25 million years (Bochenski, 1984; Mlikowsky, 1995), in the Carpathian basin, a find which we believe confirms the conclusion regarding the time of dispersal of the ancestral form and its split into two branches, Palearctic and Nearctic, as occurring before the Pleistocene (Potapov, 1985). Today the three species occupy vast territories with very different climatic conditions, from super-cold winters (the Kolyma and Yukon basins) to the warmer climates of Western Europe and the eastern states of the USA.

1.1 RUFFED GROUSE Subgenus: Bonasa (Stephens, 1819)

Stephens in Shaw, 1819: 298. Monotypical subgenus

1.1.1 *Bonasa (Bonasa) umbellus* (Linnaeus, 1766)

Attagen pennsylvaniae (Brisson, 1760): 214 (non-valid); *Tetrao umbellus* (Linnaeus, 1766): 275 (Pennsylvania, USA); *Bonasa umbellus* (Stephens in Shaw, 1819): 300; *Tetrao (Bonasa) umbellus* (Bonaparte, 1830): 389.

Sedentary forest bird, middle-sized, with slightly elongated tail and mottled colour, with strongly expressed individual and geographic variability.

Colouration

Adult male
General colour of upper body varies from red-brown to brown-grey, with dense, length-wise pattern of white or light-yellow streaks and patches. Length-wise bar stripes of different shapes and width in feathers of the nape, back, scapulars and, especially, lesser coverts have a more complicated cross-stripe pattern. These stripes are especially wide on the outer row of scapulars, forming the wide white strip in the folded wing. Feathers of the lower back, rump and uppertail coverts have oval patches in central part of feather tops, and dense narrow stripes. Patches on uppertail coverts are heart-shaped. Two bunches of elongated feathers on each side of the neck ('ruffs') of different colour – black or dark-red, with a metal-violet or greenish tint. In a vertical position these feathers form a bright collar during courtship displays. Underbody has a rough, cross-striped pattern, apart from the whitish throat, which is surrounded by small, mottled feathers. Upper breast looks dark because of a narrow cross-belt of black feathers with white terminal stripes. Tail has grey or brown background with a cross-banded pattern from blackish and light stripes with vermiculated strokes, with a wide black stripe at the top under a narrow, whitish terminal one (see Figure 33). Primaries are brown with wide, whitish cross-stripes on outer vanes. Secondaries have same colour, but on the outer ones the cross, whitish bands are hardly visible.

Male Ruffed Grouse

Female Ruffed Grouse

Adult female
As in the adult male, the main distinctions being small size of ruff feathers (half the size) and absence of a cross-belt on breast. Central pair of tail feathers differs from the others, having the same colouration as the uppertail coverts (this also occasionally seen in males, Bump *et al.*, 1947).

Male and female in first adult plumage
Differs from adults only by the colour of the two outer primaries, in which outer webs are heavily mottled with yellow-red speckles.

Juvenile
Very similar to juvenile Hazel Grouse (see below), but upper body has lengthwise, narrow stripes along quills of all feathers. Cross-stripes on tail feathers expressed more clearly. Colour of ruff feathers is more primitive, brown-blackish with red-brown tops. Sometimes there are two brown spots at feather tops, typical of colour of juvenile feathers in all grouse.

Downy chick
Upper parts of head, back and scapulars are brown–red, darker at the back, with blackish marks and a black spot on forehead. Sides of head and neck are yellow-brown with only one black stripe behind the eye (**Figure 34**). All underbody parts are pale yellow. Tarsi covered by feathers to one-third of length.

Figure 34. Head pattern of downy young Ruffed Grouse

Specific features of the colouration
Despite the large geographic variability of colour that exists in the different subspecies, there are two different colour morphs – grey and red. These are present in most populations at all times, but in different proportions. Several important studies have revealed that the proportion of specimens with differing colourations in every population depends on the severity of the previous winter: snowy winters favour 'grey' birds, and these are also longer lived (Gullion, Marshall. 1968). In an analogous study during 1963–1965 and

Male Ruffed Grouse with grey-phased plumage

2001–2002, the estimated annual survival rate is higher for grey-phased birds than for red-phased birds (Gutierrez *et al.*, 2003), i.e. the existence of the two colour morphs (dichromatism) is supported by natural selection and shows the influence of discrete climatic situations on the colouration.

Dimensions

From measurements on a total of 307 males and 151 females (Bump *et al.*, 1974), the dimensions of the birds – males, with females in brackets – are: wing length 171–196mm (165–190mm); tail 129–174mm (120–159mm); bill 24.4–31.0mm (23.5–29.3mm); tarsi 38.3–48.2mm (38.8–45.5mm); middle toe 32.4–42.2mm (31.2–39.9mm). The bill was measured from the edge of the feathering to the end of the upper mandible.

As with other grouse, adult weight fluctuates during the year. It is maximal in the autumn (November): male 660g (23.3oz), female 585g (20.6oz). Minimal weight of males is in spring (end of March, before the beginning of the intensive lek (620g/21.8oz) and at the end of August, after the intensive moult). Females have minimal weight in March, after the winter season (520g/18oz), and in June, after incubation (495g/17.5oz). The maximum weight observed for a male is 840g (29.6oz) (Bump *et al.*, 1947).

Distribution

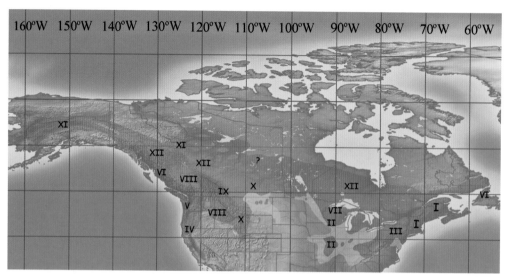

Map 1. Ruffed Grouse (*Bonasa umbellus*)
Sub-species: I – B. u. umbellus; II – B. u. mediana; III – B. u. monticola; IV – B. u. sabini; V – B. u. castanea; VI – B. u. brunnescens; VII – B. u. togata; VIII – B. u. affinis; IX – B. u. phaia; X – B. u. incana; XI – B. u. yukonensis; XII – B. u. umbelloides.
The yellow sections indicate areas from which the species has disappeared during the last 100 years.

The borders of the Ruffed Grouse range are still not well-established – see main distribution maps (Bump *et al.*, 1947; Aldrich, 1963; Johnsgard, 1973; Alsop, 2002; Rusch *et al.*, 2002). The range includes the islands of Prince Edward, Cape Breton, Nantucket and Martha's Vineyard: Ruffed Grouse were acclimatized successfully on Anticosti Island in 1911 (Bump *et al.*, 1947) and in Newfoundland in 1956 (Bergerud, 1963). The southern range border is particularly sinuous because here the disappearance of the species during the last 100 years has been most marked.

The range was much larger 100–120 years ago, the most significant decrease being in the south because of human activity. The main areas of decline were in Indiana and Illinois, between the Appalachian Mountains and the Mississippi Valley, and in Montana. Ruffed Grouse were extirpated completely in Kansas (1910), Nebraska and Colorado. Isolated parts of the range also appeared, e.g. the Black Hills in South Dakota, and in Missouri. However, Ruffed Grouse were successfully introduced to the Ruby Mountains of north-east Nevada (McColm, 1970).

Subspecies

The range includes areas with very different natural conditions, both climatic and vegetation. The sedentary mode of life, the long time for population adaptation to local environments, and other obstacles that impeded genetic changes between local populations have resulted in the appearance of many local populations that differ significantly, primarily by colouration, although the differences are highly detailed and no specific information is given here. As a result, we now have the 12 subspecies listed below. With rare exceptions these subspecies are easily distinguished and have descriptions that date from Linnaeus' time to 1943, when four new subspecies were described (Aldrich, Friedmann, 1943). It is important to add that despite the differences in colour of subspecies, most of them have, as mentioned above, two colour morphs, grey and red.

The list below follows that of Aldrich and Friedmann, 1943. The distribution of subspecies is shown in Map 1.

Ruffed Grouse vary in colour from rufous to brown-grey. This grey female was photographed in the Adirondack Mountains, New York.

Bonasa umbellus umbellus (Linnaeus, 1766)
Found in the states of Massachusetts, Rhode Island, New York, Connecticut, New Jersey, eastern Pennsylvania, mainly in broad-leaved deciduous forests.

B. u. monticola (Todd, 1940)
Distributed between lakes Michigan and Gouron, around Lake Erie and in the Appalachian woods, mainly in mixed forests with a prevalence of pines, apple, beech and hemlocks.

B. u. mediana (Todd, 1940)
Formerly distributed from the Appalachian foothills in the east to the Great Lakes to the north, and Missouri to the west, where it populated 'oak-savannah'. Now remains only as small isolated populations in eastern Missouri, southern Indiana, Wisconsin and north-eastern Minnesota, where it populates forests in which oaks and hickory dominate.

B. u. sabini (Douglas, 1829)
Occupies a narrow territory along the coasts of the Pacific Ocean from 50°N to Hamilton Bay and the Salmon River (USA). Populates lower slopes of mountain forests and along streams, with alder, maple and willows.

B. u. castanea (Aldricht and Friedmann, 1943)
Inhabits a highly restricted area on the Olympic Peninsula and the immediate vicinity of the shores of Puget Sound, western Washington. Main habitat is the wet portion of Western Red Cedar–Western Hemlock Association.

B. u. brunnescens (Conover, 1935)
Occupies Vancouver Island, British Columbia and the adjoining mainland from the vicinity of Vancouver at least to Malaspina Inlet near Lund. Habitat is subclimax woodland (alder, willow and maple communities of the Western Red Cedar-Red Hemlock Association).

B. u. togata (Linnaeus, 1766)
Occupies northern New England and Nova Scotia westward across southern Quebec and southern Ontario to central northern Minnesota, south to north-eastern Massachusetts (Manchester), east-central New York, south-eastern Ontario (Toronto), midway down the Lower Peninsula of Michigan (Midland County) and northern Wisconsin (Ashland County). Inhabits subclimax deciduous woodland (birch and aspen communities) of the White Pine-Hemlock-Sugar Maple Association.

B. u. affinis (Aldrich and Friedmann, 1943)
Ranges from Klamath and Harney, Oregon, northward – east of the Cascades, excluding the mountains of north-eastern Oregon, south-eastern and north-eastern Washington – through the interior of British Columbia to Hazelton. Habitat is subclimax deciduous woodlands (alder, aspen, poplar, birch and willow communities) of the montane and lower subalpine forests.

B. u. phaia (Aldrich and Friedmann, 1943)
Ranges from the western slopes of the Rocky Mountains in Idaho, west to south-eastern and north-eastern Washington and to north-eastern Oregon (the Blue Mountains). Inhabits subclimax deciduous woodlands (aspen and willow communities).

B. u. umbelloides (Douglas, 1829). Synonym: *B. u. canescens* (Todd, 1940)
Occupies north-western British Columbia (Atlin) southward along the eastern slopes of the Rocky Mountains to east-central Idaho and north-western Wyoming; extends eastward through the aspen parkland and spruce-fir forest of the prairie provinces of Canada north to middle Manitoba (Oxford House) and south to south-western Ontario (Lake of the Woods), across Ontario between Lake Superior and James Bay, and across Quebec to the north shore of the Gulf of St Lawrence. Habitat is subclimax deciduous woodland (aspen, poplar and willow communities) of the Rocky Mountain subalpine forest and the northern coniferous forest (White Spruce–Balsam Fir Association).

B. u. incana (Aldrich and Friedmann, 1943)

Ranges from west-central and north-central Utah, south-eastern Idaho and west-central Wyoming, north-eastward across Wyoming and the Dakotas to south-western North Dakota (Walhalla) wherever suitable habitat occurs in this predominantly grassland area. Habitat is subclimax deciduous woodland and thickets (cottonwood, aspen, and willow communities), chiefly of Rocky Mountain montane forest, and to some extent in similar subclimax deciduous communities in the lower fringe of the Rocky Mountain subalpine forest (Engelmann Spruce–Alpine Fir Association).

B. u. yukonensis (Grinnell, 1916)

Occupies western Alaska (Akiak and Nulato) eastward across Alaska, chiefly in the valleys of the Yukon and Kuskokwim rivers, and across Yukon from Selkirk and the Lewes River Valley, north to La Pierre House, east at least to the Great Slave Lake, Mackenzie, and Lake Athabasca, Alberta; extends southward along Liard River, at least to Liard, Mackenzie, and along the Athabasca River to Fort McMurray, Alberta. Perhaps from further east in the Hudsonian life zone of northern Manitoba (Brochet and York Factory). Inhabits subclimax deciduous woodlands (willow, aspen, poplar and birch communities) chiefly in White Spruce–Lodgepole Pine and Black Spruce–American Larch Associations.

Habitats

The large range of the Ruffed Grouse is the result of its adaptation to very different types of forests, due to differing climatic conditions, from the Pacific to the Atlantic, e.g. from average ambient temperatures in January and July in Alaska (-25°C/-13°F, +12°C/53°F) to those in Arkansas (+5°C/41°F, +25°C/77°F). The forest types vary from temperate coniferous rainforest to semi-arid deciduous, and from subarctic deciduous woodland communities with willows, aspens, poplars and birches among White Spruce–Lodgepole Pine and Black Spruce–American Larch Associations in Alaska, to broad-leaf deciduous in Pennsylvania or to the deciduous forests of the southern limit of the continental taiga zone, where oaks and hickory prevail. In all cases, Ruffed Grouse prefer forests where only certain types of deciduous trees grow: aspens, poplars, birches, willow, aspens, apples, hickory and hemlocks. Of these, Aspen (*Populus tremuloides*) is the most important. This is especially obvious at the northern limit of the bird's distribution, where it populates only narrow riverside deciduous forests. Deciduous trees provide the main winter food – catkins, buds and the tips of twigs. In the southern range, mixed forests with heavy shrub understory and scattered clearings are more suitable than pure deciduous forest (Edminster, 1947; Dorney, 1959).

Studies of radio-tracked females during a winter in Quebec, Canada, showed that they preferred mixed softwood/hardwood stands more than 17m (56ft) tall and 60–120 years old, with mid-story and lower-story coniferous cover (Blanchette *et al.*, 2007). The study of survival of Ruffed Grouse in different types of the forests in Minnesota showed that males survive best in hardwood stands devoid of conifers: the presence of spruce and balsam fir does not significantly detract from grouse longevity, but survival declines if the density of mature pines increases (Gullion, Marshall, 1968).

Population structure and density

The ratio between the sexes in spring is close to 1:1. Sometimes about half the birds of a population are under one year old (Eng, 1959). The proportion of young to adult birds changes constantly, depending on the success of breeding in the current year, and in different seasons because of the distinct levels of mortality in birds of different ages. The population density therefore varies within considerable limits depending upon natural conditions, seasons and favorable or unfavorable years. For example, in New York State, the breeding density varied from 3.2–8.9ha (8–22 acres) per bird near Ithaca, and from 8.5–15.4ha (21–38 acres) per bird in the Adirondacks. Maximum autumn densities varied here from 2–8ha (5–20 acres) per bird in various years (Bump et al., 1947). There is some evidence that Ruffed Grouse have a fairly synchronous 10-year population cycle at local, regional and continental levels over most of range, with the exception of the eastern United States and New Brunswick. The peak-year autumn densities ranged from 123–180 birds/sq mile in Michigan, to 353 birds/sq mile in Minnesota. The average ratio between the densities of peak years and depression years varies from 3:1 to 15:1, and in 12 cases as 8:1 (Keith, 1963), but this has not been confirmed by the studies in Minnesota during 11 subsequent years (Gullion, Marshall, 1968).

Territoriality

Ruffed Grouse are one of the most sedentary tetraonids. There has never been collection of a marked bird more than 19.3km (12 miles) from the place of marking. Broods spend the entire time from hatching to dispersion within a radius of 0.6km (0.4 mile). During dispersion, more than half of all juvenile birds cover a distance of 1.6–12km (1–7.5 miles) (Chambers, Sharp, 1958), i.e. the mobility of Ruffed Grouse is maximal in the autumn and minimal in other seasons, especially in winter. Hale, Dorney (1963) concluded that females were more mobile than males, except during the winter.

Nutrition

The main winter food is catkins, buds and twigs of deciduous trees and understory plants, among the most important, besides aspens, being several species of birch, together with willow, apple, cherry, hop hornbeam and blueberry. However, the composition strongly depends on local vegetation and climate severity and therefore differs in different areas. In Minnesota, for example, two species of aspens (*Populus tremuloides* and *P. grandidentata*) are the most important winter food, catkins being available to the bird as long as snow is on the ground (Gullion, 1969). At the same time, in Utah, chokecherry (*Prunus virginiana*) is one of the preferred winter foods, together with aspen and maple (Phillips, 1967). In Maine, winter food is mainly the buds of aspen, buds and leaves of willow, catkins and buds of hazel, and the buds of wild cherry and apple (Brown, 1946). In Alberta, where the winter is severe, 80% of the diet consists of buds and twigs of aspen and willow (Doerr *et al.*, 1974).

In spring, nutrition becomes more varied, but the main winter food remains important until May (New York State, Edminster, 1947). Other foods include the open flower buds of aspens, buds and leaves of willows and other shrubs, and the leaves of strawberries, etc. In summer, different berries began to dominate (strawberries, raspberries, blueberries, cherries and others). This diet dominates in the first half of the autumn, but the buds and catkins of trees are also taken from the beginning of August.

Insects comprise the main diet of chicks (at least 70%) during their first two weeks, but the quota decreases to 30% during the third and fourth weeks, and to only 5% by the end of July. Among the insects, ants of different species dominate, but many other insects – beetles, grasshoppers, caterpillars, etc – are also taken. As the chick diet changes, young grass leaves are taken first, then different kinds of berries, and later buds and catkins of shrubs and trees. By September, the diets of adult and young birds are identical (Bump *et al.*, 1947). Insects are never prominent in the diet of adult birds, even during the moult, and rarely exceed 10% of food intake.

The character of the autumn nutrition is transitional between summer and winter, with a gradual decrease in diversity. Berries and insects disappear first, followed by differing kinds of greenery. At the same time, the fruits of thorn apples, dogwoods, grapes, roses, etc are taken if available (Edminster, 1954). The analysis of 1,005 crop contents collected during autumn and winter in large territories of south-eastern states from Wisconsin to Maine indicated that evergreen leaves were the most common, rather than buds, twigs and catkins, in northern states. Metabolizable energy appears adequate in the north and south-east of the range, but low levels of protein and high levels of tannins may result in poorer quality winter diets along the south-eastern edge of the species range (Servello, Kirkpatrick, 1987).

Wintering

Winter life has not, as yet, been greatly studied, but because of the difference in winter climate between the northern and southern parts of the range it must differ markedly. During cold, snowy winters the birds have the same life as other northern grouse, i.e. they spend most of the time in snow burrows, with very little time foraging in the mornings and evenings. In Alberta, the birds leave their snow burrows for feeding before sunrise and after a short time (16.4 minutes on average) finish feeding and dig a new snow burrow, their crop sufficiently full to last the whole day. The bird comes out from the snow burrow again for the evening forage only after sunset and feeds for longer, 24.4 minutes on average (Doerr *et al.*, 1974). In northern Minnesota at the end of January, the volume of the full crop of a grouse just before nightfall was 105–111cm³, with a weight of 98–99g (3.46–3.49oz): to fill the crop completely required 16.5 minutes (Svoboda, Gullion, 1972).

Breeding

Ruffed Grouse are polygamous. The territorial structure of the population during the breeding season consists of a system of strips, each occupied by a solitary male who goes through his courtship displays to attract females and mate. The strips are dispersed within the forest in small groups, the grouping apparently indicating the aspiration of young males to have strips close to those of older males. The main courtship display is 'drumming', the male standing in a special place (usually on a log) in a vertical position, and beating the wings ('wingbeat display') quickly to produce a drum-like trill (**Figure 35**). All trills consist of 38–51 wingbeats: 3–4 beats per second in the first 2–3 seconds, then quickening to 20 beats per second before slowing slightly. All trills last 10–12 seconds. The drumming is audible over a distance of 400–500m (437–547yd), sometimes even to 1km (0.6 mile). On average, the male's territory is 4ha (9.9 acres), with the central area, where drumming takes place, covering 2.26ha (5.58 acres) (Marshall, 1965; Archibald, 1975; Stoll *et al.*, 1979).

Figure 35. Male Ruffed Grouse drumming
Successive studies (1–6) of a single clap of a Ruffed Grouse male during its drumming. Arrows show the direction of wing and tail movement.

The breeding density in Minnesota is nearly 3.2–4ha (8–10 acres) per male, but in most cases it is 4–6 birds/40.5ha (100 acres) (Gullion, 1969). In Ohio, the density is 2–4 birds per 100 acres (Davis, 1968), with 4.5–5.3 birds/100 acres in Iowa, and 18 males per 1.6km(1 sq mile) (the equivalent of 2.8 birds/100 acres) in Indiana (Thurman, 1966). Sometimes several males (4–8) occupy sites in close proximity, forming 'activity clusters' (Gullion, 1967), similar to the collective display grounds of capercaillies and, sometimes, Blue Grouse and Asian Spruce Grouse. Young males select their drumming places during their first autumn or winter, but only 67% of them are successful in their first breeding attempt (Dorney, Kabat, 1960).

Successful males, of any age, perform the 'rush display' – a specific ritual before copulation. In the rush, the male's body is parallel to the ground, its wings slightly spread and dropped, and its tail and ruff erect and open (Hjorth, 1970). Copulation then occurs, and is over very quickly. The female may build her nest close to the centre of the male's territory, or at a distance of up to 1km (0.6 mile) (Allen, 1934). The male takes no part in brood care, though there are unconfirmed suggestions that on rare occasions, when the chicks have been in danger, the male turns up to repel an intruder. Occasionally, a male has also been seen to replace a killed hen in caring for the young (Forbush, 1927).

The nest is usually built at the base of a tree, or tree stump, or under logs or bushes. Nest sites are chosen to provide a combination of visibility, protection and escape route – and to satisfy an apparent desire for sunlight – in middle-aged, mixed forests with deciduous and conifer trees (Edminster, 1947). The number of eggs in the clutch averages 11.5, in renesting attempts only 7.5, with females producing one egg every 36 hours. An average egg is 39x29mm. Incubation begins only after the last egg is laid and takes 23–24

A distraught female Ruffed Grouse calls to her chicks on a road in Pennsylvania, USA

A brood of Ruffed Grouse chicks attempt to cross the road.

days. During incubation, the female usually leaves the nest twice per day to feed and is away for 20–40 minutes. During stormy weather, the female will remain on the nest for much longer (Bump *et al.*, 1947). Chicks can fly at 10–12 days.

The habitats preferred by broods are mixed and regenerated clear-cut stands of trees 1.5–7m (4.9–23ft) tall and 11–20 years old, close to roads and trails (Quebec, Canada; Giroux *et al.*, 2007). In such situations, meeting a brood crossing the road in front of your vehicle is not unusual. Broods begin to disintegrate, the juveniles dispersing, when the young are 12 or more weeks old.

Hunting, recreation and conservation

Ruffed Grouse are the most important and popular game bird in North America. Autumn hunting is legal in practically all states and provinces where there are breeding populations, the exceptions being states where the species has become very rare. In 1970, for example, Ruffed Grouse were hunted in 33 American states and 10 Canadian provinces, with hunters taking 3,700,000 birds (Johnsgard, 1973). In those states/provinces where hunting is legal, its intensity is regulated by limited the hunting season. The current situation is hard to estimate because of the absence of concrete data from across the range, with annual harvests in North America being estimated only in the early 1980s (Atwater, Schnell, 1989; Storch, 2000). Later information for the states of Michigan, Minnesota and Wisconsin suggests an annual total during a population peak of about 1 million birds in each state in the late 1990s, with 300,000 annually during population lows (Dessecker, Norman, Williamson, 2006). From other information, it appears that Ruffed Grouse are one of the main terrestrial game birds across North America.

1.2 HAZEL GROUSE Subgenus: *Tetrastes* (Keyserling and Blausius, 1840)

109, 200. Type species: *Tetrao bonasia* Linnaeus, 1758. Monotypical subgenus.

The subgenus unites two species of Palearctic grouses, similar in morphology and ecology. Males of both species have a white-bordered gular spot, and shorter tail and tarsi than the Ruffed Grouse. Both species are middle-sized, forest, sedentary birds with a mottled brown-grey colour.

1.2.1 Severtzov's Hazel Grouse *Bonasa (Tetrastes) sewerzowi* (Przewalsky, 1876)

Tetrastes severzowi, Przewalsky, 1876:130. The name Severtzov's Hazel Grouse is now accepted throughout Europe, replacing Chinese Hazel and Black-breasted Hazel Grouse, which are no longer considered correct.

Sedentary forest birds inhabiting the mountain forests of central China. The only tetraonid without horny pectinations or toe feathers during winter.

Colouration

Adult male

Upper parts are, in general, olive-grey or olive-brown with transverse, interrupted black and grey stripes, wider on the back. Crown is muddy-reddish-brown with blackish spots. Forehead and nostril feathers are black. Ear coverts and post-oculars are white. Wings are dark-brown, with narrow brown-yellow transverse stripes on outer webs of primaries and same coloured tips and fringes on secondaries. Upper wing coverts as the back, but more mottled. Scapulars have whitish quill stripes. Lower body is whitish, with a reddish tinge on flanks and breast, and is covered by wide, transverse, blackish bands on breast; these are narrower on belly. Large, black, gular spot with a white border beginning in middle of forehead. Tail, which spreads fan-like during displays, differs from other species of the genus (see **Figure 33**), the feathers being black with white tips and narrow transverse white stripes (numbering 5 to 7), with only the central pair being coloured as the rump.

Male Severtzov's Hazel Grouse

Female Severtzov's Hazel Grouse

Female Severtzov's Hazel Grouse

Adult female
Similar to Hazel Grouse (see p. 81), the main difference being the colour of retrices, which are as male, but with a reddish-brown crown, darker breast, and more intense development of the transverse striping on lower parts of breast and belly. The white colour of underground is less prominent.

Male and female in first adult plumage
Main difference from adult is presence in the outer web of the 9th primary of not less than six white cross-stripes. Such stripes are absent at the 10th primary.

Juvenile
As Hazel Grouse (see below), but feathers of upper part of breast have two white cross-stripes instead of one.

Downy chick
Full description absent, but basically as Hazel Grouse, but the brown cap of crown is more expressed (Short, 1967) and black bordering of crown is absent.

Dimensions
Males (12, coll. ZIN RAN): wing length average 179mm (171–187mm); tail 127mm (117–140mm); bill 11.45mm (10.2–12.5mm); tarsi 36.7mm (36–37mm); middle toe 33.2mm (31–36mm).

Females (9, coll. ZIN RAN): wing length 173.1mm (166–181mm); tail 116.9mm (109–124mm); bill 10.9mm (9.5–11.7mm); tarsi 35.9mm (34.5–38mm); middle toe 31.6mm (31–33mm).

Weight: males during breeding season 309.9g±22.4g (10.9oz±0.7oz) (SD), n=24; during non-breeding season 341.2g±27.1g (12oz±1oz), n=16; females during egg laying and incubation 337.8g±26.4g (11.9oz±0.9oz), n=31; in non-breeding season 314.9g±20.7g (11.1oz±0.7oz), n=24 (Lianhuanshan Natural Reserve, Sun, Fang, 2010).

Moult

Moult sequences as for other grouse species, i.e. downy feathering, juvenile, first adult and final adult.

Distribution

The borders of the range are determined by the distribution of mountain boreal forests. The distance to the nearest border of the Hazel Grouse's range exceeds 1,100km (684 miles).

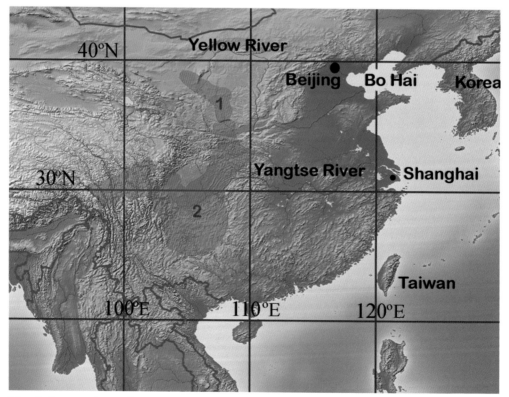

Map 2. Severtzov's Hazel Grouse *(Bonasa sewerzowi)*
Subspecies: 1 – B. s. sewerzowi; *2 –* B. s.secunda

Subspecies

At present, only two subspecies have been described:

Bonasa (Tetrastes) sewerzowi sewerzovi (Przewalsky, 1876)
Occupies the northern part of the species range, southward to the Huang He (Yellow) River.

Bonasa (Tetrastes) sewerzowi secunda (Riley, 1925)
Occupies the southern part of the range. Differs from the previous form by colouration of the tail feathers, the black transverse bands being wider, and the white, narrow stripes between them thinner and numbering 5, against 6–7 in the nominative (Potapov, 1985). The general colour is also darker.

In the ornithological collection in the Zoological Institute of Russian Academy of Sciences there are two specimens of females collected at the eastern edge of the range (Mingo Province) whose colouration differs from other specimens by the absence of the red tinge to the head, and with yellowish, not white, spots on the breast, i.e. similar to the colouration of females of western subspecies of Hazel Grouse. The labels of both specimens are handwritten by P. Sushkin (who died in 1928) and indicate a new subspecies *T. s. berezowskii* (Sushkin). However, no description of this new subspecies was made and it is assumed that Sushkin had decided to collect additional material to support his opinion.

Habitats

The main habitats are narrow valleys along streams surrounded by dense willow bushes, with steep mountain slopes covered by thick coniferous and mixed forest. All habitats are situated at an altitude of 2,400–4,700m (7,874–15,420ft), i.e. in the middle and upper parts of mountain forest belts. All 103 nests found in Gansu were situated at elevations of 2,700–3,300m (8,858–10,827ft) (Sun *et al.*, 2007). In the northern sections of the range, the species prefers forests with junipers and birches. In the western section (Tibetan mountains), forests dominated by Tibetan juniper (*Sabina tibetica*) at an altitude of 4,300–4,700m (14,108–15,420ft) are preferred, particularly riparian habitats with dense scrub (willows) and small openings for feeding and dust-bathing. The species avoids forests dominated by oak and spruce at lower altitudes (Lu Xin, 1997).

Population structure and density

Believed to be strictly monogamous. The ratio of males to females is not equal, with males dominating. The structure of any local population is based on the plots of territorial males, which are maintained in winter (see below). There is little information on the number and density of populations. In one small part of the species range, the

Lianhuanshan Natural Reserve (LNR) in Gansu Province, the biology of this species was studied extensively during 1990–2010 (Sun, Fang, 1997, 2010). The population here was stable with a density of up to 15 territorial males/km², suggesting a total of nearly 30 adult birds/km², together with some vagrant males, whose number was difficult to count. The percentage of males in local populations is 64%, but 44% of them were non-breeding and non-territorial (vagrant) (Sun, Fang, 1997, 2010).

Studies of microsatellite DNA in one of the partly isolated populations in Lianhuashan Mountains (*B. s. secunda*) indicated that this population would not persist without immigration (Larsson *et al.*, 2003).

Behaviour

The birds have a remarkable absence of fear of humans, sometimes permitting a person to approach to within 2.5m (2.7yd) and, when put up, dexterously maneuvering through dense thickets, but never moving more than 50m (55yd) (Schafer, 1938). In summer, during the intensive moult, the birds dust-bath constantly (Lu Xin, 1997).

Nutrition

The close connection of the species with habitats where birches and willows dominate testifies to the importance of these trees for forage, mainly the buds, twigs and catkins, at least during the winter. This was confirmed by data obtained in LNR, where the buds and tender twigs of willows constituted 80% of the diet from December to March (Sun, Fang, 1997). Stresemann *et al.* (1938) indicated feeding on the berries of sea buckthorn (*Hippophae rhamnoides*), this being confirmed by later studies (Sun, Fang, 1997). In summer the birds use many different foods, particularly seeds of different plants, including *Polygonum sphaerostachyum* in eastern Tibet (Lu Xin, 1997).

Wintering

Adult males maintain their territories during winter, but also occasionally form flocks, mainly during foraging on the fruits of sea buckthorn, with up to 14 birds being seen together. Spruce and fir trees serve as escape cover for feeding birds, 81% of observations indicating that the birds were within 15m of such cover. Young males and females also form small flocks. Winter flocks dissolved in March and April (Sun, Fang, 1997). The weather of the species' Central Asian range is notable for limited precipitation in autumn and winter, as a consequence of which winter snow cover is not constant, with many snow-less patches, and the snow, where it lies, rarely reaching sufficient depth to allow burrow construction. The grouse therefore roost on the branches of fir or spruce, close to the trunk. The birds also rest in the middle of the day, taking a position on the snow, usually in sunny places. At the altitude of the birds' range, heat from the sun is usually sufficient to raise the ambient temperature above 0°C (32°F), even in midwinter (Potapov, 1966). This, and the fact that the day is longer in winter (relative to that of more northerly grouse) compensates for the inability to construct the thermal refuges that are so important to other grouse species.

Breeding

The breeding season begins at the beginning of May, the same time as the Hazel Grouse close to the Arctic Circle on Russia's Kola Peninsula. This late breeding at such low latitudes (30°–38°N) is due to the climate at altitudes above 2,600m (8,530ft) in the Central Asian mountains (Potapov, 1985).

Courtship displays are poorly studied and such studies that exist include a puzzle concerning the male's nuptial voice. N. Przewalsky, in his first description, mentioned males 'whistling' in the same manner as Hazel Grouse. As Przewalsky was an experienced hunter, it is hard to imagine he was mistaken, but no other study, even those using a special whistle designed to attract male Hazel Grouse, has ever confirmed the observation. Chinese ornithologists have mentioned quiet vocalizations uttered between male and female, or between males, but have never mentioned a whistle.

Most adult males have their own territory in which they perform demonstrative flights with pronounced loud wingbeats and flutter-jumps. The size of a territory varies from 1.3–3.2ha (3.2–7.9 acres), usually 2.1–2.7 ha (5.2–6.7 acres) (Sun, Fang, 1997; 2010). Flutter-jumps, which are accompanied by loud, bi-syllabic wingbeats because of separate starting and landing phases (Scherzinger et al., 2006), reach a height of 0.5m (1.6ft) and cover 2–3m

Male Severtzov's Hazel Grouse

(6.5–9.8ft). Similar bi-syllabic wingbeats are common to both Capercaillie species (Potapov, 1985). During the performance, the male may move from tree to ground, or vice versa. This behaviour is very similar to that of the spruce grouses. Peak flutter-jump activity occurs immediately after the male leaves its roost in early morning and lasts for more than two hours (usually 5.30 a.m.–8 a.m.). The noise from the wingbeats of jumping males produce an impressive morning concert (Sun, Fang, 1997), and the description of it suggests a similarity with the 'drumming' of Ruffed Grouse (see **Figure 35**). There are also clear similarities with the behaviour of Hazel Grouse in places of high population density (Potapov, 1985).

As well as flutter-jumping, the males also perform occasional noisy territorial flights between tree crowns. If territories are close, border conflicts arise. Males defend their territories in the autumn (October–November) as well, with combat between neighbouring males being observed (Klaus *et al.*, 2001). During such conflicts, the authors mention an aggressive noise uttered by the males, a 'guttural squeaking sequence', similar to the 'rumbling sounds' of Hazel Grouse.

After mating, females move away to prepare the nest. Nests are placed on steep slopes under rocks or at the trunk base of a large tree. Clutch size is 7–8, the size of an average egg being 44.4mm (42.0–49.3mm) x 30.7mm (29.9–32.0mm), the weight varying from 16.3g to 17.1g. Egg colour is a little darker and with a more pronounced red tinge than those of Hazel Grouse (N. Nan-Shan, Beick, 1927). In more southern parts of the range (LNR), the egg size was 42.9±0.1mm x 30.4±0.08mm (n=156). The incubation period is 27–29 days, during which females took 3–7 recesses daily of 19.3±7.2 minutes (Sun, Fang, 2010).

In the northern part of the range, at about 38°N, nests with the first eggs were found no earlier than 13 June and nests with hatched eggs no later than 2 July (Beick, 1927). A nestling no older than about four weeks was collected on 22 August in Central Nan-Shan (specimens in COLL ZIN RAN, i.e. it was hatched 25–26 July. A brood of four chicks was captured in late August in LNR (Sun, Fang, 1997).

It has been established by the use of tracked females that while males remain in their territories in summer, while females with broods left the nest areas and roamed over occasionally long distances. Broods dispersed in September over distances of up to 5km (3 miles) (Sun, Fang, 2010).

Hunting, recreation and conservation

There is no information regarding hunting, but if the birds are hunted at all, the take is small and does not threaten the population. Several state reserves in China, especially in mountain regions of the south (Lianhuashan and Baishuijiang in Gansu Province, and Juitzaigou in Sichuan Province), also aid conservation. However, the number and density of birds depends on the condition of mountain forests, and exploitation of these for timber has lead to local extirpation of the species.

1.2.2 HAZEL GROUSE *Bonasa (Tetrastes) bonasia* (Linnaeus, 1758)

Tetrao bonasia (Linnaeus, 1758): 160. *Tetrao canus* (Sparrman, 1786): Table.16 (specimen with atypical colour). *Bonasa bonasia* (Bonaparte, 1830): 390. *B. europaea* (Gould, 1839) (nom. nov. pro *Tetrao bonasia*). *Tetrastes bonasa* (Olphe-Galliard, 1886): 43. '*Bonasa canescens* (sic!) Sparrman' (Mensbier, 1895): 480.

Forest bird of medium size, with comparatively short wings, moderately long tail and mottled colour, with a prevalence of grey and dark-red tinges. Sexual dimorphism in colour is moderately expressed.

Morphology

Similar to that of Severtzov's Hazel Grouse, but with slightly shorter tail and tarsi.

Colouration

Adult male

Upper body is grey with a variable reddish tinge and crossed by thin, dark-brown, narrow stripes on head, neck and upper back forming a vermiculated pattern. All feathers of the upper parts have the same design, with alternating dark and light stripes. Black gular spot is prominent, as in Severtzov's Hazel Grouse, with the same surrounding white band with narrow black bordering, well expressed on forehead and both sides of the head. Two white patches are set behind the eyes. The elongated feathers of the crest are grey with black cross-stripes. White bands on both sides of the neck base go back and down to scapulars. The male can change the form and size of these white bands and patches during courtship displays by erecting different feathers. Underbody is more mottled, the pattern formed mainly by wide, white feather tips. Breast is darker, with narrow white stripes on feather tops. These white stripes become wider towards the tail, partially joining to form the belly colour of white with small dark patches. Primaries and secondaries are brown-grey with yellowish cross-stripes on outer webs, these practically disappearing in outer primaries. Two white bands on the folded wing are formed by the white tops of scapulars and secondaries. Tail feathers have light-grey and reddish-brown bands, with a wide black band at the top, bordered by a narrow, greyish-yellow upper stripe. Central pair (sometimes two pairs) has a strongly different colour, the same as the rump (see **Figure 33**).

Male Hazel Grouse

Female Hazel Grouse

Male Hazel Grouse

Male in the first adult plumage
Differs from adult by the pattern being more diffuse because of strongly expressed thin cross-bands, especially on outer primaries. In most cases, young males have 8–9 cross-bands on the 9th and 10th primaries (Stenman, Helminen, 1974).

Adult male in summer plumage
The main peculiarity of this plumage is the absence of white bordering on the black gular spot due to new, small, mottled feathers.

Adult female
More mottled than the male, and more monotonous in character, without the bright black or white spots. Gular spot is outlined only by numerous brown patches on a grey underground. Upper body is as the male, but with a rufous or brownish tinge.

Juvenile
Upper parts, from crown to scapulars, are mottled black and dark brown with a rufous-brown or dark-brown background. Back, rump and uppertail coverts are grey with vague brown cross-stripes. Under parts are paler, with a dark, mottled breast. Tail is grey-brown, central feather pair with rufous tinge. Primaries are grey with dark cross-stripes on outer webs.

Juvenile female Hazel Grouse, N.W. Russia

Downy chick

Upper parts are brown, sometimes with an ochre tinge. Forehead is yellow-rufous, sides of head and downy parts of the body grey-yellow, sometimes with an ochre tinge on the breast. The black stripes and spots on the head form a specific pattern (**Figure 36**). The brown crown cap on the crown, seen in Severtzov's Hazel Grouse and many other grouse species, is absent.

Hazel Grouse chick, N.E. Russia

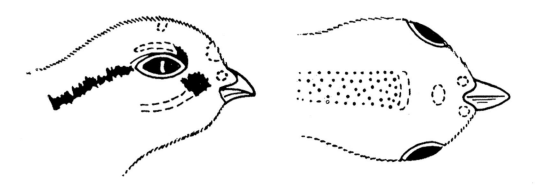

Figure 36. Head pattern of downy young Hazel Grouse
Dashed lines show the black stripes that are not present in all specimens. The dotted part shows area of brown colour.

Dimensions

Male (nominative subspecies): wing length 167.6mm (162.0–180.0mm); tail 113.5mm (104.0–122.0mm); bill 10.4mm (9.3–12.1mm); tarsi 33.5mm (28.0–36.0mm).
Female: wing length 166.6mm (162.0–171.0mm); tail 107.2mm (100.0–115mm); bill 10.9mm (10.0–12.3mm); tarsi 33.3mm (32.0–35.0mm).

Weight is maximal in the late autumn and minimal at the end of spring in males: in some cases, as in the Ruffed Grouse, the body weight of males rose again in March, up to 18%, when the first thaw appeared (Volkov, 1975). Females have minimal weight at chick hatching. In general, the weight of males is 317–580g (11.2–20.5oz), and of females 305.5–560g (10.8–19.8oz).

Moult

The plumage sequence is as for other grouse, i.e. downy, juvenile, first adult, first summer adult, second adult, etc. The brushes of juvenile feathers appear firstly on the wings. All down feathers are replaced by juvenile ones, but many juvenile feathers have no down predecessor. The moult from juvenile to first adult plumage begins at age 16–17 days with the growth of the 9th and 10th primaries. These primaries are first-generation feathers with no predecessors, and are replaced only in the autumn of the following year. These feathers allow the current year's birds to be distinguished from older birds. The male black gular spot appears first as a black stripe in the centre of the chin. Next, two black stripes appear on the sides of the neck so that the spot appears as three black stripes. Only after this stage does the full black spot become established.

The final adult plumage is reached only at the beginning of the second autumn. In all birds more than one year old there is a summer moult, these summer feathers being replaced in the autumn by the adult ones. Some feathers that fall out during the summer are not replaced, with the number of feathers being appreciably decreased during the summer moult, an adaption for the warm summer season: in more northerly populations, the summer moult is less pronounced. The male black gular spot moults at the end of August (Potapov, 1985). All moulting is finished by the end of October.

Distribution

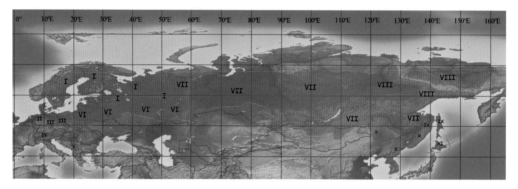

Map 3. Hazel Grouse (*Bonasa bonasia*)
Sub-species: I – B. b. bonasia; *II* – B. b. rhenana; *III* – B. b. rupestris; *IV* – B. b. styriaca; *V* – B. b. schiebeli; *VI* – B. b. volgensis; *VII* – B. b. septentrionalis; *VIII* – B. b. kolymensis; *IX* – B. b. yamashinai; *X* – B. b. amurensis; *XI* – B.b. vicinitas;

The range encompasses practically all the forest zone of Eurasia. The northern limit is defined by solid forest massifs, but in the eastern range it coincides with the distribution of the arboreal vegetation penetrating far north along the valleys of the large Siberian rivers, up to the 69°30'N in the Indigirka Basin (Perfiliev, 1975). The southern border in European Russia has moved gradually northwards as a consequence of human activity.

Subspecies

The significant differences in natural conditions across the species' huge range and the sedentary way of life have had a similar effect as in Ruffed Grouse, with numerous subspecies, these differing mainly in colour. A light grey colour is prevalent in northern subspecies, while brown, red-brown or rufous tinges dominate south-western and south-eastern populations. The distribution of subspecies is shown on Map 3.

At present there are 11 recognized subspecies:

North European Hazel Grouse *Bonasa (Tetrastes) bonasia bonasia* (Linnaeus, 1758)

Occupies Fennoscandia, Estonia and north-western European Russia. Habitats are different types of mixed and coniferous forests, mainly with birches, alders and spruces, especially along streams and cuttings.

Rhen's Hazel Grouse *Bonasa (Tetrastes) bonasia rhenana* (Kleinschmidt, 1917)
Occupies south-eastern Belgium, Luxembourg and central-western Germany (Schwarzwald, Jura). Habitat is mixed forests in hilly regions to altitudes of 100–680m (328–2,231) (Bauer, 1960).

Middle European Hazel Grouse *Bonasa (Tetrastes) bonasia rupestris* (Brehn, 1831)
Interrupted distribution in southern Germany from southern Schwarzwald east to Sudet. Habitats as the previous subspecies.

Alpine Hazel Grouse *Bonasa (Tetrastes) styriaca* (Jordans, Schiebel, 1944)
Occupies all mountain forests of the Alps and nearby mountains, including the Carpathians. Found in all kinds of mixed forests with a prevalence of coniferous trees in the mountain forests of the Alps from 600–1,900m (1,968–6,234ft), and in Carpathian Mountains at 600–2,950m (1,968–9,678ft).

Balkan Hazel Grouse *Bonasa (Tetrastes) bonasia schiebeli* (Kleinschmidt, 1944)
Occupies forests of all the mountains of the Balkan Peninsula, including western Bulgaria and northern Greece. Habitat is boreal forests at 1,200–1,700m (3,937–5,577ft). Breeds in the belt of fir-beech forests between 1,300–1,450m (4,265–4,757ft) (Matvejev, 1957).

Volga Hazel Grouse *Bonasa (Tetrastes) bonasia volgensis* (Buturlin, 1916)
Occupies the upper Volga River basin south to the limits of the species' range, west to eastern Poland, and east to the foothills of the southern Urals. Habitat in most areas is mixed forest with thick shrub understory. In Belarus it inhabits oak-pine, spruce-alder and oak forests with a well-developed shrub understory (Dolbik, 1961).

Siberian Hazel Grouse *Bonasa (Tetrastes) bonasia septentrionalis* (Seebohm, 1884)
Occupies the largest fraction of the species' range from the Pechora River and Urals to the Lena River in eastern Siberia. Habitat in the northern Urals is mixed forests with spruce, birch, willow, alder, and mountain ash. Also found in subalpine birch forests. In southern Urals, inhabits mixed birch–pine–larch forests linked to dense thickets of alder and bird cherry. In the Altai Mountains inhabits all types of taiga forest from the foothills at 400m (1,312ft) to the upper forest belt at 1,600m (5,249ft), but avoids pure pine woods. In southern Yakutia and Transbaikalia the bird prefers the sparse woodland of river flood-plains, with spruces, larches and birches and a dense understory of willow, dog rose, honeysuckle, red and black currants and other bushes.

Kolyma Hazel Grouse *Bonasa (Tetrastes) kolymensis* (Buturlin, 1916)
Occupies the river valleys from the east slopes of the Verkhoyanskiy Ridge east to the

Kolyma Ridge and south to the Iydomo–May upland region and the Djugdjur Ridge to the valley of the Ud River. Habitat is spruce and larch woods along the riverbeds with a dense understory of willow and alder bushes, dwarf birches and *Chosenia*.

Sakhalin Hazel Grouse *Bonasa (Tetrastes) yamashinai* (Momiyama, 1928)
Occupies Sakhalin Island. Habitat is sparse, mixed forests on hill slopes, mainly along rivers and near springs. In winter, the main habitats are dense thickets of willow bushes, birches and bird-cherry trees in river flood-plains. Avoids pure larch woods and thickets of pine.

Amur Hazel Grouse *Bonasa (Tetrastes) bonasia amurensis* (Riley, 1916)
Occupies the south-eastern part of the species' continental range from the Amur Valley and Great Chingan Mountains southward to southern range borders. Habitats are different types of forests (pure oak forests with a dense understory of bushes, coniferous spruce-fir forests in the mountains, etc), but as a rule the dense, wooded thickets of river flood-plains are preferred.

Japanese Hazel Grouse *Bonasa (Tetrastes) bonasia vicinitas* (Riley, 1915)
Inhabits Hokkaido Island, Japan. (Note that Hokkaido Island was connected to Sakhalin Island and through to the mainland when the ancestral *Bonasa* was creating its range). No solid data on preferred habitats.

Habitats
Hazel Grouse are forest birds, always found in arboreal vegetation, though as a result of the very large range and consequent differing climatic conditions, the species inhabits different types of forest, from pure oak with a rich understory of different bushes (southern Urals) to dense spruce-fir forests in the Siberian Mountains. But despite this variability, the optimal situation is arboreal vegetation in the valleys of small rivers, brooks and streams, especially in hilly or mountain landscapes. Among the forest types particularly preferred are those where spruce, birch and alder dominate, and the ground is wet and covered by old twigs, branches and leaves. This is particularly true near the northern limits of the range. In the subalpine belt the birds prefer birch forests, mixed birch–pine–larch forests linked to dense thickets of alder and bird cherry. Monotonous pine or larch forests are avoided everywhere, as are pine forests in sphagnum bogs. Only in southern parts of the range do the birds occasionally inhabit pine forests, but only if there is a dense fern understory. In the Carpathian Mountains, the birds inhabit beech forests; in the Ussuri region, riverbeds with bird cherry and wild vines; and in southern Korea and on Hokkaido Island, bamboo grassland (Haga, Takamata, 1986).

Population structure, density and territoriality

The male/female ratio is close to 1:1 in adult birds. However, among young birds, males usually number 12.5% more than females (Gaidar, 1974). In eastern Siberia, in winter flocks, males are 54.8% of populations on average (Murashov, 2001). Hazel Grouse are strongly sedentary: 90% of marked birds moved not more than 500m from where they had been ringed, the maximal distance being 5km (3 miles). Old females and young birds of both sexes are the most mobile (Semenov-Tianshansky, 1959; Gaidar, 1973). In another study, 34 of 37 ringed birds had moved not more than 700m from the place of ringing, the other 3 moving 1–2km (0.6–1.2 miles): one male remained in its territory for three years (Romanov, 1975). The territorial structure of the population during the breeding season consists of a system of individual territories, these occasionally forming clusters of 2–4 territories in favorable places. Such territories are also usually nesting areas, as male and female often live together throughout the year. At the end of summer, the system of territories collapses, with broods mixing and trespassing to reach the richest patches of berries (mainly raspberries, strawberries and cowberries) and other foods.

The dispersion of juvenile birds begins to the end of August. During the fall, the system of individual territories is re-established and during this phase females play a more active role than males. Female whistles, which differ from those of males, are heard much more often in the fall than in spring (Punnonen, 1954). Hazel grouse pairs are strongly attached to a single territory and may be seen in the same place year after year, though in surrounding territories the presence of birds may not be as regular (Potapov, 1985). In new pairs formed in the fall, one bird is often young. In eastern populations, east of the Yenisei River, Hazel Grouse spend the winter in flocks of 4–15 birds (3–8 in South Korea, Rhim, Lee, 2003). These flocks are also sedentary. In the north-eastern section of the range, the winter territory of such a flock is about 1km² (0.4 sq mile), decreasing to about half that in midwinter (Andreev, 1980).

Population density depends mainly on habitat quality. In especially favourable places in the southern taiga, the density can reach 20 pairs/km² (Potapov, 1985). More usually a density of 10–15 pairs/km² is reached in optimal places in spring. The density could therefore theoretically rise to 70–100 birds/km² in the fall, but in reality, brood dispersal means lower densities, the maximum observed fall density being about 50 birds/km². In less favourable habitats, the population in spring varies from 0.5 to 1.5 pairs/km². The proportion of areas of favourable and unfavourable habitat varies across the range, dependent on forest type. In Russia's Leningrad Province, for example, it is approximately 1:3, this also being typical for southern sections of the range.

The overall population of Hazel Grouse varies from year to year due mainly to climatic conditions in spring and summer. Cold rainy weather for 3–5 days or more will cause the death of most, if not all, broods in which the chicks have not reached 13–14 days of age and have no ability for thermoregulation. Also important is predator activity. Hazel Grouse predators include pine marten and sable. Though the main prey of these is rodents, during reduced rodent numbers the mustelids turn to Hazel Grouse, particularly young birds. In such situations pine martens will cache Hazel Grouse in the deep hollows of large aspen trees, such caches containing intact or partly consumed birds (Volkov, 1975). Occasionally, sable hunt Hazel Grouse intensively and during a winter each animal may eat up to 25 birds (Amur Basin, Yudakov, 1968), though in some years the remains of Hazel Grouse in sable dung was only 1.7% (Baikal region, Izmailov, Pavlov, 1975). The birds also suffer predation from foxes, and from goshawks and sparrowhawks.

A high population resulting from a successful breeding season is not maintained, with dispersion, predation and, occasionally, disease causing a reduction in numbers (Romanov, 1975). Sometimes, after a sharp population rise, numbers fall abruptly during the following winter (A. Evstafiev, pers. comm.).

Nutrition

Hazel Grouse consume a large variety of plants in different parts of their huge range, and during different seasons. Only the winter diet is monotonous, consisting of catkins, buds and twigs of birches, alders, willows and poplars. Of these, the catkins of birches and alders are the main sources across the greater part of the range. If the number of catkins is insufficient, due to a poor harvest or during severe frosts, the birds change to buds and twigs. Up to 2,000 birch buds and twig pieces have been found in the crop of a single bird (northern Siberia – Dulkeit, 1960). While feeding on alder twigs, a bird can ingest pieces up to 2cm (0.8in) long, with a diameter of 2.0–2.5mm (Potapov E., 1982). The birds also take the upper parts of shoots from bilberry during periods of thaw. In the eastern range, the main winter nutrition derives from poplars (*Chosenia* sp.) and willow. The volume of winter food taken decreases gradually as summer advances, though some is always present in the diet. In spring, as the snow disappears, Hazel Grouse change, gradually, from tree to ground feeding. The birds dig in the wet cover of old leaves, stems, etc in search of green shoots, buds, wintered seeds (including the seeds of spruce) and berries, fresh flowers, especially anemones, and the shoots and leaves of grasses. Spruce seeds fall from cones in March–April in large numbers and are so intensively taken that the birds occasionally gain small fat deposits (Formosov, 1976). Later, the seeds of different grasses and even fresh, green fir needles are added to the diet. In some localities the spring diet includes large fractions of buds and leaves of the mountain ash and aspen, these items being up to 66% of crop content (Oliger, 1973). Summer nutrition is more diverse, especially in southern populations.

As summer becomes fall, the diet includes a considerable quantity of animal matter, mainly beetles, ants, grasshoppers, different caterpillars and larvae, spiders and mollusks – a contrast to the summer diet in which animal food does not exceed 5% of the total volume for adult birds (Oliger, 1973). Berries appear in the diet from July and in August–September constitute the main fraction of the diet, especially bilberries, cowberries and raspberries. In the southern part of their range, the birds also eat other berries, taking practically all those present in its habitat.

The change to winter food sources is in September, the birds starting with the buds and catkins of different deciduous trees. In eastern areas, when there is a good harvest of Creep (Siberian Dwarf) Pine (*Pinus pumila*) nuts, the birds collect these from the ground or even peck them from the cones, swallowing them whole, the nut shell being ground in the gizzard. In the Kolyma Basin the birds take larch seeds, up to 2,500 seeds being found in a crop, the seeds permitting the bird to gain fat deposits very quickly (Andreev, 1980). As the ambient temperature falls and nights lengthen, such foods become more significant and are the main source of nutrition before the appearance of snow cover. Seeds may also be more important in years with a poor berry harvest. For example, in the area around Lake Baikal in 1971, the berry harvest was poor, all berries having been taken by August, forcing the birds to change to a winter diet one month early (Vladyshewsky, 1975b). Detailed studies of the change to winter diet were made in October 1974 in the subarctic Urals (Voyvoje River), where Hazel Grouse were numerous (26 birds/km²). Early October was relatively warm, and the year had seen a rich harvest of bilberries. The birds stayed together in small flocks of 6–10 birds and fed mainly on the berries. On 9 October, snow began to fall, and the temperature fell to -3°C (26.6°F), after which it did not rise up to freezing again, and the snow coverage thickened daily. Some birds had changed to a winter diet even before the first snow, with berries being eaten only occasionally, despite their availability (they were still above the snow under big spruce trees). In 32 crops collected from 13 October to 1 November, only five contained bilberries, and these were only solitary berries. As the diet became poorer, the quantity of food in the bird's crops increased, reaching 54g (1.9oz) on 21 October, when the birds began to roost regularly in snow burrows. Because of this change of food, the birds begin to accumulate fat quickly and one week actually became fatty (Potapov, 1985).

Animal food is important in the chick diet of chicks 1.5–2 weeks old (the sources being spiders, beetle larvae, mosquitoes, cicadas, ants, caterpillars, etc). Later the diet includes small leaves and grass seeds. At the beginning of the berry season, the chicks change to a largely berry diet, though until the beginning of September insects and spiders still compose nearly 20% of the diet. By the end of September there is no difference in the diet of adult and young birds.

Grit in the birds' gizzards is minimal at the end of summer, but increases quickly to a maximum of nearly 8g (0.3oz) in November and then decreases gradually towards the end of winter.

Wintering

During the winter, Hazel Grouse spend considerable time in snow burrows. South of 60°N in Russia's Leningrad Province, during a moderately cold weather (-10°C/14°F to

-20°C/-4°F), the birds leave their burrows for foraging either once daily as the sun rises, for 1.5–4 hours, or twice daily for about 2 hours in the morning and 30–40 minutes before sunset. For the remaining time the bird is either in a burrow, or in an open snow hollow during sunny weather. In either case, the bird spends 18–21 hours daily resting. The warmer the weather, the longer the time the bird spends foraging, with rest pauses of 40–70 minutes. During cold periods in midwinter, when the snow surface is not very hard, the bird may change its roosting position once or twice during the night, with the bird leaving its burrow, moving 5–10m on foot and digging a new burrow; though it is known that the birds will change burrows during heavy snowfall when the burrow roof thickens (Potapov E., 1982) or times of melt, the reasons for other changes are not known. If disturbed during the night, perhaps by a predator, the bird flies up from the burrow, then flies for several dozen metres before landing and excavating a new burrow.

In northern parts of the birds' range (at about 66°N), when the ambient temperature falls to -40°C (-40°F) the birds forage twice a day, in the morning and evening, for about 30–40 minutes each time, the remaining time being spent in new snow burrows. In some cases the birds will forage only once, in the morning, for about the same total time (Andreev, 1980). The lowest ambient temperature noted by Andreev was -49°C (-56.2°F): in this case the bird spent only 20 minutes feeding, its feathers fluffed. The bird stood still from time to time for 2–5 minutes, perhaps to warm the food in the crop. In extreme cold, the birds take easily available food despite its low caloric value, compensating by taking a larger quantity: during feeding in such conditions the bird takes bites from a twig at intervals of only 1.38–1.47 seconds, while to find and to eat one catkin takes 17–50 sec. In extreme cold, Snigirewsky (1946) and Dulkeit (1964) suggested that the birds may spend up to two days in a burrow before exiting to feed, though this observation had not been confirmed by later studies.

During such extreme cold conditions, the birds rarely fly, and never for more than a minute from the snow burrow to where it can feed, and about the same time to a new roost. In each case the flight distance is less than 100m. Clearly the birds are trying to reduce energy loss, and during sunny weather they will often sit in treetops sunning themselves with fluffed feathers. The birds also choose the lowest parts of river valleys for their burrows, as the ground temperatures in such areas tends to be higher (Snigirewsky, 1946). Snow burrows have an average (n=20) width of 15.69cm (6.18in); length 23.46cm (9.24in); height 14.79cm (5.82in); and roof thickness 7.06cm (2.78in) (Potapov E., 1982). The droppings excreted by a bird during the stay in the burrow causes snow melting under the bird's tail and finally forms a frozen platform.

The weight of the fresh content of a crop is maximal in the evening, before roosting, varying in different weather from 47–60g (1.7–2.1oz) (Semenov-Tianshansky, 1959; Potapov, 1985; Potapov E., 1982), with a maximum observed in the Kolyma River Basin of 81.2–84.6g (2.9–3oz) (Andreev, 1980). The average daily ration, calculated from all data, is 81.3g (2.9oz) dry weight and has a caloric value of 1,068 kilojoules (Potapov, 1985). The content of full crop is consumed completely by morning, the bird leaving the burrow for the next feed with an empty crop. Sometimes the stock of food in a full crop is insufficient and is consumed before sunrise, the unusual form of droppings (narrower and longer than usual) confirming this (**Figure 37**) (Potapov, 1982). The time between dropping excretion is more or less constant at 12 minutes, which allows the time of roosting to be calculated. During the time that the bird spends out of the burrow, the speed of excretion is higher, at 7.1 minutes between droppings (Potapov, 1982). Excrement from the caeca is produced when the bird leaves the burrow in the morning. The dry weight of the excrement is 5.13g/0.2oz (3.0–8.65g/0.1–0.3oz) daily, and its caloric value is 26.5 kJ/g (Andreev, 1980).

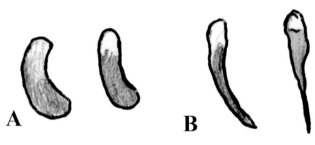

Figure 37. Winter droppings of Hazel Grouse
A – normal; B – thin type. The latter are the last produced after digestion of the crop contents. (E. Potapov, 1982).

Breeding

Hazel Grouse are strongly monogamous. In some cases pairs were observed to stay together for two years. Display activity is solitary, but in the case where the individual territories of two or three pairs are in close contact, males will meet at borders and fight in defense of their property. In aggressive situations, males raise their feathers, slightly raise a semi-open tail, extend the neck and run towards their rival, the chin feathers held vertical, resembling the 'beard' of capercaillies (Figure 36, n4), while uttering short, sharp sounds. During combat, the rivals face each other in a vertical pose, making threatening lunges and ripostes with wonderful synchrony. The rivals exchange blows to the head and neck with bill, wings and legs. Leg blows are delivered during jumps and are especially powerful (Scherzinger, 1978).

Displays begin in the first week of March in southern parts of the range and two weeks later in northern parts. Males at first walk in the snow with their wings slightly spread and lowered so that the wing tips draw lines in the snow to the sides of the bird's tracks. Sometimes males meet one another and run together in parallel at a distance of 1–2m (3.3–6.5ft) from each other ('running parallel'). Such activity is not only seen in spring, it sometimes also arises in winter flocks (15–17 birds). In such cases, the snow surface where the flock had been is covered by numerous parallel running tracks (Donaurov, 1947).

Nuptial activity reaches maximum intensity at the end of snow melting. The males utter a courtship sound, consisting of several whistled notes, two prolonged and several

Figure 38. Display postures of male Hazel Grouse

1 – alarm; 2 – singing (whistling); 3 – declaration of ownership; 4 – attacking; 5 – posture before a female (the head turns to the opposite direction)

(5–7) short ones, audible at the distance of nearly 100m (109yd) and lasting 2–3 seconds. The rhythm and number of these whistles is strongly variable in different populations and even in different individuals. The whistling male usually sits on a tree branch, or stands on the ground in a humped-up posture with the head withdrawn to the body and a widely open bill (**Figure 38**), the tail quivering with the rhythm of the song (Punnonen, 1954). This *Whistling Canto* (Hjorth, 1970) is unique among grouse. It is interesting to note that Snowcocks (*Tetraogallus* sp. of the Phasianidae) also utter similar loud whistles with a widely open bill. Sometimes during the whistling the males become so excited that they are oblivious to outside dangers.

Females also whistle, but their *Whistling Canto* is shorter and comprises only three notes, the second of which is longer and sometimes sounds as two closely connected notes. The imitation of female's whistle by a hunter in the fall is especially attractive to males.

Whistling occurs in both spring and autumn, with autumn whistling beginning in August and lasting until the end of October or through to January in southern parts of the range. Autumn performances (mainly by males only) are many times less active than those in spring.

Other elements of the male's courtship display are flutter-jumps and flutter-flights. Flutter-flights occur within an individual's territory, covering a distance of several dozen metres from one tree to another. Before the flight ends, the bird decreases the frequency of wingbeats and the wings produce especially loud flaps with the tail spreads to 125°. Flutter-jumps are rare and fulfilled in different ways in different subspecies. For example, in Finland, the male flies to a height of 1–2m and lands in the same place, the wings beating loudly and quickly. Sometimes the male produce a series of such beats without flight, its body merely taking a more vertical position (Punnonen, 1954). On occasion, the wingbeats are so rapid that they produce a loud drumming trill (sounding almost like a woodpecker), audible for a distance of up to 100m. (Teidoff, 1952; Fuschlberger, 1978). In populations of Kolyma Hazel Grouse, males make this display after finishing a flutter-flight, standing on the ground in a vertical position (**Figure 38, n3**) and utter a loud hissing (Krechmar *et al.*, 1978). Captive Western males also do this occasionally, but in a less pronounced form. Other acoustic signals, observed in captive birds only (Scherzinger, 1978), include a loud wing-beating display and foot stamping. Males in populations of Amur Hazel Grouse have a further vocalization – a series of melodious, rumbling sounds lasting about 4 seconds, uttered by males in moments of high excitement. At the same time, the male's eye-combs increase maximally and the neck is curved and strongly expanded, resembling that of the Himalayan Snowcock (Potapov, 1985; 1993). This display was observed in males near Lake Baikal (Kirpichev, pers. com.).

Before copulation, the male circles the female with his tail fanned, turning the tail towards her (**Figure 38, n5**), and simultaneously turning the head away from her. Finally there is synchronous nodding by both male and female, with simultaneous horizontal turns of the head, but in opposite directions (Scherzinger, 1978).

Nests are placed in a dry site among fallen twigs and branches, under the lower branches of a tree, near the thick base of a tree, between tree roots, in fern thickets, or even in the roots or cores of large, low stumps. In northern parts of the range, the nest is often placed in a thick moss layer. In very rare instances, nesting is in an old or partially destroyed nest of a crow or raptor. Such cases are known from Finland (Punnonen, 1954) and Russia (Potapov, 1972, Malchevsky, Pukinsky, 1983). One nest, with 9 eggs, was found in Russia's Leningrad Province (Russia) (26 May 1957), in the old nest of a Jay (*Garrulus glandarius*), in a spruce tree 4–5m (13–16ft) above the ground. Chicks can safely reach the ground from such elevated nests.

The nest is a shallow scrape excavated by the female, sparsely lined with dry leaves, grass and feathers. The scrape depth is nearly 6cm (2.4in), with a diameter of 20–22cm (7.9–8.7in). The female adds further dry leaves each time before she lays an egg (Punnonen, 1954). The number of eggs in the clutch varies from 3 to 14, usually 7–9. However, nests with 15–20 eggs have been found, though these may be the result of activity by two females. The laying of female Hazel Grouse and Black Grouse in one nest is also known (Kiselev, 1978).

Eggs are 37–43mm x 26–30mm (N.W. Russia, 103 eggs, Ivanter, 1962) or 37.9–42.4mm x 26.0–26.8mm, weight 13.1–18.8g (0.5–0.7oz), average 17.2g (0.6oz) (156 eggs, upper Volga Basin, Gaidar, 1974). The colour varies from pale to dark yellow or almost brown, with sparse brown spots of different sizes, occasionally greater than 5mm in diameter. In rare cases there are no spots. The colour of the eggs is brightest at the moment of laying, the eggs gradually becoming paler until hatching. No dependence of clutch size with latitude has been detected. The speed of laying depends on the age of the female and her nutritional state. In one case, a female laid 9 eggs in 15 days, and in another one 10 eggs in 14 days (Punnonen, 1954). One female increased the laying interval from 26 to 39 hours before the clutch was completed (Semenov-Tianshansky, 1959). Time of laying depends on latitude. In Belarus and the Baltic regions, complete clutches appear in the second half of April, whereas 800–900km (497–559 miles) north-east, in north-western Russia, this time is in the first half of May, and far to the north-east, in the Pechora Basin, complete clutches are not seen until the middle or end of June (Voronin, Beshkarev, 1995). In the extreme north-east of the range (the Kolyma Basin), complete clutches appear at the end of June (Dementiev, Schochin, 1935). Despite this, the chicks still have time to reach adult size by the end of August, such is the high speed of growth and general development during the long daylights hours of the northern summer (Potapov, 1985).

Incubation depends on weather conditions. At first, the female leaves the nest for feeding up to 5 times daily, but as hatching approaches, this reduces to 2–3 times. Feeding lasts 15–25 minutes, rarely up to 35 minutes. The duration of incubation varies from 21 to 27 days, and depends on female intensity, particularly in the early days. Hatching lasts nearly 8 hours (Dolbik, 1961). When complete, the female leads the brood away from the nest. At first the brood browses in small, sunlit openings in low grass or fern. During the first few days, the chicks are regularly brooded by the female every 5–6 minutes, even in warm weather. At 2–3 days of age, chicks can fly to a height of 1.5m (Neifeldt, 1958), and weigh 12–14g (0.4–0.5oz). The weight of the chick increases during the first 10 days at 1.8–1.9g (0.06–0.07oz) per day (Rodionov, 1963a) and by up to 9g (0.3oz) per day in the third month of life (Semenow-Tianshansky, 1959). Young birds reach adult size and weight when they are about three months old. The brood begins to disperse in August, young males leaving first, but full dispersal is sometimes completed only in October. During feeding, where there is an abundance of berries, several broods may meet and join to form a temporary aggregation of up to 30 birds.

Males take no part in incubation, but remain close to the nest during hatching. Usually the brood is led by the female, but occasionally the male will join her. In some cases, males have been seen to lead a brood after the death of the female (Danilov, 1975). When the brood leaves the nesting territory, the male usually remains in it.

Hunting, recreation and conservation

Hazel Grouse have been one of the most hunted birds in Eurasia for many years, the high quality of the meat being the main reason, with the grouse not only being sold in local markets in large cities but even exported. In Russia at the end of the 19th century, professional hunters took not less than 3 million birds annually (Menzbier, 1902). Such hunting was the reason for the disappearance of the species in many parts of central Russia; each time hunting ceased, the birds regained their original numbers within 2–3 years. In general, hunting was by snare, with the use of a whistle to attract the birds and a rifle coming into use during the 20th century. Professional hunting declined rapidly in the middle of the 20th century and ceased almost completely in the second half. Now only amateur hunting remains, though the small size of the bird is a disincentive to many. In remote regions of Russia, Mongolia and China, snare hunting is still prevalent in rural populations and is usually carried out by children (see Potapov 2001 for details of such hunting in the Altai Mountains).

In all countries where the law permits hunting, the season opens in the autumn and is restricted to a very short period. Hunting is prohibited in spring.

Management of the species in Russia is based on population monitoring, particularly when the hunting season opens, as dispersal in the autumn can complicate the counting (Fetisov, 2008; Potapov, Pavlova, 2009). Monitoring is particularly important in the western part of the range, where local populations are close to extinction. Birds are counted during spring and autumn, using whistles to attract the birds: experienced monitors can differentiate the whistles of males, females and juvenile birds. To aid conservation, hunting is prohibited in state reserves and protected areas in all countries where hunting is allowed. In Russia, education of local residents and minimal interference by dogs and cats has aided conservation considerably, and protected areas have been created that encompass the greater part of the species' range. In these, not only is hunting prohibited, but the forests that are critical to the species are maintained. In addition to such protected areas, there are also large sections of forest designated as public or municipal hunting farms, where the hunting is licensed and controlled.

CHAPTER 3

Genus 2: *Falcipennis* SPRUCE GROUSE

Canace (Reichenbach, 1853): XXIX (nom. nov. preocc., non Curtis, 1838);
Type species: *Tetrao canadensis* (Linnaeus, 1758, monotype). *Falcipennis* (Elliot, 1864):
24. *Canachites* (Steineger, 1885a): 410. *Tympanuchus* (Reichenow, 1913): 320.

The genus includes three species: *Falcipennis canadensis, F. franklinii* (Nearctic) and *F. falcipennis* (Palearctic). *F. franklinii* is considered by many to be a subspecies of *Falcipennis canadensis* because of hybridization with Canadian Spruce Grouse in the species contact zone and the absence of clear differences in the colouration of males of the two forms. However, hybridization is not unusual in grouse genus (e.g. *Dendragapus, Tetrao*), and even between representatives of different genera. Differences also exist in colouration,

Male Asian Spruce Grouse

particularly of the breast, and there are also differences in the form of the tail feathers. The two forms occupy different types of forests (mountain and plain), have different winter diets, and, particularly important, have remarkable differences in courtship displays. We therefore consider Franklin's Spruce Grouse to be a separate species (Potapov, 1970, 1985), as did some earlier American authors (Douglas, 1829; Elliot, 1864; Ridgway, 1885; Ogilvie-Grant, 1893; Peters, 1934).

All three species are mid-sized forest dwellers, with fully feathered tarsi and a comparatively short tail. Sexual dimorphism in colouration is more expressed than in *Bonasa* species.

The size of the three species is similar, though the Asian Spruce Grouse is a little larger. The shape of the spread wing in the American species is the same, but differs from that of the Asian Grouse, whose peculiarities are unique among the Tetraonidae: the Asian Spruce Grouse wing is wider, the top of the spread position falling on the 7th primary, and the outer primaries have sharp tops – a unique feature (**Figure 39**). As a result, the loading to the wing during the flight is maximal in the Asian Spruce Grouse, exceeding that of the American species by a factor of 1.5. The tail of the Franklin's Spruce Grouse male is longer and the retrices are wider than in the other species: 32.2mm (1.2in) and 26mm (1in) in males and females (on average) against the 18–23mm (0.7–0.9in) in both

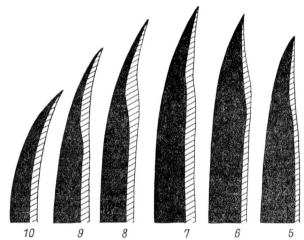

Figure 39. Adult plumages of Asian Spruce Grouse
Form of primary number 5 to 10 of Asian Spruce Grouse male during the first adult plumage (black and striped), and during all later adult plumages (only black). From specimens of COLL ZIN RAN (Potapov, 1985).

sexes of the other species. The tail feathers of Franklin's Spruce Grouse, in contrast to co-generic species, have the tops cut off straight, as in the Dusky Blue Grouse and the capercaillies, rather than rounded (**Figure 40**).

The feathering of all spruce grouse is the same. The feathers on the top of the head are slightly elongated and may be considered a rudimentary crest, but the birds never raise them as the *Bonasa* do. The naked 'eye-comb' in males is of moderate size and covered by knobs of irregular form, those in the upper row appearing as low, prolonged blades. All species have a small patch of naked skin immediately behind the eye, a little below the eye-comb. The tarsi are covered by feathers to the base of the toes. Colouration of the three species is also similar. Males have chocolate-brown backs, especially the

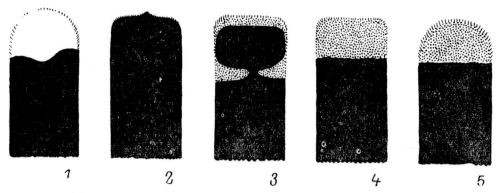

Figure 40. Tail feathers of Spruce Grouse
The form of the top of the tail feathers and their coloration in males of Falcipennis falcipennis *(1)*, Falcipennis franklinii *(2)*, Dendragapus obscurus richardsoni *(3)*, Dendragapus obscurus pallidus *(4)*, Dendragapus fuliginosus fuliginosus *(5)*. *From specimens of COLL ZIN RAN (Potapov, 1985)*.

scapulars, with dark-grey feather bordering. The lower body shows a dark chocolate gular patch with white or whitish bordering, a grey neck with dark marks and a black–brown breast plastron. Female colouration is even more similar than that of the males, the two American species more obviously similar to each other than to the Asian grouse. Nestling colouration of all three species is practically the same.

Spruce grouse colouration has similarities with the *Bonasa* species and, to a lesser degree, with Dusky Grouse and capercaillie. Indeed, there is a remarkable similarity between the colouration of the Black-billed Capercaillie subspecies *T. parvirostris stegmanni* males and *F. franklinii* (**Figure 41**). In addition, American species males (mainly *franklinii*) have a bluish, shiny tinge to fresh feathering of the black breast plastron just as in the plastrons of capercaillies and black grouse, though this disappears in preserved skins (Aldrich, Friedmann, 1946). The evaluation of similarities between colouration of Spruce Grouse and other members of the family indicates the closeness of the spruce grouses to *Bonasa* species and, to a lesser degree, to Blue and Dusky Grouse (and to a much smaller degree to *Tetrao*, *Lyrurus* and *Lagopus*).

Hybridization between Canadian Spruce Grouse and Willow Ptarmigan occurs in the north, where the two

Figure 41. Male colouration
Colouration of the males of Tetrao parvirostris stegmanni *(right) and* Falcipennis franklinii *(left) from above (left frame) and below (right frame).*

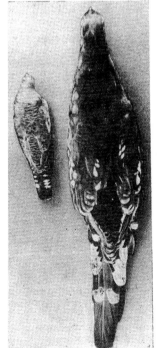
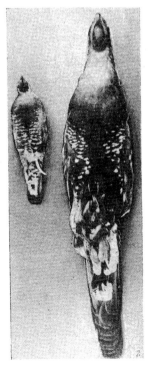

Female Asian Spruce Grouse

species inhabit neighbouring habitats (Taverner, 1931; Lumsden, 1969). The most characteristically spruce grouse features in the hybrids are pectinated toes, a white stripe behind the eye, white tips to otherwise black uppertail coverts, the black colour of the upper breast, and the generally black colour of the upper body, but with some feathers that are totally white or with white tips. Hybrid Franklin's Spruce Grouse x Dusky Grouse has also occurred, the general hybrid colouration being mainly spruce grouse-type, but the tail, coloured as Dusky Grouse, had 18 feathers with more primitive rounded tips instead of the straight cut-off seen in both parents, and colour as in Blue Grouse. No detailed descriptions of hybrids between Canadian and Franklin's Spruce Grouse have been given.

2.1 ASIAN SPRUCE GROUSE Subgenus: *Falcipennis* (Elliot, 1864)

Type species: *Tetrao falcipennis* (Hartlaub, 1855), monotype.

Single species, the main feature of which is the sharpness of the tops of the outer primaries, which increases during ontogenesis (see **Figure 39**). Within the Phasianoidea suborder, this feature is only seen in this grouse and some Cracidae species that feed, roost and nest in the trees of tropical forests (Potapov, 1983).

2.1.1 Asian[1] Spruce Grouse *Falcipennis (Falcipennis) falcipennis* (Hartlaub, 1855)

Tetrao falcipennis (Hartlaub, 1855): 39 (Stanovoy Ridge). *Tetrao canadensis var. franklinii* (Middendorf, 1851): 202-208. *Falcipennis falcipennis muratai* (Momiyama, 1928): 234 (southern Sakhalin).

Medium-sized forest bird.

Morphology

The wing is rounded at the top, with the tip of the wing coinciding with the top of the 7th, or, more rarely, the 6th or 8th primary, or even the 6th–8th primaries together. Primaries 5–10 are sharpened and curved backwards. The outer three primaries are the most sharpened, the sharpening decreasing towards the inner feathers, the 4th–1st primaries having no sharpening. The claws are long and curved. Sexual dimorphism is well expressed in colour, but is insignificant in size and weight.

Colouration

Adult male

The head is blackish-grey, with the back of the neck lighter. The back, between the scapulars, is very dark, with narrow, grey feather borders forming a scaly pattern. Lower back and rump have pale transverse stripes, with white patches along the stem in the

[1] The occasionally seen name 'Siberian Spruce Grouse' is not correct, with only a small part of the species range lying in Siberia.

Male Asian Spruce Grouse displaying in East Siberia

rump. Gular patch is black with white bordering that begins from lore and goes under eyes to the sides of neck (see **Figure 25 in Chapter 1**). Breast is black, but in collection specimens this gradually changes to dark brown. Lower breast is paler, with contrasting heart-shaped white spots. These spots became larger on belly and flanks. Undertail feathers have white tops and an indistinct cross pattern of narrow grey-yellow stripes. Primaries are black, the inner ones with whitish tips. Secondaries are paler, with thin, whitish borders and an indistinct cross pattern on the edge of the outer web, especially the inner ones. Inner secondaries have a white shaft stripe. Scapular feathers have a black–chocolate background, with a cross-pattern of thin greyish-yellow stripes and a large white spot beneath the top. Tail feathers are black with wide white tops (narrow in central pair).

The female Asian Spruce Grouse is very similar to her North American cousin.

Male in the first adult plumage
Differs from older birds by less-expressed sharpening of the outer primaries, and some details   (e.g. white tops in the central pair of tail feathers small or absent, etc).

Adult female
Upper parts are mottled brown-reddish, with ochre and grey cross-stripes and prolonged shaft patches, especially on rump and uppertail coverts. Rump feathers have two patterns, each equally frequent and independent of age. Throat is mottled whitish-ochre. Neck and upper breast are dark brown with ochre cross-stripes, and are darker than the underbody. Wing and tail are as male. Females have two colour phases, grey and ochre.

Juvenile (both sexes)
Upper parts are mottled, with ochre and brown cross-stripes and spots. Primaries are brown with whitish borders on outer webs, and rufous dots on outer webs of inner

primaries. Secondaries have clear, transverse brown and yellowish bands. Throat is white. Breast has an ochre tinge. Belly is whitish.

Downy chick
Upperbody is bright brown-yellow, in contrast to the pale yellow underparts. Black bordering of brown cap on head is indistinct or absent. The black spots on sides of the head are identical in all three spruce grouse species (**Figure 42**).

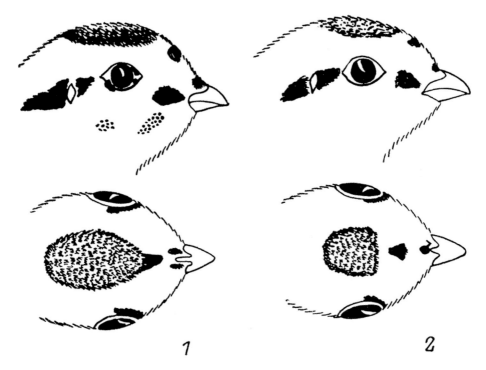

Figure 42. Spruce Grouse head pattern
Head pattern of downy young Asian (1) and Canadian (2) Spruce Grouse.

Dimensions
Males (N=34): wing length 182.7mm (174–195mm); tail 107mm (98–121mm); bill 10.7mm (8.3–12mm); tarsi 36.8mm (33–37.5mm); middle toe 36mm (34–39.4mm). Females (N=25): wing length 184.1mm (175–196mm); tail 102mm (95–106 mm); bill 10.7mm (9–12.4mm); tarsi 35mm (32–38mm); middle toe 35.3mm (32–38mm). Specimens from Sakhalin Island differ little from those of the mainland, certainly not enough to be recognized as a subspecies.
Maximum weights of an old male and female in May are 736g (25.9oz) and 730g (25.7oz) respectively, while a year-old male collected at the same place two days earlier was 662g

(25.3oz) (Potapov, 1985). Two males collected in July and August were 600g (21.1oz) and 640g (22.5oz) (Abramov, 1962); a young male in October was 635g (22.4oz). The weight of males and females from the Selemdja River (Amur River Basin) were, on average (with no division by season or age), 708g (25oz) and 636g (22.4oz) respectively (Iudakov, 1972). The difference in weight of old and year-old birds is about 100g (3.5oz).

Moult

The usual pattern for grouse. Special summer feathers are absent and the feathering is thin, as lost feathers are not replaced. Males begin the moult in mid-June and finish in mid-October. The most intensive moult is July–August. Females begin to moult after chick hatching and finish in early October. Females that lay very late begin to moult earlier. Young birds finish the moult to adult plumage in mid-September.

Distribution

The range is restricted by the distribution of a special forest type that includes fir or spruce or both. Such taiga occurs in Far East Russia, including Sakhalin Island, though the birds do not occur in the southern part of the island. The western range border is defined by the dominance of larch forests and climate severity.

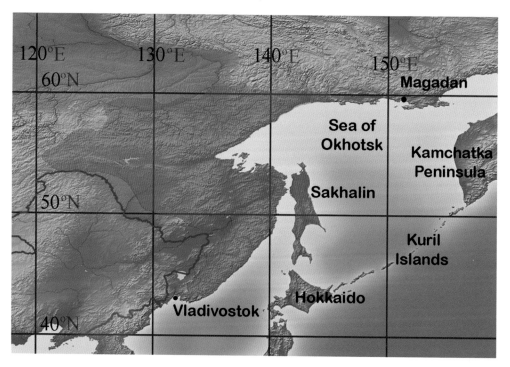

Map 4. Asian Spruce Grouse *(Falcipennis falcipennis)*.

It is difficult to evaluate the historical range, though there is some evidence for it having been larger, e.g. the Evoron Lake depression (Gusakov, 1983). A recent range map (Klaus, Andreev, 2003) suggests an absence in the range centre over an area of nearly 45,000km² (17,375 sq miles). This seemingly unrealistic situation has not been confirmed.

Subspecies

One subspecies was described based on specimens from southern Sakhalin: *F. falcipennis muratai* (Momiyama, 1928), though this was not confirmed later (Potapov, 1985; Nechaev, 1991).

Habitats

Climatic conditions across the range are severe. The average January ambient temperature varies between –16°C (3°F) and –32°C (-25°F), with +12°C (54°F) to +16°C (61°F) in July. Precipitation varies from 500–1,000mm (20–39in) annually. Snow cover varies from 170–220 days. The duration of temperatures above 0°C (32°F) is only 75–105 days. The main habitats are 'Ochotian taiga' forests, in which Ayan Spruce (*Picea ajanensis*) and White-Rind Fir (*Abies nephrolepis*) predominate, or form separate patches in larch woods. Typical sites are deep coniferous forests on mountain slopes, with moss, ledum and significant fallen branch/twig trash. During the breeding season, the birds are usually in the upper parts of the forest, close to the belt of Creep Pine, with a predominance of spruces, firs and birches, moss cover and heavily cluttered understory. The preference for steep slopes is clear throughout the range, the choice of steep, rocky ground recalling that a local Russian name for the species is 'Stone Grouse'. However, large numbers of birds are also seen in plain forests where larch predominate, with spruce and fir being present as small enclaves. Often, solitary birds, even lekking males, are seen in such forests at distances of up to a kilometre from the nearest spruce–fir enclave. In August, broods may leave the thick forest, moving to pure larch forest or even open bogs and subalpine clearings in search of cowberries and other berries, sometimes moving several hundreds metres from spruce/fir.

In winter, the main habitat is deep spruce/fir forest, usually on the lee-side of ridges, especially in deep glens, and occasionally in the brushwood of Creep Pine. In lowland area, larch forests are also used, but these must have Ayan Spruce or White-Rind Fir, the needles of which are the main winter food.

Population structure and density

It is impossible to evaluate the number of Asian Spruce Grouse because of the fragmented distribution of spruce/fir enclaves in differing types of forest. Consequently, studies only indicate a broad range of population density, from 0.25 pairs/km² (Iudakov, 1967) in the spring, to 2 pairs/km² (Potapov, 1985), to 8 birds (not pairs)/km² (Hafner, Andreev, 1998).

The autumn density is higher and can reach 13.2–14.8 birds/km² (near sources of the Amgun River Basin, Brunov et al., 1988). The total number of birds in the Bureau State Reserve (3,584km²/1,384 sq miles) in the autumn of 2000 was estimated at 13–15,000 birds, an average of nearly 4 birds/km² (Biserov, 2001).

The total population was determined as 151,800 birds at the end of 1990 (Litun et al., 1991), but there has been a decrease in population, particularly over the last 50 years. For example, in Khabarovsk Territory (824,600km²/318,380 sq miles) the population in 1976 was estimated as being up to 20,000 birds, but had decreased to 15,000 in 1981 and continues to decrease (Rosliakov, 1985). The influence of predators on the population is minimal in comparison to other species of grouse. An examination of the stomachs of 90 sables found only two with the remains of Asian Spruce Grouse, and there were no remains in 220 sampled sable droppings (Iudakov, 1967). Population decreases can therefore be said to be almost exclusively the result of human activity.

Territoriality

Asian Spruce Grouse are absolutely sedentary birds. Studies suggest that an individual bird may not move across an area of more than a few dozen square metres during an entire summer (Potapov, 1985). However, during the seasonal change of feeding areas, especially in the autumn, individual birds may cover several kilometres in search of favourable winter grounds.

The territorial structure of the population consists of the individual territories of males, whose distribution is not uniform. In favourable habitats, where several males occupy close individual territories, these may form clusters or linear structures along streams, with the edges of the bogs, etc, alternating with areas where no birds are seen.

Behaviour

Asian Spruce Grouse have no fear of man, or even of dogs, accounting for the view that this is an especially stupid bird. If a man is seen, the bird does not fly away, but either moves off slowly, or flies into the nearest tree and sits motionless even if attempts, sometimes successful, are made to catch it with a loop on a stick. Birds on the ground will often allow a man to approach closely, or even to follow close by as it moves, without apparently paying any attention. Studies in both Asia and North America indicate that this combination of fearlessness and minimal mobility is common to all three species. Birds feeding in a tree or on the ground occasionally stand still for long periods, as though they are sleeping. All movements are slow and smooth, and flying is rare. Indeed, a remarkable feature of the Asian Spruce Grouse is its preference for walking over flying, perhaps, in part, due to the specific construction of the wing.

Yet despite this 'sleeping' condition, the bird is on the alert constantly, using sound signals, as its hearing is good. That the bird is alert to predators is confirmed by a study that noted that a female with three nestlings inhabited an area close to a sable den, but suffered no losses. There are also tales of hunting dogs that regularly caught young capercaillie and black grouse, but never took young or old spruce grouse. Cryptic colouration of the birds, particularly in winter, must aid survival, and it is also the case that the male's courtship displays are the quietest of all the grouse family.

Nutrition

The main foods during winter are needles of Ayan Spruce and White-Rind Fir, which also form a proportion of the diet all year. In some regions (Sakhalin Island and Upper Amur Basin) the needles of fir are the main food (Mishin, 1959; Iydakov, 1972), while in others (Yakutia, Sikhote Alin and Lower Amur Basin) it is the spruce (Nikanorov, in litt., Andreev, 1990). In spring the diet is supplemented by fresh larch buds and later by soft larch needles, moss stem tops and the leaves of cowberry. From late summer to winter, berries are added to the diet, together with the needles of larches, firs and spruces, and the seeds of grasses. Juvenile birds also take insects (beetles, grasshoppers, ants, etc). During captive rearing it was established that chicks take few insects, feeding on larch and spruce needles from the age of two weeks (Nikanorov, in litt.).

Wintering

Winters at the borders of the range are severe, with persistent snow cover and ambient temperatures as low as -52°C (-62°F). The birds winter in small groups, or in flocks of up to 30 birds (Iudakov, 1972). It is possible that some birds in these flocks are the remains of broods not dispersed completely in the autumn. The sedentary life of the birds is maximal in winter, the entire time being spent within a very small territory among large spruce or firs that provided food, with clearings in which the birds roost under the snow. Winter life is the least studied: only in the 1980s was research carried out in the lower part of the Amur River Basin (Andreev, 1990). This indicated that adults and sub-adults of both sexes began to use snow burrows only when the ambient temperature dropped below -20°C (-4°F). At higher temperatures, the birds preferred to spend the nights in trees with dense clusters of branches 15–20m (50–65ft) above the ground. The daily schedule was very monotonous: the bird left its snow burrow at sunrise, when the light exceeded 5–7 lux, and flew to the nearest spruce to feed. The bird flies almost vertically at first, then turns between the trees to search for a suitable place.

The bird then spent all day in the tree, alternating between feeding on needles and resting. In sharp contrast to most other grouse, the bird does not dig a snow burrow during the day. The time of active feeding was 4.8 minutes on average, that of resting 19.3 minutes, the bird either motionless (slumbering) or preening. During the second half of the day, the rhythm doubles, i.e. the birds spend half the time in active feeding and resting. When resting, sat among dense branches covered by snow, the birds become almost invisible. During strong frosts, the bird spreads its feathers to maximum extent and looks like a round ball. If excavating a snow burrow, the bird comes down from the tree one hour before nightfall. Using a strong push of the legs, the bird catapults itself out of the tree, from a height of 5–7m (16–23ft), beating its wings strongly to gather speed, then gliding down on spread wings and tail to land soundless in the snow, braking by breast and tail. The bird then stands motionless, looking around for 6–17 minutes before beginning to dig. It digs its tunnel and roost chamber in about 8 minutes. The ambient temperature in the burrow rises quickly, reaching 0°C (32°F) after just a few minutes. The thickness of the chamber roof is 6.1cm (2.4in) on average, the chamber averaging 13.7cm (5.4in) high and 17.6cm (6.9in) wide. This space is large enough even if the bird fluffs its feathers. Within the chamber the bird produces droppings at a rate of 8.2 per hour, slower than during the day (11.5 per hour). As with other grouse, when leaving, the bird puts its head through the ceiling to look around, then breaks through to the surface (Hafner, Andreev, 1998).

The dry weight of the daily food intake was 39g (1.3oz) (Iudacov, 1972). However, this was only half that calculated for birds in the lower part of the Amur Basin: there it was 89g (3.1oz), dry weight, from 150g (5.2oz) of fresh spruce needles (Andreev, 1990). During feeding, the bird walks along a branch, balancing entirely with its legs (in contrast to the Hazel Grouse, which aids balance with the wings). It was noted that the bird did not tear a needle from the branch, but bit it off at the base, all the needle bases showing an accurate cut line (Iudakov, 1972, confirmed by Andreev, 1990).

Breeding

Males begin to lek in the northern part of the range from the beginning of May, and to the south from the end of April. The lek is usually, but not always, solitary: if there are clusters of individual territories, then 3 or 4 males may lek at the limits of mutual vision (observed 700km [435 miles] north of Khabarovsk, near the Uda River estuary, 54°55′N −Veprinzev, in litt.). At this site, at the end of April, several males were lekking simultaneously at a distance of not more than 100m (109yd) from each other, i.e. within both sight and hearing. However, it seemed that the males had no influence on each other, with an individual's activity provoking no activity in the others. There is therefore no reason to consider the situation a genuine collective lek. However, such a situation may well have been the forerunner of the collective lekking now seen in other grouse species.

Despite these observations, several authors have insisted that collective lekking does occur in the species. For example, studies in the southern part of the range, the Bikin River Basin in Sikhote Alin, led the authors to conclude that in spring, males concentrated at a general lekking ground, inside which each male had its own territory (of nearly 1ha) at the centre of which the owner displayed intensively, the most active males gathering 2 or 3 females. Such collective leks were said to be set on terraces of larch and spruce with lots of clearings (Puckinsky, Nikanorov, 1974). No other details support this opinion, though a similar situation has been described in the lower part of the Amur River Basin where male territories were closely situated and linearly arranged along streams, bogs and crests, and on hilltops, with clusters of 4–8 males. When close males displayed, fights often occurred.

Young males are normally tolerated within the territory of old males (Potapov, 1985; Hafner, Andreev, 1998). In one case, two males of unknown age were discovered at distances of 20m from a territorial, lekking male (Abramov, 1962). Unequivocal data regarding the possibility of one-year-old males breeding is absent, but has been conjectured (Hafner, Andreev, 1998; Andreev et al., 2001). It is possible that at favoured places for Asian Spruce Grouse, where there are aggregations of territorial males, other birds, of both sexes, are attracted, and promiscuous situations may arise.

The full courtship display of the species has only recently been described. Fragmentary information had been published (Middendorf, 1875, Yamasona, Yamada, 1939; Vorobiev, 1954), and this was analysed and linked by Potapov (1969) with additional information of his own. Further information has now been added (Pukinsky, Nikanorov, 1975; Hafner, Andreev, 1998; Möllers et al., 1995; Andreev et al., 2001) which permits a full description. At the lek, the main posture of the male is 'Wide-necked Upright' (**Figure 43, n2**), in which the neck and tail are raised, and the wings are slightly to the sides and lowered a little. The male then spreads his tail to its maximum extent and raises it vertically, fluffs the feathers of the neck, nape and throat, and begins to walk with accelerated steps. During the walk the tail is occasionally flicked open and shut synchronously with the steps, with a swishing noise. Then suddenly, the male stops, opens the tail, fluffs the neck feathers vertically, raises the rump feathers, vibrates the wings and utters a vibrating 'uuurrrrrrrrr' with a rapidly rising tone (**Figure 43, n3 and n4**) resembling wind howling in a chimney. The sound lasts nearly 2.5 seconds and while it is being made, the bill is closed and the wings are motionless. The sound is audible at 30–40m (32–43yds), but even if the observer is close to the bird, it seems to come from a distance, so that the source can be difficult to detect. After the sound ends, the bird makes two short jumps immediately, vigorously flapping the wings, both on the ground and as it leaps in the air. At the beginning of the first leap, the male produces a click, sometimes a double click. During the second leap, which immediately follows the first, the male produces two double-clicks. In summary, the clicking is 'tak...tak-tak...tak-tak', with the first click occasionally a double. The clicks are the loudest sounds of the display, audible at up to 100m (109yds). During the leaps the bird covers a distance of 0.45–1.5m (1.5–4.9ft), depending on the size of the glade. In some cases, after the second jump the bird lands and stands motionless for a moment, as though it has collided with an invisible wall, the wings partly extended and the tail near vertical (**Figure 43, n5**). The posture is very

Figure 43. Main courtship display of male Asian Spruce Grouse
1 – walking; 2 – starting position; 3 – movement of tail feathers during stops; 4 – uttering the 'urrrrrr' sound;
5 – double jump with one or two double clicks.

similar to that of Franklin's Spruce Grouse when the bird 'tips the whole body forwards' (Hjorth, 1970). Occasionally, the male turns through 180° during the first jump and moves a little to the side, but the second jump always returns to the start point (Pukinsky, Nikanorov, 1975). After finishing the display, the male stands up, closes his wings, the fluffed feathers return to the normal position and the display begins again.

Individual variations of the display have not been studied, but doubtless exist. For example, in the jumps of one male (Möllers *et al.*, 1995; Andreev *et al.*, 2001), the final posture of the bird, expressed so clearly in other cases, was absent. To date, one intriguing, unanswered question is the source of the clicks, which are very similar to those of capercaillie. Some consider them a vocal sound, while others prefer a mechanical explanation, perhaps involving the wings.

A further courtship display is a special flight by the lekking male. This starts from the lek site, the male making a vertical flight from its upright position, rising to a height of up to 3m, then descending straight down to arrive at the same point. Some authors describe the flight as silent, the rapidly vibrating wings producing only a quiet whirring (Potapov, 1969). However, others maintain the male utters a short, muffled sound, 'hrr-hrr', before starting the flight, then flies to a height of 2–3m (6–9ft) with a slight pause at the high point, 2–3 seconds, and finally making several clicks on landing (Nikanorov in litt.). Occasionally, the flight includes a landing on a branch where the male adopts an upright posture, and opens and raises the tail, before descending to the ground (Kaplanov, 1938). In one case, a lekking male made his flight in a small, mossy clearing while an observing female sat on a spruce branch 2m (6.5ft) above the ground. When an observer approached, the male, disturbed by the intrusion, performed the vertical flight 2m (6.5ft) high with the quickly beating wings held in front of him. The sound produced by this flight was a low buzz (Potapov, 1969). Other descriptions of such flutter-jumps suggest they invariably conclude with a double click (Andreev et al., 2001).

Relationships between the sexes are promiscuous. The female visits the lekking male to mate, leaving after copulation. The male then displays again, seemingly with renewed energy. The male takes no part in incubation or brood care, though the presence of the male near the brood has been observed. The nest is a shallow hole in moss near the trunk of a tree, under low branches or beneath a fallen tree, lined with dry needles, grass or leaves. One nest was 170mm in diameter and 70mm deep. The egg clutch varies from 5–12. The eggs are pale ochre and covered by numerous brown-chestnut dots and spots. The brightness of the colour decreases during incubation. The size of the eggs is 44–48mm x 33–36mm (Nikanorov, in litt.); 43–48mm x 31–32.46mm (Taka-Tsukasa, 1932). The female lays an egg every 36 hours. Incubation takes an average of 23.5 days. Egg-laying started in the Evoron Lake depression (51°3´N) in mid-May, but two weeks later in the mountains of Bureisky Ridge (Hafner, Andreev, 1998). The same dates were observed on Sakhalin Island (Gizenko, 1955), in the central Sikhote Alin (Abramov, 1965), and in the Upper Amur Basin (Selemdja River, Iudakov, 1967). The female sits tight during incubation, even permitting an observer to touch her, but during such intrusions produces a loud rustle of her tail feathers, similar to that of a lekking male, and also utters a prolonged howl resembling the male's 'song'.

A professional hunter who monitored breeding at a site over two years noted (published by Iudakov, 1972) that a nest with just one egg had six eggs six days later. After that, the number of eggs was impossible to check because the female was sitting tight and did not react even when touched. Thirty-five days after the first visit, the nest contained only eggshell and close to the nest was a brood of 12 chicks led by the female. On the hunter's approach, the female hid or moved away slowly: the chicks scattered and hid. When the hunter picked up a chick, the female moved slowly towards him, making low sounds resembling the cackle of a domestic hen. The chicks moved slowly during feeding, constantly pecking among the grass to catch insects, but never digging. On each visit, the hunter saw the male sitting motionless in a tree close to the nest. During the winter, nearby broods formed flocks that stayed close to their nest areas throughout the season. In the spring, the flock divided into pairs. On 1 July, a nest with 11 eggs was found: next day the chicks had hatched and were found close to the nest. Other broods of week-old chicks were found on the 4th, 7th and 10th July, the last one with 12 chicks.

Another careful observation resulted in the following data: in a nest of 7 eggs, the newly hatched chicks weighed 17–18g (0.5–0.6oz) and had the tubes of 7 primaries and 10 secondaries. The eye colour was dark brown, with the bill and legs light grey. The tube of the 8th primary appeared on the 8th or 9th day. The chick voice was a high peep. Short feeding periods (5–10 minutes) alternated with prolonged brooding beneath the female (10–15 minutes). The chicks were brooded until they were one month old. The chicks could make flutter-jumps at 4 days old, and at 7–8 days old could fly to lower branches. The chicks were very fearful at 3–10 days old, hiding when danger threatened, but later become trustful (A.S. Nikanorov, pers. comm. in Potapov, 1985). Isaev (2008), working in boggy area of larch forest in Yakutia in August 2004, noted that a brood of three almost fully grown chicks moved, on foot only, a distance of 120m (131yd) in a 3-hour period one afternoon, feeding on cowberries and mares-tail, and occasionally resting on the ground, despite the observer being no more than 2–3m (6–9ft) away.

Hunting, recreation and conservation

Asian Spruce Grouse were never the specific target of hunters, though they were occasionally taken by local trappers who used the birds as bait to attract fur-bearing animals (mainly sable). Hunting was completely prohibited when numbers decreased: the species was included in all issues of Red Data Book of the former USSR and is now in that of the Russian Federation. The species is protected in nine state and game reserves, covering a total area of 29,220km²/11,282 sq miles (Sokolov et al., 1997). The successful raising of birds in captivity in Novosibirsk Zoo began in 1986, the first egg being produced in 1987. In 1988 the first chicks were successfully reared, and by 2003 more than 50 chicks had been raised, allowing the planning of a programme of release in local forests. A similar programme then began in Yakutsk National Zoo ('Orto-Doidu') using birds raised at Novosibirsk (Isaev, 2008). The attention given to these programmes, and their success, suggests that it will be possible to introduce the species in taiga forest parks to compensate for losses in areas where man has influenced the landscapes to the detriment of the birds.

2.2 NORTH AMERICAN SPRUCE GROUSE Subgenus: Canachites
(Steineger, 1885)

Canace (Reichenbach, 1853): XXIX (nom. praeocc., non Curtis, 1838). *Canachites* (Steineger, 1885a): 410 (nom. nov. pro Canace).
Type species: *Tetrao canadensis* (Linnaeus, 1758), monotype.

The subgenus includes two species, very similar in colouration and morphology to the Asian Spruce Grouse, but with a prevalence in the upper, and especially in the lower, body of a cross-striped pattern. The primaries are without marked sharpness. Both subspecies were described originally as independent, species-level taxa, but were later joined by Reichenbach, 1848, on the basis that hybrids were found in contact zones.

2.2.1 Canadian Spruce Grouse *Falcipennis (Canachites) canadensis*
(Linnaeus, 1758)

Tetrao canadensis (Linnaeus, 1758): 159 (Canada, based on description of *Urogallus maculates canadensis* (Edwards, 1743–1751): 118, pl. 118 and *U. minor americanus* (Edwards, 1743–1751): 71, pl. 71). *Canace canadensis* (Reichenbach, 1853): XXIX. *Dendragapus canadensis* (Turner, 1885): 245. *Canachites canadensis* (Ogilvie-Grant, 1893): 69.

Morphology
Canadian Spruce Grouse have a comparatively narrower and sharper wing than other species of the genus. The top of the spread wing forms the top of the 8th or 7th primary, sometimes both. The tops of the tail feathers are rounded.

Colouration

Adult male
General colour of upperbody is blackish-grey with a cross-striped, sometimes bow-shaped, pattern from olive-grey stripes formed by olive-grey feather tips. The stripes are especially wide on head and neck, where they create a practically monotonous olive-grey colour. The feathers on upper body have similar colouration, with several cross-stripes

Male North American Spruce Grouse

Female North American Spruce Grouse

Male North American Spruce Grouse in Churchill, Canada

of light brown on a blackish background, and olive-grey feather tips. Black throat has, rarely, white spots, and an indistinct white border that begins behind the nostrils and goes under the eye, down to neck and around the throat patch. Prolonged white spots behind the eyes. Breast is black, striped by the narrow white ends of feathers in upper part, and with wide, white bordering of the feathers in lower part. This white feather bordering separates a black breast plastron from the black belly patch, the latter surrounded by the same white feather tops. Primaries are black-brown with whitish edges of the outer webs of 5th–8th primaries and greyish borders on the feather tops of 1st–8th primaries. Secondaries have same colour, but with wider, whitish borders on inner feather tops. Scapular feathers have white, wedge-shaped spots on tops and streaked pattern from narrow, yellowish-grey stripes. Uppertail coverts differ from rump by having a brown tinge. Tail feathers are black, with wide rufous top patches with narrow black bordering. Undertail coverts are black with wide, white tops and brown stripes at sides of webs.

Male in first adult plumage
Differs from adult only by the colour of the 10th (outer) primary, the outer web of which has a whitish, speckled pattern (Ellison, 1968).

Adult female
Upper body is mottled grey-brown, with indistinct cross pattern from wide, grey feather tips with blackish streaks, black under the tip bands, beneath which are ochreous bands. Because of wear of the grey tips, the undertip bands appear on the surface, making the upper parts of body very dark. Underbody has regular pattern of white, black-brown and

Incubating female North American Spruce Grouse

ochre-yellowish cross-stripes. White tops are especially large on belly feathers, so that occasionally belly looks almost completely white, but are very small or absent on the upper breast, which looks ochre. Wings are as male. Tail feathers are black-brown with indistinct cross design from thin ochre stripes and large rufous tops without black bordering. Central pair of tail feathers is as uppertail coverts and rump.

Juvenile (both sexes)

Almost as the Asian Spruce Grouse, but breast plastron has a more intense ochre tinge, and feathers of rump are ochre with regular dark-brown cross-stripes.

Downy chick

As Asian Spruce Grouse, but the black bordering of crown's light-brown cap is more prominent.

North American Spruce Grouse chick unusually perched on a low branch.

Dimensions

Dimensions of male and female respectively (with ranges in parenthesis) are: wing length 180.4mm (165.0–194.0mm), [177.1mm (164.0–bv191.0mm)]; tail 121.9mm (118.0–142.0mm), [106.7mm (97.0–116.0mm)]; tarsi 35.8mm (32.5–38.8mm), [34.5 (31.7–37.4mm)] (Ridgway, Friedmann, 1946),

Weight of adult males varies from 460–570g (16–20oz), and of females from 430–470g (15–16.5oz), with seasonal changes as in other grouse (Pendergast, Boag, 1973; Fig. 21).

Moult

The moult succession is as for other grouse, i.e. juvenile, first adult, first summer (partial), second autumn (second adult), etc.

Distribution

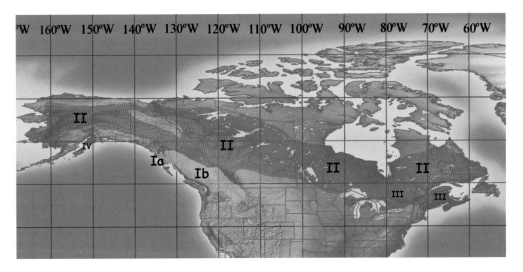

Map 5. Red – Canadian Spruce Grouse (*Falcipennis canadensis*) and Yellow – Franklin's Spruce Grouse (*Falcipennis franklinii*).
Subspecies: Ia – F. f. franklinii; *Ib –* F. f. isleibi.
II – F .c. canadensis; *III –* F. c. canace; *IV –* F. c. atratus.

The species range coincides almost exactly with the North American taiga zone, though the exact position of the border in the Rocky Mountains is unclear because of close contact with Franklin's Spruce Grouse.

Attempts to introduce the species to Kodiak Island and Newfoundland were made in 1957 and in 1964 (Long, 1981). The results are unclear, though latest range map includes Newfoundland (Alsop, 2002). Sale (2006) excluded Newfoundland from the range he presented for the species.

Subspecies

Despite the huge range, geographical variability in the species is relatively insignificant among the identified subspecies, largely because of similarity of conditions across the range. However, three subspecies have been identified:

Falcipennis (Canachites) canadensis canadensis (Linnaeus, 1758)
Colouration as described above. Occupies the entire range, apart from outlying eastern and western parts.

F. (Canachites) canadensis canace (Linnaeus, 1766)
Colouration of males is as nominative, but colouration of females of the grey phase differs by more extensive brown colour. Occupies the south-eastern part of the range west to the marshy woods of south-eastern Manitoba, Canada

F. (Canachites) canadensis atratus (Grinnell, 1910)
Colouration of males differs from that of previous subspecies by more olive-grey tinge of the back, small of the back and uppertail coverts. Females differ by brown-grey tinge of upper body. Occupies the Kenai Peninsula and nearby coastal region of Prince William Sound and Cook Bay, isolated from the main range by the high mountains of Alaska Range, Wrangell and Saint Elias. May be the same subspecies inhabiting the coastal regions close to Bristol Bay (Ridgway, Friedmann, 1946).

Habitats

The main habitat is coniferous forest of the Closed Boreal Zone, where spruce, fir or pine dominate. The dense forest understory is moss or Labrador Tea (*Ledum* sp.), with significant fallen branch, etc, debris and small, marshy clearings. Near the north-western limit of the range, the birds inhabit marginal, sparse spruce woods bordering the tundra and spreading along riverbeds (Bent, 1932). In the central part of the range (Ontario), the birds inhabit forests where Jack Pine (*Pinus banksiana*) dominates, with an understory of young white and black spruce (Lumsden, 1961a). In Michigan, USA, the usual habitat is sparse pine forest, spruce woods with poplars, aspens and birches, or bogs with sparse vegetation of black spruce and larch alternating with slightly elevated, pine-clad ridges (Amman, 1963a). In Alaska, the preferred habitat is spruce wood with a preponderance of black spruce in lower sites, and mixed white spruce, birch, aspen and poplar in the hills (Ellison, 1975).

Population structure and density

The ratio of the sexes in Alaska is equal, though one study area had 100 females to 61 males (Ellison, 1974). The ratio between adult males, females and young birds derived from the results of autumn hunting in Ontario was not constant, with significant annual changes. As a rule (with only one exception), males prevailed among adult birds (from 104 to 168 males for 100 females). Among young birds females dominated (85–92 males for 100 females): in one year the proportion was nearly equal, with males dominating in only one year (of 10) with 122 males to 100 females. The number of young birds to one adult female varied from 2.5 to 7.3 (Lumsden, Weeden, 1963). In New Brunswick, the percentage of yearlings in breeding cohorts varied from 35–58% (Keppie, 1987).

The usual density of the breeding population in Ontario was 10–22 birds/km^2 with a maximum of >50 birds/km^2 (Szuba, Bendell, 1983). Elsewhere it was 9.0–12.3 birds/km^2 in Alaska (Ellison, 1975), 5–9 birds/km^2 in Michigan (Robinson, 1980) and 1–10 birds/km^2 in New York (Bouta, Chambers, 1990). The autumn density was not counted, but the data mentioned suggest it may reach more than 50 birds/km^2. However, at the south-eastern limit of the range, e.g. Maine, the breeding success is so low (0.5–0.6 young for female) that the continued existence of the population is possible only because of immigration (Whitcomb *et al.*, 1996).

Territoriality

The Canadian Spruce Grouse is sedentary, with individuals spending their entire lives in restricted territories. In Michigan, three marked females moved no more than 2.5km (1.6 miles) from the marking area in a year, while eight males moved an average of 1.4km (0.8 miles), with a maximum distance of 5.6km (3.5 miles) (Robinson, Maxwell, 1968). In Alaska, the wanderings of young birds in the autumn averaged 3.2km/2 miles (0.2–10.5km/0.1–6.5 miles). The distances covered by 27 adult birds from their place of marking exceeded 1.6km (1 mile) in only one case, that bird moving 8km (5 miles). The mobility of the birds is maximal in the autumn, partly as a result of the search for grit.

The individual territories of adult birds varies in size from 18.6–177ha (46–437 acres) and are the most minimal during winter, 3–102ha (7–252 acres) (Ellison, 1973), though strict territorialism is peculiar to males alone, and is then only seen during the breeding season. At that time, the individual lekking arenas of males are usually in small clusters. Data from radio-tracked birds showed that males occupy territories of 1–3.5ha (2.5–8.6 acres). Young males rarely have individual territories, occupying areas of up to 8ha, though these areas are not defended and are not true territories. Usually, young males lead a nomadic life, moving freely between the territories of adult males. In one study a young male moved 1.6km (1 mile) during one day. The adult male's connection with his individual territory decreases once the females are incubating. The behaviour of one studied male is typical: the male had a territory of nearly 1.9ha (4.7 acres) between 21 April and 21 May, but then until 22 July the male roamed a territory of 12ha (30 acres) (Ellison, 1971). In summer, dispersal distances may be large (Schroeder, 1986) and in some territories emigration may exceed immigration, or vice versa. One example is a New Brunswick study where the number of young birds in the winter population changed to autumn from 18.8 to 83 birds/km² (Boag, Schroeder, 1992).

Behaviour

The main feature of the behaviour of all Spruce Grouse is the absence of fear of man, the Canadian being no exception. If threatened, chicks prefer to escape by foot, rarely flying to trees. The birds spend most of the summer and autumn on the ground, preferring to move mainly by walking. The flight is noisy, with maneuvering as in Hazel and Ruffed Grouse, but on the ground the bird is extremely quiet. Males make no vocal sounds out of the breeding season, while females only use sound during brood care, though occasionally, when in a tree, they utter a series of clucking sounds that reveal their presence (Johnsgard, 1973).

Nutrition

The main winter food throughout the range is coniferous needles, mainly spruces and pines. In Alaska, the winter food is black and white spruce (Ellison, 1966). In central Alberta, it is needles of *Pinus contorta*, and, to a lesser degree, those of spruces (Pendergast, Boag, 1970). The needles of another pine, *P. banksiana*, are the dominant winter diet of birds in Ontario and Michigan (Crichton, 1963, Gurchinoff, Robinson, 1970). In spring, after the snow cover melts, needles are replaced gradually by cowberries and blueberries, the leaves and flowers of different plants (including the leaves of blueberries and birches) and lichens. The summer diet includes the top shoots and stems of horsetail, seeds of sedges, and fresh growing bunches of spruce needles, but the dominant part is the leaves and, to a lesser degree, the flowers and berries of *Vaccinium membranaceum*. The summer diet also includes berries, insects and spiders. In the autumn, the main food is berries, but as the season ends, the fraction of needles rises and by November comprises 92.5% of the diet. In the eastern part of the range, the needles of larch are very important in the autumn (Crichton, 1963; Pendergast, Boag, 1970, 1971b). The change from the autumn diet to that of winter often happens before snow cover is established (Keppie, 1977).

Wintering

Data on the species' winter life is very scarce. The winter energy budget was studied by observations in the field and in open-air cages in central Alberta. This found that the daily ration was 40.4g (1.4oz) of pine needles (dry weight), equivalent to 899.8kJ/day. From this amount the bird used only 10.9g (0.3oz) of the dry weight, the excreted energy being 623.0kJ/day – leaving a daily energy budget of 276.8kJ (Pendergast, Boag, 1971b). Such a low level of existence energy may be explained by the fact that it was determined for birds in cages, where mobility was very restricted. However, these data are consistent with those from studies of wintering Asian Spruce Grouse in Russia's Amur Basin (Iudakov, 1972).

Breeding

Nuptial activity in males is maximal during the first half of May, when the birds are active in individual territories, situated in dense forest, but with areas of sparse trees where the male can complete its courtship displays.

There are problems in describing the courtship displays of the species, as the breeding behaviour of Franklin's Spruce Grouse has been well studied and described in detail, and in many cases descriptions for the Canadian species are actually general for the united species and therefore chiefly *F. franklinii*.

The most detailed description of the courtship display of the Canadian Spruce Grouse was given by Lumsden (1961a). The display consists of a demonstrative flight and several display acts on the ground. In the basal courtship pose, the male stands with lifted head and tail. The lower coverts of the retrices are lifted so the white tops form a specific pattern against the background of black retrices. The eyebrows are widened and rise above the head as two bright red ridges. The feathers at the front and sides of the neck, and the upper part of the breast, are raised, with the white tops of the breast feathers forming transverse bands against the black background. When moving near a female, the male takes several exaggerated steps, stops, marks time, inclines his head and utters a short, harsh hissing, followed immediately by a high, shrill sound. The tail is opened fully, closed, then opened fully again with a loud rustle during the hissing. The male then lowers its slightly spread wings to the ground.

In another courtship display, the male makes sharp movements of his head from side to side, opening and closing the tail with a loud rustle on each movement. During this ritual the male squats slightly, raises its rump, spreads the wings and rustles the breast feathers. Sometimes the male moves towards the female with pompous, but cautious, steps, with the lateral retrices of the fully open and lifted tail flicking alternatively sideways synchronously with the steps: when the left foot rises, the right retrices are rapidly flicked out and back, and vice versa. Sometimes the male also gives a slight beat or two with its wings, similar to the initial strokes in the drumming of Ruffed Grouse (Harper, 1958).

In another description, the male flew straight up, as high as the surrounding trees, 'stood' for an instant at the upper point of the flight, then dropped slowly while 'drumming' its wings, to reach the start point. This display was repeated again and again (nominate species, Bendire, 1892). In yet another description, the male flew from a branch, heading downwards, then 'paused' to flutter his wings before ascending to a branch on an adjacent tree (DeVany, 1921). A very similar, drumming flight has been described for the male of the subspecies *F. c. canace*, during which the male flew upwards with vibrating wings on a spiral course around the trunk of a large tree, all the while making a drumming sound (Brewster, 1925). Another description of a display flight by a male of the same subspecies noted that the bird 'has been seen to drum also while climbing the leaning trunk of a tree, while hovering in the air and while merely flying up or down to or from the top of a stump'. The sound of this drumming was audible at least 50m away (Forbush, 1927). Drumming flight is used by males in different situations and in different ways, but the main peculiarity of it is the momentary 'stand' at the upper point, with quick beats of the wings, and the descent to the ground or branch with the quickly flapping wings producing the drumming sound. In one case, before the landing on the ground, the male put his body into a vertical position and landed with a pronounced loud flapping that was audible at a distance of 200m (Lumsden, 1961).

Males may adopt the lek posture occasionally at any time, but particularly during the spring and autumn leks. Drumming flights are very often seen in the autumn lek (Robinson, Maxwell, 1968; Ellison, 1973).

Nests are usually placed under low spruce branches and are hidden well (Johnsgard, 1973). In some cases, the nest is made in a thick moss layer (Bent, 1932). Interestingly, although nests are usually at a distance from each other, they are sometimes set very close (Palmer, 1949). The nest is a shallow depression about 20cm (8in) in diameter, sparsely lined with dry leaves, needles, grass stems and several of the female's feathers. To aid camouflage, the cryptic female sits tight on the eggs, even permitting touching by an observer. In one study, an incubating female ignored approaching people, squirrels running close by and the approach of a Grey Jay (*Perisoreus canadensis*) (Walkinshaw, 1948).

The eggs are red-brown with a few dark brown spots and dots (Short, 1967). From a study of caged birds, it was noticed that the general colour of the eggs is practically the same as that of the young spruce buds that formed the bulk of the diet of the females, and that the greater the fraction of buds, the bright and richer the colour (Bishop, 1912). Females in captivity produce eggs at intervals of 1–3 days (Pendergast, Boag, 1971a). A full clutch is 4–12 eggs (usually 6–9) and is larger in northern parts of the range. For example, in Canada's New Scotland, the average was 5.8 eggs (39 clutches, 4–10 eggs: Tufts, 1961), while in Alaska it was 7.5 (26 clutches, 4–9 eggs; Ellison, 1973). The eggs (N=107) are 43.5mm x 31.1mm (Bent, 1932).

Females begin to lay in mid-May. Incubation lasts 23–24 days, but in caged birds it was only 21 days (Pendergast, Boag, 1971a). The female leaves the nest for feeding with an upward flight from the nest and returns to a nearby branch from where she scans for danger before flying directly to her clutch (Walkinshaw, 1948). Data from many observations indicates that the male stays close to the nest and, later, the brood, but takes no part in incubating or caring for the brood. The chicks hatch around 10 June. In Canada's New Brunswick, hatching was found to be weather-dependent, occurring between 10 June and 1 July (Quinn, Keppie, 1981). In the northern limits of the range, hatching usually begins from 12 June.

During the first two weeks of life, the chicks increase in weight by 1.61–2.55g (0.05–0.08oz) per day, then up to 5 weeks of age by 4.82–6.71g (0.17–0.23oz) per day, and up to 2 months of age by 4.31–5.93g (0.15–0.20oz) per day (Quinn, Keppie, 1981). The size of the territory the brood inhabits varies significantly, from 6.1–155ha. Disintegration of the brood begins in September, though most of the young move no great distance, the maximal movement during the first autumn not exceeding 10.5km (6.5 miles) (Ellison, 1973).

Hunting, recreation and conservation

The Canadian Spruce Grouse is a game bird in most of the provinces of Canada, including Newfoundland, where it was reintroduced in 1964, and in the US states of Alaska, Washington, Montana and Minnesota. The species is protected in Michigan, New Hampshire, New York, Oregon, Vermont and Wisconsin. In all cases where hunting is permitted, there is a defined hunting season and bag limit, and licences are required. Takes are high – in 1970, 440,000 birds were killed (Johnsgard, 1973) – but with the total population (of both the Canadian and Franklin's) estimated at more than one million, there is considered to be no need for special conservation measures. However, the success of captive rearing suggests that conservation is unlikely to be a major issue in future.

2.2.2 Franklin's Spruce Grouse *Falcipennis (Canachites) franklinii* (Douglas, 1829)

Tetrao franklinii (Douglas, 1829): 139 (the valleys of the Rocky Mountains from 50°N to 54°N near sources of the Columbia River, Canada). *T. canadensis var. franklinii* (Reichenbach, 1848): Tab. 215. *Canace franklinii* (Elliot, 1864): 23. *C. canadensis var. franklinii* (Baird, Brewer, Ridgway, 1874): 419. *Dendragapus franklinii* (Ridgway, 1885): 355. *Canachites franklini* (Ogilvie-Grant, 1893): 71. *C. canadensis franklini* (Aldrich, 1963): 533.

Similar to the previous species, but inhabits mountain coniferous forests only.

Morphology

The main morphological distinction from the Canadian Spruce Grouse are the tail, that of males being longer, and the tops of the retrices, which are cut off straight (see Figure 40) and have no spots. The upper and lower retrice coverts have the same form of top or are slightly rounded. The wings are wider.

Colouration

Adult male

While generally similar to the Canadian Spruce Grouse, *franklinii* differ by having a completely black throat (rarely with small white marks), a clearer white bordering, a wider spread of velvety black colour on the breast and upper belly, and in the colouration of tail feathers. The latter are black, sometimes with a narrow white strip on the central retrices' tops and indistinct brown specks on the lower parts. Uppertail coverts are black with large white tops and thin, yellowish streaks at the outer webs, as in the Black-billed Capercaillie. Undertail coverts are black with large white tops, sometimes with the remainder of white cross-bands on the edges of the webs and with narrow white patches on the feather shafts.

Male in first adult plumage

Differs from older males by a more prominent sharpness of the 10th primary, and the presence there of light brown specks. Uppertail coverts have narrow white tips and white cross-bands washed with brown streaks. Tail feathers are narrower and the white stripes on the tops present more often than in adult birds.

Male Franklin's Spruce Grouse

Female Franklin's Spruce Grouse

Adult female

Differs from the Canadian Spruce Grouse only by the form and colouration of the tail feathers, which are straight cut off, as in the male, and black-brown. There are indistinct rufous bands on the tops of these feathers, which are whitish along the upper edge. Central pair of tail feathers has a rufous cross-stripe pattern washed by ochreous streaks. Uppertail coverts are black with indistinct rufous stripes and dense streaks. The tops of these feathers are white, but not as large as in male.

Female in first adult plumage

Tail feathers are black with indistinct brown cross-bands and dense streaks. Uppertail coverts have the same colouration, but with narrow white strips on the tops (Zwickel, Martinsen, 1967).

Juvenile (both sexes)
Colouration as the Canadian Spruce Grouse, except the tertials and scapulars, which have a pattern due to concentric oval and cross rufous stripes (Ridgway, Friedmann, 1946).

Downy chick
As Canadian Spruce Grouse.

Dimensions
Sizes are approximately the same as Canadian Spruce Grouse. Dimensions of males and females respectively (with ranges in parenthesis) are: wing length 182.3mm (172–192mm), 179.2mm (171–190mm); tail 129.3mm (118–144mm), 107.9mm (94–119mm); tarsi 34.9mm (31.8–37.2mm), 34.2mm (32–35.8mm) (Ridgway, Friedmann, 1946).

Weight changes during the year have not been studied. Autumn weight of old males (N=65) is 492±4g (400–560g); females (N=84) 456±3g (370–513g). Autumn weight of young males (N=77) is 414±6g (213–498g), young females (N=100) is 386± 5g (158–485g). All these data are from birds collected during September and early October (Zwickel, Brigham, 1974) when a great weight increase occurs in young birds literally every week. Because of this, the maximal weight shown in parenthesis is closest to the real situation in October.

Moult
Not described.

Distribution
The range borders are not clear. The data presented in Map 5 follows Boag, Schroeder (1992).

Subspecies

Falcipennis (Canachites) franklinii franklinii (Douglas, 1829)
Occupies the entire range apart from Prince of Wales Island.

F. (Canachites) f. isleibi (Dickerman, Gustafson, 1996)
Prince of Wales Island, south-east Alaska. Differs by darker colouration, a shorter wing and longer tail and (mainly) by the narrower white tops of the uppertail coverts, these being nearly 5mm wide, rather than the 6–11mm in the nominative form.

Habitats
Mountain coniferous and mixed forest in which different kinds of pines, Engelmann Spruce (*Picea engelmannii*), firs, tsuga and junipers dominate, within altitude limits of

Male Franklin's Spruce Grouse in a spruce tree

1,500–2,700m (4,921–8,855ft) (Jewett *et al.*, 1953). Occasionally lives at lower altitudes during the summer (down to 1,050m/3,445ft) (Bent, 1932). On the eastern slopes of the Rocky Mountains in south-western Alberta, the study area was situated between 1,500m (4,921ft) and 2,000m (6,562ft) in a mountain forest of pine (*Pinus contorta*) with a mix of White Spruce, Balsam Fir and aspens.

Population structure and density

The population structure is essentially as for the Canadian Spruce Grouse. In the study area mentioned above, the density in the breeding season varied from 14.8–31.2 birds/100ha (Keppie, 1979; Herzog, Keppie, 1980), with a constant dominance of males (41–36; 55–46; 57–50; 52–39 in 1970–1973 respectively). At the same time, among young birds in the autumn, the ratio was more equal: 10–7: 21–21; 17–19; 14–13. According to the same authors, the correlation between old and young birds in 1970–1973 was 19–58; 42–59; 31–76 and 27–64. In Washington State, the ratio of young birds to one adult varied from 0.34 to 3.13 (results of autumn hunting, Zwickel, Brigham, 1974).

Territoriality

Data were obtained during a study of the movements of this sedentary species by the mass marking of birds in the same study area mentioned above. Three types of territoriality were identified: completely sedentary (61%), migratory (39%) and transit birds, not counted in common counts, and comprising 14.5% from the two groups. 'Migratory' here means that the birds remained in the territory only during the winter (75%), or only during the summer. The first birds leaving wintering places to fly to breed elsewhere during March–April were males, followed by females. The majority of migrant birds were females (79.8%), while among sedentary birds males dominated (62.4%). Radio-tracking shows that the distance of migration of females was significantly more than males (5.0±1.0km/3.1±0.6 miles and 1.7±0.5km/1.05±0.3 miles respectively). Despite these short distances, the behaviour of migrant birds was similar to that displayed by long-distance migrants: they fly in the early morning or in the evening and use the same route in spring and autumn, pausing to feed during the day. The daily distances were 1.2±0.2km (0.7±0.1 miles) in spring and 1.4±0.2km (0.8±0.2 miles) in the autumn, while sedentary birds moved only 0.11±0.2km (0.06±0.1 miles) in spring, and 1.4±0.2km (0.8±0.1 miles) in the autumn. The birds used very similar places for breeding and wintering year by year. It was also determined that of young birds leaving the territory close to their nest during their first autumn, 65.6% did not return. Of the remainder, half remained (i.e. became sedentary) within the territory, while the others left the territory in the spring, but returned in the autumn, i.e. became winter migrants. To complete a complicated picture, young birds from other nesting areas can immigrate to a territory, or become migrants to it (Keppie, 1979; Herzog, Keppie, 1980), while a further study in the same area with 93 radio-tagged birds suggested that the movements of young birds during their first dispersal were retraced at a later time (Schroeder, 1985).

Behaviour

As for the Canadian Spruce Grouse, except that a different vocal alarm call has been identified, consisting of 2–3 low notes, finished by an unpleasant squeaking sound (Douglas, 1829, it. from Jewett et al., 1953).

Nutrition

The main winter food is needles of spruces and firs, up to 5,500 needles being found in a crop (Bent, 1932). The summer diet includes different berries, leaves and the same spruce and fir needles (Jewett *et al.*, 1953). Incubating females prefer the fresh sprouts of White Spruce (McCourt *et al.*, 1973). In north-western Montana in October, the diet was chiefly the needles of larch, pines and, to a lesser degree, the needles of Engelmann Spruce and junipers, the leaves of clover, bilberry and snowberry (*Symphoricarpos rivularis*). Among insects, grasshoppers are preferred (Jonkel, Creer, 1963). In Washington State, in the autumn, the diet was mainly the needles of the pine *Pinus contorta* (47 %), larch (16 %), berries, leaves and stems of different species of *Vaccinium* (14 %). The needles of *Pseudotsuga* firs and Engelmann Spruce were taken minimally (Zwickel *et al.*, 1974).

Wintering
Apart from the winter diet, there are no details on the winter life of the species.

Breeding
Male lek activity lasts from mid–April to mid–June. Courtship displays have been well studied (MacDonald, 1968). The main peculiarity is a specific wingbeat display. In this, the male flies up from the ground to a branch of the nearest tree, in which, standing upright he '…makes three or four wing strokes like the initial movements of a drumming Ruffed Grouse. Each stroke produces an audible drum-like thump. The tail is held at an angle of about 45°, with the undertail coverts fully spread.' After this the male makes a horizontal, or slightly descending, flight for about 20m before landing on the ground with fluttering wings and a vertical body position. Just before the landing, the male makes two especially deep flaps, during which the wings strike together over his back, producing two very sharp cracks. There is another crack at the moment of landing. These cracks sound like handclapping, or the breaking of a dry branch, and are audible for a distance of 300m. During the flight, the male's tail is widely spread, and the wings produce a soft humming sound. On the ground, during a ritual that Hjorth (1970) named as 'The Rush-cum-Momentary Tail-fanning and Hiss-plus-Squeak Call', the male produces a loud rustling noise, a specific hiss and, finally, a soft low 'huuuut' (MacDonald, 1968).

Females finish laying their clutches by mid–June, with chicks hatching in the first half of July. Earlier clutches are known (e.g. 28 April in Washington State – Dawson, 1896), but the rule is for late breeding – a result of late spring and summer in the high mountains.

Egg colour is as Canadian Spruce Grouse. Clutches are 4–7, usually 5 (Bent, 1932). A repeated clutch may be 2–4 (Keppie, 1975). In one case, a female laid 5 eggs in 7 days. Egg size is (N=33) 42.7mm x 31.2mm. Incubation is intensive, the female leaving the nest for 3–4 short feeding periods daily, these not exceeding a total time of 7% of the day. When leaving the nest for feeding, the female covers the eggs with pieces of litter and thickens the lining beneath the eggs (McCourt *et al.*, 1973). Incubation is 23.5 days. Once hatched, the brood resides in a comparatively small territory, which may overlap

Female Franklin's Spruce Grouse

with a neighbor's territory. The chicks of one brood may also move to another and an entire brood may transfer on the death of its own mother (Keppie, 1977).

Hunting, recreation and conservation

Franklin's Spruce Grouse is a popular game bird and hunting is legal throughout its range, though as with the Canadian Spruce Grouse, there are defined seasons and bag limits. At present, no concerns have been raised over the population of the species and it is considered that hunting laws, and their strict enforcement, are currently sufficient in terms of conservation.

CHAPTER 4

Genus 3: *Dendragapus* BLUE GROUSE

Dendragapus (Elliot, 1864): 23. *Tympanuchus* (part) (Reichenow, 1913): 320.
Type species: *Tetrao obscurus* (Say, 1823). For consequent designation (Baird, Brewster, Ridgway, 1874: 522).

The genus includes two species of forest grouse – the Dusky Grouse (*D. obscurus*) and the Sooty Grouse (*D. fuliginosus*), both of which inhabit the coniferous mountain forests of North America's Rocky Mountains. Both species are large, needle-eating birds with comparatively long tails and legs. Males have an essentially monotonous greyish-smoky colouration, females a mottled one.

The genus was identified by Elliot as different from other North American grouse because of the presence in the Dusky (Blue) Grouse of 20 retrices. The second species, Sooty Grouse, which has only 18 retrices, was first described as a subspecies, *D. obscurus* var. *fuliginosus*, by Ridgway in 1873, one of several identified subspecies. Only in 1926 was Brooks, after careful analyses of distribution, colouration, ecology and courtship displays of all eight described subspecies, able to identify two species in the genus, each with four subspecies (Brooks, 1926). Later, an attempt was made to join the genera *Falcipennis* and *Dendragapus* into one (Short, 1967), the error of this being shown later (Potapov, 1970a, 1985), that author sharing Brooks' opinion regarding two separate species. This view was later supported by DNA analysis (Guttierez *et al.*, 2000). However, most ornithologists preferred to consider the genus as monotypic (*D. obscurus*) until 2006, when the American Ornithological Union split it into two species on the basis of the work of Brooks, together with the latest mitochondrial DNA research (Barrowclough *et al.*, 2004). A recent monograph on the biology and taxonomy of blue grouse (Zwickel, Bendell, 2004) has provided excellent information on the taxonomic structure of the genus. It is worth noting that the original defining characteristic of difference between the two species, the number of retrices, is subject to substantial variations, with many Sooty Grouse having 20 tail feathers. Such individual variations in the number of tail feathers in grouse males are rare, but are also seen in other genera, for instance the capercaillies.

The species are similar in size. Sexual dimorphism in size is more pronounced than in the genera considered in previous chapters. The pelvis of adult birds is among the narrowest and highest of the Tetraonidae, the width and height being, respectively, 76.3% and 18.4% of the length (Potapov, 1985).

Wing length, and the shape of the wing top, are similar to the Asian Spruce Grouse, i.e. 45.2–48.0% of body length, with the 7th primary the longest. Wing width (65.0–67.0% of its length in males, and 73.0% in females) is the same as in male American spruce grouse, and in female Asian Spruce Grouse, i.e. the wing of blue grouse is shorter and more rounded. The comparative length of the tail is equal in both sexes at 30.5–31.5% of body length, as in Asian Spruce Grouse. Roundness of the top of the tail is minimal, and the difference between the central and outer retrices is only 7.2–9.9% of tail length in Dusky Grouse, and 12.0–14.6% in Sooty Grouse. The length of the tarsi in both species is the same – 7.9–8.0% of body length. The central toe, as a rule, is markedly longer than the tarsi. Pectinations on the toes are minimal among American grouse, despite the large body size, usually being ≤ 2mm instead of the 2–3mm seen in Ruffed Grouse, and up to 5mm seen in Sharp-tailed Grouse (Zwickel, Bendell, 2004).

The males of both species have a specific neck morphology that permits the inflation of the skin of the lateral apteria as a large bubble. The skin is elastic and can be vastly spread during moments of sexual excitation. Normally the skin is closely compressed, appearing as a knobby surface divided by deep transverse and longitudinal fissures. The area has a well-developed muscular layer that moves the feathers around the apteria, and is lined inside by a specific muscular bag formed by strongly developed caudal portions of *M. cucullaris*. The bag has two muscular layers, the inner longitudinal, and the outer transverse. The lateral portions of *M. cucullaris* can act independently so that the bird can inflate both, or only a single, apteria. The lateral portions line all the upper part of the neck cavity and jut out as two small pockets in the centres of the stretched parts of skin (**Figure 44**).

The eye-combs of males are well developed, the surface covered by dense, thin sprouts that can be erected to a height of up to 5mm (**Figure 45, n1**).

Tarsi are feathered to the base, and the first phalanges of the toes are part feathered, as in Spruce Grouse. There is a little patch of naked skin behind the eye: this is larger in males.

The colouration of adult males is similar. Female colouration is more mottled, the colour of the upper body similar to Black-billed Capercaillie females. Juveniles differ from adults in having a white throat and a general mottled colouration, brownish tones being prevalent, and a specific longitudinal pattern from narrow white patches on the feather shafts. Downy young are ochre-brown above, yellowish-grey below, with a complex pattern of short, black stripes and spots (**Figure 46**), resembling those of capercaillie chicks.

Each species has four subspecies identified by slight differences in colouration. In some cases these differences are peculiar to the females. In general, subspecies colour is darker and more saturated in the north and paler in the south.

The range of both species is restricted to mountain forests of the North American Cordillera (see **Map 6**) from 63°N south to 33°30′N, and in general close to the Pacific

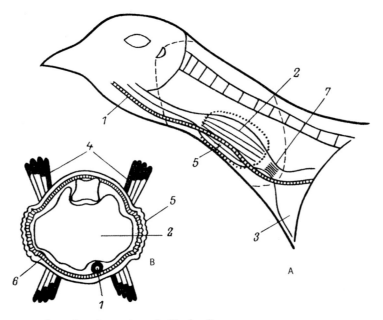

Figure 44. Construction of neck sacs in male Dusky Grouse
From the side (A), and cross-section through the sacs (B). 1 – trachea; 2 –broadened part of the esophagus (in section A it is shown in the 'calm' condition, gathered in folds); 3 – crop; 4 – surrounding rings of feathers; 5 – knobby bare skin of the neck apteria; 6 – musculature layer; 7 – sphincter. The dashed line shows the borders of the muscular bag, the dotted line the section of skin inflated during display

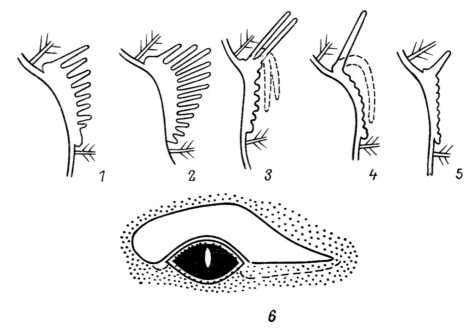

Figure 45. The eye-combs of grouse
Cross-sections of 1 – Bonasa, Falcipennis, Dendragapus, Tetrao; 2 – Lyrurus tetrix; 3 – Lyrurus mlokosiewiczi; 4 – Lagopus; 5 – Tympanuchus, Centrocercus; 6 – distribution of the red colour of the skin of Western Capercaillie around the eye and eye-comb. Dashed line – 'calm' position of the eye-comb.

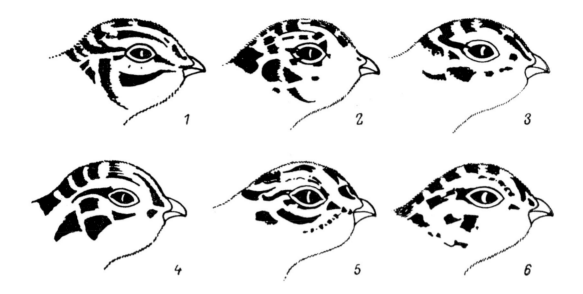

Figure 46. Head patterns of downy young Blue and Dusky Grouse
1 – D. o. obscurus; *2 –* D. o. richardsoni; *3 –* D. o. howardi; *4 –* D. f. sierrae; *5 –* D. f. atkensis; *6 –* D. f. fuliginosus *(from Moffit. 1938).*

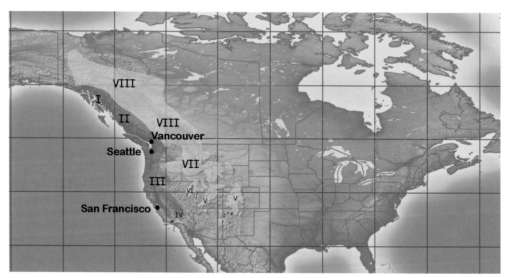

Map 6. Blue Grouse: Red – Sooty Grouse (*Dendragapus fuliginosus***) and Yellow – Dusky Grouse (***D. obscurus***).**
Subspecies: Sooty Grouse (I–IV) and Dusky Grouse (V–VIII).
I – D. fuliginosus sitkensis; *II –* D. f. fuliginosus; *III –* D. f. sierrae; *IV –* D. f. howardi; *V –* D. obscurus obscurus; *VI –* D. o. oreinus; *VII –* D. o. pallidus; *VIII –* D. o. richardsoni.
1 – Northern foothills of the Mogollon Mountains; 2 – Zuni Mountains; 3 – Taylor Mountains; 4 – Chikoma Mountains; (1–4: Bailey 1928) 5 – Toiyabe, Tonima, Monitor ridges; 6 – Ruby Mountains; 7 – Spain and Din Creek mountains; (5–7: Behle, Selander 1951); 8 – Mount Pinos (Ridgway, Friedmann 1946); 9 – South Baldy and San-Mateo mountains (Johnsgard 1973).

coast – never more than 1,600km (994 miles) from the ocean. Overall, the range has a relic character. Climatically the range is influenced by the warm Pacific Ocean and is therefore softer (i.e. more maritime) than that of the inner continent. The long, narrow range of the genus depends on the position of mountain forest belts. To the north these are lower (about 700m/2,297ft), to the south higher (1,700m/5,577ft). In general, blue grouse inhabit a range with cool, dry summers, maximum precipitation in the autumn and winter, but with a less harsh winter than those experienced by other tetraonids.

The range is unique among grouse – the parallel disposition of two species along the same mountain system for a distance of almost 3,500km (2,175 miles). The ranges of the two species are completely divided south of 49°N, but are in contact to the north, the division between them being two parallel systems of the North American Cordillera, the inner system of Rocky Mountain ridges and the coastal mountain ridges along the Pacific coast of the Pacific Ocean, including the Cascade and Sierra Nevada ridges.

Dusky and Sooty Grouse inhabit different types of mountain forests, each showing great plasticity in choice of habitats but demonstrating a constant preference for sparse forest – woodland edges and clearings with dense, tall grass, especially during the breeding season. In general, Sooty Grouse prefer denser forests. The main winter food for both species is the needles of coniferous trees.

Blue grouse behaviour is similar to that of spruce grouse. They are reticent, chiefly ground-living birds, relying on cryptic colouration for protection: when sat motionless in the crown of a tree, the play of light and shadow makes the smoky-grey birds almost invisible. Only during spring are the birds readily observable, when the males perform their nuptial songs and courtship displays. Though preferring a pedestrian lifestyle, the birds fly up easily, and have a fast, readily maneuvering flight. A flushed bird usually flies only a short distance, then sits in the upper part of a tree, becoming motionless and staying put, even if shot at. When flushed on a mountain slope, the birds prefer to glide downhill on spread wings (Bent, 1932). Young birds are relatively trusting, but older birds are wary, particularly of people. Both sexes are very silent, uttering only specific cackles when flushed.

As a rule, adult birds are solitary, though small flocks can be seen at good feeding places. The degree of permanency of such flocks is unknown. Information regarding winter life is very scarce. It is known that the birds roost in trees, and that they can stay for prolonged periods without either descending to the ground or moving from one tree to another. Only at times of intense cold, with deep snow cover, do the birds excavate snow burrows (Skinner, 1927).

Seasonal movements are usual for all populations because of the differences in breeding and wintering habitats. Specific examples are given in the species descriptions below. The ratio of sexes is usually equal. The fraction of young birds in the autumn does not usually exceed 40% of the total population. However, populations are not stable, with significant fluctuations in numbers occurring. Both species are polygamous, with rare exceptions. In spring, males occupy individual territories where they perform their courtship displays, mating with any females they attract. Generally, male territories are grouped into clusters, though the proximity of other males does not appear to influence the displays.

Female nest construction is as for other grouse – a shallow hole in the ground, about 8cm (3.2in) deep and 18cm (7in) in diameter, sparsely lined with dry grass stems, needles, etc. The nest is placed near the trunk of a large tree or under low branches, but may also be placed in tall, dense grass several hundred metres from the nearest trees. Clutch size is extremely variable, from 2–12 eggs. Egg colour is similar to spruce grouse, but with a paler background, sometimes almost white (Short, 1967). Newly hatched chicks stay together and close to the nest site for several days, feeding on different insects and the soft, green parts of grasses. Chicks can make short flights at one week, these increasing to 60m at two weeks (Mussehl, 1963). Females stop brooding the chicks when they are 11 days old. The brood stays in a territory of about 17ha, around the nest site, for about two months, with their area often overlapping the territories of other broods.

The moult of adult birds has not been well-studied. It is known that breeding females begin to change their primaries only after chick hatching (Zwickel, Dake, 1977) and finish this change at the end of September. In males, this change lasts from the end of May to the beginning of October.

Only two cases of hybridization of blue grouse with other genera of grouse are known. One was *Falcipennis franklinii* x *Dendragapus fuliginosus*. The offspring were predominantly *franklinii* in colour, but the tail was as Sooty Grouse both for the number of retrices (18), the fact they had rounded tops, and in colour (Jollie, 1955). The second hybrid, *Dendragapus fuliginosus* x *Tympanuchus (Pedioecetus) phasianellus*, was described from British Columbia, Canada (Brooks, 1907).

The close resemblance of blue grouse with the spruce grouse resulted in some authors joining the two genera under the name *Dendragapus* (Short, 1967). The close phylogenetic connection is obvious, suggesting evolution from a single ancestor, a needle-eating bird adapted to life in coniferous, mainly mountain, forests. There are some features similar to those of capercaillie (particularly the Kamchatka subspecies of *Tetrao parvirostris*), but also some with both prairie-chickens and sage-grouse. It is important to note that the main and optimal habitats of blue grouse are comparatively old types of boreal forest vegetation, with relic species of coniferous trees.

The presence in blue grouse of the deeply specialized morphological structure connected with courtship displays, i.e. the inflatable parts of naked skin of the neck, is a characteristic that is shared only by males of Nearctic grouse (7 of 11 species), being entirely absent from all Eurasian species. The development of such naked skin-based structures is incompatible with the process of adaptation to a severe winter climate, but it is, of course, possible that the ancestral blue grouse evolved in more benign, southerly conditions. Moreover, the preservation of such morphological structures was possible only in comparatively warm winters, as found along narrow coastal regions climatically influenced by a warm oceanic basin.

3.1 DUSKY GROUSE *Dendragapus obscurus* (Say, 1823)

Tetrao obscurus (Say in James, 1823): 14 (near 'Defile Creek' about 32km (20 miles) north of Colorado Springs, USA). *Canace obscura* (Bonaparte, 1857): 428. *Dendragapus obscurus* (Elliot, 1864): 23.

Medium-sized terrestrial bird with comparatively long feet and tail. There are 20 retrices (but sometimes only 18). The tops of the tail feathers are squared or truncated (see **Figure 40, n2 and n3** in Chapter 3).

Colouration

Adult male
Upper parts of the head, neck and nape are blue-grey with indistinct brown marks on crown. Back and rump are brown-grey, with an indistinct scaly pattern of light-grey borders of the feathers, and with brown streaks on scapulars. Uppertail coverts are brown with whitish streaks. Throat is white, heavily marked brown, with an indistinct white border. All underparts are ashy-grey with a light blue tinge, apart from upper breast, which is dark-brown. Feathers of base of neck and on breast are sharply bicoloured, with white bases and grey tips. Normally, the white parts are hidden by the grey tops of other feathers, but during courtship displays, when the neck apteria are inflated as bright-red bubbles, and surrounding feathers stand vertical, the white bases form white rosettes, with grey bordering. Flanks are mottled by white feather tops. Primaries are brown, patterned with whitish cross-stripes on 5th–8th, and narrow, white borders on tops of 1st–4th. Secondaries are brown, with wide white borders on tops of outer webs and indistinct cross-stripes on outer margins. Retrices are black with wide grey bands on the tops (see **Figure 40, n2 and n3** in Chapter 3) in Colorado, but are solid black in other areas. Uppertail coverts are brown with dense yellowish streaks on feather tops. Undertail coverts have wide white tops. First adult plumage has the same colouration, but the outer 9th and 10th primaries have sharp tops.

Male Dusky Grouse

Adult female

Upper parts are mottled brown, grey and yellow. Head is light-grey with brown cross-marks. Upper neck is similar, but the grey feather tops are larger, and become even larger on the back. On the lower back these grey tops decrease again, and general colouration is darker. Then, on rump and uppertail coverts the white tops increase in size again, but are whitish or brownish with thin black streaks. Underbody has a more complicated colouration: throat is as the male; neck is covered with whitish and brown marks; upper part of breast is yellowish-grey with a transverse pattern of brown and yellow stripes, and longitudinal white stripes on the feather shafts. Belly is as male. Primaries, secondaries and retrices are paler, the top bands of the retrices narrower and with blackish dots. Uppertail coverts and central pair of retrices are as rump. Undertail coverts have white tops. Females in first plumage differ from older birds only by having sharp tops to the two outer primaries.

Female Dusky Grouse

Juvenile (both sexes)

Similar to the female, but the upper body is patterned by longitudinal white strips on the feather shafts. The grey band at the top of tail is also absent, and the throat is almost completely white.

Downy chick

Underbody is greyish-yellow with an indistinct yellow-brown band across the breast. Upper body is covered by a complicated pattern of black-brown stripes and patches on a brownish-yellow background, with no sign of a brown cap on the head.

Dimensions

Males (females in brackets): wing length 201–249mm (193–229mm); tail 158.2–175.2mm (131.8–153mm); tarsi 41.0–48.3mm (36.6–44.0mm); central toe 38.4–47.5mm (35.6–43.3mm).

Weights are similar to Sooty Grouse, i.e. old males in October average 1,245g (2.7lb), old females 850g (1.87lb), first-year males and females 880g (1.94lb) and 720g (1.59lb) respectively (Bendell, 1955).

All dimensions are from Ridgway, Friedmann, 1946 and Behle, Selander, 1951.

Moult

The first juvenile feathers appear on the neck and tibia from age of 14days. At 21 days, the 9th primary appears, 2–3 days later the 10th and 1st primaries emerge. At this age (i.e. about 24 days) juvenile feathers cover most of the body, and by 28 days appear on the crown. At 35 days of age, the 3rd primary emerges, and simultaneously the secondaries

Female Dusky Grouse

and retrices change to the adult form. The change of all juvenile primaries (1–8) to the adult form is completed by 75 days of age. The development of the first adult plumage is finished when the bird is 3.5 months old. In a male specimen from British Columbia, development of the 9th and 10th primaries was not completed, while in specimens of females from the same place, gathered on the 7 and 28 September, the change of the 7th–10th primaries was not completed (Coll. Zool. Inst., St Petersburg, Russia).

Distribution

(see Map 6 and details on p. 134)

The species range stretches along the eastern ridges of the Rocky Mountains from the Selowin Mountains and South McMillan River at 63°N south to Mount Saint-Mateo, New Mexico, at 33°30′N. The main part of the continuous range is the Rocky Mountain system south to the Bitter-Rut Mountains and several nearby mountain ridges, bordered from the west and south by the Snake River Valley. Far to the south the range consists of several dozen isolated parts in high mountain groups. The largest of these are the Bighorn Mountains, Montana, and the large mountain knot around the sources of the Colorado River (Park–Reindge Ridge, Foremost Ridge, etc).

Subspecies

At present, four subspecies have been described:

D. obscurus obscurus (Say, 1823)
Tetrao obscurus (Say in James, 1823): 14
Colouration as described above. Occupies the south-eastern part of the species range southward from Bear Lake and eastward from the desert of the Great Salt Lake (Aldrich, 1963).

D. obscurus oreinus (Behle and Selander, 1951)
The back of adult males is lighter brown than in the nominative. The ends of scapulars and upper wing coverts are whiter. The streaked pattern in these feathers and on the sides of the body is paler grey. As a consequence, the general colouration is paler and grey. Females are even paler, with a prevalence of yellowish-grey, not brown. The feathers on the nape and ear coverts are grey, not grey-yellow. Inhabits partly isolated mountain groups of the Great Basin (Snake, Ruby, Shell-Creek, Tokima, Toyabe and Monitor ridges).

D. obscurus pallidus (Swarth, 1931)
The upper grey band on the tail is absent. Occupies the central part of the species' range, from Bear Lake to the north up to the Bear-Po Mountains, West-Butt and Stuart Lake (Aldrich, 1963).

D. obscurus richardsoni (Douglas, 1829)
The upper grey band on the tail is absent. Colouration of both sexes is as previous subspecies, but darker. Males have more white marks on throat and chin; the upper grey band on the tail is absent. Occupies northern section of the range, i.e. north from previous subspecies.

Habitats

In the northern range, Dusky Grouse inhabit the mountains of British Columbia close to the upper limits of the forests, especially where there are clearings with small groups of Balsam Fir (*Abies balsamea*). In more southerly mountains, in Alberta, the birds inhabit the forest belt between 1,460–1,770m (4,790–5,807ft) where dense spruce-pine forests alternate with clearings of tall grass, Pseudotsuga (Douglas firs) and rocky ground (Boag, 1966). In Washington, the highest density of birds is observed in grassland areas with an overstory of sagebrush, antelope bittersweet, snowberry and scattered clumps of aspen, with lower densities in forest clearings and close to the upper tree line. In the Blue Mountains the birds prefer the sparse forests of ridge tops, while in the canyon of the Snake River they are found in treeless, rocky places (Jewett *et al.*, 1953), or in sagebrush together with sage-grouse (Antony, 1903). In the Yellowstone National Park, the birds inhabit all types of forests and brush, from willow bushes in the foothills (1,650m) through the belts of deciduous trees (cherries and aspens) and coniferous forests (Douglas firs and pines) to the timberline (2,800m/9,186ft), and even higher in alpine meadows more than 500m 1,640ft) above the nearest trees (Scinner, 1927). Our attempts to find the grouse in the foothills here at the end of December failed, the birds being in higher, dense forests at this time. Females with broods in the Rocky Mountains prefer clearings with tall grass (17–22cm/6.7–8.7in), in the depths of dense forest with a variety of trees – pines, aspens, Douglas firs, etc (Mussehl, 1963; Boag, 1966). In the mountains of south-western Alberta, during a period of low population, the grouse evacuated low altitude habitats, occupying only those at about 1,740m (5,709ft) (Boag, 1966).

Population structure and density

Dusky Grouse populations are very variable and may sometimes reach a high level. In Colorado, during counts in three years, the researcher spotted a grouse every 42km (26.07 miles) on average, along a travelled route, the limits in different years being 16.6–62.31km (10.3–38.72 miles) (Rogers, 1968). Other counts in Montana showed that the average size of male spring territories was 7.3ha (18 acres), but with a variation between 4.8–9.7ha (12–24 acres), suggesting significant fluctuations in population (Mussehl, Schladweiler, 1969). The ratio between the sexes is close to unity. During the breeding season, old males hold territories, while young males and females move freely between them. The male breeding territory is usually at an elevated spot in a clearing with sparse trees.

Adult males have a strong connection to their territories, returning regularly to the same spot. As an example, in one study 12 of 13 males returned to their territories in the following year (Mussehl, 1960).

Behaviour

The birds are mainly terrestrial during the summer and arboreal in winter. During the breeding season, when the birds are in open habitats and spend most of the time on the ground, they are very careful and fly up at any sign of danger. In winter, the birds spend most of the time in conifers. There, if threatened, for instance by an eagle, they escape into dense branches and sit motionless, their cryptic colouration making them almost invisible.

Nutrition

The main winter food (up to 90.2% by volume) is coniferous needles, mainly those of Douglas fir (Stewart, 1944). In the northern Rocky Mountains, needles of Douglas fir were the main food in 158 samples (Martin et al., 1951). In Idaho, the crop contents of nine birds obtained in winter were found to be 99% needles and buds of Douglas fir

(Marshall, 1946). This dominance of Douglas fir was confirmed by radio-tracked birds in north-central Colorado mountain forests (2,300–4,000m/7,546–13,123ft), which showed an absolute predominance of Douglas fir and lodgepole pine (*Pinus contorta*) areas, despite the presence of other coniferous species (*Pinus flexilis, Abies lasiocarpa* and *Picea engelmannii*). The preference relates to the metabolizable energy of the first two species (1.80–1.72 kcal/g) against 1.15–1.52kcal/g for the other species (Remington, Hoffman, 1996).

The spring diet comprises green leaves (34.8%), coniferous needles (26.2%), coniferous cones (21.25%), flowers, fruits and seeds. Needles are eaten during the summer, but in smaller quantities (8.8%–12.9%), the main constituent of the diet being green leaves (up to 35.3%), mainly those of blueberry, and fruits and seeds (up to 44.6%), especially the berries of blueberry. During the autumn, the fraction of needles in the diet rises to 51%, with green leaves, fruits and seeds contributing the remainder. The diet of juvenile birds is similar in terms of vegetation, but animal matter makes up to 34.2% of the diet (Stewart, 1944).

Wintering

Little studied, especially in the northern parts of the range. The *richardsoni* subspecies spends practically all its time in coniferous trees, feeding and roosting there, resorting to snow burrows only during hard frosts and when snow cover has depth enough to allow excavation (Skinner, 1927). The radio-tracked birds of the *orheinus* subspecies of Utah fed on Douglas fir, but preferred Subalpine fir (*Abies lasiocarpa*) for roosting, the latter having greater canopy cover and so offering protection against the wind (Perkins *et al.*, 1991). If snow depth allowed, the birds would excavate snow burrows: as an example, in the Bear River Range of Utah, 53 snow burrows were found (Perkins P.J., cit. in Zwickel, Bendell, 2004), though in north-east Oregon no snow roosts were found to have been excavated by the *pallidus* subspecies (Pelren, 1997).

Breeding

The main courtship displays are hooting and strutting, the former on the ground or in trees, the latter sometimes accompanied by hooting (Blackford, 1958; 1963). In the strutting display, the head is drawn back and inflation of the neck pouches causes the ventral position of the neck to look like a hanging throat sac. The apteria are fully displayed, and where the raised feathers meet at the front, the blackish tips build a dark stripe from below the bill. The tail is fanned to 180° and well cocked (Hjorth, 1970). In this position, the male struts to and fro within its territory, this usually placed near the forest edge, perhaps near a dense conifer stand, in a grassy clearing, occasionally with rocky outcrops and old logs (Blackford, 1958; 1963). Hooting is a series of low-pitched vocalizations, usually separated into five distinct sounds – 'hoot-hoot-hoot-hoot-hoot' audible at distances of 40m, though one study suggested audibility at 75–100m (246–

Displaying male Dusky Grouse, showing the characteristic red apteria

328ft) for *D. obscurus pallidus* (Mussehl, 1963a). However, Dusky Grouse is very much quieter than Sooty Grouse. Another prominent courtship's call is the 'whoot' (pre-copulatory hoot), given at the end of a rush towards a hen. This whoot is much louder than the hoot – audible at distances up to 0.5km (0.3 mile) – and is peculiar to the male of both species (Hjorth, 1970; Degner, 1988 – cit. from Zwickel, Bendell, 2004).

Once a female is within sight, the male has a second stage of display. During this, the general appearance of the male, especially the brightly coloured, inflated neck bubbles and expanded yellow combs, alters. Blood infuses the tissues of the combs, which gradually change colour to orange and finally to crimson red (Blackford, 1958). As he approaches the female, the male jerks his head vertically and 'in synchrony with these head-jerks, the apteria facing the hen increases in size, while that far from her decreases' (Hjorth, 1970).

Also seen is the wingbeat display, a drumming flight audible at over 400m (1,312ft) (Mussehl, 1963). During this, the male flies vertically up to a height of nearly 1m (3.3ft), rapidly and loudly beating its wings, 'hangs' for a moment and then descends with a last burst of the wings before landing. During this drumming flight, the bird rotates to the left (rarely to the right) through about 180°, landing almost at the start point (Wing, 1946; Blackford, 1958, 1963). The latter author also notes a single, sharp, very loud wing note by the male during an aerial leap, though this was observed only once. The rotation noted during the drumming flight is similar to that of Asian Spruce Grouse and the Caucasian Black Grouse during its flutter-jumps. Rarer displays include a flight in which the male has erect combs and fully exposed cervical apteria, a display that was elicited by playbacks of male and female calls (McNicholl, 1978).

Male leks are essentially solitary, but situations where several males and females have gathered together, and during which collective displays occurred, have been observed (Blackford, 1958, 1963).

Nests follow the pattern of other grouse, i.e. a shallow depression in the ground, lined with dry needles, grass stems, etc. Usually the nest is hidden well, but sometimes it is set in an open clearing several hundred metres from the nearest trees. Clutch size varies from 2–9 eggs, but is usually 5–7 (Boag, 1966). The territories occupied by broods are large, and if the population is high, can partly overlap.

Hunting, recreation and conservation

Both species of Blue Grouse are among the most popular game birds in Canada and the USA, but it is not possible to differentiate between the two species in total 'Blue Grouse' takes, except in those states and provinces inhabited only by Dusky Grouse. There is a legal hunting season for the species in all states and provinces of the USA and Canada that it inhabits, with a bag limit and licensing of hunters.

The two species have relatively stable populations in most parts of their ranges, though numbers are in decline in some areas. There were 18 attempts to introduce both species of Blue Grouse to new areas between 1955 and 1976 (Zwickel, Bendell, 2004), but only 5 were successful, two on small islands near Vancouver, and 3 to separate mountains groups – one in New Mexico and two in Arizona.

3.2 Sooty Grouse *Dendragapus fuliginosus* (Ridgway, 1873)

Canace obscura var. *fuliginosa* (Ridgway, 1873): 190 (Cascade Mountains, Oregon State, USA). *Dendragapus obscurus fuliginosus* (Ridgway, 1885): 355. *D. fuliginosus* (Ogilvie-Grant, 1893): 75.

Morphology

As in the previous species, but the number of tail feathers is 18 (very rarely 20) and their tops are more or less rounded (see **Figure 40, n5** in Chapter 3).

Male Sooty Grouse

Colouration

Adult male

Similar to the previous species, but darker. Upper parts are brown–black, only the rump feathers and uppertail coverts being patterned, with whitish streaks on the upper parts. The grey upper band of the tail is narrower (15–22mm) than in southern subspecies of Dusky Grouse and has dense black marks on its lower part. The tail feathers tend to be rounded rather than cut-off as in the Dusky Grouse. Belly is grey-brown, without the scaled pattern. Feather of flanks have no clear cross-stripe pattern, but a dense, speckled one from light marks on the brown background, while the white tops and shaft stripes are more contrasting. The black of the gular patch is more intense, its white bordering more noticeable. Breast is blackish-brown, the feathers here having no white borders on the tops. The cervical apteria are tuberculate because of underlying deep fatty streaks.

Adult female

Brown is the dominant colour, particularly on the back. Only the central belly is grey, the feathers there having no white borders on the tops. Wing looks more monotonous than in Dusky Grouse because the ochre tops of the upper wing coverts are weakly marked out against the brown background.

Female Sooty Grouse

Juveniles (both sexes)
As in Dusky Grouse, but browner.

Downy chick
Lower body is sulfurous-yellow, upper body light-brown with longitudinal, blackish spots. The pattern of black stripes and spots is as Dusky Grouse (see Figure 46 on p. 134).

Dimensions

Males (females in brackets): wing length 198–248mm (178–234mm); tail 131–201mm (111–159mm); tarsi 40.2–47.0mm (36.6–42.9mm); central toe 39.7–49.5mm (34.5–42.8mm) (Behle, Selander, 1951).

Weight of adult males and females on Vancouver Island (October) averaged 1,245g (2.7lb) and 850g (1.9lb) respectively, while the weight of sub-adults was 880g (1.9lb) and 720g (1.6lb) respectively (Bendell, 1955). Autumn data from different parts of the range: adult and yearling males 1,244±11g (2.74lb±0.4oz) and 1,177±28g (2.59lb±1oz) respectively;

adult and yearling females 863±3g (1.90lb±0.1oz) and 829±6g (1.82lb±0.2oz) (Zwickel, Bendell, 2004). The same authors note that in the period from April to August, the body mass of adult males decreased slightly in May, rose in June, then decreased again during July and especially in August when the autumn moult begins.

Distribution
(See Map 6)
The three southernmost populations inhabit the isolated high mountain forests at the southern end of the Sierra Nevada Ridge (Zwickel, Bendell, 2004).

Subspecies
Four subspecies are recognized at present:

D. fuliginosus fuliginosus (Ridgway, 1873)
Colour as described. Inhabits the central part of the range, from 39°N to the Skina River in the north, including Vancouver Island. To the south-east, borders with the Sierra Nevada subspecies.

D. fuliginosus sitkensis (Swarth, 1921)
Male as nominative, but the female is more reddish. Occupies the northern part of the range, south to the coastal regions of Dickson-Entrance Sound, i.e. the species' Alaskan range.

D. fuliginosus sierrae (Chapman, 1904)
Adult males are paler, with a more developed stripe pattern. The grey upper bands on the tail feather are wider and marked black. The female is greyer, and pale in comparison to the nominative. Inhabits Clamath and Cascade Mountains north to the Winatche Mountains and Sierra Nevada, south to the Yosemite National Park.

D. fuliginosus howardi (Dickey and Van Rossem, 1923)
Adult male similar to *D. f. sierrae,* but with more developed streaks on the upper body, and with paler, more greyish tints. Tail of both sexes is longer, and tops of the tail feathers more rounded, the grey top bands wider. Inhabits the southern part of range south from the Yosemite National Park to Mount Pinos.

Habitats
Sparse mountain forest, particularly with groups of trees and clearings on mountain slopes, with a clear preference for the timberline, especially in the southern part of the range. On Vancouver Island, the birds inhabit waste ground after forest fires, particularly

Female Sooty Grouse

close to belts of Douglas fir. In the northern Cascade Mountains, the birds prefer the upper parts of the forest belt, at altitudes of 1,500–1,950m (4,921–6,398ft), where willow thickets and separate groups of spruces and Douglas firs alternate with clearings. In the mountains of Colorado, the birds live at 2,100–3,000m (6,890–9,843ft) among sparse thickets dominated by aspen, but including junipers, spruces, firs and pines, and snowberries. Summer concentrations of males are seen among groups of spruces and firs, but some solitary birds can be seen at distance of more than 2.4km (1.5 miles) from the nearest trees or bushes (Rodgers, 1963). In the southern Sierra Nevada Mountains, the birds are not seen below 2,300m (7,546ft), living close to the ridge crests among the groups of pines and Colorado Blue Spruce.

Population structure and density

The population density is not stable, showing significant fluctuations. On Vancouver Island in the summer of 1943, the density was estimated at 1.05ha (2.6 acres) per bird (Fowle, 1960). Later counts in the same area indicated the density at high and low periods was 0.93ha (2.3 acres) and 3.1ha (7.7 acres) per territorial male respectively (Bendell, Elliot, 1967). Other studies suggest a 'normal' density of, on average, 600 birds/1,000 acres (405ha) (i.e. 1.6 acres per bird), with a maximum density reaching 2,550 birds/1,000 acres, or nearly 0.4 acre (0.16ha) per bird (Bergerud, Hemus, 1975). It is estimated that nearly 40% of females may lose their brood annually, and that on average the number of young per female in the autumn is only two (Bendell, 1955). In the northern part of the species' range, young birds comprise 65% of the population in the autumn, but of these youngsters only 15–50% will survive to the next autumn (Zwickel *et al.*, 1977).

Territoriality

Southern subspecies are more sedentary than those of the northern range, though all populations exhibit a seasonal change of habitat, such changes appearing occasionally as a genuine migration. In one study, in Oregon in the early years of the 20th century, the birds were noted to migrate north–south from wintering to breeding grounds, over a distance of many kilometres, crossing several mountains. The comparatively short and rounded wings are not well adapted to distance flying, as a consequence of which the migration is carried out in an extraordinary fashion. The birds walk to a ridge crest during the day, then fly at sunset or at dawn of the next day, the flight losing height as it progresses so that the next valley is crossed to the lower slopes of the next ridge. The process is then repeated. The best flyers cover up to 2,700m (2,953yd) during a flight, simultaneously losing 120m (394ft) of height. The spring migration uses the same technique in the opposite direction (Bent, 1932). The result is that the flights bear a striking resemblance to a sledge rolling down one valley side and being hauled up the other.

On Vancouver Island, Sooty Grouse winter in pine forests near the crests of the mountain ridges and in the spring descend to breeding grounds in the foothills, the males leaving first, the females following later. In the autumn, the birds return: the maximum distance travelled by any bird does not exceed 16km (10 miles) (Bendell, Elliot, 1966; 1967). On the eastern slopes of the Cascade Mountains, the populations move north for the winter, travelling 8–50km (5–31 miles) (Zwickel, 1968). Again, the males move first, the females following (Wing *et al.*, 1944). In the mountains of Idaho, seasonal displacements are only across distances of about 3km (1.9 miles) and 600m (1,968ft) of altitude (Marshall, 1946).

Behaviour

The way of life is as in Dusky Grouse, but less solitary. After broods disperse in September, juveniles do not associate with the female or their siblings during the winter, the tendency to form flocks being low. However, groups do form increasingly until midwinter, before declining again until spring (Hines, 1986).

Nutrition

The winter diet consists mainly of coniferous needles (87.7%), presumably from fir (*Abies*) species, and Douglas fir (Stewart, 1944). In central California, the birds feed mainly on needles of the firs *Abies concolor* and *A. magnifica*, and Hemlock Spruce (*Tsuga pattoniana*), the latter being preferred (Belding, 1892, cit. in Stewart, 1944). In general, the dominant food source in the central range is needles of firs and Douglas fir, while in the southern range needles of pines are preferred. The importance of needles of Sitka Spruce (*Picea sitkhensis*) significantly increases to the north.

In the spring diet, the preponderance of needles is maintained (76.5%), but other items, such as coniferous cones, green leaves, buds and twigs, are added. During the summer, the role of needles is minimal (1.2–4.3%), the main part of the diet being flowers (54% in early summer) and fruits and seeds (47.1% in late summer). Among the flowers, those of Cats-ear (*Hypochaeris* sp.) are especially important, while the preferred green leaves are those of different species of Blueberry (*Vaccinium* sp.). In the autumn, green leaves, flowers, fruits and seeds constitute 99.1%, of the diet, the seeds mainly from Douglas fir, sedges (*Carex* sp.), berries of manzanita (*Arctostaphylos* sp.) and blueberry, and green leaves of alum-root (*Heuchera* sp.), willow, ferns and clover. The significance of animal food (insects) is minimal during the summer. Even in juveniles, insects are only a small part of the diet (4.5%), the main items being flowers, fruits and seeds (Stewart, 1944). However, the diet of downy young chicks consists mainly of insects (70%) until the end of July, when it decreases rapidly to only 4.5% (King, Bendell, 1982).

Wintering

The peculiarity of the winter diet forces the birds to spend this season in coniferous forests that grow at higher altitudes than the breeding grounds. On Hardwicke Island, British Columbia, the birds wintered in early seral stages or mature forest and avoided dense, second-growth forest, and in most cases spent midwinter in small groups, usually of 2–3 birds. In most cases, the birds associated with individuals of their own age and sex. Daily movements were small and home ranges averaged 16.8±2.3ha (41.5±5.7 acres) (Hines, 1986). On Vancouver Island, Sooty Grouse spend the winter in pine forests near ridge crests (Bendell, Elliot, 1966). Besides being the main winter food source, the dense tree crowns provide the birds with suitable roosting places. In California, White Fir (*Abies concolor*) provides the favoured winter roosts (Hoffman, 1956).

On Vancouver Island, the birds sometimes roost and rest in snow burrows. King (1971) noted that in some burrows 18–24 droppings were accumulated, while in others up to 100 were found. The author attributed the lower number to single-night occupancy, the larger, perhaps, to multiple nights. As we have noted in Chapter 1, snow burrows are occupied only once, so the true explanation is that the smaller number of droppings are associated with a resting burrow, the larger number with a roost.

Breeding

The courtship displays of Sooty Grouse differ in important respects from those of Dusky Grouse, a study of the differences being an aid to understanding how the species differ at a taxonomical level, and the degree of mutual independence for the two species' evolutionary future.

As is the case for other grouse species, the main structural feature of a population is the individual territory of the male. Males become very attached to their territories, returning to them each breeding season. In one study lasting four years, 46 marked males all returned to their breeding territories annually (Bendell, 1955). The large size of these

Displaying male Sooty Grouse, showing the characteristic yellow apteria, in Mount Ranier National Park

territories, and the constant need to defend them, are the reason for the solitary character of the male's displays. The distance between neighbouring males is usually not less than 600ft, but occasionally 7 or 8 hooting males form a 'hooting group' that usually hoots in chorus (i.e. a collective lek element).

The male courtship display is similar in general features with that of Dusky Grouse, but differs in important details. Firstly, the main advertising display, 'hooting', is much louder, audible over a distance of up to 3km (1.9 miles) in good weather (Hjorth, 1970). The 'Multiple Hoot' consists of 6 hoots rather than the 5 of the Dusky Grouse, and the frequencies of the hoots are significantly higher: 110–150Hz compared to 50–100Hz in Dusky Grouse (Hjorth, 1970). The whole canto lasts 3.2 seconds. At times of high excitement, the canto is repeated six times per minute (Bendell, Elliot, 1967). In Alaska, during the peak of the season's activity, the male uttered 627 series per hour, 8 seconds being the shortest lapse between canti (Stewart, 1967). Males will hoot from the ground or from high in a tree with equal enthusiasm. For example, in Vancouver, male preferred to hoot from the ground, despite the presence of tall trees nearby (Bendell, Elliott, 1966), but elsewhere, in British Columbia, males always sing from high in a tree (Brooks, 1926): the males of *D. f. sierrae* prefer to sing from the tops of tall trees – Hoffman, 1956).

The neck sacs of Sooty Grouse, inflated during the hoots and displays in the vicinity of females, are more heavily wrinkled and yellowish in comparison to those of Dusky Grouse. However, in northern populations during courtship displays, they are red, as in Dusky Grouse. It should, though, be noted that the colour (and size) of the apteria are lost in collection specimens and may differ in live specimens so that the colours reported by observers often differ.

The eye-combs are smaller than those of Dusky Grouse. They are lemon yellow, though sometimes they do become livid red (Bendell, Elliot, 1967). As a consequence, the display of eye-combs – bowing with head jerks in Sooty Grouse males – is not as expressive as in Dusky Grouse. The same is also true of aerial wingbeat displays, which are performed only occasionally, and when the male is flying from one branch to another. The male frequently produces loud wing noises from exaggerated wingbeats as he lands, but overall the display is less elaborate than in Dusky Grouse (Bendell, Elliot, 1967).

Nests, in construction and concealment, are as in Dusky Grouse. Clutch size varies from 6–12, averaging 6.3 (Zwickel, Bendell, 1967). On Vancouver Island, egg laying lasts throughout the first half of May, the female needing 36 hours to produce the next egg. Incubation lasts 26 days. The earliest date of hatching is 11 June. In British Columbia, broods had started to disband by late August and brood break-up was completed by 1 October. After this date no juveniles were found with siblings (Hines, 1986).

Hunting, recreation and conservation

Sooty Grouse is as popular a game bird as the Dusky Grouse, but its significance in the total hunting bag is less because of the relative size of its range. See the comments regarding Dusky Grouse for general comments on the combined Blue Grouse status.

CHAPTER 5

Genus 4: *Centrocercus* SAGE-GROUSE

Centrocercus (Swainson in Swainson, Richardson, 1831): 358, 496.
Type species, by original designation, *Tetrao urophasianus* (Bonaparte 1828).
Originally a monotype genus, becoming polytypic after designation of the
Gunnison Sage-Grouse, *C. minimus* (Young *et al.*, 2000).

Among the biological peculiarities of this genus (Swainsson, 1831), the male morphological characteristics are the most important. Among these are the unusual form and structure of two types of feathers as decorative, instrumental constructions; the apteria at the front of the neck; the unique construction of the oesophagus; the muscular system of the neck, whose activation ensures maximal broadening of the neck during courtship displays; and the unusual anatomy of the stomach/gizzard.

The decorative feathers (filoplumes) are set on both sides of the upper neck directly above the cervical apteria and are homologies of the decorative feathers of the males of Greater (*Tympanuchus cupido*) and Lesser (*T. pallidicinctus*) Prairie-Chickens, the so-called 'ears' (Potapov, 1985). It is possible to find all intermediate stages between the usual form of feather and the 'pennant' form in both adult and immature males. The maximum length of these feathers in adult males in spring in Greater Sage-Grouse is nearly 90mm (collection specimens Coll. ZIN RAN).

In Gunnison Sage-Grouse, the feathers have no 'pennant' form, are wider (3–6mm) and longer (146mm on average). The feathers also grow closer together, and during the breeding season form a dense bunch, giving the appearance of a black 'ponytail' (Young *et al.*, 2000).

Another group of feathers covering the lower parts of the sides of the neck and the upper part of the breast also have a construction unique to all Galliformes. They are short, hard, triangular white feathers with short, thick and sharpened shafts, similar to scales, which create a specific, ribbed surface. When the male moves its folded wings up and down across its breast, the feather group produces a loud noise, akin to a nail being drawn across a comb. When they appear during the moult, the feathers have long and soft black shafts with sparse short barbules, which are completely worn out by the spring, only the shaft remaining.

In addition to the usual two cervical apteria, sage-grouse have a further two small rounded ones, in the lower front of the neck. These additional apteria are well developed in adult males, developed to a lesser degree in yearling males and are either very small, or absent, in females (Honess, Allred, 1942). These apteria are formed of elastic olive-green skin, which during courtship expands into two bubbles under pressure from the inflated oesophagus. Out of the breeding season, the skin loses its elasticity, and the apteria decrease in size and are completely hidden by the surrounding feathers.

The construction of the oesophagus is as in both blue grouse and prairie-chickens, but its capability for expanding the middle part of the neck is much greater. A powerful sphincter closes the passage from oesophagus to crop and, under pressure of air forced from the lungs, the oesophagus then spreads the neck and upper part of the breast. Under this pressure, the apteria either blow up, or deflate, according to the display program.

A further unusual feature of sage-grouse anatomy is the construction of its stomach/gizzard (**Figure 47**). During adaptation to 'soft' food (the twigs and leaves of sages), the powerful stomach muscle, so characteristic of all other grouse, has atrophied to the level of a thin layer around the stomach capsule. The thickness of this muscular layer is only 2–2.8mm (Potapov, 1985), allowing the stomach to increase in diameter to 76–110mm when filled. Such a compact mass of food in the full stomach makes the mechanical work of grinding impossible, an assumption confirmed by the lack of grit in sage-grouse stomachs. The food mass therefore undergoes biochemical treatment only.

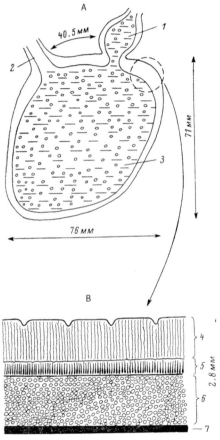

For many years it was thought that sage-grouse lacked a gizzard, making them unique among grouse. However, in the last quarter of the 20th century this was shown to be untrue. The construction of the sage-grouse stomach/gizzard was described by Potapov (1985) and confirmed by Johnson, Knuw (1989) who noted, in regard to the gizzard, that 'although the organ is relatively undeveloped...it is present.'

Among other morphological features, the lengthening and extreme sharpening of the 20 tail feathers is noteworthy.

The skulls of sage-grouse are similar to that of capercaillie in having a long bill, at 96–98% of

Figure 47. Stomach construction in *Centrocercus urophasianus* (male, sub-adult, November, 1979)
A – cross-section, B – constriction of gizzard wall. 1 – proventriculus; 2 – duodenum; 3 – content of the gizzard; 4 – keratin cover; 5 – glandular layer; 6 – muscular layer; 7 – outside cover.

cranial length compared to 110% in capercaillie. However, the skull profile resembles that of the pheasant (*Phasianus colchicus*), the nasal and frontal bones having a similar flatness.

The spread wing is rounded, the wing top being at the 7th primary. The tail is so strongly rounded that the ratio of the lengths of outer and central feathers is 30.7– 42.9%. The tarsi are feathered to their base. Importantly, sage-grouse, which never feed or escape into trees, have the same toe pectinations during the winter as most other grouse.

Colouration, and its development during ontogenesis, has similar features to the *Bonasa*, *Falcipennis* and *Dendragapus* genera. The similarity with the last genus is strengthened by the presence in males of white down feathers around the neck apteria, these forming, when the feathers are fresh, two white patches at the sides of the neck base. The colour of the undertail coverts is as in spruce grouse and capercaillie.

The specialized courtship displays, the development of some very complicated morphological structures, the relic character of the distributional range and the brightly expressed monophagy (twigs and leaves of sage only) all point to the antiquity of the genus, suggesting a very early isolation of an ancestral form from the general branch of tetraonids. However, the specializations also suggest an evolutionary similarity to blue grouse.

The image of sage-grouse as birds of open landscapes is grossly exaggerated, analyses of habitats showing that, in general, dense sage thickets, with heights up to 1.5m (4.9ft), are preferred to open, grass steppe. The turf-cereal steppes of the eastern parts of the species range are actually secondary habitats.

4.1 GREATER SAGE-GROUSE *Centrocercus urophasianus* (Bonaparte, 1828)

Tetrao urophasianus (Bonaparte, 1828):214 (North-western territories behind Mississippi, especially in Missouri, USA). *Centrocercus urophasianus* (Swainsson, Richardson, 1831): 342.

The Greater Sage-Grouse is the largest North American grouse, with strongly expressed sexual dimorphism in size, though very small in terms of colour. An entirely terrestrial bird inhabiting semi-desert and steppe habitats in inter-mountain lowlands dominated by thickets of Big Sage-brush (*Artemisia tridentata*).

Morphology

The main features are as described above. All that needs adding is that the relative length of the pelvis is maximal for grouse, especially in males, but pelvic width (as a percentage of length) is minimal (69.0% in males, 70.6% in females). The length of the caeca is minimal among grouse (see Table 2 in Chapter 1), being only 49.2% of the length of the intestines (Leopold, 1953; Potapov, 1985).

Colouration

Adult male
In spring the general colour of the upper body is dark grey with a striped pattern on the back, rump and uppertail coverts. On this background, the white cross-stripes and black tops of the vanes of some feathers are very noticeable, especially on the nape and on the frontal part of the back. The main colour pattern of upper body feathers is alternate-cross white and broad dark-brown stripes. The stripes are present either only on the feather tops, or only on the sides. The tops of most feathers are sharpened because of wear: occasionally there are only naked feather shafts above the vanes. The upper body striped pattern is

Male Greater Sage-Grouse

less pronounced on the head, which consequently looks darker. The specific decorative 'pennants' are situated above the cervical apteria and comprise bunches of 12–15 feathers.

The lower body has a more complicated colouration. Chin and throat are covered by a black patch, with insignificant white marking on the feathers, and are surrounded by an indistinct white border that begins under the eyes and is wider to the front. In turn, this white border, in its lower part, has a black outer border that appears as a small apron. The pattern is very similar to that of some other grouse. Remaining parts of the neck (lower neck and neck sides) and the breast are white, with narrow, brown, hair-like stripes on the shafts of strongly worn feathers. The base of the neck is covered by dense 'scale-form' feathers. On the sides of the body and belly, the feather form changes gradually to the normal form, each with a white lower part and a black tip. These feathers, and others situated further back which are completely brown-black, create a large brown-black patch covering the belly. The feathers on the sides of the body have a complicated pattern of asymmetric white, brown-black and yellowish stripes.

Primaries are dark brown with an indistinct white, speckled pattern on the inner vanes. Secondaries have a cross-stripe pattern, with white bordering on the tops. The striped pattern continues on the upper feathers of the rump, tail upper coverts and retrices. The retrices are strongly pointed, with black tops, the general colouration similar to those of Hazel Grouse. The grey cross-stripes of these feathers produce a streaked colouration.

In fresh, autumn plumage, adult males look paler because of the absence of wear. The upper body has a significant yellow and brown tinge, especially visible on the back, shoulders and rump, because of the corresponding colours of feather tops. The gular black spot is speckled white and brown, and its white border is not as distinct as in spring, though the black border behind the white one is well expressed. The decorative 'pennants' have more barbs in upper parts of the black shafts, most of them having a normal, though very narrow, form. Most white 'scale-form' feathers at the neck base and on the breast have black tops instead of spring's naked black shafts. Scapular feathers and inner secondaries have white patches on the shafts and a complicated asymmetric pattern from white, black and streaked grey cross-bands. All secondaries have broad white borders, with narrower ones on the first three primaries. Tail feathers have clear white tips.

Adult female

Similar to males in the autumn, especially on upper body. There is the same black belly, but with narrow white feather tips. There is a wide, predominantly white, area between the black belly and mottled breast. Tail feathers do not have black top-bands, but the white tips are present. Undertail coverts have white tops.

First adult plumage

The first adult plumage of both sexes has no clear differences from the full adult, with

Female Greater Sage-Grouse

the exception of the two outer primaries, which are sharpened and have a whitish, speckled pattern (Dalke *et al.*, 1963).

Juvenile
Similar to first adult, but paler, even whitish on the breast. Shaft stripes are well expressed on the uppertail feathers. The colour of tail feathers differs because of the white shaft tops, with a black bordering that spreads to the feather top, the edges of the vanes being olive-yellow with blackish speckles. Undertail feathers are monochromatic greyish-yellow.

Downy chick
Greyish-white tinge with whiter belly and lower part of head. The yellow and brown colours, so characteristic of the downy chicks of other grouse, are practically absent, apart from a pale yellow tinge on the nape, scapulars and back, and a brown-yellowish collar on the upper breast. Upper body has a complicated pattern of blackish spots (**Figure 48**).

Dimensions
Males (N=17): wing 303.9mm (286–323mm); tail 315.3mm (297–332mm); tarsi

56.3mm (51.3–59.0mm); middle toe 48.0mm (45.5–51.4mm).

Females (N=10): wing 260.6mm (251.0–273.0mm); tail 198.9mm (188.0– 213.0mm); tarsi 47.2mm (44.0–49.6mm); middle toe 40.3mm (36.6–41.9mm). All data from (Ridgway, Friedmann, 1946).

Figure 48. Head pattern of downy young Greater Sage-Grouse *Centrocercus urophasianus*

Weight: adult males in September 1,875g/66.1oz (1,725–2,000g/60.8–70.5oz); April–May 2,450g/86.5oz (2,250–2,725g/79.4–96.1oz); yearlings in September and April-May respectively 1,525g/53.8oz (1,400–1,600g/49.4–56.4oz) and 2,175g/76.7oz (1,975–2,275g/69.7–80.2oz). Adult females in September and April–May respectively 1,125g/39.7oz (1,050–1,200g/37.0–42.3oz) and 1,325g/46.7oz (1,175–1,400g/41.4–49.4oz). Yearlings in September and April–May respectively 1,025g/36.2oz (900–1,200g/31.7–42.3oz) and 1,250g/44.1oz (1,200–1,325g/42.3–46.7oz).

The weight of males increases in spring mainly because of the development of strongly vascularized under-skin tissue in the neck and upper parts of the breast, where there are some fat deposits (Dalke *et al.*, 1963). In young males, this weight increase is less pronounced. The maximum weight for males is 3,175g (6.99lb) and for females 1,521g (3.35lb) (Patterson, 1952).

Moult

The moult succession is as in Blue Grouse.

Distribution

The range is limited by the Rocky Mountains and Great Basin. The complicated configuration of the range borders is explained by the distribution of the species' preferred habitats, which are connected to landscape relief and specific climatic conditions that are optimal for sage-brush. During the last 50 years, the species range has seriously decreased for several reasons related to human activity, chiefly the clearing of sage-brush for irrigated farming, and the expanded use of herbicides to improve grazing conditions (Johnsgard, 1973). The last range map indicated an absence of birds in New Mexico and Arizona, with birds present only in western North and South Dakota, northern Utah, eastern California State, in the south-east corner of Alberta, and the south-western corner of Saskatchewan (Alsop, 2002).

In Alberta, numbers of displaying males have declined from about 600 in 1967 to 400 in 1987, and 122 in 1997. In Saskatchewan, counts of males have dropped from 515 males in 1987 to 61 males in 1997. Numbers of males in the two provinces have declined 80%

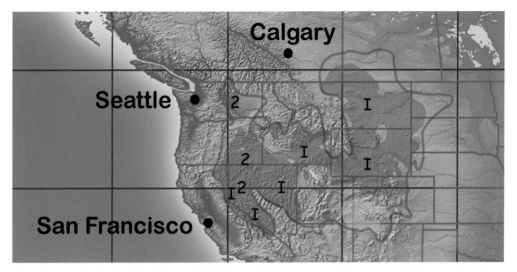

Map 7. Sage-Grouse: Red – Greater Sage-Grouse (*Centracercus urophasianus*) and Yellow – Gunnison
Sage-Grouse (*C. minimus*).
Blue line is former range.
Greater Sage-Grouse subspecies: I – C. u. urophasianus, II – C. u. phaios (in accordance with Aldrich, 1963;
Johnsgard, 1973, Schroeder et al., 2004).

from 1987 to 1997 (915 to 183). A corresponding decline of 80% has been estimated
for the total spring population over the same period (4067 to 813). In addition to the
decrease in the number of grouse, the number of active leks being used by grouse has
also declined by 56% (43 leks in 1987 to 19 leks in 1997). The current population of
sage-grouse in Canada is precarious and may be at, or very near, the minimum level for
sustaining a viable population (Aldridge, Brigham, 2003).

The revision of the contemporary sage-grouse distribution by a group of authors
(Schroeder, *et al.*, 2004) showed clearly the disastrous decline by illustrating the dramatic
difference between the pre-settlement and current range of the species. Potential habitats
originally encompassed an area of 1,200,483km² (463,509 sq miles), while the current
range encompasses 668,412km² (258,075 sq miles). The comparison of the original
and current ranges also shows that a formerly, more or less, continuous range has been
transformed into a number of isolated areas. At present there are only four large solid
areas: Oregon-Idaho-Nevada, Wyoming-Montana, Montana and Idaho. It is well known
that such a breakdown of a continuous range invariably leads to an increase of negative
factors that ultimately threaten a species' existence.

Subspecies

There are only two subspecies, differing minimally in colouration. As a consequence, the
validity of the subspecies has been contested by some authors, particularly as there is a
lack of genetic differentiation (Benedict *et al.*, 2003).

Centrocercus urophasianus urophasianus (Bonaparte, 1828)
Description as above. The nominative subspecies occupies the main part of the range, excluding only the north-western part.

Centrocercus urophasianus phaios (Aldrich, 1946)
Differs from the nominative by darker colouration. The white marks on the feathers are smaller, the grey colour is darker, the brown tinge more pronounced. Inhabits the north-western part of the range in Washington and Oregon. Local populations in north-eastern California have an intermediate colouration.

Habitats

The main habitats are hilly areas or gentle mountain slopes covered by brushes of different species of sage (mostly Big Sage-brush) of different heights and densities. Lekking birds use more or less flat places of low grass cover, without sagebrush. Nesting females prefer lower (25–50cm/9.8–19.7in), dense sage thickets. During the winter, the birds concentrate in comparatively tall and thick sagebrush, not covered by snow. Such brush offers good shelter during bad weather and, of course, is also the main food source. No connection of the species with forest vegetation has been observed.

Population structure and density

Populations undergo large, but not regular, changes. In some cases the density can reach very high levels, up to 19 birds per 100ha in spring, but the usual spring density is 3–4 birds/100ha (247 acres) (Johnsgard, 1973). Earlier sources suggested spring populations might be vary from 30–50 birds/sq mile, which equates to 11–19 birds/100ha (Edminster, 1954).

Summer counts in Idaho showed a constant and significant dominance of males (from 1:0.18 to 1:0.66), while the fraction of young birds varied from 32–60% of the population (Dalke *et al.*, 1963). A study of survival rates of females in Oregon (135 radio-tracked birds) during the autumn and winter seasons of 1989–1992 showed the average survival rate from October through February was 0.456 (SE = 0.62), with a coefficient of variation of 13.6%. It was estimated that extremely low temperatures ($\leq$ -15°C/5°F) over an eight-week period and the accumulation of snow had a negative effect on survival rates at altitudes above 1,500m (4,921ft) in comparison to low-elevation areas (Anthony, Willis, 2009).

Territoriality

Males show territorial behaviour only during the lek, with every old male occupying its own territory at collective lek grounds. Individual territories are not large, only 15–20m (16–22yd) in diameter. Females with broods move about in comparatively large territories. Local populations are mobile, transferring daily to roosting or watering places, and also seasonally, but always within defined limits. Seasonal transfers usually involve the whole population and are a change from high to low altitudes areas (the latter usually below 1,500m/4,921ft) to avoid the worst of winter's snow. The maximum distance between breeding and wintering grounds in Idaho was 160km (99 miles). The autumn migration there begins in September, when the night-time ambient temperature reaches 0°C (32°F), and lasts until snow has covered all nesting places, at which time no birds remain. The south/south-western movements are slow, with the birds flying in small flocks with prolonged stops at places with good feeding or watering. However, during heavy snowstorms, flocks of up to 150 birds have been observed. Occasionally during migration the birds also form large, but temporal, flocks of hundreds of birds.

The back migration in spring begins in the second half of March and is complete by the beginning of April (Dalke *et al.*, 1963).

Behaviour

Sage-grouse are ground dwellers, avoiding even the tops of tall sagebrushes (at only 1.5m/4.9ft) for feeding (Bent, 1932). They also avoid flight in almost all situations, attempting to evade danger on foot. Upward flight, when vital, is heavy, with loud wingbeats, and is completed very quickly. Both sexes are silent, the birds uttering a series of short cackle sounds at the moment of take-off. In summer, especially during dry and hot weather, the birds visit watering places twice daily, morning and evening, usually by walking, and flying only if the place is far off.

Nutrition

The main sources of food throughout the year are different species of sagebrush, but mainly Big Sage-brush. During the winter, more than 90% of the diet comprises leaves and twigs of this plant: only during the summer and early autumn does the fraction decline, to 31.6–63.9% (Leach, Hensley, 1954; Leach, Browning, 1958). These authors state that the summer diet includes leaves of clover and Lucerne, flowers of lettuce, and the green parts of different leguminous plants and wild cereals. Insects are not important, though grasshoppers are taken if they are abundant. The diet of newly hatched chicks during their first weeks does include insects, with these contributing up to 60% of the diet of week-old chicks. The fraction of insects in the diet decreases quickly with age, and by the time the chicks are 12 weeks old it is only 5%. Young birds begin to eat sagebrush leaves from the age of 11 weeks (Peterson, 1970). Dahlgren (2007) states that the diet of adult birds is exclusively sagebrush from mid-November to mid-May.

Wintering

The winter life of sage-grouse has not been studied in detail. It is clear that the main reason for selecting wintering quarters is the availability of sagebrush leaves and twigs. However, climate is also important. In Idaho, for example, the birds concentrated in places where the snow depth was less than 15cm (5.9in), with the birds gathering in such places in flocks of up to 1,000 (Dalke *et al.*, 1963). Roosting in snow burrows was described in Nevada (Back *et al.*, 1987), this taking place when the temperature fell below -10°C (14°F). Snow burrows are prepared in soft, unpacked drifts on the lee side of shrubs in open areas with no shrub cover visible above the snow. The average burrow was 110cm (43.3in) long and 35cm/13.8in (25–39cm/9.9–15.3in) deep, with a roof thickness of 9cm (3.5in). The average depth from the surface to the bottom of these so-called 'drift burrows' was 30cm (11.8in). The birds' use of 'open snow burrows', has also been described. These are made in soft, dry snow no more than 25cm (9.8in) deep and had a mean length of 110cm (43.3in) and mean depth of 35cm (9.9in), with a mean roof thickness of 13cm (5.1in), i.e. 'open snow burrows' are longer and deeper, and have thicker roofs than drift burrows, the differences due mainly to the available depth of snow drifts. However, in general sage-grouse prefer 'open-sky burrows', but will use typical snow-burrows if snow depths allow.

Breeding

Greater Sage-Grouse are a typical polygamous species, with characteristic grouse lek courtship displays. Lekking is more collective than for other North American grouse, with descriptions from the 19th and early 20th centuries describing gatherings of 300–400 males where populations were high, and leks of about 90 males with normal population numbers (Simon, 1940; Scott, 1942; Patterson, 1952. Dalke *et al.*, 1963, Hjorth, 1970). In Montana, the size of the lek territory varied from 0.4–40ha, with the distance between adjacent leks being an average of 2km/1.2 miles (0.5–5.8km/0.3–3.6 miles). The lek can be any flat, open, grassy place, free from tall sagebrushes, usually on the flat top of a hill or on a gentle mountain slope, but occasionally leks are placed in lowland sagebrush areas. Often these leks, and others, are at first covered by sage-brushes but are transformed into open places because of feeding, and trampling by males during intensive courtship activity.

The permanency of lek positions is very high, especially for the large ones, as is true for other grouse species with collective leks. It has been determined that some large leks have been functioning for several hundred years, the arrowheads of ancient Indian hunters having been found at the site (Dalke *et al.*, 1963).

Lek activity lasts about six weeks (**Figure 49**). Collective lek members are not equals, dividing, as a rule, into three categories. Old, dominant males occupy the central positions in the lek; younger, territorial males surround the dominant males' positions; the third category consists of young males, less than one-year old, who will not participate in mating despite their constant presence at the lek. Only if the previous breeding season was early will young males mature sufficiently to be active in the next breeding season, i.e. in their first spring (Dalke *et al.*, 1963).

In large leks, the males usually form several groups, the spatial structure looking like an aggregation of such groups (a 'porous structure'). The dominant males again occupy the central positions, attracting the majority of females and contributing more than 90% of copulations. The individual territories of these males is not large, having a diameter of 15–20m, and the borders between adjacent males is not strongly fixed (Hjorth, 1970). Every active male has several favourite places within its territory in which to carry out his courtship displays and to mate, but the

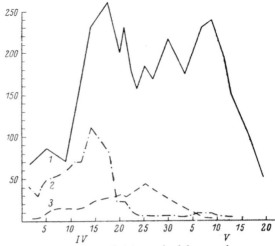

Figure 49. Intensity of visits to the lek arena by *Centrocercus urophasianus*
1 – Adult males; 2 – Adult females of all ages; 3 – Young males (Dalke et al., 1963).

connection of a male with one or another lek is not constant, with 22–52% of ringed males changing leks, moving distances of 0.5–7.0km (0.3–4.3 miles) to do so. Females may do the same. However, the really dominant males do not change leks (Dalke *et al.*, 1963).

The behaviour of females is very specific. They appear at the lek in compact groups of 10–30 birds (sometimes 50–70) and move from one group of males to another, often choosing just one, dominant male who will consequently carry out most of the mating

Female Greater Sage-Grouse

activity. Sometimes mating is interrupted by attacks from nearby males. Females may also be very aggressive one to another, with short fights resulting. At times, when many females crowd around one male, the attempts of a female to mate with another have been observed.

The main lek activity starts about 90 minutes before, and ends 90 minutes after, sunrise, with peak activity just before sunrise. During the period of maximal mating activity, males will also attend the lek in the evenings as well, usually arriving before sunset and displaying until darkness falls. At such times there is much less activity than in the mornings. Females do visit evening leks, but it appears that little attention is paid to the males.

Males leave the lek after the evening performances, moving off on foot or, occasionally, flying off, to roosting places. However, during periods of full moon, the males may stay at the lek all night, occasionally performing their displays (Scott, 1942). After mating, females leave the leks, but some do appear again. It is assumed that such females have lost their first clutch (Dalke *et al.*, 1963).

Figure 50. Main lek posture of male Greater Sage-Grouse (*Centrocercus urophasianus***)**
Before the inflation of the sacs (1); during maximum inflation (2).

Displaying male Greater Sage-Grouse, viewed from the side

The courtship display of sage-grouse males is absolutely specific: there are practically none of the vocal elements, demonstrative flights and flutter-jumps so often seen in the displays of other grouse. The main ritual is a pompous pose and several movements of feet, wings and head, accompanied by a maximum expansion of the neck and upper part of the breast by inflation of the upper cervical apteria, and by several sounds. The display lasts only three seconds. Firstly the male adopts the main posture, standing upright with the tail maximally spread and in a vertical position. The wings are lowered a little to the sides, the neck is lifted vertically, and the feathers spread to look like a huge yoke on the neck, above which the head is barely visible as a black 'T' below the bunches of pennant feathers (**Figure 50**).

During the display the male makes only three steps, during which the neck sac is expanded and lifted several times, and the cervical apteria are inflated and deflated twice.

The last expansion of the neck sac is especially strong, so that the head becomes invisible, the cervical apteria being maximally inflated. During the display, the primaries move to and fro along the spread breast five times, giving the appearance of the male stroking himself. As the primaries glide across the hard tops of the breast feathers, they produce a scratchy sound. During the last two expansions of the cervical apteria, as they deflate a loud 'cork-note' is heard, similar to that produced when a cork is sharply withdrawn from a bottle. There is also a vocal element, a series of four muffled 'coo' sounds, resembling the song of Black Grouse males.

Confrontations between males occur frequently at territorial borders. In such cases the confronting males stand close, aligned so that the head of one is opposite the tail of the other, each uttering a low grumbling sound. In a battle, the rivals hit each other with their wings, and attempt to snatch the other's 'pennants' from the back of the head with their bill (Hjorth, 1970).

Frontal view of a displaying male Greater Sage-grouse, showing the expanded neck apteria

Nests are placed beneath sagebrush cover or among tall grass at a distance from the nearest lek (Wakkinen *et al.*, 1992). In north-eastern California, the mean distance between nest and lek was greater for successful nests (3,588m/3,924yd) than for unsuccessful ones (1,964m/2,148yd, Popham, Gutierrez, 2003). It was established that the cover of tall residual grasses and medium height shrubs around unpredated nests was greater than around predated ones (Gregg *et al.*, 1994, Sveum *et al.*, 1998). This was also observed in north-eastern California (Popham, Gutierrez, 2003).

Nest litter is sparse, with eggs occasionally being laid almost on bare soil (Bendire, 1892). Clutches are of 7–8 eggs, the average size varying insignificantly within the range 7.26–7.53 (Patterson, 1952). However, clutch size in Utah averaged 6.8 eggs (Griner, 1939); in Oregon 7.13 (Nelson, 1955); and 7.5 in Colorado (Keller *et al.*, 1941). Suggestions of clutches of 10 or even 13–17 eggs have not been confirmed (Bent, 1932). Eggs have a greyish-olive background colour, with sparse brown spots and dots. Average egg size is 55mm x 38mm (Patterson, 1952). The female needs 10.5 days to lay 8 eggs. Incubation lasts 25–27 days, partly dependent on the weather, as the female spends a longer time away from the nest if feeding in bad weather.

Mass hatching occurred in Idaho during the last week of May. If the weather is bad at this time (rain, cold, wind), most chicks perish: in such cases, the number of chicks per female in July may be 2.3 instead of the 3.4–4.8 in favourable years (Dalke *et al.*, 1963). The level of predation may also be high. Summarized data on the fate of nests from eight different studies shows that from a total of 503 nests, 47.7% were destroyed by predators, the most important of these being Coyotes (*Canis latrans*), ground squirrels and badgers (Gill, 1966). It is interesting to note that data from a study of 243 radio-tracked females and 287 monitored nests showed that females who nested again had higher chick survival rates than first nests (Moynahan *et al.*, 2007).

Hunting, recreation and conservation

Sage-grouse are a very popular game bird in western North America. In the early 1970s, it was estimated that the total population was 1,500,000, and that hunters took 250,000 birds annually, four times more than in 1951 when the total US kill was less than 75,000 (Patterson, 1952: Johnsgard, 1973). In 1970, hunting was allowed in ten US States and one Canadian Province. An investigation of the influence of different levels of hunting (no hunting, limited hunting and moderate hunting) on populations in Idaho showed that areas closed to hunting had greater rates of increase of breeding population than areas open to hunting, and that these effects were more pronounced for birds occupying relatively xeric habitats close to human population centres or occupying highly fragmented habitats (Connelly *et al.*, 2003).

Hunting must now be seen in the context of the prolonged decrease of sage-grouse numbers. Habitat degradation and conversion, including the adverse affects of cultivation, dams, fragmentation, power lines, fences, expansion of the invasive plant species, changes in the fire regime, and issues related to the timing and intensity of livestock grazing, have all taken their toll on the sage-grouse population (Connelly, Braun, 1997; Braun, 1998). It was shown, for example, that ploughing even small areas of sagebrush steppe to produce cereal grains appears more detrimental to sage-grouse than chemical control of sagebrush (Swenson, 1987).

The negative response of the species to the development of the coal-bed natural gas (CBNG) fields in Wyoming and Montana is a case in point. The number of males observed at leks from 2001 to 2005 declined more rapidly than those outside the fields (Walker *et al.*, 2007). The negative influence of the development on winter habitat selection by the birds was confirmed by data from 200 radio-tracked females. In equal areas of landscape and vegetation, females avoided CBNG development in otherwise suitable winter habitat (Docherty *et al.*, 2008).

Efforts to re-establish sage-grouse populations in places where the bird had been completely extirpated, for instance in New Mexico, have failed (Schroeder *et al.*, 2004). However, an attempt in Utah during 2003–2005, when 137 females captured from two source populations were released in Strawberry Valley in which the local population was approximately 150 breeding birds prior to the release, was successful. In 2006, the peak male count for the only remaining active lek in the valley was almost four times (135 males) the six-year pre-translocation (1998–2003) average peak attendance of 36 males. This experiment shows that translocations can be an effective management tool to increase small populations when conducted during the breeding season and before the target population have been extirpated (Baxter *et al.*, 2008). Another experiment was made with human imprinted chicks to quantify the effects of three levels of forb cover in brood habitat. The results indicate that increase of forb cover in a brood area with <20% forb cover may lead to an increase in chick survival and grouse productivity (Huwer *et al.*, 2008).

In a special blueprint for preservation of this species (Braun, 2006), it was specially underlined that such strong decrease of the species' population is the result of habitat loss, fragmentation and degradation. Among the main measures is first of all the management of sage-brush steppe – the main habitat of the species – as well as management of artificial and wild fire, grazing, wildlife, fragmentation, invasive plant species, roads, structures (power lines, fences, etc) and water sources. All these measures are especially important in areas with existing sage-grouse populations.

Greater Sage-Grouse are being considered for federal listing under the Endangered Species Act in the USA. Such a listing was made in Canada in 1988 (Aldrich, Brigham, 2003). In 2000, the Canadian Species at Risk Act listed the subspecies *C. u. phaios* as extirpated in British Columbia. At the time of writing, the US Fish and Wildlife Service (USFWS) had decided that the species warranted federal listing, but this had not happened because of higher priorities.

4.2 GUNNISON SAGE-GROUSE *Centrocercus minimus* (Young, Braun, Oyler-McCance, Hupp, Quinn, 2000)

Type locality: Gunnison Valley, Colorado State, USA.

The discovery of this new species occurred not in a remote, rarely visited region, but in Colorado and Utah – States that had been carefully studied for at least 150 years. The discovery was, therefore, sensational, though perhaps not entirely unexpected, as ten years before, naturalists in south-west Colorado and south-east Utah had noticed that birds in some local populations were almost one-third smaller than those from elsewhere (Hupp, Brown, 1991; Barber, 1991). Differences in plumage and behaviour were also noticed, but it was not until the results of population genetic comparison were published (Oyler-McCance *et al.*, 1999) that the existence of a new species could be confirmed. Many aspects of the life of the Gunnison Sage-Grouse – territoriality, wintering, etc – have not been studied in detail yet. As a consequence the data presented below is somewhat limited.

Morphology

Differs from the previous species mainly by being smaller. The form, colouration and length of the retrices also differ, being narrower, more pointed and having longer tops. The black decorative feathers placed on the sides of the upper neck above the cervical apteria are not of 'pennant' form, being wider (3–6mm) and longer (146mm on average). These feathers also grow closer together, and in the breeding season form a dense bunch, suggestive of a black 'ponytail' (Young *et al.*, 2000). The length and width of the bill are less than in the Greater Sage-Grouse. The wing is shorter and more rounded because of shorter outer primaries. The roundness of the tail has not yet been measured. The skeletal peculiarities and those of the digestive tract have not yet been studied. In general, the morphological differences between this species and the Greater Sage-Grouse are similar to those between the Canadian and Franklin's Spruce Grouse, and the Dusky and Sooty Blue Grouse.

Colouration

In general, both sexes are similar to the Greater Sage-Grouse, but the tail feathers have clearly defined white or cream bars (width: 5–7mm), unlike the indistinct barring on the tail feathers of Greater Sage-Grouse (Young *et al.*, 2000).

Female Gunnison Sage-Grouse

Dimensions

The length of the wing was not given in the description of the new species, though the dimensions of the inner, 1st primary, and two outer primaries (9th and 10th) were given. Wingspan: 23in (58.42cm) against 28–38in (71.12–96.52cm) in the Greater Sage-Grouse; body length: 19–22in (48.26–55.88cm) (Alsop, 2002). Length of the bill (from nostrils): 14.3mm in males, 12.9mm in females. Length of tail feathers of males: 347mm (Young et al., 2000).

Weight: adult males 2,141g (1,727–2,435g); yearling males 1,911g (1,622–2,176g); adult females: 1,204g (1,072–1,327g); yearling females 1,131g (990–1,335g) (Young *et al.*).

Distribution

(see Map 7)

The species currently inhabits 6–7 counties of south-western Colorado (Braun, 1998; Commons, 1997) and one county of south-eastern Utah (Barber, 1991). Young *et al.*, 2000, indicate that the known historic distribution of the species in Colorado was sagebrush communities below 3,000m south of the Eagle and Colorado rivers from near Leadville (Lake County) southward, and the sage-brush dominated shrub-steppe habitat in the San Luis Valley to the boundary with New Mexico and west to the Utah state line. The species was known to occur in Grand and San Juan counties in Utah, south and east of the Colorado River. The distribution was discontinuous within this area (Rogers, 1964; Braun, 1995), separated by river valleys and high, forested mountains. In the later publications, suitable habitats were also identified in north-eastern Arizona and northern New Mexico. Potential habitats were evaluated at 46,521km² (17,962 sq miles) (Fig.1, Schroeder *et al.*, 2004). At the same time, the overall current species range was estimated to be 4,787km² (1,848 sq miles), i.e. approximately only 10% of the potential pre-settlement habitat (Map 7, Schroeder *et al.*, 2004).

Subspecies
The Gunnison Sage-Grouse is monotypic.

Habitats
In winter, the birds prefer a habitat with substantial cover (15–30%) of large, low sagebrush intermixed with native grasses and forbs, and associated riparian habitats (Hupp, Braun, 1989). The birds forage and roost in cultivated fields of alfalfa, wheat and beans (Young, 1994; Commons, 1997): these habitats differ from those of the Greater Sage-Grouse. Gunnison Sage-Grouse prefer areas with more deciduous shrubs, as well

Male Gunnison Sage-Grouse displaying at a lek

as areas invaded by pine and juniper at elevations of 1,800–2,000m (5,906–6,562ft). The preferable nesting habitats are where forbs and grass covers are found below a sagebrush canopy (Young, 1994).

Population structure and density

Eight populations are known at the moment, with nearly 5,000 breeding birds, most of them (but fewer than 3,000) in the Gunnison Basin, Colorado. Some populations are small, with fewer than 150 breeding birds, one example being the only population in Utah.

Nutrition

Sagebrush leaves are the main food from November to April. In summer, the diet expands to include forbs and insects. In disturbed and fragmented habitats, the birds forage and roost in cultivated fields of alfalfa, wheat and beans (Young, 1994; Commons, 1997).

Male Gunnison Sage-Grouse displaying

Wintering

No available data.

Breeding

Gunnison Sage-Grouse have the same mating system as Greater Sage-Grouse. Breeding lasts from March until late May. Lek courtship displays differ from those of Greater Sage-Grouse by slower rates of performance and a different mating noise (the birds pop their air sacs nine times instead of twice – Young *et al.*, 1994). Some acoustic aspects of the courtship display influence male mating success (Gibson, Bradbury, 1985: Gibson *et al.*, 1991). Only 10–15% of adult males breed on the lek each season (J.R. Young, pers. obs.). Yearling and adult females breed, but yearling males probably breed rarely (Young *et al.*, 2000). Importantly, Young observed that the females from Gunnison Basin and northern Colorado avoided playbacks of male courtship vocalizations that differed from those of their local populations. The author concluded that differences in male courtship vocalizations were likely to be a barrier to mating between Gunnison and Greater Sage-Grouse, and because of this Gunnison Sage-Grouse appear to be reproductively isolated, based on male courtship vocalization, which acts as a pre-mating isolation mechanism (Young, 1994). Divergence of mating behaviour and geographical isolation may result in the rapid evolution of a new species through sexual selection, in accordance with well-known rules in the processes of speciation.

The average clutch size is 6.8 eggs; egg size is 54.2mm x 38.0mm (Young, 1994; Commons, 1997).

Hunting, recreation and conservation

In the Gunnison Basin, the average number of males attending leks has declined by more than 60% since 1953 (J.R. Young in Young *et al.*, 2000). The Colorado Wildlife Commission prohibited hunting in areas occupied by Gunnison Sage-Grouse in 2000. However, all other available information provides nothing to encourage optimism, though the Colorado Division of Wildlife, the Bureau of Land Management and some other official agencies within the U.S. Department of the Interior, together with other local agencies and private citizens, have produced a range-wide conservation plan (Gunnison Sage-Grouse Range-wide Steering Committee, 2005), but a petition requesting listing of the species under the Federal Endangered Species Act of 1973 failed in 2006 when the USFWS declined to list the species. That decision was challenged when it became clear that it had been made as a result of political interference. In March 2011, the Service announced it was going to reconsider its position, but at the time of writing the position remains that the species will be added to the Endangered Species Act when funding and workload permit – which is not now expected until 2015 at the earliest – and in the interim will remain a State-managed species.

CHAPTER 6

Genus 5: *Tetrao* CAPERCAILLIE

Tetrao (Linnaeus, 1758): 159.
Type, by subsequent designation: *Tetrao urogallus* (Gray, 1840: 62).

The genus includes two species, the Western Capercaillie (*Tetrao urogallus*) and the Black-billed Capercaillie (*Tetrao parvirostris*), the largest birds of the Tetraonidae family. Both species inhabit Eurasian forests, from the Atlantic to the Pacific coasts, and from the tundra to the forest-steppe zone. Each has pronounced sexual dimorphism in both size and colouration. The males have long tails, and elongated feathers below the bill (the 'beard'). The species overlap in size but, in general, Western Capercaillie are larger, with a more massive skeleton and powerful musculature. The size and weight of males of both species vary widely, not only as a result of individual peculiarities but due to age and geographic position. The skeleton of males grows slowly, particularly the skull, with full size not being reached until at least 4 years of age (Kirikov, 1939, 1952; Semenov-Tianshansky, 1959; Kirpichev, 1961). However, separation of males into different age groups is difficult because of individual variations: only young males, up to 13 months old, are easily distinguished.

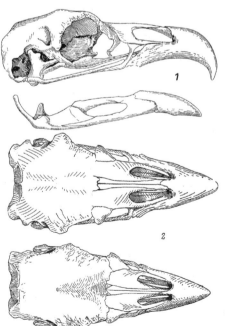

Figure 51. Skull of male *Tetrao urogallus*
1 – adult side view; 2 – adult top view; 3 – two-year-old male.

The male skull differs from that of other grouse. The dorsal-ventral projection is flattened, appearing wedge-shaped from above (**Figures 51 and 52**). The bill is very powerful, especially in *T. urogallus*, because of the need to take large quantities of pine needles and larch twigs (items firmly attached to branches) during winter. Feeding on such food also demands rapid strengthening of the maxillary apparatus (secondary prokinetism). The foramen mandibulare is larger than in other grouse, with only the Canadian Spruce Grouse being similar (Potapov, 1985). The sutures between the skull bones are visible in one-year-old birds, disappearing gradually to the age of 4.5 years (Kirikov, 1939). The frontal and nasal bones fuse during the first autumn. The frontal bones thicken towards their fusion lines with the nasal bones, forming an overhanging fold that covers the fusion line. Skull growth is faster in the Black-billed Capercaillie, with the bones knitting by the end of the third year. The skulls of female capercaillie do not show such differences, with the same proportions of mandibles to general skull size, as in other grouse species.

The morphology of the hard-palate is very different in the two species. That of the Western Capercaillie is flat, with three lengthened combs weakly expressed in females, as in other grouse species, and practically imperceptible in males. The hard-palate of the Black-billed Capercaillie is very different from other grouse species, with a powerful central comb penetrating deeply into the mouth cavity and entering a corresponding depression in the lower mandible (**Figure 53, n10-12**). Because of this, each piece of twig nipped off by the bill is broken into two parts (Potapov, 1974).

The pelvis is of usual grouse type, wide and flat. The sutures between the pelvic bones are visible in year-old birds, but have disappeared completely by the fourth year of life (Kirpichev, 1961).

The sternum keel of Western Capercaillie males has a slight notch where the bone widens to form a flat 'shelf' (see Figure 28 n3 in Chapter 1), which serves as a fulcrum when the bird roosts in a tree. Black-billed Capercaillie males also have the flat 'shelf', but the keel notch is lacking. The keel in females of both species lacks both the notch and the flat 'shelf' (Potapov, 1985).

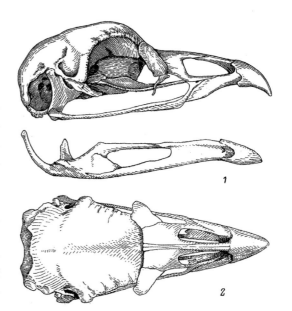

Figure 52. Skull of adult male *Tetrao parvirostris*
1 – adult side view; 2 – adult top view.

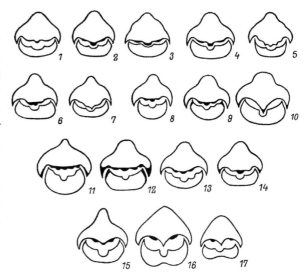

Figure 53. Cross-sections of the beaks of galliform birds at the level of the base of the operculum.
1 – Bonasa bonasia; *2 –* Falcipennis falcipennis; *3 – F. canadensis; 4 –* Dendragapus obscurus; *5 –* Lagopus mutus; *6 –* Lagopus lagopus; *7 –* Lyrurus mlokosiewiczi; *8 –* Lyrurus tetrix male; *9 –* Lyrurus tetrix, female; *10 –* Tetrao parvirostris; *11 –* Tetrao urogallus, male; *12 –* Tetrao urogallus, female; *13 –* Bonasa umbellus; *14 –* Tympanuchus phasianellus; *15 –* Gallus gallus; *16 –* Tetraogallus altaicus; *17 –* Perdix perdix.

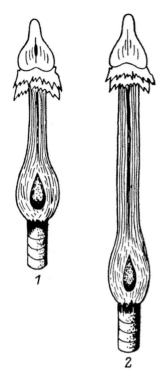

Figure 54. The trachea bend
In Tetrao urogallus *(1, 2) and* Tetrao parvirostris *(3, 4).*

Figure 55. Connection of the tongue and larynx
In Tetrao urogallus *(1) and* Tetrao parvirostris *(2).*

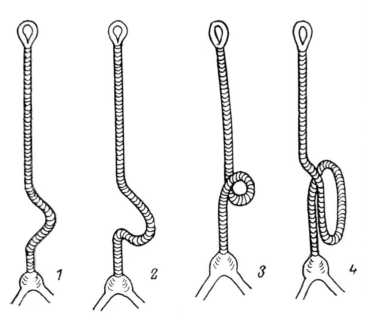

Adult male capercaillie have a long trachea which, in its lower section, forms a loop that, in *T. parvirostris*, is three times larger than in *T. urogallus* (**Figure 54**). Trachea length increases with age due to the growth of trachea rings, with full length not being attained until the bird is three years old (Potapov, 1985). In Black-billed Capercaillie, the trachea grows faster, reaching maximum length (56–58cm/22–22.8in) in the second year (Kirpichev, in litt.): the length of the looped trachea is almost half the total length (26cm/10.2in). This specific anatomy is connected with nuptial vocalizations in both species, as is the lengthening of the muscular ligament connecting the base of the tongue and the upper larynx. These consist of two muscle pairs, *mm. laryngohyoideus* and *mm. thyreoideus* (30mm in *T. urogallus* and 90–100mm in *T. parvirostris*, (**Figure 55**). The lengthening is connected with vocalization, during which the upper larynx and tongue are pulled deeply into the throat.

The wing is rounded, with the top at the end of the 7th primary. The length of tail is greater in Black-billed Capercaillie: the difference in length of the central and outer retrices is large; the fully opened tail is a semi-ellipse, rather than the semi-circle of the Western Capercaillie. The tops of the wide tail feathers are truncated, though rounded in yearling males.

Both species have extremely long pectinations on the toes in winter, with a second row in addition to the first (see Figure 1, n3 in Chapter 1). Pectination size depends on winter climate, and is largest in the northern and north-eastern populations of both species.

Hybridization

Hybridization between the capercaillie species is common in contact zones. Hybrids occur when the two species meet at the same lek. First generation hybrids may also mate. In Bargusin State Reserve (in the Lake Baikal region) in the mid-20th century, when the population density of both species was high and mixed leks and hybrids were common, hybrid females mated only with hybrid males (Kirpichev, 1958; 1974). Hybrids have been collected, described and analysed (Kirpichev, 1958; Egorov *et al.*, 1959; Potapov, 1985). They are fertile and are capable not only of crossing with other hybrids, but with pure-bred birds. Studies with caged birds suggest that second-generation hybrids have a complicated set of features, though these have not been fully described.

Hybrids of Western Capercaillie and Black Grouse are well known (and called Mejniak, 'standing between' in Russian). The main reason for such hybridization is a significant decline in one or both parental species in local populations, creating a situation in which the females of one species cannot find a mate of their own species.

Hybridization of Western Capercaillie and Willow Grouse is also known. Specimens have never been described, but have been illustrated in colour reproductions from an old Swiss book (Couturier, Couturier, 1980).

Interfamily hybrids are also known: Western Capercaillie with pheasant (seven cases in Scotland: Boag *et al.*, 1971) and with a domestic hen in captivity (Couturier, Couturier, 1980).

5.1 WESTERN CAPERCAILLIE *Tetrao urogallus* (Linnaeus, 1758)

Tetrao urogallus (Linnaeus, 1758): 159; Hartert, 1922: 1880; Johansen, 1957:233-266, Sweden.

Morphology

The largest representative of the Tetraonidae family. The males have a massive body, comparatively long neck, large head and powerful bill, with the upper mandible down-curved. The wings are rounded. The tail is long, the wide retrices with straight cut tops. The female is considerably smaller and more proportional, with a short neck and tail.

Colouration

Adult male (from two years old)
Head and neck are dark slate grey, indistinctly mottled. 'Beard' feathers are sharpened,

Male Western Capercaillie

Female Western Capercaillie

and coloured black with a green tinge on the sides. Upper body is covered by a thin, pale-grey, streaked pattern on a black or black-brown background, especially expressed on upper back. General colour of upper body is dark or paler, depending on width and density of white streaks. These streaks became narrower as the bird ages, so older males are darker. The most notable feature of the underbody is the green breast plastron with a metallic tinge formed by wide green tops of black breast feathers. Central and forepart of belly has black feathers with greenish borders, and dense, greyish streaks in younger birds. Many young birds also have white patches, the number and size of which varies with individuals and decreases with age.

Lower belly to undertail is covered by brown hair-like feathers with broad white-greyish tops. Feathers of flanks are long, with light-grey or white streaks on a chocolate background. Primaries are chocolate-brown, paler on narrow outer vane. Outer vanes of secondaries are streaked brown. The 1st, and sometimes 2nd, secondaries often have two white patches on lower feather. Of the completely white feathers under wing base, only the longest have small black tips.

Retrices are black, with white patches and stripes, whose size and number vary, and are sometimes absent in 1–3 central pairs in old males. Uppertail coverts are black, mottled light brown or whitish, with white bordering on the tops. Undertail coverts are black with white tops, spotted by black marks.

The first adult plumage of males differs by having more developed white patches and grey streaks, especially on belly and tail feathers. Undertail coverts have pure white tops.

Adult female

Upper body mottled with yellowish-brown, black, whitish and white cross-stripes. Upper back looks darker. Underbody is also mottled. Chin is whitish; throat and upper neck yellowish-brown. Breast has an ochre-yellowish background with narrow black cross-stripes. White feather tops sometimes make the belly look completely white; otherwise it appears pale with narrow, dark cross-stripes. Primaries are light-chocolate with pale top borders. Secondaries have white top borders and indistinct light-ochre cross-stripes. All upper wing coverts have white tops. Tail and uppertail coverts have white top borders, and alternate wide ochre-brown and black cross-bands. Undertail coverts have same colouration, but paler and with more wide ochre-brown bands.

Females have two colour phases, grey and reddish-brown, in practically all populations, as in Ruffed Grouse. In 'reddish-brown' females, the colour dominates, the breast plastron being pure reddish-brown, without dark cross-bands; white borders and feather top patches are narrow and weakly expressed; leg feathers are pale yellow. 'Grey' females are darker, sides of head dark with sharp white and black marks; breast plastron has clear black and white cross bands; leg feathers are dark, with brown streaks. Grey phase birds are more usual in northern populations, i.e. in colder climates; reddish-brown females are more numerous in southern populations. There is no evidence of a change from grey phase to reddish-brown during ontogenesis, i.e. the colourations are genetically fixed (Potapov, 1985).

Juvenile
Juvenile male plumage is a complicated mottled colouration with grey and brown prevalent, and a lot of white and dark marks. Most feathers have a cross-striped pattern, and many, especially on lower back, rump and upper tail, have prolonged white patches on shafts, which spread to feather tops as triangles ('juvenile patches').

Juvenile females have a more intensive reddish-brown tinge, especially on head and neck, and a pure yellowish-reddish breast plastron. No differences in colouration of primaries between the sexes, as mentioned by Höglund (1952), were found in collection samples.

Downy chick
Downy chicks are reddish-yellowish on under parts, with indistinct ochre stripe across breast. Upper parts have a complicated pattern of blackish and red-brownish stripes, with a specific pattern of black marks on crown (**Figure 56**). Bill colour differences in the sexes suggested by Höglund (1952) were not confirmed by collection specimens, or in captive-reared capercaillie (Krutowskaya, 1953; Krott, 1966).

Figure 56. Head pattern of downy young *Tetrao urogallus*

Dimensions

The size and weight of adult males varies not only with geography, but also with the age. On average, males are: body 955–992mm (Kirpitchev, 1960); wing 377–430mm; tail 247– 351mm; tarsi 62–87mm; middle toe (without nail) 59–77 mm; bill length (from nostrils) 30.0–41.4mm; bill width (at level of the front edge of nostrils) 20.4–27.5mm. Females: body 620–675mm (Kirpitchev, 1960); wing 280–322mm; tail 163–205mm; tarsi 46–59mm; middle toe (without nail) 46–58mm; bill length (from nostrils) 19–26mm; bill width (at level of front edge of nostrils) 14.2–18.2mm.

All dimensions, except body length, are from collection specimens of Coll ZIN RAN (355 males, 290 females, Potapov, 1985).

Weight: adult male 3,500–6,500g (7.71–14.33lb); adult female 1,440–2,210g (3.17–4.87lb). The average weight of birds in a given, stable population varies to a much lesser degree: males 3,900–4,300g (8.59–9.48lb), females 1,700–2,000g (3.75–4.41lb). First winter, young birds are 70% of old bird weight (males), 91% (females). In the Lake Baikal region, one-year-old males averaged 2,850g/6.28lb (2,620–4,100g/5.78–9.04lb); two-year-old males averaged 4,350g/9.59lb (4,120–4,800g/9.08–10.58); three-year and older males were 5,530–6,450g/12.19–14.22lb (Kirpitchev, 1961). Repeated capture of marked birds (Kiselev, 1971) showed that the growth of young males stopped from late autumn to the following summer, then started again until the second autumn, stabilizing through the second winter, and continuing from the following summer (**Figure 57**). The maximum confirmed weight of a male is 6.5kg (14.3lb): weights of 7–8kg (15.4–16.6lb), even 10kg (22lb), have been claimed in hunting literature, but have never been confirmed.

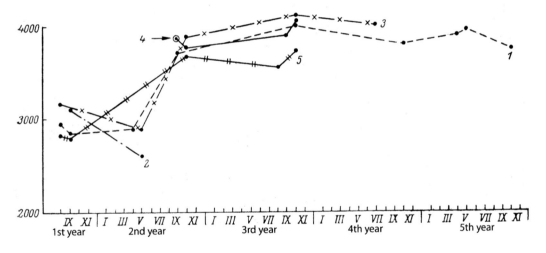

Figure 57. Changes in mass of individual *Tetrao urogallus*

Changes in mass of individual Tetrao urogallus *determined from consecutive annual captures of the same bird. Numbers represent individual birds. Vertical axis – Body mass in grams. Horizontal axis – Age of birds in years and months. (Kiselev, 1971)*

Moult

The development of the feathering and its consequent changes during the seasonal moults are well studied (Snigirevsky, 1950; Krutovskaya, Krutovskaya, 1953; Semenov-Tianshansky, 1959; Kirpichev, 1972; Potapov, 1985). The work of Kirpichev includes a unique of the development of embryo feathering. On hatching, chicks have five primary stumps 2.0–

2.5mm long. The development of chick feathering is given in Kirpitchev (1972). Feather development lasts to late autumn, by which time full, first adult plumage has formed.

The third ('summer') moult begins in males immediately after the finish of lekking (from the middle or end of May) and in females after chick hatching. This moult is short and in the male includes mainly feathers on head, neck, upper breast and front back. During this moult, many feathers that fall out are not replaced (thinning the dense winter plumage), this being especially noticeable in southern populations. In breeding females, the summer moult is weakly expressed, mainly on the head and neck (Kirpichev, 1972). In female collection specimens from the northern Urals, summer feathers were absent completely, perhaps because of the cool summers of the northern parts of the range (Potapov, 1985).

The fourth (chronologically) autumn moult is full, beginning with loss of the 1st primary (at the end of May in males, mid-June in females), and lasts until the end of September or even the end of October in northern populations, when the last feathers, the outer primary and some feathers on the neck, are changed (Potapov, 1985).

During the intensive change of wing feathers, male flight ability declines significantly, even being lost in old males (Fediushin, Dolbik, 1967).

Distribution

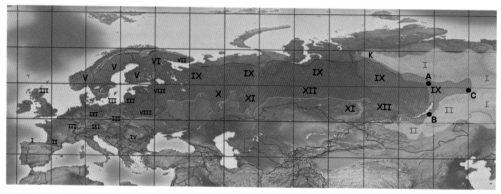

Map 8. Western Capercaillie (*Tetrao urogallus*). See also Map 9.
Subspecies (in black): I – T. u. cantabricus; II – T. u. aquitanicus; III – T. u. major; IV – T. u. rudolfi;
V – T. u. urogallus; VI – T. u. karelicus; VII – T. u. lonnbergi; VIII – T. u. pleskei; IX – T. u. obsoletus;
X – T. u. volgensis; XI – T. u. uralensis; XII – T. u. taczanowskii
K: Position of irruption of T. u. kureikensis
The yellow area represents westernmost extent of the range of Tetrao parvirostris.
A, B and C are sites where the two Capercaillie species are known to co-exist. A is the lower part of the Nakanno, Inarigda and Kothetcumo rivers (Tarasov, 1965). B is the Bargusin State Reserve on the eastern shore of Lake Baikal (Kirpichev, 1958) and C is the lower part of the Tokko and Chara rivers (Worobiev, 1963).

Western Capercaillie inhabit the greater part of the Eurasian boreal forest from the shores of the Atlantic Ocean eastwards to 122°E. It is difficult to define the western and southern range boundaries because of constant changes due to human activity, which, as a rule, decrease the species range. The northern range boundary is determined by the northern forest limit, the northernmost point being an isolated population at 70°N in northern Norway. The eastern limits of the range are determined by the limit of western taiga, where pines and spruce are replaced by larch. Capercaillie were extirpated in Britain and Ireland in the 18th century, but were reintroduced to Scotland in 1837.

Subspecies
Thirteen subspecies are currently recognized:

Tetrao urogallus urogallus (Linnaeus, 1758)
Colouration as described. Occupies most of Scandinavia, apart from southern Sweden and south–western Finland.

T. u. lonnbergi (Snigirewsky, 1957)
Distinguished by small size and dark colouration of males. Inhabits Kola Peninsula apart from north-eastern part, reaching 69°30′N near Nikel (close to the Russian–Norway border).

T. u. karelicus (Lonnberg, 1924)
Differs by paler colouration and development of the white colour in the belly. Inhabits Finland (except south-western corner) southward to Ladoga Lake. Eastern limit unknown. In western Karelian Republic (Russia) integrates with *T. u. obsoletus*.

Female Western Capercaillie in Karelia, Russia

T. u. major (Brehm, 1831)

Main features are large size, longer male tail (up to 390mm – Domaniewski, Rydzewski, 1937), which is black and usually without white spots, dark brown colouration of male back and very little white colour on the belly. Female are darkest of all subspecies. Inhabits most of Western European range: mountain forests in eastern France, southern Germany, southern Poland, the Alps and Dinar Highlands. Large isolated population exists in northern Poland. The nuptial song of the male is of the western type with a loud 'cork-note'.

T. u. aquitanicus (Ingram, 1915)

Small birds. The general colour of males is similar to nominate, but females are darker. Male nuptial song is of western type with loud 'cork-note'. Inhabits mountain coniferous forests of the Pyrénées from the sources of Ter River west to the sources of Gave d'Aspe. The distance to the nearest population of capercaillie in the Alps is nearly 500km (311 miles). The male nuptial song is of the western type.

T. u. cantabricus (Castriviejo, 1967)

Males are paler than previous race, with a shorter tail. The song of the male is the Western type, as in *T. u. major* and *T. u. aquitanicus*. Inhabits the Cantabrian Mountains from Sierra del Alba and the Picos d'Europa in the east to the Sierra de Picos Ancares 6°40′W. Separated from the Pyrénées by 300km (186 miles) of unforested, cultivated lowlands. This is the only species population to inhabit forests with no coniferous trees, the main winter food being the hard leaves of evergreen *Ilex* spp. It was assumed that conifers once grew here, but disappeared gradually due to climate change and human activity (Potapov, 1985): this is now confirmed (Rubiales *et al.*, 2009). The population decreased by up to 50% from 1982 to 1989 and there is now a serious danger of total extinction (Pollo *et al.*, 2003). The male nuptial song is of the western type.

T. u. rudolfi (Dombrowski, 1912)

Males are dark (dark than *T. u. major*) and with a shorter tail. The male's song is of the eastern type, without the 'cork-note'. Inhabits eastern and southern Carpathians, isolated localities in Bulgaria: Rhodope, Pirin, Rila, Stara planina and Vitosha (Gabrashanski, Donchev, 1970). The eastern Carpathian range, in the Ukraine, is a series of isolated populations in high mountains (Strautman, 1954). The western range border is 22°E (sources of Dniester River). The male nuptial song is of the western type, but without a 'cork-note'.

It should be noted that there is evidence of another mountain subspecies differing from the above by its small size. Some elements of the skeleton (the coracoid, scapula, humerus and sternum bones) were certainly smaller than in specimens of *T. u. major* – (Kohl, Stollmann, 1968) – but the lack of full analysis does not allow a further subspecies to be identified with any certainty.

T. u. pleskei (Stegmann, 1926)

Differs from neighbouring subspecies by details of colouration, mainly of upper body, neck, breast, tail, etc, but these can be seen clearly only in a large specimen collection, such as Coll ZIN RAN and Coll ZM MSU. Inhabits an indistinct range of narrow transition zones with four other subspecies (*T. u. major, T. u. karelicus, T. u. obsoletus* and *T. u. volgensis*). Clearest border is between this subspecies and *T. u. major* because of different male song: western with 'cork-note' and eastern without. In contact zone, both songs are heard. Width of contact zone is nearly 150km (93 miles), determined mainly from hunter information (Potapov, 1971). Range includes north-western Russia (St Petersburg, Pskov, Novgorod, Tver, Smolensk and Moscow); eastern Estonia, Latvia and Lithuania; Belorussia (excluding north-western corner); and northern Ukraine. Southern limit is limit of capercaillie range. Eastern limit is line linking south-eastern shores of Ladoga Lake to the upper Volga Basin. The male nuptial song is of the eastern type.

T. u. obsoletus (Snigirewski in Portenko, 1937): 50–51 (Archangelsk and Kyrov (now Viatka) Provinces)

One of largest and darkest subspecies. Male maximal wing length: 423mm, tail: 423mm. Belly of male has very small white patches, upper body is dull dark-brown. Females are also darker. Inhabits the northern taiga zone from Ladoga and Onega lakes eastward to the Yenisei Valley Basin. Easternmost point is in the Pogkamennaia Tunguzka (61°N) of Vilui River valley (115°E) and estuaries of Tokko and Chara rivers, Lena Basin (122°E, Vorobiev, 1963). Southern border unclear, but probably along 60°N from Ladoga Basin to the eastern range limit. The male nuptial song is of the eastern type.

T. u. kureikensis (Buturlin, 1927)

Distinguished from *T. u. obsoletus* by general dull colour with a cold-grey tinge to neck, rump and flanks (similar to *T .u. volgensis*), paler back and by smaller size and weight (male wing and tail lengths 375–390mm and 270–275mm respectively, weight averaging 3,290g (7.25lb): specimens obtained in Kureika River Valley). This is very unusual and curious bird. It was described and analysed when large numbers suddenly appeared in the lower Kureika River valley, a tributary of the Yenisei, at about 65°N, in the autumn of 1925. The birds then disappeared completely and have not been seen again. The collector, amateur hunter Dr S. Schillinger, found a population of birds of both sexes of different ages (young birds being about 25% of the total) in the second half of September. There had been no capercaillie in the area before, though *T. u. obsoletus* inhabited the Yenesei estuary. Flocks of 50–60 birds were seen, concentrated mainly on riverbanks at places where pebbles were available: the birds collected the pebbles intensively. The birds were not afraid of man or gunshots, giving the impression of never before having seen humans or been hunted. Dr Shillinger obtained 44 specimens, mainly adult males. The size and weight of the birds was similar to *T. u. lönnbergi*, i.e. smaller than *T. u. obsoletus*. Birds collected by hunters in the 1970s in the same area had weights that suggested they were *T. u. obsoletus* (Marunin, 1970). It would appear that an unknown population from an unknown site arrived in the Kureika River valley during a seasonal displacement in search of gastric pebbles, a habit that is common in the populations of the northern Siberian lowlands. The male nuptial song is unknown.

T. u. taczanowskii (Stejneger, 1885)

Male colour differs from *T. u. obsoletus* by having a paler tinge of the light-brown back, and a narrower, greenish breast plastron. The latter is similar to *T. u. uralensis*, but *T. u. taczanowskii* differs from this form by having a less white belly and central pair of tail feathers, and a longer tail. Females are very similar to *T. u. uralensis*, but darker. Inhabits the south-eastern part of the species range, eastward from the Ural Mountains, and including the mountain areas of Altai, Sayan and Baikal. At its northern border the subspecies contacts *T. u. obsoletus* at 60°N. The male nuptial song is of the eastern type.

T. u. uralensis (Nazarov, 1887)

The palest subspecies, with the shortest tail. Male upper body is light-grey, sometimes yellow-brown on the back. The belly is completely or nearly white: among 90 specimens of Coll ZIN RAN, 17 have completely white bellies, 22 have white covering less than half the belly, the remainder vary between these two extremes (Potapov, 1985). Females are similar to *T. u. taczanowskii*, but paler. The range once formed a narrow stripe through relic pine forests along the northern outlying parts of the forest-steppe zone east to 84°E (Barnaul), but in most locations the birds had disappeared by the mid-20th century. Now restricted to the south and central Urals to 60°N. The male nuptial song is of the eastern type.

T. u. volgensis (Buturlin, 1907)

Colouration is transitional between *T. u. uralensis* and *T. u. pleskei*. Inhabits the forest–steppe zone in the middle part of the Volga River Basin. The male nuptial song is of the eastern type.

Habitats

Western Capercaillie inhabit different types of forest, though in general they are seen where there are pines, especially in winter, the exceptions tending to be in southern parts of the range. In Cantabria and the forest–steppe zone of Eastern Europe, the bird inhabits pure deciduous forests, but this is almost certainly due to the disappearance of pines or other conifers as a result of human activity. In the Carpathian Mountains the birds inhabit the upper forest belt of pure spruce, at 800–1,500m (2,625–4,921ft) (Ostrovsky, 1974). The same is also true in the western Altai Mountains (Dolgushin *et al.*, 1962). In

Male Western Capercaillie in Aardal, Norway

general, the birds can live in any type of relief, plain or mountain, but in mountains they prefer the upper forest belt, right up to the timberline, which, in the Altai, is at almost 2,000m (6,562ft) (Sushkin, 1938). There is a distinct seasonal change of habitat, in most cases being from summer (spruce forest) to winter ones (pine).

Population structure and density

In the northern Urals, the ratio of males and females is 58–42%, while in broods it is 45–55% (Teplov, 1947). This change is confirmed elsewhere: in Russian Karelia there were 57.3% females among young birds, 44.8% among older ones (Ivanter, 1974); in Finland in the late summers of four consecutive years (1963–1966), the fraction of females in populations varied from 54.4–62.5% (Rajala, Linden, 1974); in central Russia during the autumn, the ratio of males to females varied from 43.7–56.3% to 65–34.9%, with males dominating in four of six years (Kiselev, 1971). The decline in the female fraction arises because of higher mortality in older females. The number of juvenile birds in populations varies considerably in the northern range, from 3–81% of the population, while in more southerly areas it is 58–80% (Semenov-Tianshansky, 1959; Romanov, 1975). We assume that the very different local climatic conditions explain this. These data suggest a large diversity in population statistics, and this is confirmed by measurements of bird density.

In areas where man's influence is minimal, this varies from 9 to 1 birds/km², and can be even lower, e.g. 0.4 birds/km² in north-western Siberia (Vartapetov, 1998).

Using data on population density, it was calculated, in 1983, that the total Eurasian population of Western Capercaillie was 2–3 million birds, half of which lived in the Russian Federation (Moss, 1983). Later data put the number of birds in Russia in 2003 at close to 3 million (Mejnev, 2004) – but see below – with a further 210,000 in Scandinavian (Marti, Picozzi, 1997). In Russia there appears to have been significant changes in population, a figure of 6–7 million birds having been calculated in the 1960s (Gavrin, 1970), falling to 1.5 million in the 1970s (Schubnikova, Nazarov, 1981), before increasing to Mejnev's figure. In Western Europe the population has decreased. The decline in Spain has already been noted; in Switzerland the population has halved in the last 30 years (Schnidrig et al., 2003); in Poland, Lithuania and Slovakia it has fallen by 33–50% over the same period. The last survey in Scotland, made in 2003–2004, gave a population of 1,980 birds (Ewing, 2009).

Territoriality

In most parts of their range, capercaillie are sedentary, spending the year in a comparatively restricted area where food resources are sufficient in all seasons. In Russia's Komi Republic, 13 of 14 ringed birds were found within 2–6km (1.2–3.7 miles) of where they were ringed – the final bird, a male, having moved 40km (25 miles) in 15 days (Romanov, 1979). In the Pechora-Ilych State Reserve (northern Urals) in August of 1980–1985, 115 capercaillie of both sexes, and different ages, were ringed. Of these, 60 were found again. One female had moved only 2.15km (1.34 miles) when found 1,123 days later. Young males after 358, 1,083 and 1,136 days were found at distances of 2.15, 0.37 and 0.05 kilometres (1.3, 0.2 and 0.03 miles) respectively. Young females were more mobile: after 412–802 days they were at distances of 4.5–12.2km (2.8–7.6 miles) (Voronin, Beshkarev, 1995). In Perm Province, of 49 marked males, almost half were captured repeatedly not more than 1km (0.6 mile) from the release point. Others moved no more than 4km (2.5 miles), with only two birds moving further: 5km (3.1 miles) and 12km (7.5 miles) (Romanov, 1973). However, in many places, especially in northern parts of the range, capercaillie are more mobile, moving greater distances, mainly because of the need to seek winter food sources and gastrolits. In north-western Siberia, capercaillie leave their breeding zone in the spruce-larch forests north from 66°N to winter in more southerly pine forests. The same seasonal migration also takes place in the vast Pechora Basin Lowlands, where the birds breed in narrow strips of spruce forests along the rivers that flow through vast treeless bogs. In the autumn, these birds fly east from their breeding grounds to the northern Urals where there are pine forests, juniper thickets and gastrolits along the banks of rivers. At this time, the number of capercaillie on the western slopes of the mountains at about 65°N increases by 10–15 times, with a prevalence of females in a ratio of 4:1 (Estafiew et al., 1973; Potapov, 1985). Intensive seasonal migrations in the northern parts of the Pechora lowlands was noted in 1921 and 1923 (Soloviev, 1927), the birds moving in flocks of 20–50 birds, or as solitary individuals. During these migrations the birds passed settlements, occasionally resting on the roofs of houses: in 1908, two trappers caught 500 birds in one hour. However, such migrations are no longer seen.

The territorial structure of a typical sedentary micro-population is centred around the lek. The same lek position may be used for hundreds of years, but leks may also disappear, or be replaced step-by-step during successive years. Yet despite this constancy of lek, there are observations that indicate that individual birds of both sexes may visit the leks of neighbouring populations.

At each lek, males will have their own territory, the size and permanency of these varying significantly, though they will forage out of this territory. In sedentary populations, birds of both sexes stay within 3–5km (1.9–3.1 miles) of the lek, females raising their broods and males moulting within those limits. Female nesting territories have not been well-studied, but in most cases it seems females nest within 2km (1.2 miles) of the lek, and there is no antagonism between adjacent hens, sometimes the hens actually choosing to nest close together. Females may also use the same nest site in successive years, occasionally even using the same nest (Krutovskaia, 1958; Potapov, 1985). Brood life, to the point of dispersal, takes place within an area of radius only 1–2km (1.2 miles) centred on the nest site (Potapov, 1985). In the autumn, the birds unite in flocks, usually by sex, and spend the winter within the same micro-population territory.

In western Siberian lowland forests, the problem of obtaining gastrolits is a serious issue for the birds, the stones only being available along the banks of many rivers. From the beginning of September, capercaillie concentrate along the pebbly bars of these rivers, with older females appearing first, followed by young females. Old males arrive in the second half of September and young males appear last. The maximum concentrations of birds occur in early October, with several dozen birds often gathering together (Nazarov, Shubnikova, 1975).

Behaviour

Though Western Capercaillie are typical forest birds, their connection to the forest is not as close as that of Hazel or Spruce Grouse. Females with broods often leave the cover of the forest for treeless bogs, water or subalpine meadows. Where forest meets steppe, the birds occasionally move 150m from tree cover to search for insects (Sushkin, 1914). In the northern Urals and Kola Peninsula along the timberline, the birds often emerge on to open mountain tundra in search of berries, being observed feeding on blueberries, sometimes in the company of Rock Ptarmigan (Semenov-Tianshansky, 1959; Potapov, 1985).

The birds are essentially ground-living from spring to autumn, especially during the intensive moult, using trees only for roosting or to escape danger. In winter, the birds feed mainly in the trees and roost in snow burrows. In Germany's Black Forest and the French

Pyrénées, it was found that in autumn/winter a hiker needed to get within 20–30m (21.9–32.8yd) of a capercaillie before it flushed, females flushing at greater distances than males, but both sexes flushing at greater distances in places where they were hunted or where there was intensive tourism (Thiel *et al.*, 2007). However, if the bird is in a snow burrow, it is possible for a skier to approach within 2–3m (2.2–3.3yd) (Potapov, 1990).

In contrast to Hazel and Spruce Grouse, capercaillie can fly above the forest, sometimes for long distances. Some observations indicate that if the birds achieve a reasonable altitude over forest, they can glide for long distances, their spread wings producing a loud whizzing sound (Semenov-Tianshansky, 1959). The speed of normal flying is nearly 60kmph (37mph), but can reach 96kmph (60mph) under pursuit by a raptor (Bannermann, 1963). In the mountains, the birds usually walk uphill, but always fly downhill (Kuzmina, 1962).

Capercaillie flock at most times of the year, forming particularly large flocks in winter, with males and females in separate groups. In former times, when the birds were abundant, such flocks numbered up to 70 for males, or 100 for females (Menzbier, 1902; Teplov, 1947; Seiskari, Koskimies, 1955; Semenov-Tianshansky, 1959). Much smaller flocks (20–50 birds) are now more common, while in places where the population is small, winter flocks may consist of both sexes, or flocks may be absent, 2 or 3 males or females gathering together, and solitary birds being seen.

Nutrition

Across the huge range, despite differences in vegetation, the main winter food is pine needles, mainly from two species, *Pinus silvestris* and *P. sibiricus*, with a small addition of new, embryo cones and twig ends. In Siberia, where both pine species are present, no specific preference is observed. At other times of the year, this food source is also used, but in minimal quantities. There is no significant difference in winter forage between the sexes. In northern Europe, males prefer to feed on the needles of diseased pines around bogs (Lobacev, Scherbakov, 1936; Teplov, 1947; Lindrot, Lingren, 1950; Kirikov, 1952) where, because of disturbances in metabolism, such needles offer higher nutritional value, more protein and less calcium (Pulliainen, 1970a). The birds will eat up to 50% of the needles from such trees, such exploitation delaying the appearance of new sprouts: as a result, the treetops have a flattened form (Potapov, 1985).

Among secondary food sources are junipers (twigs with needles and fruits) and, in Scotland, the needles of Douglas fir, a species introduced from North America (Zwickel, 1966). In southern parts of the range when there are no pines, the birds' winter food is fir or spruce needles (Teplov, 1947; Semenov-Tianshansky, 1959; Dolgushin *et al.*, 1962; Dulkeit, 1964; Ostrovsky, 1974). Capercaillie also feed on the buds, catkins and twigs of deciduous trees (birch, oak, aspen, linden, elm, willow) (Menzbier, 1902) in the Urals (Kirikov, 1952; Potapov, 1985). In some cases, birch catkins account for 15% of crop volume (South Siberia, Telepnev, 1972). In Spain's Cantabrian Mountains, the main winter food is leaves of evergreen *Ilex* spp. (Castroviejo, 1967). These examples illustrate the ability of capercaillie to adjust their main winter food if required, despite the basic monophagy. The composition of the spring, summer and autumn diets is diverse, though certain plants are especially important. First of these is bilberry (*Vaccinium myrtillus*), its stems, buds, flowers, leaves and berries being taken, especially in the summer and early autumn in most parts of the range. Other species of Vaccinium and berries of *Empetrum nigrum* are also important, to a lesser degree. In spring, females take green grasses as soon as the snow cover disappears, particularly the tubers, green leaves and winter flower buds of cotton-grass (*Eriophorum vaginatum*) (Andreev, 1978, Potapov, 1993, 2011). After the prolonged winter diet such high protein food is very important for clutch production.

Other non-winter foods include the green leaves of different trees and bushes, horsetails and fern sprouts, and the seeds of different grasses. Animal food (spiders, mollusks and insects) is not important in the diet of adult birds, being less than 10% of food volume even during the intensive moult. However, it is very important to chicks.

The use of gastrolits is very important to the birds, with their absence in breeding areas leading to large-scale migrations, though the use of hard stones from fruits such as dog rose and bird cherry have been noted (Telepnev, 1972). Gastrolits have been found to weigh up to 71g (2.5oz) in a male gizzard and 27g (1oz) in a female, but usually average 36.8g (1.3oz) in males and 24.7g (0.9oz) in females. The size of stones varies in diameter from 2–5mm, with an average of 3.5mm in males and 3.2mm in females, and its number in gizzard varies from 563 to 900 (Romanov, 1975). The quantity of gastrolits in the gizzard is not constant, being minimal in mid-summer, then increasing as the birds change to a winter diet. During the winter the number of gastrolits slowly decreases as they are removed from the gizzard with digested food, but some remain until the beginning of spring: as a consequence the birds try to add more stones in winter whenever possible. In a study in central Russia, it was noted that females outnumbered males at gastrolit collecting places in spring, being 70–80% of the total number, indicating the importance of minerals for females about to produce eggs (Kiselev, 1971).

The water needs of capercaillie are not well studied. According to some sources the birds drink regularly twice daily, in the mornings and evenings (Teplov, 1947). During winter, the birds eat snow in their burrow roosts (Potapov, 1974, 1985).

Wintering

During the winter, capercaillie are strongly sedentary, groups or flocks of males and females inhabiting restricted areas, usually not more than 2,500ha (6,178 acres), and for small groups only 0.2–50ha (0.5–124 acres) (Teplov, 1947; Ivanter, 1965; Potapov, 1985). In forests with a high fraction of pines, the birds may spend all winter in a small patch. The winter daily ration of males is 440–550g (15.5–19.4oz) of pine needles (fresh weight) (Lobachev, Scherbakov, 1936; Teplov, 1947; Semenov-Tianshansky, 1959). In the full crop of an old male collected immediately after it had constructed its snow burrow, there were 374g (13.2oz) of pine needles (fresh weight), amounting to 7.5% of the bird's body weight (Potapov, 1985). Overall, the average daily ration of a capercaillie male is 282.35g (9.96oz) of pine needles (dry weight).

The duration and number of feed periods in winter strongly depends on ambient temperature and the duration of daylight. On the Kola Peninsula, at 67°N, when daylight is minimal (December), the birds feed twice daily, sunrise and prior to sunset, when the minimum temperature reached -36.5°C (-33.7°F) (Semenov-Tianshansky, 1959). In such cold, the birds avoided feeding in the trees and fed from the snow surface on small junipers and the low branches of pines. In the northern Urals, from December to February, the birds fed only once, in the middle of the day, with feeding lasting no more than 1.5 hours. In the Altai Mountains, the temperature threshold for capercaillie feeding was -35°C (-31°F), after which the birds did not leave their snow burrows, but the duration of staying in the burrows was not ascertained (Dulkeit, 1975). Teplov (1947) suggests this might be 3–4 days, but this is unconfirmed.

As capercaillie usually walk during feeding, deep snow, especially if it is friable and dry, can be a serious problem. Because of the large pectinations and the long feathering of the tarsi, the male's winter footprint area is twice that of the summer (52cm² v 26cm²/8in² v 4in²) and, correspondingly, the loading is halved, from 80–40g/cm² (Teplov, 1947; Dulkeit, 1964). Despite this, capercaillie go through soft snow, leaving tracks consisting of two deep (up to 13cm/5.1in) trenches (Potapov, 1985). In especially deep, friable snow, males sometimes sink up to their bellies, leaving trenches 21cm (8.3in) deep (Dulkeit, 1964).

Large body size also creates problems for the bird when it excavates a snow burrow: the depth of snow must be at least 40–50cm (15.7–19.6in) for males, at least 40cm (15.7in) for females (Semenov-Tianshansky, 1959; Dulkeit, 1964). In northern parts of the range, extreme cold arrives before the snow attains these depths and the birds have to accumulate significant amounts of fat, with layers of up to 1cm forming, mainly around different parts of the intestinal tract and around the base of the tail (Romanov, 1975).

Capercaillie snow burrows start with a tunnel up to 3m long. On average, a male's burrow is 81cm (31.9in) long, 30cm (11.8in) wide and 28cm (11in) high. The burrow roof thickness is 17cm (6.7in). For females the dimensions are 57cm (22.4in), 22cm (8.7in), 37cm (14.6in) and 11cm (4.3in) respectively. The much longer length of the male burrow is to accommodate the longer tail.

The birds usually spend the middle of the day resting in snow burrows, but in sunny weather and moderate cold (say -15°C/5°F) they rest in shallow, open holes on the snow. Capercaillie also roost in trees or open snow holes if snow conditions do not permit burrow excavation. Southern populations use tree roosting more frequently: in southern

Finland the birds rarely dig burrows (Seiskari, Koskimies, 1955). Winter thaws are more frequent in western parts of the Eurasian taiga, explaining the preference for tree roosting in those areas

The bird's time budget in midwinter in a typical situation (60°N, ambient temperature -15°C to -30°C/5°F to -22°F) is: roost in snow burrow, 16.5hr, rest in hole in snow surface (middle of the day), 2.5hr, feeding, including walking and flying, 5hr. The daily weight of male droppings averages 150g/5.3oz (fresh weight), and of gut excrements, 34g (1.2oz). Capercaillie droppings differ from those of other grouse because of their great size (length 42–58mm, diameter 11–13mm, fresh weight 1.24–1.47g/0.04–0.05oz). The winter energy budget averages 5,735.1kj/day, comprising existence energy 1,558.3kj/day, excrement energy 4,185.2kj/day (Potapov, 1982; 1985). Data from northern Finland (65°N, caged birds) gave values of 8,270, 2,633 and 4,307kj/day respectively (Andreev, Linden, 1986), indicating that the energy budget is dependent on latitude, the bird's physiological condition, the weather and the diet, as would be expected.

Breeding

Western Capercaillie are a typical polygamous species, with a collective (lekking) mating process. Young male and female capercaillie reach puberty in their first year, but the chances of males breeding at that time is minimal, First-year males that do breed have very low success in terms of fertilized eggs (Kutovaya, 1976). In natural conditions, young males have no chance to breed and are completely ignored by females, this perhaps due to their inability to demonstrate the older male's full tail with its solid surface resulting from feather width (in young males, the narrow tail feathers look like the spokes of a wheel in the open tail – Potapov, 1975). Only if illegal hunting were to kill all older males at a lek could young males mate (Kirikov, 1952). At two years of age, males can maintain an individual territory at the sides of an active lek (Romanov, 1979). First-year females can breed, but data from captive birds suggests that only those with a body weight above 1.8kg (4lb) do so (Kiselev, 1971; Nemtzev et al., 1973). Such a weight requires successful wintering and the good early spring conditions, but is also influenced by hatch date: females from late broods lack the time necessary to reach a pre-winter weight that allows breeding the following spring (Potapov, 1985).

All nuptial activity takes place at the lek, the position, size and features of which vary significantly, though certain features are common. Lek arenas are under forest cover, never in the open, though the forest must not be dense and with only a little undergrowth so that activities are clearly visible over a distance of 60–70m (66–77yd). Over most of the range, lek arenas are situated in pure pine; or in mixed pine forest, usually close to a large bog; or in dry places close to the contact zone of old and young forest; or in the places with sparse arboreal vegetation in the form of short pines on swampy soil. The soil at the lek is very often swampy, usually moss soaked with water. Another important detail of a typical lek in northern parts of the range (north of 57°N) is the presence of tussocks of the cotton-grass, *Eriophorum vaginatum*, which attracts females (Potapov, 2011). In mountains, leks are usually close to the timberline, whether pine forests (e.g. the Altai), the spruce and mixed forests (oaks, birches, hornbeams, etc) of the Alps, Pyrénées and Carpathians, or even the ilex forests of Cantabria. In the Altai Mountains, large leks stretched along the crests of the ridges for several kilometres (Dulkeit, 1964).

As a rule, each local population has its own traditional lek arena (Teplov, 1947). The size of the arena varies hugely, from 10–150ha (25–371 acres), depending on the size of the local population – in optimal situations with more than 100 males, but more recently they have become smaller (perhaps 25–30 up to 50–70) (Malchevsky, Pukinsky, 1983; Potapov, 1985). In southern Finland, lek arenas vary from 6–20ha (14–49 acres), with 6–18 active males in each (Pirkola, Koivisto, 1970). In the western, central and southern part of Eastern Europe, lek arenas are small, 1–2ha (2.5–4.9 acres), with 2–5 males. Solitary lekking males began to be seen from the middle of last century, clear evidence of a serious decline in population: solitary displaying males usually precede the disappearance of capercaillie from an area.

Generally, each old male has its own territory at the lek. The size and permanency of this territory is variable, but data regarding changes is still debated. It seems that a male's individual territory has no stable, fixed borders (Pirkola, Koivisto, 1970), particularly if the number of males is high: in Western Europe, where local populations are usually small, territorial behaviour is more clearly expressed (Lumsden, 1961; Hjorth, 1970) and may even be seen outside the breeding season (Bannerman, 1963). Sometimes males maintained individual territories in the leks constantly during a period of observation of several years (Müller, 1974). Some studies suggest males may also occasionally display at neighbouring leks (Teplov, 1947; Potapov, 1985), though this has not been confirmed by data collected from marked birds (Ostrovsky, 1974; Romanov, 1979).

Male lek displays are complicated and vary with population density, the weather, and the influence of raptors and human activity. There is also considerable diversity between individuals, something that makes the reproductive behaviour of capercaillie markedly different from the 'standard' behaviour of other grouse. Courtship display consists of several specific postures (**Figure 58**), performances and sounds, the latter comprising a 'song' consisting from clicking and hissing sounds, the most important and famous element of capercaillie nuptial rituals. The description and analysis of the song has produced an extensive literature (Würm, 1885; Krudener, 1928; Boback, 1966; Marchlewski, 1962; Hjorth, 1967; 1970 and many others), but despite this, the details of sound production are still unclear or disputed. The most detailed description of capercaillie vocal apparatus and song production is that of Hjorth (1970). The song is comparatively quiet, audible up to 150–200m (164–219yd), and lasts nearly 5.5 seconds. It comprises two very different parts: the first is a series of double clicks, the tempo quickening so that they quickly

Figure 58. Lek postures of *Tetrao urogallus*
1 – main posture; 2 – rear view of fully opened tail of an old male; 3 – front view of fully opened tail of a one-year-old male; 4 – attack posture.

merge into a trilling lasting nearly 1 second. The trill stops suddenly, and the second part of the song begins immediately. This is a combination of high-pitched scraping sounds that lasts nearly 3 seconds, audible at up to 200m (219yd) (**Figure 59**), resembling the rhythmic sound of a scythe being whetted ('whetting phase'). As the first part of the song passes to the second, another sound is also heard in the background. Audible only at close distance (not more than 15m/16yd), this resembles a deep, burring grunt. In turn, in the central part of the song there are 1–5 weak accessory sounds, such as that produced by a water droplet falling into a pool ('plop'), or a doubled sound ('plip-plop').

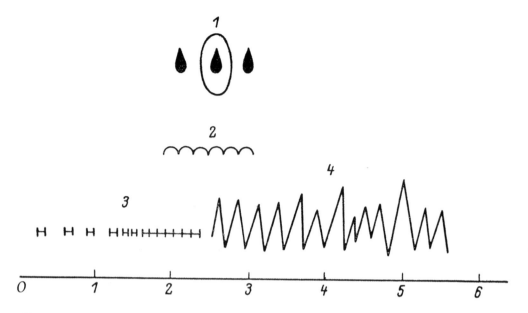

Figure 59. A graphic representation of the *Tetrao urogallus* song

1 – 'water drop' sounds (circled noise represents the cork note in western subspecies); 2 – background rumbling low note, similar to a burp; 3 – separate clicks that quickly become a united trill; 4 – a whetting noise, such as made by sharpening with a whetstone. (C) – Time in seconds.

Another prominent sound is the 'cork note' (as produced by the withdrawal of a cork from a bottle), which is louder, audible at up to 300m. This prominent element of the male's song is characteristic only for the western populations of four subspecies (*T. u. urogallus, T. u. major, T. u. aquitannicus* and *T. u. cantabricus*) and is important at that level in helping to determine the subspecies borders. The 'cork-note' develops gradually as the male ages. It is weak and indistinct in one-year-old males, more prominent and louder in two-year-old males and reaches maximum loudness in old males. The development of such a complicated structure only in western subspecies is evidence of an evolutionary advancement (Potapov, 1985).

If the male is singing on the ground, it might omit the whetting phase of the song during a flutter-jump. During singing, either in a tree or on the ground, the male adopts the 'thin-necked upright' posture (Hjorth, 1970), in which it spreads and lifts the tail, raises its neck and head to point the bill, and slightly spreads, and partly lowers, its wings (see Figure 58, n1).

A famous peculiarity of the capercaillie song is the prominent decrease in the bird's hearing while it sings. The male is deaf from the finishing of the trill to the end of the whetting phase, i.e. for nearly 3 seconds, hearing being restored completely shortly after the end of the whetting. Hunters have used this deafness over the centuries to approach males: the Russian name of the bird, *Gluhar*, derives from the feature (*gluhoi* – deaf). However, the bird is not totally deaf, being capable of hearing very loud noises: in experiments, males stop singing if there is a gunshot, a loud drumbeat or a trumpet blast (Marchlewski, 1962). The reason for the partial loss of hearing is not yet clear despite a debate lasting more than a century (Würm, 1885; Iluichev *et al.*, 1961). At present we can only say that it is connected with the mechanics of song production, which have themselves not been fully explained despite careful filming.

During maximum activity a male can sing one song after another without stopping, completing up to 500 or more songs over a 1.5-hour period, or producing 7–8 full songs a minute at sunrise. In such situations, the first part of the song may be very short or even absent (Malchevsky, Pukinski, 1983). Each song begins with clicks, with these produced almost by way of vocal testing. If the bird is disturbed during the clicks, it will pause, waiting until it has settled again, before resuming the clicks and the song.

Another vocal element of the courtship display is a raucous, guttural 'hu–achu' named the 'Belching Canto' by Hjorth. This is usually uttered by a male when landing after a demonstrative flight, during conflict or when disturbed. One more vocal element, named *skirkanie* in Russian, is rarer and has not yet been analysed by sonogram. It consists of two clicks with a specific chirping sound (like a knife against a stone) between them. This vocalization is uttered mainly in leks, especially at the end of the lekking period. It may also be uttered during flight and in the autumn if the bird is put upon by a dog (Potapov, 1985).

The male's specific display – the 'sprawl posture' – was known from imprints seen in fresh snow (Teplow, 1947) before it was observed. An old male, walking within its territory, lies on the snow, its breast in contact, the neck and head stretched forward, the wings folded, the tail partly spread and lowered. In one observation, the male spread its wings completely and held the sprawled position for several seconds (Potapov, 1975).

The 'Jump' display is observed very rarely: the male makes a vertical jump to a height of 30cm (11.8in), with the wings pressed close to the body, the head tossed back. While jumping, the male utters a short, raucous sound (Teplov, 1947).

The drumming, or flutter-jump, is made only from the ground. The bird flies up with 4 or 5 strong, short wingbeats, reaching a height of 1.5–2.0m (1.6–2.2yd), hangs momentarily with wings extended, then lands 3–7m (3.3–7.7yd) from the start point with another 4–5 wingbeats. The sound, audible at up to 100m, is heard as two bursts of wingbeats separated by a short pause. Usually flutter-jumps are made in a straight line, but sometimes the bird changes direction at the upper point by 45°–90°. During the lift, the first wingbeats hit the ground or snow, but the wings do not touch the ground on landing. Sometimes on landing, particularly on soft snow, the male falls on to its breast and remains still, its wings and tail spread, making a clear body print in the snow, exactly as Asian Spruce Grouse do, after completing its display jump (Potapov, 1969; 1985). Flutter-jumps are usually provoked by those of nearby males on the lek, or by the appearance of a female.

Another unusual collective behaviour of capercaillie, one rarely observed, is called, in Russian, *horovod* (round dance). This takes place at the beginning of the second lek stage, when females arrive and begin to walk between the males, in groups or alone. All surrounding males run to them, follow them, sometimes walking side by side in full lek posture, creating the 'round dance'. During the dance the borders between individual territories are not rigorously maintained, though conflicts are rare. However, the males do attempt to force one or more females into their own territory: occasionally a male is successful in this, gathering one or more hens (Hainard, Meylan, 1935: Hjorth, 1970; Tcherbakov, 1967).

Confrontations between neighbouring males are frequent and occasionally lead to serious combat, and rarely even result in death. During combat, usually in the contact zones of individual territories, rivals take up a range of specific postures, and make blows with bill, wings and legs. During combat, the noise from the beating wings is so loud that it has been likened by some observers to the fall of large trees.

Lek activity is clearly divided into three stages. The first is from about March, when the first signs of male nuptial activity become apparent, and lasts until males have concentrated at the lek site and the first females have appeared. The second stage is the main one, and lasts no more than 7 days, during which females visit the lek regularly and mate. The third, and final, stage is the gradual decline in male activity, lasting a week or two depending on individual males. Some individuals will also display during the winter if the weather is sunny. Often, if a group of males is feeding on snow near small pines, one will suddenly adopt a lekking pose and make several jumps with wingbeats, or walking in a distinct, pompous manner, his wings partly spread and lowered, the tips touching the snow and leaving thin furrows on both sides of his footprints. Usually such individual activity does not provoke the others (Potapov, 1985). However, as spring approaches, males in feeding groups may all start to display, and may even fight.

True activity starts with the male's regular appearance in the traditional lek site, these movements being minimal in the sedentary populations, or reverse migration in other cases. As activity increases, the males visit the lek more frequently and begin to roost at the site. Once roosting has started, if the weather is good, the males begin singing and will also feed close to the site, mainly from the ground. As more males gather, arena activity increases, but at this stage individual territories have not been established, with the males moving freely around the site: judging by the battle traces, the situation is not entirely harmonious. At this stage, activity is weather dependent, with bad weather interrupting proceedings. The birds can sense the approach of both good and bad weather, with activity in good weather slowing as the males sense approaching bad weather and speeding up in bad weather as they sense the arrival of better times. Males usually arrive in the evening, with older males displaying first, followed by two-year-olds and then juveniles (Kirikov, 1947; 1952).

As snow-free patches form, the second stage of lek activity begins, the males becoming strongly territorial. Birds (arriving usually in the evening) perch in trees and utter the 'Belching Canto', then make flights that define their territorial limits, taking them from tree to tree over distances of 20–30m (22–33yd), with slow, loud wingbeats. The loud wingbeats of such flights are provocative, one male's flights immediately making other males at the lek respond with flights of their own. Usually each male will make 3–5 flights each evening, the day's final songs being after nightfall. In general, singing males sit on thick branches, occasionally feeding between songs. Females may be present, but are inactive and quiet.

Morning activity begins while it is still very dark. The male begins to click, then sings. Singing is now intense, with most males singing 600–700 times, some up to 1,300 times as dawn breaks (Pukinsky, Roo, 1966; Müller, 1974). Females arrive at around daybreak, their presence betrayed by their characteristic 'ak…ak…ak'. The females usually land in individual territories, having selected their males during previous visits. As soon as a female arrives, the males fly down and start to display. Mating then occurs on the ground, the male being careful to guard his territory against intruders. Usually intruders retreat, but combat may occur, the winner usually being the territory owner (Würm, 1885; Hjorth, 1970, Potapov, 1975). Females do not arrange themselves evenly around the lek, most concentrating at central territories. Consequently, the male owners of these favoured sites have several hens, with the owners of peripheral territories often having none. At a central territory, 4–7 females will peacefully feed around an actively lekking cock.

Once the sun has risen, the females begin to fly away, some of the males following them. The status of these males is unclear – are they those from the bottom of the male hierarchy who have not mated? As there is no confirmed case of mating outside the lek, the most likely answer to the question is they probably are unmated males, and the pursuit is futile. The most active cocks do not follow the females, remaining and continuing to display, mainly by singing, on the ground at first, then from trees. If the lek is not disturbed, some males may stay and sing to 9 a.m. or 10 a.m. After that, those males still present begin to forage and gradually move away from the lek.

Although the second stage ritual described above is of the same basic form everywhere, there are differences in local populations (Teplov, 1947; Potapov, 1975). The second stage of lekking lasts 7–10 days (Teplov, 1947, Pircola, Koivisto, 1970). As soon as females cease to visit, and begin to prepare nests and to lay, male activity declines, though males may continue to visit the arena for a further 3–4 weeks. During this period, males arrive at the lek long before sunset, feed for hours, then roost in the same trees. In the absence of females, they do not descend to the ground in the morning, and sing less enthusiastically. In cold summers in the northern parts of the range, males can sing until mid-June when the moult begins. However, males do display in summer, autumn and even in winter. Autumn display activity begins after the main stage of the moult is completed, i.e. from the end of August, with the males displaying in trees, on the ground, at lek or feeding sites, and often in the mixed sex flocks. In the Rhine Basin, males display in their territories to the end of November and are regularly visited by females (Müller, 1974). The testicles of males collected in the autumn on the Kola Peninsula and in the northern Ural showed a clear size increase in September (Semenov-Tianshansky, 1959). Winter displays are rare, and information on them in the wild is scarce. In open cages in Belarus, young males leked throughout the winter (Kutovaia, 1976).

Choice of mate is entirely decided by the female. After the hen has made her choice, the two birds are ready to mate immediately. Observations suggest that despite several females surrounding a male, he will mate only in the morning and only with one of them (Pukinsky, Roo, 1966; Nemtzev et al., 1973). However, in open cages females sometimes mated again with the same male after 20–30 minutes (Kutovaya, 1976). Females usually nest and rear their broods within 1km (0.6 mile) of the lek, occasionally nesting within 40–50m (44–55yd) of each other (Belarus, Dolbik, 1961). Nests are placed under the cover of low branches, mainly of spruce; under a fallen trunk; between exposed roots; occasionally in more open places near a trunk, but very rarely in open clearing. Nest construction is simple –a shallow scrape in soil or moss, sparsely lined with dry grass, needles, leaves, moss and feathers. If spring is late, females may lay eggs directly on the snow. In one study, a female laid four eggs on snow in Finland (at 61°15′N), but only after the fourth egg, moss lining appeared. Snow had disappeared when the ninth (final) egg was laid. Despite this, chicks hatched successfully (Pulliainen, Rajala, 1973).

Females begin to lay 3–4 days after mating and lay, on average, an egg every 24 hours, or perhaps a little longer – 5 eggs in 6 days (Höglund, 1952; Semenov-Tianshansky, 1959). In captivity, in open cages, females lay eggs from every 30–35 hours to every 46–48 hours, the latter period being more usual. Very rarely, the laying interval can be 4 days (Kutovaia, 1976).

Egg colour varies significantly even within a local population, and changes during incubation. Colour depends on the female's diet: the more conifer sprouts and buds, and cotton-grass stems, the browner and brighter the egg. Eggs have numerous, evenly distributed, dark-brown dots and spots, with several larger patches. Egg size on the Kola Peninsula was (N=29) 57–58mm x 41–43mm, average weight: 53.2g (1.87oz) (Semenov-Tianshansky, 1959); in the northern Urals the average size was 58.4x41.2mm (56.2–60.5mm x 40.5–42.1mm) (Teplov, 1947); in the Pyrénées – 59.9x41.1mm (Couturier, 1980). Egg sizes from different regions in Coll ZIN RAN (N=22) were: 54.0–63.7mm x 39.1–46.0mm, average 57.2x41.7mm. Among them, one egg from the Barnaul region of western Siberia was especially large at 63.7x46.0mm (Potapov, 1985). Egg size partly depends on the age of the female.

Clutch size varies within a population, as it depends on the ratio of young to old females, and on weather conditions in winter and early spring. For example, in the

Western Capercaillie nest in Karelia, Russia

southern Urals in a propitious spring in 1946, clutches were very large, one nest having 16 eggs: broods of 12 nestlings were observed many times. But during cold and rainy springs, the average clutch is five (Kirikov, 1952). A slight tendency for clutch size to decrease from south to north, 7.7 to 5.8, was noticed in Finland (Linden, 1983). The smallest clutches have 4–5 eggs, the largest observed being 16 (South Ural, Kirikov, 1952). In European Russia and Belarus, the average size of the clutch varies from 6.2 (northern Ural, Teplov, 1947a) to 8.3 (Belarus, Gavrin, 1969a).

Incubation begins before the laying of the last egg, and is intensive, females leaving the nest for feeding usually twice daily, in morning and evening, for only 10–35 minutes. In warm weather, absences are shorter, in cold weather, more frequent – up to 5 times daily (Swedish Lapland, Lennerstedt, 1966). At one nest under video surveillance in Finnish Lapland, with an ambient temperature of -0.5°C (31.1°F) to +29°C (84.2°F), the hen left the nest for feeding three times daily for 20–70 minutes (average – 34 minutes). She turned the eggs with her bill about every 100 minutes. All the chicks hatched safely during one day, and left the nest, together with the hen, early the next morning, but returned after 16 minutes. The hen brooded them for nearly 30 minutes, and after a further 20 minutes they all left the nest for the final time (Pulliainen, 1971). In the Alps, an observed female left the nest three times daily, each time for 20 minutes (Krott, 1966). It seems that periodic cooling of the eggs during the hen's absence is necessary for normal development of the embryo: during the absence of the female, temperatures as low as 14.6°C (58.2°F) have been observed. Egg temperature during incubation varies from 34.0°C (93.2°F) to 36.4°C (97.5°F), but temperatures as high as 43.6°C (110.5°F) have been recorded (Gruner, 1951; Lennerstedt, 1966).

During incessant rain the female will sit continuously throughout the day but, never, it seems, for more than 36 hours. Incubation varies from 20–30 days, with an average of 26 days (Höglund, 1952; Semenov-Tianshansky, 1959; Ivanter, 1965, Pulliainen, 1971). However, the claimed 20-day incubation period of Uschkov (1887) has never been confirmed.

The weights of newly hatched nestling have been measured as 35.8g (1.26oz) (Karelia; Ivanter, 1965); 36–37g (1.27–1.3oz) (Kola Peninsula: Semenov-Tianshansky, 1959); 33g (1.16oz) (Viatka Province, Russia; Efremov, 1940); 38–45g (1.34–1.59oz) (Krasnoyarsk Territory; Krutovskaya, Krutovskaya, 1958); and 38.2g (1.35oz) (Sweden, Höglund, 1955). Such remarkable variations are evidence of significant differences of the egg size and weight. Despite actively searching for food after the first few hours of life, chicks lose 2–3g (0.07–0.10oz) in weight during the first 24 hours post-hatching (Höglund, 1955; Semenov-Tianshansky, 1959). Searching for food is instinctive, the chicks pecking at insects (preferably on the lower surfaces of leaves), drops of dew and bright spots. In the first days of life, the colour green is especially attractive, but the chick soon learns to prefer flowers (Höglund, 1955).

The dependence of the brood's well-being on the weather has been studied experimentally. The body temperature of newly hatched chicks is 37.6°C (99.7°F), this increasing gradually to 41.6°C (106.9°F) at 18 days old when the chicks can fully regulate their temperature. Young chicks cool very quickly. **Figure 60** shows the minimal ambient temperature during dry weather at which a chick can feed for 20 minutes without needing brooding by the hen (Höglund, 1955). Clearly, the lower the ambient temperature, and the higher the air moisture, the quicker the chicks chill and the more frequently they need to be brooded, reducing the time for feeding. During cold, rainy weather the number of available insects also decreases. As a result, in persistent poor weather chicks younger than 18 days often perish. In rare cases, such chicks do survive if there is abundant food: in one example on the shores of Lake Baikal, survival in bad weather was assured by an abundance of Chironomid larvae. Though older chicks can regulate their temperature, persistent foul weather also affects them: six-week-old chicks were found to have halved the normal daily increase in body weight and delayed the moult process in such conditions (Kirpitchev, 1968).

Chicks begin to fly short distances at 4–5 days. At 5 days, they can to fly to a height of 30cm (11.8in), and at 8 days up to 1m (3.3ft). At 18 days, chicks fly 10m (11yd) (Krutowskaya, Krutovskaya, 1953; Krott, 1966). During the first 10 days of life, chicks react to danger by hiding and becoming still, not moving even if handled (Teplov, 1947). When older (10–12 days), they fly up and travel as far as possible before hiding. From three weeks of age, in general chicks fly into trees and hide in the crowns. The hiding chick sits motionless, stretching its neck and head along the branch, and does not react to any

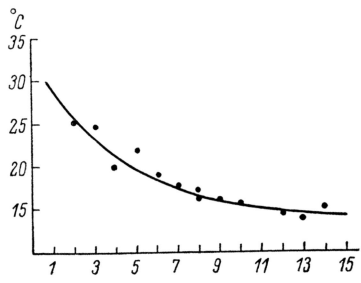

Figure 60. Variation of minimum outside temperature required for a baby chick in order to feed for more than 20 minutes without sheltering under the hen.
Vertical axis – outside temperature. Horizontal axis – age of chick in days (Höglund, 1955).

noise, even a gunshot (Efremov, 1940).

Embryo mortality is low, brood size equalling clutch size. Complete clutch destruction occurs due to predation or desertion of female (usually a young bird) during bad weather. Exact data on chick losses are scarce. During the first month broods prefer to stay in spruce forests, by streams, in glades, and particularly near large bogs, mainly along the borders of these, on more elevated ground where, often, reeds grow.

Such places are attractive because of the rich insect life. Brood disintegration begins when the juveniles reach about 80 days of age, the males leaving first. At this age, juvenile males show aggressive behaviour and also make attempts to mate with females (Krutowskaya, 1953; Krott, 1966). The males form small groups of 2–7, these occasionally joining with females to form mixed flocks in the late autumn.

Hunting, recreation and conservation

Three main factors influence the capercaillie population: hunting (trade and sport), destruction and fragmentation of forests, and prolonged climatic changes. The hunting take has never been high in comparison to that of Hazel, Willow or Black Grouse. Even when the population was far higher than today, and there were game markets in all large Russian cities, capercaillie were less popular than the other grouse because of their tough, slightly unpalatable meat (Menzbier, 1902).

Capercaillie are only hunted for sport, especially at spring leks, this developing mainly in Western and Central Europe several centuries ago. During the 19th century, the sharp decline in population meant that hunting became the privilege of nobles (Würm, 1885). In Great Britain, lek hunting was never practiced, professional hunters considering it 'ungentlemanly' (Bannerman, 1963). Today Britain is the only country where capercaillie hunting is banned, though hunting at leks is prohibited in Scandinavian countries. In other countries, the duration of the capercaillie hunting season has decreased. In Finland, hunting is only allowed in the autumn, and the season is shortened, or closed, depending on conditions, and an agreed quota of birds per hunter is set (Ranta *et al.*, 2008). In the Russian Federation, the number of hunters in remote areas has decreased, and state control over the purchase and use of weapons has increased.

Forest destruction is now the main reason behind the decline in capercaillie numbers, especially in the Russian Federation: for example, in Leningrad Province, the area of forest declined from 41,000km (25,476 sq miles) to 34,000km (21,127 sq miles) over the last 20 years (Potapov, Pavlova, 2009). Forest fires are particularly disastrous for capercaillie because the comparatively dry pine forests burn first. Fires occur throughout the bird's range, but have maximum effect in the main part of the range, the Russian Federation, particularly in the remote taiga forests that are the greatest stronghold of the species.

Global climate change also influences the capercaillie population. At present, the data on capercaillie numbers are insufficient to reach definite conclusions, and the attempt to connect the disappearance of the species in Great Britain with the global cooling of the so-called Little Ice Age (Watson, Jenkins, 2009) failed.

Attempts to halt the decline in capercaillie numbers are entirely dependent on man. Several developments are underway, and each may be very effective. One is the avoidance of disturbance by giving the birds due consideration in nearby settlements, e.g. avoiding interference by domestic animals, dogs and cats, as well as banning hunting. Studies in Russia show that capercaillie can survive close to people if the forest is continuous or even partially fragmented as long as interference is minimized: a small lek was found in a suburb of St Petersburg that had been active for at least ten successive years at the distance of about 500m (547yd) from the nearest home (Potapov, 2008b). Another development is improvement of conditions for the birds in protected areas, for instance by creating artificial places where gastrolits are available. Regular supplies of high-calorie food – grains and berries – also help. Such practices, begun at first in hunting 'farms' in the Urals, gave rapid results, the population density doubling in comparison to natural areas, with up to 1.82 birds/km² (Gubin, 1981). In the best of the State or private hunting farms, the density can reach 36 birds/km², with the cost of maintaining such densities being sustained by charging high prices for a licence to hunt. Of course, reserves in which there is total protection of the birds also aid conservation.

Rearing capercaillie in captivity and the release of young birds to the wild in places where numbers have seriously declined is also worthwhile. The first attempts to do this were in Russia in 1860, but serious attempts began during the USSR era (Larin, 1941; Krutovskaya, Krutovskaya, 1953, Kutovaya, 1976; Nemtzew, 1981; Nemtzev *et al.*, 1973; Pavliushik, Malutina, 1981) in official farms in central European Russia, western Siberia and Belorussia, and later in eastern Siberia and in Moscow. Attempts were also made from 1975 in Bulgaria (Kolev, 1981). Eggs were collected from wild nests and hatched in incubators or under domestic hens, but such rearing is expensive in both labour and equipment. At the same time, the Central Hunting Laboratory in Moscow was carrying out successful experiments in domesticating wild-caught adult birds (Valkovich, 1981), something that had already been done in Sweden at the end of the 19th century. The stock of more or less domesticated capercaillie allowed populations to be re-established in places where the birds had disappeared or had never before bred. The most successful attempt was that in Scotland, where the last bird had been shot in 1785 (Bannerman, 1963). Attempts at reintroduction were attempted several times, using birds from Sweden, with success being achieved in 1837 in Scotland. Another successful attempt was in northern Kazakhstan in 1965 (Cherepanov, 1981): the species had been extirpated here at the beginning of the 20th century (Stegmann, 1934). In Russia, the well-known grouse specialist Sergey Kirpichev has been successfully rearing and releasing birds without any support from government or hunting organizations.

However, there have been many failures, in Ireland and England (Long, 1981) and in both Canada and the USA (Long, 1981).

The latest information on the number of capercaillie in Russia, based on winter counts in 2002–2003 (Mejnev, 2004), suggests a population of about 2,750,000 birds, but this figure is approximate as the counts included regions occupied by both capercaillie species, which were not distinguished by the counters. Our opinion is that the Russian population is perhaps 2.2 million and represents the bulk of the world population.

5.2 BLACK-BILLED CAPERCAILLIE *Tetrao parvirostris* (Bonaparte, 1856)

Tetrao parvirostris (Bonaparte, 1856): 880 (nom. nov. pro *T. urogalloides* Middendorf, 1851). Synonym: *Tetrao urogalloides* Middendorf, 1851.

Morphology

Large size, only a little less than the Western species. The male's tail is particularly long (41% of body length), longer than any other tetraonid. In north-eastern populations, wintering birds have very thick feathering of the tarsi and well-developed pectinations, the length of which exceed those of all other grouse, reaching 12–13mm.

Colouration

Adult male
General colour is dark-brown to black, with large white patches, mostly drop-like shapes,

Male Black-billed Capercaillie

on tops of secondaries, median and lesser wing coverts, and on flank feathers. Head and upper body are black, or brown-black, partly with a metallic tinge. Upper parts of two-year-olds are lighter because of grey-yellowish streaks: these may also be present in older birds, especially in south-western populations. Underparts are dark-brown, apart from the dark-green chin and breast plastron with a metallic tinge. Feathering of lower belly and legs is black-brown, sometimes with white tips or narrow white cross-bands. Primaries are brown with white bordering on outer vanes of 5th and 6th, rarely on 7th and 8th. Secondaries, greater, median and lesser wing coverts are darker, with large white tips that form two white crossed bands in folded wing. Dark-brown scapulars also have white tops that form two longitudinal white bands on both sides of the back. Tail feathers are blackish-brown; uppertail and undertail coverts are black with wide white tops. Bill and nails are black.

First adult plumage differs from subsequent dress by being browner and having no metallic tinge to upper body, a less distinct tinge to chin and a markedly narrower breast plastron. Streaking also develops in most feathers of mantle and uppertail coverts, and, to a lesser degree, along borders of tail feathers, with 3–4 pairs of tail feathers and 1–4 primaries (sometimes all primaries) having narrow white borders on the tops. Outer vanes of secondaries are covered by light brown streaks. In many cases, inner secondaries of young males are unchanged from juvenile plumage.

Adult female

Colouration is very similar to Western species, differing mainly by absence of reddish-brown breast plastron. Belly centre looks darker and monotonous. On breast, the stripes beneath feather borders are narrow, have a metallic tinge and, as a result, form a specific colour pattern on the breast plastron, which has a metallic tinge. Throat and neck front look more ochreous than other body parts. Leg feathers are greyish-white. Primaries are dark-brown with indistinct cross-striped pattern on outer webs and white bordering on tops. Secondaries are darker, sometimes black, with white borders on tops. Speckled design of folded wing is created by wide white tops of greater, median and lesser wing coverts. The big white tops of scapulars form two white longitudinal, interrupted stripes along sides of the back. Tail and uppertail feathers are dark brown with ochreous cross-stripe pattern and white tops. Undertail coverts have same colour, but white top patches are especially large.

Female Black-billed Capercaillie

Juvenile

Juvenile plumage of males and females is similar. General colour is greyish-ochre, a little darker on mantle, with a cross-striped pattern and additional, whitish feather shafts on the darker back. Pattern is formed by dark-brown and yellowish cross-stripes. Brown stripes beneath feather borders are often divided in the centre, forming two side patches. In some feathers, especially on wing and tail, there are white patches on feather shafts, these spreading towards the top to form triangular spots. Primaries are dark-brown with indistinct yellowish cross-stripe on outer vane.

Downy chick

Yellowish-brown above, sulfur-yellow below. Upper part of the head is brownish-yellow, nape and back more ochreous, with an indistinct ochreous-brown pattern. **Figure 61** shows specific pattern of black marks on head. Distinct brown cap with black bordering on crown, very similar to those of spruce grouse, black grouse and ptarmigans (Potapov, 1985).

Figure 61. Head pattern of a downy young *Tetrao parvirostris*

Dimensions

Size of old males (two years and older): body length 960–990mm; length of folded wing 372–410mm; tail 310–421mm; length difference between the central and outer tail feathers 67–150mm; bill length and width 23.8–29.2mm and 16.4–21.0mm; tarsi 56–66 mm; central toe 57–65mm. The length of the tail as a fraction of the length of the wing averages 81.6% in Kamchatka, and up to 97.3% in mainland birds. In several specimens (Lake Baikal region), the length of the tail exceeded the length of the wing. The difference in size between birds across the range is small, though birds from central Yakutia are largest, while those from Kamchatka are smallest. In the area around Lake Baikal, the size of yearling sub-adults and older males were, respectively: body length 886mm (866–900mm), 988mm (972–1,017mm), 1,007mm (1,000–1,015); wing 355mm

Black-billed Capercaillie chicks in Magadan, Siberia

(340–370mm), 364mm (355–390mm), 381mm (362–400mm); tail 269mm (260–275mm), 371mm (350–395mm), 383mm (361–414mm) (Kirpichev, 1961; Potapov, 1985).

Females: length of folded wing 288–327mm; tail 172–240mm; length difference between the central and outer tail feathers 22–54mm; bill length and width 17.0–23.5mm and 13.0–16.0mm; central toe 45.0–52.0mm.

The weight of males varies through the year between 3,350–4,580g (7.4–10lb). Female weight: 1,700–2,200g (3.7–4.8lb).

Moult

As in previous species, apart from the synchronicity of primaries and secondaries in the right and left wings (which sometimes breaks), and replacement of inner secondaries, which may be preserved to the next autumn moult (Kirpichev, 1972).

Distribution

The northern border coincides with the northern limits of forests, going beyond the Arctic Circle only along the valleys of the great rivers. The western border of the range is situated within the range of Western Capercaillie, and is not clear. Map 9 gives the best current position.

The range also has two isolated parts, one on the Kamchatka Peninsula, the other on Sakhalin Island. On Kamchatka, the northern range limit is defined by the distribution of arboreal vegetation (59°N – Potapov, 1985). On Sakhalin, the birds occupy the northern part, once south to 48°N (Voronov etc, 1975), but now only to 49°30′(Nechaev, 1991).

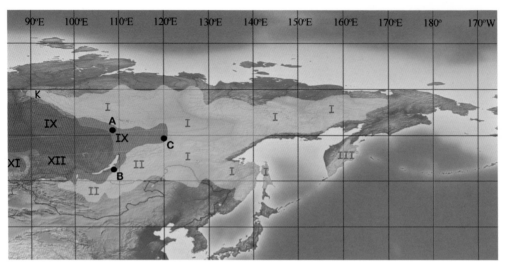

Map 9. Black-billed Capercaillie (*Tetrao parvirostris*). See also Map 8.
Subspecies (in purple): I – T. p. parvirostris; II – T. p. stegmanni; III – T. p. kamtschaticus.
The red area represents easternmost extent of the range of Tetrao urogallus.
A, B and C are sites where the two Capercaillie species are known to co-exist. A is the lower part of the Nakanno, Inarigda and Kothetcumo rivers (Tarasov, 1965). B is the Bargusin State Reserve on the eastern shore of Lake Baikal (Kirpichev, 1958) and C is the lower part of the Tokko and Chara rivers (Worobiev, 1963).

Subspecies

The geographical variability of the species is not significant, despite the isolated populations, with one exception – the population of Kamtchatka differs from that of the mainland not only in colour and morphology but also in mode of life, including nutrition.

Tetrao parvirostris parvirostris (Bonaparte, 1856)
Synonyms: *Tetrao urogalloides* (Middendorf, 1851); *T. urogalloides* var. *sachalinensis* (Bogdanov, 1884); *T. parvirostris janensis* (Tugarinov in Grote, 1932); *T. urogalloides kolymensis* (Buturlin, 1932); *T. urogalloides turensis* (Buturlin, 1932).
All local colour variations, once described as subspecies, were synonymized by Kirikov, 1952. Colour and size as described above. Inhabits the main part of the species range, with the exception of its south-western part and the Kamchatka Peninsula.

T. p. stegmanni (Potapov, 1985)
Male colour differs by the presence of white cross-stripes on the sides of the belly and lower part of the breast (see **Figure 41 in Chapter 3**), making the bird similar to male Franklin's Spruce Grouse. The white strips are formed by white feather tops. Inhabits the

mountain taiga regions of northern Mongolia and south-eastern Transbaikal (Selenga's Dauria), i.e. eastern Sayan Mountains westward to the sources of the Oka River at 99°E. The main habitats are different types of the mountain taiga, chiefly with pines, including Creep Pine, rather than larch forests, the latter being smaller and well scattered, and composed only of Siberian Larch (*Larix sibirica*), which cannot grow on permafrost.

T. p. kamtschaticus (Kittlitz, 1858)
T. kamtschaticus (Kittlitz, 1858): 353 (Kamchatka).
Colouration and body proportions are so different from the other subspecies that Kittlitz described it as a new species. The form preserves many ancestral features because of its long isolation from the main species range, a period of not less than 65,000 years. The male's general colour is dark-grey, with only the head and the front of the neck being black. The breast plastron has a green tinge, and the feathers of the lower part of the breast have a white, heart-shaped patch, as in Asian and Franklin's Spruce Grouse, or cross-stripes, or shaft spots. The flank feathers have white patches under the tops, very similar to *Dendragapus* species, as is the whole colouration of the lower part of the body (Potapov, 1985). Female colouration also has many differences from the other subspecies, and a more pronounced similarity to female Western Capercaillie. This is the smallest form of capercaillie. The length of the folded wing of males (N=6): 382.2mm (range 375–391mm); tail length: 322.5mm (295–350mm). Male body weight: 3,709g/8.18lb (3,500–3,800g/7.72–8.38lb) (Kirpitchev, 1960). Inhabits all the forests of the Kamchatka Peninsula.

Habitats

The main habitat is larch forest, the species range coinciding, to a large degree, with the distribution of *Larix cajanderi* and *L. gmelini*, whose distribution is determined by the distribution of permafrost. The favoured habitat is sparse, mature forest, those alternating old trees with young, and including areas of blueberry and cowberry, fire recovery areas and bogs. In the southern parts of the range, the birds inhabit mixed mountain and pine forests, In Mongolia, the birds live in any forest type, provided there is an abundance of cowberry. In northern parts of the Sikhote-Alin Mountains, the species prefers larch forests in depressions, sometimes swampy areas, or in bogs between ridges clothed by thick spruce and Creep Pine (Potapov, 1985). The most unusual habitat is on the Kamchatka Peninsula, where the birds inhabit forests of a local species of birch – the Stone birch (*Betula etmanii*). The species avoids dark, thick coniferous taiga dominated by spruces and firs, to an even greater degree than Western Capercaillie.

Population structure and density

Data on population structure is very scarce. In the upper Kolyma Basin during the winter of 1935/1936, females dominated hugely, with one male to 7–10 females, but by the following autumn males dominated broods, with one female to 5–7 males (Dementiev, Shochin, 1939). It is possible that the winter observation was unknowingly in an area where females preferentially gathered, but the second observation, on the prevalence of males, has not been confirmed by other observations.

In most parts of the range the population is low. Some data suggest that the density of birds fluctuates to a far greater degree than the Western species: during a population peak the density can reach 8.3birds/km², but such high densities are very rare now. On the Kamchatka Peninsula, the average density of nesting females is 0.3–2.0birds/km², the maximum seen (in spruce forests) being 6.1birds/km². In many places the birds were absent. In the Kronotsky State Reserve, the density of wintering birds in Stone birch forests during 1971–1982 fluctuated between 0.028 and 1.64birds/km² (Lobkov, 1986).

There is some information suggesting that population fluctuations have a 10-year periodicity (Andreev, 1974). The peak density was in the Vilui and Olekma River Basins in 1952–1953, in the Vilui Basin in 1961–1962 (Andreev, 1974), then in the Olekma Basin in 1963 (Benthen, 1967), but again in Vilui in 1968 (Perfiliev, 1975). The reasons for such fluctuations are unknown, but in Vilui in 1953 an unknown disease caused the birds to lose feathers, and for weight to decline seriously, with the weight of old females being only 800–1,000g (1.76–2.20lb) (Egorov *et al.*, 1950). Such epidemics may account for local population fluctuations.

Territoriality

Information is scarce. In many places there is a distinct mosaic distribution of the birds, with a large forest having areas where there are no birds alternating with areas of normal population density and others where the density is high. The pattern is not stable, implying that it is a much more mobile species than the Western Capercaillie. One study noted large numbers of Black-billed Capercaillies moving east in the upper part of the Vilui River Basin in the autumn (Perfiliev, 1975). In Amur Province, the birds crowded together in some places during the winter, with flocks of up to 100 birds being seen, but then the flocks disappeared suddenly (Benthen, 1965; Barancheev, 1965) with no apparent cause, although forage was still available. Ringing of birds has been minimal, but has shown that the birds travel up to 250km (155 miles) (Kirpichev, pers. com.). In mountain areas, there is insignificant vertical movement: in the mountains of Sakhalin Island, the birds move to the subalpine zone during the autumn and return to gently sloping lowlands in the spring (Mishin, 1960), while in the Baikal Mountains the birds move up to the subalpine zone, where the lek arenas are situated, in the spring (Kirpichev, 1960). On the Kamchatka Peninsula, broods move up to the Creep Pines at 600–700m, but as soon as there is snow cover, they retreat back to lowland forests (Averin, 1948; Markov, 1968; Lobkov, 1986). However, winter excrements were found on the slopes of the Krasheninnikov volcano at a height of 900m (2,953ft) (Lobkov, 1986).

Behaviour

The birds spend most of the time on the ground, but in flight may ascend to considerable altitudes: when the birds were moving from one mountain ridge to another, they were seen at heights of 1,000m (3,281ft) (Kirpichev, pers. com.). Kirpichev also reports that the birds can fly almost vertically upwards at great speed, and make long flights, maneuvering skillfully between the trees. Such flights, and the large size of the bird, may explain its preference for sparse forest.

Vocal sounds are not well studied. A disturbed male utters light, irregular clicks (Kozlova, 1930), while A. Kretchmar heard spring sounds resembling those of Willow Ptarmigan (pers. comm.).

Nutrition

The close connection of the species with larch is especially clear in winter, when the tops of twigs and buds, and sometimes the cones, of larch comprise the main, sometimes the only, source of nutrition across most of the range in winter when the average ambient temperature is below 0°C (32°F) for up to 8 months. The ends of larch twigs, with large quantities of buds, have a thick layer of rind, beneath which is a layer of cambium (under-rind cellulose). When this forage reaches the gizzard, gastrolits work to remove the layer for further digestion. As a result, the twigs become 'naked' central rods about 1mm in diameter rather than 3–5mm when they are on the tree, and these rods comprise the main content of bird's hard excrements. In mixed coniferous forests with pines or firs, the birds take the needles of all species, but prefer the needles of Siberian Pine, so much so that it is the main food in places such as Transbaikal and Amurland (Kirpitchev, 1960; Filonov, 1961). In places with minimal snow cover, the birds take the berries and green leaves of cowberry and bearberry throughout the winter. On the Kamchatka Peninsula, the populations in birch forests take buds and catkins as their main winter food, with small additions of willow buds (Averin, 1948). Another important winter food is the fruit of dog roses. Near the Omolon River (67°N), the fruits constituted 80% of all food items from November to February: only in March did the birds begin to feed exclusively on larch (Andreev, 1975).

In spring, the birds eat bearberry, cranberry, cowberry, etc, and fresh greens – flowers, different grasses, fern sprouts and the new needles and inflorescences of larch – as they appear. In the crops and gizzards of males obtained during spring on the shores of Lake Baikal, the needles, sprouts and inflorescences of larch, dominated, with lesser amounts of needles, buds and twigs of Siberian pine, berries, grass, etc (Novicov, 1941).

During the summer, the quantity of twigs, buds and needles of larch decline, the forage consisting of seeds, the flowers and green parts of various grasses and, in the second half of summer, different berries. Among the berries, great bilberry, cranberry, and *Empetrum* spp. are important, and, in the late autumn and winter, dog-rose fruit. The summer diet also includes insects, the most important being ants, their eggs and larvae, and *Orthoptera* spp.

In the autumn, as well as berries, the diet includes the nuts of Siberian and Creep Pine, the sprouts and buds of bushes, and larch needles. In Amur Province during September, the birds were taking 200g (7oz) of larch needles during a feeding session.

Wintering

Both males and females spend the winter in flocks, with the higher the local density, the larger the number of birds in the flock. In places with low density, groups are of 3–5 birds. The winter way of life is as in Western Capercaillie, but occurs in the coldest part of the range of either species, including the famous 'Pole of Coldness' in Russia's Verkhoyansk region, where the ambient temperature can fall to -70°C (-94°F). There, the birds roost in snow burrows, leaving them in the mornings to feed. The birds begin feeding immediately, either flying to the nearest larches or walking on the snow between low larch branches. The deeper the snow cover, the more the tops of the trees are used, with the clipping producing larches with a specific spherical form. Such trees then attract even more birds because of the high density of twigs (Mejennyi, 1957).

In the Omolon River valley of the Kolyma Basin Andreev (1980), it was noted that after morning feeding, the birds spent the middle of the day in snow burrows, feeding again before nightfall. In midwinter, the birds decrease the length of the evening feed by feeding intensively in larch crowns, filling their crops maximally before retreating to a snow burrow. However, there are variants to this general scheme: sometimes, after morning feeding, the birds walk about in search of delicacies such as dog-rose fruits, catkins or twigs of birches, or great bilberries if the stems protrude from the snow. Walking is not a problem, even if the snow is deep and soft, with the average load foot loading being $24.5g/cm^2$ and $22.3g/cm^2$ in male and female respectively. During a day's feeding, males cover 350–440m (383–481yd) on foot.

Roost places are usually in clearings. The depth of male and female snow burrows are 39–42cm (15.3–16.5in) and 32–35cm (12.6–13.8in) respectively, the thickness of the snow roof is 11–15cm (4.3–5.9in) and the length of the tunnel is 80–150cm (31.5–59in). Flying is usually minimal, with a winter day's flying lasting no more than two minutes, including flights to feeding and roosting places. During feeding, the bird spends no more than 0.2% of its daily energy budget, and at an ambient temperature below -10°C (14°F) was seen to clip food items by taking 27–30 bites in a 13-second period. In the frozen air, it was possible for the observer to hear the sounds produced by the feeding bird at a distance of 50–70m (55–77yd), a double click accompanying each bite, the first when the palate crest breaks the twig in two, the second when the twig detaches from the stem. The interval between the clicks when a male was feeding was 0.8±0.4 seconds. During warmer weather, when the twigs are less brittle, the bird has to spend more time and effort obtaining forage. This means that the temperature at which the bird foraged is discernible when examining crop content, low temperatures indicated by a clean fracture of the twig, higher temperatures by a break more akin to the greenstick fracture of a child's bones. The minimum temperature at which the birds were observed to feed was -53°C (-63.4°F) (Omolon River, Andreev, 1980).

In the Kolyma River Basin and regions north of the Sea of Okhotsk, where the birds winter in the severe conditions, a wonderful adaptation of the males, allowing them to increase their potential for feeding, has been discovered. Because of their weight, males have difficulty feeding in trees, as most branches will not support them: females, being only half the weight, have no such problem. Males therefore prefer to feed from the ground (i.e. from snow cover), but that it only really possible where there are young larches, whose tops emerge from the snow. Constant feeding on these young trees forces the trees to produce new sprouts and delays growth so that the trees grow slowly and

Female Black-billed Capercaillie in winter

have heavy growth at their crowns which, of course, is advantageous to the birds. This restricted, and 'crown-heavy', growth pattern is so characteristic of male winter-feeding areas that the areas have been termed 'Capercaillie gardens' by Tarchov (1988), who first described the trees. When initially reported, some experts were sceptical, but the existence of these gardens has now been confirmed by other researchers (e.g. Potapov (personal visits), Andreev, 1991).

The number of twig pieces in a crop is large, up to 13,350 (Egorov et al., 1959). The daily ration in midwinter in the Omolon River valley, at 68°N, was 142g/5.0oz (dry weight: 338g/11.9oz fresh weight) for males and 97g/3.4oz (231g/8.1oz) for females, 40% of which were the dog-rose fruits and the remainder larch twigs, producing 967.2Kj/day for males, 745.3Kj/day for females. The bird expends 10–11% of its energy warming the food to body temperature (Andreev, 1980). The real daily energy expenditure is actually a little higher than the energy input, as the bird gradually burns fat reserves accumulated in the autumn. Such accumulation of fat prior to winter, though usual for many bird species, is unusual in grouse. The fat accumulates under the skin of the rump, around the crop, on the thighs, under the breast and shoulder pterylies, and on the neck and belly. On inner parts of the body, fat accumulates mainly around the stomach and, sometimes, the trachea loop (Egorov et al., 1959; Perfiliev, 1975; Potapov, 1985). Birds collected in the Verkhoyansk region during winter had especially large fat deposits, up to 250g (Egorov et al., 1959). Near Lake Baikal, females preserved some fat deposits to the spring, exceeding those of males, and representing up to 12% of body weight (Kirpichev, 1960).

Large fat deposits are obviously connected with the necessity to thermoregulate, particularly at the start of winter, when strong frosts are seen before an adequate thickness of snow accumulates to allow snow burrow construction. In such situations the birds are forced to roost in the crowns of trees, hiding among the thick bunches of twigs, or in shallow scoops in the snow. Occasionally, the birds will dig deeply into frozen soil if the snow cover is thin (Andreev, 1980). On very cold days when the snow cover is thin, the birds move to warmer areas. At such times, the birds lose their natural caution, and become easier prey to hunters (Egorov et al., 1959; Snigirevsky, 1946).

Breeding

Lek activity starts at the beginning of April in Kamchatka and the Amur region, in the middle of the month in the Omolon Valley and on Sakhalin Island, and at the end of April in Mongolia. In all cases it is still wintry, with snow cover and ambient temperatures often below -20°C (-4°F). As usual, peak male activity coincides with female visits to the lek becoming regular. In the Lake Baikal region this is mid-May, in the Omolon Valley 16–22 of May, in the Kolyma Uplands 15–19 May (Andreev et al., 2006). Breeding is also completed at different times, up to mid-June or even early July in the Amur region (Barancheev, 1965).

Lek sites are usually among sparse larch, perhaps near a clearing created by fire, on the terrace of a river valley or on a gentle mountain slope (Nordmann, 1861; Mishin, 1960; Andreev, 1977; Potapov, 1985). In the Lake Baikal region, lek sites are situated in larch or pure pine forests on the mountain slopes, right up to ridge crests at 1,000–1,300m (3,281–4,265ft). The largest leks on Baikal Ridge are situated at larch timberline (Kirpichev, 1960). Where the density of birds is very high, as many as 200 males may gather (Nordmann, 1861; Andreev, 1953; Benthen, 1965; 1967), but in most cases the number is 6–10. As with other grouse species, leks are traditional. In one well-documented case in Kamchatka, a new forestry settlement was set up deep within a larch forest, and when spring came the birds began to gather, the site being a traditional lek site. The forestry staff did what they could to minimize disturbance and the birds quickly became accustomed to them, ceased to be afraid and continued with their courtship displays occasionally with men at only 3–4m (10–13ft) away (Kirpichev, pers. comm.).

Male courtship displays are very similar to those of Western Capercaillie, but less complicated. The male has a principal posture ('Upright posture' – Hjorth, 1970), used on the ground or in a tree. In it, the head and the neck are vertical, the wings half spread, with the wing tips lightly brushing the ground. The full, spread tail is also upright, with the central pairs of retrices perpendicular to the back and the two sides of the tail forming

Displaying male Black-billed Capercaillie are unusual in that they often display in trees.

Figure 62. Postures of *Tetrao parvirostris*
1 – Singing posture of Tetrao parvirostris, *2 – Confrontational postures of male (Andreev 1977a).*

a right–angle around this central pair so that the tail looks very like an open book. In this posture what is remarkable is the projected crop (**Figure 62**). Male flutter-jumps are as Western Capercaillie, with four flaps upward and four downward. The height of the flutter-jump is 1–3m (3–10ft), and during it the bird covers a distance of 4–20m (13–66ft). Flutter-jumps occur often during displays, but are never seen when the bird is singing.

The male's song consists of a series of clicking sounds, and short cackling trills. The clicks are very similar to the sound of castanets (Kozlova, 1930). The song has two parts. The first part is 'tak–trrrack–tack–tack', repeated 3–4 times and increasing in speed. The second part is alternating clicks and rasping sounds, finished by four almost merged clicks, during which the male becomes partially deaf (Barancheev, 1965; Kirpichev, in litt.). The entire song lasts nearly 3 seconds, and is audible at long distances, up to 1km (0.6 mile) or even further (Andreev, 1977). The hierarchical structure of the lek has three levels, as in other grouse species.

Males begin to sing at feeding places, roosts and day resting places, and then gradually begin to visit the lek arena. Lek activity is then as Western Capercaillie, with males appearing at the lek in the evening, either by walking or, in mountain areas, by flying. In the latter, the birds glide down on spread wings with no wingbeats. Immediately after arriving, males begin to sing, continuing into the night. At high altitudes north of the Arctic Circle, males can sing all night, though with a decrease in activity at midnight (Andreev, 1977). Usually the birds spend the night in the trees, but some roost on the snow. Females arrive at dawn, by which time the males are singing on the ground. The appearance of the females produces maximal activity among the males, each of them, especially the leaders, attempting to attract as many females to its individual territory as possible. Such territories are 20–50m (22–55yd) in diameter, with males displaying, and mating occurring, at the centre. Females gather around the leaders, with up to ten hens around a single male, even though such males will mate only once or twice during a morning (four matings have been seen rarely) with the same or different females. Males defend their territories vigorously. During conflicts, the males assume the 'Upright Posture' and circle each other as though dancing, moving backwards and forwards synchronously and make threatening movements of their wings while withdrawing their heads to avoid being struck. Though such posturing is often seen, serious battles are rare, though blood spots and neck feathers on the snow – and neck wounds on captured birds – are occasionally seen (Andreev, 1977).

Autumn lekking behaviour occurs from August to the end of November. During it, males sing from trees or the ground, often in different places each day, dependent on their feeding schedule (Egorov et al., 1959; Mishin, 1960; Perfiliev, 1975).

Females nest close to the lek, with the nest usually being set close to the base of a tree, under a fallen tree or in heaps of brushwood. The shallow nest (diameter nearly 21cm/8.3in) is lined with dry leaves or trash, pieces of larch rind and some feathers. In one case, a nest in Kamchatka was a construction of old leaves, dry grass, pieces of birch rind and some feathers, resembling an upturned hat 10cm deep (Lobko-Lobanowsky, Jilin, 1962). This unusual construction may be explained by the ground being saturated after snow melting.

Females begin to lay long before the last frosts are over, in early May in the southern parts of the range and to mid-June in northern parts. Eggs are light-brown or even whitish-brown with thick dark-brown dots and some black-brown patches. Egg size (N=19, Coll

Female Black-billed Capercaillie with newly hatched chicks in Magadan, Siberia

ZIN RAN) is 56.7 x 40.7mm (52.6–60.5mm x 39.0–42.3mm) (Potapov, 1985). The weight of fresh eggs is 46.65g (1.65oz) (Lobko–Lobanovsky, Jilin, 1962). Clutch size is 5–10, usually 6 or 7, but in the north-eastern part of the range (Putoran Plateau) clutches are smaller: 3–5 (Romanov, 2006). Incubation lasts 26–28 days (Kirpichev, 1960). Hatching in the wild has been observed only once: it began in the morning and finished at 14.00. The weight of the newly hatched chick was 31g (1.1oz) (Schubnikova, Morosov, 1950).

Information on brood life is scarce. The chicks begin to flutter when they are 6–7 days old (Kirpichev, 1960). Broods feed in grassy glades and water meadows, taking different insects, the fresh green parts of grasses, and seeds, until berries ripen. On Kamchatka, females with broods moved down to coniferous valley forests. The chicks feed on berries from August, but insects still remain a significant fraction of the diet until autumn.

Hunting, recreation and conservation

Concrete data is absent, though it is known that local people hunt the birds regularly throughout the year. In the 1960s and 1970s there was even an international trade in the species, professional hunters taking birds in Mongolia and exporting them to the former USSR where it was possible to buy Black-billed Capercaillie in Moscow shops. This trade has now ceased. At about the same time, some authors were noting significant population decreases in Kamchatka, Sakhalin Island and Amur Province (Nechaev, 1975; Voronov et al., 1975; Lobkov, 1986). On Kamchatka during winter, counts in State hunting farms in four successive years from 2000–2003, the stock was 164,200, 77,700, 42,000 and 34,100 birds (Mejnev, 2004).

The temporary prohibition of hunting on Sakhalin and Kamchatka allowed the number of birds to increase quickly, but after the ban was revoked, the population rapidly declined again (Lobkov, 1986). As a consequence, only protection in State and Game reserves offers any optimism for the future of the birds. Fortunately, there are now more than 30 such reserves, in all of which hunting and logging is banned. As with the Western Capercaillie, captive breeding, now achieved by S. Kirpichev in Barguzin State Reserve, may aid conservation.

The total number of Black-billed Capercaillie was estimated in 2003 as approximately 1,225,000 (Mejnev, 2004).

CHAPTER 7

Genus 6: *Lagopus* PTARMIGAN

Lagopus (Brisson, 1760): 181. *Oreias* (Kaup, 1829): 177, 193 (type species *Tetrao scoticus* (Latham, 1787) (for monotype). *Attagen* (Kaup, 1829): 170, 193 (type species for the primary designation '*Tetrao montanus* and *islandicus*').

The genus includes three species: Willow Grouse (*Lagopus lagopus*), Rock Ptarmigan (*Lagopus mutus*) and White-tailed Ptarmigan (*Lagopus leucurus*). All three are medium-sized, terrestrial birds of open or semi-open landscapes dominated by grass and bush vegetation in the tundra, tundra-forest and forest-steppe zones, subalpine and alpine mountain belts.

The three species unite several morphological features that differ from other tetraonids. Firstly, the white winter colour. An exception is the British Isles' Willow Grouse subspecies – the Red Grouse – though white feathering exists in the genome of this form and is seen from time to time in some specimens. The presence of such a specific winter dress complicates the moult process, with four plumages, each relating to a season, and colouration being in accord with the colours of habitat landscape. This moult ability results from most of the feather follicles being able to produce two or even three feathers during the year. After feather loss, the feather's follicle may remain non-active for a while (Salomonsen, 1939; Snigirevsky, 1950), with the colour of the new feather from that follicle depending on the bird's hormonal situation (Novikov, 1939). As a consequence, different feather follicles are active during the moult in different ways and produce different feathers at different times. Seasonal plumages transform one to another gradually, each plumage including feathers of the previous dress. Only the winter plumage appears entirely complete, and even then, in southerly populations some coloured autumn feathers are maintained until the next spring moult.

The second morphological feature is full feathering of the toes rather than the growth of pectinations, the latter being only partly preserved, as rudiments, in White-tailed Ptarmigan and, rarely, in some specimens in southern populations of Willow Grouse. Only 3–6 distal scales on the toes are not replaced by feathers.

A third morphological feature is the differing proportions of the pelvis (**Figure 63**). The length of the postacetabular part is shorter than in other grouse, constituting 34.7–41% of general pelvis length, instead of the 41.8% in other species (Potapov, 1985). The width of the pelvis is maximal between the lawteral surfaces of the antitrochanters, though that between the lateral surfaces of the *os pubis* may be equivalent, whereas in other grouse the maximal width is always between the lateral surfaces of the *os pubis* (see Table 1 in Chapter 1). The width of the ptarmigan pelvis exceeds 80% of its length. Another interesting feature of ptarmigan anatomy is the extra-large size of the intestines, due mainly to the volume of its caeca, the size of which is a maximum for tetraonids (see Table 2 in Chapter 1).

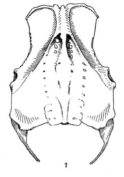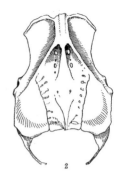

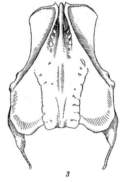

The preferred habitats of the three species sometimes overlap. However, in places where one or other species is absent, the resident species occupies all habitat types. In the High Arctic New Siberian Islands, where there are no Rock Ptarmigan, Willow Grouse occupy habitats usually associated with that species, while in Greenland, where Willow Grouse are absent, the situation is reversed. In the Alaskan

Figure 63. Pelvis bone of ptarmigans *1* – Lagopus lagopus; *2* – L. mutus; *3* – L. leucurus.

mountains, where all three species are found together, they occupy different habitats during the breeding season. In winter, they occupy the same habitat but utilize different food resources, or the same resource on different days (Moss, 1974).

All three species are monogamous, though polygamy occurs rarely in northernmost populations of both Rock and Willow Ptarmigans. The territorial structure in the breeding season is similar, with males who hold territories mating. Both sexes reach puberty in the first year of life, but males can realize their reproductive potential only if they hold individual nesting territories.

Size, the level of sexual dimorphism in colour, nestling colour and the number of tail feathers link ptarmigans with the spruce grouse: the rough black-and-white colouration of the breast feathers of White-tailed Ptarmigan is very similar to that of spruce grouse. Dark *Lagopus lagopus scoticus* males are reminiscent of one-year-old *Lyrurus tetrix*, while *L. mlokosiewiszi* has eye-combs of ptarmigan form. The same eye-comb form is also seen in the three *Tympanuchus* species and the two sage-grouse (**Figure 45, n4** in Chapter 4). Male Greater Prairie-Chickens, during their short courtship flights, also utter a series of short sounds reminiscent of the first part of the Willow Grouse's 'song'. Rock and White-tailed Ptarmigans also illustrate a curious behaviour with respect to man that is shared by spruce grouse. Sometimes, especially in thinly populated areas, it is possible to approach to within 2–3m (6.5–9.8ft) before the birds move slowly away on foot.

Hybrids between ptarmigans (mainly Willow Grouse) and capercaillie, black grouse and Canadian Spruce Grouse are known, both in the wild and in captive birds. The hybrids usually inherit the white colouration on the belly, though other body parts are only partially white, and a ptarmigan eye-comb form. The feathering of hybrid toes is not complete, with feathers covering only the first two phalanges, the third having horny pectinations.

6.1 WILLOW GROUSE *Lagopus lagopus. Tetrao lagopus* (Linnaeus, 1758)

Synonyms: *T. albus* (Gmelin, 1788; *T. lapponicus* (Gmelin, 1788): 751 (Lapland). *T. albus* (non Gmelin): (Latham, 1790); *T. rehusak* (Bonnaterre, 1791); *T. cachinnans* (Retzius, 1800); *T. saliceti* (Temminck, 1815); *T. subalpinus* (Nillson, 1817); *Lagopus lapponicus* (Stephens in Shaw, 1819); *L. brachydactylus* (Gould, 1837); *L. albus* (Keyserling, Blausius, 1840).

Mainly a terrestrial bird of medium size with white colouration in winter (except for populations in the British Isles). In North America, the species is known as Willow Ptarmigan.

Morphology

The open wing is partially sharpened, with the top of the wing at the 8, or 8th and 7, primaries. The number of retrices is 16, rarely 18. All tail feathers have the same length, the open tail being semi-circular. Occasionally, if the moult is delayed, the central pair of feathers may be shorter, with the length of the other feathers increasing to the outside, as a result of which the open tail looks the same as a Black Grouse female (**Figure 64**). Rarely, the length of the retrices increases from the centre through the next 4–5 pairs, then decreases again. The toes are feathered to the last, marginal 3–5, scales: the number

Figure 64. Forms of the open tail of *Lagopus lagopus*
1 – normal; 2, 3 – abnormal.

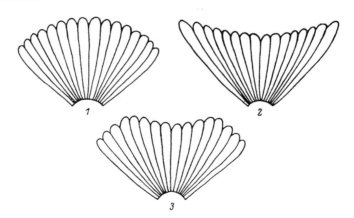

of scales depends on the severity of the local climate. The claws are whitish, strong, long and curved.

Colouration

The description here is general for all subspecies except *L. l. scoticus, L. l. hibernicus,* and *L. l. variegarus,* which are considered below.

Adult male

Winter plumage: General white colour; only the retrices, apart from central pair, are black with white tops (**Figure 65, n1 and n2**). Most tail feathers have white bases. Central pair is white and hides the black tail feathers, improving camouflage. Occasionally, the central pair has an indistinct cross-striped pattern or is black with especially large white tops: in these situations camouflage is assured by long, white uppertail coverts.

Spring plumage: The head, neck, breast and front of the back are reddish-brown, a contrast to the white of the remaining body. On the head there are three contrasting white areas: nostrils, base of bill and rings around the eyes. In European populations, to the southern Urals and west Siberia, the males have a second stage of spring plumage, with reddish-brown feathers covering all the back, rump and upper tail.

Summer plumage: Comprises white winter feathers, spring feathers and specific summer feathers. General colour is ochre-brown, with black cross-stripes and patches. Head and back are darker, almost black. Rump feathers are similar, but with narrow white top borders, these wearing out by autumn. White primaries and secondaries remain to full autumn moult, when they are replaced by new white ones, apart from the four inner secondaries, which are yellowish-brown with black-brown cross-stripes and white top edges. Middle wing coverts have the same colouration: in the folded wing these feathers cover the white primaries, secondaries and white greater coverts almost completely, providing camouflage. Breast and belly feathers are yellow, with brown cross-stripes. In northern populations, some white belly feathers remain until the moult to winter plumage.

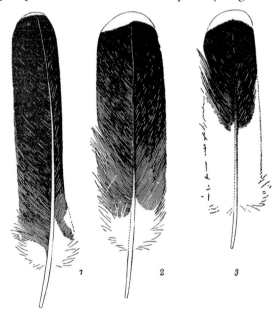

Figure 65. Winter tail feathers of *Lagopus lagopus*
1 – outer tail feather of male; 2 – central tail feather of male; 3 – central tail feather of female.

Male Willow Grouse

Autumn plumage: Colouration is browner than in summer, with the feather bases usually white. First adult autumn plumage of young males differs from adult in being a combination of juvenile (see below) and some adult autumn feathers, those covering the breast and being scattered among other feathers.

Adult female

Winter plumage: Similar to male, but the tail feathers have completely white lower halves (**Figure 65, n3**).

Summer plumage: There are no specific spring feathers, with winter plumage changing to that of summer. Upper body is mottled, with large black patches of different shapes,

Female Willow Grouse

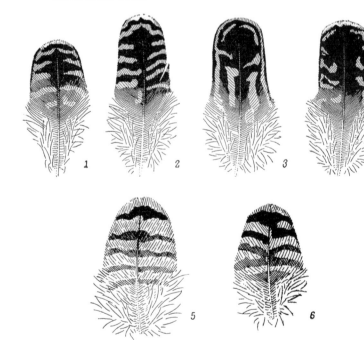

Figure 66. Female summer feathers of *Lagopus lagopus*
1 – 4 from the back, 5 – 6 from the breast.

and light ochreous and whitish cross-stripes on a yellowish background (**Figure 66**). The narrow white borders on feather tops wear out by the autumn, the upper body becoming darker. Underparts are paler, yellow or yellowish-brown, with contrasting black-brown cross-stripes.

Autumn plumage: A combination of summer, autumn and winter feathers. The autumn feathers are yellow-brown or a brown background patterned by thin grey cross-stripes. These feathers appear mainly on the breast, neck and head, and sometimes hide the summer feathers. On the back and rump, the number of autumn feathers is less than those of summer.

Young females in first autumn plumage differ from young males by having fewer adult autumn feathers, scattered among the juvenile ones.

Juvenile (both sexes)

Mottled, with light-brown patches and stripes of different shapes on a yellowish-ochreous background. As the bird grows, large numbers of new juvenile feathers appear, with diverse patterns. The characteristic pattern is parabola- or oval-shaped brown stripes, reflecting the shape of the feather top, in combination with other stripes, close to the shafts, and an upturned white triangle at the top (**Figure 67**).

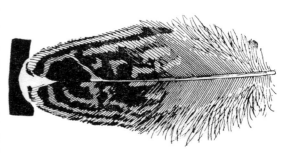

Figure 67. Juvenile feather from the shoulder of a Willow Ptarmigan showing the characteristic upturned white triangle at the tip

Downy chick

Sulfur-yellow underparts and flanks. Upper parts have wide brown stripes with black borders across the back and rump. Red and black spots form a specific pattern on the wings. Head has brown cap with black bordering, which connects to bill ridge and back with black stripes, and a row of black spots on sides of the head (**Figure 68**). However, there are many deviations from this scheme, even among chicks of the same brood.

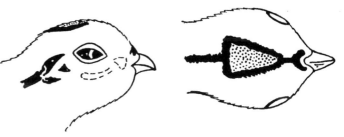

Figure 68. Head pattern of a downy young *Lagopus lagopus*
The dotted area is brown, while the dotted lines indicate black stripes and patches seen in some specimens.

Dimensions

Despite the huge species' range, variations of size are minimal, dependent only on the sex, age and the individual. Basic data are given here from 942 specimens of Coll ZIN RAN, with ranges for both males and, in parenthesis, females: wing length 189–230mm (178–220mm); tail 98–120mm (90–123mm); bill (from the front edge of the nostrils) 9.3–14.1mm (8.9–13.6mm); bill width (at the level of the front edge of the nostrils) 7.1–11.2mm (7.3–10.8mm); tarsi 30–41mm (28–42mm); middle toe 24–34mm (22–34mm).

The weight of both sexes changes during the year as in other grouse. The maximum recorded body weight is 900g (31.7oz) (male, subspecies *L. l. major*), the minimum 410g

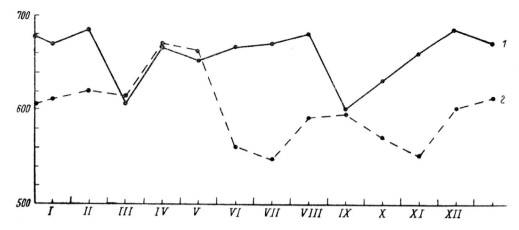

Figure 69. The dynamics of body mass in *Lagopus lagopus scoticus*
1 – average male mass; 2 – average female mass (Leslie, 1911). Vertical axis – mass in grams; horizontal axis – time in months.

(14.5oz) (female, subspecies *L. l. brevirostris*). Body weight in males varies from a maximum in January of 677.2±8.3g (23.9±0.2oz) to a minimum in June (568.2±0.3g/20.0±0,01oz), and in females from 619±13.6g (21.8±0.4oz) in November to 471.4g (16.6oz) in July (Russian tundra, Voronin, 1978); male winter average is 724g (25.5oz), 627g (22.1oz) in June and 571g (20.1oz) in July/August (Taimyr Peninsula, Pavlov, 1975); male winter (December) maximum is 800g (28.2oz), minimum (June) 590g (20.8oz); female maximum (December and March) 750g (26.4oz) (Yakutia, Perfiliev, 1975). Analogous data has also been published for Alaskan birds (West, Meng, 1968). In the 'softer' climatic conditions of the British Isles, the weight of an individual is more uniform (**Figure 69**).

Moult

Newly hatched chicks are completely covered by down feathers, but with the follicles of the first 7 juvenile feathers on the wings, which unroll on the fifth day of life. Juvenile feathers appear first on the wings, tail and back, then on other body parts. Down disappears by 33–35 days of age. The growth of juvenile feathers lasts at least two months, with the last feathers being throat, chin and sides of the neck, which appear in early autumn. Feathers of the first adult plumage (white) appear on 15th day of life (1st primary), with the last ones replacing the feathers on the head, shoulders and breast in the late autumn.

The next, first spring, moult of young birds begins in April, as in adult birds. Male spring nuptial plumage covers the head and neck, and forms in only 7–10 days. The moult then pauses for 3–4 weeks during lekking, then resumes again in populations of subspecies *L. l. lagopus, L. l. pallasi,* and *L. l. major,* with the first feathers moulted being those of the back.

The summer moult begins in northern populations in the first half of June, 'summer' feathers appearing on the back, rump, flanks and belly, together with the central pair of tail feathers, and among the spring feathers of the head and breast. The maximum level of summer plumage is seen in males in the second half of July.

The autumn moult begins in July. It is partial, producing few feathers of autumn colouration, these mainly on the upper body. Finally, at the beginning of August, the complete winter moult of contour feathers begins. These appear first on the belly, covering it completely by end of August/beginning of September. The last coloured contour feathers disappear only in October, though in southern populations (forest-steppe zone) some may be preserved all winter on the head, neck and (very rarely) the back (**Figure 70**). Change of white primaries for new ones, from the 1st to 10th, lasts more than 3 months, from June to September.

The female moult follows the same scheme, but begins later and completes to a lesser degree. The summer stage begins earlier, and is almost completed by the time the chicks hatch. The autumn stage begins in July and is less expressed than in males.

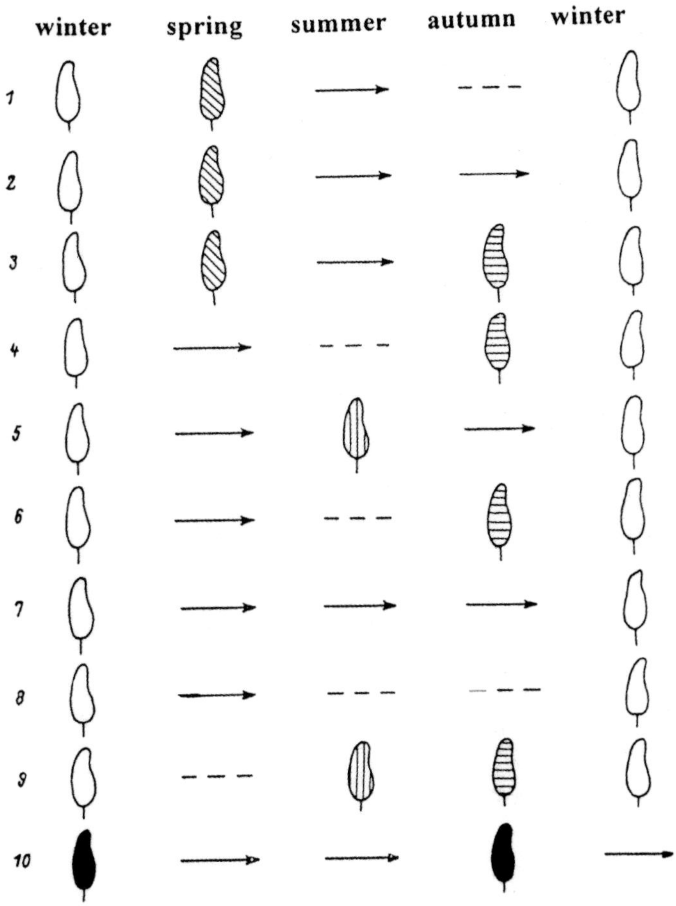

The tarsi and toe feathers in

Figure 70. Various moult sequences for *Lagopus* feathers

Figures 1–9 are the change of white winter feathers to white winter feathers with the various possible intermediate steps through spring, summer and autumn moults. In each case the solid arrow indicates the continued presence of a feather through the next season, while the dotted line indicates loss of the feather, but that it is not replaced until the following season. Feather 10 is the black tail feather of L. lagopus and L. mutus, though in both species differences in the sequence are noted between individuals. In L. leucurus there are no black tail feathers, the sequence being as No. 7.

both sexes wear and are lost from April, the toes being naked by June. New feathers appear from the end of July and are fully developed by the end of September. The horny cases of the claws fall off in July, new ones appearing and reaching full length by November. Moult of the horny cover of the bill begins in April and is completed by the beginning of September.

There are significant differences in both the duration and the start dates of the whole moult process, and of the different stages, between different populations, especially between the northernmost and southernmost ones, of up to 3–4 weeks in each case.

In addition, the start time of moult may change, by 2–3 weeks on the tundra, within a population as a result of weather conditions (Voronin, 1978).

Distribution

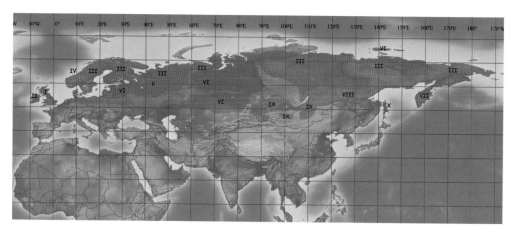

Map 10. Willow Ptarmigan (*Lagopus lagopus*)
Eurasia
Subspecies: I – L. l. scoticus; *II* – L. l. hibernicus; *III* – L. l. lagopus; *IV* – L. l. variegatus; *V* – L. l. pallasi; *VI* – L. l. major; *VII* – L. l. kamtschatkensis; *VIII* – L. l. sserebrowsky; *IX* – L. l. brevirostris; *X* – L. l. okadai.

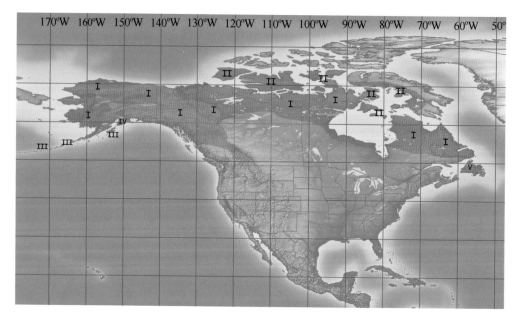

Map 11. Willow Ptarmigan (*Lagopus lagopus*)
North America
Subspecies: I – L. l. albus; *II* – L. l. leucopterus; *III* – L. l. muriei; *IV* – L. l. alexandrae; *V* – L. l. alleni.

The Willow Grouse's range is the largest among the grouse and occupies a vast area of the northern parts of Eurasia and North America. The northern limit of the range is defined by the shores of the Arctic Ocean, failing to reach that shore in only three places – the Arctic peninsulas of Gydan, Yamal and Taimyr. Willow Grouse inhabit many islandvs of the Polar Basin and have been introduced to the Shetland Isles, at the end of the 19th century/beginning of the 20th century, and Newfoundland.

The North American range is more compact, with few isolated sections, and these only on islands. According to Alsop (2002), the western border is the shore of the Pacific Ocean, south to Douglas Bay (53°N). The species inhabits the whole of Newfoundland Island, reaching the southernmost point of its North American distribution there at 46°50′N.

Subspecies

The specialization of different populations to the different natural conditions across such a huge range, together with differences resulting from isolation, has led to a large number of subspecies. It must be borne in mind that distribution of many of these subspecies, as indicated on the map, is not well studied because of the scarcity of specimens in summer plumage (the most important diagnostic) in collections.

L. l. lagopus (Linnaeus, 1758)
Colour and size as given above. Occupies all the tundra and forest-tundra zones of Eurasia and the taiga zone of eastern Siberia south to 60°N.

L. l. albus (Gmelin, 1788)
Colouration as nominative: differs only by being slightly smaller. Inhabits the continental tundra of North America, except the north-eastern parts of the Canadian Arctic Archipelago.

L. l. leucopterus (Taverner, 1932)
Differs from other subspecies by white colouration of the rods of primaries and secondaries. Occupies the islands of Canada's Arctic Archipelago south to Southampton Island, and the Melville peninsula.

L. l. pallasi (Portenko, 1972)
Male colouration differs from nominative by more prominent red tint of brown common parts and full development of the spring colouration on the back. Female summer plumage is paler. Occupies the south-western part of the European range.

L. l. major (Lorenz, 1904)
Differs by large body size and the presence of autumn feathers in the winter plumage. Occupies the self-isolated part of the south-western part of the species' range in

the forest-steppe zone from the Ural River Basin up to the foothills of the Altay-Sayan mountains.

L. l. brevirostris (Hesse, 1912)
Differs from other subspecies by the smaller beak size, which is minimal for the species. Occupies many isolated areas in subalpine belt of the Altai, Sayan, Hangai and Tannu-Ola mountains.

L. l. sserebrowsky (Domaniewski, 1933)
Differs by the very intensive dark tint of the male's summer colouration and by the shortness of the wing. Inhabits the subalpine zones of the East-Siberian mountains from Russia's Baikal region and Mongolia's Chantey Ridge up to the northern part of China's Great Hengan Mountains.

L. l. okadai (Momiyama, 1928)
Described as a separate subspecies because of the shorter wing and longer beak and tail, but this was not confirmed in Russian collections. However, the male's summer colour differs by the more pronounced red-brown tint of the upper body. Inhabits Sakhalin Island.

L. l. kamtschatkensis (Momiyama, 1928)
Similar to the Sakhalin subspecies but with smaller wing, tail and beak. The male's summer plumage is also not as bright. Restricted to the Kamchatka Peninsula, but the northern border is not yet clear.

L. l. alexandrae (Grinnell, 1909)
Differs from other North American subspecies by the darker brown colouration of the male's summer plumage. Occupies the narrow Pacific seashore regions of Alaska and British Columbia from Alaska's Kenai Peninsula south to Porter Island (Canada), including all islands situated close to this seashore and isolated from continental subspecies in Alaska and Canada by the high Saint-Ilea and Coastal ridges.

L. l. muriei (Gabrielson and Lincoln, 1959)
Colouration is similar to that of the previous subspecies, but brighter and with a more pronounced red tint to the brown parts of the male plumage. Inhabits islands from Kodiak Island and the Shumigan Islands westward to the Aleutian Atka Island (175°W).

L. l. alleni (Stejneger, 1884)
Colouration similar with that of *L.l. albus* but differs by having brown rods to the primaries and some other wing feathers. It is interesting to note that in museum collections there

Male Willow Grouse. It is spring and the male is moulting to breeding plumage in Manitoba, Canada.

are some specimens of this subspecies that cannot be differentiated from a specimen obtained on the Kamchatka Peninsula (Potapov, 1985). Restricted to Newfoundland.

L. l. scoticus (Latham, 1787)
Tetrao scoticus (Latham, 1787). Synonyms: *Lagopus persicus* Grey, 1849; *Tetrao dresseri* (Kleinschmidt, 1919).

L.l. hibernicus (Kleinschmidt, 1919)
Both these subspecies inhabit the British Islands, the first all of Great Britain and surrounding islands, the second all of Ireland. The two differ weakly from each other by colouration only, but differ sharply from all other subspecies by the absence of a white winter plumage and the constant black-brown colour of the flight feathers.

L. l. variegatus (Salomonsen, 1936)
Inhabits four islands by Trondheim Fjord, north-east Norway, the largest of them, Hitra Island, being 750km² (290 sq miles). All the islands are, climatically, strongly influenced by the Gulf Stream and so have little or no snow cover in winter, and winter temperatures

that rarely fall below 0°C (32°F). As a result, the winter plumage consists of coloured and white feathers in equal numbers.

Habitats

The ecological plasticity of Willow Grouse exceeds that of all other tetraonids. But despite the great diversity of climate and vegetation across its vast distribution, there are important features common to all populations. The first is the preference for open or semi-open habitats, even in the taiga (moss bogs, fire-affected areas and water meadows beside rivers). The second is the presence in abundance of willow, birch or alder bushes – the main sources of winter food. In Eurasia, such habitats are common in four natural zones: tundra, taiga, forest-steppe and mountain subalpine belts.

On southern tundra and forest-tundra, the birds prefer hummock moss–bush habitats alternating with thick willow bushes by streams or around lakes, and hummock bogs where they are found not only in lowlands but also on watersheds. In the High Arctic, the birds prefer riverside polygonal tundra with mature grass and dwarf willows.

In taiga forest, the vast upriver moss bogs are the preferred habitat. These hummock bogs form tundra-lake landscapes, with dense thickets of willow and birch bushes, bilberries, Labrador tea, etc, and sparse, undersized pines and birches. Large areas of heather that appeared after forests had been denuded by human activity have become the main

Female Willow Grouse in Manitoba, Canada – a good example of the camouflaged colouration of female grouse.

habitat for Willow Grouse in the British Isles and, partially, in Scandinavia. In the Hibins Mountains of the Kola Peninsula, the birds inhabit a mountain forest belt that differs from other mountain forests of the Eurasian taiga-forest zone by being more sparse, with large spruces growing to the timberline at 500–600m (1,640–1,968ft), allowing a very rich understory of birches and willows (Novikov, 1952; Semenow-Tianshansky, 1959).

In the forest-steppe zone, the main habitats are areas of pines, birches, aspens, alders, alternating with open spaces covered by tall grass and bushes. In these areas, the birds will occasionally place nests in open steppe areas far from the nearest tree/bush vegetation.

In the subalpine belt, the birds prefer dense thickets of willow and birch bushes on flat or gently sloping ground between springs and lakes, or on high, flat passes. In Russia's Far East, along the coasts of the Pacific Ocean, dense thickets of Siberian Dwarf Pine (*Pinus pumila*), a bush-like tree that grows to the timberline in the mountains, are interspersed with stone scree and open spaces with tundra-like vegetation, forming a perfect habitat. The upper limit of the subalpine habitat varies with latitude. In the mountains of the Kola Peninsula, at 67°40′N, the birds are found to the timberline at 600m (1,968ft); in the Urals, at 67°N, they are found at 300–500m (984–1,640ft) (Morozov, 1989); on the Putoran Plateau, at 69°N, to 600–900m (1,968–2,953ft); on Kamchatka, at 54°–56°N, at 350–1,100m (1,148–3,609ft) (Lobkov, 1986).

These habitat types are primarily nesting areas used during the short breeding period of 2–3 months. At all other times Willow Grouse have a nomadic way of life, especially during the winters when flocks sometimes move long distances in search of places where there is sufficient winter forage. In most cases, such places – in tundra, forest-tundra and taiga zones – are huge tracts of willow bushes in river valleys, with the birds occasionally congregating in flocks of up to several thousand birds.

Population structure and density

The sex ratio in populations is rarely equal, with males usually exceeding females. On the Pechora River Basin, the fraction of males during ten consecutive years varied from 40.3–67.1%, with a prevalence of males in seven years (Voronin, 1978). A similar situation was found in the British Isles (Jenkins *et al.*, 1963). In Finnish Lapland the fraction of males in populations increased with age, from 46.7–57.1% among young birds to 51.3–75.6% in adults (Pulliainen, 1975a). The ratio of young and adult birds in populations varies greatly, especially in northern ones, from almost 0–87% (Voronin, 1978). In north-eastern European tundra, two female phenotypes were found, these differing by the presence (Type 1) or absence (Type 2 – as in males) of brown patches on the tail feathers. The ratio of these types changed from year to year, but Type 1 always dominated, from 52–66% (Voronin, 1978).

Population numbers fluctuate considerably from year to year: some studies have indicated that these changes may be cyclic (MacKenzie, 1952, Watson, Moss, 2008 in the

British Isles, Myrberget, 1972, in Norway, Bergerud, 1970 in Newfoundland, and Andreev, 1988 in the Kolyma region of Siberia). Periods from 3–10 years have been suggested by these studies, the most frequently suggested period being 3–4 years. However, these suggestions were not confirmed by other studies (Marcstrom, Hoglund, 1980; Jenkins, Watson, 1970; Potapov, 1985). Fluctuations in numbers are dependent on a number of factors, the most significant of which is the weather, particularly at chick hatching.

Another cause, one that affects Willow Grouse more than other grouse species, could also account for cyclic fluctuations. Lemmings are the main food source for many tundra predators, including Arctic Foxes, Rough-legged Buzzards, Snowy Owls and some gulls. During 'lemming years', when the rodent population rises steeply, predator numbers also rise. Then, when the lemming population crashes, the predators switch to other prey and that invariably means Willow Grouse. Because of the presence of reproductive cycles in lemming, these can therefore be reflected in the Willow Grouse population. For further details of this potential cycling mechanism see Potapov and Sale (2013). When on the European tundra, lemming disappeared completely in 1971, by the beginning of August only 25% of brood chicks survived (Myrberget, 1974, Voronin, 1978). However, a relationship between grouse and lemming numbers cannot, for instance, explain the apparent cyclical nature of fluctuations seen in British populations, where there are no lemmings. Hudson (1992) suggested that periodicity in the British Isles might be driven by parasitism.

The density of birds in an area at the end of the breeding season can vary hugely, for example, from 2–3 to 2,150 birds per 1,000ha (2,471 acres) (see **Table 5** in Chapter 1). In taiga forest and forest-steppe zones, the periods of high and low densities are not regular and vary during the breeding season between 2–50 pairs/1,000ha and in winter between 1–82 birds/1,000ha) (Potapov, 1985). The highest spring density seen to date was on the tundra of Newfoundland – 806 pairs for 1,000ha – (Mercer, McGrath, 1963). On the tundra between the Pechora River and the Ural Mountains, the maximum density reached 262 pairs/1,000ha, but the minimum, between density peaks, was only 29 pairs/1,000ha (Voronin, 1978).

Territoriality

The territorial structure of populations during the breeding season comprises individual nesting territories, these being established by males or by newly formed pairs at the beginning of the season. At that time, males demonstrate strong territoriality with differing nuptial, aggressive and defensive behaviours. Females stay close to their nests, but show no aggressive territorial behaviour. Female/brood life is essentially sedentary, but as the birds change from a summer to an autumn and winter diet, they change habitat and become nomadic. However, despite this change, males still occasionally demonstrate territorial displays, particularly on calm, clear mornings: the more sedentary the population the more likely the displays. In the practically sedentary populations of the British Islands, male territorial displays cease during the intensive summer moult, but resume in the autumn and continue on sunny mornings throughout the winter. Dispersion of young birds takes place in the autumn with attempts to find free plots between those of old males who still maintain their territorial behaviour (British Isles, Watson, Jenkins, 1964). There is no information regarding the autumn territorial activity of old males in other sedentary populations in the forest zone. The nomadic way of life in flocks during the winter throughout the species' range usually decreases territorial instincts, even if there is such activity in the autumn (Potapov, 1985).

The most settled way of life is that of the populations of the British Isles, Aleutians and Newfoundland. In Scotland, 95% of marked young birds were collected within a radius of 1.5km (0.9 miles), with only rare movements of 16km (10 miles) or more. The mobility of old birds was only a little higher, with 88% of marked birds not moving more than 1.5km (0.9 miles) from the point of ringing (Watson, Jenkins, 1968).

Regular seasonal migrations are characteristic only of tundra and forest-tundra populations. On the tundra, only a very small fraction of birds remain for the winter, but if the snow cover becomes very deep, the entire population will leave. The birds that remain are mostly males (Miheev, 1948; Andreev, 1980; Weeden, 1964). Among the 316 birds collected during the winter near the southern foothills of Alaska's Brooks Range, 73% were males, while of 60 collected in more southerly, wooded areas, 92% were female (Weeden, 1964). On the tundra areas of the Yamal, Gydan and Tazowsky peninsulas, where winters usually bring comparatively thin snow cover, and willow bushes remain available, some birds winter as far north as 72°30′N (Nazarov, Shubnikova, 1971), but the majority migrate south to areas with rich, bush-arboreal vegetation. On the New Siberian Islands, where most birds leave the archipelago in October/November to spend the winter on mainland tundra, some birds overwinter regularly, despite the absence of any bush vegetation, with the only available forage being dwarf willow.

The most prominent seasonal migrations are those of the tundra of the Yamal, Gydan and Taymyr peninsulas, and of Alaska, with the timing of the autumn migration and its intensity varying with the establishment of true winter conditions. Migration is slow, step-by-step, if the autumn is (relatively) warm and there is little snow, but becomes very intense if the temperature drops and there is significant snowfall. In the northern Pechora Basin, when winter began in 1931, small groups of birds left first, with mass migration several days later. Birds passed in flocks of 100–300 birds, at heights of 50–200m (164–656ft), one after the other, for five days (Miheev, 1948). In Alaska, around 50,000 birds migrate across the Brooks Range (Anaktuvuk Pass) each year: on one spring day 10,000 birds passed on northward passage (Irving et al., 1967). In general, the birds choose migration routes that connect north–south running along valleys of large rivers, but clearly wind strength and direction also affect the flights.

Distances covered by migrating birds vary enormously, some travelling only a few kilometres, while others move 800–1,000km (497–621 miles) (Snyder, 1957; Gagina, 1958). Some birds fly across the sea, with unsuitable winds then causing high mortality. An example, during the autumn migration from Kolguev Island to the mainland in 1926 or 1927, many dead birds were found in the estuary of the Indigirka River (Miheev, 1948). On some of these cross-sea migrations from Kolguev, the birds arrived on the mainland so exhausted that they could be readily picked up (Soloviev, 1927). There is evidence that in 1915–1916, strong winds had caused havoc among a huge flock of migrating birds, with the pile of dead bodies washed up on the shore forming a bank 2m high (Soloviev, 1927). In Kuskokwim Bay, Alaska, a flock of Willow Grouse flew around a boat, some landing on it to rest, and at least 10 birds were also seen to land on the water (the sea was calm at the time), resting there before easily taking off and continuing the migration flight (Zimmerman *et al.*, 2005). This is the first evidence that the birds can use the sea to rest, at least in favourable conditions.

Migrating Willow Grouse that cross open sea from the New Siberian Islands do so after the sea has frozen. The birds have been seen gathering on the south coast of Kotelny Island waiting for the sea to freeze. Some birds actually rest, and even roost, in the snow covering the sea ice during the flight (Pleske, 1928). To the north of the archipelago, Willow Grouse also migrate from breeding grounds on Bennett Island to the nearest New Siberian Island (Faddeevsky Island, 170km/106 miles SSW) when the sea freezes. On this route, numerous traces of the birds were observed on the snow covering the sea ice, and two birds were actually collected (Birula, 1907; Coll ZIN RAN).

The reverse, spring migration, begins in March, the routes coinciding with those of the autumn migration if weather conditions allow.

Behaviour

Willow Grouse are essentially terrestrial, walking on the ground or the snow cover during winter to feed from the low branches of willows or birches. For most of the time throughout the year the birds live in flocks, the size of these varying from a few birds to several hundred. Specific winter behaviour is considered below. During seasonal displacements, the birds show a light, quick flight and, as noted above, fly significant distances without stopping. In both Taimyr and Alaska, the birds follow herds of migrating reindeer, using places where the animals had dug in the snow to search for their own forage (Krechmar, 1966). Similar behaviour has also been observed on the New Siberian Islands.

Nutrition

The main winter food, from tundra to steppe, is twigs and buds of different species of willow, birch and, to a lesser degree, *Chosenia arbutifolia* and alder. Catkins of birch and alder are an

Red Grouse female (left) and male

additional food source. In the European forest zone, and in Newfoundland, the chief winter diet is the dwarf birches *Betula nana*, *B. tortuosa*, and *B. exilis* (Peters, 1958; Potapov, 1985). At the start of winter, when the snow cover is thin, the green stems of the bilberry are also consumed. The exception to these general dietary comments are the British Red Grouse subspecies, whose main food source, not only in winter but for practically the whole year, is heather shoots: only in Scandinavia is this food source also utilized in some populations, but to a much lesser degree (Nordhagen, 1928; Seiskari, 1957; Tanhuanpaa, Pulliainen, 1969; Höglund, 1970). Another exception is the New Siberian Island population, where wintering birds feed on twigs and buds of dwarf willow that is usually still visible above the minimal snow cover, as well as on the green parts of different grasses and flowers that remain fresh, but frozen, throughout the winter. The Russian Polar Expedition of 1903 stated that the crops of wintering birds were completely filled with young shoots and buds of *Salix polaris*, seed capsules of *Papaver nudicaule* and a *Stellaria,* together with small leaves of *Potentilla intermedia* and seed capsules of *Saxifraga caespitosa*. Such a diet is more commonly associated with Rock Ptarmigan that are not found on the archipelago.

Where snow cover is invariably deeper, the birds gradually progress up the trees as snow accumulates, finishing in the crowns – a progression observed in Russia (Semenow-Tianshanski, 1959; Kishinski, 1975; Andreev, 1980) and Alaska. In Russia, the movement towards the crowns was accelerated by competition from hares and elk (moose) (Kalinin, 1974; Andreev, 1980), the crown feeding moving to thicker twigs as the supply of more easily managed twigs dwindled (Andreev, 1980). In Alaska, the birds also switched food items, eating the shorter willows first (*Salix glauca, S. richardsoni, S. pulchra*) then progressing to the tall *S. alascensis* as the snow depth grew (West, Meng, 1966). The study suggested that with equal availability of willow and poplar species, the birds preferred willow.

The change from winter to spring diet begins as soon as the first thaw patches appear, with the diet becoming wider as leaves and berries of the cowberry, leaves of *Andromeda*, the stems of horse-tails, etc, are added. As the weather improves, the fraction of winter forage in the diet declines as catkins, flowers, fresh green stems, the shoots of blueberry, etc, become available. Feeding on blueberries is a characteristic of populations in the European and west Siberian forest zone: on the Kola Peninsula, for example, blueberry shoots often constitute more than half the crop content in May and June (Semenov-Tianshanski, 1959). In eastern Siberia and in Alaska, the birds feed on the shoots of whortleberry (*Vaccinium uliginosum*) and, in Yakutia, the leaves and buds of cowberry (Perfiliev, 1975).

The summer diet of adults mainly comprises fresh green leaves and stems, berries, seeds and, to a lesser extent, moss and mushrooms. Among the most important seeds are those of ledums, dryads, sedges and *Andromeda*. For Alaskan birds, the axil bulbs of *Polygonum viviparum* are important. Of the berries, cowberry, whortleberry, crowberry and the fruits of dog roses are the most important. Cranberries are also taken, but in general only during the early spring. The quantity of animal material is insignificant, even in southern populations. Some birds do eat snails, grasshoppers, caterpillars, etc, but in general this is only occasionally, when the animals occur in great numbers. However, the rougher, arboreal food – sprouts, buds and catkins of willows and birches – is still taken (Rodionow, 1969; West, Meng, 1966), even the needles of larches and spruces (Yakutia – Perfiliev, 1975). Berry, leaf and seed consumption declines as September approaches, the fraction of arboreal food increasing. However, in the autumn, in the European range, the importance of the blueberry stems rises again, with up to 6,000 pieces of them having been found in a single crop (Novikov, 1952).

Animal material is very important to chicks, but only in the first few days of life when the diet includes spiders, cicadas, diptera, butterfly caterpillars, small mollusks, etc. By the time the chick is a month old, the fraction of animal material in the diet has fallen almost to zero, with the chick diet becoming much as that of older birds. This is especially noticeable in chicks from northern populations: chicks from southern populations may not start to take chiefly arboreal food until the second month of life (Iurlov, 1960).

The birds use gastrolits at all times, but especially in winter, these constituting 20–30% of the gizzard contents (Kishinski, 1975). In most places the number of gastrolits decreases towards the end of the winter, especially in the regions with deep snow cover. On the Kola Peninsula at the end of the winter, 14% of collected birds had no gastrolits at all. Stones are replenished as soon as they become available: on the Timan tundra of north-eastern Europe, in March/April, all collected birds had gastrolits (Micheev, 1948), while in eastern Siberia at the same time, gastrolits were found in 90% of birds – in many cases the birds used the hard seeds of cloudberries (Perfiliev, 1975). The size of stones utilized increases in spring, with stone weights being 110–160mg; the number of stones increases up to July, but individual stone size decreases (Semenow-Tianshansky, 1959). However, in one study on the Timan tundra during the summer, 20% of birds had no gastrolits (Micheev, 1948).

Wintering

Across most of their range, Willow Grouse live in severe winter conditions for 7–9 months of the year, with adaptation to these conditions being observable in both morphology and behaviour. The bird has two main aims: to decrease energy expenditure and to maintain body temperature. The first aim is aided by decreasing the time for feeding by more intense feeding, and the second by spending long periods (16–17 hours daily) in a snow burrow. Usually the bird leaves its burrow in the early morning and begins foraging immediately, or after a short flight, feeding in a small flock from the snow cover, and moving from one bush to another in one direction, leaving a wide track behind them. Then, after two hours of feeding, the birds rest on the snow, under bushes, before feeding again before sunset. If the wind is strong, or the temperature low, the birds will excavate a snow burrow in the middle of the day. After the evening feed, the flock flies to a new roosting place, usually no more than 400–500m (437–546yd) away, though if the flock is small (3–5 birds), they may roost where they have fed.

When the birds roost in flocks, their snow burrows are close together, within 1–1.5m (3.3–4.9ft). The roosting chamber is about 25cm (9.8in) long, 16–18cm (6.3–7.1in) wide

Male Willow Grouse in winter plumage

Male Willow Grouse in winter plumage, southern Alaska

and 14–21cm (5.5–8.3in) high, with a roof 9–11cm (3.5–4.3in) thick. The length of the tunnel to the chamber is usually about 50cm (19.6in), but it can sometimes be 2m (6.5ft). Willow Grouse droppings measure 23–29mm x 6.5–8.5mm, with a dry weight of 0.34–0.39g (0.012–0.013oz), and comprise pieces of twigs 0.5–1.5mm in diameter, from which the bark and cambium have been stripped.

Usually the total daily time for feeding is 3–6 hours, with the mid-day rest being 2–5 hours, but if the day is short, the birds feed without resting (Pavlov, 1975). Extreme cold (-50°C [-58°F] and below) does not prevent feeding, but the birds are very sensitive to the wind. A wind speed of greater than 7m (23ft) per second may delay the start of feeding, decrease the feeding time to 1.5 hours, or even stop feeding altogether. If low temperatures coincide with a significant wind, the birds may not leave their burrows for two days or even more (Pavlov, 1975). In low temperatures, during feeding the birds fluff up their feathers, looking like white balls.

The daily ration of the birds is approximately the same throughout their range. In the Kolyma River Basin in midwinter, the daily ration was 139g/4.9oz (fresh weight), i.e. 64.5g/2.3oz (46%) dry weight of buds and twigs (Andreev, 1980); on the Kola Peninsula it was 104.5g/3.7oz fresh or 54.3g/1.9oz dry (Semenov-Tianshansky, 1959); on Taimyr and the Bolshezemelskaya Tundra 120–130g/4.2–4.6oz fresh (Pavlov, 1975; Voronin, 1978); in the Leningrad region 132g/ 4.7oz fresh (Potapov, 1985). On the Kola Peninsula during the winter, the maximum number of food items (*Betula verrucosa* and *B. nana*) found in a crop was 6,337 (Novikov, 1952). In the Kolyma region, the birds prefer twigs of diameter 0.8–1.5mm, which they bite into pieces 4.5–15mm in length. As the availability of such twigs declines, the birds are forced to use thicker twigs, up to 2.6mm in diameter and 10–27mm in length. The weight of twig pieces taken therefore increases during the winter, from 12mg to 31mg, but the nutritional values of each decreases in proportion (Andreev, 1980).

Although winter forage is abundant, reserves are not infinite, and its lack limits local populations. In Leningrad Province, each bird consumes almost 12kg (26.5lb) of twigs, catkins and buds of willows and birches during the six months of winter, with reserves of food being the main factor restricting the population density and influencing its mobility: the winter density is 0.9–1.2 birds/km² (Rodionov, 1966).

The caloric equivalent of the bird's daily ration is 1,415–1,754kJ, from which the bird uses only 33% (481–586kJ) for life support, the remaining energy being excreted. On average, the birds lose 0.68g (0.02oz) a day in body weight, amounting to 12.2kJ daily. Most of the remaining energy is spent in thermoregulation, the expenditure in moving, etc, being minimal. Daily flying is restricted to no more than two minutes, while feeding on foot for four hours expends only 19.7kJ (Andreev, 1980). Andreev calculated the energy that the bird spent in biting its food from branches, this being minimal – 1.2kJ/day – if the ambient temperature was -40°C (-40°F) because of the brittleness of the twigs. When the ambient temperature rises to about 0°C (32°F), the elasticity of the twigs is restored and more effort is required to bite pieces off. It has been suggested that this may be one of the main reasons the south-west section of the species' range has decreased in size as the climate has warmed (Volkov, 1970). But, at -40°C (-40°F), more energy is required to heat the food in the bird's crop, that taking 49.4kJ/day, 9.6% of the daily energy budget.

Breeding

Males begin to display as soon as the first red feather appears on the neck, this usually occurring during the spring flock migration. On the tundra, arrival at the breeding area usually coincides with the appearance of snow-free patches, the males immediately dispersing and acquiring territories, a process accompanied by almost non-stop display activity, this usually initiated by one bird and immediately taken up by neighbours, though at this stage there are few battles. Once begun, activity is interrupted only by short feeding sessions, or bad weather.

The main courtship display is a nuptial flight that advertises both the male and his territory. The actual form of the flight and vocal sounds during it varies between subspecies. The simplest flight is that of *L. l. scoticus*, in which the male flies steeply up to a height of 8–10m, then descends with the beating wings curved slightly back and down, the tail widely spread, the feet straight forward and the head and neck held up. During the lift, the male produces a barking 'a', while during the descent he utters a series of 8–12 abrupt guttural sounds 'ka-ka-ka-ka-ka…'. After landing, the male finishes the display with a series of cries: 'ko-va…ko-va…ko-va' (Watson, Jenkins, 1964). In

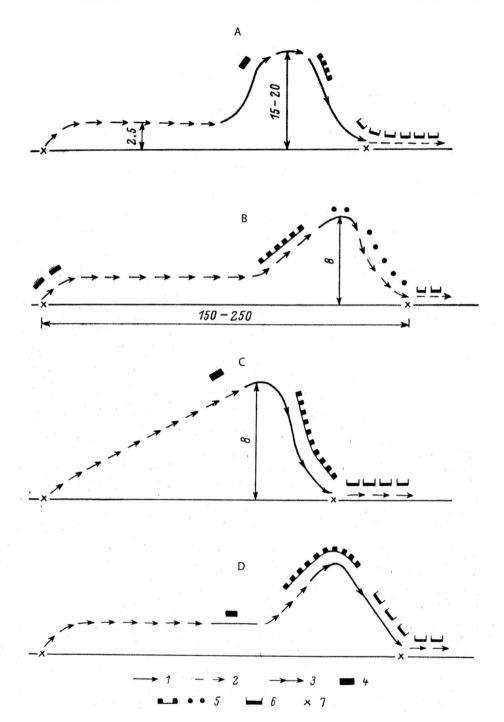

Figure 71. Courtship flight patterns of *Lagopus lagopus* according to different sources from different locations

A – Miheev, 1948; B – Estafiev (in litt.) C – Watson, Jenkins, 1964; D – E. Potapov (in litt). 1 – active flight; 2 – running on the ground; 3 – gliding flight; 4 – point of first call; 5 – laughing; 6 – special sounds produced during landing 'kabào…kabào…kabào'; 7 – landing point. Vertical measure – height of flight apex (m).

continental subspecies the flight is more complicated, the male initially flying to the right, 2–3m (6.5–9.8ft) above the ground, for about 200m (218yd), then flying sharply upwards (the 'steep climb' – maximum height 15–20m [49–66ft], Miheev, 1948) before descending steeply from the high point with spread and back-curved wings, fanned tail and hidden head. After completing the flight the bird runs 3–4m (9.8–13ft) (**Figure 71**). When making the 'steep climb', the male raises his head and flattens his back 2–3 times simultaneously. The duration of the flight is 12–15 seconds, of which the descent and landing takes 4.3 seconds (Potapov E., in litt.). Vocal sounds during the flight are constant, but differently described, perhaps reflecting real differences in different populations. The first sound is a loud, sharp 'gau…' which, after one second is followed by rolling 'laughter' produced by short, merged syllables 'ke-ke-ke-ke rrrrrrrrrrrrrrrr', and, finally, on landing, the characteristic species cry, a repeated 'kabào…kabào…kabào' (Figure 71), this uttered as the male spreads and closes his tail. On the ground, or on an observation post, the male may also move his head, with neck thrust up and forwards, and utter a tremulous, trilling 'ko-ko-ko-kokrrrrrrr' (Semenow-Tianshansky, 1959).

Two neighbouring males may also perform the 'parallel flight', flying close to the ground and side by side, while making large circles that can cover several kilometres. During the flight, the distance between the males remains constant at 30–50m (33–55yd). On the ground, neighbouring males may also perform the 'parallel duel' at the border of their territories, walking side by side for a short distance, each uttering the 'kabào' cry. Occasionally, this 'duel' may occur outside the territories and draw 5–6 birds into the display (Watson, Jenkins, 1964).

During courtship displays, the males are very noisy, signalling that their territory is occupied or reacting to neighbouring display activity with a loud 'krrrrrrrr', 'krrrrrow' or 'kak-ka-ka-ka-ka-krrrrow'. They also make similar sounds if danger threatens. During combat, rivals also utter a loud, abrupt 'kok'. Females are more silent, though they do occasionally make sounds, the most usual being a 'ka-ka-ka-ka…' similar to the cackle of a domestic hen.

During male display activity, females tend to be alone or in small groups. Pairs form very quickly, in just a few days, as the land becomes snow-free. Both males and females attempt to regain the previous year's territory, new partners usually being chosen only if a former partner has died. Willow Grouse are strongly monogamous: even in rare cases in which two or three females settle in a male's territory, the male will stay with one female rather than dividing his time between them. It has been shown experimentally that females in these cases do not demonstrate mutual aggression (Yamal Peninsula – Tarasov, 2001), though contrasting behaviour was noted in Canada (Hannon, 1984; Martin et al., 1990) where, in some cases, not only were females antagonistic, but male aggression to a second female was seen, the female being chased away much as a rival male would be. This difference seems related to individual characteristics, some males being more 'peace loving' to other females and even to the strange males. In experiments, such males reacted listlessly, even to stuffed males in full spring plumage, this reaction being seen in successive years (Tarasov, 1995). Tarasov suggests that a form of 'behavioural polymorphism' exists in tundra populations, perhaps offering enhanced reproductive success in certain population density situations. However, some males are less peaceable, and after pair formation, border disputes may lead to combat, males using observation points as sentry posts and being ready to fight at any time, with any approaching male being immediately driven away.

Both sexes reach maturity during the first year of life. There are also no differences in reproductive potential between young and old birds, though the eggs of older females are a little larger and the chicks correspondingly larger than those of young females (Myrberget, 1970). The timing of breeding varies significantly across the huge range, full clutches being seen, on average, in later May/early June in tundra and forest-tundra zones, a period when the mid-day ambient temperature reaches about 5°C (41°F). What is remarkable is the synchronicity of breeding time across areas with latitudinal differences of 10°–12° (e.g. East Siberia and Canada), indicating that day length is insignificant in terms of timing. Incubation lasts 18–22 days, with chicks hatching in late June/early July. However, these timings may vary by up to three weeks if the spring is early or late. In the northern range, the effect of delayed hatching may be catastrophic, with chicks from late clutches having no time to complete the growth necessary for winter survival: a brood of 12 seven-day-old chicks found on 17 August on Bennett Island (Uspenski, 1963), the northernmost point of the species' range (74°40′N), had no more than 20 days to prepare for winter and almost certainly perished. By contrast, on more southerly tundras, if spring is early and summer warm, females will re-nest after brood loss (Kirby, Smith, 2005).

In the forest zone, the earliest breeding dates are to the west. In Britain, females begin laying in April (early, middle or end, depending on the exact location – Watson, Moss, 2008), while in Scandinavia, European Russia, Estonia and Belorussia laying starts in early May, though again late springs may cause a delay (Rodionov, 1969; Viht, 1975; Fomenkov, 1975; Potapov, 1985). In the eastern part of the Eurasian range, laying starts at the end of May/early June (Nechaev, 1975; 1991), though in Siberian mountains and Russia's Far East laying may occur in mid-June (Folitarek, Dementiev, 1938, Potapov, 1985; Pavlov, 1948; Kishinski et al., 1982). In Alaska, hatching peaks occur from 20 June to 5 July, but are later in July in the Canadian Arctic Archipelago (Weeden, 1963).

The nesting territory is selected, acquired and defended by the male and may be held for several subsequent years. The size of the nesting territory depends on the local population density. In the most favourable places on southern tundra when the population is high, territories may be as small as 0.23ha (0.56 acres), with nests being close together. With more usual population densities the average is 0.86ha (2.1 acres), but may be up to 7ha (17.2 acres) at other times (Voronin, 1978). In the forest zone when the breeding density is low, there may be only 0.5–2.5 pairs/km², with neighbours being so far apart that it is difficult to detect the territory a male is defending. Again, with a more usual population density territories are 1–3ha (2.5–7.4 acres) (Ivanter, 1974).

The female builds her nest within the male's territory, often using the same site as the previous year, or one very close to it (Alison, 1976). The nest is a simple, shallow depression sparsely lined with dry grass, moss, etc. Nest sites differ across the range, but the female usually tries to place the nest among low bushes for camouflage, the site allowing a good view of any approaching danger. Dry ground is preferred, but if it is damp, the nest base will be thicker. On tundra, in rare cases, the base of the nest may be up to 10cm (3.9in) thick with walls 2cm (0.8in) thick. The diameter of such nests may be up to 18cm (7in) (Miheev, 1948). In the forest zone, nests are usually on top of dry tussocks in moss bogs or, in the forest itself, under the low-hanging branches of spruces.

Clutch size depends on the physiological condition of the female, which in turn depends on conditions during the previous winter and other, as yet unclear, issues apparently connected to population size: it was, for instance, noted that clutch size was higher during population depressions than in times of high bird density: 7.8±0.26–8.46±0.25 and 6.0±0.79–6.9±0.39 respectively (Russia's Bolshezemelskaya tundra, Voronov, 1978). Such differences make it difficult to define a dependence of clutch size on latitude. The maximum number of eggs seen in a clutch is 20, the minimum 4, while in most cases clutch size is 8–12. On Newfoundland, for example, clutch size averages 10.2 eggs (106 nests, Bergerud, 1970) and in Alaska 6.8–7.8 eggs (5 and 8 nests respectively, Johnsgard, 1973).

A second clutch, if the first is lost, is always smaller. Clutch loss results from predation or human activity, the number of second clutches reflecting the size of such losses (6–25% in Sweden, Parker, 1981; 17.5–55.2% as a consequence of agricultural activity in the forest-steppe, Ulianin, 1939; Jurlov, 1960). New clutches must be laid within about 10 days of a loss, as the female can produce fertilized eggs only in the period 3–14 days after mating, unless she mates again (Parker, 1981). In the tundra zone, it was found that the male's gonads decreased quickly in size after mating and ceased to function about halfway through the incubation process (Voronin, 1978). In more southerly areas, male sexual potential is preserved longer, allowing more time for unfortunate hens to attempt to raise a brood even if the chicks of the first brood were about a week old when they were lost (Kirby, Smith, 2005).

Egg size varies insignificantly across the range. On Russia's European tundra, the eggs were 42.8mm±0.54 (39.5–47.0mm) x 30.8mm±0.15 (28.0–32.0mm) (Voronin, 1978). The eggs are generally whitish-ochreous with numerous scattered brown spots and patches of different sizes. Fresh eggs have a rich reddish tinge, which disappears during incubation. Females produce eggs at intervals of about 24 hours. During the laying, the female stays at the nest for 1–2 hours (Voronin, 1978). Incubation begins once the last egg is laid. Up to that time, the eggs usually lay open to the weather, though this does not seem damaging, despite morning frosts down to -3°C (26.6°F). If there are a large number of eggs, they sometimes form two layers. In such situations, the sudden flight of the female may cause one or more eggs to roll out of the nest. If that happens, the female will restore them when she returns.

The daily incubation schedule depends on the weather, the female's condition and her experience. Usually the female leaves the nest for 3–6 times daily to feed, but will avoid leaving during rain or if the ambient temperature is low. Feeding excursions last 5–48 minutes: the absence of the female in the nest lasts from 40–120 minutes each day, usually 60–80 minutes (Semenov-Tianshansky, 1959; Voronin, 1978; Pulliainen, 1978b). When the female leaves the nest in calm conditions, she will cover the eggs with dry trash from the nest lining. From the beginning of the second week of incubation, the female turns the eggs regularly to ensure even heating, the embryo's sensitivity to cooling increasing with time. For the same reason, the female is more reluctant to leave the nest as incubation progresses, even allowing an observer to touch her rather than abandon the eggs. On the last day of incubation, the female does not leave the nest to feed. Incubation lasts 18–22 days, usually 21–22 days.

During incubation the male stays close to his observation place at all times, though he will feed close to the nest or accompany the feeding female. During such combined feedings, the male often leaves the female for a short time to inspect the nest site, though he avoids approaching closer than a distance of 10m (10.9yd) so as not to disclose its location (Pulliainen, 1978b). In very rare cases, males whose partner has died will finish the incubation and even successfully rear the brood (Allen et al., 1978). The male's behaviour changes remarkably towards the end of incubation: he keeps concealed, often hiding if danger approaches, but will attack without hesitation if detection is unavoidable.

Hatching takes place in the morning and is very rapid, all chicks emerging in about 2–3 hours (Iurlow, 1960; Voronin, 1978). The weight of newly hatched chicks is 10.7–13.7g (0.4–0.5oz) on the tundra, 14.5–15.8g (0.5–0.6oz) in the forest-steppe zone, with chick weight varying not only across a population, but also within the same brood (Jurlov, 1960). The body temperature of newly hatched chicks is 39.4±0.5°C (102.9±1°F) (Myhrberget et al., 1977). After hatching, the chicks dry in the nest for several hours and are then led slowly away by the female, with the brood forming a tight group and being occasionally brooded. Brood life is nomadic; the group, led by the female ahead, the male behind her, moves at about 160m (175yd) an hour, not allowing for stops (Dixon, 1927). For the first two weeks the brood wanders within, or close to, the nesting territory limits. Broods then begin gradually to unite into flocks: after a successful breeding season, several hundred birds may flock prior to the autumn migration.

At 10 days old the chicks can flutter their wings: when they are two weeks old they can

Male Willow Grouse in spring, beginning the moult from winter plumage, in Northwest Territories, Canada

fly 50–80m (55–87yd). By the age of one month, the chicks behave as the adults. However, there is a significant difference between the speed of growth of chicks in the northern and southern parts of the range. On Eurasian tundra, with its short summer but continuous daylight, young birds are full-grown in 70 days (weight on average 617.5g [21.7oz]), while in the forest-steppe zone, young birds of this age weigh only 480–513g (16.9–18.1oz) and are not full grown until they are 100–110 days old (Voronin, 1978; Jurlov, 1960).

Hunting, recreation and conservation

At present, Willow Grouse is the only grouse species whose numbers allow unlimited hunting in many areas of the tundra and forest-tundra zones, though this situation is changing. Hunting in those areas is concentrated in the autumn and winter seasons and is essentially amateur in nature. The one exception is the hunting of Red Grouse in Britain, where it is, in essence, an industry with regular, controlled burning of heathland and moorland carried out with the aim of increasing grouse densities so that hunting gives good returns for the hunters and landowners. The density of local populations of Red Grouse on these moors reaches a much higher level than would be expected in normal conditions, with up to 331 bird/km² in spring (Watson *et al.*, 1984a). Many of these birds will become the victims of hunters during the traditional autumn hunting season.

Until recently, hunting was organized in Russia, with annual autumn season takes being several hundred thousand, and the birds reached big city markets. For example,

30,000–200,000 birds were obtained from the Pechora River Basin (Voronov, 1978), 300,000 from the lower parts of the Ob River Basin (Formozov *et al.*, 1963), 150,000 from the Taimyr Peninsula (Pavlov, 1975). Because of the high expense of transporting the birds from these remote areas, this professional hunt ceased at the end of the 20th century. Local, amateur hunting is not thought to greatly influence population numbers.

The same situation prevails in North America, where the annual kill of all three species of ptarmigan (though predominantly Willow Grouse) in the 1970s was about 300,000 (Johnsgard, 1973). From other calculations, the hunting activity of First Nation peoples in 61 Alaskan villages during the period 1954–57 was 53,000 birds annually (Weeden, 1963).

In most parts of its Eurasian range, both the number and density of the species are stable, though with regular fluctuations. However, there has been a decrease in both range and bird numbers in the south-western part of the range, beginning in the 19th century and still continuing, despite hunting bans in Estonia, Belarus, and Russia's Leningrad Province. One reason for the decrease is global warming. Winters now are much less snowy and occasionally the large bogs that are the main winter habitat for the birds are snow-free, making the birds in their white plumage very conspicuous to raptors. Another cause for the decline has been an increase in agricultural activity: in such situations, illegal hunting adds pressure to an already serious situation. Throughout the range, the main measures for conservation are hunting laws and the setting up of different kinds of protected areas – State Reserves, sanctuaries, National Parks, etc. In Russia, re-introduction of birds into areas of the former range has proved completely ineffective, as the released birds disperse widely: between 1955 and 1965, more than 6,000 birds were released in European Russia without a positive result (Osmolovskaya, 1969).

6.2 ROCK PTARMIGAN *Lagopus mutus* (Montin, 1781)

Tetrao mutus (Montin, 1781). Synonyms: *Tetrao lagopus* (non Linnaeus) (Fabricius, 1780); *Tetrao alpinus* (Nilsson, 1817); *Lagopus mutus* (Forster, 1817); *Lagopus cinereus* (MacGillivray, 1837).

Small birds, with a terrestrial way of life on stony tundra and alpine–subalpine belts.

Note: The genus *Lagopus* was described by Brisson (1760), who wrote 'white in winter, variable in summer, lateral tail feathers are blackish with white tips'. Though the description fits both *Lagopus lagopus* and *L. mutus*, Brisson clearly had *L. mutus* in mind as the type species of the genus. *L. mutus* was the accepted scientific name for the species for two centuries until David and Gosselin (2002a, 2002b) proposed a change to *L. muta* on the basis that *lagopus* was a feminine Latin noun and that Brisson had consistently used feminine adjectives in combination with Lagopus. The name was subsequently changed by the American Ornithological Union (Banks *et al.*, 2004).

However, the *lagopus* derives from the Greek compound word λᾰγώ-πους ('hare foot', a reference to the birds' feathered feet and toes), a combination of an adjective (λᾰγώ) and a noun (πους), each of which is masculine (Lindell and Scott, 1996, p. 1023 and p. 1456), though the compound word may be masculine or feminine. We therefore consider David and Gosselin's view that *lagopus* was a feminine Latin noun to be erroneous. Furthermore, Article 30.1.2 of the International Code of Zoological Nomenclature (2000) states that 'a genus-group name that is or ends in a Greek word transliterated into Latin without other changes takes the gender given for that word in standard Greek dictionaries', while Article 30.1.4.2 states that 'A genus-group name that is or ends in a word of common or variable gender (masculine or feminine) is to be treated as masculine unless its author, when establishing the name, stated that it is feminine or treated it as feminine in combination with an adjectival species-group name'.

We therefore consider 'lagopus' to be masculine and the species name *Lagopus mutus* to be valid, and we have used it in this book. We have also used names ending in '*-us*' rather than '*-a*' in subspecies names.

Morphology

Rock Ptarmigan possess the narrowest and most sharpened wing of any grouse. The top of the wing is formed by the end of the 8th primary, in rare cases the 8th and 7th. The width of the wing is 53.1% of its length against 61.8% in the Willow Grouse. The relative length of the wing in this species is larger than in the Willow Grouse, forming 48.6–53.1% of the body length (48.6–50.4% in the Willow Grouse). Other parts of the body (tail, bill, tarsi and middle toe) have the same proportions as in Willow Grouse, though the bill is thinner.

The remarkable morphological feature is the structure of the male trachea that acts as a resonator during spring breeding vocal activity. As well as inflating the oesophagus during vocalization, the male uses an inflatable membranous pocket, about the size of a small walnut, on the dorsal surface of the trachea just below the larynx (MacDonald, 1970). The tracheal rings here are incomplete from the dorsal and ventral sides, and are joined by a thin membrane that functions as a hinge, allowing the rings to extend laterally and to flatten their curvature when the dorsal membrane is inflated. This description has not, as yet, been confirmed since, but such structures are present in other birds, e.g. the Emu (*Dromiceius novaehollandiae*) (Teresa, 1930).

Male Rock Ptarmigan

Colouration

Adult male

Winter plumage (October–May): Almost all body feathers are white, apart from black stripes on both sides of head from the base of the bill to, and a little behind, the eyes. The tail is as *L. lagopus*, but the black feathers have white bases and tops, with more white than that species.

Spring plumage (May–June): White still dominates, but many coloured feathers appear on head and neck, and, later, on breast (these forming a broad, blackish necklace) and back. Maximal development of spring feathering is reached in early June. General spring appearance is mottled, with blackish spring feathers dispersed between white ones. In extreme northern populations spring colouration develops very late and males spend the lek time in winter feathering.

Summer plumage (end of June–mid–September): Upper body is grey, with separate black patches and thin sinuous cross-stripes on some feathers. The tops of these feathers have a cross design resulting from white stripes on a black background. Most upper body, breast and flank feathers are grey with thin, yellowish streaks. Chin, throat and neck are covered by white and yellowish spots. Some breast feathers have a black-and-white cross pattern, and some flank feathers have narrow white tops and a cross pattern from blackish and yellowish stripes. Central pair of retrices and, sometimes, the coverts are dark-grey with narrow white top borders and very small blackish streaks, these occasionally flowing together to form blackish patches. By mid-August, only central and lower belly remain white. On the wings, coloured feathers replace white only on the shoulders, 4–6 inner secondaries, inner great coverts and nearly all the median and outer coverts, these being grey with narrow tops and thin streaks of white.

Autumn plumage (September–October): Plumage is a mix of summer feathers, new autumn ones, and the occasional new white feathers that appear at this time. Autumn feathers have a white base, the colouration differing from that of summer by having a thinner, softer, streaked pattern on a lighter background. Summer feathers tend to dominate on the head, neck and upper breast.

Adult female

Winter plumage (October–May): Plumage is white, as males, but as a rule, females do not have a black stripe on the head, though this is present in the most northerly populations. However, in these cases the stripe is not sharply expressed, and has many white spots (Salomonsen, 1939; Johnsen, 1941). In northern Alaska and northern Scandinavia, only 1.4–6.8% of females have this stripe, while 21.1–34.3% have separate black feathers in the same place (Weeden, 1964; Pulliainen, 1970c). Tail feathers are never solid black, the central pair having brown marks, the remainder brown cross-bands. However, this feature is not enough to distinguish the sexes, as about one-third of males are similarly coloured (Pulliainen, 1970c).

Summer plumage (May–July): Highly mottled. Upper body is predominantly black, the feathers having white top borders, with a cross-stripe pattern developing mainly on scapulars, rump, uppertail and nape of neck. Inner secondaries have the same cross-stripe pattern, but with a black background that occupies all the upper part of the inner web. Lower body is lighter, especially the belly, because of wide, white feather tops. The area of

Female Rock Ptarmigan

the crop looks darkest because the brown stripes are close together there. Primaries and secondaries remain white all summer, apart from the four inner secondaries and greater, lesser and distal median wing coverts. Central pair of tail feathers also remains white. During incubation, the white top borders wear out and the female becomes very dark, especially on head and back, which look almost completely black.

Autumn plumage (August–September): Autumn plumage is a mix of summer, autumn and winter feathers, with the proportions varying significantly between southern and northern populations, as well as between individual birds. Autumn feathers, light grey in colour and very thin, appear mainly on neck, back and breast and are hardly visible against the background of dark, worn summer plumage. A uniform streaked colouration is a characteristic of the feathers of the back and, especially, of some breast feathers that have a regular pattern of thin brownish cross-stripes on a light-grey background. The white bases of autumn feathers, so characteristic in males, does not occur in every feather, being seen only on those that appear at beginning of winter. Maximal development of autumn plumage takes place at the beginning of September, when new white winter feathers cover belly, back parts of flanks and throat.

Female Rock Ptarmigan of the subspecies L. m. captus, *the most northerly nesting breed of grouse. The photograph was taken in autumn in N.E. Greenland. The bird is moulting to winter plumage.*

Juvenile

General background is yellowish-grey, with black-brown patches covering the central, upper part of the feathers, and with cross-stripes of same colour below or to the sides of the patch. Most juvenile feathers have the triangular white spot at feather tops seen on all juvenile grouse. The earliest juvenile feathers to appear have a greater contrast pattern, the blackish and yellow colours being brighter, the white triangles more distinct, so that upper parts look gold-black.

For young males and females in the first adult (autumn) plumage, the lower body is 70% white, with breast and neck maintaining juvenile feathering, the first adult autumn feathers covering practically all the upper body and then appearing on the breast. These feathers have a regular black cross-stripe pattern on a light-grey background. There are numerous variations, but always with a large black field on upper part of the feathers.

Downy chick

As Willow Grouse, apart from the natal down on the tarsi being longer and thicker (**Figure 72, n1**).

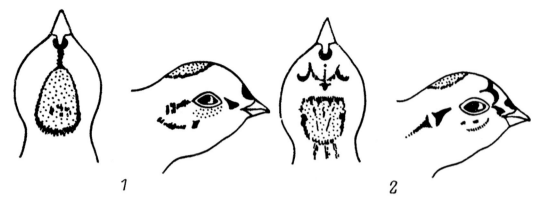

Figure 72. Head patterns of *Lagopus* nestlings
1 – Lagopus mutus; *2* – Lagopus leucurus.

Dimensions

Body length varies from 370–400mm in males and 365–390mm in females. Other dimensions of 285 specimens of males and 197 specimens of females (Coll ZIN RAN) are males (females in brackets): wing length 182–216mm (175–204mm); tail 80–120mm (82–103mm); bill length (from nostril ends) 8.0–13.0mm (7.2–12.0mm); bill width at the same place 7.5–9.6mm (6.2–9.0mm); tarsi 27–38mm (26–38mm); middle toe v19–32mm (21–30mm).

Both body size and weight are greatest in the northernmost populations, i.e. in northern Greenland and Svalbard subspecies: the length of the male's wing and tail are 222–237mm and 130–155mm respectively, and body weight can reach 880g (31oz), almost double that of other subspecies. In other areas the maximal body weight of males reaches only 515–615g (18–22oz), and also varies significantly with the season. As in the Willow Grouse, minimal body size and weight are seen in the high-mountain populations of southern Siberia.

Moult

As Willow Grouse, with such differences that occur being only in the details.

The moult to first autumn plumage (the growth of the 1st white primary) begins when the chick is four weeks old, before many of the juvenile feathers have completed their growth. During the whole period from hatch to late autumn, the young bird is in an uninterrupted process of moult, ending only when the bird has acquired its white winter plumage. The white plumage appears first on the belly when the chick is about six weeks old, then spreads to the flanks and lower part of the breast. After this, the white feathers begin to appear among the yellowish-grey ones on all the upper parts of the body, and finally cover the bird completely. The last feathers to change are on the head, back and upper breast.

The general scheme of the moult in adult birds then follows. In males, the spring moult is partial, and varies with individuals and latitude. In northernmost populations, males lek in complete winter plumage. In other parts of the range, the coloured spring feathers appear in large quantities on the head and breast, creating a mottled colouration from early May to early June. The spring moult gradually becomes a summer moult that finishes in early July when the autumn moult begins. In the most cases, white feathers are preserved only on the belly and chin, but in some individuals, especially in southern populations, coloured plumage covers almost the whole body. In northern populations the last coloured feathers disappear at the beginning of October, but in southern populations they may remain until December or even through to the next spring (Salomonsen, 1939; Jakobsen *et al.*, 1983).

The female moult has no spring phase, with the birds changing from white to summer plumage in a short time. Females begin incubation in full summer plumage, at least on the upper body. The autumn stage of the moult begins two weeks later than in males and, as a result, is shorter and partial. In northernmost populations, autumn feathers comprise no more than 10% of all coloured feathers. The moult finishes at the same time as in males.

Full replacement of primaries lasts 2.5–3.0 months in both sexes, but timing is strongly influenced by climatic and individual physiological effects.

Distribution

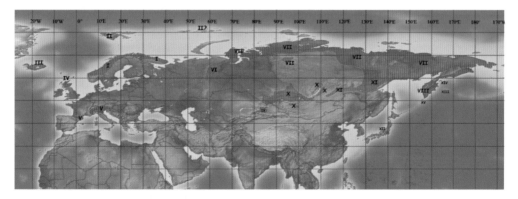

Map 12. Rock Ptarmigan (*Lagopus mutus*)
Eurasia
Subspecies: I – L. m. mutus; *II* – L. m. hyperboreus; *III* – L. m. islandorum; *IV* – L. m. millaisi; *V* – L. m. helveticus; *VI* – L. m. comensis; *VII* – L. m. pleskei; *VIII* – L. m. krasheninnikowi; *IX* – L. m. macrorhynchus; *X* – L. m. nadezdae; *XI* – L. m. transbaicalicus; *XII* – L. m. japonicus; *XIII* – L. m. ridgwayi; *XIV* – L. m. gerasimovi; *XV* – L. m. kurilensis.

The species range is very complicated, with its circumpolar character more fully expressed than in Willow Grouse, as the range includes Greenland. Among all grouse, the Rock Ptarmigan has the most northerly distribution, reaching a claimed, but unconfirmed,

83°24′N (Pirie Land and Lockwood Island, in northern Greenland; 81°40′N (Rudolf Island, Franz Josef Land); about 77°N (Ellesmere Island); and 77°40′N on the continental mainland (Taymir Peninsula). However, the species is absent from all islands of the Eurasian Arctic from Kolguev Island eastward to Wrangel Island. To the south, the species reaches 35°N in Japan, though in mountainous areas the range is much further north, e.g. 46°55′N in the Mongolian Altai, 49°30′N in the coastal mountains of western Canada.

Map 13. Rock Ptarmigan (*Lagopus mutus*)
North America
Subspecies: I – L. m. yunaskensis; *II* – L. m. atkensis; *III* – L. m. sanfordi; *IV* – L. m. chamberlaini; *V* – L. m. gabrielsoni; *VI* – L. m. townsendi; *VII* – L. m. evermanni; *VIII* – L. m. nelsoni; *IX* – L. m. dixoni; *X* – L. m. rupestris; *XI* – L. m. captus; *XII* – L. m. saturatus; *XIII* – L. m. welchi

Subspecies

As with Willow Grouse, *L. mutus* forms many subspecies, but because of its adaptation to more habitats across the vast distributional range, in places represented by isolated populations, the number of subspecies is much greater, with 28 having been identified. Most of these subspecies are minimally differentiated, clear differences only being seen in *L. m. hyperboreus* (large body size) and *L. m. japonicus, L. m. ridgway* and *L. m. evermanni* (darker summer plumage). In all the other subspecies, differences in colouration and body size are very weakly expressed and, as a consequence, confirmation of existence requires a good series of collected specimens in summer and autumn plumage, and this is far from being the case for all named subspecies. In general, all subspecies can be divided into a few groups on the basis of the general colour tone of the male plumage (Buturlin, Dementiev, 1935). The first group includes those with dark summer colouration, as mentioned above. The second group includes those with a general grey tone (European subspecies and the Aleutian *L. m. sanfordi*). The third group has a brown tone (south Siberian mountain subspecies: *L. m. nadezdae, L. m. transbaicalicus* and *L. m. macrorhyncus*). In the fourth group there is a yellowish tint to the male's summer plumage (almost all Aleutian, American, Greenlandic and north Siberian). Such a grouping provokes a temptation to transfer the unifications to the field of phylogenetic connections (Höhn,

1969), but that may produce mistaken conclusions. It is enough, therefore, to note that, in general, grey tones increase towards the north, brown towards the south. Body size also increases towards the north. Subspecies distributions are indicated on Maps 12 and 13.

L. m. mutus (Montin, 1781)
Occupies the mountains and coastal tundra of Scandinavia and the Kola Peninsula.

L. m. millaisi (Hartert, 1922)
Inhabits the mountains and hills of Scotland from the northern coast southward to 56°N. In the south, inhabits only mountains above 900m.

L. m. helveticus (Thienemann, 1829)
Inhabits the mountains of central Europe (Alps and Pyrénées).

L. m. comensis (Sserebrowsky, 1929)
Distribution restricted to the subalpine and alpine belts of the northern Urals from the northernmost point (Osovei Lake, 68°36´N, Coll ZIN RAN, Potapov, 1985) southward to the Konjakov' Stone Mount, 59°36´N (Sabaneev, 1874; Danilov, 1975).
L. m. pleskei (Sserebrowsky, 1926)
Range includes all the northern part of Asia, from Yamal to Chukotka and south at least to the sources of the Yana River at 68°N. In the southern parts of the east Siberian range it adjoins the range of the trans-Baikal subspecies, but the position of the border between the two is unknown.

L. m. nelsoni (Stejneger, 1884)
Occupies all of mainland Alaska, Kodiak, Afognak, Hinchinbrook, Montague and Ushagat islands, and the eastern Aleutian Islands – Unimak, Unalaska and Amak. To the east, this subspecies shares a border with the Canadian subspecies *L. m. rupestris*: the border in not clear, but may be placed approximately along the line between the Mackenzie River Delta, through Fort Eagle to the sources of the Kuskokwim River (Aldrich, 1963).

L. m. rupestris (Gmelin, 1788)
Inhabits northern North America from the middle part of the Yukon River eastward to Labrador, all islands of the Canadian Arctic Archipelago (excluding only the north-eastern part of the Ellesmere Island), and the southern part of Greenland's northern shores to 65°N in the west and 69°N in the east. Several authors (Gabrielson, Lincoln, 1959; Todd, 1963) have expressed serious doubts about the existence of clear differences between *L. m. nelsoni* and *L. m. rupestris*.

L. m. welchi (Brewster, 1885)
Range restricted to Newfoundland, where the birds dwell sporadically on the rocky tops of the hills where they are not numerous.

L. m. saturatus (Salomonsen, 1950)
Inhabits the north-western coast of Greenland from Upernavik southward to Egedesminne. In the south, forms a transitional zone to *L. m. rupestris*, but well isolated from north Greenland's subspecies *L. m. captus* by the ice wall of the Stenstrup Glacier, which is 500km (311 miles) wide.

L. m. captus (Peters, 1934)
Inhabits all north-western, north and north-eastern coasts of Greenland, from Thule in the west to Scoresbysund in the east. The northernmost subspecies of Rock Ptarmigan.

L. m. islandorum (Faber, 1822)
Found only on Iceland, where it is seen across the island.

L. m. nadezdae (Sserebrowsky, 1926)
Range includes the Altai and Sayan mountains, adjacent mountains of northern Mongolia (Mongolian Altai, Hangai Ridge and Han-Taiga Ridge) and Baikal's Hamar-Daban Ridge.

L. m. macrorhynchus (Sserebrowsky, 1926)
Restricted to the Saur Ridge, and eastern parts of the Tarbagatai mountain system. An isolated subspecies, separated from the nearest populations of *L. m. nadezdae* (in the Altai Mountains) by 200km (124 miles).

L. m. transbaicalicus (Sserebrowsky, 1926)
A revision of collection specimens (Potapov, 1985) determined a range from the Baikal Ridge eastward to coastal ridges of the Sea of Okhotsk (Djugdjur Ridge) and from the Tukuringra, Iam-Alin and Dusse-Alin ridges in the south of east Siberia northward to the southern parts of Verkhoyansk Ridge and the Kolyma Plateau, where the specimens with transitional features to *L. m. pleskei* appear (Kishinski, 1968).

L. m. krascheninnikowi (Potapov, 1985)
Occupies the Kamchatka Peninsula. Isolated from the nearest mainland subspecies (*L. m. pleskei*) by 100km (62 miles) of lowlands at the peninsula's neck and from the nearest island subspecies on the Karaga, Commander and Kuril Islands by the sea.

L. m. gerasimovi (Redkin, 2005)
Inhabits only Karaga Island, 50km (31 miles) from the eastern shore of the Kamchatka Peninsula.

L. m. kurilensis (Kuroda, 1925)
Inhabits the northern Kuril Islands from Shumshu to Shikotan islands inclusive.

L. m. ridgwayi (Stejneger, 1885)
Inhabits the Commander Islands of Bering and Medny.

L. m. japonicus (Clark, 1907)
Inhabits the mountains of central Honshu, Japan (two isolated populations in the mountain areas of Akaishi and Chida).

L. m. evermanni (Elliot, 1896)
Inhabits only the Aleutian Attu Island. The distance to the nearest other subspecies, *L. m. townsendi,* is 300km (186 miles).

L. m. townsendi (Elliot, 1896)
Restricted to the Aleutian islands of Kiska and Little Kiska.

L. m. chamberlaini (Clark, 1907)
Inhabits only the Aleutian Adak Island.

L. m. sanfordi (Bent, 1912)
Restricted to the two Aleutian islands of Tanaga and Kanaga.

L. m. atkhensis (Turner, 1882)
Found only on the Aleutian Atka Island.

L. m. gabrielsoni (Murie, 1944)
Inhabits the Aleutian islands of Amchitka, Rat and Little Sitkin, and perhaps also nearby islands (Gabrielson, Lincoln, 1959).

L. m. yunaskensis (Gabrielson, Lincoln, 1959)
Restricted to the Aleutian island of Yunaska Island, but possibly also on Amutka Island.

L. m. dixoni (Grinell, 1909)
Inhabits coastal regions of southern Alaska from the coasts of Glacier Bay and the nearest

islands to Baranov and Chichagov islands. The eastern border is conditionally drawn along the eastern slopes of the Coastal Range.

L. m. hyperboreus (Sundevall, 1845)
Inhabits the Svalbard archipelago including Bear Island and, perhaps, Franz Josef Land.

Habitats
Rock Ptarmigan prefer more open places than Willow Grouse, with their habitats often being completely devoid of trees or bushes. In mountains and on Arctic tundra, the birds select areas with scarce vegetation cover – lichens, mosses, dwarf Arctic birch, different grass and berry plants, interspersed with stony or rock ground. In such areas, the bird's cryptic colouration can make it difficult to locate. In a clear contrast to Willow Grouse, the species avoids moss tussock tundra with thick willow bushes. The favoured habitats on islands (not only the Kuril, Commander and Aleutian islands, but much larger islands such as (southern) Greenland, Iceland, Japan, Newfoundland and also the Kamchatka Peninsula) are more diverse, the birds nesting not only on bare, stony places, but in areas more typical of Willow Grouse, i.e. damp lowlands with grass cover and sparse bushes, though these are only utilized if Willow Grouse are absent. During the autumn and winter, habitat depends chiefly on the availability of food, so places where the snow is blown away by strong winds, or bush thickets between sparse trees in subalpine belts or the forest-tundra zone, are favoured.

Population structure and density
As a consequence of choosing areas with scarce food supplies, Rock Ptarmigan are rarely high in either number or density. In places where both Willow and Rock Ptarmigan are seen together, numbers of the latter are always lower. Only in the most suitable places can the density reach 2–5 pairs/km² (Gizenko, 1968; Voronov, 1968; Lobkov, 1986), i.e. maximal density only reaches mean Willow Grouse density (**Table 5 in Chapter 1**). On wintering grounds, if food resources are sufficient, the density can approach summer levels: in subalpine habitats of the coastal mountains near Magadan, by the Sea of Okhotsk, where the birds spend the winter in small flocks, densities of almost 8 birds/km² (Potapov, 1988) have been recorded.

Most researchers believe species populations are cyclical, with a period of 10 years, though supporting data for this is scarce (Jenkins, Watson, 1970; Weeden, Theberge, 1972; Gudmundsson, 1972), and even when cycles are tentatively observed, they do not appear synchronous, even across relatively small areas (e.g. in Scotland).

The population of birds in any area depends on the percentage of older females and their condition, which depends on the severity of the previous winter, weather conditions, hunting and predation pressure, etc. In Iceland, most raptors' deaths are due to Gyrfalcon (Gudmundsson, 1970), while in Alaska the main culprit is the Stoat, which annually predates 15–45% of nests. In general, predation and disease kills 10–34% of the chicks in any brood, a rate which means that only two or three nestlings of the average clutch will live long enough to be able to fly (Weeden, 1965).

In most populations, males exceed females. In Scotland, males were 58.5% of the total population (Watson, 1965). However, in extreme northern populations, such as Canada's Bathurst Island and northern Greenland, females dominate, in some cases males having 2 or 3 nesting females within their territories (Salomonsen, 1950b, MacDonald, 1970). The winter mortality of the species is significant, with percentages of 40–67% usually quoted, but despite this, populations remain stable: Weeden (1965) noted that, provided the mortality does not exceed 60%, any individual population would remain stable. However, increased female mortality is a characteristic for populations in danger of extinction, as is feared in the mountains of Japan where the ratio of males to females is 2:1 (Sakurai, Tsuruta, 1972; Chiba, Shinji, 1972).

Territoriality

In terms of both attachment to a nesting territory (particularly of females) and large-scale wandering in search of food in other seasons, Rock Ptarmigan are almost identical to Willow Grouse, though in each case to a lesser degree. In mountain areas, there are no significant vertical displacements, and only during prolonged heavy snowfalls do the birds descend to the foot of the hills. There are horizontal displacements, especially in northern populations, with the birds chiefly moving to open, hilly areas that are swept clear of snow by constant winds, or to forest-tundra habitats with rich bush vegetation. In general, island populations are sedentary, though those of islands of the Canadian Arctic archipelago are an exception.

In the places where the species population is high, such seasonal displacements may be considered true migrations: as an example, on the Taymir Peninsula between the Lena and Khatanga rivers, autumn displacements are short (5–16 days) and intensive, with flocks of birds flying high over unfrozen lakes (Sdobnikov, 1957). However, some birds, mainly males, remain on their breeding territories throughout the winter: those males that do move tend to leave last and return first.

The timing of the birds' return (the spring 'migration') is dependent on altitude and local climate. In some places the birds can appear several days before the appearance of the sun (e.g. German Land, Greenland at 77° N, 4–8 February, Eta, 78°N, 13 February, Salomonsen, 1950b) or immediately on its appearance (northern Taymir, 5–21 February, Sdobnikov, 1957), though in each case the mass arrival of migrant birds occurs later.

Migration of Rock Ptarmigan is most noticeable in Greenland, where the seasonal movement is concentrated into two narrow coastal corridors (between sea and glacial ice) on the west and east coasts, each 2,000km (1,243 miles) long (see, for example,

Salomonsen, 1950b). On the continental mainland, migrations are much smaller, both in terms of bird numbers and distance. As an example, birds from the northern Gydan Peninsula move to the Taz River valley, a distance of nearly 600km (373 miles) (Sdobnikov, 1957).

Nutrition

The diet of *L. mutus* has not been studied in many parts of the range and is well documented only in Alaska, Finnish Lapland, north-east Russia and Scotland. The winter diet is better understood than that of breeding birds. Plasticity of the diet as been noted, especially in winter, when the birds change their food sources dependent on local conditions: when deep snow covered the short willow bushes in Finnish Lapland, the birds fed on birch catkins, as Black Grouse do (Pulliainen, 1970b).

Differences between the diet of Willow and Rock Ptarmigan generally appear small: in those few places where the ranges of the birds overlap, the species use different parts of the same plants, though simultaneous feeding of the two is very rarely observed. Rock Ptarmigan prefer soft, tender parts of the plants, probably because the thin bill is weaker in comparison to that of Willow Grouse. In the Kolyma River Basin, the birds prefer to feed on alder catkins, which constitute up to 44% of the winter diet, these rarely forming part of the Willow Grouse's diet (Andreev, 1980). The remaining diet was thin twigs (0.5–1.3mm in diameter) of birch and willow bushes. The dry weight of the twig pieces averaged 7.4mg and 5.4mg for males and females respectively, i.e. 3–4 times less than for Willow Grouse. Alder catkin pieces were larger, averaging 78mg (range 51–115mg): the caloric value of these is much higher, but the time taken to search for them (20–100 seconds) is also much greater. It was noted that on days of particularly low temperatures, the percentage of catkins in the bird's daily ration increased (Andreev, 1975a, 1980). In some areas of Scotland, twigs do not form any part of the winter diet, the main constituent being soft shoots and leaves of different species of *Vaccinium*, crowberry, saxifrage and heather (Watson, Moss, 2008). In Alaska, in places where both ptarmigans wintered, the *L. mutus* diet was considerably restricted in comparison to *L. lagopus* (Weeden, 1969), seemingly a further indication that the Rock Ptarmigan bill is less versatile than that of the Willow Grouse.

The species' diet does occasionally include unusual food items, for example, the nuts of Creep Pine obtained from cones. To acquire these, the bird pecks at the upper scales covering the nuts, an activity that takes a considerable time. Eventually, when the nuts are exposed, they are swallowed whole and broken down in the stomach. When examined, the droppings of the birds include numerous micro-pieces of nutshell. Such unusual feeding was observed on mountain ridges near Magadan, where these pines form the upper limits of the timberline. The birds were also feeding on young pine sprouts (Potapov, 1988).

In summer, *L. mutus* uses green food items to a lesser degree than *L. lagopus*, but utilizes a greater range of seeds and, especially in the northern parts of the range, the axil bulbs of *Polygonum viviparum*, the stems, leaves and berries of crowberry, different flowers (mainly thunderberry, andromeda, blueberry and whortleberry), the leaves and young shoots of willow, the catkins of dwarf birch, and different berries. Insects form almost no part of the diet, even of nestlings, the diet of the latter being much as that of adults, with the addition of seed capsules of polytrychous mosses (Semenov-Tianshansky, 1959).

In northern Taymir, the diet of local birds based on a study of the contents of 346 crops of specimens collected from early spring to late autumn detected 86 species of plants, including 8 species of moss and 11 lichens (Tichomirov, 1955). The most important food items were the leaves of *Dryas punctata*, the buds, leaves and twigs of willows (*Salix polaris, S. arctica* and *S. reptans*) and, in summer, the buds and flowers of some species of saxifrage, *Polygonum viviparum* and many others. The author, the famous Russian botanist B.A. Tichomirov, noted particularly that most of the plants utilized belonged to the Arctic-alpine flora, while those utilized by Willow Grouse belonged to the boreal forest flora.

Wintering

Throughout most of the range there is little data on species wintering. In the Kolyma Basin, the birds spent the winter in the upper reaches of small rivers and streams, in areas overgrown by low alders and dwarf birches, and on mountain slopes near the timberline at altitudes of 850–900m (2,789–2,953ft) where larch was sparse. However, the birds in such high areas occasionally descended in groups to valley terraces and, on rare occasions, even to the valley bottoms, where they joined wintering Willow Grouse. Such upland areas usually see temperature inversions that make the valley bottoms colder than the higher areas, and are more frequently snow-bound. In some cases, the ambient temperature on high ground can be 12–15°C (24–30°F) warmer than in the valley bottoms (Andreev, 1975a) and the birds can decrease their energy expenditure by basking in the sun. Snow on the upper slopes is also easier for the birds to manage, as wind tends to create a harder crust, allowing the birds to walk more comfortably on the surface. The wind also creates deeper, softer snow banks on lee sides, which makes excavation of snow burrows easier. The species' use of temperature inversions is also well known in north-east Greenland, where the birds form large flocks and move to mountain slopes at altitudes of 300–1,000m (984–3,281ft) where the ambient temperatures are higher (Salomonsen, 1950a).

In the northern Urals, the birds winter in very different conditions, staying above the timberline on flat areas of mountain tundra (rather than slopes) where there are small patches of larch and thickets of birch bushes. On the tundra of the Kola Peninsula's Hibin Mountains, the birds always winter above the timberline, concentrating in places where the wind has scoured the snow and left bare ground. There is no bush vegetation in these places, the birds feeding on the green parts, buds and frozen berries of alpine plants. Only

Male Rock Ptarmigan moulting from winter to spring plumage, Skaftafell, Iceland.

heavy snowfall forces the birds to descend to the dwarf birch forests, where they feed on buds and catkins (Semenov-Tianshansky, 1959).

In general, the winter strategy of Rock Ptarmigan differs markedly from that of Willow Grouse, with Rock Ptarmigan favouring areas with few thickets and wintering in small groups (rarely more than 5–9 birds), or often just a single pair, or even a solitary bird. Gatherings of 20 or more birds are very rare. Only in Greenland, where Rock Ptarmigan occupy the adaptive zone of Willow Grouse in the southern part of the island, do the birds gather in large numbers.

The bird's daily schedule is similar to that of Willow Grouse, and equally monotonous. At latitudes of 65°–70°N, a bird spends nearly 18 hours in snow burrow, leaving the burrow in morning twilight and walking to the nearest food source, where it feeds for about 2 hours. In the middle of the day, the bird rests for 3–4 hours in an open snow hollow or a new burrow. The bird then forages again for about 2 hours until the light fades. As the day lengthens, the feeding time increases. While foraging, the bird moves at 125–250m (137–273yd) an hour and covers no more than 600–800m (656–875yd) during the day, usually moving across the slope or along a stream in search of low bushes. In extreme cold, the birds feed quickly, each bite of a twig making an audible click (MacDonald, 1970). Flights are very short, with a bird spending no more than 2–3 minutes flying.

Foraging activity and its bioenergetics were studied in Kolyma River Basin by Andreev (1980). Searching and biting of a single twig piece requires 1.5–2 seconds on average, but the search for an alder catkin requires much more time: 20–100 seconds. The rate of food consumption in the snow burrow averages 1.6g (0.05oz) an hour (0.93–2.27g/0.03–0.08oz dry weight), the daily ration averaging 48.6g/1.7oz (29.8–63.2g/1.05–2.2oz, damp weight 82g/2.9oz) for the bird of 436–516g (15.4–18.2oz). These data are in good agreement with others obtained in Alaska (1.46–1.5g/0.051–0.052oz an hour: Moss, 1973) and Greenland (1.25–1.68g/0.04–0.06oz an hour: Gelting, 1937). Crop weights from birds obtained just before roosting were 13g (0.4oz), 17g (0.6oz), 24.5g (0.9oz) and 36.3g (1.3oz) (dry weight). The weight of droppings in snow burrows was 14.4±1.3g (0.5±0.04oz), with 11.4±2.3g (0.4±0.08oz) of gut excrement. The average value of excretion energy is 795.9kJ/day, compared to an existence energy of 207.7–439.6kJ/day (Andreev, 1980). Such an unusual correlation between these energies suggests that the winter energy expenditure of Rock Ptarmigan is both low and stable.

As with other grouse, the Rock Ptarmigan roosts in snow burrows for energy efficiency, with roosting in shallow hollows being very rare. The bird selects the position of the burrow during its foraging walk. Once selected, excavation is very rapid, the process lasting not more than 15–20 seconds. The bottom of the roosting chamber is usually 25–28cm (9.8–11in) below the snow surface, the ceiling 7–10cm (2.8–3.9in) deep, with a chamber width of about 16cm (6.3in) (Andreev, 1980).

There is little data on the winter life of Rock Ptarmigan in the extreme northern habitats on Svalbard and in northern Greenland. Greenlandic birds can move southward to latitudes below 60°N, but there is some evidence that birds remain as far north as 77°N on the east coast and 75°N on the west, compared to the known wintering position of 75°N on the Taymir Peninsula of the continental mainland. Clearly, in terms of foraging, the duration of winter daylight is crucial, and this is a particular issue for Svalbard birds which have no opportunity to move south of 76°40′N, as that would require a flight of 700km (435 miles) above a stormy, partially frozen, sea. Svalbard birds (L. m. hyperboreus) are therefore forced to survive a dark period of at least four weeks when they live on fat deposits accumulated in the autumn, the ability to accumulate such deposits being an extreme development for grouse (Potapov, 1985). A careful analysis of body weight, fat deposits and the quantities of food in crops of 224 specimens collected in all seasons during a two-year period (Mortensen et al., 1983) showed that accumulation of fat occurred during October, with maximal amounts (250g/8.8oz on average, and in some cases up to 350g/12.3oz in adults and 100g/3.5oz in young birds) being reached by the beginning of November. These large reserves were spent by the beginning of February, when the sun re-appeared and regular foraging could begin. Experiments with caged Svalbard birds in artificial conditions indicated fat deposits began in August, and that in October the reserves composed up to 30% of body weight (Mortensen *et al.*, 1982).

Our calculations suggest an energy expenditure of birds in snow burrows of 314kJ, so that the average fat reserve (9,943.3kJ) is sufficient for the bird to survive without additional forage for 31 days, a time almost exactly equal to the dark period at the latitude of Svalbard birds. However, we consider it more likely that the birds utilize the weak Arctic twilight, which can be as long as two hours at the start and end of the dark period, to forage: there is some evidence to suggest that Svalbard birds utilize the feeding activity of local reindeer – themselves a subspecies, *Rangifer tarandus platyrhynchus*, of the mainland reindeer – that break up the snow cover with their hooves to reach

Female Svalbard Ptarmigan L. m. hyperboreus *in Ossian Sars, Kongsfjorden, Spitsbergen. Found only on Svalbard, this smaller subspecies is one of the rarest of all grouse.*

Male Svalbard Ptarmigan L. m. hyperboreus *in Forlandsundet, Spitsbergen*

the underlying vegetation. Indeed, the content of the crops is, on average, 57g (2oz) in November, 18g (0.6oz) in December, 11g/0.4oz(!) in January and 30g (1oz) in February (Mortensen *et al.*, 1983), the bird's fat reserves therefore only compensating for the deficiency of gathered food, rather than replacing it entirely (Potapov, 1985). Such an excellent adaptation for life cannot have appeared quickly, no doubt developing gradually over the period from when the archipelago was close enough to the mainland, at the start of the Pleistocene epoch, to have acquired its population.

Breeding

Monogamy is less sharply expressed than in Willow Grouse, polygamy being more prevalent on Arctic tundras. Despite this, however, the breeding habits of the species have all the attributes of monogamy – the establishment and defense of nesting territories and the apparent stability of pairs. Evidence of polygamy is based, in part, on the observation of males leaving the nesting territory towards the end of hatching, but in detailed observations on Greenland it was found that such males usually return to their broods within one month (Salomonsen, 1950a), their absence being due to intensive moulting. More obvious cases of polygamy have been observed on northernmost tundras of Bathurst Island and northern Greenland, where two or three females were seen nesting within a single territory, but here the explanation may be simply the preponderance of females in the population. In such cases, as for Willow Grouse, males give maximal attention to one female, though they do not entirely ignore the others (MacDonald, 1970; Salomonsen, 1950a). Importantly, it was noticed that in cases where there were two or three females per male, the males differed from their peers in being noticeably highly active: such males are more likely to become the victims of raptors, natural selection apparently working for the preservation of monogamy (MacDonald, 1970). In 'normal' situations, each male has only one female within its nesting territory.

Both sexes are sexually mature at the end of their first year and take equal part in breeding during the following spring. However, some young birds from late clutches do not breed, spending the breeding season in small groups, or alone. The sex ratio in such groups is unknown. When the population density is high, some birds may not breed as a result of not acquiring a nesting territory. In an experiment in Scotland, 15 territorial males were removed: most were replaced by other birds (Jenkins, Watson, 1970).

The territorial structure of the population is as in Willow Grouse, i.e. the nesting territories of males. Territories are larger, because of the lower population density, and their borders are less clear. In the Canadian Arctic Archipelago, males defend territories of almost 2.5km²/0.9 sq miles (250ha/618 acres) (MacDonald, 1970), though in places where the population density is higher, the distance between the centres of adjacent territories may be as low as 300–400m (984–1,312ft) (Greenland, Salomonsen, 1950a), and an individual nesting territory cannot exceed 12.5ha (31 acres). Similar nesting territory sizes have been observed in Russia's Kolyma highland area (Kischinsky, 1968), while those on the Taymir Peninsula measure 25–30ha (62–74 acres). The minimum size of nesting territory, 3ha (7 acres), was observed in Japan (Sakurai, Tsuruta, 1972).

Male sexual activity starts weakly, but increases sharply after the appearance of the first patches of bare ground, the eye-combs becoming much exaggerated.

The male's courtship ritual includes a nuptial flight and several specific postures and displays, which are well described by MacDonald (1970). The basal courtship posture is similar to that of other grouse: the head and tail are raised up, tail opened maximally, but the wings slightly open and held in such a way that the tops of outer primaries are between the bases of the outer retrices. The male maintains this posture at its territorial sentry posts, as he walks, or even as he makes short runs, uttering a short series of jerky, cackling sounds. The courtship flight begins with a jump and vigorous wingbeats, the tail opened maximally, and accompanied by a loud, guttural cry. At first the male flies low, following the contours of his territory. Then he shoots steeply upwards on spread wings (making a 'hill') and, close to the upper point of the flight, fluffs his neck feathers and begins to utter the first part of a 'song' which resembles that of the Corncrake (*Crex crex*). The male then apparently hangs motionless in the air before descending along a very steep parabola, with fluttering wings, and while uttering the second part of the song – the same sounds but lasting twice as long. During the descent the spread tail is lowered steeply down, but after the landing it is raised again as the male begins walking. One interesting feature of the song is its audibility, the noise seeming very similar irrespective of the distance: a bird at a distance of 100m (109yd) or so can, in fog, appear very much closer (Andreev, 1971). The duration and distance of courtship flights vary significantly. Firstly, they are short and low (sometimes not exceeding 1m/3.3ft), but during maximal activity may cover 400m (437yd), the male rising to 75m (246ft). In most cases the flight follows a straight line, with only one 'hill', but more complex flights occur, with the male flying in a wide circle with several 'hills'.

During the establishment of territories, neighbouring males often come into conflict. Typically, the two males will make 'parallel runs', with spread tails in a horizontal position, their bright red bill-combs vertical, the necks elongated, the heads bowing repeatedly. From time to time the birds stop suddenly, confront each other and, with necks curved and bills opened, utter long, rasping, cackling sounds. The rivals beat each other with their wings and also peck at one another. Sometimes battles are so vigorous that rivals roll across the ground as a single feather ball. The winner pursues his rival over a considerable distance, on the ground or in the air. Conflicts may also occur between females within the same nesting territory of a male.

Nests are situated in open places with sparse, low grass, and scattered, lichen-covered rocks and stones. The nest may be placed under a large stone: in very rare cases, among thick heath or grass or in tussocks among the sphagnum-cotton-tail bogs (Sdobnikov, 1957; Watson, 1965). The nest is a shallow scrape in the ground with some dry litter lining (grass stems, the hen's feathers, etc), or without any lining. Clutch size varies in different years and populations, but in general clutches are much smaller than for Willow Grouse, averaging 6.5–7 (Watson, 1963; Weeden, 1965) and are minimal in Japan (5.6–6.0, Sakurai, Tsuruta, 1972). In extreme northerly populations, egg-laying begins in the first half of June. Breeding is earlier in springs with rapid snow thaw, chicks hatching at the end of June, as in Scotland (Watson, 1965) and even in Japan, i.e. despite the latitudinal differences, breeding time differences are not great and overlap as a consequence of fluctuations due to local weather. In Scotland, in the very early spring in 1961, the first nestlings appeared at the end of May (Watson, 1963).

The female's incubation schedule is as Willow Grouse (Watson, 1963). Incubation varies from 21 to 23–24 days (Salomonsen, 1950b; Watson, 1963; MacDonald, 1970; Sakurai, 1972). The weight of a newly hatched chick is 15–21g (0.5–0.7oz) (Sakurai, 1972). The chicks begin flutter-flight activity from 10 days old, and by the age of two weeks can cover a distance of up to 2.5m (8.2ft) (MacDonald, 1970). After leaving the nest, the brood wanders mainly within the limits of the nesting territory (Scotland, Japan), but on northern tundra displacements are larger, though even here some broods show very little mobility: one brood in Alaska covered 12.5km (7.8 miles) during a five-day period, while another stayed practically in one place during the same period (Weeden, 1965).

Males aid the protection of young hatchlings, but once the chicks are a few days old, some leave the brood and move to another habitat for the intensive moult phase (Semenow-Tianshansky, 1959; Vorobiev, 1963; Watson, 1963; Kishinski, 1968; Perfiliev, 1975). These males return a month later, by which time the chicks have a body weight of about 350g (12.3oz). Young birds attain adult size in the southern parts of the range by the time they are three months old (Sakurai, 1972), but in northern populations growth is much more intensive and finishes at two months of age (Salomonsen, 1950b).

Broods begin to amalgamate into flocks at the end of August. During the autumn, such flocks can be large, up to 300 birds, but later such large gatherings divide into smaller groups and disperse. Data on autumn lek activity is very scarce, but was observed between 15–17 October in a study on the Kola Peninsula (Novikov, 1952a).

Hunting, recreation and conservation

At present, most populations are remote from significant human activity, and are relatively untroubled. Where Rock Ptarmigan come into close contact with man, populations are rapidly reduced or eliminated, in part because of the species' inherent trustfulness and absence of fear. In North America, the species was listed as Legal Game in 1970 in Alaska, British Columbia, Newfoundland, Quebec, Alberta, Manitoba, Ontario and Saskatchewan (Johnsgard, 1973). Local people in remote parts of the range also take the birds for eating and for use as trap bait for fur-bearing animals. However, in the main continental parts of the species' range, the human population density is so low that hunting influence is considered minimal in comparison to other causes of mortality. In these areas, the highest bird mortality is almost certainly as a result of the importance of species as a food source for High Arctic raptors: the species is, for instance, a very important resource to the Gyrfalcon (Potapov, Sale, 2005), as well to mammal predators, chiefly the Arctic Fox.

In Iceland, management of Rock Ptarmigan numbers means that hunting is banned in years of low numbers (Nielsen, Peterson, 1995) and there is total protection in reserves totalling 29,220km² (11,282 sq miles).

6.3 White-tailed Ptarmigan *Lagopus leucurus* (Swainon, 1831)

Tetrao (Lagopus) leucurus (Swainson in Swainson, Richardson, 1831): 356 (Rocky Mountains, 54°N)
The smallest representative of the grouse family.

Morphology

Generally similar to the Rock Ptarmigan, but differing chiefly in having a completely white winter plumage, including the tail feathers. The wing is wider than in the Rock Ptarmigan (60.7% of wing length). Important features are the narrower, higher pelvis, and the presence of rudimentary pectinations (1.0–1.5mm long, among the feathering of the toes), and longer feathers closer to the toe ends (Potapov, 1985).

Colouration

Adult male
Winter plumage: The feathering is completely white.
Spring plumage (April–May): Plumage is mottled, scattered brown-blackish feathers occurring among the white winter feathers. These coloured feathers appear firstly on head and neck, later on breast and upper back. As the year progresses, more coloured feathers appear.
Summer plumage: All upper body is dark, almost black, with a rough, streaked design from thin greyish-yellow and whitish cross-stripes. Some coloured feathers have white top borders that wear off by summer's end. Lower body is pale yellowish-grey, apart from central belly and thighs, which remain white. All flying feathers are white, only the central pair of tail feathers having the same grey-yellowish colour as the rump.
Autumn plumage: Upper parts vary from yellowish to reddish-yellow, mixed with grey, and with thin blackish streaks. The blackish cross-stripes on head are wider and form a more or less regular pattern. Sides of head, chin and throat are white with thin dark-brown stripes, with these wider on breast feathers. Flanks are yellowish-grey with blackish-brown spots. Legs are white with small number of grey feathers.

Adult female
Winter plumage: As in male.
Summer plumage: As male, but more saturated by an ochreous-yellowish tint.
Autumn plumage: Similar to male, but upper body, throat and breast are more ochreous, with blackish streaks.

Male White-tailed Ptarmigan

Female White-tailed Ptarmigan

Male and female in first adult (autumn) plumage
Similar to adult female autumn plumage, but less yellowish/more grey. The two central pairs of tail feathers are pale yellow with dark-brown cross-stripes. Third central pair has coloured inner web, but white outer web. All primaries and secondaries are dark-brown, only the two outer primaries being white.

Juvenile (both sexes)
Similar to first autumn plumage, but top of head is covered by grey-yellow, white and black patches, and many feathers on back and rump have large blackish and whitish spots. Chin and throat are white.

Downy chick
Crown is yellowish-brown with black bordering. Forehead and nostril feathers are white with black spots. Sides of head are white with black stripes from bill back through eye (see Figure 72, n2). Another interrupted stripe goes from bill base across lower sides of head. Nape and interscapular space are reddish-brown; middle of back, rump and uppertail coverts are yellowish-brown with blackish-brown stripes on both sides of upper body. Wings are yellow-grey with reddish-brown spots and stripes. Underbody is yellowish-greyish-white, with an indistinct yellow tint to breast and belly centre. Flanks have dark-brown patches.

All colourations are in accordance with Ridgway, Friedmann (1946).

Dimensions
Male: wing length 176.7mm (range 164–188mm); tail length 97.8mm (85–106mm); tarsi 32.7 (30.5–34.7mm); middle toe 25.6mm (23.8–28.3mm) (N=28 for all measurements). Females (36): wing length 173.1mm (155–183mm); tail length 88.5mm (84–106mm); tarsi 32.2mm (29.8–34.7mm); middle toe 25.1 (23.6–28.3mm) (N=36 for all measurements). All data from Ridgway, Friedmann, 1946.
Specimens from Coll ZIN RAN gave: male (N=2): wing length 173mm and 172mm; tail length 82mm and 94mm; bill length 8.4mm and 9.8mm; bill width 6.9mm and 7.0mm; tarsi 29.0mm and 29.5mm; middle toe 26mm and 28mm. Female (N=2): wing length 179mm and 184mm; tail length 89mm and 95mm; bill length 7.8mm and 9.7mm; bill width 6.4mm and 6.9mm; tarsi 29.5 and 32.0mm; middle toe 28.0mm and 29.5mm. Male weight: 323g/11.4oz (maximum 430g/15.2oz, N=24, Johnson, Lockner, 1968). Female weight: 329g/11.6oz (maximum 490g/17.3oz, N=14, Rogers, in Johnsgard, 1973). The average weight of males and females in Alaska: 355±11g/12.5±0.3oz (N=5, captured 19 October); 363±9g/12.8±0.3oz (N=12, captured 20 December); 369±8g/13±0.3oz (N=10, captured 6–8 March) (Moss, 1974).

Moult

Similar to other ptarmigans, but a detailed description is as yet unavailable. From photographs taken on 30 May in the southern range (mountains of Colorado), the moult begins very late, only at the end of May (Bent, 1932). In another photograph (Montana, 18 June), a male has already almost completed the moult to summer plumage. In general, though, coloured feathers appear in May and are not divided into spring and summer types, as they are in other ptarmigans. Most coloured feathers appear firstly not on the head, as in Rock Ptarmigan, but on the breast (photos in Johnsgard, 1973). Two males from Coll ZIN RAN, collected 24 and 25 July in different parts of the Rocky Mountains, show clear moult to autumn plumage. Nearly all of the upper parts of the bodies are covered by autumn feathers, under which are hidden well-worn summer feathers. Primaries 6 and 7 have also changed. A male from Ashnola River, British Columbia, taken 4 October, had completed the moult to winter plumage: primary 10 and half the feathers of the upper body are white, the remaining being autumn and a few summer feathers. The underbody is white, apart from the sides of the breast, where many autumn feathers remain, and the centre breast, which has a few autumn feathers. The times of the moults to autumn and winter plumage appear similar to those in Rock Ptarmigan (Potapov, 1985).

A rare case has been described (Braun, Martin, 2001) of two females found in the Colorado Mountains in August in full winter plumage without any signs of moult. Despite the conspicuous colouration, the behaviour of both birds appeared normal (and clearly the birds had survived for some time). The authors consider the reason for such an unusual event was failure of the hormones that initiate the winter–summer change.

Distribution

Inhabits only the subalpine and alpine belts of North American Cordilleras from the Alaska Range and Nahanni Mountains (66°N) south to 36°N (Sangre de Cristo Mountains, New Mexico). There is some doubtful information about the range's northern borders in Alaska and Canada. According to the Cornell Laboratory Map, the northern range includes only the Alaska Range in Alaska and Mackenzie Mountains north to 68°N (the south-eastern end of the Richardson Mountains) with two large protuberances to the north-west and north from 60°N. In another, newer, map (Alsop, 2002), the northern border is a straight line along the 64°N latitude line from the Alaska Range east to the centre of the Mackenzie Mountains. In a third, older, map (Johnsgard, 1973) the range border from the eastern end of the Alaska Range goes south-east to the Coastal Range, the Mackenzie Mountains range being isolated from the main range and covering all the mountains north-west to the sources of Porcupine River at 67°N. Of the numerous islands in the Pacific Basin, the species inhabits only Vancouver Island and the Alexandra Archipelago.

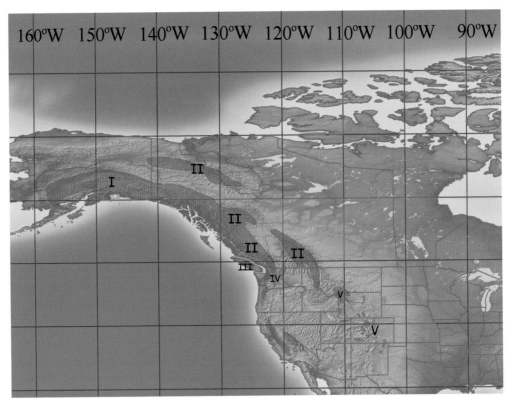

Map 14. White-tailed Ptarmigan (*Lagopus leucurus*).
Subspecies: I – L. l. peninsularis*; II –* L. l. leucurus*; III –* L. l. saxatilis*; IV –* L. l. rainierensis*; V –* L. l.
altipetens.
1 – Population introduced.

Subspecies

At present five subspecies are recognized, three of which differ only in the colouration of
the male's summer plumage (in comparison to the nominative): *L. l. peninsularis* is greyer,
L. l. rainieriensis is darker; with two differences in size – *L. l. saxatilis* has a longer wing and
a larger, steeply curved bill, while *L. l. altipetens* has a longer wing and tail.

L. l. leucurus (Swainson, 1831)
Inhabits all the northern part of the species' range, excluding the coastal mountain ridges
of Alaska, south to the Canada–USA border.

L. l. peninsularis (Chapman, 1902)
Inhabits the coastal mountain system of south-western Alaska from the Kenai Peninsula
through the Alaska Range and St Elias Mountains south to the Admiralty archipelago
and the sources of the Iskur River.

L. l. saxatilis (Cowan, 1939)
Found only in the mountains of central Vancouver Island.

L. l. rainierensis (Taylor, 1920)
Found only in a small area of the Rocky Mountains in Washington State, from Mount Jack (47°50′N) south to Mount Adams (46°12′N).

L. l. altipetens (Osgood, 1901)
Inhabits the most elevated ridges in the southern Rocky Mountains: Bighorn Ridge, Absaroka Range, Gallatin and Madison in the Yellowstone National Park, Savage Ridge in the western part of San-Juan Mountains, and the Sangre de Cristo Mountains, New Mexico, south to 35°59.08′N.

Habitats

White-tailed Ptarmigan inhabit upper mountain belts above the timberline. The birds prefer sloping ground, steep or gentle, and flat passes with rocks and patches of wet alpine grass, not tall enough to hide a bird, and where dwarf bushes are no higher than 45cm (17.7in). The birds avoid bush-tree vegetation and swamps. In winter, they descend to bush thickets at the timberline, but do not descend further. In most areas of Colorado, for example, the birds prefer rich thickets of alpine willow. There are no marked seasonal displacements, as are observed in the other ptarmigan species.

Population structure and density

Population densities, particularly in autumn, may be high, but never reach the levels of the other ptarmigans. The normal density during the breeding season is 5.9–7.5 birds per 100ha (247 acres), with an observed maximum of 19.5 birds/100ha (Johnsgard, 1973). There are no data on the sex ratio in populations. The percentage of young birds in autumn populations varies from 33–47%. The annual mortality of young birds is 63%, that of adults 29%. Data from marked birds suggests a comparatively long life, 12 of 36 females, and 16 of 31 males still being alive after 5 years (Choate, 1963).

Territoriality

Of the three ptarmigan species, the White-tailed Ptarmigan is the most sedentary, not only during the breeding season, but also during winter. In Colorado, birds covered about a mile each day during the winter, roaming from place to place in search of forage and moving up to 24km (15 miles) in total over the season. However, during the breeding season the birds rarely move more than 457m (500yd) per day. After incubation, males and broodless females move to higher elevations close to melting snow patches. Females with broods also move higher, but only by about 549m (600yd) to summer brood-rearing areas (Braun, Rogers, 1967b). Sometimes, broodless females may cover longer distances, up to 16km (10 miles), during autumn displacements (Braun, 1969).

Nutrition

The winter diet in southern parts of the range consists mainly of willow twigs and buds, the bushes of which remain available above the snow cover. Among other plants, males take grasses on hilltops from which the snow has been scoured by wind, while alder buds and catkins are eaten by females wintering in the upper parts of the forest belt (May, Braun, 1972). In Alaska, the winter diet consists of alder catkins and buds (up to 77%), willow buds and twigs (up to 57%) and buds and catkins of birches (up to 46%). Stems of grass and the berries of crowberry are also eaten (Weeden, 1967). The author believes that this diversity of food items avoids competition in those areas of the species' wintering range where it overlaps with one or both of the other ptarmigan species.

The autumn diet chiefly comprises willow leaves, these making up to 98% of crop contents. The same food source is also the main constituent of the summer (June) diet of birds in the coastal areas of British Columbia. In the northern part of this province, and in Alberta, buds, twigs and leaves of willows are the main food items from May to September. Willow is therefore the most important item in the nutrition of the species over its entire range. That said, the summer diet is more varied, about 50% of the food intake comprising the green leaves, stems, flowers and seeds of *Stellaria, Potentilla, Ranunculus, Dryas, Saxifraga* species, and bulbils of *Polygonum viviparum*, most of which have high protein contents. Much the same list of food plants has been shown to comprise the autumn diet in the northern part of range, with the addition of seeds of *Draba* spp. In the southern part of the range (Colorado), a difference in the summer diet of males and females has been observed, bulbils of *Polygonum viviparum* being the major constituent of the female diet, while sedge and cereal seeds are most important in males (Weeden, 1967; May, Braun, 1972).

Wintering

In the southern part of the range, White-tailed Ptarmigan winter near the timberline, females in areas in which alder and willow bushes dominate, at altitudes of 2,550–3,000m (8,366–9,843ft), and males at a higher level, 3,300–3,600m (10,827–11,811ft), where dwarf trees dominate. However, this division of the sexes, which lasts from the end of November through to the end of March, is not absolutely complete. The winter life of the species in the northern part of the range is not, as yet, well studied.

The birds are minimally active during winter days, spending most of the time motionless in open snow holes. During walks to forage, the birds move slowly, keeping their bodies close to the snow cover, and in open places, in contrast to summer days, are very cautious. Wintering flocks can reach 50–60 birds, but these flocks are rarely compact, the birds tending to disperse in small groups. Activity is minimal at midday, though the birds tend to rest and feed more or less simultaneously at all times. By late afternoon the birds often need to move to a different feeding area, which they usually do with a short flight. Before the flight the birds stop feeding, turn their heads, presumably to watch for danger, then fly up simultaneously. After the flight, the birds resume feeding, moving quickly as they do, occasionally travelling up to 900m (984yd) in 30 minutes. Occasionally, the birds take buds from higher branches, jumping to reach them, as the buds from lower branches have already been consumed. Such activity makes them less cautious, allowing an observer to move within 3–6m (3.3–6.6yd). The birds roost overnight in snow burrows, excavating these very quickly by digging and by side-to-side body movements. Burrow tunnels are sometimes 60cm (24in) long, with the bird, as other grouse, occasionally putting its head out to control depth and to observe the surroundings. Observations suggest that the birds are never short of winter forage: in Colorado, they maintained fat deposits throughout the winter and, indeed, had actually accumulated greater reserves as spring approached, in sharp contrast to the other two ptarmigan species, despite the fact that ambient temperatures in January can fall to –36°C (–33°F), the average January temperature being –16°C (3°F) (Braun, Schmidt, 1971; May, Braun, 1972).

A group of male White-tailed Ptarmigan in Gunella Pass, Colorado

Breeding

White-tailed Ptarmigan are monogamous, though occasionally two, or even three, females have been observed to nest in a male's territory. Males return to the breeding grounds first, nuptial activity beginning with the appearance of snow-free ground and increasing sharply when the females arrive. Males establish individual territories, the size of which increases as snow melts. On average, individual territories vary from 6.4 –18.8ha (15.8–46.4 acres), though only about 20–30% is used and truly defended. Males demonstrate territorial behaviour up to the time of brood hatching.

Male courtship displays are similar to those of other ptarmigan species, though there are specifics. The first of these concerns the demonstrative flight, which does not include a 'hill', and is accompanied by very different vocalizations. At the start, the male utters a short, four-syllable raucous 'ku-ku-kiiiii-kiiierrrr', this being repeated 3–4 times at intervals of 1–3 seconds. The third syllable is similar to the cry of terns. Similar vocalizations may also be made by females. Male courtship displays near the female, i.e. those that precede mating, are similar to those of Rock Ptarmigan (R. Schmidt cited in Johnsgard, 1973). In the main courtship posture, the neck and head, and the tail, are raised. The male then approaches the female with a series of short, quick steps and inclines his head and neck to her side. But though the display is similar to the Rock Ptarmigan, the male White-tailed Ptarmigan looks very different from his Rock cousin, there being no colours to contrast the white plumage, apart from the bright red, and maximally broadened, eye-combs, and several black patches on head, neck and breast. The Rock Ptarmigan male in this posture has strongly contrasting black tail feathers, raised vertically and spread to look like the spokes of a wheel, but the same broadened red eye-comb and blackish spots on the head, neck and breast (though without spots in the far north). The Willow Grouse male differs from both in having a red-brown head, neck and breast.

The nest is a shallow scrape with a diameter of about 12.5cm (4.9in), lined with grass stems, leaves, the hen's feathers, etc. When incubating, the female is well camouflaged, the colouration of the upper body merging with the surrounding, lichen-covered stones. The clutch is usually 6–8 eggs, but can vary from 4–15. Eggs are, on average, 43.0–29.5mm. The shell colour is whitish or red-yellowish, rarely marked or patched with brown. Incubation is 22–23 days. Males usually stay near the nest to protect it until hatching, after which they leave their territory for higher grounds, close to melting snow patches to moult: here they are joined by broodless females.

Females and broods move slowly within the limits of the nesting territory, the size of which varies in different years from 8–16ha (20–40 acres). The female and brood stay within a few hundred metres of the nest site during the first month of chick life, then gradually move to green sedge meadows at higher altitudes, though they do not reach the altitudes where the males are moulting (Braun, Rogers, 1967b). All the birds begin to join

Female White-tailed Ptarmigan

flocks towards the end of August (Choate, 1963; Braun, Schmidt, 1971; May Broun, 1972; Johnsgard, 1973).

In Montana, mating was at the beginning of June, egg laying in mid-June, the chicks hatching at the beginning of July: by the end of July the chicks could fly (Choate, 1963). Changes to this schedule will, of course, occur due to weather conditions in different years: later or repeated clutches may hatch as late as 18 July.

Hunting, recreation and conservation

White-tailed Ptarmigan is a legal game bird across practically all its range – hunting is banned only on Canada's Vancouver Island and in Washington State, USA. Hunting is permitted, with seasonal and bag limits in the remaining US states where the species is found, despite the fragmented nature of its range, which has led to concerns over the long-term viability of some populations. General opinion is that hunting for such a small bird at high altitude in remote areas strongly restricts the likelihood of adverse results and so there is no need for a ban (Braun *et al.*, 1993).

The reasons for the decline in numbers of the species include overgrazing by livestock and the building of ski areas. Management of the species in these, and other areas, requires the regulation of hunting, the seasonal closure of high mountain roads, limits on hunting bag, etc, but definitive information on hunting activity is scarce. The situation regarding the populations introduced to California's Sierra Mountains (southward from Sonora Pass at 38°25′N) in 1971–71 is better as the species has been well studied. During the subsequent 18 years, the species colonized the alpine habitats along the main ridges northwards for 79km (49 miles) and southward for 114km (71 miles). Despite the low population densities, the sex and age ratios were similar to native populations (Frederick, Gutierrez, 1992).

CHAPTER 8

Lyrurus (Swainson in Swainson, Richardson, 1831): 497. *Tetrao* (Short, 1967): 32.
Type, by original designation, *Tetrao tetrix* (Linneaus).

The genus comprises two Palearctic species, the Black Grouse, with its vast, trans–Palearctic range, and the Caucasian Black Grouse, with a very small, relic range. The Black Grouse was removed from the genus *Tetrao* by Swainson (1831) because of the unique shape of the male's tail feathers. However, the new genus was not initially recognized, and when the Caucasian Black Grouse was first described in 1875, it was placed in the genus *Tetrao*, only being redefined in *Lyrurus* much later (Ogilvie-Grant, 1893; Satunin, 1907; Nesterow, 1911 and others). Some authors continue to consider the new genus as incorrect, either on the basis of argument (Short, 1967), or with no supporting argument (Glutz von Blotzheim *et al.*, 1973; Watson, Moss, 2008, etc). Short placed the capercaillies and the black grouses in one genus – *Tetrao* – on the base of similarities in size and colour; the prominent sexual dimorphism; the feathering of the tarsi and toes; the number (18) and length of tail feathers; and the colour of eggs and nestlings. But close examination reveals flaws in these arguments: male capercaillie are twice the length and four times the weight of male black grouse; colour similarities are restricted to the Western Capercaillie (and not all subspecies of that); tarsi and toe feathering are similar in all grouse species; several grouse have 18 tail feathers and in some species individuals may have 14–24 feathers, making use of retrices to differentiate or unite species difficult; the length of the tail feathers in grouse is strongly dependent on the role of the tail in mating displays; and the Tetraonids have a single egg colour (yellow-brown background and brown markings) and downy chicks of essentially similar colour and similar brown, black–bordered, head 'caps' (though this is absent in *Tetrao urogallus* (**Figure 73**).

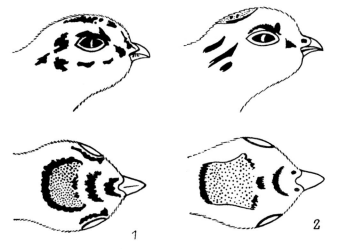

Figure 73. Head pattern of downy young *Lyrurus tetrix*
1 – Western populations; 2 – Eastern populations.

1

2

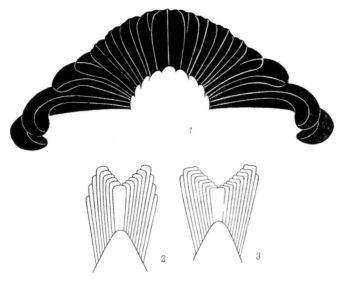

Figure 74. Tails
Tails of the male (1) and female (2) Lyrurus tetrix, *and female L. mlokosiewiczi (3).*

In addition, the skull shape of capercaillie males is unique, as is the form of the male's outer retrices in black grouse, and the preferred habitats of capercaillie and black grouse differ markedly.

The plumage of adult Black Grouse males (both species) is black, with only minor white and grey additions. The first year-old male plumage differs, especially in Caucasian Black Grouse: in the first description of the species a one-year-old male was described as female (Taczanowski, 1875). Males of both species also have a specific summer plumage, mainly on the head and neck, distinguishing the genus from others of the family apart from the *Lagopus*. However, the clearest characteristic of males of the genus is the bifurcated tail and unique curved form of elongated lateral retrices. In Black Grouse (which normally have 18 tail feathers), the most elongated and curved are the outer, 9, pair, the curvature and length decreasing to the 6th pair: the remaining feathers have the normal form, the central pair being the shortest (**Figure 74**). The outer retrices are twice the length of the central pair. The tail of male Caucasian Black Grouse is also bifurcated, but the difference between the length of the outer and central retrices is smaller, a factor of 1.33. The form of the retrices is also very different: in Black Grouse the curved part of the feathers is in the same plane, while in Caucasian males, each feather is curved downwards and has the vanes diverging from the shaft at an angle of nearly 95° to form a 'gutter' (**Figure 75**).

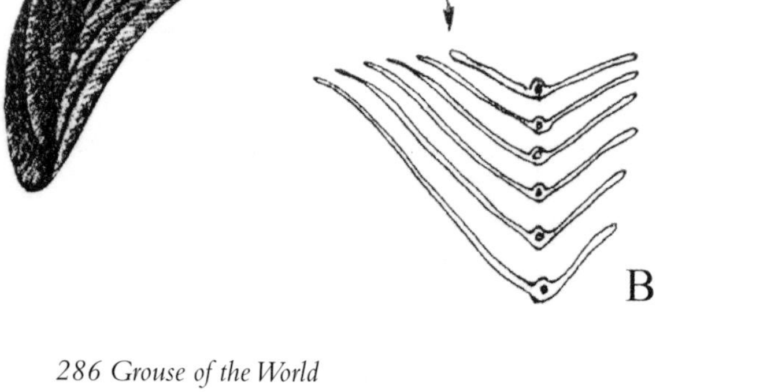

Figure 75. Caucasian Black Grouse tail
'B' is a section through the tail ('A') showing the 'gutter-like' construction of the feathers.

The development of final adult colouration in Black Grouse takes several years, evidence of a primitive characteristic since rapid development implies a more advanced character. Stegmann (1932) and Potapov (1985; 2005) showed that *L. t. viridanus* has the most primitive adult male colouration, with the most advanced being *L. t. britannicus*. Some ancestral features, such as the black throat spot with indistinct white bordering in first adult plumage, are present in the first subspecies (see Figure 25, n4 in Chapter 1). Androgynous females (i.e. females with limited female sexual hormones) in *L. tetrix* are very dark, but not black, and look like one-year-old *L. t. danus* males, but with more ancestral features. This is important phylogenetic information, as male colouration, hidden in the female's genome, is removed from the pressure of natural selection and so may preserve ancestral features.

The aberrant colouration of many Black Grouse specimens also offers interesting data regarding the content of the species' genome. Kots (1937) described 27 such aberrations, 9 for males and 18 for females, but no aberrations were found in *L. mlokosiewiczi*. The most remarkable feature in the colouration of all aberrant males is the development of depigmentation (white colour) of feathers in different parts of the body, expressed to a various degree and occasionally resulting in complete albinism. One of these aberrant forms, named *marginata* by Prof. Kots, suddenly appeared in southern Norway in large numbers: males of one local population were so different in colouration, they were described as a new subspecies, *L. tetrix bjerkreimensis* (Schaanning, 1921). The distribution of this mutation was restricted to a small area and its future is unknown. The colour of the aberrant males was similar to the spring plumage of male Willow Ptarmigan.

Hybrids of Black Grouse with other grouse species are rare, though hybrids with both capercaillie, the two Eurasian ptarmigans, Asian Spruce Grouse and even pheasant and domestic hen have been described. The most stable features of these hybrids are the bifurcated tail, the white 'mirror' on the wing, and the black upper body. Most feathers also possess a white fringe at the apex. In male *L. tetrix* x *Lagopus lagopus* hybrids, the eye-combs are of *Lagopus* form, and under the thick toe feathering, pectinations are preserved, as in the White-tailed Ptarmigan. This is interesting as the Caucasian Black Grouse eye-comb has the same structure as in ptarmigans, while in *L. tetrix* the eye-comb is of the same type as in *Bonasa, Falcipennis, Dendragapus* and *Tetrao* (see Figure 45, n2 and n3 in Chapter 4).

Both black grouse species prefer open or semi-open habitats with a prevalence of deciduous trees (birches, alders, aspens, willows, etc). The birds avoid closed coniferous forests, and also have a specific winter diet, dominated by the twigs, buds and catkins of deciduous trees, chiefly birch.

7.1 BLACK GROUSE *Lyrurus tetrix* (Linneaeus, 1758)

Tetrao tetrix (Linnaeus, 1758). Synonyms: *T. betulinus* (Scopoli, 1769); *T. ericaceus* (Brehm, 1831); *Lyrurus tetrix* (Swainson, Richardson, 1831).

Morphology

Medium-sized bird with significant sexual dimorphism in size and colouration. The most remarkable feature is the deeply bifurcated tail, in which the outer retrices are the longest and have tops that curve outwards (see **Figure 74**). The tarsi are feathered to the base, and the base of the central toe is also feathered. The species has a reduced ability to survive very low winter temperatures, this being the reason for its absence from the sparse larch forests of eastern Siberia, despite the presence there of significant numbers of birch trees and the species' ability to feed on the buds and twigs of larches, as it does in the upper forest belt of the European Alps (Zettel, 1974).

Colouration

Adult male

General colouration is black with a violet-blue gloss on the head, neck, rump, breast and, to a lesser degree, the back. There is a large white patch ('mirror') on the wing and undertail coverts. Lower belly is brown, with wide whitish tops on hair-like feathers. Primaries are dark-brown with whitish shafts and whitish margins of the outer webs of Nos. 4–6, and wide white patches on the lower half of Nos. 1–5. These white patches, together with the white secondaries bases, form the 'mirror' (**Figure 76**). Secondaries are white, with broad black bands occupying most of the upper half, but white margins at the tops. The white bases decrease in size towards the inner secondaries and are absent on the last of these. The width of the black band increases from the outer to the inner secondaries and the innermost one or two feathers are completely black. There are white patches on the great coverts, which form a separate white stripe visible on the open wing (**Figure 76**). Secondary coverts and

Figure 76. Opened wing of male *Lyrurus tetrix*

Male Black Grouse

alula feathers have white lower parts. Underwing coverts are mostly white, this creating the white underwing that is clearly visible during flight. All retrices are black.

Adult male

In first adult plumage: Differs by having a less pronounced gloss to black feathers and presence of brown stripes on most scapulars, secondaries, inner primaries and uppertail coverts, the latter also having blackish-brown tops.

In second adult plumage: The brown stripes practically disappear, remaining only partially on the inner wing. Some stripes remain even in the third adult plumage, but not beyond that age.

In summer plumage: Present only on head and neck, especially in southern populations. Summer feathers are a mottled pattern due to light-brown cross-stripes on a brown background. Feathers on throat and upper part of neck front are completely white

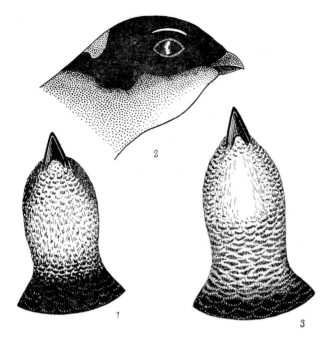

or have broad white tops, these forming a white throat patch in most cases (**Figure 77**).

Adult female
Mottled overall with a brown nuance and cross-stripe pattern. Upper body is yellow-brown with grey and black cross-stripes and patches. Sometimes the black-brown stripes combine, the yellow-brown stripes that divided them preserved only as two small patches along the vane edges. The design of the feathers varies greatly. Retrices have wide black and brown cross-bands, as

Figure 77. Summer plumage pattern
On the neck of male Lyrurus tetrix *(1, 2) and* L. mlokosiewiczi *(3).*

Female Black Grouse

in wing coverts. Greater ones are brown with a white base to outer vanes, and blackish, with weak stripes to the main parts. Primaries are brown with unclear white bordering and whitish stripes on outer vanes, and large white patches at inner vane bases, these decreasing toward the outer ones and absent on the four outer primaries. Secondaries are white with broad, brown top bands, and brown streaks covering almost the entire upper feathers. Lower body has a more even cross-striped pattern, especially on breast where dark-yellow and brown stripes alternate. Some birds have an indistinct, whitish gular patch. Lower breast and belly have two types of colouration. In the first, the belly is black-brown, with the surrounding feathers covered by a pattern that is whitish, created by broad, untwisted white feather tops. In the second, the entire underbody has an even cross-stripe pattern. Base of undertail is white, the undertail coverts having broad white tops and brown cross-bands. Tarsi feathering is light-grey or whitish.

Juvenile
Mottled overall, with dark-brown, black, yellow-brown and white stripes and patches creating a complicated design. Breast feather shafts are white and form an indistinct longitudinal pattern. On secondaries, upperwing coverts and scapular feathers, the cross-stripe design is cut off by a longitudinal white shaft stripe that spreads towards the feather tops and is finished by a characteristic white patch in the form of an inverted triangle. In some populations (forest-steppe of western Siberia), the secondaries have white bases. Primaries are brown with thin white top borders, an indistinct cross-stripe pattern on the outer vanes, and brownish inner vanes. Retrices are cross-striped, with the little white triangle top patches.

Downy chick
Sulphur-yellow below with darker breast. Upper body is brown-yellow with indistinct longitudinal and thin cross-stripes. Brown cap on crown has black bordering and a horseshoe patch in front of it (see Figure 73).

Dimensions
Significant sexual dimorphism in size and weight. There are also differences between birds of differing ages, and geographical variations. Males take three years to attain full size, the change being especially prominent between the second and third years. Females are full-grown at two years. In each case, however, there are significant individual variations, these depending on the time of hatching, and local conditions during growth periods. Dimensions of 152 adult males and 109 adult females (in parenthesis) in Coll ZIN RAN are: wing length 257–296mm (219–254mm); tail 93–270mm (88–123mm); difference between central and outer retrices 45–113mm (10–36mm); bill 13.5–18.4mm (12.3–18.0mm); bill width 10.5–13.6mm (9.8–12.4mm); tarsi 40–49mm (37–45mm);

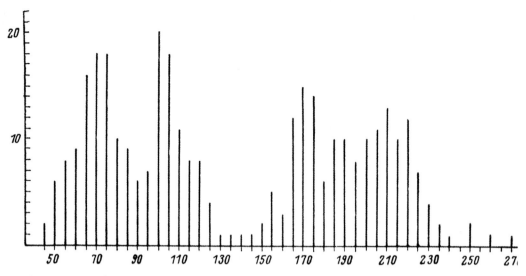

Figure 78. Length of male *Lyrurus tetrix* tails (Coll ZIN RAN)
Vertical axis – number of specimens, horizontal axis – length in mm. The graph shows distinct peaks at bird ages of one, two and three years, clearly indicating that tail length increases as the bird ages (Potapov, 1985).

central toe 40–50mm (39–45mm). The length of the tail in males increases with age (**Figure 78**).

In general, seasonal changes in body weight are as other grouse species. In Western Europe, the usual body weight of adult males in the spring is 1,100g–1,250g (2.42–2.76lb), and in autumn is 1,200g–1,350g (2.65–2.98lb). In both seasons, birds with weights of 1,500–1,600g (3.31–3.53lb), and even 1,800g (3.97lb), are found (Couturier, 1980). More rarely, males with weights to 2,000–2,100g (4.41–5.63lb) are seen (Wurm, 1897; Fuschlberger, 1956).

In Finland, the average weight of males was: 1,220g/2.69lb (September) and 1,270g/2.80lb (October–December). Maximal weight was 1,540g/3.39lb (N=1,065, Koskimies, 1958).Young males may reach the weight of the adults very quickly, sometimes even during their first autumn. In Finland, young males averaged 1,100g/2.42lb (September); 1,190g/2.62lb (October); 1,250g/2.76lb (November–December) (Koskimies, 1958).

In the Pechora Basin, the highest weight seen in autumn/early winter was 1,650g/3.64lb (A. Estafiev, pers. comm.). In northern Kazakhstan, male weights were similar, but in Tian-Shan Mountains, they were higher (Kuzmina, 1962).

Data on the weight of females is scarce. In Finland, average female weight in September was 900g/1.98lb; 960g/2.12lb (October); 990g/2.18lb (November); and 980g/2.16lb (December) (N=774, Koskimies, 1958).

Moult

The moult sequence is similar to that of most grouse species. The downy plumage of newly hatched nestlings changes to juvenile plumage at about two weeks, and 1–2 days later juvenile primaries begin to change into adults (Rodionow, 1963c). The contour feathering of first adult plumage appears firstly on the sides of the breast, the rump, the centre and sides of the belly; then the back, the breast centre, head and neck. The change of juvenile to adult retrices occurs with the change of the 6th primary, when the bird is 50 days old. This moult to first adult plumage finishes when the birds are 110–120 days old (end of September), though occasionally the innermost secondaries are preserved until December, and several small juvenile feathers on the breast and the neck until January (Rodionov, 1963b; Potapov, 1985). The next moult, in summer, is only partial, with loss of the 10th primary (end of May), and involves feathers of the head, neck and, partly, the breast. It lasts until early August, and is combined partly with the autumn moult. The latter is better expressed in southern populations than northern ones. The summer moult in females is less prominent. The full autumn moult, during which all feathers (including summer ones) are changed, begins in males with the 1st primary and ends as winter begins. Females start the full moult immediately after chick hatching, but finish at the same time as the males.

Distribution

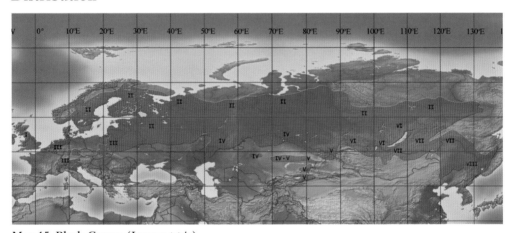

Map 15. Black Grouse (*Lyrurus tetrix*)
Subspecies: I – L. t. britannicus; *II* – L. t. tetrix; *III* – L. t. juniperorum; *IV* – L. t. viridanus; *V* – L. t. mongolicus; *VI* – L. t. jenisseensis; *VII* – L. t baikalensis; *VIII* – L. t. ussuriensis.

The species range covers practically all the forest and forest-steppe zones of Eurasia from the Atlantic (in Britain and Scandinavia) almost to the Pacific, the eastern limit being as close as 100–150km (62–93 miles) to the ocean (Shulpin, 1936; Austin, 1948). In the west, along the 30°E longitude line, the range width is from 51°N to 69°N, a distance of nearly 2,100km (1,305 miles). In general, the range borders are determined by the northern edge of the taiga zone and southern distribution of the forest-steppe zone. The northernmost point of the range is in Scandinavia, where it reaches 70°N.

There is little doubt that in Western Europe the range was originally solid, but it now consists of more than a dozen isolated parts. The decrease in the species' range has occurred in the last 200–300 years (both in Western Europe and across the entire forest-steppe zone) as a result of human activity.

Subspecies

Across the range, colouration, particularly of females, varies significantly. In most cases, such variations are not clinal. The size and weight of birds also varies, but to a lesser degree. Both increase towards the south of eastern Siberia, where they reach maximal extent. Among the many subspecies that have been described, only the following eight are currently recognized by taxonomists.

Lyrurus tetrix tetrix (Linnaeus, 1758)
Occupies all the range within the limits of the taiga zone from Scandinavia to Yakutia. The western and southern borders are not sharp, with wide transmission zones to neighbouring subspecies.

Lyrurus tetrix britannicus (Witherby and Lönnberg, 1913)
Inhabits the British Isles, chiefly Scotland, but also northern England and Wales. The British subspecies has the darkest colouration and the smallest size of the white 'mirror' on the wing in both sexes.

Lyrurus tetrix juniperorum (Brehm, 1831)
Colouration of males similar to British subspecies, but with more white on the secondaries. Females have more black-brown than British females. Restricted to Western and Central Europe, east to approximately the line from Luga (28°E) to Smolensk (32°E).

Lyrurus tetrix viridanus (Lorenz, 1891)
Colouration of males and females differs from all other subspecies. The development of the white colour on the wing is maximal. White bases to the retrices exist in 50% of males and 60% of females. The metallic gloss on the breast and rump is more green than violet. The males have brown streaks on the upper body, especially the secondaries and tertials at all ages, these areas never being completely black. Most females (79%) have a well-expressed white gular patch, 74% have a red-brown breast and 79% a black-brown patch at the centre of the belly. In both sexes, the difference in length between the central and outer retrices is greater than in any other subspecies. Inhabits the Forest-Steppe Zone from the valley of the Volga River eastward to Tomsk Province, and southward to the species' range border, except in eastern Kazakhstan, where the subspecies is contiguous with *L. t. mongolicus* and a

wide transmission zone between them runs from Mount Kyzyl-Ray (75°E) to Tchingiz-Tau (80°E).

Lyrurus tetrix jenisseensis (Sushkin, 1925)
Males are slightly darker than the previous subspecies and do not differ from that of the next subspecies. Female colouration is lighter and less brown than *L. t. mongolicus*. The range is not yet clear. In general, it is restricted to the Sayan-Altai Mountain system, northwards to the Yenisey mountain-ridge (57°N), eastward to the Hubsugul Lake region, westward to the Tigirinsky, Listviaga and Holzun ridges and southward to the species' range border.

Lyrurus tetrix mongolicus (Lönnberg, 1904)
The first designation regarding sites in Mongolia (Bain-Gol and Chan-Tengry mountains) was a mistake and was later corrected by the author – Lönnberg, 1905a). Now known to inhabit the south-eastern Altai (Tarbagatay ridge, mountains around Marka-Kul Lake), Kalbin, Tarbagatay-Saur, Dzungarian Ala-Tau, Boro-Khoro, Ketmen ridges and northern Tian-Shan Mountains.
Females have more dark brown above, and are darker grey with thick stripes below.

Lyrurus tetrix baikalensis (Lorenz, 1911)
Males and most females are distinguished by their very large size. In males, the shiny plumage has a more light-blue gloss than in the two previous subspecies. Females differ from previous subspecies by paler colour of the under body and the presence there of a cross-stripe pattern. Occupies the southern Baikal region eastward to the Great Khingan Mountains and Zeya River estuary in the Amur River valley (Potapov, 1985).

Lyrurus tetrix ussuriensis (Kohts, 1911)
Males are smaller than the Baikal subspecies and lack the stripe pattern on the upper body from the age of two years. Females are darker, with a more intensive red-brown tint. Occupies the south-eastern part of the species' range. The territories of constant nesting are mainly the central parts of the Amur River Basin, and the valleys of the Sungari and Ussuri rivers. Inhabits NE China south to 41°N and the NE corner of the Korean Peninsula south to 40°N.

Habitats
The optimal habitat is a combination of groves, bush thickets or large clearings in the Eurasian taiga and forest-steppe zones. In the taiga, the preferred habitat includes large bog areas or, in the western part of the range, heathland. The latter is especially important in Great Britain and coastal regions of the North and Baltic seas. Other habitats are sparse

Female Black Grouse

pine-birch woods in river valleys, fire-damaged areas, agricultural fields and the forest edges. In the forest-steppe zone the favoured habitat has birch and pine groves mixed with willow, dog rose, etc, thickets, alternating with agricultural fields.

Occasionally, the birds also occupy bush thickets in northern part of the steppe zone. In western Kazakhstan, where there were thickets of steppe cherry and blackberry, Black Grouse even penetrated semi-desert areas, where the berries of *Eleagnus* sp. thickets were an important source of winter nutrition, and co-existed with Stone Curlew (*Burhinus oedicnemus*) and Houbara Bustard (*Chlamydotis undulata*) (Sushkin, 1908).

In mountains, Black Grouse occupy upper forest limits or the lower margins of the forest belt in the foothills. In the Altai Mountains, for example, the birds live at the upper and lower forest edges, separated by the solid forest belt. This situation may formerly have been more common, but human activity at the lower forest margins has forced populations in many areas to extinction.

Seasonal changes in habitat occur only in the south of the species' range, with the birds there moving into forested areas with a high percentage of tall, old birches for the winter, as these trees are the main source of food.

Population structure and density

The sex ratio in adult birds is not constant. That said, in general, males tend to outnumber females in the northern part of the range, the reverse being the case in southern parts (Couturier, 1980 [France]; Ellison, 1978 [France]; Johnstone, 1969 [Great Britain]; Jurlov, 1960 [Kazakhstan]; Viht, 1975 [Estonia]; Rajala, 1974 [Finland]).

The ratio of young to old birds in a population depends entirely on breeding success in the current year. The normal ratio is 1.9–3.0 young birds per adult female, but if breeding success declines, this may fall to 0.3 per female (Rajala, 1974; Ellison, 1978).

The total number of birds in a population is higher in the southern range, particularly in eastern parts of the forest-steppe zone, where human activity has had less of an impact. But the high mobility of Black Grouse hampers evaluation of the results of local monitoring of the number of birds, because of the impossibility of differentiating the effect of immigration and emigration. Data on the maximum population density varies significantly across the range, but shows a clear tendency for a decline. In southern Finland and Russia's Pskov Province, maximum densities observed in the mid-20th century were 28.6–30.7 birds/km² in the autumn, and up to 15 birds/km² in spring (Rajala, 1966a, b; Rusakov, 1971). The latest data shows that such high values are much reduced, both in Russia and European countries: in Leningrad Province, for example, numbers have halved in the last 40 years from a value that was already lower – down from 3.3 birds/km² to 1.5 bird/km² (Ivanov, Potapov, 2008). A marked decline in overall numbers was noted in many places towards the end of the 20th century (Snow, Perrins, 1998), with some countries now having very small populations.

Territoriality

Black Grouse differ from other Palearctic forest grouse in having high mobility, with displacement of both individual birds and whole flocks being a feature of the species throughout its range. The displacements of entire populations is not uncommon, and are as likely to occur during times of a decline in population numbers as when numbers are increasing. Though movements are most often seen in the autumn, in general they are random events with no regular rhythm, apparently precipitated by local conditions. As an example, in southern Kola Peninsula, after a successful breeding season in 1965, the Black Grouse population moved west in October when vermin attacked the local birch trees, potentially reducing the availability of winter forage. Single females moved first, soon followed by massed flocks. The flocks rested near the shore of Kandalaksha Bay before crossing (a distance of 15km/9.3 miles), with the birds massing on the roofs of buildings, aerials, the cranes in the port, etc. In total, it took six weeks for the population to move, the remaining population in the area being very considerably reduced for several years (V. Biankhi, pers. info. in Potapov, 1985). A similar situation, but with a north–south transfer, was seen in the Pechora River Basin in 1895 (Reztzov, 1904). As a consequence of such movements, winter population densities may occasionally increase by up to 14 times the normal density (Teplov, 1947b), this being observed near Tomsk in eastern Siberia (Kareev, 1928), and in China's Sungary River Valley (Shulpin, 1936).

Similar movements are not possible in isolated parts of the range, as alternative habitats do not exist. In such areas, Black Grouse are forced to accept a more sedentary life, and the stability of leks, and even of individual territories, year on year, is observed (e.g. de Vos, 1983). The individual territories of males in Western European populations can be very large: 90–120ha (222–297 acres) in the Alps (Pauli, 1974), and up to 303–689ha (749–1,703 acres) in Scotland and Holland (Robel, 1969; de Vos, 1983). Such individual territories may be separated one from another, but usually overlap. The territory of a female and brood is considerably less: in the Pskov Province of western Russia, it varied in different years from 2.22–4ha (5.49–9.88 acres) (Rusakov, 1976).

Behaviour

During the summer, Black Grouse are mainly terrestrial. The preferred habitat is then thick grass or bushes, open places being avoided, especially in areas where the species is hunted. In such areas the birds are extremely careful, becoming very elusive. The birds' eyesight and hearing are excellent, which allow them to evade hunters: they are also confident and adroit in trees. If danger threatens from a terrestrial predator, males utter a low, guttural 'ghuk…ghuk…ghuk'. If the danger is from the air, a different sound is used 'tiutt-tiutt-tiutt-tiutt…tiut' (Boback, Müller-Schwarze, 1968). Males also have another alarm call, a low, guttural 'ku-karrr', when in a feeding flock or at the lek. Females in flocks also utter a low, guttural alarm call – 'krruagg'. When with her brood, the female makes a low 'kok…kak…kok' as re-assurance, with the frequency increasing if danger appears. If the birds are unable to avoid danger, both sexes make a low hissing (Potapov, 1985).

If forced to fly, the flight differs with circumstances. On occasions, the birds make swift, vertical flights, these being seen particularly in winter when escaping danger directly from a snow burrow, with the bird bursting through the snow roof and rising vertically in a cloud of snow. Once airborne, Black Grouse are fast fliers (speeds exceeding 100kmph [62mph] having been registered – Couturier, 1980), though sometimes not fast enough to avoid the attentions of a Goshawk (*Accipiter gentilis*). They can also travel considerable distances without resting, for example crossing sea inlets up to 25km (15.5 miles) wide (Jenning, 1956).

Nutrition

The species' diet is well studied only within Europe and parts of western Siberia, though the scarce information from other areas confirms the general results. The basic winter nutrition is buds and catkins of birch, this being clearly reflected in the German name of the species – *Birkhuhne* (Birch Grouse). Birch twigs are used when catkins are not available, with good harvests of catkins usually occurring only once every 3–4 years. Preponderance of birch is also, of course, dependent on local conditions: in the European Alps, where birch are rare or absent, the main constituent of the diet is evergreen stems of blueberry, larch twigs and rhododendron leaves. In some areas of the range, alder catkins and buds, and the needles, buds and young cones of Dwarf Mountain Pine (*Pinus mugo*), have been noted as winter forage (Zettel, 1974), occasionally being the main constituent (e.g. Haker, Myrberged, 1969).

On the Kola Peninsula, northern Urals, western Siberia and Transbaikalia, the forage included pine needles and cones when these were particularly abundant (Potapov, 1985). Similarly, in central western Russia, the main winter forage is sometimes juniper needles and berries (Lobachev, Scherbakov, 1933). The berries of dog rose have been noted as important in the Siberian forest-steppe zone (Iurlov, 1960), while willow buds and twigs have formed the main diet of birds in Russia's Far East (Shulpin, 1936). Spruce needles are the winter forage in the spruce forests of Tian-Shan main forage (Zverev, 1962)

In warmer seasons, the diet is much more diverse. Young grass and last year's berries are eaten in spring, followed by the green stems, leaves and seeds of different grass and, in the second half of the summer, berries. In agricultural regions, wheat and millet are taken (Ulianin, 1949; Kirikov, 1952; Iurlov, 1960). The main food of nestlings during the first days of life is insects, with small amounts of tender green parts of grass, seeds and berries. In Western Europe, insects composed 76% in the diet of 12-day-old nestlings, but by the age of two months this had declined to 6.25% (Brüll, 1961). In Finland, in September, insects made up 2.1% of the crop content of males, 6.7% in females, 15.8% and 21.8% of male and female juveniles respectively. By October the differences between the diets of old and young birds had disappeared (Helminen, Viramo, 1962). In western Siberia's forest-steppe zone, the diet of newly hatched nestlings was primarily insects, with vegetable food such as the green leaves of clover entering the diet when the chicks were 5–7 days old. The percentage of vegetable food then increased, reaching 33.2% by the age of two weeks, and dominating the diet of six-week-old chicks. Birch leaves were taken from June, but the buds, twigs and catkins of birch and other plants were found in only 5.3% of crops in July and 10.2% of crops in August (Jurlov, 1960).

In the forest zone, winter foods are found in the diet through the spring, disappearing from the diet only at the beginning of June. For example, in Leningrad Province (at 60°N) during a sudden cooling at the beginning of May, males finished their morning lek early and flew to the nearest birch forests to feed just as they had done in winter (Potapov, 1985).

Gastrolits are constantly present in the birds' stomachs, though in southern populations stones may be replaced by the hard seeds of fruits, these beginning to be seen in examined stomachs from late summer/autumn, but being the major or only gastrolits by February.

Wintering

Black Grouse begin to form flocks from mid-autumn, flock size and make-up depending on local population density. In the southern Urals, most flocks comprise old males (Kirikov, 1952), while in Western Europe, in sedentary populations, adult males prefer a solitary way of life, flocking being restricted to young males, and females of all ages (de Vos, 1983). In Estonia, where 348 winter flocks were analysed, 35 flocks comprised only males, 5 only females, the others being mixed (Viht, 1975). In eastern Leningrad Province, during years of 'normal' population, flocks (97–123 birds) comprised both sexes (Potapov, 1985). In some cases, winter flocks may be 200–300 birds (Kirikov, 1975). Usually, such winter flocks lead a sedentary way of life: in Leningrad and Novgorod Provinces, for example, a flock of nearly 100 birds spent the entire winter in an area of 30–40km² (12–15 sq miles) (Potapov, 1985).

Black Grouse are more sensitive to the low ambient temperatures than capercaillie or ptarmigan, and when the temperature falls below -20°C (-4°F) spend 23 hours each day in snow burrows, emerging to feed for an hour, or even less. Experiments have established that Black Grouse plumage has limited insulation properties, its thermal conductivity being 1.151kJ/°C/hour, about double what would be expected (Hissa *et al.*, 1982), explaining the absence of the species from the continental northern parts of east Siberia.

The normal winter life of the birds, i.e. when the ambient temperature is below zero, but not greatly so, and the snow is deep, is monotonous. The birds leave their snow burrows at sunrise and fly to a feeding place, usually no more than several hundred metres (maximally 2km/1.2 miles) away. Feeding time is temperature dependent, but is rarely more than 0.5–1.5 hours, the birds foraging in upper tree crowns, then flying to a new roosting place in open areas – usually large bogs, old agricultural fields, openings along the forest edge, or cuttings. Total flight times are rarely more that 3–5 minutes. During periods of thaw, the birds always rest and roost in trees. As winter draws to an end, and the day lengthens, the birds feed twice daily, morning and evening, spending the middle of the day in snow burrows or in the open holes in the snow surface, depending on the temperature.

The quantity and composition of the forage is dependent on weather and availability. If the temperature is low and feeding time is reduced, the birds mainly take twigs and buds, as searching for catkins needs more time. When the catkin harvest is good, the bird's ration consists almost exclusively of them. The dry weight of the bird's daily ration is nearly 120g (4.2oz) for males and 100g (3.5oz) for females. The number of droppings in a snow burrow after a long stay is 95–111. The quantity of caecal excrement strongly depends on ambient temperature: during strong frosts it is 17.6g/0.62oz (dry weight) in males and 7.1g (0.25oz) in females, instead of the usual 47g (1.66oz) and 37.4g (1.32oz) if the temperature is moderate. For example, the daily energy budget of a male Black

Grouse in winter in Russia's Leningrad Province with an ambient temperature of -20°C was 2,472.2kJ. The excreted energy was 1,787.6kJ, meaning the assimilated energy was 735.6kJ: for females the figures were 2,101.4kJ, 1,519.5kJ and 625kJ (Potapov, 1982).

The size of a typical snow burrow chamber is 19–28cm x 30–41cm (7.5–11in x 11.8–16.1in), height 16–25cm (6.3–9.8in) and snow ceiling thickness 7–11cm (2.8–4.3in). In most cases, the bird excavates a short, 15–50cm (5.9–19.7in) tunnel before preparing the roosting chamber, but tunnels may reach 4m (13.1ft), and may even have a 90° turn at their centre. Interestingly, if the snow crust is hard, perhaps as a result of thaw/freeze, the bird may utilize the track of elk (moose) to aid excavation. These heavy animals punch holes in the snow surface that the bird can use as the start point of a tunnel. However, such usage is very rare (Potapov, 1985).

Breeding

Black Grouse are polygamous, and males take no part in the rearing of chicks. Males have common leks at which they gather daily from the beginning of the breeding season to the time of hatching. Despite the collective character of Black Grouse and capercaillie leks, they differ significantly. Black Grouse leks are placed in open habitats (bogs, meadows, glades, clearings, even on lake ice), but never far (50–100m/55–109yd) from the forest edge, similar to those of *Tympanuchus phasianellus*. In the forest-steppe zone, leks are usually close to tall bush thickets: there is only one example of a lek in open, feather-grass sandy steppe (Naurzum State Reserve, Northern Kazakhstan), 5–6km (3.1–3.7 miles) from the nearest forest (Ulianin, 1949). In mountains, leks are usually at the forest-free tops of watershed ridges, but may sometimes be among sparse, tall birches (Kirikov, 1952; Jurlov, 1960). In the Alps, Carpathians and northern Urals, leks are on open, flat spots near passes, or the open gentle slopes above timberline, each often being subalpine meadows (Teplova, 1952; Couturier, 1980). In the Tian-Shan and Altai mountains, leks are usually on southern slopes, occasionally surprisingly steep slopes, close to trees (Kuzmina, 1962).

The number of males at the lek varies considerably, dependent mainly on local population density and the extent of predation (including hunting). Formerly leks of 100, even 200, males were mentioned (Menzbier, 1902) – 100 birds were seen in south-east Kazakhstan even in the mid-20th century (Kuzmina, 1962) – but more recently, lower numbers (perhaps 3–7) are more usually seen. Males may also lek alone, this usually happening when the population density is low, and is often the precursor of the complete disappearance of the birds from an area (Potapov, 1985).

The size of lek arenas depends on local topography and the number of males. A lek with 10–15 active males will occupy 0.3–0.5ha; with more birds, this may rise to 1–2ha. Neighbouring leks may be close (1,100m/1,203yd in Leningrad Province, 900m/984yd in west Siberian: Potapov, 1985; Jurlov, 1960), but 3–4km (1.9–2.5 miles) is more usual in places with normal population densities. Arenas are not constant, as they are in capercaillie, rarely occupying the same spot (more or less) over a ten-year period. This lack of constancy usually results from human activity, though Black Grouse mobility also plays a part, the plasticity it engenders undoubtedly having aided species survival in periods of changing natural conditions as well as those due to human interference. In mountain areas, changes in lek position reflect changing spring conditions. Interaction between adjacent populations is also a contributory factor, as in most localities in southern parts of the forest zone, isolated populations have more stable leks.

As well as the main lek, the birds may also have 'spare leks', the functioning and significance of which are poorly studied and understood. In cases when there are no clear boundaries between adjacent populations, these spare leks may complicate research, as the same group of males may use two or even three leks. In one study area of western Siberia, the same group of males changed lek position during a single morning, at other times changing every few days (Jurlov, 1960). Studies showed that the territorial structure of the population consisted of several territories of micro-populations, each with 6–18 males and the same number of females occupying territories of 12–40km² (5–15 sq miles). During the lek, the males were distributed between 3–7 lek arenas (each with 1–8 males), with each such lek adjoining 1–6 female nesting territories. The lek arenas did not have equal status, there always being a main, largest, lek at a central position, around which flocks of 25–48 birds formed in the autumn (Shinkin, 1966; Shilo, 1972). Within the lek, older, more experienced males have individual territories close to the arena's centre. New leks may be formed when an experienced male selects a new site for himself: if it is a good site, his displays will attract other males who will establish territories around him. Such a new lek may then become established as the main lek. If the population density falls, and the lek is abandoned, it may be re-established if the population rises again: in one area, the birds disappeared for three years, but occupied the same arenas when they returned (Potapov, 1985).

The start of nuptial activity depends on local conditions, but usually begins in March, males 'mumbling' (see below) during quiet, sunny weather. Excitement grows daily and by the beginning of April all males begin mumbling or uttering a special hissing cry. They also chase one another with spread wings, and even fight, and make demonstrative flights. These activities happen spontaneously at first, often near feeding sites, and with no female audience. They are also weather-dependent, with bad weather ending displays. But eventually, usually after the main lek arena is snow-free and the females appear, true lekking begins, usually in late April/early May, and usually lasts 10–12 days.

During the main lek, old males arrive first, usually an hour before daybreak, and begin their courtship activity immediately. The males may roost close to the arena after the evening lek and sometimes, with a full moon and calm weather, they begin to mumble and hiss in the middle of the night. Females also appear at the arena in darkness, but always about 15 minutes after the males. Female behaviour is not standard – they may sit in the trees for several minutes, either alone or in groups of 2–3, and then descend to the arena; go straight to the arena centre, walking between lekking males; or fly around the arena. A lek of medium size will usually be visited by 1–4 females at a given time, presumably different ones.

Male morning lek activity is occasionally interrupted as if by command, with displays and songs ceasing and the birds staying motionless for several seconds, then all flying from the arena in one direction, and remaining absent for 15–20 minutes before returning and resuming. Such interruptions may happen simultaneously in 2–3 nearby leks across an area of 2–3km (1.2–1.9 miles), which makes it unlikely that raptors cause the cessation. It has been suggested (Potapov, 1985) that the breaks might be due to the need for foraging, as males arrive at the lek straight from roosting (i.e. hungry), but the behaviour remains puzzling.

Morning leks last 2–3 hours from sunrise, the actual time depending on the number of birds, especially females, in arena, and the weather. There may also be evening leks during the main phase of lek activity, but these never reach a high level of activity and females rarely visit. Evening leks begin at sunset and continue into full darkness, but in the north of the range, during the 'white nights' of long Arctic days, they may continue through until morning. Lek behaviour has also been observed in early winter, in northern Mongolia, with males leaving their roosts at sunrise, flying to the lek arena, and landing in nearby trees. They 'mumbled' (see below) several times before descending to the lek arena, where they walked in full posture along paths trampled in the snow during previous visits, mumbled and hissed for nearly an hour, then left the arena to forage. All the specimens collected were adult males: no females were observed (Kozlova, 1930).

Competition for the best spots at leks may lead to conflict between male Black Grouse.

At the lek, males are strictly territorial, each one performing only in its own territory, though the permanence of such territories varies: sometimes, individual males will occupy the same territories at the centre of the arena from year to year, while other males will divide the surrounding area differently each year (Sweden, Hjorth, 1970), or the complete structure may vary annually (Leningrad Province, Potapov, 1985). The size of individual territories also varies considerably: with a large number of males, they are small, about 100m² (120yd²) at the arena centre (Lack, 1946; Höhn, 1953), but with fewer males, they may be 170–350m² (203–419yd²) at the centre and up to 4,000m² (4,784yd²) at its outskirts (Kruijt, Hogan, 1967; Hjorth, 1970; Potapov, 1985). Experimental studies confirm what would be expected – that females attempt to position themselves where there is a maximal concentration of males, i.e. at the arena's centre (Kruijt et al., 1972).

The hierarchical structure of the lek has not been rigorously studied, but Koivisto (1965), working in Finland, suggests that each lek has three ranks, with the upper rank consisting of males aged three years or more occupying the central arena. Places near the centre are occupied by two-year-old, second-rank males. At the periphery are young, third-rank birds. However, this suggested structure is at odds with earlier work by Kirikov (1952), who suggested that the central arena is very often occupied not only by older males, but also by some only 11 months old, i.e. birds from the earliest broods of the previous spring that are in their own first spring. This implies that the structure comprises two ranks, not three, the first comprising highly active males of different ages that occupy the central arena and probably account for 98% of mating, and a second rank comprising all other males. That implies that age is not the dominant factor, though it appears to be the case that when males reach five years of age, they are unable to maintain their dominant position at the arena centre and are pushed aside by rivals (de Vos, 1983). Battles occur between adjacent territory holders. The males, facing each other, make several deep bows, sometimes to the ground, or move in the same direction, staying close to each other and singing ('parallel duel'). Males attack and retreat in turn, with exact synchrony, with the distance between them not altering. Battles also occur between females, usually when two meet close to a male.

The main male courtship display is the famous 'song' – the 'mumbling' that can actually be heard at any time during the year, but particularly in spring. The song is the loudest lek sound, audible at distances up to 3.5km (2.2 miles)! It consists of 3–5 series of soft gurgling sounds lasting 2.2–2.4 seconds. The first 2–3 sounds are short, 0.3 seconds long, followed by a more prolonged final series with a slightly rising tone, lasting 1.5 seconds and consisting of 15–18 guttural sounds. During this final series, the oesophagus is expanded maximally and the bird shudders from bill to tail, as if convulsing. Between the neck feathers, the white apteria skin is visible. The male exhausts air through its nostrils as it completes the song, then, after completion, the bill remains open, just as it is open for the moment before the production of the first series of the song. During active lekking, males often sing many times without interruption. The song differs between populations. Though this has not been fully studied, it seems the song is longer in Leningrad Province than in Sweden (sonograms in Hjorth, 1970; Potapov, 1985), while it is quieter in the Tian Shan Mountains than in plains' populations (Zverev, 1962). In some cases males may utter a guttural 'ku – kararara' after finishing the song, a noise also made occasionally during conflict or when feeding in trees.

The other vocalization, the hissing 'tchuffy' call, is an aggressive signal, used during displays as a sign of strong excitement. When uttered by one male, it is immediately repeated by the surrounding males. When uttering the call from the ground, the neck and head are lifted upright, with the spread tail thrown back and the half-spread wings making short, not full, flaps (mainly with only the shoulders being moved). The neck twitches, the head is raised a little more, the bill opens widely and the feathers of the chin are raised vertically to form a 'beard'. The sound lasts only 0.9–1.1 seconds, with a rise of tone towards the end. Males also sometimes utter a prolonged, loud hissing during a battle or when they fly one against another during demonstrative flights.

Male Black Grouse displaying at a lek

Figure 79. Lek jumping flight of male *Lyrurus tetrix*

In the basic courtship posture, the male straightens his head and neck forward, parallel to the ground, similar to the posture of ptarmigan. The head is lowered slightly so that the bright-red and maximally extended eye-combs protrude like horns. The tail is held vertical, even slightly inclined, and spread so that the tops of the laterally curved retrices touch the ground, while the white undertail coverts protrude above the shortened central retrices so that there is a sharp contrast of white against black. From behind, the tail looks like an opened white flower with a partly black bordering (**Figure 79**). The wings are spread to the sides and lowered slightly. The neck is dilated, not only by inflation of the oesophagus but from raised feathers, with the tops overlying one another to form a sleek surface.

Flutter-jumps, accompanied by a loud hissing 'tchuffy', may be simple, accompanied only by convulsive wing quivering, or may be a vertical flight to a height of 0.5m (1.6ft) with a turn through 45°–180°, but landing at the start point.

Flutter-flight starts with loud wingbeats, the bird rising steeply with 3–4 wingbeats, then descending (**Figure 79**). From the highest point, the bird makes a short horizontal flight, landing with very loud wingbeats. Demonstrative flights, seen only during maximal lek activity, differ only by covering longer distances. During the flight, the male usually travels from one side of its territory to the other. During all these jumps and flights, the white wing patches are clearly visible, since one reason for the flights is to demonstrate them.

In those areas where a solitary male leks, the same overall process is maintained. In some cases solitary males have been observed lekking within hearing distance of a collective lek, perhaps even within just a few hundred metres. In such cases the solitary male may be visited by a female, perhaps even by two simultaneously (Potapov, 1985). De Vos (1983) observed a reverse situation, with females preferentially mating only with solitary males, despite making regular visits to a collective lek: this is considered to be a very rare occurrence.

Lek activity decreases rapidly once females stop visiting, and the males start their moult (Kirikov, 1952). Females may appear in the arena at this late stage (usually June) if their first clutch was a failure: some females collected in leks at such times showed brood patches and had follicles indicating two clutches (Jurlow, 1960).

A widely held opinion maintains that mating takes place outside the lek arena, this based on observations of females flying from the arena and being pursued by young males from the periphery (Sabaneev, 1876; Menzbier, 1902; Ulianin, 1949; Iurlow, 1960; Chelzov-Bebutov, 1965; Hjorth, 1970). However, actual mating beyond arena limits has never actually been observed, with all observed mating taking place at the arena centre (Koivisto, 1965; Kruijt et al., 1972; de Vos, 1983; Potapov, 1985). Nests are placed under the cover of thick vegetation, very rarely being in open positions among the low grass of a forest glade. In the forest-steppe zone, nests are similarly placed, though they may also be placed in feather-grass steppe away from the nearest trees (Ulianin, 1949). One female used the old nest of a raptor or raven at a height of 7m (23ft) (Witherby et al., 1949). Ground nests are a shallow scrape up to 10–11cm (3.9–4.3in) deep and 23–28cm (9.1–11in) in diameter.

The usual clutch size is 7–9 eggs and, in repeated clutches, 4–6. The maximum observed clutch is 13 eggs (Ivanter, 1968). Eggs are usually laid every 1.5 days (Siivonen, 1957). In one case a hen laid 9 eggs in 13 days (Couturier, 1980). The basic egg colour is yellow to light-ochre, with small quantities of brown dots and spots, occasionally with more intensive speckling. Egg size varies considerably (length: 46.0–58.4mm, width: 33.2–42.8mm) and is dependent on the age of the hen as well as her physiological condition. The weight of fresh eggs averages 33.9g/1.20oz (28.8–37.8g/1.02–1.33oz, N=128: maximal weight 40.96g/1.44oz – Couturier, 1980) and during incubation decreases by 3.6–3.7g/0.12–0.13oz) (Jurlov, 1960).

Incubation takes 23–25 days (Ulianin, 1949; Semenov-Tianshansky, 1959, Jurlov, 1960), but sometimes up to 28 days (Couturier, 1980). The incubating hen turns her eggs regularly, up to 34 times daily (average 25 times). The female feeds 1–4 times daily, with each absence lasting 10–20 minutes, though sometimes up to 60–70 minutes. In general, the female feeds only a few dozen metres from the nest, though she can move as much as 400m (Semenov-Tianshansky, 1959; Robel, 1969). In general, the time of the female's absence from the nest is 2.4–5.3% of the incubation period. Before hatching begins, the female will not leave the nest for 19–20 hours.

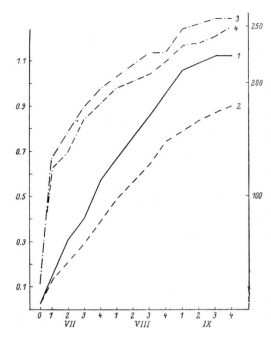

Figure 80. *Lyrurus tetrix viridannus* nestling growth

Left vertical axis – mass in kg; right vertical axis – wing length in mm. Horizontal axis – time in months and weeks. 1 – Male mass; 2 – Female mass; 3 – Male wing; 4 – Female wing (Yurlov, 1960).

The weight of a newly hatched chick is 24–25g (0.85–0.88oz) (Jurlov, 1960; Fediushin, Dolbik, 1967). Soon after hatching, the brood leaves the nest to lead a nomadic life in areas of bush/trees growth with rich and tall grass, in water-meadows with bush clusters, in field edges, in forest glades with raspberry and dog-rose thickets, in wide forest cuttings, in old forest fire's areas, and in the edges of the large bogs. The speed of the brood's movement in the first day is nearly 10m (11yd) per hour (Semenov-Tianshansky, 1959). By the third day the brood has moved up to 900m (984yd) (Robel, 1969). Chick growth is illustrated in **Figure 80**.

Within their territory, broods usually choose sunny spots where the soil is light and favourable for dust bathing. The chicks begin to flutter short distances at 10 days. At first, if danger threatens, the chicks hide while the female runs, dragging a wing in an attempt at distraction. If flushed, chicks flutter or run, uttering a thin peep, and then try to hide again. When they have reached 25–30 days old, the chicks and female will all attempt to hide from danger, usually in thick grass, but if flushed they will all fly, often in many different directions, landing several hundred metres away, with the brood then gradually reforming.

At this time males are solitary or form small groups of 2–5 birds in remote areas where they moult. If flushed, males fly short distances, landing in thick vegetation where they move quickly away on foot; they avoid landing in trees.

Hunting, recreation and conservation

Black Grouse was once an important game bird, particularly in Russia and the Scandinavian countries, with hundreds of thousands of them being hunted and delivered to city markets. By the 1960s, this trade had ceased, the birds now being the target of amateur hunters, though for some country dwellers they are still a valuable source of nutrition.

But even without professional hunting, amateur hunting takes remain high (Couturier, 1980) and Black Grouse numbers, particularly in Western and Central Europe, and along the southern border of the species' range in Russia, are declining, with human activity and range reduction the major cause. When the human population was low and agriculture was one feature of a mosaic landscape, man and the Black Grouse could co-exist, but the increase in population has made life difficult for the birds. Rykowski (1959) has shown that just the daily flush of a brood on successive days will lead to death. Only in the Scandinavian countries and in north and east Russia (i.e. Siberia) is the population more or less stable. In all other countries of the species' range, the situation is worrying, and over recent years, five conferences have been held in Europe dedicated to Black Grouse conservation; a sixth conference was held in Sweden in September 2012. However, it has to be said that, despite international efforts to conserve the species, Black Grouse numbers continue to decline.

7.2 Caucasian Black Grouse *Lyrurus mlokosiewiczi* (Taczanowski, 1875)

Tetrao mlokosiewiczi Taczanowski, 1875. Synonym: *Tetrao mlokosyewitzii* Dinnik, 1884.

Morphology

Large terrestrial bird, a little smaller than previous species and differing from it by being a monotonous black or brown-grey colour. The wing is short and wide, the width, as a percentage of length, being 76% and 71% in males and females respectively. The wing top is more rounded than in Black Grouse. The male wing width is greater because of the length of the secondaries, the comparative length of which, as a percentage of wing length, is greater than in the Black Grouse: 60.1% against 46.5%. The reason is the way the male *L. mlokosiewiczi* flies. Males spend most of their time on the ground, using the 'standard' grouse horizontal flight if they need to move (usually over short distances only) to feeding or resting places. But if they move greater distances downhill, they glide. This flight form, first described only in 1977 (Potapov, Pavlova, 1977) and fully by Potapov (1978; 1983; 1985, 1986b), is unique among galliforms, though normal for high mountain species. In a downhill glide, the birds utilize gravity, converting potential to kinetic energy for a very energy-efficient flight in comparison to the 'standard' grouse method (Potapov, 1966; 2002; 2004a, b). The flight trajectory is a spiral, descending parallel to the mountainside approximately 100m above it. Gliding phases account for 75% of total flight time and is interrupted every 3–4 seconds by 5–8 wingbeats (**Figure 81**). Flight speed decreases during these strokes, with the flight becoming more horizontal. The flight is accompanied by a whistling sound during the glide phase and interrupted regularly by 5–8 shorter whistles during the wingbeats: the same sound is produced by the wings during male flutter-jumps in courtship display. The glide sounds were described and analyzed morphologically (Potapov, Pavlova, 1977), and were first

Figure 81. Downhill flight pattern of the
Caucasian Black Grouse
*Straight lines indicate gliding, groups of vertical lines
indicate wingbeats.*

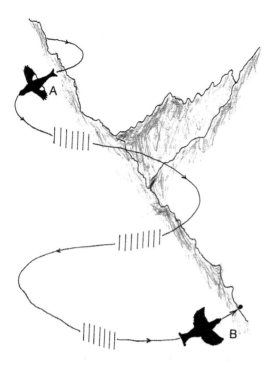

recorded in 1989 (Bergmann *et al.*, 1991).
The structure of the primaries indicates
that the sounds are produced by the outer
primaries, particularly the outermost. This
feather is shorter and narrower than in *L.
tetrix,* and has no broadening at its base
(**Figure 82**), which is unusual in galliform
birds. The five outer primaries shows wear
on the inner web margins (**Figure 83**)
resulting from high air pressure during
gliding (Potapov, 1978).

The wings of one-year-old males are
as adult males, but the primaries of females
show no sign of wear, with female flight
being the 'standard' grouse form of a series
of flaps alternating with short glides on spread wings. In addition,
female *L. mlokosiewiczi* fly rarely, and then only for short distances.
Unlike males, they have never been observed in downward flight.
This sexual dimorphism in flight is the only one observed to date
among grouse species (Potapov, 1978; 1985; 2004).

As noted above, the inner and outer webs of the male tail
feathers are angled to resemble a gutter, a form that would seem
associated with the main adult male habitat – alpine and subalpine
meadows with tall grass and thick bushes. When it rains, or there
is a heavy dew, the vegetation becomes wet, and the males keep
their tails parallel to the ground during feeding, with the gutter
shape helping to drain water. The tail is, of course, used during
courtship displays, its length meaning it can occasionally be seen
like a flag above tall grass, alerting the observer to the position
of a lek arena. The tail appears to offer no flight advantage –
during sharp turns, air pressure distorts the long, soft tail feathers
(Potapov, 1985; 2004b).

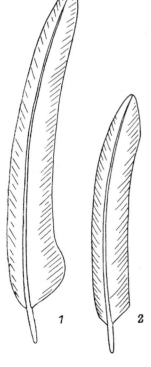

Figure 82. Distal primary feathers
Of Lyrurus tetrix *(1) and* L. mlokosiewiczi *(2).*

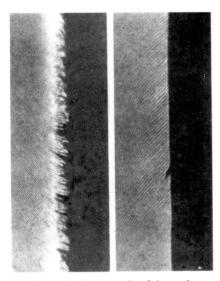

Figure 83. Outer web of the male
10th primary
In left –L. mlokosiewiczi *(ragged edge)*
and right – L. tetrix *(smooth edge)*

Caucasian Black Grouse have the longest legs of any grouse species, being similar in length to those of the high mountain *Tetraogallus* snowcocks. Snowcocks are also similar in movement, going uphill by foot, but fly downhill in the same way. *L. mlokosiewiczi* also have long feet, an adaptation to walking on steep slopes with the numerous mounds and stones among thick, tall grass and bush vegetation (Potapov, 1978).

Three other morphological features are connected with male sexual activities. Male eye-combs are a similar structure to those of ptarmigan, consisting of a flat surface covered by low knobs, and with a high blade along the upper margin formed by long, finger-like papilla inosculated at the bases and disposed in two rows, one above the other (see **Figure 45 in Chapter 4**). The height of the erected blade is 4.6–4.8mm, the general width of the eye-comb with raised blade is 11–12mm and the length is 19–20mm. Normally the blade hangs down passively and covers the flat surface of the eye-comb. In turn, the naked eye-comb is hidden by feathers in cold weather, becoming practically invisible. Potapov (2004b) considered the species a relic mountain form, the structure of the male eye-comb being an ancestral feature.

The second feature is the absence of lek vocalizations due to the reduced size of the male syrinx (**Figure 84**). This size reduction is evidence of long-term evolution in high mountains, where low-frequency vocalizations do not carry as well in the lower atmospheric pressure (Potapov, 1966).

The third feature is the significant difference in colouration between the first and second adult male plumage. The first is grey-brown, similar in colour to adult females, while the second is completely black. Some collection specimens have a single black feather, i.e. the colour is possible at a genetic level, but is not supported by natural selection (Potapov, 1985, 2005). The colour difference undoubtedly results from natural selection to better camouflage inexperienced young males and so avoid raptor predation. One-year-old males spend the

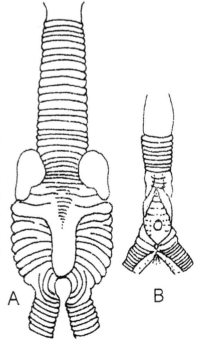

Figure 84. The syrinx
Of Lyrurus tetrix *(A) and* Lyrurus mlokosiewiczi *(B). After Lorenz, 1887.*

A   B

winter in female flocks in the upper parts of the forest belts, separate from the older, black males (Vitovich, 1986), which winter in separate flocks above the timberline. Cryptic colouration also helps one-year-old males to avoid attack in open lek arenas, where experienced, older, males are less vulnerable (Vitovich, 1986).

Colouration

Adult male

In final (third) adult plumage: General colour is black, with a slight metallic gloss on breast, head, neck and back. Primaries and secondaries are black-brown: in very old birds the primaries and leg feathers are black, and there is a metallic gloss on the belly and along the primary shafts (Potapov, 1985).

In first black (second adult) plumage: Differs from third adult only in presence of brown speckles and stripes on inner secondaries, inner great and middle upperwing coverts, rump and retrice edges. Nostril feathers and some on the forehead are dark-brown. Leg feathers are brownish-grey.

Male Caucasian Black Grouse

In the first adult plumage: General colour is grey-brownish, without black feathers (except in rare cases). Upper body is grey with a striped pattern and uniform brown spots. Underparts are generally grey, apart from a white chin patch and a black-brown patch on the belly. Most feathers have a complicated pattern of grey and whitish cross-stripes and whitish vane bordering. Some feathers have the typical features of juvenile design.

In summer plumage: Summer plumage appears only on head and neck (see **Figure 77**) and only in two-year-old or older birds. The chin is white and surrounded by brown spots. Other parts are covered by dark-brown feathers with pale yellow and whitish stripes and spots.

Adult female

In adult plumage: Colouration and design are similar to the male first adult plumage, i.e. mottled brown-grey. The cross-stripe patterns of contour feathers are more prominent, the stripes wider, but not covering the tops of all feathers where the streaked design prevails. The pattern on the retrices is as a spruce tree drawn by a child.

In the first adult plumage: Almost as adult, but the two outer primaries have sharpened tops. This feature is useful in distinguishing young females no older than 14 months, when the tops are lost due to wear.

Female Caucasian Black Grouse

Juvenile

Uniformly mottled brownish-yellow. Most contour feathers have a cross-stripe pattern with prolonged, narrow shaft-stripes on upper breast feathers. Outer primaries are brown with white tops and an indistinct cross-pattern on the outer webs. Retrices have a cross-striped pattern with reversed triangle white patches on the tops.

Downy chick

Sulphurous-yellow underparts and brown upper parts, with a brown crown cap surrounded by black bordering, and a complicated pattern of black stripes and spots on both sides of the head (**Figure 85**).

Figure 85. Head pattern of downy young *Lyrurus mlokosiewiczi*

Dimensions

Data from specimens in the Coll ZIN RAN and Coll ZM MSU, from Potapov, 1985.

Adult male (N=30): wing length 214.4mm (200–229mm); tail length 201.2mm (187–219mm); difference between central and longest outer retrices 47.8mm (34–68mm); bill length 14.7mm (13.5–16.1mm); bill width 10.5mm (9.6–11.2mm); tarsi length 47.2mm (43–50mm); middle toe length 46.1mm (44–49mm).

Young male (N=6): wing length 210.3mm (202–216mm); tail length 153.5mm (146–163mm); difference between central and longest outer retrace 10.8mm (6–21mm); bill length 14.7mm (13.7–15.7mm); bill width 10.4mm (9.3–11.0mm); tarsi length 46mm (42–48mm); middle toe length 44.1mm (42–46mm).

Adult female (N=7): wing length 197.8mm (196–206mm); tail length 134.6mm (127–145mm); difference in retrice length 7.2mm (2–13mm); bill length 13.4mm (12.9–14.0mm); bill width 9.7mm (8.8–10.3mm); tarsi length 43.5mm (42.0–45.5mm); middle toe length 41.2mm (39–44mm).

The weight of adult males varies, but in spring (March–June) averages 862.2g/30.41oz (820–1,005g/28.9–35.4oz); of young males (February–April): 766g/27.0oz (770–900g/27.1–31.7oz); of young females in September: 750–916g/26.5–32.3oz

The characteristic white underwing of a male Caucasian Black Grouse in Great Caucasian Ridge, Georgia

(Hanmamedov, 1965); of young females in November: 722–728g/25.5–25.7oz (Noska, Tschusi, 1895).

Moult

The moult sequence is as for Black Grouse. Summer feathers are present from mid-June to mid-August (for birds reared in captivity – Vitovich, 1986). Vitovich determined that if a first-year ('grey') male lost one or more feathers casually, i.e. for non-moult reasons, the replacement feather would be black, not grey. This is a clear indication that each feather follicle is pre-programmed to a strict succession through juvenile, first, second, etc, plumage. Vitovich removed grey feathers from different areas of captive birds, and in all cases the replacement feather was black, allowing him to conclude that the colour of a feather depended not on age, but on the number of feather generations.

Distribution

The range covers all the Caucasian Mountains: the Greater Caucasus, the Lesser Caucasus, and adjacent mountain systems of the Armenian Highlands and Asia Minor Peninsula. There is no information on whether the species also occupies the neighbouring areas of Dagestan in Russia, the Karadag Mountains in Azerbaijan, the mountains of eastern

Turkey, and the north-eastern Karadag Ridge in Saradjar–Tepe, northern Iran (Scott and Adhami Mirhosseyni, 1975), but it is possible that isolated populations exist.

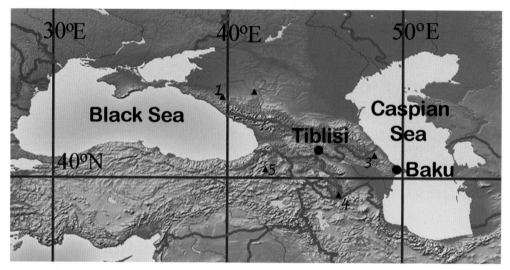

Map 16. Caucasian Black Grouse (*Lyrurus mlokosiewiczi*).
1 – Mount Schessi; 2 – Mount Bermamyt; 3 – Mount Dubrar; 4 – Kara-Dag Mountains (Iran); 5 – Kara-Urgan (Turkey).

Subspecies

This species is monotypic.

Habitats

The main habitat is areas of bush thicket alternating with subalpine meadows close to the timberline. The preferred bushes are low birches, junipers, dog roses and rhododendron. Almost any degree of steepness will be occupied if the habitat is suitable, only females with broods preferring gentle slopes or flat places near stream sources, passes, etc. The species avoids solid forest areas, even in winter. In the Lesser Caucasus, where birch and rhododendron are usually absent, the birds inhabit areas along the timberline where oak and hornbeam are interspersed with thickets of juniper and dog rose.

The preferred habitats do not extend for more than 400–500m (1,312–1,640ft) vertically (Tkatchenko, 1966; Molamusov, 1967; Potapov, Pavlova, 1974). Across the range, the habitat occurs at altitudes from 1,500–3,300m (4,921–10,827ft). The nesting zone is more compressed, from 2,000–2,600m (6,562–8,530ft) in the Greater Caucasus, and a little higher in the Lesser Caucasus – 2,450–2,705m (8,038–8,875ft) on Armenia's Pambak Ridge (Liaister, Sosnin, 1942).

In the Teberda State Reserve, northern Caucasus males occupied an area at 2,300–2,700m (7,546–8,858ft) in winter, with females occupying 2,200–2,400m (7,218–7,874ft).

In summer the females nested and reared broods at 2,200–2,600m (7,218–8,530ft), while males moulted at 2,400–2,700m (7,874–8,858ft) (Vitovich, 1986). During the summer, males often visit alpine meadows at heights of up to 3,200m (10,499ft) (Chunichin, 1964).

Population structure and density

Data on the ratio of males and females in populations is inconsistent. Averin (1938) found 50.8% males and 49.2% females, but a study in the Teberda State Reserve found that females comprised only 20–25% of the population (Tkatchenko, 1966). Later information from the same reserve found 1.3 males to 1 female (Vitovich, 1986). All these authors noted the difficulty of distinguishing one-year-old males from females, even at short distances, and the potential error this introduced to counts. However, the distinct difference in colour of young and adult males allowed the ratio of these in the spring leks to be more accurately assessed, this ratio giving a good guide to the previous year's breeding success. In the Teberda Reserve, the percentage of young males during 12 years of observations varied from 3.6–44.4% (Vitovich, in litt., Potapov, 1985).

Data of numbers and population densities are scarce, with precise information having been collected only from the Teberda Reserve when it was noted that the population doubled in the seven years after reserve creation, from 1.4 birds/km² in 1960 to 3.8 birds/km² in 1968 (Vitovich, 1977; 1986). Later (1998), close to the borders of the Caucasian State Reserve, the summer density was estimated at 2.3 adults/km² (Drovetski, Rohwer, 2000).

Territoriality

No available data, but the general impression is of a highly sedentary species.

Behaviour

The Caucasian Black Grouse is secretive and silent. The birds spend most of the time on the ground, in the thick, tall grass or bushes. They move uphill on foot, but fly downhill. The male gliding flight is described above. Females have a typical grouse flight pattern – short glides alternating with flapping flight. The species is very trusting of humans, especially in places where they have not been hunted. In such places it is no problem to approach females to 10m (11yd) or so, and to within 7–8m (7.6–8.7yd) of males at the lek. When flushed, the birds try to escape by flying downhill. The birds prefer to be in groups during all seasons, though solitary old males may be encountered, particularly during moult periods (Chunichin, 1964; Vitovich, 1986).

Nutrition

The diet of the species differs between populations in the Greater and Lesser Caucasus. In the Greater (northern) range, the winter diet consists of the buds, catkins and twigs of

Female Caucasian Black Grouse

birch, needles and fruits of juniper, fruits of dog roses, and willow twigs. Additional items include pine needles, twigs, buds and berries of mountain ash, buds of maple, berries of currants, and leaves and berries of cowberries (Averin, 1938; Kutubidze, 1961; Tkatchenko, 1966; Vitovich, 1986). In the Lesser Caucasus (southern) range, the main winter forage is juniper fruits and needles. The winter diet is usually maintained until early May. During spring and summer, to mid-August, the main forage is fresh green grass stems, leaves, flowers and, later, seeds. Because of the richness of the Caucasian subalpine flora, the birds utilize several dozen grasses. From mid-August, berries and fruits of different plants are taken, particularly those of the *Vaccinium* species. As with other grouse, the change to winter forage is dependent on ambient temperature and snow cover.

Chicks feed eclectically, taking everything from flies to green leaves, though insects form 95% of the diet during the first three weeks of life (Averin, 1938).

Wintering

Winter life has been studied only in the northern Caucasus (Averin, 1938; Vitovich, 1986). There, the importance of snow cover was noted, 35–40cm (13.8–15.7in) of snow being the main determinant for habitat preference. As already noted, in winter the birds divide into two groups – old males, and females and young males. Each group occupies a different habitat, with old males occupying the upper limits of birch forests with nearby subalpine meadows and dense thickets of rhododendron and juniper at heights of 2,300–2,700m (7,546–8,858ft), where the depth and quality of the snow depends on constant winds. The birds usually roost on northern slopes above the timberline, 50–150m (164–492ft) below a ridge crest, in places where the snow is generally dry and loose so that excavation of a snow burrow is easy. Such places are rare and the males may roost in them in successive years, roosting elsewhere only after heavy snowfalls.

Females with young males roost in birch forests at 2,200–2,400m (7,218–7,874ft). Such forests are snow-bound all winter, but the tree branches prevent snow compression and burrow excavation is easy. Interestingly, even where their habitats overlap, the two groups live separately, rarely meeting.

The bird's daily activity is determined by day length and weather conditions. They leave their roosts in deep early morning twilight, an observer knowing this only because of the noise they make as they emerge from burrows. Most birds begin to feed immediately, with morning feeding lasting about 1.5 hours. Feeding is from the snow surface, with food items being pecked from low branches. Only rarely do the birds fly up into a birch to feed. After feeding, the birds then rest for four hours, either in a sheltered, sunny spot or a new burrow. In open places they turn occasionally, this being especially true of old males whose black feathering absorbs heat effectively. Evening feeding lasts 2.5–3 hours. The birds then fly to the roosting place, spend several minutes perched on a tree or rock to scan for danger and then construct a burrow. The roosting chamber is 15–25cm (5.9–9.8in) high, 30cm (11.8in) long and 15–20cm (5.9–7.9in) wide (Averin, 1938). During bad weather (strong winds or heavy snowfalls), most birds feed only in the morning, usually for up to 3 hours, then roost until the next day.

Life in the southern range, where winters are 'softer', has not yet been studied.

Breeding

Females can breed in their first spring (aged 9–10 months), males in their second spring, with breeding in the first spring being an exception: the size of the testicles of first spring males is less than half that of adult birds (Kutubidze, 1961). Spring breeding activity may begin in March and visits to lek arenas become regular only from the second half of April. Maximal lek activity occurs in the second half of May, when visits by females become regular. After the females cease to visit, male activity decreases quickly and ends completely in early June.

Most lek arenas are on southern mountain slopes (occasionally on ground to 45°), covered by thick grass and 300–400m (984–1,312ft) above the timberline. The micro-relief of such slopes is usually a series of small terrace-like steps, these perhaps from old landslips or old paths. Sometimes arenas may be on subalpine meadow, surrounded on two or three sides by short birches or bushes. The grass of the arena is tall enough for the stem tops to fold over, such 'curtains' offering shelter from bad weather and cover in the event of raptor attacks. Arena size depends on local relief, vegetation and the number of males. In most cases, 2–7 males will visit regularly, and will occupy a space extending for 150m (492ft) up the slope and 400–600m (1,312–1,968ft) along it. In larger leks, where the number of males can reach 20–30 birds, the lek can be 500m (547yd) in diameter, though arenas of that size and number of birds are now rare. Arenas have a high degree of permanence, with instances where they have been in use for at least 17 years being known (Averin, 1938; Potapov, Pavlova, 1977; Potapov, 1985; Vitovich, 1986).

In the early stages of the lek, the males display in twilight, but as activity increases, the time shifts back towards full darkness, with males arriving 1–1.5 hours before sunrise. Some males will spend the night close to the arena. Arriving males start their courtship displays immediately after arriving, and stop at 8–9 a.m., dispersing on foot, or by flying, to feed. They return to the arena at 2–4 p.m. and display again. In the first phases of the lek, evening displays last until it is dark, and towards the end of lek activity the males finish earlier. Bad weather curtails or even stops lek activity, particularly at the start and end of the lek period; at peak activity some males may not leave the arena.

In large leks, a hierarchical structure of three ranks, postulated as likely for the Black Grouse, is apparent. As usual, the arena's centre is prime real estate and males with territories there defend them carefully, even to the extent of roosting on them. Males at the centre begin displaying earlier (both in season and day) and end later. Available evidence indicates that these first-rank birds are not less than three years old. In a Teberda Reserve lek of 18, the oldest males were five. The second-rank birds are two- or three-year-old males that display later and finish earlier than first-rank males. The lowest rank is young males in the first adult (grey) plumage. They do not have fixed territories and wandering freely around the arena, displaying rarely and never pursuing females. Old males are indifferent to these grey males, threatening only if one approaches too closely: grey males retreat speedily if threatened. However, grey males are sometimes accepted by older males almost as pupils, being allowed to stand close by with no negative reaction (Potapov, Pavlova, 1977). Only one observation of a grey male battling an old male has been noted: the young male triumphed (Vitovich, pers. comm.).

A typical first-rank male's lek territory is 50 x 80m (55 x 87yd), with the longer axis along the slope. Neighbouring males will be about 30m (33yd) apart and peripheral males about 200–300m (219–328yd) from the centre. The centre of the lek arena is set close to the arena's downhill border, so that females reach it first after arriving uphill on foot. During maximal lek activity, females visit the arena daily, both morning and evening. In the morning they arrive at daybreak, approaching from the nearest forest edge uttering (only in the mornings) a loud five-syllable vocal signal – 'ke-ke-ke-ki-ki'

Figure 86. Main lek postures
Of Lyrurus tetrix *(1) and* L. mlokosiewiczi *(2).*

– audible at up to 1km (0.6 mile). Females rarely visit the lek simultaneously, with not more than 2–3 females being seen together at either morning or evening leks. Mating was observed only in the morning (Vitovich, 1986).

In the basic male lek position (**Figure 86**), the breast is expanded, protruding both up and forwards. The neck is curved, bringing the head back so it lies behind the ball-like breast. The tail is raised, but only slightly opened. The wings are lowered slightly. In this position, the male either stands still or turns to show different sides. Usually the pose precedes a flutter–flight, the species' main courtship display (**Figure 87**). Before the flight, the male stands vertically, the expanded breast still up and

Figure 87. Lek jumping flight of a male *Lyrurus mlokosiewiczi*
View of the back (6) during rotation (3).

forward (looking similar to the English Pouter pigeon – **Figure 87, n1**). The eye-combs are maximally widened, and the male then flies vertically up to 1–1.5m (3.3–4.9ft) with 4–5 wing flaps, making a turn of 90–180° at the high point and then landing passively at a point close to the start. The number of wingbeats is very easy to count, as each produces a whistling sound audible to 150m (164yd). The main purpose of the flutter-flight is to demonstrate the white patches on the lower surfaces of the wings – as the bird turns in the air these are clearly visible, against the black plumage background, to all surrounding females, even in the darkness of early daybreak. Sometimes the male will make a flight without turning, though usually only if the ground is flat (Vitovich, 1986). After landing, the male remains motionless for several seconds, then returns to his start point if he has missed it. Early observers stated that the motionless state is a form of trance, it being possible to capture the bird by hand (Noska, Tschusi, 1895). Flutter-flights are often repeated, their frequency reflecting the male's level of sexual excitement (Averin, 1938). The appearance of females or a new male in the arena will both provoke males to start the flights.

During conflicts between males, the birds run at each other, their heads and necks straight out ahead, the tail parallel to the ground (**Figure 88**). As with other grouse species, there is also a 'parallel duel'. To start this, the males take up a posture used when patrolling a territory, particularly if females or rival males are close by – the male lifts and expands his breast, raises his tail to 45–60° and opens it slightly so it resembles a lyre (Figure 88). As a result, as the male walks in tall grass, the tail is clearly visible. Sometimes, during pursuit of a female, the male opens his tail far wider, but only for a few seconds.

Figure 88. Aggressive postures of *Lyrurus mlokosiewiczi*
Aggressive posture (1), along with postures in parallel duels (2).

In the parallel duel, the two males move at 1.5–2m (4.9–6.6ft) from each other (Figure 88). With exact synchrony they move, speed up, stop and make flutter-flights. Usually the bills of both males are open during the duel. The motivation for such duels, which may cross the entire lek arena, is unclear, but is presumably associated with territory defense. Rivalries between males occasionally take the form of a male appearing close to the territory of a lekking male and performing synchronous courtship displays at a distance of 3–7m (9.8–23ft). The males may then threaten each other, but such events rarely end in conflict, as the territory owner usually succeeds in driving the other away by threat alone (Potapov, Pavlova, 1977). True battles between males are rare. If they occur, the two males beat one another with bills, legs and wings.

One characteristic of species leks is the relative absence of the loud vocalizations that are the norm in the lekking of most other grouse. That of females has already been described. Males are quieter, only two sounds having been recorded to date. The first is a short, low raucous sound uttered during confrontations, when the bill is open (Noska, Tschusi, 1895; 1895; Averin, 1938). The male may also utter such sounds when circling around a female. The sound is audible only at distances of 30m, yet the male shudders with the effort of vocalizing (Vitovich, 1986). Interestingly, the sound has been described as very similar to the raucous lek sound of hybrid *L. tetrix* x *T. urogallus* birds (Potapov, 1985). The other sound is the click, described first as being produced by the bill during male confrontations (Averin, 1938). Later the clicks were described as resembling castanets, and being uttered only in one situation – during the flutter-jump. This is a rare display, a jump with a single wingbeat reaching a height of 60–80cm (23.6–31.5in), the male uttering the click at the high point, and again after landing. The click is very loud – audible at 200m/219yd (Vitovich, 1986) – and resembles the clicks of Black-billed Capercaillie (Potapov, 1985).

As with Black Grouse, *L. mlokosiewiczi* can demonstrate lek behaviour all year, except for the time of heavy moult (July–August). During autumn/winter leks, males of different ages gather at the arenas, though activity is restricted to older birds (Tkatchenco, 1966; Vitovich, 1986).

Mating is simple. The female chooses her mate and approaches him slowly, stopping occasionally. When the female is just a few metres away, the male puffs up like a ball, raises its folded tail vertically and walks to her. The female adopts the invitation position and the male jumps on to her. Mating takes 10–15 seconds, during which the male's long tail is against the ground. His wings remain folded and he does not grasp the female's crown feathers with his bill (Vitovich, 1986).

The nest is placed on south- or east-facing slopes under the cover of bushes or high tussocks with overhanging grass. Sheltered positions are chosen, as frosts occur often at the high altitudes favoured by the species. The female also chooses a spot where she has good visibility down the slope. In particularly suitable places, the female will nest several years in succession (Vitovich, 1986). The nest is 19–21cm (7.5–8.3in) in diameter and 5–9cm

Caucasian Black Grouse Nest, Teberda State Reserve, Karachai, Cherkes Republic, North Caucasian Federal Region, Russia

(2–3.5in) deep, lined with dry grass. The size of the clutch varies from 4–12, averaging 7 (N=44). Clutches with 4 eggs belong to the young females, or females who have lost a first clutch (Vitovich, 1986). The average size of eggs is 52.7mm x 35.0mm (Averin, 1938); 50.1mm x 35.8mm (Tkatchenko, 1966); 47.5–50.5mm x 35–37mm (Kutibidze, 1961); 49.7 x 35.3mm (N=80) (Vitovich, 1986). The eggs are yellowish-grey with numerous small brown spots.

Egg laying begins in mid-May in the north of the range and late April in the south. The earliest clutch – 10 eggs – was found on 10 May in north-western Azerbaijan (Hanmamedov, Aslanbekhova, 1985). In a unique case in Swanetia (Georgia), a nest with 10 fresh eggs was found on 15 August (Kutubidze, 1961). Incubation lasts 25 days, the female sitting so tight she will allow a human observer to approach to 1–1.5m (3.3–4.9ft). Hatching a brood takes about two days. Embryo mortality, on the basis of 15 nests during a 5-year period, was 30%, as a result of predation or chilling at the beginning of incubation. In well-placed nests with experienced females, mortality was zero. The brood leaves the nest the day the last chicks hatch, spending 3–4 hours close to it, then leaving the area, never to return, even in bad weather. The chicks are regularly brooded by the hen. Chicks begin to flutter short distances at 10 days, fluttering away to hide in the grass at any sign of danger. When they can fly well, chick response to danger varies, some taking flight, others hiding in tall grass (Vitovich, 1986). The female cares for her brood until mid-August, when the young begin to disperse. The young birds complete the moult to first adult plumage by early September. They are then 80% of adult weight. At this time the birds also begin to form flocks, these reaching maximal size as winter begins.

Many authors have suggested that chick mortality is very high (Averin, 1938; Chunichin, 1964; Tkatchenko, 1966), mainly because of the cold, wet weather. Others dispute this, maintaining that the result is due to incorrect counting. Vitovich (1986) considers the behaviour of the chicks (some flying, some hiding) makes it impossible to count broods accurately in mid-summer, giving one good example: he flushed a brood and observed only two chicks flying up with the female, but with the aid of a trained dog then found five chicks hidden in the grass. He considers that only such careful counts can give a true measure of chick mortality. The latest study of chick mortality suggests that broods lose one chick, on average, every 10 days (Drovetski, Rohwer, 2000).

Hunting, recreation and conservation

Caucasian Black Grouse are not a significant game bird in any of the countries that its range embraces. Even in the remote past, the species was only sought by a very small number of hunters, though it was snared by some local people (Radde, 1884). As a consequence, hunting cannot be considered a reason for the decline in range or population. The species is included in the Red Data Books of the Russian Federation, Georgia, and Azerbaijan, but such a measure defends the birds only against hunting: as has been known for some time, the main reason for the decline is overgrazing of the subalpine and alpine belts during the summer by cattle, the cutting of forests, especially near the timberline, and the influence of raptors. Cattle begin to graze the subalpine meadows in May/June, a time that coincides with nesting: that habitat is also the one favoured by broods. The cattle are also accompanied by herdsmen and dogs, adding to the birds' problems. Cessation of cattle grazing, for example in the Teberda State Reserve, has resulted in a slow but steady increase in the population. However, in most parts of the species' range, a decrease in cattle grazing would be in conflict with the interests of the local human population and, consequently, is unlikely.

Deforestation, especially in the southern part of the species' range, has an important negative effect on the species. Laws are enacted, but in general there is insufficient control of forest activities. The control of foxes aids the birds, but martens, Golden Eagles and herdsmen's dogs all take their toll.

On the positive side, one form of agriculture – the creation of hay-fields – is very favourable to the species. Such fields are scarce in the southern mountains, but very important as they provide the main source of cattle winter forage. As a consequence, hay fields are strictly guarded in summer, both from cattle and other animals, and become a haven for grouse broods. In such places the density of grouse population may be 4–16 times higher than in surrounding pastures (Sihkarulidze, 1974).

Captive rearing, and release, of the grouse may also support populations in which bird numbers have become dangerously low. Attempts have shown (Mlokosievich, 1925; Kalinovsky, 1900; Vitovich, 1986) that captive rearing of Caucasian Black Grouse is much easier than, say, that of *L. tetrix*, and does offer a significant possibility for limiting further decline, though there has been no real development of the idea so far. Large reservations – the Caucasian and Teberda State Reserves in Russia, the Lagodechi State Reserve in Georgia, the Zakataly State Reserve in Azerbaijan and the Dilijan State Reserve in Armenia – and other, smaller local reserves are also, of course, immensely helpful in species conservation. In that regard, the establishment of the Erzi State Reserve in central Greater Caucasus in 2000 (Ingushetia Republic, Russian Federation) was to be applauded.

CHAPTER 9

Genus 8: *Tympanuchus* PRAIRIE-CHICKENS

Tympanuchus Gloger, 1842:358. *Cupidonia* (Reichenbach, 1853).Type species: *Cupidonia americana* Reichenbach, 1852 = *Tetrao cupido* Linnaeus, 1758 for original designation. Type species: *Tetrao cupido* Linnaeus, 1758, by monotypy.

The genus unites three species of grouse, the Greater Prairie-Chicken (*Tympanuchus cupido*), the Lesser Prairie-Chicken (*T. pallidicinctus*) and the Sharp-tailed Grouse (*T. phasianellus*). Originally only *T. cupido* was considered as the monotypic genus *Tympanuchus* because of the presence of cervical sacs in the neck's apteria that inflate during lek performances. The Sharp-tailed Grouse was initially placed in the genus *Centrocercus* along with the Sage-Grouse because of its long tail (Swainson, Richardson, 1831), but later it was placed in a new, monotypic genus, *Pedioecetes* (Baird, 1858). The Lesser Prairie-Chicken was originally described as a subspecies of the Greater Prairie-Chicken, but careful study of the two forms then revealed features that defined it as separate species. This conclusion is confirmed by the overlap of the ranges of the two forms in Texas, Colorado, Kansas and Oklahoma in the not-so-distant past (Ridgway, Friedmann, 1946), the different colour of the gular sacs (Jones, 1963; 1964) and differences in courtship displays (Hjorth, 1970). The objection that the small differences between Greater and Lesser Prairie-grouse, and the greater ones between those two and the Sharp-tailed Grouse, is intolerable within one genus (Short, 1967) is easily removed if we accept the existence of two subgenus, the nominate subgenus *Tympanuchus* and the subgenus *Pedioecetus* (Potapov, 1985). The close relationship of Prairie-Chickens and Sharp-tailed Grouse was shown very early on the basis of osteological features (Shufeldt, 1882), and later on the basis of other details (Short, 1967). Among skeletal peculiarities, the presence of sesamoid ossification in *m. flexor hallicus breves* is absent in other genera of grouse (Hudson *et al.*, 1959). Other common features for the three species are: medium body size; the practically complete absence of sexual dimorphism in the monotonous plumage colouration, and yet, despite this, the presence of collective leks; the one-blade construction of the yellow or red eye-comb and its small size (see Figure 45, n5 in Chapter 4); the presence of brightly coloured naked apteria that is inflated during displays; the number of retrices (18); the colour and design of the outer vanes of the primaries; the dark colour of the crown; and the white colour of the throat and chin. The colour and design of downy chicks is also the same, without any trace of a black cap on the crown. The significant differences between the colouration of juvenile and adult plumage does not permit us to consider the latter as primitive. The unique elongated feathers above the cervical apteria in Greater and Lesser Prairie-Chickens, and the prominently elongated central retrices of the Sharp-tailed Grouse that are absent in other grouse species, are clear evidence of the deep specialization of feathering in the three species.

All three species also prefer open habitats. The courtship displays of the three have their own characteristics, but also have two common features – the run and the song, the latter consisting of hooting and gurgling sounds. Among other elements of courtship displays, there are elements shared with Asian Spruce Grouse, Blue and Dusky Grouse, Willow Ptarmigan and Black Grouse that, following Potapov (1985), we consider evidence of the ancient phylogenetic relationship with ancestors of the genera *Dendragapus*, *Falcipennis*, *Lagopus* and *Lyrurus*.

Hybridization of the *Tympanuchus* grouse with other grouse genera is rare, though, and the overlap of ranges and habitats may be the main reason for this. To date, only hybrids between Sharp-tailed Grouse and Sage and Dusky Grouse have been observed. In the first case, the colour and pattern of the Sage-Grouse dominated the hybrid upper body, while the breast was identical with that of the Sharp-tailed Grouse. Especially interesting was the colour and pattern of tail feathers – black with the grey tops, as in some forms of *Dendragapus*. In the case of hybridization with a (male) Dusky Grouse, the features of the latter dominated the upper body and tail, but the underbody was as the Sharp-tailed Grouse (Brooks, 1907; Eng, 1971).

The clear evidence of a close relationship between the Greater Prairie-Chicken and the Sharp-tailed Grouse became indisputable in the mass hybridization between the two species that occurred at the beginning of the 20th century during the large-scale agricultural development of virgin prairies and adjacent forest-steppe landscapes. Human agricultural activity quickly destroyed all habitat barriers that had existed between the two species (Johnsgard, Wood, 1968), after which even the significant differences in courtship displays failed to prevent hybridization. In newly appearing sympatric areas, the two species formed mutual leks in which males of both species, and hybrid males (from several generations, including reciprocal crossings), performed their displays. But despite this occurrence, the hybrids did not develop into a new form, absorbed crossings meaning that in most places, where the Sharp-tailed Grouse were more numerous, Greater Prairie-Chickens eventually disappeared even where the areas had been part of their original range. Today there are still areas where the ranges of the two species overlap or touch, and in these, though mutual leks are not observed, leks are often placed close together. In such cases female Sharp-tailed Grouse sometimes visit Greater Prairie-Chicken leks and mate there (Svedarsky, Kalahar, 1980).

The behaviour of an adult hybrid male in a Greater Prairie-Chicken lek in Colorado has been observed. Neither species dominated the appearance of the hybrid, its form being intermediate between the two: the tail was rounded, but the central pair of retrices was slightly elongated; the 'pinnae' (see below) were very short; and the air sacs were purple, as in Sharp-tailed Grouse, but much larger when inflated than in that species. The courtship display of the hybrids was also intermediate. The hybrid stamped its feet faster and for longer than a Greater Prairie-Chicken, but ran less than a Sharp-tailed Grouse. The bird controlled a larger territory than a male Prairie-Chicken, but not at the centre of the lek arena, and he was not approached by any Prairie-Chicken female. He pursued females, leaving his territory to do so, but as this required entering the territories of other males, he was rapidly chased back to his own territory, or occasionally chased so vigorously that he was forced to fly away (Evans, 1966).

8.1 PRAIRIE-CHICKENS Subgenus: *Tympanuchus* (Gloger, 1842)

Tympanuchus (Gloger, 1842): 358.
Type species: *Tetrao cupido* Linnaeus.

Terrestrial birds of middle size, inhabiting the open landscapes of the steppe and forest-steppe zones of North America. Both sexes have cryptic colouration on the upper body and a cross-stripe pattern on the lower. Both sexes have a bunch of elongated feathers on each side of the neck. Sexual dimorphism in both size and colouration is weakly expressed.

8.1.1 Greater Prairie-Chicken *Tympanuchus (Tympanuchus) cupido* (Linnaeus, 1758)

Tetrao cupido (Linnaeus, 1758): 160 (Virginia). *Bonasa cupido* (Stephens, 1819): 299. *Cupidonia americana* (Reichenbach, 1852): XXIX (nom. nov. pro *Tetrao cupido* Linnaeus, 1758, see Reichenbach 1848: (4), tab. 339, fig. 1896-1898). *Cupidonia cupido* (Baird, 1858b): 628.

Morphology

The proportions and size of the body are as for most grouse. The wings are rounded with the top of the open wing formed by the 7th primary. The tarsi feathering in southern populations (*T. c. attwateri*) does not fully reach the base (Potapov, 1985), and in one of the specimens of the extinct subspecies *T. c. cupido* (a male obtained 29.12.1886 on Martha's Vineyard), only the central toe has pectinates (Coll ZIN RAN). Both sexes have bunches of elongated feathers ('pinnae') on the sides of the neck above the cervical apteria, but in males the pinna are twice the length of those in females. Pinnae are formed by 12 feathers, the length of which increases from the front of the bunch to its rear. The skin of the inflated air-sacs is orange-yellowish.

Colouration

Adult male

Mottled yellowish-brown, the pattern darker and more complicated on the upper body. The colouration is formed by alternate whitish and black-brown stripes. Feathers of the nape and back have a regular pattern of black-brown and yellowish-light-brown stripes. A black stripe runs through the eye to the neck, where it adjoins the black of the pinnae. Chin, throat and cheeks are yellowish-white with some small brown spots at the bill base. On each side of the upper neck are the elongated pinna feathers: most of these are black with

Male Greater Prairie-Chicken

narrow white tips, the frontal feathers having long white stripes on the ends. Under body is paler with a regular pattern of narrow, light-brown stripes. The rear belly and undertail coverts are white. Primaries and secondaries are grey-brown with sparse white cross-stripes on outer webs. Only on inner secondaries is the colour brighter, and the pattern more symmetric. The outer tertials have the same colour and design, but the top white spots are triangular. All wing upper coverts have a simple cross-stripe pattern. Retrices are black-brown with narrow white borders at the tops and an indistinct cross-stripe pattern on the central feather pair. Undertail coverts are black-brown with wide white tops.

Adult female

Similar to male, but pinnae are only half the length and mostly white. The black stripes at sides of the head are only weakly expressed. Retrices are patterned by yellow-brown

Female Greater Prairie-Chicken

stripes. Undertail coverts have a pattern of alternating brown and white stripes, and white feather tops to the feathers.

Juvenile (both sexes)
Juvenile plumage is even more mottled than that of adult (Ridgway, Friedmann, 1946). Rufous-yellow dominates the upper body colour, but with speckling of numerous brown or black spots, marks and strokes. Back feathers have thin white shaft stripes that form an indistinct pattern. Upper wing coverts and primaries are as adults, but primary tips are sharpened. Secondaries are a more intensive brown. Back, rump and uppertail coverts are as adults, but more rufous and with paler feather tops. Retrices are blackish and have seven or eight thin white cross-stripes and white borders. The dark head stripes link the angles of the mouth through the eye to the ears. Chin, throat and lower cheek parts are white, tinged cream. Breast feathers are white with a yellowish tinge and thin, brown cross-stripes. Body sides have broad, brown cross-bands. Belly and thighs are whitish, with thin, brown cross-stripes, with only the belly centre being completely white. Undertail coverts are white with traces of brown cross-stripes.

Downy chick
Lower body is yellowish-grey with a light brown tint on breast. Upper body is yellowish-brown with a more intensive reddish tint on rump, and with many black spots, especially on crown, nape and middle of back. Single black spot on the forehead, and three little spots form a small stripe behind the eye. Upperwing coverts and secondaries are brown with white tips, these forming white cross-stripes on the folded wing (Ridgway, Friedmann, 1946; Johnsgard 1973).

Dimensions
Male (N=17): wing length 226mm (range 217–241mm); tail 96.2mm (90–103mm); tarsi 49.7mm (46.5–51.5mm); middle toe 45mm (43–47mm).
Females (N=11): wing length 219mm (208–220mm); tail 90.3mm (87.5–93.5mm); tarsi 49.1mm (46–52mm); middle toe 43mm (41–44.6mm) (Ridgway, Friedmann, 1946).
From specimens in Coll ZIN RAN: Males (N=8): wing 216–242mm; tail 76–102mm; length of retrices 31–33mm (Coll ZIN RAN); length of bill (from the front edge of nostrils) 12.3–14.9mm; width of bill (at front edge of nostril) 8.7–10.0mm; tarsi 37.5–48mm; middle toe (without claw) 39–48mm.
Average weight of 22 males (taking no account of season): 992g (35oz); maximum weight: 1,361g (48oz). From 16 females, the data are 770g (27oz) and 1,020g (36oz) respectively (Johnsgard, 1973).

Moult

The moult succession is as the Black Grouse. Summer feathering appears only on the head and neck. The 1stdefinite primary appears at 28 days of age, growth being completed at 56 days; timings of the 2nd primary are 35and 56days respectively; for the 3rd – 41and 65 days; 4th – 49 and 77 days; 5th – 55 and 84 days, 6th – 60 and 86 days; 8th – 82 and 126 days (Johnsgard, 1973).

Distribution

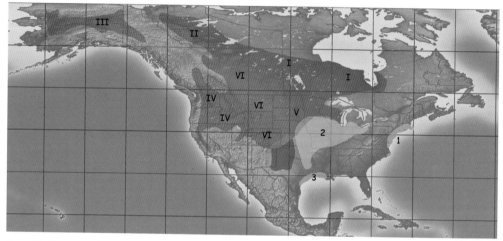

Map 17. Ranges of *Tympanuchus* species at the end of the 19th century.
The range of Tympanuchus phasianellus *is indicated in red.*
Sub-species: I – T. phasianellus phasianellus; *II –* T. ph. kennikotti; *III –* T. ph. caurus; *IV –* T. ph. columbianus; *V –* T. ph. campestris; *VI –* T. ph. jamesi.
The range of Tympanuchus cupido *is indicated in yellow.*
The overlap of T. phasianellus *and* T. cupido *is indicated in orange.*
Subspecies: 1 – T. cupido cupido; *2 –* T. c. pinnatus; *3 –* T. c. attwateri.
The range of Tympanuchus pallidicinctus *is indicated in blue.*
The overlap of T. phasianellus *and* T. pallidicinctus *is indicated in purple.*

The range of the Greater Prairie-Chicken has undergone significant changes over the last 200 years as a consequence of the transformation of the prairies due to both agriculture and industry: indeed, it is now difficult to reconstruct the original range. It is believed that the birds once inhabited the oak savannah (or oak-steppe) of what are now the states of Minnesota, Iowa, Illinois, Missouri, the eastern parts of Texas, Oklahoma, Kansas, Nebraska, the north-western corner of Arkansas, and the northern parts of Indiana and Ohio. An isolated part of the ancient range occupied the coastal regions of the Atlantic Ocean from New Hampshire south to Maryland. There may also have been an isolated population in the coastal regions of the Gulf of Mexico between the estuaries of the Mississippi and Nueces rivers (**Map 17**). Following the intensive cultivation of the oak savannah and

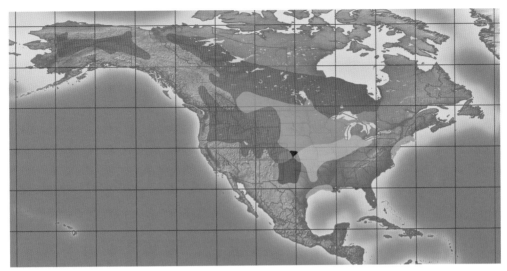

Map 18. Ranges of *Tympanuchus* species in 1920s.
The range of Tympanuchus phasianellus *is indicated in red.*
The range of Tympanuchus cupido *is indicated in yellow.*
The overlap of T. phasianellus *and* T. cupido *is indicated in orange.*
The range of Tympanuchus pallidicinctus *is indicated in blue.*
The overlap of T. phasianellus *and* T. pallidicinctus *is indicated in purple.*
Black indicates where all three species overlap.
Subspecies are as indicated on Map 17.

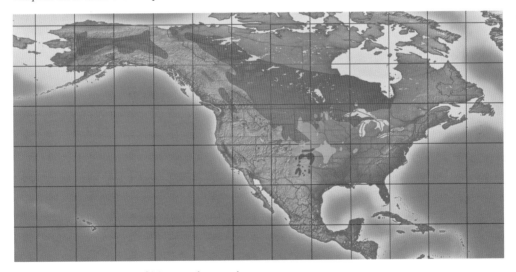

Map 19. Modern ranges of *Tympanuchus* species.
The range of Tympanuchus phasianellus *is indicated in red.*
The range of Tympanuchus cupido *is indicated in yellow.*
The overlap of T. phasianellus *and* T. cupido *is indicated in orange.*
The range of Tympanuchus pallidicinctus *is indicated in blue.*
Subspecies are as indicated on Map 17.

prairies, the species broadened its initial range to the west and north-west, and by the 1920s had completely populated North and South Dakota, Nebraska, Kansas and even the Canadian prairies of southern Manitoba, Saskatchewan and Alberta (**Map 18**). Then the population went into sharp decline, due to both uncontrolled hunting and habitat destruction, reaching minimal size in the 1950s. By 1932, the eastern isolated form (*T. c. cupido*) had disappeared, while the southern isolated (Gulf of Mexico) form (*T. c. attwateri*) had been reduced to a few isolated sites. The largest parts of the former range now remain only in South Dakota, Nebraska and Kansas, and nearby parts of Oklahoma and Missouri. Several small populations also exist, and are protected, in North Dakota, Minnesota, Wisconsin, Michigan, Illinois, Missouri, Oklahoma and Colorado. The species has now completely disappeared from Canada (**Map 19**).

Subspecies
The geographical variation in both size and colouration are minimal.

Eastern Greater Prairie-Chicken (Heath Hen) *T. cupido cupido* (Linnaeus, 1758)
Originally distributed along a narrow strip of the Atlantic from the southern part of Maine to the estuary of Potomac River and perhaps even to Virginia and North Carolina (the latter the probable reason for Linnaeus' reference to the position of the type specimen). Human activity in the 1870s left a small population on Martha's Vineyard that was protected in 1908 when the estimate was about 50 birds. The protection was very effective, and there were nearly 2,000 birds by 1916. Unfortunately, a great fire that year destroyed virtually the entire habitat, as well as nests with clutches. That, and the severe winter which followed, reduced the population to 150 birds, mainly males. Infection originating in turkeys reduced the population still further, and attempts at conservation failed: by 1928 only one male was known to be alive. The bird survived alone for 4 years, but disappeared in 1932 (Bent, 1932; Anonymous, 1932). All that is now known of the subspecies derives from the observations at Martha's Vineyard, and from the study of rare specimens. The single, male, specimen in Coll ZIN RAN had a wing length of 222mm (the 8th primary was the longest); alula 89mm; tail 91mm; length and width of bill at front end of nostrils 12.0mm x 9.5mm; tarsi 39mm; central toe + nail 41mm +14mm. The pinnae are narrow and 65mm long. Pectinations are only present on the central toe. The distance between the ends of the 2nd secondary and the longest (8th) primary is 85mm, i.e. the width of the open wing is slightly wider than that of other subspecies (Potapov, 1985).

From the work of Bent (1932), the lekking of the species did not differ from other subspecies.

Western Greater Prairie-Chicken *T. c. pinnatus* (Brewster, 1885)
In comparison to the previous form, the general colouration is greyish, with less of an ochreous tinge. Occupies the main part of the current species' range. The general characteristics of this subspecies' biology are given below.

Southern Greater Prairie-Chicken *T. c. attwateri* (Bendire, 1893)

Differs by slightly darker colouration and slightly smaller size. At the beginning of the 20th century (to the 1920s), the subspecies inhabited the coastal regions of the Gulf of Mexico from Abbeville (92°W) west to the mouth of Nueces River (97°30′W) (Ridgway, Friedmann, 1946). At present the subspecies is on the verge of extinction. In 1967, only approximately 1,000 birds occupied a territory of 58,500ha (144,557 acres) (Johnsgard, 1973) and the bird was added to the Endangered Species List. However, the population continued to decline, with only 42 birds being counted in 1996. A captive breeding and reintroduction program then began at Houston Zoo under the supervision of the US Fish and Wildlife Service. As almost the entire range of the birds was in private (rancher) hands, the landowners were encouraged to become involved in the program. In the years to 2007, 1,147 birds were returned to the wild and refuges were set up for their protection, the combination rescuing the subspecies from almost certain extinction.

Habitats

Formerly, the main species habitats were damp, tall-grass prairies, alternating with oak forest and flood-land forests. A close connection with arboreal vegetation was seen only in winter, when most of the birds moved from the prairie to forested areas, sometimes travelling distances of more than 400km (249 miles) (Johnsgard, 1973). No such habitat now exists except in the eastern part of the original range. The best current habitat is cultivated land with different kinds of cereals, especially sorghums, the tall stems of which are not covered by snow in winter. The now-extinct eastern subspecies inhabited open habitats in coastal sand dunes covered by bilberries and tall oaks. On the shores of the Gulf of Mexico the birds prefer the same habitats, occupying plots of prairie that have escaped destruction, cultivated fields and oak stands.

Population structure and density

The population density of the species across its original range is not known with any certainty. Yeatter (1963) gives a density of male birds of 13/km², but today the density in the most suitable habitats is much reduced, varying from 1.8–2.3 birds/km², though it has been known to reach 19–20 birds/km² when population levels are high, and remained at 5–6 birds/km² over a period of several years in Kansas (Johnsgard, 1973). In Oklahoma the density in the mid-20th century was 5–7 birds/km² (Jones, 1963). Very little is known about population structure. Males comprised 54.9% of juvenile birds and 56.4% of adults. Juveniles were 50.2% of the autumn population, while the annual survival rate was 28–38% (Hamerstrom, Hamerstrom, 1949; Johnsgard, 1973). The mortality of 10-week-old chicks is 56% (Bowman, Robel, 1977).

The number of birds in both South Dakota and Nebraska varies significantly from year to year. In South Dakota the population was estimated at 80,000 in 1968, as 39,000 in 1982 and 65,000 in 1997. In Nebraska the population rose from 100,000 in 1968 to 200,000 in 1979, declined to 130,000 in 1997, but then rose to its former level. The increase in numbers in both states was the result of a Federal Conservation Reserve Program initiated in the mid-1980s to conserve water, soil and wildlife resources by paying farmers to plant and maintain perennial cover crops of grasses, forbs and shrubs (Fredrickson *et al.*, 1999; Svedarsky *et al.*, 2000; Westemeier *et al.*, 1999: Robb, Schroeder, 2005).

Territoriality

In general, the species is strongly sedentary, birds spending their entire lives within a comparatively small territory, with limited seasonal displacements. Only in northern parts of the range when the population was high were birds seen making regular seasonal movements (southwards in winter), this being particularly noticeable when winters were severe with significant snowfall. In Wisconsin, for example, flocks of up to 300 birds crossed the western part of Upper Lake, which is nowhere less than 24km (15 miles) wide, during spring and autumn migrations. In Iowa the birds also regularly moved south in the autumn, returning in March. These movements were seen until the end of the 19th century, but when cereals began to be cultivated in the State, the birds changed to a more sedentary way of life. Regular seasonal movements were also observed in North Dakota, these appearing as real migrations in severe winters (which are common), with large flocks flying one after another at a considerable height (Bent, 1932).

Today, with the sharp decrease in both range size and overall population numbers, such movements are rarer, though they are seen, for example, in northern Nebraska, where most birds move south, with just a few males remaining behind (Kobriger, 1965). In most other areas, seasonal movements look to be no more than everyday changes of roosting places to feeding grounds and vice versa. In one study, 87% of ringed birds spent the entire year in a territory with a radius of 1.5–3.0km (0.9–1.9 miles), though the remaining birds made flights of 46–160km (29–99 miles), and in doing so fulfilled the important role of increasing genetic diversity (Hamerstrom, Hamerstrom, 1949).

Radio telemetry indicates that the individual territories of old males are maximal in March (averaging 506.8ha/1,252 acres) and minimal in August (31.6ha/78 acres). Young males follow the same pattern, though some birds moved to other areas of population (Robel *et al.*, 1970).

Behaviour

Greater Prairie-Chickens are among the most terrestrial of all grouse, with the birds spending most of their time on the ground among thick, tall vegetation. Only in winter, when the main source of food is arboreal, are the birds seen in trees. Despite having good flying ability, the birds prefer to move on foot, with flight only being used when moving

Female Greater Prairie-Chicken

to a new area for roosting or feeding, or to escape danger. In those cases, in general the distance flown is small.

Nutrition

Throughout spring, summer and autumn, the main dietary items comprise three food groups: fresh green parts of grasses, different seeds, and insects. The percentage of insects in the diet can be up to 30% of food intake, the most important species being *Othoptera*, particularly different kinds of grasshopper and locust. Locusts may be consumed in large quantities during invasions. During the autumn, in some places acorns are a main constituent of the diet, these being swallowed whole. In winter, the main food in recent times has been cultivated cereals, mainly maize and sorghums. When available, the green leaves of clover and lespedeza, and soya beans are added to the diet (study in Missouri and Oklahoma – Korschgen, 1962; Jones, 1963). The main source of winter forage before cultivation of the prairies is unknown, but the fact that the birds can utilize the twigs and buds of deciduous trees during severe winters suggests that these items once formed the main diet, just as in other grouse species, although even then, in areas where the winter was softer, the seeds of wild cereals and beans, different berries, and the fruits of dog roses would have been taken, just as they are today (Bent, 1932).

Wintering

The species' winter life depends on the season's character. If the snow depth exceeds 30cm (11.8in), the birds roost in snow burrows, as other grouse, but if the snow cover is shallower, or is covered by an icy crust, or during periods of thaw, the birds roost in the thick, tall grasses or reeds. If conditions allow, the birds spend all winter in large flocks in small territories. In north-west Minnesota, areas of forbs, especially alfalfa and goldenrod (*Solidago* spp.), appeared to provide the best conditions for roosting in snow burrows (Rosenquist, 1996). After leaving their roosting place, the flock flies a short distance (usually not more than 1.6km/1 mile) to the nearest feeding place in a field of cereals. Interestingly, each flock used the same field throughout the winter, despite of the presence of other, similar fields (Hamerstrom, Hamerstrom, 1949). In North Dakota, the birds roost in snow burrows only when soft, deep snow cover allows, otherwise they roost in bowl-like depressions excavated in the snow, or among dense, snow-free vegetation (Toepfer, Eng, 1987).

Data on the wintertime budget and energy requirements of the species are absent, though the maximum fresh content of a crop was 63g in a study by Bent (1932).

Breeding

Lek activity begins early. In Oklahoma males begin to visit lek arenas and to display in February, while near the shores of the Gulf of Mexico they may start in January. The period of maximum lek activity, when females participate, is much later – at the end of March in the southern range (Hamerstrom, Hamerstrom, 1955; Robel *et al.*, 1970), or in April (Wisconsin, Hjorth, 1970) in the north. Female participation begins gradually, rising to a peak over about three weeks, then remains high for about two weeks, during which period nearly 90% of mating occurs. Female activity then ceases over just a few

Conflict between neighbouring male Greater Prairie-Chickens at a lek

Male Greater Prairie-Chicken displaying

days. However, there is another peak of female participation about three weeks later, with radio-marking of females suggesting this was due either to the loss of first clutches and the need to mate again, or involved young females whose pubescence was delayed. Overall, female participation at the lek arena was one month shorter than that of males: in Kansas, for example, it lasted, on average, from 30 March to 10 June, the peaks of visits being in early May and early June (Robel *et al.*, 1970).

Lek arenas are in open places, mostly on the gentle slopes or tops of low hills, covered by sparse, low (no higher than 15cm/5.9in) grass (Anderson, 1969). Arenas are stable, existing without change for 30–40 years, even in places where buildings or roads appear nearby. However, such disturbances have also been known to cause arenas to be moved several hundred metres or even to disappear. Though stable in position, some lek arenas may actually function only when the density of birds is high, being unused during periods of depressed population.

The number of males at the lek is now much reduced from former times, averaging 12 males (range 2–42). Solitary leks are very rare. The lek's hierarchical structure has two levels: the first is the most active males, aged 3 years or more, which occupy the arena's centre; the second comprises males with less prominent activities, the number of whom may exceed the number of the first group. First-category males maintain individual territories throughout the lek, driving off rivals, actively displaying and mating with females who appear in their plots. Second-category males have individual territories at the periphery of the arena, but do not defend these as readily, even moving to other areas during the same day. The size of a male's territory is, on average, 185m²/221yd², varying from 55m²/66yd² (at the arena centre) to 350m²/419yd² (at the periphery). Markers of the borders between neighbouring territories are different details of the micro relief and vegetation: Anderson (1971) showed that it was possible to alter territory borders by artificially replacing such details.

Radio tracking has also established that some males do not hold territories: these males may be young or old, and may visit several lek arenas in turn. Many females do the same. In one study, a female who lost two clutches visited a different lek each time to mate (Robel *et al.*, 1970).

During the active phase of lekking, males appear about 45 minutes before the sunrise. Maximum activity lasts until about an hour after sunrise, after which it decreases before stopping completely 1–2 hours later. The evening lek is not as firmly fixed. Usually males appear 1.5–2 hours before sunset and are maximally active at the moment of sunset. After sunset, activity continues until it is dark, at which point the males fly away to roost. However, as for all other grouse species, the weather has an influence on lek timings and activity.

In the main lek courtship posture the male's head and neck are stretched forward, parallel to the ground, as in Black Grouse, with the air sacs partially or fully inflated (**Figure 89**). The tail is held upright and partially open, the wings slightly opened to the sides. The pinnae are upright and pointed slightly forward, looking like horns. The nuptial song, the main element of the courtship display, is uttered in this posture, with the singing accompanied by a series of specific movements carried out in strict sequence. The bird firstly makes a short run (up to 3m/3.3yd), accelerating towards the end, then stamps its feet for about 2 seconds, stopping suddenly. The bird immediately opens its

Figure 89. Basic lek posture of *Tympanuchus cupido*

tail widely, folds it with two loud clicks, then utters its song of three low, hooting notes, 'hooom–aaa–hooom', that lasts 2 seconds. In sonograms, these hoots look like one uninterrupted sound with three pulsations.

During the foot stamping, the feet hit at 20 blows/sec, producing a noise akin to a low drum roll, audible at distances of up to 30m (33yd) as the stamping sound is amplified due to the resonance effect of the bird's body (Hjorth, 1970). During the hooting, the bird's air sacs are inflated twice, at the end of the first syllable/beginning of the second. The hooting song is audible at distances of more than 3km (1.9 miles), comparable to that of the Black Grouse. During the third syllable of the song, the male's tail is spread maximally and then closed again. The entire song is uttered with the bill closed; it then opens at the end of the performance. The entire ritual of run, stamping and song lasts about 5 seconds.

The male's courtship flight is very short and low, no higher than 1m (3.3ft) and with 2–3 wingbeats. Immediately after landing, the male utters a specific 'laughter' sound, resembling the first part of the Willow Ptarmigan's song (Hjorth, 1970).

Male lek activity increases sharply when females appear, the male performing the rituals as it circles a female, occasionally adopting a posture in which the bill, breast and tops of spread wings touch the ground, while simultaneously the rear of the body is elevated – a similar posture to that of capercaillies and spruce grouse (Potapov, 1985). There are also specific postures and movements during confrontations with rival males, the birds performing the 'parallel duel', as has been described for other grouse species. If confrontations result in battles, the wings are the main weapon (Hjorth, 1970).

Autumn lek activity takes place regularly from mid-September to December, males gathering at the arena and performing their activities in order to defend individual territories. Young males are also involved at this time (Hjorth, 1970).

During the spring lek, females arrive later than males, usually appearing in groups, rarely singly or in twos. They will often mate several times during the morning. Most couplings are with first-category males, but among these only 67% will actually mate. In some cases a single male will actually achieve 70–75% of all mating (Robel, 1966). Before mating, females usually visit the arena three days (but not more) in succession.

Once mated, a female prepares a nest a short distance from the arena, in general no more than 1.6km (1 mile) from it (Anderson, Toepfer, 1999), though occasionally at a more remote site, or even close to another lek arena (Robel et al., 1970). As a rule, the nest is placed in thick, tall grass in an open area, or among bushes, and even trees. The nest is always well-concealed, but a study in Missouri noted that the use of woody vegetation sites lowers the nest success rate: 57.7% of clutches hatched when the woody cover was <5%, but only 17.6% when woody cover was >5%, because such areas attract mammalian predators, and assist avian predators by providing perch sites (McKee et al., 1998). Shade from strong sunlight is a necessary condition of the nest's position (Bent, 1932).

The nest is of usual grouse form, i.e. shallow scrape of 18–20cm (7.1–7.9in) in diameter, about 5cm (2in) deep and sparsely lined with dry grass. Egg laying begins in the first decade of May and lasts for almost a month. The t of laying depends on the hen's physiological conditions, but usually the interval between eggs is more than 24 hours. In one study a female laid the next egg 7 days after the first one, taking 18 days in total to lay 11 eggs (Bent, 1932). When leaving the nest during the egg-laying phase, the hen covers the eggs with dry grass.

The eggs are olive-grey in colour, with large quantities of small brown spots. In some cases the spots may be larger, up to 2mm in diameter, and occasionally all spots are faint. The average size of eggs (N=100, Wisconsin) is 44.86mm x 33.59mm (Bent, 1932). The number of eggs in a clutch varies from 7–17, averaging 11.5 (Bent, 1932) or 12 (Hamerstrom, 1939). Incubation averages 25 days (McEven *et al.*, 1969), but sometimes may be only 23 or 24 days. During incubation, the female leaves the nest to feed only twice daily, in the morning and evening, never leaving during the hottest time of the day. Brood hatching may take up to 2 days. The mass appearance of nestlings begins from the end of May and lasts through the first decade of June. The latest date seen for newly hatched nestlings from a repeated clutch is 7 July (Bent, 1932).

The weight of newly hatched nestlings is 15.9g (0.56oz) (Bent, 1932). As with other grouse, the nestlings are very sensitive to cold and are brooded by the female regularly, during the day as well as at night. After hatching, broods often join together, even where they are of different ages. Broods begin to disperse from the end of August/early September, though in general the young birds do not travel far from their place of birth, radio tracking suggesting a maximum distance of 1,218m (1,332yd) (Bowman, Robel, 1977).

Hunting, recreation and conservation

Greater Prairie-Chickens were a very popular game bird during the second half of the 19th century: in 1874 alone, market hunters shipped not less than 300,000 birds from Nebraska to eastern cities (Vodehnal, 1999). But the popularity of the hunt fell in the 1920s as the population declined. As population numbers declined, hunting was prohibited in several States, though the hunting take was still significant: in 1967, for example, hunting was allowed in six States, the estimated annual kill in these reaching 85,000 birds (Johnsgard, 1973). Hunting is now prohibited or very restricted across the species range. However, populations have continued to decline – for example, in Missouri the population density declined from 225 birds/100ha (247 acres) in 1960–1965 to close to zero in 2010 (Jamison, Alleger, 2009).

8.1.2 Lesser Prairie-Chicken *Tympanuchus (Tympanuchus) pallidicinctus*
(Ridgway, 1873). *Cupidonia cupido* **var.** *pallidicinctus* (Ridgway, 1873): 190 (south-western prairies).

Morphology

The main differences from the previous species are the dull red tinge of air-sac skin and the bright yellow eye-combs that are nearly twice the width and more conspicuously enlarged during displays. All other proportions of the body, including the shape of wing and tail, are the same, apart from the central pair of retrices, which are narrower. Reduction of pectinations has not been mentioned.

Colouration

Adult male
The general colouration is as for the Greater Prairie-Chicken, differing mainly by having a clearer, but thinner, cross-stripe pattern, with most stripes bicoloured brown and black. The brown cross-stripe pattern is well developed on the central pair of retrices.

Adult female
As the previous species.

Female Lesser Prairie-Chicken

Male Lesser Prairie-Chicken

Female Lesser Prairie-Chicken

Juvenile (both sexes)
Similar to the previous species, but a more rufous general tone.

Downy chick
As the previous species, but pale below, less rufous above. The black spots on the upper parts and the sides of the head are paler (Sutton, 1968).

Dimensions
Males (N=5): wing length 212mm (range 207–220mm); tail 92.4mm (88–95mm); tarsi 44.4mm (43–47mm); middle toe 39mm (36.5–40.0mm). Females (N=4): wing length 198mm (193–201mm); tail 84.2mm (81–87mm); middle toe 38.4mm (36–40mm). (All data from Ridgway, Friedmann, 1946).
Average weight of male (with no allowance for seasonal changes): 780g/27.51oz (maximum: 893g/31.50oz). For females: 722g (25.47oz) and 779g (27.48oz) respectively (Johnsgard, 1973).

Moult
Sequence and timings as in Greater Prairie-Chicken.

Distribution
(See Maps 17–19)
The original range of the species is unknown, but is assumed to have covered the prairies of northern Texas, eastern New Mexico, western Oklahoma, western Kansas and south-eastern Colorado, where, in isolated patches, the birds are still seen today. It is unclear if the ranges of Greater and Lesser Prairie-Chickens overlapped in the past. Aldrich (1963) maintains they did not, but Ridgway, Friedmann (1946) consider the original Lesser Prairie-Chicken range went further north and east, including parts of Nebraska and Missouri, where it must have overlapped the Greater Prairie-Chicken range. Today the greater part of the species' range is on the border of New Mexico and Texas, and in central and southern parts of Kansas.

Subspecies
The species is monotypic.

Habitats
The basal habitat was dry prairie, usually with sandy soils and a prevalence of grass, dwarf oak and *Andropogon* sp. stands, sometimes together with sagebrush (Jones, 1963). This habitat extended across the species' range. Where dwarf oak is absent, the birds choose places with tall scrub sage and *Andropogon* sp. (Hoffman, 1963).

Population structure and density

The sex ratio in populations changes constantly, though the dominance of males is generally seen, with the percentage of males varying from 44.5–65.7%. The percentage of young birds among the males of a population varies from 28.4–65.7%. The percentage of young birds in a population in the autumn varies from 37.3–68.6%. The number of chicks per female at the end of summer varies hugely, from 1.4–10.2. The annual mortality of males is 65%, with full replacement of the population occurring every five years (New Mexico: Campbell, 1972; Johnsgard, 1973).

Formerly, the density of birds was very high in some areas, especially during summer and autumn, when flocks of several hundred concentrated in cereal fields (Bent, 1932). In more recent times, the density in the most suitable habitats has been 26–58 birds/km². The overall population of the species in the 1960s was evaluated as 36,000–43,000 birds (Johnsgard, 1973), but the current size of the overall breeding population may now be less than 10,000 birds (M. Schroeder, pers. com. in Storch, 2000).

In general, the species is terrestrial, but is much less sedentary than its larger cousin, being strong, swift fliers. The birds form flocks and lead a relatively mobile life.

Nutrition

The main winter food of the species is seeds of different cultivated cereals and soy beans. The diet of the birds before agriculture changed the face of their habitat is not known, but the species' close connection with bush vegetation allows us to suppose that the birds took buds and twigs in oak thickets, probably supplementing these in snow-free periods with the seeds of different grasses, much as they do today. In the warmer seasons, the fresh green parts and seeds of grasses are important, but insects are especially so, constituting 41.8–48.6% of the daily ration, i.e. double that of Greater Prairie-Chickens. Insects are also taken in winter in areas where softer conditions allow them to be found. Interestingly, berries are almost absent from the summer and autumn diets.

Wintering

The winter life of Lesser Prairie-Chickens differs significantly from that of other grouse because the range is an area of warm and, mostly, snow-free winters. However, on the rare occasions when severe cold and snowfall occurs, the birds are able to excavate and roost in snow burrows as other grouse. The preservation of this behavioural feature, together with a complex of adaptations for survival in severe winters, such as pectinates on the toes, indicates that the species formerly inhabited areas with a more severe climate (Jones, 1963).

Breeding

The breeding processes are as for the Greater Prairie-Chicken, though large leks with many participants are unknown and do not appear to have existed in the past. The average number of males at a lek arena is 13.7, the maximum being 43. In areas with a normal population density, each lek services an area of 1.7km² (0.6 sq mile) (Jones, 1963). Lek activity begins very early, even in midwinter. The most active lek period is during the first half of April, when 80% of all mating occurs (in Kansas), or late April/early May in Texas (Crawford, Bolen, 1975). Morning lek activity begins while it is still dark, reaching a maximum an hour before sunrise (Kansas –Hjorth, 1973). However, in Texas, maximum activity was found to be 27 minutes after sunrise and evening lek activity was maximal 49 minutes before sunset (Crawford, Bolen, 1975). Females visit the arenas both in the morning and the evening, but mating has never been observed during the evening lek. Autumn lek activity never reaches the intensity of spring and the arrival of the cold of winter ends proceedings.

The courtship displays of the two Prairie-Chicken species are similar (**Figure 90**). The song ('booming' – some American authors have referred to it as 'gobbling', a term usually reserved for the vocalization of male turkeys) of the Lesser Prairie-Chicken is a very short vocalization lasting only 0.7 seconds and consists of three soft notes that practically merge together, followed by a louder, vibrating note, audible at distances of up to 2km (1.2 miles). During the song, the air sacs are inflated only once, to a smaller size than in the Greater Prairie-Chicken. The tail is also only opened and closed once, with a loud rustle. The posture of the singing Lesser male is the same as for the Greater male, and the singing is preceded by the same short run and concluded with foot stamping, though the latter is slower at 16–17 stamps per second (Hjorth, 1970).

The Lesser male's song is preceded by several flutter-jumps to a height of about 0.5m. During the jump, the male's body is orientated parallel to the ground: he may or may not turn through 180° during the jump. Such flutter-jumps may transform into a flutter-flight, as in Black Grouse, during which the male utters a specific cackling sound resembling that of the Willow Ptarmigan (Hjorth, 1970). The main specific of courtship display, one unique among grouse, is an antiphonal singing, described, and named as a 'duet', by Hjorth (1970). The duet is performed by two males standing close together at the border between their territories. The males sing in turn, with accurate pauses of fractions of a second. The song's sequence is as for the

Figure 90. Basic lek posture of *Tympanuchus pallidicinctus*

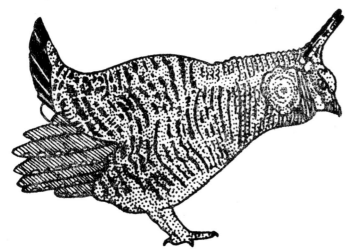

Male Lesser Prairie-Chicken in typical display posture, showing the characteristic inflated apteria

solitary display. Such duets may last 3–4 seconds, and the two males may be joined by other nearby males, each trying to sing synchronously with one of the duet singers.

Another sound, produced by males when they are close to a female, is a short series of soft, but abrupt notes: 'chilk', lasting 0.3 seconds and sounding very similar to those of the male Sharp-tailed Grouse (Hjorth, 1970).

Females nest close to the lek arenas, placing the nest under the cover of tall bunches of grass or the branches of bushes. The average clutch is 10.7 eggs (range 6–18, Johnsgard, 1973). The eggs are pure white or have a grey-yellowish tinge. There may be a few small brown spots, but these may be absent. The size of eggs, on average, is 42.0mm x 32.5mm (Johnsgard, 1973); 41.9mm x 32.0mm (Bent, 1932). Incubation lasts 25–26 days (Johnsgard, 1973). The process of incubation is as in the previous species. The female and her brood inhabit a territory of 64–102ha (158–252 acres). A study of female mortality, based on the annual and seasonal radio tracking of 227 marked females, showed a lower daily survival rate during incubation and brood rearing, i.e. this time is the most dangerous for the birds due to predation, by both mammals and raptors (Hagen *et al.*, 2007). The probability of a nest surviving was 0.72 and for a brood surviving, reared by adults and sub-adults, was 0.49 and 0.05 respectively (Fields *et al.*, 2006).

Hunting, recreation and conservation

During the last several years the species has become a high priority for the U.S. Fish and Wildlife Service and hunting is significantly restricted. There is no hunting season for the birds in New Mexico, Oklahoma and Texas, while in Kansas only limited numbers of permits are issued with a two-bird bag limit.

The birds have been successfully reared in captivity, which encourages the possibility of re-introduction.

8.2 SHARP-TAILED GROUSE Subgenus: Pedioecetes (Baird, 1858)

Pedioecetes (Baird, 1858): XXI. Type specimen: *Tetrao phasianellus* (Linnaeus, 1758), (Baird, 1858), by monotype.

This subgenus includes only one species, which differs from the other species of the genus by the presence of a small crest and a sharply elongated central pair of retrices.

8.2.1 Sharp-tailed Grouse *Tympanuchus (Pedioecetes) phasianellus* (Linnaeus, 1758)

Tetrao phasianellus (Linnaeus, 1758): 160 (Hudson Bay). *Pedioecetes phasianellus* (Elliot, 1865): pl. 15.

Morphology

Middle-sized terrestrial grouse with insignificant sexual dimorphism in both colouration and size. The sharply elongated central pair of retrices is narrow and have rounded tops. The other retrices are short and decrease in length significantly from the central pair to the outer ones. The retrices, apart from the central pair, are slightly curved inwards

Figure 91. Tail feathers of *Tympanuchus phasianellus*
Of juvenile (A) and adult (B). Numbers represent the feather pairs

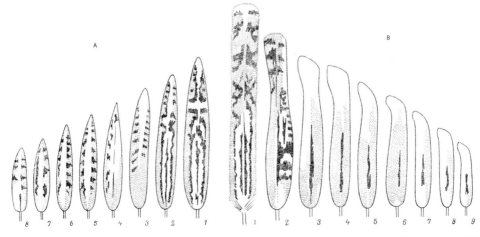

in their upper parts (**Figure 91**): in black grouse, retrice curvature is in the opposite direction and length increases from the central pair . Juveniles have only 16 retrices (cf 18 in adults – Figure 91). The air sacs are small, with a reddish or pale-violet colour. There are no pinnae. The toes have well-developed pectinates during the winter.

Colouration

Adult male

Uniformly mottled sandy-yellow, grey, brown and white. Upper body is yellowish-grey with small black-brown spots. Nape and upper back are darker, with numerous brown and whitish spots. The top of the head is greyish-brown. The sides of the head have the same colouration as female Greater Prairie-Chickens. Crest feathers are blackish-brown with grey tips. Feathers of back and rump have a complicated pattern formed by black, grey and white patches and stripes in different combinations. Underbody has a lancet pattern that disappears in the centre, the lower belly and undertail being almost all white. Chin and throat are light yellow with sparse brown marks. Primaries and secondaries have the same colouration as the other species of the genus, but the white cross-stripes on the primary's outer webs are both more numerous and more contrasting. The central pair of retrices has a complicated pattern of longitudinal and cross black stripes against a grey-yellow background (**Figure 91**). On the other retrices, white dominates, each having only one black longitudinal stripe on the shaft. Undertail coverts are white with black patches on the shafts.

Female Sharp-tailed Grouse in flight

Adult female

As the male, but the crest feathers have a cross-striped pattern, and the pattern of the central retrices is simpler with cross-stripes and a large blackish-brown patch beneath a white top.

Male Sharp-tailed Grouse

Female Sharp-tailed Grouse

First adult plumage (both sexes)
Both males and females are as adults.

Juvenile (both sexes)
Upper parts are mottled by alternate black-brown and yellowish-grey cross-stripes, these darker on the head, nape and upper back. Whitish feather shafts and a top spot of triangular shape form a specific juvenile pattern of longitudinal stripes on all parts of the upper body. Underparts are white, apart from the breast feathers, which have brown spots and cross-stripes. Primaries and outer secondaries are as adults, but differing by having mainly pointed tops. Retrice colouration is simpler than in adults, with a longitudinal pattern on the lower part of the feathers, and a crossed one on the upper part.

Downy chick
Very similar to the two previous species, differing only by being paler brown above and with fewer black spots and stripes on the head (**Figure 92**).

Figure 92. Head pattern of downy young *Tympanuchus phasianellus*

Dimensions

Males (N=7): wing length 207.5mm (range 205–212mm); tail 120.4mm (110–124mm); bill 11.6mm (10.5–12.7mm); tarsi 43.9mm (43.0–45.5mm); middle toe 39.8mm (35.5–41.8mm).

Females (N=11): wing 201.2mm (195–208mm); tail 117.3mm (113–126mm); bill 11.3mm (10.1–11.9mm); tarsi 42.8mm (40.0–44.4mm); middle toe 38.3mm (36.3–40.5mm).

All data from Ridgway, Friedmann (1946).

There are no data regarding seasonal variation of weight. The average weight of 236 males was 951g (33.55oz), the maximum being 1,087g (38.34oz). The same data from 247 females was 815g (28.75oz) and 997g (35.17oz) respectively (Nelson, Martin, 1953).

Moult

The succession of moults is as in other species of genus.

Distribution

(see Maps 17–19)

As with the other species of the genus, the range of the Sharp-tailed Grouse has altered significantly over the last 70–80 years. In former times the species was distributed over a considerable portion of the continental interior, though the range was not continuous, consisting of two isolated areas, with the main area covering the continental centre and a smaller part occupying central Alaska and the upper Yukon Valley in Canada. In this smaller area, the species has maintained its original distribution, reaching the Arctic Circle, both along the valley of Koniukuk River (Bent, 1932) and in the lower Mackenzie River valley (Aldrich, 1963), each of which represents the northern forest limit. The northernmost point reached by the species is Fort McPherson, on the border between the Canadian provinces of Yukon and North-West Territory, 98km (61 miles) north of the Arctic Circle (Godfrey, 1986). The two parts of the range were separated by high mountains, which the species avoids; the western limit of the range was also defined by high mountain ridges. To the south, the species was distributed to 37°N, and occupied three main vegetation zones: forest, forest-grassland and grassland. The eastern limit of the species was defined by the western limit of the temperate deciduous forest.

During the last 70–80 years, major changes have occurred in the southern half of the main part of the range, mainly in the forest-grassland and grassland zones, as a consequence of human activity. Initially, as agriculture developed, Sharp-tailed Grouse extended their range eastward, occupying Iowa, Minnesota, Wisconsin and northern parts of Illinois and Michigan. But the rapid intensification of agriculture soon forced the species to abandon these States, and to reduce its former range, with about 25% of the range, mainly in the south-west, disappearing. In the south-west, by the 1970s the range had been transformed into a series of small, isolated patches (Johnsgard, 1973). The latest range map (Alsop, 2002) indicates that only two of these patches remain, one small area on the Oregon/Idaho border and a narrow strip along the western border of Wyoming. The westernmost part of the range is now isolated, though unfragmented, with the birds occupying the inter-mountain (Great Basin) region of British Columbia, an area of 62,000km² (23,938 sq miles) (Ritcey, 1995) stretching from 54°N to 50°N.

Subspecies

The large size of the species' range and the fact that it covers different climatic and vegetation zones, from northern boreal forests to southern grasslands, has resulted in local adaptations and, consequently, a number of subspecies.

Hudson Sharp-tailed Grouse *Tympanuchus (Pedioecetes) phasianellus phasianellus*
(Linnaeus, 1758)
Nominative, as described above. Occupies an area surrounding Hudson Bay, the northern part of Ontario and north-eastern Manitoba, south to 53°N. The preferred habitats are meadows with bushes along the riverbeds, bogs, glades, etc, fire-damaged areas in mixed and coniferous forest, and the outskirts of the agricultural fields.

Western Sharp-tailed Grouse *Tympanuchus (Pedioecetes) phasianellus, campestris*
(Ridgway, 1884)
Differs from other subspecies by having a significant rufous tinge to the plumage. Occupies south-west Ontario, the southern half of Manitoba, and the States of Minnesota, Michigan, Iowa, Wisconsin and Illinois. The main habitat is 'oak savannah' and openings in broad-leaved deciduous forests (Aldrich, 1963).

Alaskan Sharp-tailed Grouse *Tympanuchus (Pedioecetes) phasianellus caurus*
(Friedmann, 1943)
General colouration is paler, with a grey shade to the plumage. Inhabits the isolated range section in Alaska and the Canadian provinces of Yukon, British Columbia and Alberta (Ridgway, Friedmann, 1946; Aldrich, 1963). Prefers bogs, glades and fire-damaged areas, broad water meadows along rivers in northern coniferous forests, and thickets of willow and dwarf birch bushes among the sparse trees of the forest-tundra zone.

Mackenzie Sharp-tailed Grouse *Tympanuchus (Pedioecetes) phasianellus kennicotti*
(Suckley, 1861)
Differs from other subspecies by being very dark. Occupies the basin of the Mackenzie River, the Great Slave and Great Bear lakes, northward to the Anderson and Lockhart Rivers, i.e. north of the Arctic Circle, where forest-tundra landscapes dominate, continuous coniferous forest being seen only along the Mackenzie Valley (Bent, 1932).

Prairie Sharp-tailed Grouse *Tympanuchus (Pedioecetes) phasianellus jamesi*
(Lincoln, 1917)
Similar to the Alaskan subspecies, but paler above. Occupies prairies from the southern border of species' range northward to central parts of Canada's Alberta and Saskatchewan provinces, and from South and North Dakota west to Montana in the USA. Inhabits bush thickets of different types, sometimes with arboreal vegetation along rivers.

Columbian Sharp-tailed Grouse *Tympanuchus (Pedioecetes) phasianellus columbianus* (Ord, 1815)
Colouration similar to the previous subspecies, but less brown, and with a greyer tinge.

Occupies the Great Basin and lowlands of the Rocky Mountains, northward to 54°N. The subspecies is currently isolated from the main range. The chief habitats are open grasslands and deciduous woody vegetation (Ritcey, 1995).

Habitats

The high adaptability of Sharp-tailed Grouse has permitted it to assimilate a large number of different habitats, from hot, dry prairies in the Great Basin to cold, damp areas in the forest-tundra zone north of the Arctic Circle. That said, despite its wide distribution, and the different vegetation zones, the species prefers open habitats with bush and sparse arboreal vegetation, the most suitable habitats being a combination of open places with low grass (where lek arenas can be placed) and dense bush thickets, with the grass between these being tall enough to hide nests and broods. Even on prairies and sage semi-deserts, the birds prefer places with some bush or tree vegetation, while in woodlands it chooses clearings (glades, water meadows, bogs, agricultural fields, etc), avoiding dark, dense woods, particularly coniferous ones, with broods never penetrating more than about 50m (55yd) from the forest edge (Hamerstrom, 1963). In general, Sharp-tailed Grouse habitats resemble those of Black Grouse in Eurasia.

Population structure and density

Studies have shown a small prevalence of males in populations – 56% of males among young birds and 60% among adults. In Wisconsin during 1941–1942, in suitable habitats, on average there were 1–2 birds/km² (converted from acreages in Grange, 1948). A later study estimated the normal autumn density as 2–10 birds/km² (converted from 14–23 birds per square mile, Edminster, 1954)

Territoriality

In former times, when the population of Sharp-tailed Grouse was high, seasonal displacements were significant, though the data on distances and regularity are insufficient to quote values. Bent (1932) noted the birds flying southward from the lower Mackenzie (Fort Norman) in October and reappearing on 12 March near Fort Simpson. Dice (1920) notes that the species did not move from the valleys of the Tanana and Yukon rivers (at 65°N) during the winter, indicating that southern displacements were not regular. Such seasonal habitat changes apparently also occurred in prairie populations, the birds leaving the grasslands for forest edges in search of arboreal forage. With the appearance of agricultural fields, such movements ceased. Radio tracking of birds in Wisconsin showed that 81% of 162 marked birds spent the whole year within the same territory, moving no more than 3km (1.9 miles) from the place of marking: only 10% of the birds moved more than 8km (5 miles), the maximum being 33.6km (20.8 miles)

(Hamerstrom, Hamerstrom, 1951). In Nebraska, 35 marked males spent the winter no more than 5.3km (3.3 miles) from their lek arenas (Kobriger, 1965).

Behaviour

In general, the species has a terrestrial way of life during the warm seasons of the year. Lek activity, nesting, brood rearing, resting and roosting, feeding, dust bathing, moulting, indeed all activities, take place on the ground. The only time the birds move to the trees is in late autumn and winter, when they spend most of the time in trees, feeding and resting, and also roosting if the weather prevents the use of snow burrows. However, the birds do fly away at a sign of danger, rather than running and hiding as other grouse. The flight of the Sharp-tailed Grouse is light and quick. When lifting off, they often utter a call similar to the cackle of domestic hens; the call is also occasionally heard during feeding. The birds gather in flocks, particularly during winter: in former times flocks of several hundred birds were not uncommon.

Nutrition

The main winter food is mainly twigs, buds and catkins of birches, willows, aspens, poplars and even larch. In Ontario and Minnesota, the main winter food was the buds and catkins of birch, the buds of aspen, willow, ash, and blueberry (Snyder, 1935). In other cases, for instance in North Dakota, the main winter diet was buds of willows and, in addition, of chokecherry and poplar, and rose hips (Aldous, 1943). In Utah, the winter forage chiefly comprised the buds of chokecherry, maple and serviceberry (Johnsgard, 1973). In southern parts of the range during winter, the most important food items are the seeds of cultivated cereals, these constituting up to 55% of the daily ration (Harris, 1967).

In the spring, the main forage is the fresh green parts of different grasses, particularly wild cereals, with these items also being the preferred diet in summer. In Washington State, this forage comprised up to 75% of the summer diet (Jones, 1966). Insects do not form a significant part of the spring or summer diet, but are important in the autumn, when the birds moult. At that time, insects, especially grasshoppers, comprise more than 35% of the daily ration (Jones, 1966). In the northern range, the autumn forage chiefly comprises different kinds of berries, especially of *Vaccinium* sp. Berries are also important in the southern part of the range, dog rose, snowberry, wolfberry, bearberry, blueberry and mountain ash being taken (Johnsgard, 1973).

Wintering

In northern parts of their range, Sharp-tailed Grouse spend the winter in much the same way as other grouse. The birds feed twice daily, morning and evening, spending the rest of the time resting or roosting in a snow burrow. To the south, where the winter weather is warmer and snow may be absent, the birds are active all day, usually resting during the middle of the day. The winter energy budget has been studied in captive birds in open cages, the results indicating that the bird's existence energy is more or less stable: in winter it is about 420kJ ME/day (Evans, Dietz, 1974).

Breeding

Sharp-tailed Grouse are polygamous, with ritual breeding displays at lek arenas. Both males and females are capable of breeding during their first spring.

Lek arenas are set in open habitats, usually on upper slopes or at the tops of hills, occasionally far away from the forest edge. Arenas are maintained from year to year, and are visited throughout the year (except for short intervals during the active moults in summer and midwinter), an interesting outcome of this being the fact that the grass in the arenas is low and sparse due to constant trampling. In areas with a normal population density, arenas are set 0.8–2.4km (1.5 miles) from each other.

In Michigan and Minnesota, males start to appear at the lek during good weather as early as February. As soon as they arrive the males will start to display and to defend territories from rivals. Males arrive at the lek about an hour before sunrise. In the middle part of the range, females begin to visit the leks from mid-March, but regular visits begin only in mid-April/early May. Females arrive 15–30 minutes after the males, and leave soon after sunrise. Most mating occurs just before or at sunrise.

The number of males at a lek is usually 10–20 birds, the average number from 1,664 observed leks being 12.9 (Johnson, 1964, cit. from Johnsgard, 1973). Individual male territories are a minimum at the arena's centre (averaging only 21m²/25yd²) and larger at the periphery (up to 150m²/179yd²). In one studied lek, the arena was only 100m in diameter, with central territories not exceeding 50m² (59yd²) (Hjorth, 1970). Central territories are occupied by the most active males. The age of these birds is debated: Hjorth (1970) considered they could be birds as young as one year old, but usually were two-year-old birds, but Lumsden (1965) considered that the birds were at least two years' old. Though the latter may be correct, it is clear that one-year-old males can and do breed, though it seems likely that experienced, older birds are responsible for most mating activity (the most active bird accounting for some 75% of all couplings). In an experiment in which males were removed from a lek, it was found that only when the number of males at the arena had been halved were new males recruited, with young males joining during March. No new replacements arrived during April (Rippin, Boag, 1974).

Male activity at the lek decreases sharply after females cease to visit (i.e. after laying and incubation begin), though some activity continues until early July. Then, in August, the males begin to visit the lek again, the autumn lek being particularly active in September and October, but continuing until December.

The main male courtship display is a dance consisting of active and passive elements, these lasting equal times, though towards the end of the lekking period the passive part becomes longer. During the first, active, phase, the male adopts a posture resembling a toy airplane, with the wings stretched out horizontally, the head and neck stretched forward and lowered slightly and the tail vertically erect (**Figure 93**). In this pose, the male stamps the ground at great speed (18.6 stamps per second – Hjorth, 1970) while moving slowly ahead or in a circle. The stamping sounds like a drum roll, and is audible at up to 200m. While the male is moving, his tail opens and shuts alternatively from one or other side with a loud rustling sound. During the dance the male stops suddenly from time to time (only briefly, for about 0.08 seconds). At these times he opens and shuts his tail twice and utters a short vocal signal that resembles a short flicking sound, 'chilk', the loudest noise of the display. The male also utters several low sounds resembling the 'cork-note' of capercaillie, but audible only over a few metres. The active part of the dance then stops abruptly, to be followed by the passive part, during which the male ceases stamping, folds his wings, apart from the outer primaries, and utters a tremolo of soft, cooing sounds that decrease in volume. The full dance lasts 18–19 seconds. Invariably, the dancing of one male provokes neighbouring males to follow suit, with dances occasionally being performed synchronously by several males (Lumsden, 1965; Hjorth, 1970).

The male flutter–flight is short (distances of about 6m/6/6yd), low (no higher than 1m/3.3ft) and without turns. Sometimes, especially if a female is close by, the male makes a shorter flutter-jump, then vibrates his wings where he lands. During confrontations, males occasionally stand in front of each other: their tails are vertical, the crests on their heads are raised slightly and the birds incline and raise their heads quickly. During each of these bows, the birds utter a low, short, cooing sound, and inflate their air sacs to two bright purple balls. The low sound lasts 0.25 seconds and is audible at distances of up to 1,200m (1,312yd). Another vocal sound uttered during confrontations is a gurgling 'lok-a-lok', during which the bill opens for a moment and the air sacs inflate slightly. Rivals will also dance in front of each other or adopt a 'frozen' posture, lying with their breasts on the ground, their rumps and tails

Figure 93. Dancing pose of male *Tympanuchus phasianellus*

Displaying male Sharp-tailed Grouse in Crookston, Minnesota

raised, their wings spread: males may remain for up to half an hour in this 'frozen' state. If battles occur, the males attempt to beat one another with open bills or their legs.

Nests are similar to other grouse species, the scrape having a diameter of 17.5–20cm (6.9–7.9in) and depth of 7.5–10cm (3–3.9in) (Bent, 1932). The number of eggs in a clutch varies from 5–17, with an average of 12.1 (Hamerstrom, 1939). The size of eggs (N=27, nominative subspecies) is 43.1mm x 32.3mm (Bent, 1932). The eggs are yellow-grey or chocolate, with or without small quantities of brown 'sparkles'. Incubation lasts 24–25 days (captive birds in open cages, McEwen *et al.*, 1969), but sometimes only 21 days (Bent, 1932). In northern parts of the range, incubation begins in the first decade of May, in southern parts at the beginning of April. Once hatched, broods stay first in a very restricted area of open grassland, where there is a large population of insects and copious fresh green grass. The brood territory is rarely more than a half-mile in diameter (Edminster, 1954). Chicks begin to flutter when they are 10 days old, with the brood beginning to disperse when the chicks they are about 6 weeks old (Johnsgard, 1973).

Hunting, recreating and conservation

Sharp-tailed Grouse are the only representative of the genus whose numbers do not give cause for concern. In 12 States of the USA and 6 Provinces of Canada, the species is an important game bird. The estimated annual kill in 1970 was approximately 312,000 in the USA and 328,000 in Canada (Johnsgard, 1973). Connelly *et al.* (1998) concluded that although fluctuations in harvest were seen, similar numbers were taken in later years.

The species was introduced successfully in the Lower Peninsula in Michigan, but the number of birds there then decreased mainly through the habitat losses (Amman, 1963b).

CHAPTER 10
Grouse: Present and Future

POPULATIONS AND FACTORS INFLUENCING POPULATIONS

Data on the population density of grouse species are given in **Table 5 in Chapter 1**. From time to time most grouse species reach maximal density levels, but these cannot be sustained for long periods, as they inevitably lead to food shortage, and a shortage of suitable breeding territories. Moreover, high population densities attract predators and may also lead to disease epidemics or helminth invasions. Consequently, a sharp decrease in density usually follows a peak, and may persist for several years. These fluctuations are peculiar to all grouse species and sometimes form regular, repeated cycles with periods of 3–10 years; such cycles are particularly seen in tundra and northern taiga populations. However, despite the cycles having been observed by many researchers, the exact reasons for them are not well understood and may differ in different species.

Factors that influence grouse numbers, though not cyclically, have been identified. Of these one of the most serious is bad weather. Cold and rain, and the so-called 'cold returns' (i.e. when a cold snap occurs out of season) – particularly if they occur around the time of chick hatching or rearing – can be devastating. Grouse chicks acquire full ability to thermoregulate at the age of 2–3 weeks, and before full ability is achieved the chicks need regular additional heating from the female. This is especially important during cold and rainy weather, but a consequence is a reduction in feeding time, so if such weather persists, the chicks may perish from starvation or hypothermia. Cold, rainy weather also reduces the number of insects available as food – the main chick dietary requirement during the early weeks of life. That weather is a major reason for chick mortality has been attested in numerous studies (e.g. Kirikov, 1952; Höglund, 1952. 1955; Marchström, 1960; Krott, 1966; Volkov, 1968; Semenov-Tianshansky, 1970; Gullion, 1970; M ller, 1974). Such unfavourable, and persistent, weather is a feature of northern climates. In such situations, populations in which there is a spread of incubation times among females have higher chances of survival. If the bad weather is prolonged, or the spread of incubation periods is small, up to 80% of females may leave their broods, and the number of young birds in the autumn may be only 1 for every 4–5 adult females (Gullion, 1970; Danilov, 1975). Other natural disasters – forest fires, winter 'icings', etc – may also result in serious decreases in population numbers.

It is known that the productivity of old, experienced females is higher than that of young females, so the fraction of females in the population as a whole – and the ratio of old to young birds – are also extremely important in determining population numbers. Young females may not breed or may produce fewer eggs, or breed later so that their chicks do not achieved the required level of maturity before the start of winter (Porat, Vohns,

1972). Birds originating from late broods also have less vitality, particularly the females, which often do not breed the following year. The number and quality of eggs produced by females is also not constant, even in the same population, changing according to the age spread of females, weather conditions during the winter and early spring, etc. Bird mortality may also differ from year to year due to predation. Predator population size will clearly affect predation rates, but equally important is the population density of other prey species. As an example, the Mustelidae – martens, sable, etc – which are rodent predators, will hunt grouse, particularly young birds, if rodent numbers crash. In the Siberian taiga, in some localities, sable may take as many as 40% of Hazel Grouse during the winter months.

One more interesting input to the equation determining grouse numbers is bird lifetime. This can be hard to establish, but ringing has provided some information. At the moment, the maximum known age for a grouse is 15 years (male *Lagopus leucurus*, Colorado, USA, Braun *et al.*, 1993), with 14 years for a male *Dendragapus obscurus richardsoni* (Sheep River, Alberta, Canada, Zwickel *et al.*, 1989) and 13.5 years (sex unspecified) (*Tetrao urogallus*, Germany, Müller, 1974), though available information suggests that the average life span of birds surviving their first year is 3–4 years (Yudakov, 1968).

THE FUTURE

Grouse have existed for not less than 4–5 million years. During this time, though short on a geological timescale, they have survived a period of intense global cooling that culminated in the Pleistocene Ice Ages. The period was interrupted several times by periods of warming, and saw the appearance and rapid development of mankind. The deep, multivalent adaptations grouse developed during global cooling helped them not only to survive during the Ice Ages, but to occupy all the terrestrial ecosystems of the northern hemisphere from the forest-steppe zone north to the tundra of the High Arctic. The appearance of man and his hunting activities did not, at first, disturb the birds' lifestyle: grouse numbers were great, the populations being barely impacted by the scarce prehistoric hunters whose main interest was, in any case, larger mammals – from reindeer to mammoth. The availability of grouse and the relative ease with which they could be captured probably helped prehistoric man survive hard times: the number of ptarmigan bones in many Paleolithic sites is clear evidence of this. But grouse were never a main item of ancient man's diet. As well as a food source, grouse may also have been watched and their winter shelters copied. To this day, people of the Chukotka Peninsula take shelter in rapidly constructed snow refuges if they are overcome by a storm while travelling: the Chukchi people call these shelters 'ptarmigan houses' (Potapov and Sale, pers. comm. and pers. practice). Perhaps grouse shelters were also the inspiration for the igloos of Inuit hunters.

But the rapid development of human civilization changed the situation completely within just a few hundred years. Until the medieval period in Eurasia, the balance between the growth of the human population and its influence on the natural world (and, therefore, the welfare of grouse) was more or less acceptable. But change was to come, and the spread of agriculture and the destruction of forests for industry and fuel, at first in Eurasia, had a significant, negative impact on grouse species. The first to suffer were Black Grouse and southern populations of Willow Ptarmigan. Though it occurred a little later in North America, the same changes did occur there: there, most of the prairie and shrub-steppe had been taken into agricultural use by the beginning of the 20th century. The human population of the Nearctic also increased and spread, the main impact being on the *Tympanuchus* species. In Western Europe, destruction of the forests led to the disappearance from some areas of Hazel Grouse and Western Capercaillie: by the beginning of the 20th century these species remained only in mountain forests.

As the human population increased and spread, hunting – particularly professional hunting and trade in captured birds – increased, with big cities being supplied with grouse that offered cheap meat to their citizens. In Scandinavia and Russia where this trade flourished, thousands of Hazel Grouse, Black Grouse, capercaillie and Willow Ptarmigan appeared during the winter seasons in the markets in St Petersburg, Moscow and other large cities, the killing resulting in local populations, particularly of Hazel Grouse and

Male Western Capercaillie in a forest in Aardal, Norway

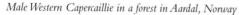

capercaillie, being regularly extirpated and then restored by natural dispersion processes after several years (Menzbir, 1902). In North America, trade hunting was only a problem for a short time, in the late 19th/early 20th centuries, with the most popular species being Ruffed Grouse (Bump *et al.*, 1947). Amateur hunting was also widespread, taking its own toll, and although this has decreased as a result of a change in habits (especially in Russia) or legislation, illegal hunting still continues, particularly in the northern areas of both the Palearctic and the Nearctic.

As a consequence of these changes, i.e. of habitat destruction and hunting, the situation of all tetraonids across most of their ranges is far from ideal. Only in the northern taiga and tundra zones of each continent can it be claimed to be satisfactory, though in the tundra the development of gas and oil industries threatens the two Arctic-dwelling ptarmigan species. For species with a tiny distributional range, the situation is perilous.

For all grouse species, the twin threats of global warming and mankind suggest a hazardous future. Global warming may be a danger for some, if not all, grouse species because of their adaptations to a cold climate and a well-defined winter, though it is clear that during their history grouse have survived several periods of global warming that were more significant than that which is currently occurring. The last such period of warming, the Eemian interglacial, lasted 10,000 years and ended about 120,000 years ago. During the Eemian, the forests of Europe reached 71°N (the shores of the Arctic Ocean), but grouse – even the ptarmigan – survived. During the Eemian, grouse survived in colder localities, northern parts of the continents, the upper belts of mountains, etc, or in the same areas because of their adaptive capabilities: even today several species, for example the Western Capercaillie and Hazel Grouse, can survive successfully both in super-cold regions (north-east Siberia), as well areas with a 'softer', even snow-free winter (Western Europe). But it must be remembered that the Eemian warming took place over a more protracted period than some experts are now predicting for the present warming, and that during the Eemian the grouse were not also contending with the pressure of human activity.

The problem of the co-existence of grouse and mankind is unresolved and depends exclusively on man. Human society has already made progress, but it is still far from having developed measures that will solve the problem. There are many ways to optimize the preservation of grouse, the most important of which, we believe, are:

- strong control and even the complete prohibition of hunting
- the creation of protected areas in the most optimal localities for the different species. It is also important that protected areas are connected in order to increase the species gene pool.
- special biotechnical measures within grouse habitats, including the practice of providing additional, protein-rich food (for example, cereals), especially during the breeding season.

- the rearing of grouse in captivity in special farms and their release into suitable habitats, the augmentation of numbers in areas of low population density and the reintroduction of grouse to places from which they have disappeared in the near or remote past. This suggestion will inevitably be controversial, as captive rearing (of both grouse and other species) has not always been successful. However, both captive breeding and the translocation of birds from areas of high population to augment areas of depressed population have had successes.

It is our view that the regulation of hunting, including limiting the hunting season, regulating the number of birds killed are important measures and, most importantly, guaranteeing regulation enforcement, as its impact is, more or less, immediate. At present, only three nations have respectable and enforced hunting regulations – the UK, Canada and the USA. Full prohibition of hunting during the spring lek is critical, something which is especially important in the 'civilized' countries of Europe, where it is frequently practiced. Any disturbance of the mating system is disastrous for any grouse population and should be considered absolutely unacceptable, whatever the opinion of the hunting fraternity. We need to recall the opinion of the famous British ornithologist David Armitage Bannerman, who stated that for the British hunter it was hard to imagine a more ungentlemanly way of hunting than pursuing capercaillie during the lek (Bannerman, 1963).

The evidence suggests that if human activities can be controlled or limited, grouse can live in close connection with man, though the species will never become synanthropic in the way that the House Sparrow (*Passer domesticus*) or others have become. But grouse can live very close to humans if they are left untroubled. There are many examples of this: we have watched Rock Ptarmigan in Iceland foraging close to the buildings of Reykjavik in winter and Willow Ptarmigan doing the same close to buildings in the suburbs of Petrozavodsk to the north of St Petersburg. The latter species have been seen equally close to other settlements in Russia's forest-tundra zone. Some grouse may also be seen near settlements during the breeding season. A capercaillie lek was observed only 500m (547yd) from the nearest houses of St Petersburg, 1 or 2 displaying males being present regularly over a period of several years, with equally regular visits by several females (Potapov, 2009). Hazel Grouse are also known to winter regularly in the wooded areas between properties, with only the activity of domestic animals such as cats and dogs preventing nesting in such places. What is clear from these examples is that it is the actions of people that will undermine the attempts of grouse at co-existence.

The authors remain hopeful that with continued progress in the understanding of the great importance of wildlife preservation among people, the care given to grouse will reflect their uniqueness. Grouse are a marvellous collection of birds, a wonderful creation of nature and we must do all we can to protect them.

REFERENCES & BIBLIOGRAPHY

Aanes, S., S. Engen, B-E. Sæther, T. Willebrand and V. Marcstrom, 'Sustainable harvesting strategies of Willow Ptarmigan in a fluctuating environment', *Ecological Applications,* vol. 12, 2002, 281–290.

Abramov, K.G., 'Observations of Spruce Grouse in Amurland', *Ornithologia,* vol. 4, 1962, 182–184 (in Russian).

Aldrich, J.W. and H. Friedmann, 'A revision of the Ruffed Grouse', *Condor,* vol. 45, no.3, 1943, 85–103.

Aldrich, J.W., 'New subspecies of birds from western North America', *Proc. Biol. Soc. Washington,* vol. 59, 1946, 129–136.

Aldrich, J.W., 'Geographical orientation of American Tetraoidae', *J. Wildlife Management.,* vol. 27, no. 4, 1963, 529–545.

Aldrich, J.W., 'Historical background' in O.H. Ewitt (ed.), *The Wild Turkey and its Management,* The Wildlife Society, Washington D.C., 1967, 3–16.

Aldridge, C.L. and R.M. Brigham, 'Distribution, status and abundance of Greater Sage-Grouse, *Centrocercus urophasianus,* in Canada', *Canada Field Nat.,* vol. 117, 2003, 25–34.

Aldous, S.E., 'Sharp-tailed Grouse in the sand dune country of north-central North Dakota', *J. Wildlife Management,* vol. 7, 1943. 23–31.

Alison, R.M., 'Female Ptarmigan re-occupying nest site', *Auk,* vol. 93(3), 1976, 657.

Alpheraki, S.P., 'The birds of the eastern Asov Region', *Ornithol. Bull.,* vol. 4, 1910. 245–252 (in Russian).

Allen, A.A., 'Sex rhythm in Ruffed Grouse (*Bonasa umbellus* Linn.) and other birds', Auk, vol. 51(2), 1934, 180–199.

Alsop, F.J. III, *Birds of North America,* New York, 2002.

Alsop, F.J. III, *Birds of Canada,* Dorling Kindersley Limited, Canada, 2002.

Amman, G.A., 'Status of Spruce Grouse in Michigan', *J. Wildlife Management,* vol. 27, 1963a, 591–593.

Amman, G.A., 'Status and Management of Sharp-tailed Grouse in Michigan', *J. Wildlife Management,* vol. 27 (4), 1963b, 802–809.

Anderson, R.K. and J.E. Toepfer, 'History, status and management of the Greater Prairie-Chicken in Wisconsin', in W.D. Svedarsky, R.H. Hier, N.J. Silvy (eds.), *The Greater Prairie-Chicken, a National Look.* Agricult. Experiment. Station, Univ. of Minnesota, St Paul, Minnesota. miscellaneous publ. 99, 1999, 39–58.

Anderson, R.K., 'Prairie-Chicken responses to changing booming-ground cover type and height', *J. Wildlife Management,* vol. 33(6), 1969, 636–643.

Anderson, R.K., 'Orientation in Prairie-Chickens', *Auk,* vol. 88 (2), 1971, 286–290.

Andreev, B.N., *The Birds of the Vilui Basin,* Yakutsk (in Russian), 1974.

Andreev, V.N. (ed.), *Seasonal and Weather Dynamics of Phytomass in Subarctic Tundra.* Novosibirsk (in Russian), 1978.

Andreev, A.V., 'Specifics of the ecology of Rock Ptarmigan (*Lagopus mutus*) in the Commander Islands', *Zool. J.,* vol. 50 (8), 1971, 1260–1262.

Andreev, A.V., 1975a. 'The winter life and nutrition of the Rock Ptarmigan (*Lagopus mutus*) in the extreme North-East of the USSR', *Zool. J.,* vol. 34 (5), 727–733.

Andreev, A.V., 'On the energy spent by Black-billed Capercaillie in obtaining winter forage', *Ecology,* vol. 6, 1975b, 90–92.

Andreev, A.V., 'Courtship displays of Black-billed Capercaillie in north-eastern Siberia', *Ornithologia,* vol. 13, 1977, 110–116.

Andreev, V.N. (ed.), *Seasonal and weather dynamics of phytomass in the subarctic tundra,* Novosibirsk (in Russian), 1978.

Andreev, A.V., *Adaptation of birds to the winter conditions of the subarctic,* Moscow (in Russian), 1980.

Andreev, A.V., 'The ten year cycle of the Willow Grouse of Lower Kolyma', *Oecologia,* vol. 76, 1988, 261–167.

Andreev, A.V., 'Observations of the winter biology of the Asian Spruce Grouse in Amur Land. ', *Zool. J.,* vol. 69 (3), 1990, 69–80.

Andreev, A.V., 'Winter habitat segregation in the sexually dimorphic Black-billed Capercaillie *Tetrao urogalloides' Ornis Scandinavica,* vol. 22 (3), 1991, 287–291.

Andreev, A.V., F. Hafner, S. Klaus and H. Gossow, 'Displaying behaviour and mating system in the Siberian Spruce Grouse *Falcipennis falcipennis', J. Ornith.,* vol. 142, 2001, 404–424.

Andreev, A.V., H. Linden, 'Winter energetics of Capercaillie – a methodological approach', *Ornis Fennica,* vol. 71, 1994, 33–42.

Anonymous, 'Notes and news', *Auk,* vol. 49 (4), 1932, 524.

Anthony, A.W., 'Migration of Richardson's Grouse', *Auk,* vol. 20, 1903, 24–27.

Anthony, R.G. and M.J. Willis, 'Survival rates of female Greater Sage-Grouse in autumn and winter in south-eastern Oregon', *J. Wildlife Management,* vol. 73 (4), 2009, 538–545.

Archibald, H.L., 'Temporal patterns of spring space use by Ruffed Grouse', *J. Wildlife Management,* vol. 39 (3), 1975, 472–48.

Austin, O.L., 'The birds of Korea', *Bull. Mus. Compar. Zool.,* vol. 101 (1), 1948, 1–301.

Averin Iu, V., 'Caucasian Black Grouse', *Proc. Caucasus State Reserve,* Moscow, vol. 1, 1938, 56–86.

Averin Iu, V., 'Black-billed Capercaillie in the Kamchatka', *'Protection of Nature',* Moscow, vol. 5, 1948, 12–16.

Babenko, V.G., *Birds of the Lower Amur River Basin,* Moscow, 2000.

Back, G.N., M.R. Barringto and J. K. McAdoo, 'Sage-Grouse use of snow burrows in north-eastern Nevada', *Wilson Bull.,* vol. 99 (3), 1987, 488–490.

Baird, S.F., *Catalogue of North American birds, chiefly in the Museum of the Smithsonian Institute,* Smiths. Inst., 1858, 17–56.

Baird, S.F., T.M. Brewer and R. Ridgway, *A History of North American Birds,* vol. 3, Boston, 1874.

Balachonov, V.S., 'Some ornithological observations on the eastern slopes of the sub-polar Ural Mountains', *Proc. Institute Ecology of Plants and Animals,* Sverdlovsk, vol. 15, 1978, 57–63.

Ballard, J.W.O. and M.C. Whitlock, 'The incomplete natural history of mitochondria', *Molecular Ecology,* vol. 13, 2004, 729–744.

Bannerman, D.A., *The Birds of the British Isles,* vol. 12, 1963.

Barancheev, L.M., 'The number and ecology of the Black-billed Capercaillie in Amur Province', *Ornitologia,* vol. 7, 1965, 92–96.

Barber, H.A., 'Strutting behavior, distribution and habitat selection of Sage-Grouse in Utah', Thesis, Brigham Young University, Provo, Utah, 1991.

Barrowclough, G.F., J.G. Groth, L.A. Mertz and R.J. Gutiérrez, 'Phylogeographic structure, gene flow and species status in Blue Grouse *(Dendragapus obscurus)', Molecular Ecology,* vol. 13, 2004, 1911–1922.

Baxter, R.J., J.T. Flinders and D.L. Mitchell, 'Survival, movements and reproduction of translocated Greater Sage-Grouse in Strawberry Valley, Utah', *J. Wildlife Management,* vol. 72 (1), 2008, 179–186.

Beck, T.D. and C.E. Braun, 'Weights of Colorado Sage-Grouse', *Condor,* vol. 80, 1978, 241–243.

Behle, W.H. and R.K. Selander, 'New race of the Dusky Grouse *(Dendragapus obscurus)* from the Great Basin', *Proc. Biol. Soc., Washington,* vol. 44, 1951, 125–128.

Beick, W, 'Die Eier von *Tetrastes sewerzowi,'* Przew, *Ornith. Monatsber.*, vol. 35, 1927, 176–177.

Bendell, J.F., 'Disease as a control of a population of Blue Grouse *Dendragapus obscurus fuliginosus* (Ridgway)', *Can. J. Zool.,* vol. 33, 1955c, 195–223.

Bendell, J.F. and P.W. Elliott, 'Habitat selection in Blue Grouse', *Condor,* vol. 68, 1966, 431–446.

Bendell, J.F. and P.W. Elliott, 'Behavior and the regulation of numbers in Blue Grouse', *Canadian Wildlife Serv. Report Series No. 4,* 1967.

Bendire, C.E., 'Life histories of North American birds', *U.S. Nat. Mus. Spec. Bull.,* vol. 1 (1), 1892.

Bendire, C.E., *Forest and Stream,* vol. 11, 1893, 20 (cit. from Ridgway, Friedmann, 1946).

Benedict, N.G., S.J. Ouler-McCance, S.E. Taylor, C.E. Braun and T.W. Quinn, 'Evaluation of the eastern *(Centrocercus urophasianus urophasianus)* and western *(Centrocercus urophasianus phaios)* subspecies of Sage-Grouse using mitochondrial control-region sequence data', *Conservation Genetics,* vol. 4, 2003, 301–310.

Bent, A.C., 'A new subspecies of Ptarmigan from the Aleutian Islands', *Smiths. Misc. Collect.*, vol. 56, no. 30, 1912, 1–2.

Bent, A., 'Life histories of North American Gallinaceous birds', *US Nat. History Bull.,* vol. 163, 1932, 1–490.

Benthen, P.V., 'The Galliform birds of the northern part of Chita Province', *Papers of IV All-Union Ornith. Conf.,* Alma-Ata, 1965, 26–28.

Benthen, P.V., 'Resources of Game animals and perspective of the hunting farm development in Kalar District, Chita Province', *Proc. Irkutsk Agricultural Inst.,* vol. 25, 1967, 100–147.

Bergerud, A., 'Newfoundland wildlife management and annual report 1962–1963', *Ann. Report Dept. Mines, Agricult. and Resources for year ending 31st March, Newfoundland,* 1963, 68–126.

Bergerud, A.T., 'Population dynamics of the Willow Ptarmigan *(Lagopus lagopus alleni* L.) in Newfoundland, 1955 to 1965', *Oilos,* vol. 21 (2), 1970, 299–325.

Bergerud, A., 'Demography and behaviour of insular Blue Grouse populations', in A. Bergerud and M. Gratson (eds), *Adaptive strategies and population ecology of northern Grouse,* vol. 1–2, University of Minnesota Press, 1987, 29–77.

Bergerud, F. and H.D. Hemus, 'An experimental study of the behavior of Blue Grouse *(Dendragapus obscurus)* 1. Differences between the founders from three populations', *Canad. J. Zool.*, vol. 53 (9), 1975, 1222–1237.

Bergerud, A. and M. Gratson 'Survival and breeding strategies of Grouse', in A. Bergerud and M. Gratson (eds). *Adaptive strategies and population ecology of northern Grouse,* vol. 1–2, University of Minnesota Press, 1987, 473–577.

Birkenmajer, K. and E. Zastawniak 'A new late Palaeogene macroflora from Bellsun, Spitsebergen', *Acta Palaeobotanica,* vol. 45 (2), 2005, 145–163.

Birula, A., 'A sketch of the life of birds in polar seashores of Siberia', in *Scientific Results of Russian Polar Expedition in 1900–1903.* Division E, Zoology, St Petersburg, vol. 1 (2), 1907.

Biserov, M.F., 'On the summer biology of Spruce Grouse in the upper Bureia River Basin', *Abstracts of the XI Russian (International) Ornith. Conf.,* Kazan, 2001, 93–94.

Blackford, J.L., 'Territoriality and breeding behavior of a population of Blue Grouse in Montana',

Condor, vol. 60 (2), 1958, 145–167.

Blackford, J.L., 'Further observations on the breeding behavior of a Blue Grouse population in Montana', *Condor,* vol. 65 (6), 1963, 485–513.

Blanchette, P., J-C. Bourgeous and S. St-Once, 'Ruffed Grouse winter habitat use in mixed softwood–hardwood forests, Quebec, Canada', *J. Wildlife Management,* vol. 71 (6), 2007, 1758–1764.

Boag, D.A., 'Population attributes of Blue Grouse in south-western Alberta', *Canad. J. Zool.,* vol. 44(5), 1966, 799–814.

Boag, D.A., A. Watson and N. Rousfield, 'Characteristics of Pheasant–Capercaillie hybrids', *Scottish Birds,* vol. 6 (6), 1971, 313–316.

Boag, D.A. and M.A. Schroeder, 'Spruce Grouse *(Dendragapus canadensis)* in *The Birds of North America,* No. 5 (A. Poole, P. Stettenheim and F. Gill, eds). The Academy of Natural Sciences, Philadelphia, and The American Ornithologists' Union, Washington, D.C., 1992.

Boback, A.F., 'Das Auerhuhn', *Die neue Brehm-Bucherei,* no. 86, 1966, 118.

Boback, A.F. and D. Müller-Scwarze, 'Das Birkwild *(Lyrurus tetrix L.)*', *Die neue Brehm-Bucherei,* no. 397, 1968, 102.

Bobrov, E.G., 'The history and systematics of larches', *Komarov's Readings,* Issue 25, 1972, 1–90.

Bochenski, Z., 'Middle Pleistocene remains of birds from Kozi Grjbiet in the Swietokrzyskie Mountains', *Acta Zoologica Cracoviensia,* vol. 27, 1984, 177–186.

Bochenski, Z., 'Pliocene Grouse of the genus *Lagopus* from Poland', *Acta Zoologica Cracoviensia,* vol. 34 (2), 1991, 563–577.

Boev, Z., 'Middle Villafranchian birds from Varschets (Western Balkan Range–Bulgaria', *Courier Forschiungsinstitut Senckenberg,* vol. 181, 1995, 259–269.

Boev, Z., 'Fossil birds of Dorkovo – an early Pliocene site in the Rhodope Mts (Southern Bulgaria)', *Geologica Balcanica,* Vol. 28, No. 1–2, 1998, 53–60.

Boev, Z., 'Early Pliocene Avifauna of Musielevo (Central Northern Bulgaria)', *Acta Zoologica Cracoviensia,* vol. 44 (1), 2001, 37–52.

Boev, Z., 'Tetraonidae Vigors, 1825 (Galliformes – Aves) in the Neogene–Quaternary record of Bulgaria and the origin and evolution of the family', *Acta Zoologica Cracoviensia,* vol. 45 (special issue), 2002, 263–282.

Bogdanov, M.N., 'Biogeographical essay on Black Grouse *(Tetrao tetrix)*', in *The proceedings of the 1st Congress of the Russian naturalists,* St Petersburg, 1868, 189–210.

Bogdanov, M.N., 'List of the birds of the Russian Empire', St Petersburg, 1884.

Bonaparte, C.L., 'Notice of a non-descript species of Grouse from North America', *Zool. Journ.,* London, vol. 3, no. 10, 1828, 212–214.

Bonaparte, C.L., 'General observations on the birds of the genus *Tetrao,* with a synopsis of the species hitherto known', *Phil. Soc. Trans. Philad.,* vol. 3, 1830, 383–394.

Bonapate, C.L., 'Tableaux paralléliques de l'Ordre des Gallinacés', *Compt. Rend. Hebdom. Acad. Sci.,* Paris, vol. 42, 1856, 874–884.

Bonaparte, C.L., 'Tableaux des genres des Gallinaces dispose en series paralleles', *Compt. Rend. Acad. Sci.,* Paris, vol. 41 (1), 1857, 425–429.

Boulter, M.C. and S.B. Manum, '15. Oligocene and Miocene vegetation in high latitudes of the North Atlantic: Palynological evidence from the Hovgård Ridge in the Greenland Sea (Site 908)', *Proceedings of the Ocean Drilling Programme, Scientific Results,* vol. 151, 1996, 289–296.

Bouta, R.P. and R.F. Chambers, 'Status of threatened

Spruce Grouse population in New York; a historical perspective, ecosystem management. Rare species and significant habitats', *New York State Mus. Bull.*, vol. 471, 1990, 82–91.

Bowman, T.J. and R.J. Robel, 'Brood break-up, dispersal, mobility and mortality of juvenile Prairie Grouse', *J. Wildlife Management*, vol. 41 (1), 1977, 27–34.

Braun, C.E., 'Distribution and status of Sage-Grouse in Colorado', *Prairie Naturalist*, vol. 27, 1995, 1–9.

Braun, C.E., 'Sage-Grouse decline in western North America: what are the problems?', *Proceedings of the Western Association of State Fish and Wildlife Agencies*, vol. 67, 1998, 134–144.

Braun, C.E. and K. Martin, 'Unusual summer plumage of White-tailed Ptarmigan', *Wilson Bull.*, vol. 113 (4), 2001, 373–377.

Braun, C.E., K. Martin and L.A. Robb, 'White-tailed Ptarmigan (*Lagopus leucurus*)', in *The Birds of North America*, No. 68 (A. Poole and F. Gill, eds)., The Academy of Natural Sciences, Philadelphia, and The American Ornithologists' Union, Washington, D.C., 1993.

Braun, C.E. and G.E. Rogers, 'Habitat and seasonal movements of White-tailed Ptarmigan in Colorado', Abstr. papers presented at meeting Colorado-Wyoming Ac. Sci., April 28, 1967 (cit. from Johnsgard, 1973).

Braun, C.E. and R.K. Schmidt, 'Effects of snow and wind on wintering populations of White-tailed Ptarmigan in Colorado', in *Snow and Ice Symp.*, Colorado, 1971, 238–250.

Brehm, C.L., *Handbuch Naturgesichte aller Vögel Deuschland*, Illmenau, 1831.

Brewster, W., 'The Heath Hen of Massachusetts', *Auk*, vol. 2, no.1, 1885a, 80–84.

Brewster, W., 'The Rock Ptarmigan of Newfoundland', *Auk*, vol. 2, no.2, 1885b, 193–195.

Brewster, A., 'The birds of the Lake Umbagog region of Maine', *Bull. Mus. Comp. Zool.*, vol. 41, 1925, 1–241 (cited from Hjorth, 1970).

Brisson, A.B., *Ornithologie*, Paris, vol.1, 1760.

Brodcorb, P., 'The Pleistocene avifauna of Arredondo, Florida', *Bull. Florida State Mus. Biol. Sci.*, vol. 4 (9), 1956, 269–291.

Brodcorb, P., 'Catalog of fossil birds: Part 2 (Anseriformes through Galliformes)', *Bull. Florida State Mus. Biological Sciences*, vol. 8, 1964, 195–335.

Brooks, A.A., 'A Hybrid Grouse, Richardson's X Sharp-tailed', *Auk*, vol. 24 (2), 1907, 167–169.

Brooks, A.A., 'The display of Richardson's Grouse, with some notes on the species and subspecies of the genus *Dendragapus*', *Auk*, vol. 43 (3), 1926, 281–287.

Brown, C.P., 'Food of Maine Ruffed Grouse by seasons and cover type', *J. Wildlife Management*, vol. 10 (1), 1946, 17–28.

Brüll, H., 'Birkwildforschung und Birkwildhege in Schleswig-HolsteIn', *Ztschr. Iagtwiss.*, vol. 7 (3), 1961, 104–126.

Budanzev, L. Iu., 'Some problems of studying Early Cenozoic Arctic flora', in A. Tholmachev (ed.), *The Polar Ocean and its seashores in the Cenozoic*, 1970, 76–86 (in Russian).

Bump, G., R.W. Darrow, F.C. Edminster and W.F. Crissey, *The Ruffed Grouse*, New York, 1947.

Burchal-Abramovich, N.I. and B.I. Zalkin, 'The study of birds in the lower Amur Daria River: from materials of archeological excavations of ancient Choresm', *Uzbek's Biol. J.*, vol. 1, 1971, 47–49 (in Russian).

Buturlin, S.A., 'Neue paläarctischen Formen', *Ornith. Monatsber.*, jg. 15, no. 5, 1907, 81–82.

Buturlin, S.A., 'The birds of the Far East', *Ornithol. Bull.*, no. 4, 1916, 209–228 (in Russian).

Buturlin, S.A., 'Kureika's light-beaked Capercaillie',

Uragus, vol. 3, no. 2, 1927, 1–2 (in Russian).

Buturlin, S.A., 'Sur les races du Becasseau cincle (on varibles) et du Tetras a bec noir', *Alauda*, ser. 2, 4 (3), 1932, 261–270.

Buturlin, S.A. and G.P. Dementiev, *A Complicated Key to the Birds of the USSR*, vol. 2, 1935 (in Russian).

Buxton, P.A., *Animal Life in Deserts*, London, 1928.

Campbell, H., 'A population study of Lesser Prairie-Chicken in New Mexico', *J. Wildlife Management*, 36 (4), 1972, 689–699.

Castroviejo, H., 'Eine neue Auerhuhnrasse von der Iberischen Halbinsel', *J. Ornithol.*, Jg. 108, no. 2, 1967, 220–221.

Chambers, R.E. and W.M. Sharp, 'Movement and dispersal within a population of Ruffed Grouse', *J. Wildlife Management*, vol. 22, 1958, 231–239.

Chapman F.M., 'A New Grouse from California', *Bull. Amer. Mus.*, vol. 20, 1904, 159–161.

Chelzov-Bebutov, A.M., 'Biological significance of the Black Grouse's lek in the theory of sexual selection', *Ornithologia*, vol. 7, 1965, 389–397.

Cheng, Tso-Hsin, *A Synopsis of the Avifauna of China*, Beijing Science Press, 1987.

Cherepanov, N.T., 'On the experience of the artificial settlement of Capercaillie in the Borovskoe Hunting Farm', International Capercaillie meeting, Moscow, Abstracts, 1981, 18–21 (in Russian).

Chiba, S. amd E. Suhinji, 'Food analysis of the Japanese Ptarmigan, *Lagopus mutus japonicus*', in *Japanese Rock Ptarmigan*, Tokyo, 1972, 114–140 (in Japanese, English resumé).

Choate ,T.S., 'Habitat and population dynamics of the White-tailed Ptarmigan in Montana', *J. Wildlife Management*, vol. 27 (4), 1963, 684–699.

Christophovich, A. 'Development of botanical geographical districts of the Northern Hemisphere from the beginning of the Tertiary period', in N. Shatskiy (ed.) *A Question of Geology*, Moscow, 1955, 824–844 (in Russian).

Chunichin, S.P, 'The Caucasian Black Grouse', *Hunting and Hunting Farm*, vol. 8, 1964, 22–23 (in Russian).

Clark, A.H., 'Eighteen new species and the new genus of birds from Eastern Asia and Aleutian Islands', *Smiths. Inst. Nat., Mus. Proc.*, vol. 32, 1907, 467–475.

Commons, M.L. 'Movement and habitat use by Gunnison Sage-Grouse (*Centrocercus minimus*) in south-western Colorado', MS. Thesis, University of Manitoba, Winnipeg, 1997.

Conover, H.B., 'A new race of Ruffed Grouse from Vancouver Island', *Condor*, vol. 37, no. 4, 1935, 204–206.

Connelly, J.W. and C.E. Braun, 'Long-term changes in Sage-Grouse *Centrocercus urophasianus* populations in western North America, *Wildlife Biology*, vol. 3, 1997, 229–234.

Connelly, J.W., M.W. Gratson and K. Preese, 'Sharp-tailed Grouse (*Tympanuchus phasianellus*)' in *The Birds of North America*, no. 354 (A. Poole and F. Gill, eds)., The Birds of North America, Philadelphia, 1998.

Connelly, J.W., K. Preese and M.A. Schroeder, 'Monitoring of Greater Sage-Grouse habitats and populations', *Station Bulletin 80*, College of Natural Resources Experiment Station, University of Idaho, Moscow, Idaho, 2003.

Cough, J.R., H.L. German, D.R. Knight, P. Sparks and P.B. Pearson, 'Importance of the caecum in intestinal synthesis in the mature domestic fowl', *Poultry Sci.*, vol. 29, no. 1, 1950, 52–58.

Couturier, M.A., *Couturier Les Coqs de Bruyére*, Boulogne, t. 1, 2, 1980.

Cowan, J.M., 'The White-tailed Ptarmigan of Vancouver Island', *Condor*, vol. 41 (1), 1939,

82–83.

Cramp, S., K.E.L. Simmons and C.M. Perrins, *Birds of the Western Palearctic*, vol. 4, 1980, Oxford University Press, Oxford.

Crawford, J. and E. Bolen, 'Spring lek activity of Lesser Prairie-Chicken in West Texas', *Auk*, vol. 92 (4), 1975, 808–810.

Crichton, V., 'Autumn and winter foods of Spruce Grouse in Central Ontario', *J. Wildlife Management*, vol. 27 (4), 1963, 597–598.

Cronin, T., *Paleoclimates: Understanding Climate Change Past and Present*, Columbia University Press, 2010.

Crowe, T.M., P. Bloomer, E. Randi, V. Lucchini, R.T. Kimball, E.L Braun and J.G. Groth, 'Supra-generic cladistics of landfowl (Order Galliformes)', *Acta Zoologica Sinica*, vol. 52 (supplement), 2006a, 358–361.

Crowe, T.M., R.C.K. Bowie, P. Bloomer, T.G. Mandiwana, T.A.J. Hedderson, E. Randi, S.L. Pereira and J. Wakeling, 'Phylogenetics, biogeography and classification of, and character evolution in Gamebirds (Aves: Galliformes): effects of character exclusion, data partitioning and missing data', *Cladistics*, vol. 22 (6): 2006b, 495–532.

Dalke, P.D., D.B. Pyrah, D.C. Stanton, J.E. Crawford and E.F Schlatterer, 'Ecology, productivity and management of Sage-Grouse in Idaho', *J. Wildlife Management*, vol. 27 (4), 1963, 811–841.

Danilov, N.N., 'Ural and Trans-Ural', in S.V. Kirikov *The Tetraonid Birds*, Moscow, 1975, 59–82 (in Russian).

Davies, R. and A. Bergerud, 'Demography and behaviour of Ruffed Grouse in British Columbia', in A. Bergerud and M. Gratson (eds), *Adaptive Strategies and Population Ecology of Northern Grouse*, vol. 1–2, University of Minnesota Press, 1987, 78–121.

Davis, J.A., 'The post-juvenal wing and tail molt of the Ruffed Grouse (*Bonasa umbellus monticola*) in Ohio', *Ohio Journ. of Science*, vol. 68, 1968, 305–312.

Dawson, W.L., 'Notes on the birds of Okanogan Co. Washington', *Wilson Bull.*, vol. 8 (10), 1896, 1–4.

Dementiev, G.P. and A.N. Schochin, 'On the avifauna of Kolyma River', *Proc. Zool. Mus. Moscow Univ.*, vol. 2, 1935, 56–60 (in Russian).

Derevyanko, A.P., A.K. Agadzhanyan, G.F. Baryshnikov *et al.*, 'Denisova cave, multi-layer archaeological site in the north-western Asia', in A.P. Derevyanko (ed.) *Archaeology, Geology and Paleogeography of the Pleistocene and Holocene of the Altai Mountains*, Novosibirsk, 1998 (in Russian).

DeVany, J.L., 'The Spruce drummer', *Can. Field Nat.*, vol. 35, 1921, 16–17.

Dice, L.R., 'Notes on some birds of interior Alaska', *Condor*, vol. 22 (1), 1920, 176–185.

Dickerman, R.W. and J. Gustaffson, 'The Prince of Wales Spruce Grouse: a new subspecies from south-eastern Alaska', *Western Birds*, vol. 27, 1996, 41–47.

Dickey, D.R. and A.J. Van Rossem, 'Description of a new Grouse from Southern California', *Condor*, vol. 25, no. 2, 1923, 168–169.

Dimcheff, D.E., S.V. Drovetski and D.P. Mindell, 'Phylogeny of Tetraonidae and other Galliforme birds using mitochondrial 12S and ND2 genes', *Molecular Phylogenetics and Evolution*, vol. 24, 2002, 203–215.

Dinnik, N. Ia., 'Caucasian Black Grouse (*Tetrao mlokosyewytsii Tacz.*)', *Nature and Hunting*, March, 1884, 15–20 (in Russian).

Dixon, J.S., 'Contribution to the life history of the Alaska Willow Ptarmigan', *Condor*, vol. 29 (5), 1927, 213–223.

Doerr, P.D., L.B. Keith, D.H. Rusch and C.A.

Fischer, 'Characteristic of winter feeding aggregations of Ruffed Grouse in Alberta', *J. Wildlife Management*, vol. 38 (4), 1974, 601–615.

Doherty, K.E., D.E. Naugle, B.L. Walker and J.M. Graham, 'Greater Sage-Grouse winter habitat selection and energy development', *J. Wildlife Management*, vol. 72 (1), 2008.

Dolbik, M.S., 'Results of ecological study of the most important galliforme birds of Belarus', *Ecology and migration of birds in Baltic republics, Proc. IV Baltic conf.*, Riga, 1961, 85–90 (in Russian).

Domaniewski, J., 'Contribution à la conaissance des Oiseaux de la Transbaicalie du sud-ouest et de la Mongolie du Nord', *Acta Ornith. Mus. Zool. Polon.*, vol. 1, no. 6, 1933, 147–179.

Dombrowski, R., *Ornis Romaniae*, Bucharest, 1912.

Donaurov, S.S., 'The Hazel Grouse in the Pechora-Ilych State Reserve', *Proc. Pecora-Ilych State Reserve, M.*, issue 4, part 1, 1947, 77–122 (in Russian).

Dorney, R.S. and C. Kabat, 'Relation of weather, parasitic disease and hunting to Wisconsin Ruffed Grouse population', *Wisconsin Conserv. Dept. Techn. Wildl. Bull.*, vol. 20, 1960, 1–64.

Douglas, D., 'Observations on some species of the genera *Tetrao* and *Ortyx*, natives of North America', *Trans. Linn. Soc.*, London, vol. 16, 1829, 133–149.

Drovetski, S.V., 'Plio-Pleistocene climatic oscillation, Holarctic biogeography and speciation in an avian sub-family', *Journ. Biogeography*, vol. 30, 2003, 1173–1181.

Drovetski, S.V. and S. Rohwer, 'Habitat use, chick survival and density of Caucasian Black Grouse *Tetrao mlokosiewiszi*', *Wildl. Biol.*, vol. 5, 2000, 233–240.

Dulkeit, G.D., 'Hunting animals: Problems and evaluation methods of Altai-Sayan mountain taiga hunting territories' productivity', *Proc. State Reserve "Stolby"*, issue 4, 1964, 1–352 (in Russian).

Dulkeit, G.D., 'Altai and Sayans', in S.V. Kirikov (ed.) *The Tetraonid Birds*, Moscow, 1975, 83–99 (in Russian).

Edminster, F.C., *The Ruffed Grouse: Its Life History, Ecology and Management*, New York, 1947.

Edminster, F.C., *American Game Birds of Field and Forest*, New York, 1954.

Edwards, G., *A Natural History of Birds*, parts 1–4, London, 1743–1751.

Efremov, P., 'Summer observation of Capercallie and its harvest in the Kay Region, Kirov District', *Scientific Papers of Mari Pedagogical Institute*, vol. 1 (1), 1940, 147–174 (in Russian).

Egorov, O., Yu. Labutin and A. Mezenniy, 'On the biology of the Black-billed Capercallie', *Proc. Inst. Biology*, Yakutian Academy of Sciences, vol. 6, 1959, 97–105 (in Russian).

Elliot, D.G., 'Remarks on a proposed arrangement of the family of Grouse, with new genera added', *Proc. Acad. Nat. Sci.*, Philadelphia, vol. 16, 1864, 23.

Elliot, D.G., *A Monograph of the Tetraonidae, or Family of the Grouse*, New York, 1865.

Elliot, D.G., 'Descriptions of an apparently new species and subspecies of Ptarmigan from the Aleutian Islands', *Auk*, vol. 13 (1), 1896, 24–29.

Elliot, D.G., *The Gallinaceous Game Birds of North America*, New York, 1897.

Ellison, L.N., 'Seasonal foods and chemical analysis of the winter diet of Alaskan Spruce Grouse', *J. Wildlife Management*, vol. 30 (6), 1966, 729–735.

Ellison, L.N., 'Sexing and aging of Alaska Spruce Grouse by plumage'. *J. Wildlife Management*, vol. 32 (1), 1968, 12–16.

Ellison, L.N., 'Territoriality in Alaskan Spruce Grouse', *Auk*, vol. 88 (4), 1971, 652–664.

Ellison, L.N., 'Seasonal social organization and

movements of Spruce Grouse', *Condor*, vol. 75 (4), 1973, 375–385.

Ellison, L.N., 'Populational characteristics of Alaskan Spruce Grouse', *J. Wildlife Management*, vol. 38 (3), 1974, 383–395.

Ellison, L.N., 'Density of Alaskan Spruce Grouse before and after fire', *J. Wildlife Management*, vol. 39 (3), 1975, 468–471.

Ellison, L.N., 'Black Grouse population characteristics on a hunted and three unhunted areas in the French Alps', in *Woodland Grouse Symposium*, Inverness, 1978, 64–73.

Ellsworth, D.L., R.L. Honeycutt and N.J. Silvy, 'Systematics of Grouse and Ptarmigan determined by nucleotide sequences of the mitochondrial cytochrome-b gene', *Auk*, vol. 113, 1996, 811–822.

Emslie, S.D., 'The Early and Middle Pleistocene Avifauna from Porcupine Cave', in A.D. Barnosky (ed.), *Biodiversity Response to Climate Change in the Middle Pleistocene: the Porcupine Cave Fauna from Colorado*, University California Press, Berkeley, 2004.

Eng, R.L., 'A study of the ecology of male Ruffed Grouse (*Bonasa unbellus L.*) on the Cloquet Forest Research Center, Minnesota', PhD dissertation, University of Minnesota (cit. from Johnsgard, 1973), 1959.

Eng, R.L., 'Two hybrid Sage-Grouse x Sharp-tailed Grouse from central Montana', *Condor*, vol. 73, no. 6, 1971, 491–493.

Estafiev, A.A., N.M. Polejaev and S.S. Beliaev, 'Annual autumn roaming of Capercaillie in the sub-polar Urals from adjacent regions of the Pechora lowlands', in *Protection of the Living Nature in the Komi ASSR*, Syktyvkar, 1973, 19–22 (in Russian).

Evans, K., 'Observations on a hybrid between the Sharp-tailed Grouse and the Greater Prairie-Chicken', *Auk*, vol. 83 (6), 1966, 128–129.

Evans, K. and D. Dietz, 'Nutritional energetics of Sharp-tailed Grouse during winter', *J. Wildlife Management*, vol. 38 (4), 1974, 622–629.

Ewing, S., 'Scottish Capercaillie survey', *Grouse News*, vol. 38, 2009, 3.

Faber, F., *Prodromus der islandischen Ornithologie oder geschichte der Vögel Islands*, Copenhagen, 1822.

Farner, D., 'Digestion and digestive system', in *Biology and Comparative Physiology of Birds*, vol. 1, 1960, 411–468.

Fediushin, A.V. and M.S. Dolbik, *The Birds of Belorussia*, Minsk (in Russian), 1967.

Fenna, L., D.A. Boag, 'Adaptive significance of the caeca in Japanese Quail and Spruce Grouse', *Canad. J. Zool.*, vol. 52, no. 12, 1974, 1577–1584.

Fenna, L., D.A. Boag, 'Filling and emptying of the galliforme caecum', *Canad. Journ. Zool.*, vol. 52, no. 4, 1974, 537–540.

Fetisov, S.A., 'The count of Hazel Grouse *Tetrastes bonasia* with a hunter's whistle', *Russian Journ. Ornith.*, vol. 17 (441), 2008, 1421–1428 (in Russian).

Fields, T.L., G.C. White, W.C. Gilbert and R.D. Rodgers, 'Nest and brood success in Lesser Prairie-Chicken in west-central Kansas', *J. Wildlife Management*, 2006, 70.

Filonov, K.P., 'Winter in the life of birds in the Bargusin State Reserve', *Proc. Bargusin State Reserve*, vol. 3, 1961, 39–98 (in Russian).

Folitarek, S.S. and G.P. Dementiev, 'Birds of the Altai State Reserve', *Proc. Altay State Reserve, Moscow*, vol. 1, 1938, 7–91 (in Russian).

Forbush, E.H., *Birds of Massachusetts and Other New England States*, Boston, vol. 2, 1927.

Formosov, A.N., *Mammals, Birds and their Inter-relations with the Surrounding Habitats*, Moscow, 1976 (in Russian).

Formosov, A.N., Iu. A. Isakov, S.V. Kirikov, 'Terrestrial game animals', in *The Natural Resources of the Soviet Union, Its Utilization and Reproduction*, Moscow, 1963, 180–209 (in Russian).

Fowle, C.D., 'A study of the Blue Grouse (*Dendragapus obscurus* Say), on Vancouver Island, British Columbia', *Can. J. Zool.*, vol. 38, 1960, 701–713.

Frederick, G.P. and R.J. Gutiérrez, 'Habitat use and population characteristics of the White-tailed Ptarmigan in the Sierra Nevada, California', *Condor*, vol. 94, no. 4, 1992, 889–902.

Fredrickson, L.F., B. Crouch and G.L. Heismeyer, 'Status and management of the Greater Prairie-Chicken in South Dakota', in W.D. Svedarsky, R.H. Hier, N.J. Silvy (eds), *The Greater Prairie-Chicken, a National Look*, Agricult. Experiment Station, University of Minnesota, St Paul, Minnesota. Miscellaneous Publ., vol. 99, 1999, 75–80.

Friedmann, H., 'A new race of the Sharp-tailed Grouse', *J. Wash. Acad. Sci.*, vol. 33, 1943, 189–191.

Furbringer, M., *Unterzukhengen zur morphologie und systematic der fogel.* Amsterdam, vol. 1, 1888.

Fuschlberger, H., *Das Hahnenbuch. 2. Aufl*, München, 1956.

Gabrashansky, P. and S. Donchev, 'Subspecies, habitats and factors influencing numbers in Bulgaria', *Finnish Game Research*, vol. 30, 1970, 152–155.

Gabrielson, I.N. and F.C. Lincoln, *The Birds of Alaska*, Harrisburg, Washington, 1959.

Gaidar, A.A., 'Marking of Hazel Grouse and the results', *Bull. Moscow Soc. of Naturalists (MOIP), Biol. Section*, vol. 78, issue 6, 1973, 120–124 (in Russian).

Gaidar, A.A., 'On the biology of Hazel Grouse reproduction near the Viarka and Kama rivers', Proc. 2nd All-Union Ornith. Conf., Moscow, part 2, 1974, 44–45 (in Russian).

Galtier, N., B. Nabholz, S. Glémin and G.D. Hurst, 'Mitochondrial DNA as a marker of molecular diversity: a reappraisal', *Molecular Ecology*, vol. 18, 2009, 4541-4550.

Gambarian, G.P., 'Some peculiarities of the mandibles of galliform birds', *Zool. Journ.*, vol. 57, no. 11, 1978, 1699–1705 (in Russian).

Gardarsson, A., 'Cyclic predation changes and some behaviour events in Rock Ptarmigan in Iceland' in A. Bergerud and M. Gratson (eds), *Adaptive strategies and population ecology of northern Grouse*, University of Minnesota Press, vol. 1–2, 1987, 300–329.

Gavrilov, V.M., 'Energy of existence in galliform birds: dependence on ambient temperature, season and body size', *Ornithologia*, no. 15, 1980, 73–79 (in Russian).

Gavrin, V.F., 'The density and dynamics of tetraonid birds in the mixed forest sub-zone', in *The natural productivity of the hunting lands of USSR*, Kirov, part 1, 1969a, 38–43 (in Russian).

Gavrin, V.F., 'The ecology of Hazel Grouse in Beloweje Forest' in *The State Reserved Hunting Farm 'Beloweje Forest', Minsk*, vol. 3, 1969b, 146–172 (in Russian).

Gelting, P., 'Studies on the food of the East Greenland Ptarmigan, particularly its relationship to vegetation and snow cover', *Medd om Gr nland*, vol. 116, 1937, 101–196.

Gibson, R.M. and J.W. Bradbury, 'Sexual selection in lekking Sage-Grouse: phenotypic correlates of male mating success', *Behavioral and Ecological Sociobiology*, vol. 18, 1985, 117–123.

Gibson, R.M., J.W. Bradbury and S.L. Vehrencamp, 'Mate choice in lekking Sage-Grouse revisited: the roles of vocal display, female site fidelity, and copying', *Behavioral Ecology*, vol. 2, 1991, 165–180.

Giroux, W., P. Blanchette, J-C. Bourgeois and G. Cabana, 'Ruffed Grouse brood habitat use in mixed softwood-hardwood Nordic-temperate forests', Quebec, Canada, *J. Wildlife Management*, vol. 71 (1), 2007, 87–95.

Giesen, K.M., 'Lesser Prairie-Chicken (*Tympanuchus pallidicinctus*)', in *The Birds of North America* (A. Poole and F. Gill, eds.), The Birds of North America, Philadelphia, no. 364, 1998.

Gill, R.B., 'Weather and Sage-Grouse productivity', Colorado Game, Fish and Parks Department Outdoor Information Leaflet, Denver, 1966.

Gisenko, A.I., 'On the biology and number of Willow and Rock Ptarmigan in Kamchatka' in *Populations of tetraonid birds in the USSR*, Moscow, 1968, 12–13 (in Russian).

Godfrey, W.E., *The Birds of Canada*, Ottawa, 1986.

Gloger, C.W.L., *Hand- und Hilfs-buch der Naturgeschichte*, Breslau, Bd. 1, 1842.

Glutz von Blotzheim, U.N., K.M. Bauer and E. Bezzel, *Handbuch der Vögel Mitteleuropas*, Bd. 5, Frankfurt am Main, 1973.

Gmelin, J.F., *Linnaeus Sistema Naturae*, 13th edition, Lipsiae, vol. 1, 1788.

Gofman, D.N., 'On the ancestral features in feathering of *Lyrurus* and *Tetrao* (and the problems of the phylogeny of the family Tetraonidae)', *Zool. J.*, vol. 23 (2/3), 1944, 82–89 (in Russian).

Golovneva, L.B., 'Palaeogene climates of Spitsbergen', GFF 122, 2000, 62–63.

Gould, J., *The Birds of Europe*, London, vol. 4, 1837.

Grange, W.R., 'Some observations on the Ruffed Grouse in Wisconsin', *Wils. Bull.*, vol. 48, 1936, 104–110.

Gratson, M., 'Spatial patterns, movements and cover selection by Sharp-tailed Grouse', in A. Bergerud and M. Gratson (eds), *Adaptive strategies and population ecology of northern Grouse*, University of Minnesota Press, vol. 1–2, 1987, 158–192.

Gray, G.R., *A List of the Genera of Birds*, London, 1840.

Greenwood, D.R., J.F. Basinger and R.Y. Smith, 'How wet was the Arctic Eocene rain forest? Estimates of precipitation from Paleogene Arctic microfloras', *Geology*, vol. 38, 2010, 15–18.

Gregg, M.A., J.A. Crawford, M.S. Drut and A.K. Delong, 'Vegetational cover and predation of Sage-Grouse nests in Oregon', *J. Wildlife Management*, vol. 58, 1994, 162–166.

Griner, L.A., 'A study of the Sage-Grouse (*Centrocercus urophasianus*) with special reference to life history, habitat requirements and numbers and distribution', M.S. thesis, Utah State University, Logan, 1939.

Grinnell, J., 'The birds of the 1908 Alexander expedition to Alaska', *Berkeley Univ. Calif. Publ. Zool.*, no. 5, 1909, 181–244.

Grinnell, J., 'Birds of the 1908 Alexander Alaska expedition with a note of the avifaunal relationships of the Prince William Sound District', *Berkley Calif. Univ. Publ. Zool.*, no. 5, 1910, 361–428.

Grinnell, J., 'A new Ruffed Grouse from the Yukon Valley', *Condor*, vol. 18, no. 4, 1916, 166.

Grote, H., 'Phaenologische daten aus dem Gebiets des Kältepols', *Ornith. Monatsb.*, vol. 40 (5), 1932, 141–145.

Gruner, A.M., 'The limits of temperatures in a Capercaillie nest during incubation', *Nature*, vol. 5, 1951, 68–69.

Gubin, N.T., 'Capercaillie in the Sverdlovsk Province', International Capercaillie Meeting, Moscow, Abstracts, 1981, 22–24 (in Russian).

Gudmundsson, F., 'The predator-prey relationship of the Gyrfalcon (*Falco rusticolis*) and the Rock Ptarmigan (*Lagopus mutus*) in Iceland' in Abstract of the XV Intern. Ornithol. Congress, Hague, 1970, 113–114.

Gullion, G.W., 'Selection and use of drumming sites by male Ruffed Grouse', *Auk*, vol. 84 (2), 1967, 87–112.

Gullion, G.W., 'Aspen-Ruffed Grouse relationship', Abstr. of Papers at 31 Mid-West Wildlife Conf., 1969, 1–3.

Gullion, G.W., 'Factors influencing Ruffed Grouse populations', Trans. N. Amer. Wildlife Conf., 1970, no. 35, 1970, 93–105.

Gullion, G.W., W.H. Marshall, 'Survival of Ruffed Grouse in boreal forests', *Living Birds*, vol. 7, 1968, 117–168.

Gunnison Sage-Grouse Range-wide Steering Committee, 2005.

Gurchinoff, C. and W.L. Robinson, 'Chemical characteristics of jack-pine needles, selected by feeding Spruce Grouse', *J. Wildlife Management*, vol. 36 (1), 1972, 80–87.

Gusakov, E., 'Siberian Spruce Grouse', in A.M. Kozlov (ed.) *Red Data book of the RSFSR: Animals*, Moscow, 1983, 232–233 (in Russian).

Gutiérrez R.J., G.F. Barrowclough amd J.G. Groth, 'A classification of Grouse (Aves: Tetraoninae) based on mitochondrial DNA sequences', *Wildlife Biology*, vol. 6, 2000, 205–211.

Gutiérrez, R.J., G.S. Zimmerman amd G.W. Gullion, 'Daily survival rates of Ruffed Grouse in northern Minnesota', *Wildlife Biol.*, vol. 9, 2003, 351–356.

Hafner, F. amd A.V. Andreev, *Das Sichelhuhn*, Naturwissenschaftlicher Verein f. Kärnten, Klagenfurt and St Petersburg, 1999.

Haga, R. amd S. Takamata, 'Ecology and breeding biology of the Hazel Grouse *Tetrastes bonasia* in captivity', *Tori*, vol. 34, no. 4, 1986, 105–125.

Hagen, C.A., J.C. Pitman, B.K. Sandercock, R.J. Robel and R.D. Applegate, 'Age-specific survival and probable causes of mortality in female Lesser Prairie-chickens', *J. Wildlife Management*, vol. 71 (2), 2007, 518–525.

Hale, J.B. and R.S. Dorney, 'Seasonal movements of Ruffed Grouse in Wisconsin', *J. Wildlife Management*, vol. 27 (3), 1963, 648–656.

Han, S.H. and Y. Fujimaki, 'Review of the distribution of Hazel Grouse in the Korean Peninsula', *Grouse News*, vol. 12, 1996, 11–15.

Hainard, R. and O. Meylan, 'Notes sur le Grand Tetras', *Alauda*, Ser. 3, 7 (3), 1935, 282–327.

Haker, M. and S. Myrberget, 'Browsing by *Lyrurus tetrix* on Pinus mugo – var. arborea', *Sterna*, vol. 8, 1969, 243–237.

Hamerstrom, F.N., 'A study of Wisconsin Prairie-Chicken and Sharp-tailed Grouse', *Wilson Bull.*, vol. 51 (1), 1939, 105–120.

Hamerstrom, F.N., 'Sharp-tail Grouse brood habitat in Wisconsin's northern pine barrens', *J.Wildlife Management*, vol. 27 (4), 1963, 793–802.

Hamerstrom, F.N. and F. Hamerstrom, 'Daily and seasonal movements of Wisconsin's Prairie-Chickens', *Auk*, vol. 66 (2), 1949, 313–337.

Hamerstrom, F.N. and F. Hamerstrom, 'Mobility of the Sharp-tailed Grouse in relation to its ecology and distribution', *Amer. Midl. Nat.*, vol. 46 (1), 1951, 174–226.

Hannon, S.J., 'Factors limiting polygyny in the Willow Ptarmigan', *Animal Behaviour*, vol. 32, 1984, 153–161.

Hannon, S.J., P.K. Eason and K. Martin, 'Willow Ptarmigan (*Lagopus lagopus*)', in *The Birds of North America*, no. 369 (A. Poole and F. Gill, eds), The Birds of North America, Philadelphia, 1998.

Hanmamedov, A.I., 'On the Galliforme birds in north-eastern Azerbaidjan', *Proc. Zool. Inst. Azerbaidjan Acad. Sci.*, Baku, vol. 25, 1965, 98–110 (in Russian).

Hanmamedov, A.I. amd F.A. Aslanbekova, 'Breeding of the Caucasian Black Grouse', *Proc. Azerbaidjan Acad, Sci.*, 1965, 59–64 (in Russian).

Harper, F., 'Birds of the Ungava Peninsula', University of Kansas Museum Nat. Hist., miscellaneous publ., no. 17, 1958, 1–171.

Harris, S.W., 'Fall foods of Sharp-tailed Grouse in Minnesota', *J. Wildlife Management*, vol. 31 (3), 1967, 585–587.

Hartert, E., *Die Vögel der paläarktishen Fauna*, Berlin, Bd. 3, 1922, 1755–2328.

Hartlaub, G., 'Über *Tetrao falcipennis*, nov. sp.', *J. Ornithol.*, Jg. 3, no. 1, 1855, 39–42.

Hartzler, J. and D. Jenni, 'Mate choice by female Sage-Grouse', in A. Bergerud and M. Gratson (eds), *Adaptive strategies and population ecology of northern Grouse*, University of Minnesota Press, vol. 1–2., 1987, 240–269.

Herzzog, P. and D. Keppie, 'Migration in a local population of Spruce Grouse', *Condor*, vol. 82, no. 4, 1980, 366–372.

He, F. and Y-Zh. Ceng, 'Present status of the Chinese Hazel Grouse in north-western Yunnan' in T. Lovell and P. Hudson (eds). Proc. 4th Intern. Grouse Symp, Lam, West Germany, September 1987, 199–202.

Helminen, M. and J. Viramo, 'Animal food of Capercaillie (*Tetrao urogallus*) and Black Grouse (*Lyrurus tetrix*) in autumn', *Ornis Fennica*, vol. 39 (1), 1962, 1–12.

Hesse, E., '*Lagopus lagopus brevirostris*', *Ornith. Monatsber.*, Jg. 20, no.6, 1912, 101–102.

Hines, J.E., 'Social organization, movements, and home ranges of Blue Grouse in fall and winter', *Wilson Bull.*, vol. 98 (3), 1986, 419–432.

Hines, J.E., 'Winter habitats relationships of Blue Grouse on Hardwicke Island, British Columbia', *J. Wildlife Management*, vol. 51 (2), 1987, 426–435.

Hissa, R., H. Rintamaki, S. Saarela, A. Marjakangas, E. Hohtola and H. Linden, 'Energetics and development of temperature regulation in gallinaceous birds', *Suomen Riista*, vol. 29, 1982, 29–39.

Hjorth, I., 'Fortplantningsbeteenden inom hönsfågelfamiljen Tetraonidae (Reproductive behaviour in male Grouse)', *Vår Fågelvärld*, vol. 26, 1967, 195–243.

Hjorth, I., 'Reproductive behaviour of Tetraonidae', *Viltrevy*, vol. 7, no. 4, 1970, 184–596.

Hoffman, R. S., 'Observations on a Sooty Grouse population at Age Hen Creek, California', *Condor*, vol. 58, 1956, 321–333.

Hoffman, D.M., 'The Lesser Prairie-Chicken in Colorado', *J. Wildlife Management*, vol. 27 (4), 1963, 726–732.

Höglund, N., 'Capercaillie reproduction and climate', *Papers on Game Research*, vol. 28, 1952, 78–80.

Höglund, N., 'Body temperature, activity and reproduction of Capercaillie', *Viltrevy*, vol. 1, 1955, 1–87.

Höglund, N., 'On the ecology of the Willow Grouse (*Lagopus lagopus*) in a mountainous area in Sweden' in VIII International Congress of Game Biologists, Helsinki, 1970, 118–120.

Höhn, E.O., *Das Schneehühner*, Neue Brehm-Bücherei, 1969.

Holder, K. and R. Montgomerie, 'Rock Ptarmigan (*Lagopus mutus*)', in *The Birds of North America*, no. 51 (A. Poole and F. Gill, eds.), The Academy of Natural Sciences, Philadelphia, and The American Ornithologists' Union, Washington D.C., 1993.

Honess, R.F. and W.J. Allred, 'Structure and function of the neck muscles in inflation and deflation of the oesophagus in the Sage Cock', *Wyoming Game and Fish Dept. Bull.*, vol. 2, 1942, 5–12.

Hörnell-Willebrand, M., 'Temporal and Spatial Dynamics of Willow Grouse *Lagopus lagopus*', unpublished doctoral thesis, Swedish University of Agricultural Sciences, Faculty of Forest Sciences Department of Animal Ecology, Umeå (cit. from Watson, Moss, 2008), 2005.

Hudson, P.J., *Grouse in Space and Time*, Game Conservancy Trust, Fordingbridge, 1992.

Hudson, G.E., P.J. Lanzilotti and G.D. Edwards, 'Muscles of the pelvic limb in galliforme birds', *Amer. Midl. Nat.*, vol. 61 (1), 1959, 1–67.

Hulten, E.A., *Outline of the history of Arctic and boreal biota during the Quaternary Period*, Stockholm, 1937.

Hulten, E.A., 'The distributional conditions of the flora of Beringia', in Pacific basin biogeography, Honolulu, 1963, 42–48.

Hupp, J.W. and C.E. Braun, 'Topographic distribution of Sage-Grouse foraging in winter', *J. Wildlife Management*, vol. 53, 1989, 823–829.

Huwer, S.L., D.R. Anderson, T.E. Remington and G.C. White, 'Using human-imprinting chicks to evaluate the importance of forbs to Sage-Grouse', *J. Wildlife Management*, vol. 72 (7), 2008, 1622–1627.

Iahontov, V.D., 'The birds of Penjina District' in *The birds of the north-east Asia*, Vladivostok, 1979, 135–162 (in Russian).

Iakovlev, B.P., 'The animals of Manchuria in collections of the Museum of the Society of Explorers of Manchuria (Birds)', Section of Natural Sciences, Ser. A., Harbin, 1929 (in Russian).

Ilyichev, V.D., 'Regarding the deafness of the Capercaillie during the lek', *Hunting and Hunting Farm*, vol. 4, 1961, 25–26 (in Russian).

Ingram, C.A., 'A few notes on *Tetrao urogallus* and its allies', *Ibis*, vol. 3, no. 1, 1915, 128–133.

International Code of Zoological Nomenclature, Fourth Edition, International Commission on Zoological Nomenclature, 2000.

Irwing L., G. West, L.J. Peyton and S. Paneak, 'Winter feeding program of Alaska Willow Ptarmigan shown by crop content', *Condor*, vol. 69, no. 1, 1967, 69–77.

Isaev, A.P., 'The Asian Spruce Grouse in Yakutia', *Yakutsk*, vol. 48, 2008 (in Russian).

Ivanov, V.S. and R.L. Potapov, 'The ecology of the Black Grouse (*Lyrurus tetrix*) and fluctuations in its population density during last 50 years in Gatchina District, Leningrad Province', *Russian J. Ornithol.*, 2008, vol. 17, no. 448, 1632–1638 (in Russian, with English resumé).

Ivanter, E.V., 'On the ecology of the Hazel Grouse in Karelia', *Ornithologia*, no. 4, 1962, 87–98 (in Russian).

Ivanter, E.V., 'Ecology and number of Capercaillie in Karelia', Materials of the IV All-union Ornith. Conf., Alma-Ata, 1965, 139–141 (in Russian).

Ivanter, E.V., 'Capercaillie and Willow Ptarmigan in Karelia', *Ornithologia*, vol. 2, 1974, 206–226 (in Russian).

Iydakov, A.G., 'Spruce Grouse in upper Amurland' in *Preservation, management and reproduction of the natural resources in Amurland*, Khabarovsk, 1967, 186–187 (in Russian).

Iydakov, A.G., 'Influence of raptors on the number of Hazel Grouse in the Upper Amur Basin', in *Populations of tetraonid birds in USSR*, Moscow, 1968, 86–88 (in Russian).

Iydakov, A.G., 'Biology of the Spruce Grouse (*Falcipennis falcipennis*) in Amur Province', *Zool. Journ.*, vol. 51 (4), 1972, 620–622 (in Russian).

Izmailov, I.V. and M.P. Pavlov, 'Areas west and east from Baikal', in *The Tetraonid Birds*, S. Kirikov (ed.), 1975, 100–112 (in Russian).

Jacobsen, J.R., C.M. White and W.B. Emison, 'Molting adaptations of Rock Ptarmigan on Amchitka Island, Alaska', *Condor*, vol. 85 (4), 1983, 420–426.

James, E., 'Account of an expedition from Pittsburgh

to the Rocky Mountains, performed in the years 1819, 1820', by Order of the Hon. J.C. Calhoun, Secretary of War, under the command of Maj. S.H. Long, of the U.S. Top Engineer. Compiled from the notes of Major Long, Mr. T. Say and other Gentleman of the Party, by Edwin James, Botanist and Geologist to the expedition. In three volumes. vol.2, 1823, Philadelphia.

Janossy, D., 'Upper Pliocene and lower Pleistocene bird remains from Poland', *Acta Zool. Cracoviensia*, vol. 19 (21), 1974, 531–566.

Janossy, D., 'Plio-Pleistocene bird remains from the Carpathian Basin, Galliformes. 1. Tetraonidae, *Aquila*, vol. 82, 1976, 13–36.

Janossy, D., 'Diejungmittelpleistozäne Vogelfauna von Hunas (Harmannshof)', in F. Heller et al. (eds), 'Die höhlenruie Hunas bei Hartmannshof (Landkreis Numberger Land). Eine paläontologische und urgeschichtliche Fundstelle aus dem Spät-Riss)', *Quartär-Bibliothek*, vol. 4, 1983, 265–288.

Jehl, J.R., 'Pleistocene birds from Fossil Lake, Oregon', *Condor*, vol. 69 (1), 1967, 24–27.

Jehl, J.R., 'Fossil Grouse of the genus *Dendragapus*', *Trans. San Diego Soc. Nat. Hist.*, vol. 15, 1969, 165–171.

Jenkins, D. and A. Watson, 'Population control in Red Grouse and Ptarmigan in Scotland', in VIII International Congress of Game Biologists, Helsinki, 1970, 121–141.

Jenning, W., 'Verksamheten vis Ottenby fagelstation, 1955', *Vär Fägelvarld*, vol. 15 (3), 1956, 151–176.

Jewett, S.G., W.T. Taylor, W.T. Shaw and J.W. Aldrich, *Birds of Washington State*, 1953, Seattle.

Jitkov, B.M., 'The birds of the Yamal Peninsula', *Ann. Zool. Museum Imp. Acad. Sci.*, vol. 17 (3–4), 1912, 311–369 (in Russian).

Johansen, G., *On the ornithofauna of the Tomsk Province*

steppe, Tomsk, 1907 (in Russian).

Johansen, H., *Revision und Enstehung der arctischen Vogelfauna*, Kobenhavn, 1956.

Johansen H., 'Rassen und Populationen des Auerhahuhns (Tetrao urogallus)', *Viltrevy*, vol. 1, 1957, 233–266.

Johnsen S., 'Remarks on the Svalbard Ptarmigan (*Lagopus mutus hyperboreus* Sundev.)', *Bergens. Mus. Arbok.*, vol. 7, 1941, 1–29.

Johnsgard, P.A., *Grouse and Quails of North America*, University of Nebraska, Lincoln, 1973.

Johnsgard, P.A., *The Grouse of the World*, London, 1983.

Johnsgard, P.A. and R.F. Wood, 'Distributional changes and interactions between Prairie-Chickens and Sharp-tailed Grouse in the Mid-West', *Wils. Bull.*, vol.80 (2), 1968, 173–188.

Johnson, M.D. and J. Knue, *Feathers from the Prairie*, Bismarck, North Dakota, 1989.

Johnstone, G., 'Ecology, dispersion and arena behaviour of Black Grouse, *Lyrurus tetrix* (L.) in Glen Dye, N.E.. Scotland', Phil. Thesis, University of Aberdeen, 1969.

Jollie, M.A., 'A hybrid between the Spruce Grouse and the Blue Grouse', *Condor*, vol. 57 (3), 1955, 213–215.

Jones, R.E., 'Identification and analysis of Lesser and Greater Prairie-Chicken habitats', *J. Wildlife Management*, vol. 27 (4), 1963, 757–778.

Jones, R.E., 'Spring, summer and fall foods of the Columbian Sharp-tailed Grouse in eastern Washington', *Condor*, vol. 68, 1966, 536–540.

Jonkel, C.J. and R.R. Creer, 'Fall food habits of Spruce Grouse in north-west Montana', *J. Wildlife Management*, vol. 27 (4), 1963, 593–596.

Jordans, A. and C. Schiebel, '*Tetrao bonasia styriacus*, form. Nova', *Falco*, no. 40, 1944, 1.

Jurgenson, P.B., 'The summer drought of 1938 in Kuibyshev's State Reserve', *Science-Methodic*

Memories of the State Reserve's Committee, vol. 3, 1939, 200–203.

Kalinin, M.V., 'Why Willow Grouse are disappearing', *Hunting and Hunting Farm*, vol. 10, 1974, 22–23 (in Russian).

Kapitonov, V.I., 'Ornithological observations on the Lower Lena River', *Ornithologia*, vol. 4, 1962, 40–63 (in Russian).

Kaplanov, L.G., 'On the biology of the Dikusha Black Hazel Grouse (*Falcipennis falcipennis*)', *Bull. Far-East Branch Ac. Sci., USSR*, vol. 32, 1938, 148–150 (in Russian).

Kaplanov, L.G., 'On the specificity of Capercaillie and Pheasant ranges in Sikhote-Alin', *Bull. Moscow Soc. Testers of Nature*, vol. 84, 1979, 35–37.

Kareev, S.A., 'Invasion of Black Grouse', *The Hunter*, vol. 7, 1928, 23–24 (in Russian).

Kaup, J.J., *Skizzirte Entwickelungs. Geschichte und naturliches System der Europaischen Thierwelt*, Darmstadt. Th. 1, 1829.

Keller, R.J., H.R. Sheperd and R.N. Randall, 'Survey of 1941 North Park, Jackson County, Moffit County, including comparative data of previous seasons', Sage-Grouse Survey, Colorado Game and Fish Dept., Denver, 1941.

Kennamer, J.E., M. Kennamer and R. Brenneman, 'Chapter 2, History' in *The Wild Turkey* (J.G. Dickson, ed.), Southern Forest Experiment Station, 1992, 2–5.

Keppie, D.M., 'Clutch size of the Spruce Grouse, *Canachites canadensis franclinii* in southern Alberta', *Condor*, vol. 77 (1), 1975, 91–92.

Keppie, D.M., 'Snow cover and the use of trees by Spruce Grouse in autumn', *Condor*, vol. 79, no. 3, 1977, 91–92.

Keppie, D.M., 'Dispersal, overwinter mortality and recruitment of Spruce Grouse', *J. Wildlife Management*, vol. 43 (3), 1979, 717–727.

Keppie, D.M., 'Impact of demographic parameters upon a population of Spruce Grouse in New Brunswick', *J. Wildlife Management*, vol. 51 (4), 1987, 771–777.

Keyserling, A. and J.H. Blausius, *Wirbelthiere Europas*, Braunschweig, 1840.

Khristophovich, A.N., 'The development of the botanical-geographical areas of Northern Hemisphere from the beginning of the Tertiary', in *The Problems of Asian Geology, Collected Articles*, Issue 2, 1955 (in Russian).

King, R.D. and J.F. Bendell, 'Food selected by Blue Grouse (*Dendragapus obscurus fuliginosus*)', *Canad. J. Zool.*, vol. 60 (12), 1982, 3268–3281.

Kirby, A.D. and A.A. Smith, 'Evidence of re-nesting after brood loss in Red Grouse *Lagopus lagopus scoticus*', *Ibis*, vol. 147, 2005, 221.

Kirikov, S.V., 'On changes with age in Capercaillie and age composition in leks', *Scient. Method., Newsletters of the Reservation's Committee*, vol. 2, 1939, 98–109 (in Russian).

Kirikov, S.V., 'The lek and biology of breeding of south Ural Capercaillie', *Zool. J.*, vol. 26 (1), 1947, 71–84 (in Russian).

Kirikov, S., *Birds and mammals in the landscapes of the southern Urals*, Moscow, 1952 (in Russian).

Kirikov, S.V., 'The southern part of the Forest Zone', in S.V. Kirikov (ed.), *The Tetraonid Birds*, Moscow, 1975, 157–202 (in Russian).

Kirpichev, S.P., 'Hybrids between Western and Black-billed Capercaillie', *Sci. Transactions of Moscow University*, vol. 197, 1958, 217–221 (in Russian).

Kirpichev, S.P., 'The Black-billed Capercaillie', *Hunting and Hunting Industry*, vol. 5, 1960, 22–24 (in Russian).

Kirpichev, S.P., 'On changes in the constitution, size and plumage with age in Capercaillie', *Proc. Barguzin State Reserve*, vol. 3, 1961, 127–154 (in Russian).

Kirpichev, S.P., 'Observations on the influence

of low temperatures on tetraonid birds', in *Resources of tetraonid birds in the USSR*, Moscow, 1968, 35–36 (in Russian).

Kirpichev, S.P., 'On the molt of Capercaillie', *Ornithologia*, vol.10, 1972, 303–319 (in Russian).

Kirpichev, S.P., 'On the distribution of Western and Black–billed Capercaillie in the Yenisey region of Siberia', Materials of the All-Union Ornithol. Conf., Moscow, 1974, 63–65 (in Russian).

Kiselev, Iu. N., 'The catching and marking of Capercaillie as a method of studying species biology', *Proc. of the Oka State Reserve*, vol. 7, 1971, 133–178 (in Russian).

Kiselev, Iu. N., 'Factors determining population dynamics in Grouse birds', *Proc. Oksk. State Reserve*, Issue 14, 1978, 50–122 (in Russian).

Kishinski, A.A., *The birds of the Kolyma Highlands*, Moscow, 1968 (in Russian).

Kishinski, A.A., 'Tundra: New Siberian Islands, northern Far East', in S.V. Kirikov (ed.), *The Tetraonid Birds*, Moscow, 1975, 113–135 (in Russian).

Kishinski, A.A., V.E. Fomin, A. Bold and N. Zevenmiadah, 'Birds of the Munk-Hairchan-Ula Mountains' in *Biological resources and natural conditions of Mongolian People's Republic, Moscow*, vol. 18, 1982, 62–81 (in Russian).

Kittlitz, F.H., 'Denkwirdigkeiten einer Reise nach em russischen Amerika, nach Micronesia und durch Kamtschatka', *Gotha*, vol. 2, 1858.

Klaus, S. and A.V. Andreev, '*Falcipennis falcipennis* (Hartlaub, 1855), Sighel Huhn', in *Atlas der Verbreitung Palaearctischer Vogel*, 20 Lieferung, 2003, 1–8.

Klaus, S. and Y-H. Sun, '*Bonasa severzowi* (Prjewalski, 1876) China Hasel Huhn' in *Atlas der Verbreitung Palaearctischer Vogel*, 20 Lieferung, 2003, 1–6.

Kleinschmidt, O., 'Ornis Hermanica', Part Bellage zu Falco, *Falco*, Jg. 15, 1917, 1–10.

Kleinschmidt, O., 'Die farbungen des schottischen Moorhuhns', *Falco*, Jg. 15, no. 1, 1919, 2–4.

Kleinschmidt, O., 'Hazelhühner', *Falco*, no. 37, 1941, 18.

Kobriger, G.D., 'Status, movements, habitats and foods of Prairie Grouse on a Sandhill refuge', *J. Wildlife Management*, vol. 29 (4), 1965, 788–800.

Kohl, S. and A. Stollmann, 'Verschiedenheiten in Knochenbau Karpatischer Auerhähne (T. urogallus rudolfi Dombrowski, 1912 und T. u. major Brehm, 1831)', *Zool. Listy, Praga*, vol. 17 (3), 1968, 237–244.

Kohts, A., 'On homologous rows in the colouration of feathering in Tetraonidae and Phasianidae', in Collected Papers in Memory of Academician Menzbier, 1937, 211–234 (in Russian).

Kohts, A., 'Die neue Subspecies of Birkhuhn *Tetrao tetrix ussuriensis*', in Lorenz, 1911.

Koivisto, J., 'Behaviour of the Black Grouse, *Lyrurus tetrix* (L.), during the spring display', *Riist. Julkais*, vol. 26, 1965, 3–60.

Kojevnikovn, Iu. P., 'Historic perspective on the vegetation cover of northern Asia', St Petersburg, 1996 (in Russian).

Kolev, I.V., 'Ecology, biology and artificial rearing of Capercaillie in Bulgaria', International Capercaillie Meeting, Moscow, 1981, 34 (in Russian).

Korschgen, L.J., 'Food habits of Greater Prairie-Chicken in Missouri', *Amer. Midl. Nat.*, vol. 68 (2), 1962, 307–318.

Koskimies, J., 'Seasonal, geographical and yearly trends in the weight of Capercaillie (*Tetrao urogallus*) and Black Grouse (*Lyrurus tetrix*) in Finland', *Ornis Fennica*, vol. 35, 1958, 1–18.

Kozlova, E.V., 'The birds of south-western Transbaikalia, Northern Mongolia and Central Goby', in *Notes for the study of the Mongolian and*

Tuva Republics, no. 12, 1930 (in Russian).

Krechmar, A.V., 'The birds of western Taimyr', *Proc. Zool. Inst. Acad. Sci.*, USSR, vol. 39, 1966, 185–312 (in Russian).

Krechmar, A.V., A.V. Andreev and A.F. Kondratiev, *Ecology and distribution of birds in the North-East of the USSR*, Moscow, 1978 (in Russian).

Kretzoi, M., 'Vogelreste aus der altpleistozänen Fauna fon Betfia', *Aquila*, vol. 67–68, 1962, 167–174.

Krott, P., 'Das Schicksal eine Auerhuhngesperres', *Bonner Zool. Beitr.*, vol. 17, 1966, 53–86.

Krudener, A., 'Auerwild Naturgeschichte und Jagt, Neudamm', 1928.

Kruijt, J.P. and J.A. Hogan, 'A social behaviour on the lek in Black Grouse (*Lyrurus tetrix tetrix* (L.)', *Ardea*, vol. 55, 1967, 203–240.

Kruijt, J.P., G.J. de Vos and L. Bossema, 'The arena system of Black Grouse', in Proc. XV Intern. Ornith. Congr., Leyden, 1972, 399–423.

Krutovskaya, E.A., 'The birds of the Stolby State Reserve', *Proc. of State Reserve "Stolby"*, vol. 2, 1958, 206–285 (in Russian).

Krutovskaya, E.A. and E.V. Krutovskaya, 'The experience of domesticated and semi- free rearing of Capercaillie', in *The Transformation of Vertebrate Fauna of Our Country* (collection of articles), Moscow, 1953, 201–234 (in Russian).

Kuroda, N., 'Description of three new races from the Kuril Islands, Hokkaido and Formosa: *Lagopus mutus kurilensis*, *Passer rutilans kikuchii* and *Certia familiaris ernsti*', *Bull. Brit. Ornith. Club.*, vol. 45, no. 29, 1925, 15–17.

Kutovaya, T., 'The rearing of Capercaillie in Beresina State Reserve', *Hunting and hunting management*, no. 6, 1976, 30–32 (in Russian).

Kutubidze, M.E., 'Ecology and distribution of the Caucasian Black Grouse in Georgia', *Proc. Institute Zoology Acad. Sci. Georgian SSR*, vol. 18, 1961, 8–38 (in Georgian).

Kuzmina, M.A., 'Order Galliformes' in *The Birds of Kazakhstan*, vol. 2, 1962, 389–487 (in Russian).

Kuzmina, M.A., 'Comparative characteristics of nutrition of tetraonid and phasianid birds in the USSR', *Proc. Inst. of Zoology Ac. Sci. Kazach*, SSR. Y29, 1968, 76–152. Alma-Ata (in Russian).

Larin, S.A., 'The rearing of Capercaillie and Black Grouse in captivity', *Proc. Moscow Ins. Zootechnology*, vol. 1, 1941, 166–181 (in Russian).

Latham, J., 'A natural history, or general synopsis, of birds', *Supplement*, 1787, London.

Latham J., *Index ornithologias*, London, vol. 2, 1790, 467–920.

Leach, H.R. and B.M. Browning, 'A note on the food of Sage-Grouse in the Madeline plains area of California', *Calif. Fish and Game*, vol. 44 (2), 1958, 73–76.

Leach, H.R., A.L. Hensley, 'The Sage-Grouse in California, with special reference to food habits', *Calif. Fish and Game.*, vol. 40 (4), 1954, 385–394.

Lennerstedt, I., 'Egg temperature and incubation rhythm of a Capercaillie (*Tetrao urogallus* L.) in Swedish Lapland', *Oikos*, vol. 17 (2), 1966, 169–174.

Leopold, A.S. 'Intestinal morphology of gallinaceous birds in relation to food habits', *J. Wildlife Management*, vol. 17 (2), 1953, 197–203.

Leopold, E.B. and M. Denton, 'Comparative age of grassland and steppe east and west of the Northern Rocky Mountains, USA', *Annals of the Mo. Bot. Garden.*, vol. 74, 1987, 841–867.

Levin, V., 'Reproduction and development of young in a population of California Quail', *Condor*, vol. 65, no. 4, 1963, 249–278.

Liaister, A.F. and G.W. Sosnin, *On the avifauna of the Armenian SSR*, Erevan, 1942 (in Russian).

Lindell, H. and R. Scott, *A Greek–English Lexicon*, Clarendon Press, Oxford, 9th ed, 1996.

Linden, H., 'Variations in clutch and egg size of Capercaillie and Black Grouse', *Suomen Suomen Riista*, vol. 30, 1983, 44–50.

Lindrot, C.H., 'The Aleutian Islands as a route for dispersal across the North Pacific', in *Pacific basin Biogeography*, Honolulu, 1963, 121–131.

Lindrot, H. and L. Lingren, 'On the significance for forestry of the Capercaillie *Tetrao urogallus* L., feeding on pine needles', *Suomen Riista*, vol. 5, 1950, 60–68.

Lincoln F.C., 'A review of the genus Pedioecetes', *Colorado. Proc. Biol. Soc. Washington*, vol. 30, 1917, 83–86.

Linnaeus, C., *Systema naturae*, 10th edition, Holmae, 1758.

Lobachev, S.V. and F.A. Scherbakov, 'The natural forage of Black Grouse', *Bull. Moskow Soc. Testers of Nature, biology division*, vol. 42, no. 1, 1933, 42–61 (in Russian).

Lobachev, S.V. and F. A. Scherbakov, 'The natural forage of Capercaillie during the year', *Zool. J.*, vol. 40 (2), 1936, 307–320 (in Russian).

Lobko-Lobanovsky, M.I. and A.F. Jilin, 'Breeding biology of Kamchatka's Black-billed Capercaillie', *Ornithologia*, vol. 5, 1962, 164–165 (in Russian).

Lobkov, E.G., *The nesting birds of Kamchatka*, Vladivostok, 1986 (in Russian).

Long, J.L., *Introduced birds of the World*, Sydney, 1981.

Lönnberg, E., 'Ein Beitrage zur Kenntnis der geographischen Variation des Birkwilds (*Tetrao (Lyrurus) tetrix*)', *Ornith, Monatsber*, vol. 12 (7–8), 1904, 105–109.

Lönnberg, E., 'Short notes on a collection of birds from Tianshan', *Arkiv Zool.*, vol. 2 (9), 1905, 1–23.

Lönnberg, E., 'Nagot om tjaderrasen', *Flora*, vol. 19, 1924, 66–74.

Lorenz, T., 'Über *Tetrao tetrix* subspecies *viridanus*', *J. Ornith., Jg.* 39, 1891, 366–368.

Lorenz, T., *Beitrage zur Kenntnis der ornithologischen Fauna an der Nordseite des Kaucasus*, Moscow, 1887.

Lorenz, T., 'A visit to the Kuban region', *Nature and Hunting*, March, 1889, 55–62 (in Russian).

Lorenz, T., '*Lagopus albus* (L.) nov. subsp. major.', *Ornith. Motatsber.*, Jg. 12, no. 11, 1904, 177–178.

Lorenz, T., *Die Birkhühner Russlands, deren Bastarde, Ausartungen und Varietäten*, Wien, 1911.

Lu Xin, 'A new distribution area of Chinese Grouse in Tibet', *Grouse News*, no. 14, 1997, 18–20.

Lucchini, V., J. H glund, S. Klaus, J. Swenson and E. Randi, 'Historical Biogeography and a Mitochondrial DNA Phylogeny of Grouse and Ptarmigan', *Molecular Phylogenetics and Evolution*, vol. 20, no. 1, July 2001, 149–162.

Lukhtanov, A.G. and N.N. Berezovikov, 'Data on the avifauna of the Bukhtarma Valley, South-Western Altai', *Russian Journ. Ornith.*, Vol. 12, Express–issue no. 239, 2003, 1130–1146 (in Russian).

Lumsden, H.G., 'Displays of the Spruce Grouse', *Canad. Field Nat.*, vol. 75, 1961a, 152–160.

Lumsden, H.G., 'The display of the Capercaillie', *Brit. Birds*, vol. 54 (7), 1961b, 257–272.

Lumsden, H.G., 'Displays of the Sharp-tailed Grouse', in *Ontario Dept. of Lands and Forests Research Rep.*, vol. 66, 1965, 1–68.

Lumsden, H.G., 'A hybrid Grouse *Lagopus* x *Canachites* from northern Ontario', *Canad. Field Nat.*, vol. 83 (1), 1969, 23–30.

Lumsden, H.G. and R.B. Weeden, 'Notes on the harvest of Spruce Grouse', *J. Wildlife Management*, vol. 83 (4), 1963, 587–591.

MacDonald, S.D., 'The courtship and territorial behaviour of Franklin's race of the Spruce Grouse', *The Living Birds*, vol. 7, 1968, 5–25.

MacDonald, S.D., 'The breeding behavior of

Rock Ptarmigan', *The Living Birds*, vol. 7, 1970, 195–238.

MacGinitie, H.D., *The Kilgore Flora, a late Miocene flora from northern Nebraska*, University of California Press, Berkeley and Los Angeles, 1962.

Mackenzie, J.M., 'Fluctuations in the numbers of British Tetraonids', *J. Animal Ecol.*, vol. 21 (1), 1952, 128–153.

Malchevskii, A.S. and Y.B. Pukinskii, *The birds of Leningrad Province and adjacent territories*, Leningrad, vol. 1, 1983, (in Russian).

Marchlewski, J.H., 'Gluszec. Studia Soc. Scien. Torunensis.', *Ser. E (Zoologia)*, vol. 4(3), 1962, 1–39.

Marchström, V., 'Studies on the physiological and ecological background to the reproduction of Capercaillie (*Tetrao urogallus* Linn.)', *Viltrevy*, vol. 2, 1960, 1–85.

Marchström, V. and E. H glund, 'Factors affecting reproduction of Willow Grouse (*Lagopus lagopus*) in two highland areas of Sweden', *Viltrevy*, vol. 11 (7), 1980, 285–314.

Marco, A.S., 'New Iberian Galliforms and reappraisal of some Pliocene and Pleistocene Eurasian taxa', *Journ. Vertebrate Paleontology*, vol. 29 (4), 2009, 1148-1161.

Marshall, W., 'Cover preferences, seasonal movements and food habits of Richardson's Grouse and Ruffed Grouse in southern Idaho', *Wilson Bull.*, vol. 58 (1), 1946, 42–52.

Marshall, W.H., 'Ruffed Grouse behavior', *Bioscience*, vol. 15, 1965, 92–94.

Marti, C. and N. Picozzi, 'Capercaillie, *Tetrao urogallus*', in *The EBCC Atlas of European Breeding Birds* (W. Hagemejer and M.J. Blair, eds), London, 1997.

Martin, K., S.J. Hannon and S. Lord, 'Female-female aggression in White-tailed Ptarmigan and Willow Ptarmigan during the pre-incubation period', *Wilson Bull.*, vol. 102, 1990, 532–536.

Matvejev, S.D., 'Tetrebska divjiac (fam. Tetraonidae) u istochoj Jugoslaviji', *Ann. Inst. Recherches Sci. concernant la Chasse de l'ânne 1956*, 1957, vol. 3, 1957, 5–95.

May, T.A. and C.E. Braun, 'Seasonal foods of adult White-tailed Ptarmigan in Colorado', *J. Wildlife Management*, vol. 36 (4), 1972, 1180–1186.

Mayr, G., 'A new basal galliform bird from the middle Eocene of Messel', *Senck. Leth.*, vol. 80, 2000, 45–57.

McColm, M., 'Ruffed Grouse', *Nevada Outdoors*, vol. 4 (3), 1970, 27.

McCourt, K.H., D.A. Boag and D.M. Keppie, 'Female Spruce Grouse activities during laying and incubation', *Auk*, vol. 90 (3), 1973, 619–623.

McKee, G., M.R. Ryan and L.M. Meclin, 'Predicting Greater Prairie-Chicken nest success from vegetation and landscape characteristics', *J. Wildlife Management*, vol. 62, 1998, 314–321.

Mejenny, A.A., 'The influence of Black-billed Capercaillie on the form of the crown of larches', *Botanic J.*, vol. 42 (1), 1957, 84–85 (in Russian).

Mejnev, A.P., 'Capercaillies, Hazel Grouse, Black Grouse', *Hunting animals of Russia, Issue 6: The condition of hunting animal resources in the Russian Federation in the years 2000–2003*, 2004, 168–189 (in Russian).

Menzbier, M.A., *The Birds of Russia*, vol. 1, 1895 (in Russian).

Menzbier, M.A., *The hunting birds of European Russia and the Caucasus*, Moscow, vol. 2, 1902 (in Russian).

Mercer, E. and R.A. MacGrath, 'A study of a high Ptarmigan population on Brunette Island, Newfoundland, in 1962', Dept. of Mines, Agriculture and Resources., St. John's, 1963.

Middendorpff, A. Th., *Sibirische Reise. Th. 2:*

Säugethiere, Vögel und Amphibien, 1851.

Miheev, A.V., *The Willow Ptarmigan*, Moscow, 1948 (in Russian).

Miller, A.H., 'An avifauna from the lower Miocene of South Dakota', *Univ. Calif. Publ. Bull. Dept. Geol. Sci.*, vol. 27 (2), 1944, 85–100.

Milne-Edwards, A., 'Sur les oiseaux fossiles des depots eocenes de phosphate de chaux du Sud de la France', in P.L. Sclater (ed.), *Comptes Rendus du Second Congres Ornithologique International*, 1892, 60–80.

Mishin, I.P., 'On the nutrition of Spruce Grouse on Sakhalin Island', *Ornithologia*, vol. 2, 1959, 197 (in Russian).

Mishin, I.O., 'On the biology of tetraonid birds on Sakhalin Island', *Ornithologia*, vol. 3, 1960, 251–258 (in Russian).

Mizkevitch, I., 'Black Grouse (*Tetrao tetrix*) in the Kuban Region', *Nature and Hunting*, February 1897, 1–7 (in Russian).

Mlikowsky, J., 'Early Pleistocene birds from Stranska skala: 1 Musil'stalus cone', in R. Musil (ed.), *Stránská Skála Hill: excavation of open-air sediments 1964–1972, Anthropos (Brno)*, vol. 26, 1995, 111–126.

Mlikowsky, J., *Cenozoic Birds of the World. Part 1: Europe*, Prague, 2002.

Moffit, J., 'The downy young of Dendragapus', *Auk*, vol. 55, no.4, 1938, 589–595.

Molamusov, H.T., *The birds of the central part of the northern Caucasus*, Nalchik, 1967 (in Russian).

Möllers, F., W. Engländer, Z. Klaus and A.V. Andreev, 'Ein Rauhfusshuhn in Dichten Wald – Variabilität im Ausdrucksverhalten des Sichelhuhns' *Falcipennis Falcipennis*', *Journ. Ornithol.*, vol. 136 (4), 1995, 389–399.

Montin, L., *Physiographica Saelskapets Handlinger*, Stockholm, vol. 1, 1781.

Momiyama, T.T., 'A catalogue of the bird-skins made by Mr. Matakiti Tatibana in Southern Sakhalin from May 1926 to January 1927', *Annot. Ornithol. Orient.*, vol. 1, no. 3, 1928, 201–239.

Morosov, V.V., 'Birds of the western macro-slope of the Polar Ural', in *Distribution of birds in the Urals*, Sverdlovsk, 1989, 69–72 (in Russian).

Mortensen, A., S. Unander and M. Kolstad, 'Seasonal changes in body composition and crop content of Spitsbergen Ptarmigan *Lagopus mutus hyperboreus*', *Ornis Skand.*, vol. 14 (14), 1983, 144–148.

Moss, R., 'Effects of captivity on gut lengths in Red Grouse', *J. Wildlife Management*, vol. 36, no. 1, 1972, 99–103.

Moss, R., 'The digestion and intake of winter foods by wild Ptarmigans in Alaska', *Condor*, vol. 75, no. 3, 1973, 293–300.

Moss, R., 'Winter diet, gut lengths and interspecific competition in Alaskan Ptarmigan', *Auk*, vol. 91 (3), 1974, 737–746.

Moss, R., 'Gut size, body weight and digestion of winter foods by Grouse and Ptarmigan', *Condor*, vol. 85, 1983, 185–193.

Moss, R., D. Weir and A. Jones, 'Capercaillie Management in Scotland', *Woodland Grouse Symposium*, Inverness, 1978, 140–155.

Mossop, D., 'A relation between aggressive behaviour and population dynamics in Blue Grouse', in A. Bergerud and M. Gratson (eds), *Adaptive strategies and population ecology of northern Grouse*, University of Minnesota Press, vol. 1–2, 1987.

Mourer-Chauvire, C., 'Les oiseaux du Pleistocene moyen et superieur de France', *Documentes des Laboratoires de Geologie de la faculte des Sciences de Lyon*, vol. 64, 1975, 1–624.

Mourer-Chauvire, C., 'Les Galliformes (Aves) de Phosphorites du Quercy (France)', in K.E. Campbell (ed.), *Papers in avian paleontology honoring Pierce Brodkorb, Natural History Museum* of Los Angeles County Science Series, vol. 36, 1992, 37–95.

Mourer-Chauvire, C., 'Dynamics of the avifauna during the Paleogene and the early Neogene of France: setting of the recent fauna', *Acta Zoologica Cracoviensia*, vol. 38, 1995, 325–342.

Moynahan, B.J., M.S. Lindberg, J.J. Rotella and L.W. Thomas, 'Factors affecting nest survival of Greater Sage-Grouse in north-central Montana', *J. Wildlife Management*, vol. 71 (6), 2007, 1773–1783.

Müller, F.G., 'Territorialverhalten und siedlungsstruktur einer Mitteleurpaishen Population des Aerhuhns *Tetrao urogallus major* C.L. Brehm', thesis dissertation, Marhurg, 1974.

Murie, O.J., 'Two new subspecies of birds from Alaska', *Condor*, vol. 40, no. 3, 1944, 121–123.

Mussehl, T.W., 'Blue Grouse production, movements and populations in the Bridger Mountains, Montana', *J. Wildlife Management*, vol. 24 (1), 1960, 60–68.

Mussehl, T.W., 'Blue Grouse brood cover selection and land-use implications', *J. Wildlife Management*, vol. 27 (4), 1963, 547–555.

Mussel, T.W. and P. Schladweiler, 'Forest Grouse and experimental Spruce budworm insecticide studies', *Mont Fish and Game Tech. Bull.*, no. 4, 1969.

Murashov, I.P., 'Data on the structure of Hazel Grouse flocks in autumn', Abstracts of the XI Russian (International) Ornith. Conf., Kazan, 2001, 454 (in Russian).

Myrberget, S., 'Reproductive success of young and old Willow Ptarmigan *Lagopus lagopus*', *Riistatietell*, vol. 30, 1970, 169–172.

Myrberget, S., 'Fluctuations in a north Norwegian population of Willow Grouse', in *Proc. XV Intern Ornith. Ongr.*, Hague, 1972, 107–120.

Myrberget, S., K.E. Erikstag and T.K. Spids , 'Variations from year to year in growth rates of Willow Grouse chicks', *Astarte*, vol. 10, 1977, 9–14.

Nasarov, P.S., 'Zoological Research on the steppes of Kirguis', *Bull. Soc. Mat. Moscow*, vol. 62, pt. 2, 1887, 338–382 (in Russian).

Nasarov, A.A. and O.N. Shubnikova, 'Migration of Willow Grouse in Yamalo-Nenezk's National Region', *Bull. Mosc. Soc. Testers of Nature*, vol. 76 (6), 1971, 22–30.

Nasarov, A.A. and O.N. Schubnikova, 'The Northern Taiga', in S.V. Kirikov (ed.), *The Tetraonid Birds*, Moscow, 1975, 31–40 (in Russian).

Naumov, S.P., 'Mammals and birds of the Gydan Peninsula (north-western Siberia)', *Proc. Polar Comiss. Acad. Sci. USSR*, vol. 4, 1931, 1–106 (in Russian).

Nechaev, V.A., 'Amur-land and Primorie', in S.V. Kirikov (ed.), *The Tetraonid Birds*, Moscow, 1975, 241–250 (in Russian).

Nechaev, V.A., *The Birds of Sakhalin Island*, Ac. Sci., USSR, Vladivostok, 1991 (in Russian).

Nechaev, V., 'The Siberian Spruce Grouse *Falcipennis falcipennis* (Hartlaub, 1855)', in D.S. Pavlov, L.N. Mazin, V.V. Rozhnov and V.E. Flint (eds), *Krasnaya kniga Rossiyskoy Federatsii (Zhivotnye)* [*Red Data Book of the Russian Federation (Animals)*], Aginskoye: AST and Balashikha: Astrel, 2001, 465–466 (in Russian).

Neifeldt, I.A., 'On the ornithofauna of southern Karelia', *Proc. Zool. Inst. Ac. Sci.*, USSR, vol. 25, 1958, 183–254 (in Russian).

Nelson, A.L. and A.C. Martin, 'Gamebird weights', *J. Wildlife Management*, vol. 17 (1), 1953, 36–42.

Nelson, O.C., 'A field study of the Sage-Grouse in south-eastern Oregon with special reference to reproduction and survival', M.S. Thesis 1955, Oregon State University, Corvallis, Oregon.

Nemtzev, V.V., 'The rearing of Capercaillie in Darwin

State Reserve', International Capercaillie Meeting, Moscow, 1981, 35–37 (in Russian).

Nemtzev, V.V., V.V. Krinitzky and E.K. Semenova, 'The rearing of tetraonid birds in open-air cages', *Proc. Darwin State Reserve*, issue 11, 1973, 187–248 (in Russian).

Nesterov, P.V., 'Notes on the avifauna of south-eastern Transcaucasia and the north-eastern part of the Asia Minor', *Ann. Zool. Museum Imperator's Acad. Sci.*, vol. 16 (3), 1911, 311–408 (in Russian).

Nielsen, O.K. and G. Pétursson, 'Population fluctuations of Gyrfalcons and Rock Ptarmigan: analysis of export figures from Iceland', *Wildlife Biology*, vol. 1, 1995, 65–71.

Nordhagen, R., 'Rupeaar og Bareaar', *Berg. Mus. Aarbok Naturv, Rekke*, vol. 2, 1928, 1–52.

Nordmann, A., *Observations sur la Faune Pontique. Vouage dans la Russie meridionale et la Crime, execute en 1834, sous la direction de M. Demidoff*, 1840, Paris.

Nordmann, A., 'Eine beobachtungen ueber den Auerhahn am Amur', *Bull. Soc. Imp Nat., Moscow*, vol. 34 (3), 1861, 261–266.

Noska, M. and V.R. von Tschusi zu Scmidthoffen, 'Das Kaucasiche Birkhuhn, *Tetrao mlokosiewiczi*' *Ornithol. Jahrber.*, vol. 6, 1895, 2 (100–125); 3 (129–150); 4 (189–162); 5 (209–243).

Novikov, B.G., 'Sexual hormone and signs of sex in *Perdix perdix*', *Proc. Acad. Sci., USSR, ser. biol.*, vol. 3, 1939, 422–444 (in Russian).

Novikov, G.A., 'The ecology of birds in Hibin's Mountains', *Proc. Zool. Inst. Acad. Sci., USSR*, vol. 9 (4), 1952, 1155–1198 (in Russian).

Ogilvie-Grant, W.R., *Catalogue of the birds in the British Museum (Nat. Hist.)*, London, vol. 22, 1893.

Oliger, N.M., 'Data on the nutrition of tetraonid birds in the forest zone of the European part of the RSFSR', *Proc. Darwin State Reserve*, Issue 9,

1973, 151–157 (in Russian).

Olson, S.L., 'The Fossil Record of Birds', in D.S. Farner, J.R. King and K.C. Parkes (eds), *Avian Biology*, vol. 8, New York, 1985, 79–238.

Ord, G., 'North American zoology', in W.A. Guthrie *New Geographical, Historical and Commercial Grammar*, 2 edition, Philadelphia, vol. 2, 1815, 290–361.

Osgood, W.H., 'New subspecies of North American birds', *Auk*, vol. 18, no. 2, 1901, 179–187.

Osmolovskaia, V.I., 'Artificial introduction of game birds as the way of maintaining and increasing numbers', *Bull. Moscow Soc., Testers of Nature*, vol. 74 (1), 1969, 15–24 (in Russian).

Ostrovsky, A.I., 'Factors influencing Capercaillie number in the Ukrainian Carpathians', Materials of the All-Union Ornithol. Conf., Moscow, 1974, 288–289 (in Russian).

Page, R. and A. Bergerud, 'A genetic explanation for ten-year cycles of Grouse', in A. Bergerud and M. Gratson (eds), *Adaptive strategies and population ecology of Northern Grouse*, vol. 1–2, University of Minnesota Press, 1987, 423–438.

Parker, H., 'Duration of fertility in Willow Ptarmigan hens after separation from the cock', *Ornis Skand.*, vol. 12 (3), 1981, 186–187.

Patterson, R.L., *The Sage-Grouse in Wyoming*, Denver, 1952.

Pauli, H., 'Zur Winteröcologie des Birkhuhns Tetrao tetrix in den Schweizer Alpen', *Ornith. Beobachter*, vol. 71 (4), 1974, 247–278.

Pavliusshik, T.E. and N.V. Maliutina, 'Artificial rearing of Capercaillie in Berezina State Reserve', International Capercaillie meeting, Moscow, 1981, 38–40 (in Russian).

Pavlov, B.A., 'Taymyr Peninsula' in S.V. Kirikov (ed.), *The Tetraonid Birds*, Moscow, 1975, 17–26 (in Russian).

Pavlov, E.I., *Birds and Mammals of Chita Province*,

Chita, 1948, (in Russian).

Pemberton, J.R., 'The nesting of Howard's Grouse', *Condor*, vol. 30, 1928, 347–348.

Pendergast, B.A., 'Nutrition of Spruce Grouse of the Swan Hills', Alberta. M.S. Thesis, 1969, University of Alberta.

Pendergast, B.A. and D.A. Boag, 'Seasonal changes in diet of Spruce Grouse in Central Alberta', *J. Wildlife Management*, vol. 34 (3), 1970, 605–611.

Pendergast, B.A. and D.A. Boag, 'Maintenance and breeding of Spruce Grouse in captivity', *J. Wildlife Management*, vol. 35 (1), 1971a, 177–179.

Pendergast, B.A. and D.A. Boag, 'Nutritional aspects of the diet of Spruce Grouse in Central Alberta', *Condor,* vol. 73 (6), 1971b, 437–443.

Pendergast, B.A. and D.A. Boag, 'Seasonal changes in the internal anatomy of Spruce Grouse in Alberta', *Auk*, vol. 90, no. 2, 1973, 307–317.

Pereira, S.L. and A.J. Baker, 'A molecular timescale for galliform birds accounting for uncertainty in time estimates and heterogeny of rates of DNA substitutions across lineages and sites', *Molecular Phylogenetics and Evolution*, vol. 38, 2006, 499–509.

Perfiliev, V.I., 'Yakutia', in S.V. Kirikov (ed.), *The Tetraonid Birds*, Moscow, 1975, 113–135 (in Russian).

Peters J.L., *Check-list of birds of the world*, vol. 2, 1934.

Peters, S.S., 'Food habits of the Newfoundland Willow Ptarmigan', *J. Wildlife Management*, vol. 22 (4), 1958, 381–394.

Peterson, J.G., 'The food habits and summer distribution of juvenile Sage-Grouse in Central Montana', *J. Wildlife Management*, vol. 34 (1), 1970, 147–155.

Phillips, R.L., 'Fall and winter food habits of Ruffed Grouse in Northern Utah', *J. Wildlife Management*, vol. 31 (4), 1967, 827–829.

Pirkola, M.K. and J. Koivisto, 'The main stages of the display of Capercaillie and their phenology', in *VIII Intern. Congr., Game Biology*, Helsinki, 1970, 177–184.

Pleske, Th., 'Birds of the Eurasian Tundra', *Memories Boston Soc. Nat. Hist.,* vol. 6 (3), 1928.

Pollo, C.J., L. Robles, J. Seijas, A. Garcia-Mirand and R. Otero, 'Cantabrian Capercaillie *Tetrao urogallus cantabricus* population size and range trend. Will the Capercaillie survive in the Cantabrian Mountains?', *Grouse News*, vol. 26, 2003, 3–5.

Poole, E.L., 'Weights and wing areas of North American birds', *Auk*, vol. 55 (3), 1938, 511–517.

Popham, G.P. and R.J. Gutiérrez, 'Greater Sage-Grouse *Centrocercus urophasianus* nesting success and habitat use in north-eastern California', *Wildlife Biology*, vol. 9, 2003, 327–334.

Porath, W.R. and P.A. Vohns Jr, 'Population ecology of Ruffed Grouse in north-east Iowa', *J. Wildlife Management*, vol. 36, no. 3, 1972, 793–802.

Portenko, L.A., *Birds of the sub-polar Northern Urals*, Moscow, Leningrad, 1937 (in Russian).

Portenko, L.A., *Birds of the Chukotka Peninsula and Wrangel Island*, Leningrad, vol. 1, 1972 (in Russian).

Pospelova, G.A., A. Kapichka, V.P. Liubin and S.V. Sharonova, 'The use of scalar magnetic parameters of the bedrocks for the reconstruction of paleoclimate at the time of formation of the deposits in Kudaro-I and Kudaro-III caves (South Osetia, Georgia)', *Physics of the Earth*, vol. 10, 2001, 76–86 (in Russian).

Potapov, E. 'Winter Ecology of Hazel Grouse', MSc thesis, 1982, University of Lenigrad, Dept. of Vertebrate Zoology (in Russian).

Potapov, E. and R.G. Sale, *The Gyrfalcon*, T&AD Poyser London/Yale University Press, 2005.

Potapov, E. and R.G. Sale, *The Snowy Owl*, T&AD Poyser, London, 2013.

Potapov, L.P., *The hunting trade of Altai people*, Russian Ac. Sci., St Petersburg, 2001 (in Russian).

Potapov, R.L., 'The birds of Pamir', *Proc. Zool. Inst. Ac. Sci., USSR*, vol. 39, 1996, 1–119 (in Russian).

Potapov, R.L., 'The courtship displays of the Asian Spruce Grouse (*Falcipennis falcipennis*)', *Zool. J.*, vol. 48 (6), 1969, 864–870 (in Russian, with English resumé).

Potapov, R.L., 'Comparative review of Spruce Grouse (genera *Falcipennis* and *Canachites*, Tetraonidae) of Asia and North America', *Proc. Zool. Inst. Ac. Sci.*, USSR, vol. 47, 1970a, 205–235 (in Russian).

Potapov, R.L., *The role of Beringian land in the history of family Tetraonidae: The Arctic Ocean and its seashores in the Cenozoic*, Leningrad, 1970b, 537–541 (in Russian).

Potapov, R.L., 'Some details of the evolution and distribution of Capercaillie (*Tetrao urogallus*) during anthropogenic times', *Zool. J.*, vol. 50 (6), 1971, 875–885 (in Russian, with English resumé).

Potapov, R.L., 'Adaptations of the family Tetraonidae to the winter season', *Proc. Zool. Inst. Ac. Sci., USSR*, vol. 55, 1974, 207–251 (in Russian).

Potapov, R.L., 'Specificity of the nuptial behavior of Capercaillie, *Tetrao urogallus obsoletus* Snigir., in northern Karelia', *Proc. of Kandalaksha State Reserve, Murmansk*, vol. 9, 1975, 159–170 (in Russian).

Potapov, R.L., 'New data for the Caucasian Black Grouse *Lyrurus mlokosiewiczi* (Taczanowski)', *Proc. Zool. Inst. Acad. Sci., USSR*, vol. 76, 1978, 24–35 (in Russian).

Potapov, R.L., 'Bioenergetics of the Tetraonidae during the winter', *Proc. Zool. Inst. Ac. Sci.,*

USSR, vol. 113, 1982, 57–67 (in Russian).

Potapov, R.L., 'Parallelism in structure and colouration in different representatives of the Order Galliformes', *Proc. Zool. Inst. Ac. Sci., USSR*, vol. 116, 1983, 34–45 (in Russian).

Potapov, R.L., 'Order Galliformes, family Tetraonidae', *Fauna of the USSR*, new series, no. 133, 1985 (in Russian).

Potapov, R.L., 'On the avifauna of the Mongolian Altai and adjacent territories', *Proc. Zool. Inst. Acad. Sci., USSR*, vol. 156, 1986a, 57–73 (in Russian).

Potapov, R.L., 'New data on the Caucasian Black Grouse, *Lyrurus mlokosiewiczi* (Taczanowski)', *Ornith. Studies in USSR*, vol. I, 1986b, 101–120 (in English; translation of Potapov, 1978).

Potapov, R.L., 'The feeding of Rock Ptarmigan on nuts of Creep Pine', *Proc. Zool. Inst. Acad. Sci., USSR*, vol. 182, 1988, 137–139 (in Russian).

Potapov, R.L. 'Systematic position and taxonomic level of Grouse in the order Galliformes', *Bull. Brit. Ornithol. Club, Centenary*, vol. 112a, 1992, 251–259.

Potapov, R.L., 'Adaptation of birds to the life in the high mountains of Eurasia', Abstract 23 Intern. Ornith. Congress., Beijing, 2002, 7–8.

Potapov, R.L., 'Adaptation of birds to life in the high mountains of Eurasia', *Acta Zoologica Sinica.*, vol. 50 (6), 2004a, 970–977.

Potapov, R.L., 'Adaptation of the Caucasian Black Grouse *Lyrurus mlokosiewiczi* to life in high mountains', *Russ. J. Ornith.*, vol. 13, Express-issue no. 263, 2004b, 507–525 (in English).

Potapov, R.L., 'Genus Lyrurus Swainson, 1831 (Black Grouse): taxonomic position, composition, distribution, phylogenetic relationship and origin', *Russ. Journ. Ornith.*, vol. 14, express-issue no. 296, 2005, 723–741 (in English).

Potapov, R.L., 'On the time and routes of penetration

of of the Caucasian Black Grouse's ancestor into the Caucasus', *Russ. J. Ornith.*, vol. 17, express-issue no. 473, 2008a, 1295–1307.

Potapov, R.L., 'A lek of the Capercaillie *Tetrao urogallus* near suburban settlement Komarovo on the Karelian Isthmus', *Russ. Journ. Ornith.*, vol.17, express-issue no. 440, 2008b, 1400–1406 (in Russian, with English resumé).

Potapov, R.L. and A.V. Andreev, 'On the bioenergetics of Black Grouse *Lyrurus tetrix* L. during winter season', *Reports Ac. Sci., USSR*, biol. ser., vol. 210, no. 1973, 499–500 (in Russian).

Potapov, R.L. and E.A. Pavlova, 'The specificity of the nuptial display of the Caucasian Black Grouse', *Ornithologia*, vol. 13, 1977, 117–126 (in Russian).

Potapov, R.L. and E.A. Pavlova, 'The Hazel Grouse *Bonasa bonasia* in Leningrad Province', *Russian Journ. Ornith.*, vol. 18, express-issue no. 473, 2009, 491–500 (in Russian, with English resumé).

Potapov, R.L., 'Capercaillie lek within the city limit of St. Petersburg, Russia', *Grouse News*, Issue 42, 2011, 29–31.

Potapova, O.R., 'The Pleistocene Ptarmigans, Lagopus, from the northern Urals', *Proc. Zool. Inst. Acad. Sci., USSR*, vol. 147, 1986, 46–58 (in Russian, with English summary).

Przewalsky, N.M., *Mongolia and the land of the Tanguts*, St Petersburg, vol. 2, 1876 (in Russian).

Pukinsky, Iu. B. and S.S. Roo, 'On the behavior of Capercaillie in the lek period', *Bulletin Leningrad State Univ., Ser. Biology*, vol. 21, 1966, 22–28 (in Russian).

Pukinsky, Iu. B. and A.S. Nikanorov, 'Spruce Grouse', *Hunting and hunting industry*, vol. 7, 1974, 42–43 (in Russian).

Pulliainen, E., 'Composition and selection of food in winter by Capercaillie in north-east Finnish Lapland', *Suomen Riista*, vol. 22, 1970a, 67–73.

Pulliainen, E., 'Winter nutrition of the Rock Ptarmigan *Lagopus mutus* (Mont.) in north-eastern Finland', *Ann. Zool. Fenn.*, vol. 7 (3), 1970b, 295–302.

Pulliainen, E., 'Colour variation and sex identification in the Rock Ptarmigan (*Lagopus mutus*) in Finland', *Suomal. Tiedeakat. Toim. Biol.* (Ser. A), vol. 160, 1970c, 1–6.

Pulliainen, E., 'Behavior of a nesting Capercaillie (*Tetrao urogallus*) in north-eastern Lapland', *Ann. Zool. Fenn.*, vol. 8, 1971, 456–462.

Pulliainen, E., 'Structure of two Willow Grouse populations in Finnish Lapland in the winters of 1972–1974', *Ann. Zool. Fenn.*, vol. 12 (4), 1975, 263–267.

Pulliainen, E., 'Behaviour of a Willow Grouse *Lagopus lagopus lagopus* at the nest', *Ornis Fennica*, vol. 55 (3), 1978, 141–148.

Pulliainen, E., 'Food selection in the tetraonid hybrids *Lyrurus tetrix* x *Tetrao urogallus*, *Lyrurus tetrix* x *Lagopus lagopus*, *Tetrao urogallus* x *Lagopus lagopus*', *Ornis Fennica*, vol. 54 (4), 1982, 170–174.

Pulliainen, E. and P. Rajala, 'Observations on the nesting of birds in snow', *Ornis Fennica*, vol. 50 (2), 1973, 89–91.

Punnonen, A., 'Beitrage zur Kenntnis des Lebensreise des haselhuhn *Tetrastes bonasia*', *Pap. Game Research*, vol. 12, 1954, 1–90.

Quevedo, M., R. Rodriguez-Mu os, M. Ba uelos and A. Fernandes-Gil, 'A captive Breeding programme for Cantabrian Capercaillie: does it make any sense?' *Grouse News*, vol. 30, 2003, 10–13.

Quinn, N.W.S. and D.M. Keppie, 'Factors influencing growth of juvenile Spruce Grouse', *Canadian Journ. Zool.*, vol. 59 (9), 1981, 1790–1795.

Radde, G.I., *Ornithological fauna of the Caucasus*, Tiflis, 1884 (in Russian).

Radeff, T., 'Uber die Rohfaserverdauung beim

Huhn und die hierbei dem Blinddarm zukommende Bedeutung', *Biochem. Z.,* vol. 193, 1928, 192–196.

Rajala, P., 'Finnish population of the tetraonids in 1966', *Suomen Riista*, vol. 19, 1966c, 156–161.

Randi, E., G. Fusco, R. Lorenzini and T.M. Crowe, 'Phylogenetic Relationships and Rates of Allozyme Evolution within the Phasianidae', *Biochemical Systematics and Ecology*, vol. 19, no. 3, 1991, 213–221.

Ranta, E., J. Lindström, H. Linden and P. Helle, 'How reliable are harvesting data for analyses of spatio-temporal population dynamics?', *Oikos*, vol. 117, no. 10, 2008, 1461–1468.

Ravinski, L., *Description of the economy of Astrakhan and Kazan Provinces in the base of its civilian and natural conditions*, St Petersburg, 1807.

Redkin, Ya. A., 'New subspecies of Rock Ptarmigan *Lagopus mutus* (Montin, 1776) (Tetraonidae, Galliformes) from Karaginsky Island', *Ornithologia*, vol. 32, 2005, 6–12 (in Russian).

Reichenbach, L., 'Die Vollständigste Naturgeschichte des In- und Auslandes'. *Dynopsis Avium,* no. 3, Gallinacea, Leipzig, 1848, 281–389.

Reichenbach, L., *Avium systema naturae*, Dresden and Leipzig, 1853.

Reichenow, A., *Die Vögel; Handbuch der Systematischen Ornithologie*, Stuttgart. Bd.1, 1913.

Reztzov, S.A., 'The birds of the Perm Province (northern part: Verchotursky and Cherdynski districts)', in *The Fauna and Flora of the Russian Empire*, Zool. Division., Moscow, issue 6, 1904, 43–225 (in Russian).

Rhim, S-J. and W-S. Lee, 'Winter sociality of Hazel Grouse *Bonasa bonasia* in relation to habitat in a temperate forest of South Korea', *Wildlife Biology*, vol. 9 (4), 2003, 365–370.

Remington, T.E. and R.W. Hoffman, 'Food habits and preferences of Blue Grouse during winter',

J. Wildlife Management, vol. 60 (4), 1996, 808–817.

Ridgway, R., 'The birds of Colorado', *Bull. Essex Inst.*, vol. 5, 1873, 174–195.

Ridgway, R., 'Description of some new North American birds', *Proc. Biol. Soc., Washington*, vol. 2, 1984, 89–95.

Ridgway, R., 'Some amended names of North American Birds', *Proc. US Nat. Museum*, vol. 8, 1885.

Ridgway, R. and H. Friedmann, *The birds of North and Middle America*, Smithsonian Institute, Part X (Galliformes), 1946.

Riley, J.H., 'Description of three new birds from China and Japan', *Proc. Soc. Biol.*, vol. 28, 1915, 161–164.

Riley, J. H., 'Description of a new Hazel Grouse from Manchuria', *Proc. Soc. Biol.*, vol. 29, 1916, 17–18.

Riley, J.H., 'A new Hazel Grouse from the Province of Szechuan, China', *Auk*, vol. 42, no. 3, 1925, 422–423.

Rippin, A.B. and D.A. Boag, 'Recruitment to populations of male Sharp-tailed Grouse', *J. Wildlife Management*, vol. 38 (4), 1971, 616–621.

Ritcey, R., 'Status of Sharp-tailed Grouse in British Columbia', *Wildlife Working Report No. WR–70*, 1995.

Robb, L.A. and M.A. Schroeder, 'Greater Prairie-Chicken (*Tympanuchus cupido*): a technical conservation assessment', *Washington Dept. Fish and Wildlife*, 2005.

Robel, R.J., 'Booming territory size and mating success of the Greater Prairie-Chicken (*Tympanuchus cupido pinnatus*), *Anim. Behav.*, vol. 14, 1966, 328–331.

Robel, R. J., 'Nesting activities and brood movements of Black Grouse in Scotland', *Ibis*, vol. 111, 1969, 395–399.

Robel, R.J., J.N. Briggs, J.J. Gebula, N.J. Silvy, C.E.

Viers and P.G. Watt, 'Greater Prairie-Chicken ranges, movements and habitat usage in Kansas', *J. Wildlife Management*, vol. 34 (2), 1970, 286–306.

Robinson, W.L. and D.E. Maxwell, 'Ecological study of Spruce Grouse on the Yellow Dog Plains', Jack-Pine Warbler, vol. 46, 1968, 75–83.

Rodionov, M.A., 'On the biology of Hazel Grouse (*Tetrastes bonasia* L.) in Leningrad Province', *Transactions of Leningrad State Pedagogical Inst.*, vol. 230, issue 9, 1963a, 139–165 (in Russian).

Rodionov, M.A., 'The molt and age peculiarities of Black Grouse (*Lyrurus tetrix* L.)', *Transactions Leningrad State Pedagogical Inst.*, vol. 230, 1963b, 167–178.

Rodionov, M.A., 'On the biology and ecology of the Black Grouse in Leningrad Province', in Proc. VI Pribaltic Ornith. Conf., Vilnius, 1966, 135-137.

Rodionov, M.A., 'On the biology of the Willow Ptarmigan in Leningrad Province', *Ann. Nature Testers of Estonia*, 1969, 37–78.

Rogers, G.E., 'Sage-Grouse investigations in Colorado', *Colorado Dept. Game, Fish and Parks, Tech. Publ.*, no. 16, 1964.

Romanov, A.A., 'Willow Grouse in Lena-Hatanga region', *Proc. Arctic Inst.*, Moscow, Leningrad, vol. 2, 1934, 45–54 (in Russian).

Romanov, A.A., 'Species, numbers and habitat disposition of birds in the Severnaya River Basin', in A.A. Romanov (ed.), *Bird and animal communities of the Putoran Plateau: studies and conservation*, 2006, 9–70 (in Russian).

Romanov, A.N., 'The North-East Russian Plain', in S.V. Kirikov (ed.), *The Tetraonid Birds*, Moscow, 1975, 45–58 (in Russian).

Romanov, A.N., *The Western Capercaillie*, Leningrad, 1979 (in Russian).

Rosenquist, E.L., 'Winter aspects of Prairie-Chicken ecology in north-west Minnesota', M.S. thesis.

St. Cloud State University, Minnesota, 1996.

Rubiales, J.M., F.J. Ezquerra, F. Gomez-Manzaneque, S.G. Alvarez, I.G. Amorena and C. Moria, 'The long-term evolution of Cantabrian mountain landscapes and its possible role in the Capercaillie drama', *Grouse News*, vol. 38, 2009, 9–11.

Rusakov, O.S., 'The structure and dynamics of the Black Grouse population', in Conference on Game Birds, Moscow, 1976, 96–100 (in Russian).

Rusch, D.H., S. De Stefano, M.C. Reynolds and D. Lauten, 'Ruffed Grouse (*Bonasa umbellus*)', in *The Birds of North America*, no. 515, 2000 (A. Poole and F. Gill, eds.), The Birds of North America, Philadelphia.

Rykovski, A.S., 'On the reasons for the decrease of Black Grouse in populated regions', in *II Ornith. Conference., Moscow*, vol. 3, 1959, 91–93 (in Russian).

Sabaneev, L.P., *The vertebrate animals of the Central Ural and their distribution in Perm and Orenburg Provinces*, Moscow, 1874 (in Russian).

Sabaneev, L.P., *Black Grouse: the hunting monography*, Moscow, 1876.

Sakurai, N., 'Fluctuations of body weight and clutch size in *Lagopus mutus japonicus* Clark', in *Japanese Rock Ptarmigan*, Tokyo, 1972, 141–159 (in Japanese, with English resumé).

Sakurai, N. and S. Tsuruta, 'Population studies of the Japanese Ptarmigan (*Lagopus mutus japonicus* Clark) in the Murode area, Tateyama, Japan Alps, from 1967 to 1969', in *Japanese Rock Ptarmigan*, Tokyo, 1972, 184–215 (in Japanese, English resumé).

Sale, R., *A Complete Guide to Arctic Wildlife*, Christopher Helm, London, 2006.

Say, T., in E. James *Account of an expedition from Pittsburg to the Rocky Mountains*, Philadelphia, vol. 2, 1823, 14.

Salomonsen, F., 'Notes on a new race of the Willow Grouse, *Lagopus lagopus variegatus*, subsp. *nova*', *Bull. British Ornith. Club*, vol. 56, no. 394, 1936, 99–100.

Salomonsen, F., 'Molts and plumage sequence in the Rock Ptarmigan *Lagopus mutus* (Montin)', *Videnskabelige Meddelelser fra dansk Naturhistoriks forening*, vol. 103, 1939, 1–491.

Salomonsen, F., *Grønlands Fugle*, part 2, 1950, 159–348, København.

Satunin, K.A., 'On cognition of birds in the Caucasus Region', *Transactions of Caucasian Dept. of Russian Geographical Society*, vol. 26 (3), 1907, 1–144 (in Russian).

Schaaning, H.T., 'Bjerkreim-orren *Lyrurus tetrix bierkreimensis subsp nova*', *Stavanger Mus. Arshhefte*, vol. 31 (2), 1921, 1–27.

Schäfer, E., 'Ornithologische Ergebnisse zweier Forschunsreisen nach Tibet', *J. Ornith.*, jg. 47, no. 2, 1938, 1–349.

Scherbacov, I.D., 'Specificity of the courtship displays of Capercaillie in Mordova State Reserve', *Proc. Mordova State Reserve, Saransk*, vol. 4, 1967, 8–52 (in Russian).

Scherzinger, W., 'Courtship postures of the Hazel Grouse: studies in captivity', Woodland Grouse symp., Inverness, 1978, 131–133.

Schmidt, R.K., 'Behaviour of White-tailed Ptarmigan during the breeding season', in A. Bergerud and M. Gratson (eds), *Adaptive strategies and population ecology of northern Grouse*, University of Minnesota, vol. 1–2, 1987.

Schnigrid, R.S., P.P. Mollet and K. Bollmann, 'Capercaillie conservation in Switzerland', *Grouse News*, vol. 25, 2003, 12–13.

Schroeder, M.A., 'Behavioral differences of female Spruce Grouse undertaking short and long migrations', *Condor*, vol. 87, 1985, 281–286.

Schroeder, M.A. and L.A. Robb, 'Greater Prairie-Chicken (*Tympanuchus cupido*)', in *The Birds of North America*, no. 36, (A. Poole, P. Stettenheim, F. Gill (eds.), The Academy of Natural Sciences, Philadelphia and The American Ornithologists' Union, Washington, D.C., 1993.

Schroeder, M.A., J.R. Young and C.E. Braun, 'Sage-Grouse (*Centrocercus urophasianus*)', in *The Birds of North America*, no. 425, (A. Poole, P. Stettenheim and F. Gill (eds), The Academy of Natural Sciences, Philadelphia and The American Ornithologists' Union, Washington, D.C., 1999.

Schroeder, M.A., C.L. Aldridge, A.D. Apa, J.R. Bohne, C.E. Braun, S.D. Bunnell, J.W. Connelly, P.A. Deibert, S.C. Gardner, M.A. Hilliard, G.D. Kobriger, S.M. McAdam, C.W. McCarthy, J.J. McCarthy, D.L. Mitchell, E.V. Rickerson and S.J. Stiver, 'Distribution of Sage-Grouse in North America', *Condor*, vol. 106, 2004, 363–376.

Schulpin, L.M., *The game-birds and the birds of prey of Primorie (Russian Far East)*, Vladivostok, 1936 (in Russian).

Schumacher, S., 'Die blinddarme waldhuhner mit besonderer Berucksichtigung eigentumlicher secretionserscheinungen in denselben', *Z. fur Anatomie und Entwicklungsgeschichte*, vol. 64, 1922, 76–95.

Scopoli, J.A., *Historico-Naturalis Annus 1: Descriptiones avium Lipsiae*, 1769.

Scott, D.A. and A. Adhami Mirhosseyni, *The Birds of Iran*, Teheran, 1975, 410.

Scott, J.W., 'Mating behavior of the Sage-Grouse', *Auk*, 59, 1942, 472–498.

Sdobnikov, L.P., 'The Siberian Rock Ptarmigan (*Lagopus mutus kellogae* Grin.) at the northern limit of its distribution', *Proc. Arctic Inst.*, vol. 205, 1957, 63–71 (in Russian).

Seebohm, H., 'On Tetrao griseiventris, a recently

discovered species of Hazel Grouse from North-East Russia', *Ibis*, 1884, 430–431.

Seiskari, P., 'On the winter feeding of the Willow Ptarmigan', *Suomen Riista*, vol. 11, 1957, 43–47.

Seiskari, P. and J. Koskimies, 'Ecological evidence of racial divergence in the Capercaillie *Tetrao urogallus* L in Finland', *Pap. Game Research*, vol. 16, 1955, 1–11.

Semenov-Tianshansky, O.I., 'Ecology of the Tetranoid birds', *Proc. of the Lapland State Reserve*, issue 9, 1959, 1–319 (in Russian).

Semenov-Tianshansky, O. I., 'Some trends in ecological research in Tetraonids in Russian Reserves', *Finn. Game Research*, vol. 30, 1970, 142–145.

Servello, F.A. and L.L. Kirkpatrick, 'Sexing Ruffed Grouse in the south-east using feather criteria', *Wildlife Soc. Bull.*, vol. 14 (3), 1986, 280–282.

Shilo, A.A., 'Quality evaluation of different kinds of habitats in the country between the Ob and Yenisey Rivers', in *Population of Tetraonid Birds in the USSR*, Moscow, 1968 (in Russian).

Shilo, A.A., 'Within–species groups of Black Grouse in the country between Ob and Yenisey Rivers', in *Zoological problems of Siberia, Novosibirsk*, 1972, 344–345 (in Russian).

Shinkin, N.A., 'Population of Black Grouse in Kemerovo Province's forest-steppe', in *Matters of Zoology*, Tomsk, 1966, 165–166 (in Russian).

Short, L.L., 'A review of the genera of Grouse', *Amer. Mus. Nov.*, no. 2289, 1967, 1–39.

Shubnikova, O.N. and Iu. V. Morosov, 'Some ornithological observations in central Yakutia', *Bull. Moscow Soc. Nature Testers Biology*, vol. 64 (5), 1959, 142–144 (in Russian).

Shufeldt, R.W., 'Osteology of the North American Tetraonidae', in the *12th Ann. Rep U.S. Geol. and Geog. Surv., Washington*, 1882, 643–718.

Shufeldt, R.W., 'Tertiary fossils of North American birds', *Auk*, vol. 8, 1891, 365–368.

Shufeldt, R.W., 'A study of the fossil avifauna of the Equus beds of the Oregon Desert', *J. Acad. Phil.*, vol. 9, 1892, 389–425.

Shufeldt, R.W., 'Review of the fossil fauna of the desert region of Oregon, with a description of additional material collected there', *Bull. Amer. Mus. Nat. Hist.*, 1913, 32.

Shufeldt, R.W., 'Fossil birds in the Marsh Collection of Yale University', *Conn. Trans. Acad. Arts. Sci.*, vol. 19, 1915, 1–110.

Siivonen, L., 'The problem of the short-term fluctuations in numbers of tetraonids in Europe', *Pap. Game Research*, vol. 19, 1957, 1–44.

Sibley, Ch. G. and J.E. Ahlquist, *Phylogeny and classification of birds: A Study in Molecular Evolution*, Yale University Press, 1990.

Sicharulidse, Z.D., 'On the biology of the Caucasian Black Grouse', *Ornithologia*, vol. 11, 1974, 410–415 (in Russian).

Simon, J.R., 'Mating preference of the Sage-Grouse', *Auk*, vol. 57 (2), 1940, 467–471.

Simpson, G.G., *The major features of evolution*, Columbia University Press, 1973.

Sinitzyn, V.M., *The Paleogeography of Asia*, Leningrad, 1962 (in Russian).

Skinner, M.P., 'Richardson's Grouse in Yellowstone Park', *Wilson Bull.*, vol. 39 (4), 1927, 208–214.

Sluijs, A., S. Schouten, M. Pagani, M. Woltering, H. Brinkhuis, J.S.S. Damsté, G.R. Dickens, M. Huber, G.J. Reichart, R. Stein, J. Matthiessen, L. Lourens, N. Pedentchouk, J. Backman, K. Moran and the Expedition 302 Scientists, 'Subtropical Arctic Ocean temperatures during the Palaeocene/Eocene thermal maximum', *Nature* 441 (7093), 2006, 610-613.

Snigirewsky, S.I., 'The Tetraonidae birds of the USSR', PhD. thesis, Leningrad, 1946 (in Russian).

Snigirewsky, S.L., 'The molt of tetraonid birds

(Family Tetraonidae, order Galliformes)', in *Memoriam of the Academician P.P. Sushkin*, 1950, 215–236 (in Russian).

Snigirewsky, S.L., 'Description of the subspecies *Tetrao urogallus lonnbergi* in Johansen H., Rassen und Populationen des Auerhahuhns (*Tetrao urogallus*)', *Viltrevy*, 1957, 253.

Snow, D.W. and C.M. Perrins (eds), *The Birds of the Western Palearctic* (Concise Edition), vol. 1, Non-Passerines, Oxford University Press, 1998.

Snyder, L.L., *Arctic Birds of Canada*, Toronto, 1957.

Soloviev, D., 'On the displacement of Capercaillie in Pechora Land', *The Hunter*, 4, 1927, 25 (in Russian).

Sserebrowsky, P.V., 'Neue Formen des Moor Schneehuhnes (*Lagopus lagopus* (L.)', *J. Ornith.*, jg.74, no. 3, 1926a, 511–515.

Sserebrowsky, P.V., 'Übersicht der in Russland vorcommenden Formen von *Lagopus mutus* Montin', *J. Ornith.*, vol. 74 (4), 1926b, 691–698.

Sserebrowsky, P.V., 'Züsatze zur Übersicht der paläarctischen Schneehüchner (*Lagopus*)', *J. Ornithol.*, vol. 77 (4), 1929, 521–524.

Stangel, P.W., P.L. Leberg and J.I. Smith, 'Systematic and population genetics', in *The Wild Turkey* (J.G. Dixon, ed.), *Wild Turkey Federation and USDA Forest Service Book*, 1992, 18–28.

Steadman, D.W., 'A review of the osteology and paleontology of Turkeys (Aves: Meleagridinae)', *Contrib. Sci. Nat. Hist. Mus., Los Angeles Co.*, vol. 330, 1980, 131–207.

Stegmann, B., 'Eine neue Auerhuhnform', *Compt. Rend. Ac. Sci.*, USSR, Ser. A, 1926a, 65–66 (in Russian).

Stegmann, B., 'Uebersicht der geographischen Formen von Tetrao parvirostris Bp', *Compt. Rend. Ac. Sci.*, USSR, Ser. A, 1926b, 229–231.

Stegmann, B., 'Die geographischen Formen des Birkhuhns (*Lyrurus tetrix* L.)', *J. Ornithol.*, vol. 80 (3), 1932, 342–354.

Stegmann, B., 'The birds of Kokchetav's pine forests', *Proc. Kazakhstan Acad. Sci., USSR*, vol. 1, 1934, 5–34 (in Russian).

Stegmann, B., *Basics of the ornithological division of the Palearctic*, Moscow, 1938 (in Russian).

Steineger, L., 'A new subspecies of Willow Grouse from Newfoundland', *Auk*, vol.1, no. 4, 1884, 369.

Steineger, L., 'Diagnoses of new species of birds from Kamchatka and the Commander Islands', *Proc. Biol. Soc., Washington*, vol. 2, 1885, 97–99.

Stenman, O. and M. Helminen, 'Ageing method for Hazel Grouse (*Tetrastes bonasia*) based on wings', *Suomen Riista*, vol. 25, 1974, 90–96.

Stephens, I. F., in *Shaw's General zoology or systematic natural history*, vol. 11, part 2, 1819, 265–646.

Stewart, P.A., 'Hooting of Sitka Blue Grouse in relation to weather, season and time of day', *J. Wildlife Management*, vol. 31, 1967, 28–34.

Stewart, R.A., 'Food habits of Blue Grouse', *Condor*, vol. 46, 1944, 112–120.

Stewart, J., 'Intraspecific variation in modern and quaternary European Lagopus', *Smithson. Contr. Paleobiol.*, vol. 89, 1999, 159–168.

Stoll, R.J., M.W. McKlain, R.L. Boston and G.P. Honchul, 'Ruffed Grouse drumming site characteristics in Ohio', *J. Wildlife Management*, vol. 43 (2), 1979, 324–333.

Storch, I., *Grouse: Status Survey and Conservation Action Plan 2000–2004*, UICN, 2000.

Strautman, F.I., *The birds of the Soviet Carpathians*, Kiev, 1954 (in Russian).

Stresemann, E., W. Meise and M. Schonwetter, 'Aves beickianae', *J. Ornith.*, vol. 86 (2), 1938, 171–221.

Suckley, G., 'Description of a new species of North American Grouse', *Proc. Acad. Nat. Sci. Philad.*, 1861, 361–363.

Sun, Y.H. and Y. Fang, 'Notes on the natural history

of the Chinese Grouse *Bonasa sewerzowi*', *Wildlife Biol.*, vol. 3, 1997, 265–268.

Sundevall, G., 'Plate XXXVIII', in P. Gaimard, *Voyages de la Comission Scientifique du nord en Scandinavie, en Laponie du Spitzberg et aux Feroe Pendant les annees 1838, 1839 et 1840, sur la corvette la Recherche Zoologie*, vol. 1, Paris, 1845.

Suomalainen, A. and E. Arhimo, 'On the microbial decomposition of cellulosa by wild gallinaceous birds (family Tetraonidae)', *Ornis Fennica*, vol. 22, 1945, 21–23.

Sushkin, P.P., 'The birds of the central Kirgisian Steppe', in *The Fauna and Flora of the Russian Empire*, vol. 8, 1908, 1–803 (in Russian).

Sushkin, P.P., 'The birds of the Minusinsk Province, Western Sayan and Urianchay Land', in *The Fauna and Flora of the Russian Empire*, vol. 13, 1914, 1–551 (in Russian).

Sushkin, P.P., *The list and distribution of birds in the Russian Altai and nearby territories of north-west Mongolia, with a description of the new or less familiar forms*, Leningrad, 1925 (in Russian).

Sushkin, P.P., *The birds of the Soviet Altai and adjacent territories of north-western Mongolia*, Moscow and Leningrad, vol. 1, 1938 (in Russian).

Sutton, G., *Birds Worth Watching*, Oklahoma Press, 1986.

Svedarsky, W.D. and T.J. Kalahar, 'Female Sharp-tailed Grouse copulates with Greater Prairie-Chicken in Minnesota', *Wilson Bull.*, vol. 92 (2), 1980, 260–261.

Svedarsky, W.D., R.L. Westemeier, R.J. Robel, S. Cough and J.E. Toepfer, 'Status and management of the Greater Prairie-Chicken *Tympanuchus cupido pinnatus* in North America', *Wildlife Biology*, vol. 6, 2000, 277–284.

Svoboda, F.J. and G.W. Gullion, 'Preferential use of aspen by Ruffed Grouse in northern Minnesota', *J. Wildlife Management*, vol. 36, no. 4, 1972, 1166–1180.

Swainsson, W.G. and G. Richardson, *Fauna Boreali-Americana*, London, 1831.

Swarth, H.S., 'The Sitkan race of the Dusky Grouse', *Condor*, vol. 23, no. 2, 1921, 59–60.

Swarth, H.S., 'Report on a collection of birds and mammals from the Atlin region, Northern British Columbia', *Univ. Calif., Publ. Zool.*, vol. 30, no. 4, 1926, 51–162.

Swarth, H.S., 'Geographical variation in the Richardson Grouse', *Proc. Calif. Acad. Sci.*, vol. 20 (4), 1931, 1–7.

Swenson, J.E., 'Decrease of Sage-Grouse *Centrocercus urophasianus* after ploughing of sage-brush steppe', *Biological Conservation*, vol. 41, 1987, 125–132.

Sweum, C.M., W.D. Edge and J.A. Crawford, 'Nesting habitat selection by Sage-Grouse in south-central Washington', *J. Range Management*, vol. 51, 1998, 265–269.

Sych, V.F., *Morphology of the locomotor apparatus in birds*, Ulyanovsk, 1999 (in Russian).

Szuba, K.J. and J.F. Bendell, 'Population densities and habitats of Spruce Grouse in Ontario', in *Resources and dynamics of the boreal zone, Proc. Conf., Thunder Bay, Ontario*, August 1982, Association of Canadian Universities for Northern Studies, Ottawa, 1983, 199–213.

Tachtadjan, A., 'Main phitochtoria of the later Cretaceous and the Paleogene in the territory of the USSR and adjoining countries', *Botanical Journal*, vol. 51 (9), 1966, 1217–1230 (in Russian).

Taczanowski, L., 'Description d'une nouvelle espece de Coq de bruyer (*Tetrao mlokosiewiczi*)', *Proc. Zool. Soc.*, London, 1875, 266–269.

Taibel, A.M., 'Caratteristiche e peculiarita anatomische nei vari membri ella famiglia Cracidae', *Suppl. alie Ricerche di Biol. Della*

Selvaggina, vol. 7, suppl. 1, 1976, 677–726.

Taka-Tsukasa, N., *The birds of Nippon*, vol. 2, part 1, 1932, London.

Tanhuanpää, E. and E. Pulliainen, 'Major fatty acid composition of some organic fats in the Willow Grouse (*Lagopus lagopus*) and the Rock Ptarmigan (*Lagopus mutus*)', *Ann. Acad. Sci. Fenica*. Ser. A, IV, biol., vol. 141, 1969, 1–14.

Tarasov, V.V., 'Territorial conservatism in Willow Ptarmigan in the north of Yamal Peninsula', *Ecology*, vol. 3, 1995, 215–221.

Tarasov, V.V., 'Sexual interrelations in Willow Ptarmigan in the northern limit of its range', in *Problems of the study and protection of birds in Eastern Europe and Northern Asia*, Materials of XI Orn. Conf. Kazan, 2001, 587–588 (in Russian).

Tarasov, P.E., J.W. Williams, A.A. Andreev, T. Nakagawa, E. Bezrukova, U. Herzschuh, Y. Igarashi and H. Müller, 'Satellite- and pollen-based quantitative woody cover reconstructions for northern Asia: verification and application to late-Quaternary pollen data', *Earth and Planetary Science Letters*, vol. 264, 2007, 284–298.

Tarchov, S.V., 'Winter nutrition of Black-billed Capercaillie in connection with the ecology of Larches', *Ornithologia*, vol. 23, 1988, 138–146 (in Russian).

Taverner, P.A., 'A new hybrid Grouse *Lagopus lagopus* (L.) x *Canachites canadensis* (L.)', Nat. Mus. of Canada, Ann. Report, 1931, 90–91.

Taverner, P.A., 'A new subspecies of Willow Ptarmigan from the Arctic islands of America', *Bull. Nat. Mus. of Canada*, vol. 68, 1932, 87–88.

Taylor, W.R., 'A new Ptarmigan from Mount Rainier', *Condor*, vol. 22, 1920, 146–152.

Teidoff, E., 'Das Haselhuhns', *Neue Brehm-Bücherei*, h. 77, 1952.

Telepnev, V.G., 'Some peculiarities in the feeding of south-siberian Capercaillie', *Collect. Science-Technical Information of Inst. Of Hunting Farm and Fur-breeding.*, *Kirov*, vol. 37–39, 1972, 58–61 (in Russian).

Teplov, V.P., 'The Capercaillie in the Pechora–Ilych State Reserve', *Proc. Pechora-Ilych State Reserve*, vol. 4 (1), 1947a, 3–76 (in Russian).

Teplov, V.P., 'On the ecology of the forest game of Pechora–Ilych State reserve', *Proc. Pechora-Ilych State Reserve, Moscow*, vol. 4 (1), 1947, 123–167 (in Russian).

Teplova, E.N., 'Birds of the Pechora-Ilych State Reserve', *Proc. Pechora-Ilych State Reserve, Moscow*, vol. 6, 1957, 5–115 (in Russian).

Teresa, S.I., 'Construction of the vocal apparatus in birds', *Proc. Sci. Research Inst., Moscow State Univ.*, vol. 1–2, 1930, 1–88 (in Russian).

Thienemann, F.A.L., *Systematische Darstellung der Fortpflanzung der Fögel Europa*, Abth. 3, Leipzig, 1829.

Thiel D., E. Menoni, J-F.Brenot and L. Jenni, 'Effects of recreation and hunting on flushing distance of Capercaillie', *J. Wildlife Management*, vol. 71 (6), 2007, 1784–1792.

Thurman, J.R., 'Ruffed Grouse ecology in southeastern Monroe County, Indiana', M.S. thesis 1966, Purdue University (cit. from Johnsgard, 1973).

Tichomirov, B.A., 'On the influence of animals on the vegetation of the Taymyr tundra', *Bull. Moscow Soc. of Nature Testers.*, New Series, Biology division, vol. 60 (5), 1955, 147–151 (in Russian).

Todd, W.E.C., 'Eastern races of the Ruffed Grouse', *Auk*, vol. 57, no. 3, 1940, 390–397.

Todd, W.E.C., *Birds of the Labrador Peninsula and adjacent areas*, Toronto, 1963.

Toepfer J.E. and R.L. Eng, 'Winter ecology of the Greater Prairie-Chicken on the Cheyenne National Grassland, North Dakota', in A.J.

Bjugsrag (technical coordinator), *Prairie-Chickens on the Cheyenne National Grassland*, 1988, 32–48.

Tolmachev, A.I., 'On the natural conditions of Tertiary Arctic flora existence', *Journal of Botany*, vol. 29 (1), 1944, 17–28 (in Russian).

Tolmachev, A.I., *'On the history of the origin and development of the dark-coniferous taiga*, Moscow-Leningrad, 1954 (in Russian).

Tkatchenko, V.I., 'Ecology of the galliforme birds in the north-western Caucasus highlands', *Proc. Teberda State Reserve, Stavropol*, vol. 6, 1966, 5–144 (in Russian).

Tugarinov, A. Ia., 'Birds of the Würmian Glaciation in the Crimea (from the results of excavations in Crimean caves)', *Proc. Soviet Section of Intern. Assoc. Quaternary Studies, Leningrad*, vol. 1, 1937, 97–114 (in Russian).

Turner, L.M., 'On *Lagopus mutus* Leach, and its allies', *Proc. U.S. Nat. Mus.*, vol. 5, 1882, 225–233.

Turner, L.M., 'List of the birds of Labrador', *Proc. U.S. Nat. Mus.*, vol. 8, 1885, 233–254.

Tyrberg .T., *Pleistocene birds of the Palearctic: a catalogue*, Cambridge, 1998.

Uhl D., C. Traiser, U. Greisser and T. Denk, 'Fossil leaves as palaeoclimate proxies in the Palaeogene of Spitsbergen (Svalbard)', *Acta Palaeobotanica* 47, 2007, 89–107.

Ulianin, I.S., 'Biology of the Willow Ptarmigan in northern Kazakhstan', *Proc. Zool. Museum of Moscow State Univ.*, vol. 5, 1939, 109–126 (in Russian).

Ulianin, I.S., 'On the ecology of Black Grouse, Willow Ptarmigan and Grey Partridge in northern Kazakhstan', *Proc. Naursum State Reserve*, vol. 11, 1949, 108–139 (in Russian).

Uspenski, S.M., 'Birds and Mammals of Bennett Island', *Proc. Inst. Arctic and Antarctic., Leningrad*, vol. 224, 1963, 180–205 (in Russian).

Valkovich, M.V., 'Domestication of Capercaillie caught in the wild to create parental stock in a hunting farm', International Capercaillie meeting, Moscow, 1981, 16–17 (in Russian).

Vartapetov, L.G., *The Birds of the West-Siberian Taiga*, Novosibirsk, 1998 (in Russian).

Vasilchenko, A.A., 'New data regarding the avifauna of Hamar-Daban', *Ornitologia*, vol. 17, 1882, 130–134 (in Russian).

Vaskovsky, A.P., 'Review of the stratigraphy of the anthropogenic deposits of the extreme Asian North East', in *Notes on Geology and Raw Materials of North-East USSR*, vol. 16, 1963, 74–96 (in Russian).

Viht, E.A., 'Estonia', in S.V. Kirikov (ed.), *The Tetraonid Birds*, Moscow, 1975, 203–215 (in Russian).

Vigors, N.A., 'On the natural affinities that connect the orders and families of birds', *Trans. Linnean Soc., London*, vol. 14, 1825, 395–517.

Vitovich, O.A., 'The ecology of the Caucasian Black Grouse', *Proc. Teberda State Reserve*, vol. 10, 1986, 165–309 (in Russian).

Vladyshewsky, D.V., 'Ukrainian Karpaty', in S.V. Kirikov (ed), *The Tetraonid Birds*, Moscow, 1975, 233–240 (in Russian).

Vodehnal, W.L., 'Status and management of the Greater Prairie-Chicken in Nebraska', in W.D. Svedarsky, R.H. Hier and N.J. Silvy (eds.), *The Greater Prairie-chicken: a national look*, 1999, 81–98.

Volkov, N.I., 'Changes in the number of Hazel Grouse in winter', in *Populations of tetraonid birds in the USSR*, Moscow, 1968, 8–9 (in Russian).

Volkov, N.I., 'Data on the feeding of Willow Ptarmigan during the winter', *Bull. Moscow Soc. of Nature Testers.*, vol. 75 (1), 1970, 123–127 (in Russian).

Volkov, N.I., 'The upper part of the Western Dvina River Basin', in S.V. Kirikov (ed.), *The Tetraonid*

Birds, Moscow, 1975, 224–232 (in Russian).

Vorobiev, K.A., *The birds of Ussuri Land*, Moscow, 1954 (in Russian).

Vorobiev, K.A., *The birds of Yakutia*, Moscow, 1963 (in Russian).

Voronin, N.R., 'Notes on the ecology of Willow Ptarmigan in Pechora', in *Populations of tetraonid birds in the USSR*, Moscow, 1968, 9–10 (in Russian).

Voronin, N.R., *The Willow Ptarmigan of the Bolshezemelskaya Tundra*, Leningrad, 1978 (in Russian).

Voronin, N.R. and A.P. Beshkarev, 'Genus Tetrao, Capercaillie', in R.L. Potapov (ed.), *Fauna of north-eastern Russia. Birds*, vol. 1, 1995, 146–156 (in Russian).

Voronov, V.G., G.A. Voronov and V.P. Vshivzev, 'Sakhalin and Kuril Islands', in S.V. Kirikov, (ed.), *The Tetraonid Birds*, Moscow, 1975, 251–258 (in Russian).

Vos G., de. 'Social behaviour of Black Grouse: an observational and experimental field study', Ardea, vol. 71, 1983, 103.

Wakkinen, W.L., K.P. Reese and J.W.Connelly, 'Sage-Grouse nest locations in relation to leks', *J. Wildlife Management,* vol. 56, 1992, 381–383.

Walker, B.L., D.E. Naugle and K.E. Doherty, 'Greater Sage-Grouse population response to energy development and habitat loss', *J. Wildlife Management*, vol. 71 (8), 2007, 2644–2654.

Walkinshaw, L.H., 'A nest of the Spruce Grouse in East-Central Saskatchewan', *Wils. Bull.,* vol. 60, 1948, 118.

Watson A., 'A study of Ptarmigan in the northern Highlands', in D.A. Bannerman, *The birds of the British Isles*, vol. 12, 1963, 321–331.

Watson, A., 'Food of Ptarmigan (*Lagopus mutus*) in Scotland', *Scot. Nat.*, vol. 71, 1964, 60–66.

Watson, A., 'A population study of Ptarmigan in Scotland', *J. of Animal Ecology*, vol. 34, 1965, 135–172.

Watson A. and D. Jenkins, 'Notes on the behaviour of Red Grouse', *British Birds*, vol. 57, 1964, 137–170.

Watson A. and D. Jenkins, 'Experiments on population control by territorial behaviour in Red Grouse', *J. Animal Ecology*, vol. 37, 1968, 595–614.

Watson A. and R. Moss, *Grouse*, London, 2008.

Weeden, R.B., 'Management of Ptarmigan in North America', *J. Wildlife Management*, vol. 27 (4), 1963, 673–683.

Weeden, R.B., 'Spatial separation of sexes in Rock and Willow Ptarmigan in winter', *Auk*, vol. 81 (4), 1964, 534–541.

Weeden, R.B., 'Breeding density, reproductive success and mortality of the Rock Ptarmigan of Eagle Creek, Central Alaska, from 1960 to 1964', in Trans. 30th N.A. Wildlife and Natural Resources Conf., Washington, 1965, 336–347.

Weeden, R.B., 'Seasonal and geographic variation on the foods of adult White-tailed Ptarmigan', *Condor*, vol. 69, 1967, 303–309.

Weeden, R.B., 'Foods of Rock and Willow Ptarmigan in Central Alaska with comments of inter-specific competition', *Auk*, vol. 86 (2), 1969, 271–281.

Weeden, R.B. and J.B. Therberge, 'The dynamics of a fluctuating population of Rock Ptarmigan in Alaska', in *Proc. XV Intern. Ornithol. Congress, Hague*, vol. 15, 1972, 90–106.

Wereshagin, N.K. and R.L. Potapov, 'Mejniak (hybrid *Tetrao urogallus* x *Lyrurus tetrix*)', *Hunting and hunting industry*, vol. 7, 1981, 12 (in Russian).

West, G.C., 'Seasonal differences in metabolic rates of Alaskan Ptarmigan', *Comp. Biochem and Physiol.*, vol. 42a, 1972, 867–876.

West, G.C. and M.S. Meng, 'Nutrition of Willow

Ptarmigan in northern Alaska', *Auk*, vol. 83 (4), 1966, 603–615.

West, G.C. and M.S. Meng, 'Seasonal change in body weight and fat and effect of diet on fatty acid composition of Alaskan Willow Ptarmigan', *Wilson Bull.,* vol. 80, 1968, 426–441.

Westemeier, R.L. and S. Cough, 'National outlook and conservation needs for Greater Prairie-Chicken', in W.D. Svedarsky, R.H. Hier and N.J. Silvy (eds), *The Greater Prairie-Chicken: a national look*, 1999, 169–187.

Wetmore, A., 'Notes on certain Grouse of the Pleistocene', *Wilson Bull.*, vol. 71, 1959, 178–182.

Whitcomb, S.D., F.A. Servello and A.F. O'Connell, 'Patch occupancy and dispersal of Spruce Grouse on the edge of its range in Maine', *Canad. J. Zool.*, vol. 74, 1996, 1951–1955.

Wiley, R.H., 'Territorialty and non-random mating in Sage-Grouse *Centrocercus urophasianus*', *Anim. Behav. Monogr.*, vol. 2, 1973, 87–169.

Wiley, R.H., 'Evolution of social organization and life history patterns among Grouse', *Quart. Rev. Biol.*, vol. 49, no. 3, 1974, 210–227.

Witherby, H.F., F.C. Jourdian, N.F. Ticehurst and B.W. Tucker, *The Handbook of British Birds*, London, vol. 5, 1947.

Witherby, H.F. and E. Lönnberg, 'The British Black Grouse, *Lyrurus tetrix britannnicus subsp. nova*', *British Birds*, vol. 6, no. 9, 1913, 270–271.

Wolfe, D.H., 'Nesting documentation for the White-tailed Ptarmigan in the Sangre de Cristo Mountains, New Mexico', *Oklahoma Biol. Survey, 2nd Series*, vol. 7, 2006, 21–23.

Würm, W., *Das Auerwild, dessen Naturgeschichte, Jagt und Hege. Eine ornithologische und jagliche Monographie*, Wien, 1885.

Wu Yi Peng Jitai Gao Hong, 'Study on the breeding ecology of the Pheasant Grouse (*Tetraophasis obscurus*)', *Acta Ecologica Sinica*, vol. 14, no. 2,

1994, 221–222.

Yamasina Y. and S. Yamada, 'The habits of *F. falcipennis* and the experience of the species in captivity', *Tori*, vol. 2 (41), 1935, 13–18.

Yeatter, R.E., 'Population responses of Prairie-Chickens to land-use changes in Illinois', *J. Wildlife Management*, vol. 27, 1963, 739–757.

Young, J.R., 'The influence of sexual selection on phenotypic and genetic divergence of Sage-Grouse', PhD dissertation, Purdue University, 1994.

Young, J. R., C.E. Braun, S.J. Ouler-McCance, J.W. Hupp and T.W. Quinn, 'A new species of Sage-Grouse (*Phasianidae: Centrocercus*) from south-western Colorado', *Wilson Bull.*, vol. 112 (4), 2000, 445–453.

Young, J. R., J.W. Hupp, J.W. Bradbury and C.E. Braun, 'Phenotypic divergence of secondary sexual traits among Sage-Grouse *Centrocercus urophasianus* populations', *Anim. Behav.*, vol. 47, 1994, 1353–1362.

Yudakov, A.G., 'Spruce Grouse in upper Amurland', in *Preservation, Management and Breeding of the Natural Resources in Amurland*, Khabarovsk, 1967, 186–187 (in Russian).

Yudakov, A.G., 'Influence of raptors on the number of Hazel Grouse in the Upper Amur Basin', in *Populations of tetraonid birds in the USSR*, Moscow, 1968, 86–88 (in Russian).

Yudakov, A.G., 'Biology of the Spruce Grouse (*Falcipennis falcipennis*) in Amur Province', *Zool. Journ.*, vol. 51 (4), 1972, 620–622 (in Russian).

Yurlov, K.T., 'On the ecology of Willow Ptarmigan and Black Grouse in Barabin and Kulunda steppes', *Proc. Biol. Inst. Sibir. Division Acad. Sci. USSR*, 1960, 3–85 (in Russian).

Zabolotny, N., 'The nest of a Hazel Grouse in a tree', *Hunting and the hunting industry*, no. 5, 1979, 24–25 (in Russian).

Zettel J., 'Nachrungsőcologische Untersuchungen am Birkhuhn, *Tetrao tetrix*, in dem Schweizer Alpen', *Ornith. Beobachter*, vol. 71 (4), 1974, 186–246.

Zimmerman, C.E., N. Hillgruber, S.E. Burril, M.A. St Peters and J.D. Wetzel, 'Offshore marine observation of Willow Ptarmigan, including water landings, Kuskokwim Bay, Alaska', *Wilson Bull.*, vol. 117, 2005, 12–14.

Zink, R. and G. Barrowclough, 'Mitochondrial DNA under siege in avian phylogeography', *Molecular Ecology*, vol. 17, 2008, 2107–2121.

Zubakov, V.A., *Global climatic events of the Pleistocene*, Leningrad, 1986 (in Russian).

Zverev, M.D., 'On the ecology of Tianshan's Black Grouse (Zailiisky Ala-Tau)', *Ornithologia*, vol. 5, 1962, 208–211 (in Russian).

Zwickel, F.C., 'Winter food habits of Capercaillie in north-east Scotland', *British Birds*, vol. 59 (8), 1966, 325–336.

Zwickel, F.C., 'Blue Grouse (*Dendragapus obscurus*)', in A. Poole, P. Stettenheim and F. Gill (eds), *The Birds of North America*, no. 15, 1992, The Academy of Natural Sciences, Philadelphia, and The American Ornithologists Union, Washington, D.C.

Zwickel, F.C. and C. Martinsen, 'Determining age and sex in Franklin's Spruce Grouse by tails alone', *J. Wildlife Management*, vol. 31 (4), 1967, 760–763.

Zwickel, F.C., D.A. Boag and J.H. Brigham, 'The autumn diet of Spruce Grouse: a regional comparison', *Condor*, vol. 76, no. 2, 1974, 212–214.

Zwickel, F.C. and J.H. Brigham, 'Autumn weights of Spruce Grouse in North-Central Washington', *J. Wildlife Management*, vol. 38 (2), 1974, 315–319.

Zwickel, F.C., J.H. Brigham and I.O. Buss, 'Autumn structure of Blue Grouse populations in north-central Washington', *J. Wildlife Management*, vol. 39, 1975, 461–467.

Zwickel, F.C. and J.F. Bendell, 'Early mortality and the regulation of numbers of Blue Grouse', *Canad. J. Zool.*, vol. 45 (5), 1967, 817–851.

Zwickel, F.C. and J.F. Bendell, *Blue Grouse: their Biology and Natural History*, NRC Research Press, Canada, 2004.

Zwickel, F.C., D.A. Boag and J.F. Bendell, 'Longevity in Blue Grouse', *North Amer. Bird Bander*, vol. 14, 1989, 1–4.

Zwickel, F.C. and J.A. Dake, 'Primary molt of Blue Grouse (*Dendragapus obscurus*) and its relation to reproductive activity and migration', *Canad. J. Zool.*, vol. 55 (11): 1977, 1782–1787.

INDEX

tailed Ptarmigan *and* Willow
Grouse
neck sacs 42, 53, *133*, 144, 153, *166*,
358
nesting 38-9, 69, 78, 93, 111, 122, 136,
145, 153, 169, 191, 202, *203*, 221, 248-
9, 273, 283, 307, 323, *324*, 341, 348, 359
North American Spruce Grouse **113**;
114-16, *133*
North European Hazel Grouse *84*
nostrils 13, *14*, 48
nutrition 27-31, 49, 50-1
    Asian Spruce Grouse 107
    Black-billed Capercaillie 28,
    215-16
    Black Grouse 298-9
    Canadian Spruce Grouse 120
    Caucasian Black Grouse 317-18
    Dusky Grouse 142-3
    Franklin's Spruce Grouse 128-9
    Greater Prairie-Chicken 337
    Greater Sage-Grouse 27, 163
    Gunnison Sage-Grouse 174
    Hazel Grouse 28, 88-9
    Lesser Prairie-Chicken 27, 346
    Rock Ptarmigan 266-7
    Ruffed Grouse 27, 66-7
    Severtzov's Hazel Grouse 76
    Sharp-tailed Grouse 356
    Sooty Grouse 27, 150-1
    Western Capercaillie 192-3
    White-tailed Ptarmigan 281
    Willow Grouse 27, 240-3

O
operculum 13-14
Oreias 223
origins and evolution 40-55, 361

P
palaeontological record 40-4, 53, 55, 57
Palearctic grouse 10-11
    see also Asian Spruce Grouse;
    Black-billed Capercaillie; Black
    Grouse; Caucasian Black Grouse;
    Hazel Grouse; Rock Ptarmigan;
    Severtzov's Hazel Grouse; Western
    Capercaillie *and* Willow Grouse
parallel duels 247, 304, 322-3, 341
parallel flight 247
parallel runs 91, 273
Pedioecetes subgenus 349
plumage
    courtship 38, 57
    seasonal 53, 223, 226-8, *243-4*,
    253-4, *255*, 256, *257*, 268, 275,
    289, *290*
    see also feathers *and* moult
population factors 360-4
population status *see* hunting and
population status
population structure and density
    Asian Spruce Grouse 105-6
    Black-billed Capercaillie 37,
    213-14
    Black Grouse 37, 297
    Canadian Spruce Grouse 37,
    118-19
    Caucasian Black Grouse 37, 317

Dusky Grouse 142
Franklin's Spruce Grouse 127-8
Greater Prairie-Chicken 37, 335-6
Greater Sage-Grouse 37, 162
Gunnison Sage-Grouse 174
Hazel Grouse 37, 87-8
Lesser Prairie-Chicken 37, 346
Rock Ptarmigan 37, 264-5
Ruffed Grouse 37, 66
Severtzov's Hazel Grouse 75-6
Sharp-tailed Grouse 37, 355
Sooty Grouse 37, 149
Western Capercaillie 37, 189-90
White-tailed Ptarmigan 37, 280
Willow Grouse 37, 237-8
postures, display 69, *92*, 109, 122, *166-8*,
197, 199, 219, *220*, 272, 306, *321*, *340*,
341, *347-8*, *358-9*
Prairie-Chickens **326-59**; 52, *133*, 362
Prairie Sharp-tailed Grouse *332*, 354
predation 35, 87-8, 106, 142, 169, 205,
206, 238, 265, 274, 324, 341, 348, 361
Ptarmigan, Willow *see* Willow Grouse
ptarmigans **223-84**; 12, *14*, 53-4, *133*
pterylosis 16

R
range *see* distribution
Red Grouse 21, 223, 224, 226, *230*,
232, 235, *241*, 245, 251
re-introduction
    Greater Sage-Grouse 170
    Sooty Grouse 145
    Western Capercaillie 206-7
    see also introduction
reproduction *see* breeding
rhamphotecae 20, *21*
Rhen's Hazel Grouse *84*, 85
Rock Ptarmigan **223-5**, **252-3**; 53, 54,
191, 364
    breeding 271-4
    colouration 254-8
    dimensions 258
    distribution *259-60*
    habitats 264
    hunting and conservation 274
    morphology 18, 24, *177*, *224*, 253
    moult *255*, *257*, 258-9, *268*
    nutrition 266-7
    population structure and density
    37, 264-5
    sexes (female) 255, *256-7*; (male)
    253, *254-5*, *268*
    subspecies *257*, 260-4
    territoriality 265-6
    wintering 267-71
    young *257*, *258*
roosting 76, 107, 143, 151, 177, 194,
218
    see also snow burrows
Ruffed Grouse **56-7**; 363
    breeding 38, *39*, 57, 68-70
    colouration 38, 43-4, 50, 58-61
    dimensions 61
    distribution *62*
    habitats 65-6
    hunting and population status 70
    morphology 18, 24, *48*, *56-7*, *177*
    nutrition 27, 66-7

population structure and density
37, 66
sexes (female) *59*, 60, *63*, *69*; (male)
58, *59*, 60, *61*, 68
subspecies 62-5
territoriality 66
wintering 67-8
young *60*, *70*

S
Sage-Grouse **154-75**; 38, 44, 52, *133*
Sakhalin Hazel Grouse *84*, 86
seasonal changes
    feeding 28
    plumage 53, 223, 226-8, *243-4*,
    253-4, *255*, 256, *257*, 268, 275,
    289, *290*
    body weight 28, *30*
Severtzov's Hazel Grouse 50
    behaviour 76
    breeding 36, 77-8
    colouration 71-3
    dimensions 73-4
    distribution *74*
    habitats 75
    hunting and conservation 78
    morphology 13, *56-7*
    moult 74
    nutrition 76
    population structure and density
    75-6
    sexes (female) *72-3*; (male) 71, *72*,
    73, 77
    subspecies *74*, 75
    wintering 76-7
    young 73
sexes
    breeding roles 36-8
    ratios *see* population structure and
    density
sexes (female)
    Asian Spruce Grouse *99*, *102*
    Black-billed Capercaillie *209*,
    217, *221*
    Black Grouse *286*, *290*, *296*
    Canadian Spruce Grouse 115-16
    Caucasian Black Grouse *286*, *313*,
    318
    Dusky Grouse 138, *139-40*
    Franklin's Spruce Grouse *125*, *130*
    Greater Prairie-Chicken *330*, *337*
    Greater Sage-Grouse 158, *159*, *165*
    Gunnison Sage-Grouse *172*
    Hazel Grouse *80*, *81*, *82*
    Lesser Prairie-Chicken *343*, *344*
    Rock Ptarmigan 255, *256-7*
    Ruffed Grouse *59*, 60, *63*, *69*;
    Severtzov's Hazel Grouse *72-3*
    Sharp-tailed Grouse *350*, *351*
    Sooty Grouse 146, *147*, *149*
    Western Capercaillie *180*, *181*, *185*
    White-tailed Ptarmigan 275, *276*,
    277, *284*
    Willow Grouse 226, 227, *228*, *236*
sexes (male)
    Asian Spruce Grouse *96*, 100,
    101, 102
    Black-billed Capercaillie *177*, *207*,
    208, 219-20